THE WORLDS OF EXISTENTIALISM

A Critical Reader

THE WORLDS OF EXISTENTIALISM

A Critical Reader

EDITED

With Introductions and A Conclusion

BY

MAURICE FRIEDMAN

The University of Chicago Press
Chicago and London

The University of Chicago Press, Chicago 60637
The University of Chicago Press, Ltd., London

 Phoenix Edition Published 1973

International Standard Book Number: 0–226–26348–7
Library of Congress Catalog Card Number: 63–11627

Printed in the United States of America

ACKNOWLEDGMENTS

GRATEFUL acknowledgment is made to the following publishers, authors, and translators for permission to reprint selections from copyright material:

George Allen & Unwin Ltd., London, for permission to reprint selections from Friedrich Nietzsche, *Thus Spake Zarathustra,* trans. by Thomas Common; *The American Journal of Psychoanalysis,* Harold Kelman, editor, for Silvano Arieti, "What Is Effective in the Therapeutic Process?" Vol. XVII, No. 1 (1957), and Viktor E. Frankl, "On Logotherapy and Existential Analysis," Vol. XVIII, No. 1 (1958); *The American Journal of Psychotherapy* for Silvano Arieti, "Recent Conceptions and Misconceptions of Schizophrenia," Vol. XIV, No. 1 (January, 1960); Silvano Arieti for permission to quote from the two articles above and "The Two Aspects of Schizophrenia," *The Psychiatric Quarterly* Vol. XXXI (July, 1957); Professor John F. Bannan, Dept. of Philosophy, Loyola University, for his translation of Maurice Merleau-Ponty, "What Is Phenomenology?" *Cross Currents,* Vol. VI, No. 1 (Winter, 1956); to Basic Books, Inc., London and New York, for Ludwig Binswanger, *Being-in-the-World. Selected Papers,* ed. by Jacob Needleman, copyright © 1963 by Basic Books and for Medard Boss, *Psychoanalysis and Daseinsanalysis,* copyright © 1963 by Basic Books. Beacon Press, Boston, for Viktor Frankl, *From Death-Camp to Existentialism,* copyright © 1959 by Viktor E. Frankl; A. & C. Black Ltd., London, for Gabriel Marcel, *Being and Having,* 1949; Basil Blackwell, publisher, Oxford, England for Kathleen Freeman, *Ancilla to the Pre-Socratic Philosophers,* 1956; Geoffrey Bles Ltd., London, for Nicolas Berdyaev, *Freedom and the Spirit,* 1935, and the British Commonwealth (including Canadian) rights to Nicolas Berdyaev, *The Destiny of Man,* 1955; T. B. Bottomore of The London School of Economics and Political Science for his translation of Karl Marx, "Alienated Labor" in Erich Fromm, *Marx's Concept of Man* (New York: Frederick Ungar Publishing Co., copyright © 1961 by Erich Fromm); Professor Martin Buber of Jerusalem, Israel, for "Distance and Relation," "Elements of the Interhuman," and "Guilt and Guilt Feelings," *Psychiatry,* Vol. XX, No. 2 (May 1957) copyright 1951 and 1957 by Martin Buber and for the "Nachwort" to Martin Buber, *Die Schriften über das dialogische Prinzip* (Heidelberg: Verlag Lambert Schneider, 1954); André Deutsch Ltd., London, for Gustav Janouch, *Conversations with Kafka,* 1953; for Rollo May, "Dangers in the Relationship of Existentialism to Psychotherapy" from the book *Psychoanalysis and Existential Philosophy* edited by Hendrik M. Ruitenbeek, copyright © 1962 by Hendrik M. Ruitenbeek, Dutton Paperback edition, reprinted by permission of the author and E. P. Dutton & Co., Inc.; Ferdinand Enke Verlag, Stuttgart, for Viktor von Weizsäcker, *Fälle und Probleme. Anthropologische Vorlesungen in der medizinischen Klinik,* 1947 ("Beiträge aus der allgemeinen Medizin," Heft 3, 2nd ed., 1951); *Faith and Freedom* (England) for Paul Tillich, "The Theological Significance of Existentialism and Psychoanalysis," Vol. IX, No. 25 (Autumn, 1955); Farrar, Straus & Cudahy, Inc. for Karl Jaspers, *Reason and Existenz,* trans. by William Earle, copyright © 1955 by the Noonday Press, for Franz Rosenzweig, *Understanding the Sick and the Healthy,* ed. by N. N. Glatzer, trans. by T. Luckman, copyright 1954 by the Noonday Press, and for Jean-Paul Sartre, *The Transcendence of the Ego,* trans. by Forrest Williams and Robert Kirkpatrick, copyright © 1957 by the Noonday Press; A. Francke Verlag, Bern, for Martin Heidegger, *Platons Lehre von der Wahrheit. Mit einem Brief über den "Humanismus,"* 1947; Free Press of Glencoe for Rollo May, "The Context of Psychotherapy" in Morris I. Stein, ed., *Contemporary Psychotherapies,* copyright © 1961 by the Free Press of Glencoe, and for Erwin M. Straus, *The Primary World of Senses,* copyright © 1963; Librairie Gallimard, Paris, for Gabriel Marcel, *Journal Métaphysique* (*Metaphysical Journal*), © Editions Gallimard, 1928; Grune & Stratton, Inc., New York, and J. L. Moreno, coordinating editor, for Ludwig Binswanger, "Existential Analysis and Psychotherapy" and for J. L. Moreno, "The Philosophy of the Third Psychiatric Revolution" in Frieda Fromm-Reichmann and J. L. Moreno, eds., *Progress in Psychotherapy,* Vol. I, Grune & Stratton, 1956, and for Medard Boss, " 'Daseinsanalysis' and Psychotherapy" in Jules H. Masserman and J. L. Moreno, eds., *Progress in Psychotherapy,* Vol. II, Grune & Stratton, 1957; Harcourt, Brace & World, Inc., New York, for Helen Merrell Lynd, *On Shame and the Search for Identity,* © 1958; Harper & Row Publishers, Inc., New York, for Nicolas Berdyaev, *The Beginning and the End,* copyright 1952 by Y.M.C.A. Press, for the American rights to Nicolas Berdyaev, *The Destiny of Man,* copyright © 1960 by Harper & Brothers, for Raymond Blakney, *Meister Eckhart: A Modern Translation,* copyright 1941 by Harper & Brothers, for Martin Buber, *Eclipse of God,* copyright 1952 by Harper & Brothers, for Martin Buber, *Pointing the Way,* ed. by Maurice Friedman, copyright © 1957 by Martin Buber, copyright © 1963 by Maurice Friedman, for Wilhelm Dilthey, *Pattern and Meaning in History,* copyright © 1962 by George Allen & Unwin Ltd., London, for Martin Heidegger, *Being and Time,* copyright © 1962 by SCM Press Ltd., for Søren Kierkegaard, *Purity of Heart Is to Will One Thing,* copyright 1938, 1948 by Harper & Brothers, for Paul Tillich, *Dynamics of Faith,* copyright © 1957 by Paul Tillich (by special permission), and for special permission to cite the Torchbook editions of these works where they exist; the Harvill Press Ltd., London, for Gabriel Marcel, *The Mystery of Being,* Vol. I—*Reflection and Mystery,* 1950, Vol. II—*Faith and Reality,* 1951; Hippokrates Verlag, Stuttgart, for

Viktor E. Frankl, *Das Menschenbild der Seelenheilkunde,* copyright © 1959; The Horizon Press, New York, for Martin Buber, *The Tales of Rabbi Nachman, Hasidism and Modern Man, The Origin and Meanings of Hasidism,* ed. by Maurice Friedman, copyright © 1956, 1958, and 1960 respectively by Martin Buber; to Houghton Mifflin Co. for Carl R. Rogers, *On Becoming a Person,* copyright 1961 by Carl R. Rogers; Humanities Press Inc., New York, for Maurice Merleau-Ponty, *Phenomenology of Perception,* copyright © 1962 by Routledge & Kegan Paul Ltd., London; *International Journal of Sociometry,* J. L. Moreno, ed., for J. L. Moreno, "The Dilemma of Existentialism, Daseinsanalyse and the Psychodrama," Vol. I, No. 1 (September, 1956); Ernst Klett Verlag, Stuttgart, for Hans Trüb, *Heilung aus der Begegnung,* 1952, and for Hans Trüb, "Vom Selbst zur Welt," *Psyche,* Vol. I (1947); Vittorio Klostermann Verlag, Frankfurt am Main for Martin Heidegger, *Holzwege,* 1950, and *Vom Wesen des Grundes,* 1955; Alfred A. Knopf Inc., New York, for Albert Camus, *The Rebel,* copyright © 1956 by Alfred A. Knopf, Inc., *The Myth of Sisyphus,* copyright © 1955 by Alfred A. Knopf, *The Plague,* copyright 1948 by Stuart Gilbert, and for Jean-Paul Sartre, *No Exit and Three Other Plays,* copyright 1946 by Stuart Gilbert, copyright 1948, 1949 by Alfred A. Knopf, Inc., *The Devil and the Good Lord,* copyright © 1960 by Alfred A. Knopf, Inc., *The Age of Reason* and *The Reprieve,* copyright 1947 by Eric Sutton, and for Viktor E. Frankl, *The Doctor and the Soul,* copyright © 1955 by Alfred A. Knopf; K. F. Koehler Verlag, Stuttgart, for Viktor von Weizäcker, *Arzt und Kranker,* Vol. I, 3rd ed., 1949, and *Diesseits und jenseits der Medizin,* 1950; Kösel-Verlag, Munich, for Ferdinand Ebner, *Das Wort und die geistigen Realitäten* (Innsbruck: Brenner-Verlag, 1921), published by Kösel as part of Ebner, *Fragmente, Aufsätze, Aphorismen* (1963), the first of a three-volume edition of Ebner's work; *Liberation* and Dwight MacDonald, trans., for Albert Camus, *Neither Victims nor Executioners.* A Liberation Pamphlet, 1961; the *Journal of Existential Psychiatry,* copyright 1960 by Libra Publishers, 1133 Broadway, New York 10, N. Y., for Viktor E. Frankl, "Beyond Self-Actualization and Self-Expression," Vol. I, No. 1 (Spring, 1960); *The Library of Living Philosophers,* Paul Arthur Schilpp, ed., for Gabriel Marcel, "I and Thou" in Paul Arthur Schilpp and Maurice Friedman, eds., *The Philosophy of Martin Buber* (Wilmette, Ill.: Open Court, 1964); the Macmillan Co., New York, for Martin Buber, *Between Man and Man,* first published by Kegan Paul, London, 1947; Dr. Rollo May for "Some Comments on Existential Psychotherapy," written expressly for this anthology; Meridian Books, The World Publishing Company for Martin Heidegger, "The Way Back into the Ground of Metaphysics," trans. by Walter Kaufmann, published in *Existentialism from Dostoevsky to Sartre,* edited and introduced by Walter Kaufmann, Meridian Books, copyright © 1956 by The World Publishing Co.; *Modern Age,* Eugene Davidson, ed., for Maurice Friedman, "Existential Psychotherapy and the Image of Man," Vol. VI, No. 3 (Summer, 1962); Thomas Nelson & Sons for the Revised Standard Version of the Holy Bible copyright 1946 and 1952 by the Division of Christian Education of the National Council of the Churches of Christ in the U.S.A.; New Directions, Publishers, New York, for *Poems from the "Book of Hours"* by Rainer Maria Rilke, trans. by Babette Deutsch, copyright 1941 by New Directions; Ernst Reinhardt Verlag, Munich, for Ludwig Binswanger, *Grundformen und Erkenntnis menschlichen Daseins,* first published by Max Niehans Verlag, Zurich, 1942; Martinus Nijhoff Boekhandel for Edmund Husserl, *Cartesian Meditations,* copyright 1960; W. W. Norton & Co., Inc. for Rainer Maria Rilke, *Duino Elegies,* copyright 1939, and *Letters to a Young Poet,* rev. ed., copyright 1954; the Open Court Publishing Company, Wilmette, Ill., for Friedrich Schelling, *Of Human Freedom,* copyright 1936; Oxford University Press, London, for Søren Kierkegaard, *Point of View, Etc.,* edited by Dr. Walter Lowrie, 1939; Pantheon Books for Jacques Maritain, *Existence and the Existent,* copyright 1948; *Partisan Review* for José Ortega y Gasset, "In Search of Goethe from Within," in William Phillips and Philip Rahv, eds., *The New Partisan Reader, 1945-1953,* copyright 1953 by Harcourt, Brace & Co.; to Philosophical Library, New York, for Gabriel Marcel, *The Philosophy of Existentialism,* copyright © 1956 by Philosophical Library, for Karl Jaspers, *The Perennial Scope of Philosophy* (London: Routledge & Kegan Paul, 1950); for Jean-Paul Sartre, *Being and Nothingness,* trans. by Hazel E. Barnes, New York, Philosophical Library, 1956, copyright 1956 by Philosophical Library, and for Jean-Paul Sartre, *Existentialism,* copyright 1947 by Philosophical Library; Princeton University Press for Søren Kierkegaard, *The Concept of Dread, Concluding Unscientific Postscript, Fear and Trembling,* and *Sickness unto Death,* copyright 1944, 1941, 1951, and 1954 respectively by Princeton University Press; *The Psychiatric Quarterly* for Silvano Arieti, "The Two Aspects of Schizophrenia," Vol. XXXI (July, 1957); *Psychiatry* for Leslie H. Farber, "The Therapeutic Despair," Vol. XXI, No. I (February, 1958); *Psychologia,* Kyoto University, Dr. Koji Sato, ed., for "Dialogue between Martin Buber and Carl Rogers," Vol. III, No. 4 (December, 1960); Random House, New York, for Fyodor Dostoevsky, "Notes from the Underground" in *The Best Short Stories of Dostoevsky,* Modern Library, for Maurice Friedman, *Problematic Rebel: An Image of Modern Man,* copyright © 1963 by Maurice Friedman, and for Rollo May, "Existential Bases of Psychotherapy" in Rollo May, ed., *Existential Psychology,* copyright © 1961; Henry Regnery Co., Chicago, for the United States rights and Vision Press Ltd., London, for the British Commonwealth rights to Martin Heidegger, *Existence and Being,* 1949; the *Review of Existential Psychology and Psychiatry,* Dr. Adrian van Kaam, editor, for Medard Boss's "Anxiety, Guilt, and Psychotherapeutic Liberation" and the Comments on this paper by Sabert Basesču, Louis de Rosis, and Henry Elkin, Vol. II, No. 3 (September, 1962), for Leslie H. Farber, "Despair and the Life of Suicide," Vol. II, No. 2 (May, 1962), "Schizophrenia and the Mad Psychotherapist," Vol. II, No. 3 (September, 1962), and "Will and Willfulness in Hysteria," Vol. I, No. 3 (November, 1961); for Carl R. Rogers, "The Loneliness of Contemporary Man," Vol. I, No. 2 (May, 1961), and for Paul Tillich, "Existentialism and Psychotherapy," Vol. I, No. 1 (January, 1961); the *Review of*

Metaphysics, Dr. Paul Weiss, ed., for Martin Buber, "What Is Common to All," Vol. XI, No. 3 (March, 1958); Professor Carl R. Rogers, Madison, Wisconsin, for his "The Loneliness of Contemporary Man" and his *On Becoming a Person* (see above under *Review of Existential Psychology and Psychiatry* and Houghton Mifflin Co.); Routledge & Kegan Paul for Martin Buber, *The Way of Man according to the Teachings of Hasidism,* 1950, and for H. A. Hodges, *Wilhelm Dilthey, An Introduction,* 1944; Dr. Guido Schneeberger, Hochfeldstrasse 88, Bern, Switzerland, for Guido Schneeberger, *Nachlese zu Heidegger. Dokumente zu seinem Leben und Denken,* published by Guido Schneeberger, Bern, 1962; Verlag Lambert Schneider, Heidelberg, for Franz Rosenzweig, *Der Stern der Erlösung,* 3rd ed., 1954; Schocken Books, Inc., New York, for Martin Buber, *Tales of the Hasidim,* copyright 1947, 1948 by Schocken Books, Inc., for Nahum N. Glatzer, *Franz Rosenzweig. His Life and Thought,* copyright 1953, 1961 by Schocken Books, for Franz Kafka, *Parables and Paradoxes,* copyright 1946, 1947 by Schocken Books, Inc., for Franz Kafka, *The Great Wall of China,* copyright 1946, 1948 by Schocken Books, Inc., for Franz Kafka, *Dearest Father,* copyright 1954 by Schocken Books, Inc., for Franz Kafka, *Diaries,* copyright 1948, 1949 by Schocken Books, Inc., for Kurt Goldstein, Foreword-1963 to *Human Nature in the Light of Psychopathology,* Schocken Books, Inc., 1963, copyright © 1940, 1963 by the President and Fellows of Harvard College; Charles Scribner's Sons for selections from *I and Thou* by Martin Buber, translated by Ronald Gregor Smith (Copyright © 1958 Charles Scribner's Sons); from *Good and Evil* by Martin Buber, trans. by Michael Hale Bullock (Copyright 1953 Martin Buber); from *Slavery and Freedom* by Nicolas Berdyaev, trans. by R. M. French (Copyright 1944 Charles Scribner's Sons); Springer-Verlag, Berlin, Göttingen, Heidelberg, for Karl Jaspers, *Psychologie der Weltanschauungen,* Berlin, 1931, and his *Philosophie,* Berlin, 1932, Vol. I—*Philosophische Weltorientierung,* Vol. II—*Existenzerhellung,* Vol. III—*Metaphysik;* SCM Press, Ltd., London, for British Commonwealth rights to Karl Jaspers, *Reason and Anti-Reason in Our Time,* 1952; Georg Thieme Verlag, Stuttgart, for Viktor von Weizsäcker, *Der Gestaltkries. Theorie der Einheit von Wahrnehmen und Bewegen,* 4th ed., 1950; The University of Chicago Press for Maurice S. Friedman, *Martin Buber: The Life of Dialogue,* copyright © 1955, 1960 by Maurice S. Friedman, for Paul Tillich, *Systematic Theology,* Vols. I and II, copyright 1951 and © 1957 by the University of Chicago, and for Paul Tillich, *Biblical Religion and the Search for Ultimate Reality,* copyright © 1955 by the University of Chicago; the University of Michigan Press for selections reprinted from Jacob Boehme, *Six Theosophic Points* with an Introductory Essay by Nicolas Berdyaev, copyright © by the University of Michigan 1958; and Yale University Press for selections reprinted from Martin Heidegger, *An Introduction to Metaphysics,* copyright © 1959 by Yale University Press, Inc., for the American rights to Karl Jaspers, *Reason and Anti-Reason in Our Time,* copyright 1952 by Yale University Press, Inc., and for Paul Tillich, *The Courage to Be,* copyright 1952 by Yale University Press.

TABLE OF CONTENTS

Part II: *Phenomenology and Ontology*

Part III: *The Existential Subject*

Part IV: *Intersubjectivity*

Part V: *Atheist, Humanist, and Religious Existentialism*

Part VI: *Existentialism and Psychotherapy*

Part VII: *Issues and Conclusions*

PREFACE

THE AIM of this anthology is to bring out the critical issues that exist among the existentialists in their treatment of such subjects as phenomenology, the existential subject, intersubjectivity, religion, and psychotherapy. In order to accomplish this aim it presents a large number of short selections from the most important existentialist writers and their forerunners. The selections from these authors are subsumed under the themes rather than presented separately by authors. At the same time, the authors within each section are listed separately and the titles of the selections taken from them appear in the Table of Contents. Thus, it is possible for the reader to use this anthology in two ways. First, he can read it through as I have organized it in order to understand the basic issues; but then he may also go back and, using the Table of Contents as a guide, read together the selections from any author who interests him particularly.

This work has been some years in the making and has proved a monumental task. One of the most important aspects was supervising the translation of a good deal of material from the German, all except one item of which had never before been translated. This includes several selections from Martin Heidegger translated by Dr. Edith Kern, who also rendered a new and more satisfactory translation of a selection from Heidegger's "Letter on Humanism"; many selections from Karl Jaspers' *Philosophie* and his *Psychologie der Weltanschauungen,* translated by Marga Franck and Arthur Newton in cooperation with the Jaspers scholar Dr. Eva Reinitz Gossman and myself; translation of Ludwig Binswanger's basic theoretical work *Grundformen und Erkenntnis menschlichen Daseins* by the Binswanger scholar Dr. Jacob Needleman of San Francisco State College; passages from Franz Rosenzweig's central work *Der Stern der Erlösung* by Professor William Hallo of Yale University, who also translated the documents of Heidegger's Nazi periods and selections from important works by the European psychotherapists Hans Trüb, Viktor von Weizsäcker, and Viktor Frankl; passages from Ferdinand Ebner's central work *The Word and The Spiritual Realities,* Martin Buber's "History of the Dialogical Principle," and Hans Trüb's "Individuation" by myself; Ludwig Feuerbach's path-breaking "Basic Principles of the Philosophy of the Future" by Dr. Leonie Sachs of Hunter College; and selections from three of Viktor von Weizsäcker's books by my former student Katherina Englesing von Rhau in cooperation with myself. I have gone over all these translations and take final responsibility for them.

When an author of a collection or anthology is given permission by various publishers or other authors to reprint articles, essays, parts of books, or any material in copyright, the material must be reprinted exactly and without change except for the correction of typographical errors. In the present volume, deletions are indicated by ellipses, insertions are bracketed, and the spelling of the original—whether American or British—is retained. For the sake of clarity and consistency, punctuation has been standardized. Thus, because the material contained in this book was drawn from a wide variety of sources, the reader will be aware of variations in spelling, grammatical usage, and style. Editorial footnotes are numbered consecutively in each of the seven Parts; those notes which appeared in the original editions of the texts used are marked within the articles with asterisks, daggers, etc.

I am particularly grateful to my friend and Sarah Lawrence colleague Dr. Eva Reinitz Gossman for her generous and painstaking help over many weeks in the revision of the Jaspers translations. I must also record my pleasure that my friend and former colleague Dr. William Hallo's translation of passages from Rosenzweig's "Star of Redemption" has had the happy result of our finding in him the translator of Rosenzweig's great work that the Franz Rosenzweig Society has long awaited.* Finally I wish to thank my friend Dr. Rollo May for writing expressly for this anthology the essay, "Some Comments on Existential Psychotherapy."

Rather than give full citations in the text for the sources of the selections, I have given brief titles the complete citations of which can be found in the Bibliography of Selections at the end of the book.

MAURICE FRIEDMAN
Professor of Philosophy
Sarah Lawrence College

Bronxville, New York
November, 1963

* Rosenzweig's *Star of Redemption,* trans. by William Hallo, should appear in 1966 or 1967, published by Holt, Rinehart & Winston.

THE WORLDS OF EXISTENTIALISM

Introduction

"GIVE ME a one-sentence definition of existentialism." This statement is often more a ritual defense against the insecurity aroused by not being *au courant* than a genuine desire for knowledge. It typifies more than any other the phenomenal popularization *and* distortion that the movement called existentialism has undergone since Jean-Paul Sartre's widely publicized visit to the United States in 1946. The very notion that existentialism is something that can be defined in a catch phrase, or that one can merely know *about* it without understanding it from within, has made it, for some people, into an intellectual fad and robbed it of its proper seriousness. Yet existentialism is not merely a fad any more than it is a single, well-defined movement within philosophy. It is a powerful stream, welling up from underground sources, converging and diverging, but flowing forward and carrying with it many of the most important intellectual tendencies and literary and cultural manifestations of our day.

It is time, therefore, that a mature view of existentialism replace the easy definitions and the popular oversimplifications. Such a view can only come from looking at the existentialist writers themselves, understanding them in their uniqueness, their similarities and differences concerning the issues they have in common. This is the purpose of this book. "The *Worlds* of Existentialism" indicates that existentialism is not one world but many; "A *Critical* Reader" indicates that the most pressing need at the moment is for an anthology which will bring out the issues among the existentialists.

"Existentialism" is not a philosophy but a mood embracing a number of disparate philosophies; the differences among them are more basic than the temper which unites them. This temper can best be described as a reaction against the static, the abstract, the purely rational, the merely irrational, in favor of the dynamic and the concrete, personal involvement and "engagement," action, choice, and commitment, the distinction between "authentic" and "inauthentic" existence, and the actual situation of the existential subject as the starting point of thought. Beyond this the so-called existentialists divide according to their views on such matters as phenomenological analysis, the existential subject, the intersubjective relation between selves, religion, and the implications of existentialism for psychotherapy. In addition to these major issues, with which this book shall be concerned, there are a number of other issues that will arise in the course of our readings and which we shall develop in our conclusion—existentialism and social problems, existentialism and sex, the relation between existentialism as philosophy and existentialism as literature, and finally, existentialism as phenomenological analysis of existence *vs.* existentialism as pointing to the concrete.

This last issue serves to illustrate further the difficulties of defining existentialism. The fact is that many existentialist philosophers have proliferated philosophies as abstruse and verbose as any they have attacked. Many of these philosophers are existentialists in the very different senses of analyzing existence according to general existential categories and of pointing to the unique and the concrete in existence which lies beyond all analysis. Recently, I lectured to the John Dewey Philosophy Club of the University of Vermont on "The Existentialism of Martin Buber." At an informal discussion before my lecture, a student said to me, "I know nothing of Martin Buber, and I know nothing of existentialism. But I have an idea that the latter is important for the former. So could you give me a brief definition of existentialism?" "Would it not be better," I replied, "if I told you something directly about Buber instead of offering you a general category from which you deduce something about him?" After a pause I added, "And I have given you a definition of existentialism in what I just said." Insofar as one can define existentialism, it is a movement from the abstract and general to the particular and the concrete. The understanding of a particular existentialist thinker in his particularity would be more important, therefore, than any amount of general definition. Pascal won early fame as a mathematician. But existentialist that he was, he revolted against being understood by means of a category or a classification. " 'Such an one is a good mathematician,' it is said," writes Pascal, referring to himself, and adds, "But I have nothing to do with mathematics, he would take me for a proposition."!

It may surprise some that I refer to Pascal as an existentialist, but the fact is that there is no easy dividing line between the so-called modern existentialists, beginning with Søren Kierkegaard, and their forerunners, going all the way back to the Bible and the Greek philosophers. Existentialism is a direction of movement toward particulars, but it is not and can never be an espousal of the particulars at the expense of all generality and abstraction. Therefore, existentialism is actually a relative thing—a tendency rather than a platform. Compared to Parmenides' insistence on the unchanging one, Plato is an existentialist. Compared to Plato's insistence on the reality of timeless forms or ideas, his disciple Aristotle is an existentialist. Compared with both Plato's and Aristotle's concern with the metaphysical, Socrates' insistence on human life and human values is existentialist. Compared to St Augustine, St. Thomas Aquinas may be seen as existentialist. Compared to the modified "realism" of St. Thomas, the "nominalism" of Duns Scotus may be regarded as existentialist. Yet Jacques Maritain regards St. Thomas himself as an existentialist.

Thus, Part I of *The Worlds of Existentialism* will be devoted to a selection of some of the most important forerunners of modern existentialism, including a number of thinkers who are not properly labelled existentialists but who have marked existentialist strains. Pointing out those strains through the selections we have chosen and our comments on them will be a more useful way of continuing our definition of existentialism than elaborating generalities before looking at any specific writer. This whole book, in fact, is an extended definition of existentialism. Or rather it is a pointing finger which should help the reader recognize the strains of existentialism when he encounters them and at the same time avoid the easy labelling which distorts and oversimplifies. Among the forerunners we have selected, for example, are a number of men who are more properly called mystics than existentialists—Meister Eckhart, Jacob Boehme, the Hasidim, and Dostoevsky—and some, like Nietzsche, who might best be called vitalists. Yet they have often made an important contribution to the converging and diverging stream that has issued into this modern movement, and they bear strong marks in themselves of the tendency toward valuing the particular and concrete.

The list of those who might be considered forerunners of modern existentialism is inexhaustible, especially if one considers the whole range of literature, which has always had a strong tendency toward the particular and the personal. Whitman celebrates a leaf of grass as "no less than the journey-work of the stars." Under the influence of Jacob Boehme, Blake celebrates both reason and energy, the contraries from which arise progression, the unity of body and soul, every bird as "an immense world of delight." His "Auguries of Innocence" are

> To see a world in a grain of sand,
> And a heaven in a wild flower;

Hold infinity in the palm of your hand,
And eternity in an hour.

Similarly, Gerard Manley Hopkins, under the influence of the medieval nominalist Duns Scotus, never tired of celebrating "pied beauty"—"dappled things," "all things counter, original, spare, strange."

Each mortal thing does one thing and the same:
Deals out that being indoors each one dwells;
Selves—goes itself; *myself* it speaks and spells;
Crying *What I do is me: for that I came.*

There is perhaps no more moving existentialist confession in poetry than that of the aging Irish poet, William Butler Yeats, who sees the rich fantasies and occult symbols that filled the poetry of his early and middle period as his "circus animals . . . on shows."

Heart-mysteries there, and yet when all is said
It was the dream itself enchanted me:
Character isolated by a deed
To engross the present and dominate memory.
Players and painted stage took all my love,
And not those things that they were emblems of.

Now that he is old Yeats recognizes, in contrast to Proust, that one cannot live in the ideal world the imagination has created, however beautiful and engrossing it may be. The "pure mind" has its start in "refuse," and in the end one is thrown back from the essential to the existential:

Those masterful images because complete
Grew in pure mind, but out of what began?
A mound of refuse or the sweepings of a street,
Old kettles, old bottles, and a broken can,
Old iron, old bones, old rags, that raving slut
Who keeps the till. Now that my ladder's gone,
I must lie down where all the ladders start,
In the foul rag-and-bone shop of the heart.*

The root of "existentialism" is, of course, "existence." That might seem to include just about everything, and by the same token to say nothing, were it not for the traditions in the history of religion and the history of philosophy which have tended to look away from the "passing flux" of existence to a realm of true

* "The Circus Animals' Desertion" in *The Collected Poems of W. B. Yeats,* Definitive Edition, with the Author's Final Revisions (New York: The Macmillan Co., 1956), p. 335f.

"Being," unchanging and eternal, a world of ideal essences or a formless absolute beyond these essences, in comparison with which the particulars of our earthly life are seen as merely phenomena—the shadows in Plato's cave which at best reflect in wavering and unsteady fashion, and more usually obscure, that essential reality which is not directly accessible to man through "the life of the senses." It is true that "religion has always been existentialist," as Walter Kaufmann puts it, but this is only a half truth and is confusing if taken as a whole one. Religion has never been simply a detached observation of reality for its own sake. Rather it has always been a way of life, a way of man. It has always stood in need, therefore, of existential verification in the lived life of men. On the other hand, through the dual need of expressing religious reality and of handing it down, religion has inevitably produced many manifestations which have led in very opposite directions from man's concrete existence. Religion is neither an objective philosophy nor a subjective experience. It is lived reality which is ontologically prior to its expression in creed, ritual, and group. At the same time, it is inseparable from these expressions and cannot be distilled out and objectified in itself. What begins as a basic attitude or relationship, arising in the encounter with the whole reality directly given to one in one's existence, ever again leads, in the history of religion, to a progressive movement away from the concrete and particular toward the abstract and general—the codification of ritual and moral codes, the conversion of spontaneous hymns into fixed prayers, of dramatic myth into fixed creed and systematic theology. It is understandable, therefore, that the life of every religion depends not only upon its continuation but upon those men within it who will bring it back to the concrete reality from which it began—often through relating to the traditional forms in such a way that they point back to the lived religious life rather than lead away from it, sometimes through breaking through these forms to new central experiences and the new forms that arise from them. In this dialectic those who insist on the incessant return to the lived religious life and on the superior reality of the religious meeting with reality over any formulations concerning the nature of religious reality may properly be called existentialist.

The same holds true in the history of philosophy. It is customary to glimpse the crucial beginning of Western philosophy in the tension between Parmenides' assertion that only the unchanging One is real and Heracleitus' assertion that all is flux. The great accomplishment of Plato lay in combining these two opposites in such a manner as to retain both the One and the Many, the unchanging and the changing. Whatever the variations, all Western philosophy has really proceeded from the problem that Plato set for himself. It is no more possible to have the One without the Many than the Many without the One. In this sense, as we have seen, even what we may recognize as existentialist trends within the history of philosophy are nothing more than matters of emphasis.

This matter of emphasis is by no means an unimportant one, however. Though in Plato's later dialogues he recognizes increasingly the irreducible reality of the many, irrational matter, and necessity (*ananke*), in his best-known dialogues of the middle period, such as the *Republic,* the *Phaedo,* the *Phaedrus,* and even the *Symposium,* existence is seen as an uneasy combination of unchanging ideal forms and the flux of becoming in matter, and the life of man is seen as a progress from the visible and the particular to the invisible and the general, with the final product of the dialectic a more or less mystical direct knowledge of the absolute Good (or Beautiful). Insofar as any philosopher has turned away from the tendency to locate the really real in a separate metaphysical sphere of essences in favor of the greater reality of personal existence in the here and now, he stands for an existentialist trend within the history of philosophy.

If the seventeenth-century thinker Pascal may be called the first truly modern existentialist, it is the nineteenth-century theologian Søren Kierkegaard who stands as the founder of the philosophy of existence proper. This means that modern existentialism must be understood as occupying a very special place in the never-ending dialogue that makes up the history of philosophy. On the one hand, it grows directly out of German idealism—Kant, Fichte, and Hegel—and on the other it is a reaction against this idealism. In particular it is a reaction against the universal historical approach of Hegel, which dominated European thought in the first part of the nineteenth century. Kierkegaard, Feuerbach, and Marx in the nineteenth century, like Franz Rosenzweig in the twentieth, were all Hegelians who rebelled against the master even while standing on the foundation he provided.

One part of this foundation is phenomenology, the attempt to understand not simply through causal formulae and analyses but through openness to the whole range of phenomena that manifest themselves. This is particularly important in the understanding of man. Part II of *The Worlds of Existentialism* will be devoted to the development of phenomenology and its transformation into what Martin Heidegger calls "fundamental ontology" (the study of being) or what Karl Jaspers calls the "encompassing." A second part of this foundation is the emphasis upon the subject. This emphasis goes back not only to the German idealists but to Descartes, who followed his method of universal doubt by the assertion that in his inability to doubt that he doubted he found the one unshakable basis for his existence. Those who see modern existentialism as a continuation of the subjectivity of Descartes are not wrong, but those who see it as a reaction against Descartes are also not wrong. Practically every existentialist philosopher has undertaken a fundamental critique of Descartes' *cogito;* almost all of them have objected to the impoverishment and objectification of subjectivity that has resulted from identifying the "I" with a "thinking thing" rather than with the whole person, seen from within. Thus Kierkegaard's particular revolt against the world-historical system of Hegel and the revolt of all modern existentialists against the Cartesian *cogito* must be seen as an emphasis upon the existential subject in all his wholeness and concreteness—the willing, feeling, thinking person who decides and acts and does so from the limited perspective of his particular life-situation rather than from some universal vantage point provided by reason or history. Part III of *The Worlds of Existentialism* will be devoted to "The Existential Subject."

It is in this emphasis upon the existential subject that the crucial distinction is found between existentialism and the various brands of empiricism, positivism, and instrumentalism that also emphasize the particular, the concrete, and the here and now. For these latter the particular is still seen from without, from the standpoint of the detached observer, rather than from within, from the standpoint of lived life. Nietzsche recognizes that values are relative to land and sea and sky, as does the modern cultural relativist, but Nietzsche knows, as no empiricist or positivist does, that "man is the valuing animal" and that "without valuing the nut of existence is hollow." Nietzsche recognizes that life must be lived from within—from the standpoint of the person or the self. This does not mean introversion or subjectivism, but it does mean that there is a crucial and inescapable distinction between authentic and inauthentic existence. Man's task in life is to authenticate his existence, and to the existentialist this can never mean the mere adherence to external moral codes, on the one hand, or the romantic's deification of passion and feeling, on the other, nor even the vitalist's emphasis on the organic flow of life. Instead it means personal choice, decision, commitment, and ever again that act of valuing in the concrete situation that verifies one's truth by making it real in one's own life—in one's life with man and the world.

Existentialism cannot be limited merely to a reaction against Hegel and the German idealists, for that battle was largely won in the nineteenth century yet existentialism has continued to grow and flower in a large variety of ways in the twentieth. Indeed, what was a few isolated streams in the nineteenth century has become a broad confluence of streams in the twentieth. In part this development must be explained as the result of a general and growing emphasis upon the dynamic, of which evolutionism, vitalism, and pragmatism are also a part. "An invisible current causes modern philosophy to place . . . a certain longing after the restlessness of life . . . above . . . a settling down into easy intelligibility," writes Henri Bergson in *An Introduction to Metaphysics*. "It thus tends . . . to advance in an opposite direction to ancient thought." If Bergson's statement hardly applies to the school of logical analysis which dominates so much of American and British philosophy, it is true of the pragmatism of a William James, modern personalism, and Bergson's own vitalism, as well as of existentialism. In fact, it is difficult to make clear and precise distinctions between these various trends of modern philosophy, even when the difficulty is not further complicated in the case of thinkers like Nietzsche who are both vitalists and existentialists.

In vitalism, however, there is more the sense of flowing with the stream and far less that of the urgency of personal decision, personal authentication of existence, and with it, when necessary, that aloneness that enables one to stand as a genuine person, or "Single One," in the face of the crowd. Similarly, James' pragmatism has less of that sense of tension, crisis, and personal choice, less personal anguish and more "will to believe" than in existentialism. Personalism comes closest of all, and various existentialist thinkers such as Berdyaev and Buber may also be called personalists. However, existentialism tends to ground the person in existence, in his relation to being, or in his relation to other persons in a more thoroughgoing way than personalism in general does.

The existentialists have not been able to follow the basic tenet of philosophical idealism, namely, that reality corresponds to thought, that a clear idea is necessarily a true one. They complain, like Nietzsche's Zarathustra, against those who would make existence "smooth and thinkable." Without being irrationalist, vitalist, or demonic, existentialism has left the door open for the concrete reality which cannot be reduced to human categories of thought, for the "nothing" and the "absurd." "The world is founded upon the absurd," says Ivan Karamazov in Dostoevsky's great novel, and many modern existentialists would come close to admitting this.

Another objection to Descartes' *cogito* is that it begins by assuming the reality of one's own "I" while doubting the reality of all other selves. With the partial exception of Kierkegaard, every modern existentialist has taken exception to this aspect of the *cogito* in favor of the recognition that we live in a world of intersubjectivity. "I challenge you to show me where one personality ends and another begins," wrote Dostoevsky, who also said, "I love, therefore I exist." Even Sartre and Camus, who explicitly accept the *cogito* as the starting-point of philosophy, affirm intersubjectivity. "I rebel, therefore *we* exist," says Camus. At the same time, there is an important difference, as we shall see, between those existentialists who regard the relations between subjects as an additional dimension of the self but see existence primarily in terms of the self and those who see the relations *between* selves as the fundamental reality. Part IV of *The Worlds of Existentialism* will be devoted to the different positions that these thinkers have taken on intersubjectivity.

In the Introductory Essay to his anthology *Existentialism from Dostoevsky to Sartre*, Walter Kaufmann explains his omission of the religious existentialists, such as Berdyaev, Buber, Bultmann, Tillich, and Marcel, first, on the all-too-true ground that "religion has always been existentialist" (which would seem to us more a reason for including them than for excluding them), second, on the palpably false ground that "not one of the later religious existentialists has so far left a mark, like Kierkegaard, on literature or on philosophy," and third, on the rather whimsical note that an anthology "is not a collection of flowers or a meadow on which we pick a blossom here and there" but "an attempt to tell a story and follow a path." "The religious existentialists have not played an important part in our story," * he adds—for the reason, we might note, that he has arbitrarily shaped his story to exclude all of them but Kierkegaard. The fact is that there is no one story to tell, and any attempt to reduce existentialism to a single story is an unwarranted oversimplification of a tremendously complex group of interrelated phenomena.

Today no mature anthology of existentialism can omit the religious existentialists. Not only is Kierkegaard himself a basically religious existentialist, but, for all the fame of Sartre and Heidegger, it is the religious existentialists who make up the large majority of those who are properly considered existentialists. That none of these thinkers have made a philosophical contribution worthy

* New York: Meridian Books, 1956, p. 49f.

of consideration is refuted not only by Kaufmann himself (in the case of Martin Buber) * but by an ever-growing testimony here and abroad to the significance of such thinkers as Buber, Nicolas Berdyaev, Gabriel Marcel, Franz Rosenzweig, Paul Tillich, Jacques Maritain, and Ferdinand Ebner. What is more, the easy contrast between "atheist" and "religious" existentialists breaks down on the careful examination of their thought. What is demanded instead is a progressive shading from anti-theistic humanism to non-theistic humanism to theistic humanism and to theism. Part V of *The Worlds of Existentialism* will be devoted to tracing this gradual shading through sixteen different thinkers. To speak of shadings does not mean that there are no real issues or conflicts here. On the contrary, along with intersubjectivity and possibly phenomenology, the most important issues among the various existentialists arise just here. Since these issues are fundamental to the views of each author, this is all the more reason why an anthology which aims to do justice to the real situation in existentialism today must devote considerable attention to this field.

Psychotherapy is not an issue but a field. At the same time, it represents one of the most exciting and significant applications of existentialism in our time. Through that very unclarity which attends the birth of new movements, existential psychotherapy makes manifest the important issues that are still unresolved among the major existentialist thinkers. Part VI of *The Worlds of Existentialism* will be devoted to a comprehensive (though by no means exhaustive) coverage of the contributions of existentialist philosophers to psychotherapy and the applications by psychotherapists of existentialist philosophies.

In a "Critical Reader" such as this, a Conclusion is necessary in which the issues that arise in each of the Parts be underlined and discussed and in which other, related, issues be posed. The very nature of existentialism makes it impossible to select only systematic philosophers at the expense of the unsystematic. By the same token, it is not possible to restrict existentialism to philosophy alone. A literary writer like Franz Kafka has as much claim to

* In his essay on "Buber's Religious Significance" in *The Philosophy of Martin Buber* volume of *The Library of Living Philosophers*, Kaufmann proceeds to a systematic attack on Kierkegaard, Jaspers, Heidegger, and Sartre—the very figures who occupy the central place in his *Existentialism from Dostoevsky to Sartre*—and finishes with the statement, "In the end one must conclude that there is only one existentialist, and he is no existentialist, he is Martin Buber."! (Paul Arthur Schilpp and Maurice Friedman, editors, *The Philosophy of Martin Buber* [Wilmette, Ill.: The Open Court Publishing Co., 1964].)

being considered an existentialist as any philosopher—not because he reads any existentialist philosophy into his novels and stories, as one sometimes feels that Sartre does, but because he deals with concrete existence itself and arrives at a unique understanding of it. For the same reason, I have included in Part V not only one of the letters of the German poet Rainer Maria Rilke, but also several of his poems. They speak the existential better than any abstract statement of his could possibly do.

The method of this anthology follows from its goal. If Part I deals with Forerunners and Part VI with applications to psychotherapy, Parts II to V (and really Part VI too) are basically concerned with the essential issues between the principal existentialist thinkers. For this reason, I have not organized the chapters according to separate thinkers, as has invariably been the case in all earlier anthologies, but according to these central issues. What is more, it was neither possible nor desirable in most cases to include whole chapters or sections from the works of these thinkers. With a few exceptions, such as Rilke's "Letter to a Young Poet," Marx's "Alienated Labor," and Ortega y Gasset's "In Search of Goethe from Within," the selections for each thinker have been from no one part of a book and usually not even one book. Rather, they represent my choice of the quintessence of each thinker—what is necessary to present his position in its uniqueness, and at the same time show his place in relation to the particular part of this anthology under which the given selection is subsumed. These selections should serve to illuminate the central issues in "the worlds of existentialism."

I have not followed those who wish to reduce existentialism to the hegemony of one thinker, as in particular some of the followers of Heidegger tend to do. "We can only hope to find a path out of the hopelessly tangled growth of contemporary 'existentialist' thought," writes Medard Boss, "if we start again from the clear and unambiguous source of modern 'existentialism,' i.e., from the fundamental insights of Martin Heidegger's 'analysis of Dasein'." * Contemporary existentialist thought is indeed a tangled growth, but dogmatic and one-sided pronouncements such as those of Boss offer us no way out of this situation. Whether we like it or not, existentialism remains a complex converging and diverging of streams. The reader of this anthology will understand how untrue it is to speak of Heidegger or any other one figure, even Kierkegaard, as "the clear and unambiguous source of modern existentialism." Only an approach that is faithful to the actual com-

* Medard Boss, *Psychoanalysis and Daseinsanalysis*, trans. by Ludwig B. Lefebre (New York, London: Basic Books, Inc., 1963), p. 3f.

plexity and that illuminates it can be of any real help in our present situation. For this reason, I have presented insofar as I could, the whole range of existentialist thinkers, whether I happen to agree with them or disagree with them. I do not claim to understand all these thinkers equally well or to be entirely impartial in regard to them. But I believe that I have presented the essential in their thought and the issues between them with sufficient clarity to enable the reader to judge for himself.

An important aspect of this presentation of issues is the inclusion, wherever possible, of the criticisms that one existentialist thinker has made of another, such as the criticisms of Sartre by Heidegger, Buber, Marcel, Maritain, and Berdyaev; Buber's critique of Heidegger and Jaspers; Jaspers' and Tillich's (implicit) and Marcel's (explicit) critique of Buber; Sartre's critique of Heidegger; Heidegger's implicit critique of Jaspers; and José Ortega y Gasset's comparison between Heidegger and himself.

A special problem facing any anthologist who is seriously involved with his subject, is that he has a position of his own and at the same time must properly appreciate and impartially present all positions, those that run counter to his own as well as those he sees as complementary. I have tried to handle this by including some selections from my own writings in three parts of the book while limiting myself in my introductions and conclusion to clarification of the issues that I see. In other words, I see my role as a critical anthologist very much as the college teacher sees his. I hope that just for this reason *The Worlds of Existentialism* will be of value to many teachers and students and, in fact, to anyone who—recognizing that existentialism is more than a fad—is ready to trade in one-sentence definitions for "a critical reader."

Part I

FORERUNNERS

Although we have said that all Western philosophy begins with the problems set by Plato, it is to the pre-Socratic Greek philosopher Heracleitus of Ephesus, who was in his prime about 500 B.C., that we turn as our forerunner among the Greek philosophers. It is no accident that existentialists such as Friedrich Nietzsche, Martin Heidegger, and Martin Buber have turned increasingly to Heracleitus to rediscover what they feel to have been lost in the stream of Greek philosophy since Plato. His sayings about universal flow, the continual newness of all things, real listening and speaking, the dynamism of the "ever-living Fire" of which the universe consists, the harmony of opposites, of the bow and the lyre, the importance of being really awake and present and of following the common, and character as destiny—all have a striking existentialist quality. In a very different tradition—that of the Bible—there are also clear presages of existentialism: from the distinction between authentic and inauthentic existence in Psalm 1, the creation as speech in Psalm 19, and "a heart of wisdom" as the right response to the transiency of life in Psalm 90, to the sacrifice of an upright existence in Micah, the famine for the words of the Lord in Amos, the vanity of the ceaseless round of existence in Ecclesiastes, and the contending of Job—the true existentialist who refuses to give up the facts of his sufferings and innocence or the terrible and unique reality of God in favor of his friends' generalities concerning God's punishment of the wicked and reward of the good. The call for authentic existence which is placed in such ringing tones by the Psalms and repeated, on the social level, by the prophets, is taken up anew in Jesus' "Sermon on the Mount" (Matthew 5-7). Man is the salt of the earth, but if he has lost his savour—his authenticity—then there is nothing that can make up for this loss.

The great German mystic Meister Eckhart (1260-1328) has been called "the father of German idealism," but he might still more validly be called a father of existentialism. His mysticism is of that direct, concrete kind that focuses the attention back on one's personal existence. Rejecting spiritual techniques in favor of shining "with the divine Presence without having to work at it," he emphasizes that personal will—the "aristocrat" within the soul—that enables the One to be born of God "today, within time, in human nature." The need of a beggar is more important than the highest rapture, action from the core of the soul than any "why" which gives reasons for life, the direct knowledge of God—"the greatest self-sharer"—than any knowledge *about* God, the mastery of life than the mastery of books, the body and soul united than the soul alone, the uniqueness of the "I" than any general ideal, the unity of I and Thou than any abstract oneness beyond time and space.

Another great mystic who must also be considered both prototype and source of existentialism is the Lutheran gnostic Jacob Boehme (1575-1624). Like Eckhart, Boehme emphasizes will. As Eckhart speaks of the spark within the soul and the Godhead behind God, so Boehme speaks of the fire of desire and the *Ungrund,* or abyss of nothingness, out of which all being comes. But Boehme, partly under the influence of the medieval Kabbala, is still more dialectical in his attitude toward evil than Eckhart, and this teaching of progression through the energy of contraries has had a strong influence on a vast range of thinkers, including such existentialists as Nietzsche, Dostoevsky, Buber, Heidegger, Berdyaev, and Tillich. Although Boehme also had enormous influence on the German idealists, he is not, as Berdyaev points out, an idealist but a realist. "He has not lost the living touch with real existence; he has not locked himself in the world of abstract thought, apart from being, nor in the world of subjective personal experiences . . . Knowledge is realized in existence itself . . . entirely of experience and of life, born of torments about the fate of man and of the world." Boehme's greatest contribution, according to Berdyaev (who in his own thinking carries this idea further than even Boehme himself) is his conception of freedom as deeper than and prior to all nature.

> Boehme was perhaps the first man in the history of human thought to recognize that the foundations of being, prior to being, are unfathomable freedom, the passionate desire of nothing to become something, the darkness in which fire and light are burning; in other words, he was the founder of an original metaphysical voluntarism that is unknown to medieval and classical thought.[1]

[1] Nicolas Berdyaev, "Unground and Freedom," Introductory Essay to Jacob Boehme, *Six Theosophic Points and Other Writings* (The University of Michigan Press, Ann Arbor Paperbacks, 1958, p. xxf.).

Blaise Pascal (1623-1662) has left us in his famous *Pensées* reflections about the "misery and grandeur of man," who is neither all nor nothing but is a finite middle between the infinitely large and the infinitesimally small—a "thinking reed" who is terrified before the silence of the infinite spaces yet *knows* that he dies as the Universe that crushes him does not. Pascal sees the contradictions of human existence with a clarity that impels us to call him the first modern existentialist. He is at the same time a religious existentialist who rejects the God of the philosophers—the God Descartes "proves"—in favor of the living God—"the God of Abraham, Isaac, and Jacob."

Hasidism, the popular communal mysticism of East European Jewry in the eighteenth and nineteenth centuries, does not stand in the same stream of intellectual influence as the other forerunners we have selected, though it has played a major role in shaping the thought of Martin Buber and through him of other existentialist thinkers. It is, however, a this-worldly mysticism whose concern for "hallowing the everyday,"—for authenticating existence in the here and now—gives the utterances of the Hasidic masters a startlingly modern and strikingly existentialist ring. The Hasidic feeling for the uniqueness of each person, for the importance of the present moment, for serving God with the "evil" urge, for performing outer action with inner intention, gives Hasidism an original strain of existentialism that, through Buber's retelling, still speaks with power to us today.

With Friedrich Schelling (1775-1854) we return to the main stream of Western European thought and with it to that transitional stage that eventually led to a revolt within and against German idealism and produced the first conscious philosophies of existence. Schelling, partly under the influence of Boehme, began the movement beyond German idealism in his "Of Human Freedom" (1809). A still more decisive breakthrough came with his later thought leading to his famous Berlin lectures on "The Philosophy of Revelation." Summarizing this latter development in Schelling's thought the Canadian existentialist philosopher Emil Fackenheim writes:

> The idealist philosopher seeks to absorb in an Absolute not just existence in general, but his own personal existence. . . . Thus the problem has suddenly shifted from a contradiction in ideas to a contradiction in the existence of the philosophizing person. And just as the crisis of thought reveals the limits of an autonomous reason, so the crisis in existence reveals the limits of an autonomous life. . . . If God is radically outside human reason, feeling and will, then He can become accessible only if He reveals Himself. . . .

> The leap merely enables the philosopher to recognize and understand a revelation if it has in fact taken place. . . . If Christianity is a real relation to God, it will also be a true relation, a relation to God as He truly is.[2]

The Philosophy of Revelation, according to Fackenheim, is a metaphysical system whose unity is shattered at crucial points by acts of freedom—by *a posteriori* facts such as that of existence and creation which must be accepted as given without further explanation. Schelling's metaphysical system left no lasting mark, but Kierkegaard, who attended Schelling's Berlin lectures, may have been stirred by them toward his "leap of faith," and Schelling's philosophy of human freedom has strongly influenced the thought of both Tillich and Berdyaev.

The decisive break from German idealism and particularly from that of Hegel comes not only with Kierkegaard but also with two German philosophers who are usually thought of in quite other terms than those of existentialism—Ludwig Feuerbach (1804-72) and Karl Marx (1818-83). Feuerbach is usually classified as a materialist, yet his *Basic Principles of the Philosophy of the Future* (1843) (much of which is presented here for the first time in an English translation) is clearly existentialist in its rejection of the "old philosophy" which sacrificed the true existential subject to abstract, absolute mind and in its presentation of a "new philosophy" based on the concrete existence of the whole body-soul person, the "I" and the other I, the "Thou." If Feuerbach gave a decisive impetus to Marx's dialectical materialism, he also had an important effect on Martin Buber's later formulation of the philosophy of "I and Thou." (One might say that Kierkegaard presented the I-Thou relation with God, Feuerbach with man, and that Buber put the vertical and horizontal together and made them two dimensions of one reality.) Marx himself took from Feuerbach not only the theoretical bases of his socialism but that theme of the alienation of man's freedom and creativity that has occupied so many nineteenth- and twentieth-century thinkers from Nietzsche and Freud to Heidegger and Sartre. Although his remedy points to a new set of abstractions, Marx's analysis of the human condition in "The Alienation of Labor" (1844) is an important document that applies existentialist insights to concrete social problems.

There are a number of existentialist motifs in Herman Melville's great American novel *Moby Dick* (1851) and still more in

[2] Emil L. Fackenheim, "Schelling's Philosophy of Religion," *The University of Toronto Quarterly*, Vol. XXII, No. 1 (October, 1952), Secs. IV & V.

Fyodor Dostoevsky's novels: *Notes from the Underground* (1864), *The Possessed* (1872), and *The Brothers Karamazov* (1880). The awareness of the *Angst* of human existence, its anguish and dread, the recovery of man's alienated freedom, the emphasis upon the particular fact and upon the absurd, and the "man-god's" proclamation of self-will in remarkable anticipation of Nietzsche and Sartre—all justify inclusion of passages from these novels in this section. The inclusion of passages from Friedrich Nietzsche's *Thus Spake Zarathustra* (1883) needs no justification, unless it be an explanation of why (with the exception of the selection in Part V on "Atheist, Humanist, Religious Existentialism,") they are not placed among those of other existentialist philosophers. No one would deny Nietzsche a place as one of the foremost proto-existentialists. His teaching of "will to power," of "the death of God"—the loss of any absolute base for values—of the importance of the self, of man as a valuing animal, of the uniqueness of each man's way—all bring him clearly within our focus. Yet there is too much of the vitalist in Nietzsche to justify classifying him entirely as an existentialist philosopher, as we do Kierkegaard. For a similar reason, we have not placed Dostoevsky among the existentialists proper, as has Walter Kaufmann. Dostoevsky's questions are existential, as Paul Tillich would put it, but his answers are not: they are taken from the realm of orthodoxy, on the one hand, and devotional mysticism, on the other. For all this, both Nietzsche and Dostoevsky stand with Kierkegaard as nineteenth-century giants who deeply influenced twentieth-century existentialism.

Heracleitus of Ephesus[3]

2. Therefore one must follow (the universal Law, namely) that which is common (*to all*). But although the Law is universal, the majority live as if they had understanding peculiar to themselves.
4. If happiness lay in bodily pleasures, we would call oxen happy when they find vetch to eat.
6. The sun is new each day.
8. That which is in opposition is in concert, and from things that differ comes the most beautiful harmony.
18. If one does not hope, one will not find the unhoped-for, since there is no trail leading to it and no path.
19. Men who do not know how to listen or how to speak.
30. This ordered universe (*cosmos*), which is the same for all, was not created by any one of the gods or of mankind, but it was ever and is and shall be ever-living Fire, kindled in measure and quenched in measure.
32. That which alone is wise is one; it is willing and unwilling to be called by the name of Zeus.
34. Not understanding, although they have heard, they are like the deaf. The proverb bears witness to them: 'Present yet absent.'
45. You could not in your going find the ends of the soul, though you travelled the whole way: so deep is its Law (*Logos*).
49. One man to me is (*worth*) ten thousand, if he is the best.
49*a*. In the same river, we both step and do not step, we are and we are not.
51. They do not understand how that which differs with itself is in agreement: harmony consists of opposing tension, like that of the bow and the lyre.
54. The hidden harmony is stronger (*or*, 'better') than the visible.
73. We must not act and speak like men asleep.
75. Those who sleep are workers and share in the activities going on in the universe.

[3] Kathleen Freeman, *Ancilla to the Pre-Socratic Philosophers*, pp. 24-33.

76. Fire lives the death of earth, and air lives the death of fire; water lives the death of air, earth that of water.
85. It is hard to fight against impulse; whatever it wishes, it buys at the expense of the soul.
89. To those who are awake, there is one ordered universe common (*to all*), whereas in sleep each man turns away (*from this world*) to one of his own.
91. It is not possible to step twice into the same river. (*It is impossible to touch the same mortal substance twice, but through the rapidity of change*) they scatter and again combine (*or rather, not even 'again' or 'later', but the combination and separation are simultaneous*) and approach and separate.
93. The lord whose oracle is that at Delphi neither speaks nor conceals, but indicates.
101. I searched into myself.
107. The eyes and ears are bad witnesses for men if they have barbarian souls.
119. Character for man is destiny.
124. The fairest universe is but a dust-heap piled up at random.

The Old Testament[4]

The Psalms

1 Blessed is the man
who walks not in the counsel of the wicked,
nor stands in the way of sinners,
nor sits in the seat of scoffers;
2 but his delight is in the law of the LORD,
and on his law he meditates day and night.
3 He is like a tree
planted by streams of water,
that yields its fruit in its season,
and its leaf does not wither.
In all that he does, he prospers.
4 The wicked are not so,
but are like chaff which the wind drives away.

[4] Revised Standard Version.

[5] Therefore the wicked will not stand in the judgment,
nor sinners in the congregation of the righteous;
[6] for the LORD knows the way of the righteous,
but the way of the wicked will perish.

19 The heavens are telling the glory of God;
and the firmament proclaims his handiwork.
[2] Day to day pours forth speech,
and night to night declares knowledge.
[3] There is no speech, nor are there words;
their voice is not heard;
[4] yet their voice goes out through all the earth,
and their words to the end of the world.

90 [4] For a thousand years in thy sight
are but as yesterday when it is past,
or as a watch in the night.

[5] Thou dost sweep men away; they are like a dream,
like grass which is renewed in the morning:
[6] in the morning it flourishes and is renewed;
in the evening it fades and withers . . .
[9] For all our days pass away under thy wrath,
our years come to an end like a sigh.
[10] The years of our life are threescore and ten,
or even by reason of strength fourscore;
yet their span is but toil and trouble;
they are soon gone, and we fly away . . .
[12] So teach us to number our days
that we may get a heart of wisdom.

Micah

6 [6] "With what shall I come before the Lord
and bow myself before God on high? . . .
[7] Shall I give my first-born for my transgression,
the fruit of my body for the sin of my soul?"
[8] He has showed you, O man, what is good;
and what does the Lord require of you
but to do justice, and to love kindness,
and to walk humbly with your God?

Amos

8 [11] "Behold the days are coming," says the Lord God,
"when I will send a famine on the land;
not a famine of bread, nor a thirst for water,
but of hearing the words of the Lord."

Ecclesiastes or the Preacher

1 2 Vanity of vanities, says the Preacher,
vanity of vanities! All is vanity.
3 What does man gain by all the toil
at which he toils under the sun?
4 A generation goes, and a generation comes,
but the earth remains forever . . .
8 All things are full of weariness;
a man cannot utter it;
the eye is not satisfied with seeing,
nor the ear filled with hearing.
9 What has been is what will be,
and what has been done is what will be done;
and there is nothing new under the sun.

2 11 Then I considered all that my hands had done and the toil I
had spent in doing it, and behold, all was vanity and a striving
after wind, and there was nothing to be gained under the sun . . .
15 Then I said to myself, "What befalls the fool will befall me
also; why then have I been so very wise?" And I said to myself
that this also is vanity. 16 For of the wise man as of the fool there
is no enduring remembrance, seeing that in the days to come all
will have been long forgotten. How the wise man dies just like
the fool! 17 So I hated life, because what is done under the sun
was grievous to me; for all is vanity and a striving after wind.
18 I hated all my toil in which I had toiled under the sun, seeing
that I must leave it to the man who will come after me;
3 For everything there is a season, and a time for every matter
under heaven:

2 a time to be born, and a time to die;
a time to plant, and a time to pluck up what is planted;
3 a time to kill, and a time to heal;
a time to break down, and a time to build up;
4 a time to weep, and a time to laugh;
a time to mourn, and a time to dance;
5 a time to cast away stones, and a time to gather stones together;
a time to embrace, and a time to refrain from embracing;
6 a time to seek, and a time to lose;
a time to keep, and a time to cast away;
7 a time to rend, and a time to sew;
a time to keep silence, and a time to speak;
8 a time to love, and a time to hate;
a time for war, and a time for peace.
9 What gain has the worker from his toil?

12 Remember also your Creator in the days of your youth, before
the evil days come, and the years draw nigh, when you will say,
"I have no pleasure in them"; 2 before the sun and the light, and
the moon, and the stars are darkened and the clouds return after
the rain; 3 in the day when the keepers of the house tremble, and
the strong men are bent, and the grinders cease because they are
few, and those that look through the windows are dimmed, 4 and
the doors on the street are shut; when the sound of the grinding
is low, and one rises up at the voice of a bird, and all the daughters
of song are brought low; 5 they are afraid also of what is high, and
terrors are in the way; the almond tree blossoms, the grasshopper
drags itself along and desire fails; because man goes to his eter-
nal home, and the mourners go about the streets; 6 before the sil-
ver cord is snapped, or the golden bowl is broken, or the pitcher is
broken at the fountain, or the wheel broken at the cistern, and
the dust returns to the earth as it was, and the spirit returns to
God who gave it. Vanity of vanities, says the Preacher; all is van-
ity.

Job

3 20 "Why is light given to him that is in misery,
and life to the bitter in soul,
21 who long for death, but it comes not,
and dig for it more than for hid treasures;
22 who rejoice exceedingly,
and are glad, when they find the grave?
23 Why is light given to a man whose way is hid,
whom God has hedged in?
24 For my sighing comes as my bread,
and my groanings are poured out like water.
25 For the thing that I fear comes upon me,
and what I dread befalls me.
26 I am not at ease, nor am I quiet;
I have no rest; but trouble comes."

7 7 "Remember that my life is a breath;
my eye will never again see good.
8 The eye of him who sees me will behold me no more;
while thy eyes are upon me, I shall be gone.
9 As the cloud fades and vanishes,
so he who goes down to Sheol does not come up;
10 he returns no more to his house,
nor does his place know him any more . . .
17 What is man, that thou dost make so much of him,
and that thou dost set thy mind upon him,

18 dost visit him every morning,
and test him every moment?
21 Why dost thou not pardon my transgression
and take away my iniquity?
For now I shall lie in the earth;
thou wilt seek me, but I shall not be."

13 7 Will you speak falsely for God,
and speak deceitfully for him?
8 Will you show partiality toward him,
will you plead the case for God?
9 Will it be well with you when he searches you out?
Or can you deceive him, as one deceives a man?
10 He will surely rebuke you
if in secret you show partiality.
11 Will not his majesty terrify you,
and the dread of him fall upon you?
12 Your maxims are proverbs of ashes,
your defences are defences of clay . . .
15 Behold, he will slay me; I have no hope;
yet I will defend my ways to his face.

40 6 Then God answered Job out of the whirlwind:
7 "Gird up your loins like a man;
I will question you, and you declare to me.
8 Will you even put me in the wrong?
Will you condemn me that you may be justified?

42 4 "Hear, and I will speak;
I will question you, and you declare to me."
5 I had heard of thee by the hearing of the ear,
but now my eye sees thee . . .

The New Testament

The Gospel According to Matthew

THE SERMON ON THE MOUNT

5 13 "You are the salt of the earth; but if salt has lost its taste, how
shall its saltness be restored?"

6 21 For where your treasure is, there will your heart be also.
22 "The eye is the lamp of the body. So, if your eye is sound,
your whole body will be full of light; 23 but if your eye is not sound,
your whole body will be full of darkness. If then the light in you
is darkness, how great is the darkness!
24 "No one can serve two masters; for either he will hate the one
and love the other, or he will be devoted to the one and despise
the other. You cannot serve God and mammon.
25 "Therefore I tell you, do not be anxious about your life, what
you shall eat or what you shall drink, nor about your body, what
you shall put on. Is not life more than food, and the body more
than clothing? 26 Look at the birds of the air: they neither sow nor
reap nor gather into barns, and yet your heavenly Father feeds
them. Are you not of more value than they? 27 And which of you
by being anxious can add one cubit to his span of life? 28 And
why are you anxious about clothing? Consider the lilies of the
field, how they grow; they neither toil nor spin; 29 yet I tell you,
even Solomon in all his glory was not arrayed like one of these.
30 But if God so clothes the grass of the field, which today is alive
and tomorrow is thrown into the oven, will he not much more
clothe you, O men of little faith? 31 Therefore do not be anxious,
saying, 'What shall we eat?' or 'What shall we drink?' or 'What
shall we wear?' 32 For the Gentiles seek all these things; and your
heavenly Father knows that you need them all. 33 But seek first his
kingdom and his righteousness, and all these things shall be yours
as well.
34 "Therefore do not be anxious about tomorrow, for tomorrow
will be anxious for itself. Let the day's own trouble be sufficient
for the day.
7 16 You will know them by their fruits. Are grapes gathered from
thorns, or figs from thistles? 17 So, every sound tree bears good
fruit, but the bad tree bears evil fruit. 18 A sound tree cannot bear
evil fruit, nor can a bad tree bear good fruit."

Meister Eckhart[5]

Because he has *only* God and thinks only God and everything is nothing but God to him. He discloses God in every act, in every place . . .

One ought to keep hold of God in everything and accustom his mind to retain God always among his feelings, thoughts, and loves. Take care how you think of God. As you think of him in church or closet, think of him everywhere. Take him with you among the crowds and turmoil of the alien world. (8)

Of what does this true possession of God consist, when one really has him? It depends on the heart and an inner, intellectual return to God and not on steady contemplation by a given method. It is impossible to keep such a method in mind, or at least difficult, and even then it is not best. We ought not to have or let ourselves be satisfied with the God we have thought of, for when the thought slips the mind, that God slips with it. What we want is rather the reality of God, exalted far above any human thought or creature. Then God will not vanish unless one turns away from him of his own accord. (9)

So a man should shine with the divine Presence without having to work at it. He should get the essence out of things and let the things themselves alone. That requires at first attentiveness and exact impressions, as with the student and his art. So one must be permeated with divine Presence, informed with the form of beloved God who is within him, so that he may radiate that Presence without working at it. (10)

The impulse to sin is not sin but to consent to sin, to give way to anger, is indeed sin. Surely, if a just person could wish such a thing, he would not wish to be rid of the impulse to sin, for without it he would be uncertain of everything he did, doubtful about what to do, and he would miss the honor and reward of struggle and victory. Because of the impulse to evil and the excitement of it, both virtue and its rewards are in travail born. (12)

Good will is not less powerful for good than bad will is for evil. Be sure of it, that even if I never do evil and yet, if I hold bad will,

[5] A Modern Translation by Raymond B. Blakney.

I shall have sinned just as much as if I had done the deed. With a will that is purely bad, I commit as great sin as if I were to murder all the people in the world, even though I did not lift a finger toward the crime. Why should not the same power reside in good will? It does—and much, incomparably more!

In fact, I may do anything at all with my will. I may bear the burdens of mankind, feed the poor, do the world's work and anything else I please. If I lack the power but not the will to do, then before God I have done it and no one may deny or dispute it for a moment. To will to do something as soon as I may, and to have done it, are the same in God's sight. Furthermore, if I choose that my will shall be a match for the total will of the world, and if my desire is perfect and great, then it shall be so; for what I will have I have. And so, if I really want to love as much as the world has ever loved, and thereby I mean to love God, or what you please, then it is so, when my will is perfect. (13)

. . . If a person were in such a rapturous state as St. Paul once entered, and he knew of a sick man who wanted a cup of soup, it would be far better to withdraw from the rapture for love's sake and serve him who is in need. (14)

So I say that the aristocrat is one who derives his being, his life, and his happiness from God alone, with God and in God and not at all from his knowledge, perception, or love of God, or any such thing. . . . This much is certain: when a man is happy, happy to the core and root of beatitude, he is no longer conscious of himself or anything else. He is conscious only of God.

To be conscious of knowing God is to know *about* God and self. As I have just been explaining, the agent of the soul which enables one to see is one thing and the agent by which one knows that he sees is another. (80)

. . . The same One, who is begotten and born of God the Father, without ceasing in eternity, is born today, within time, in human nature. . . .

. . . This birth is always happening. And yet, if it does not occur in me, how could it help me? Everything depends on that. (95)

Do all you do, acting from the core of your soul, without a single "Why." . . . For, truly, if you imagine that you are going to get more out of God by means of religious offices and devotions, in sweet retreats and solitary orisons, than you might by the fireplace or in the stable, then you might just as well think you could seize God and wrap a mantle around his head and stick him under the table! To seek God by rituals is to get the ritual and lose God in the process, for he hides behind it. On the other hand, to seek God without artifice, is to take him as he is, and so doing, a person "lives by the Son," and is the Life itself.

For if Life were questioned a thousand years and asked: "Why live?" and if there were an answer, it could be no more than this: "I live only to live!" And that is because Life is its own reason for being, springs from its own Source, and goes on and on, without ever asking why—just because it is life. Thus, if you ask a genuine person, that is, one who acts [uncalculatingly] from his heart: "Why are you doing that?"—he will reply in the only possible way: "I do it because I do it!" (127)

I am as sure of this as I am that I am alive: nothing is as near to me as God is. God is nearer to me than I am to myself. My being depends on God's intimate presence . . . Man is not blessed because God is in him and so near that he *has* God—but in that he is aware of how near God is, and knowing God, he loves him. (129)

. . . *"If you want the kernel, you must break the shell."* And therefore, if you want to discover nature's nakedness, you must destroy its symbols and the farther you get in, the nearer you come to its essence. . . .

Many years ago, I did not exist, but shortly thereafter, because of my father and mother who ate bread and meat, and garden vegetables, I became a person. To this end, my parents were not able to contribute much but God made my body without any help and created my soul like that which is supreme. Thus I came to possess life (*possedi me*). (148f.)

If the soul knows God in creatures, night falls. If it sees how they have their being in God, morning breaks. But if it sees the Being that is in God himself alone, it is high noon! See! This is what one ought to desire with mad fervor—that all his life should become Being. . . .

Thus we say that it is good to die in God so that he may give us instead that Being which is better than life, a being in which our life subsists even now. (172)

I say that humanity is just as perfect in the poorest, most despised person as it is in the Pope or the emperor, for humanity is really dearer to me than even the person I am myself. (177)

I have been thinking for some time that the fact that *I am a person* is something others hold in common with myself. That I see and hear and eat and drink—this I have in common with other animals, but the fact that *I am* pertains only to me and not to other men or angels, nor even to God, except as I am one with him. (189)

Ego, the word "I," is proper to no one but God alone in his uniqueness. *Vos* means "you" to the extent that all of you have achieved unity in [God's] uniqueness. Thus, Ego and Vos, I and you-people, together stand for the unity of which I have spoken.

That we may be unique and that our uniqueness may remain, may God help us all! Amen. (191)

Any devotion to any practice that limits your freedom to wait upon God in this present moment and to follow him into the light, by which he may show you what to do and what not to do—how to be as new and free with each moment as if you had never had, or wanted, or could have another—any such commitment or premeditated practice that limits your freedom—I now call "married life." In it, your soul will bring forth no fruit other than the discipline to which you are so anxiously committed and you will trust neither God nor yourself, until you are finished with it. In other words, you will find no peace, for no one can be fruitful until he is done with his own work. I put this down as an interval [of effort] from which the yield is small, because it has to come out of self-designed bondage and not out of freedom. (208)

Some authorities maintain that the soul is in the emotions only but it is not so. Many great scholars make that error. The soul is whole and undivided, at once in the foot and the eye and every other member. Or take a section of time, it may be today or yesterday: the present Now-moment gathers all parts of time up into itself. That present Now in which God created the world is as near to this bit of time as any moment is and the Last Day is as near to it as yesterday . . . He is neither this nor that. As one saint says: "If anyone imagines that he knows God and his knowledge takes form, then he may know something but it is not God!" Thus when I say that God is not being and that he is above being, I have not denied him being but, rather, I have dignified and exalted being in him. . . .

God is the great self-sharer. (219f.)

Meister Eckhart spoke this way: One person who has mastered life is better than a thousand persons who have mastered only the contents of books, but no one can get anything out of life without God. (236)

Meister Eckhart said that no person in this life may reach the point at which he can be excused from outward service. Even if he is given to a life of contemplation, still he cannot refrain from going out and taking an active part in life. (238)

What is truth? Truth is something so noble that if God could turn aside from it, I could keep to the truth and let God go. (240)

I have sometimes said that if a man goes seeking God and, with God, something else, he will not find God; but if one seeks only God—and really so—he will never find only God but along with God himself he will find all that God is capable of. If you seek your own advantage or blessing through God you are not really seeking God at all. Thus Christ says: "True worshipers shall worship the Father"—and that is well said.

If you ask a good man: "Why are you seeking God?"—he will reply: "Just because he *is* God!"

"Why are you seeking truth?"

"Just because it *is* truth!"

"Why are you seeking justice?"

"Just because it is justice!" And such people are quite right. For everything in time has a reason. For example, ask any man: "Why are you eating?" You will get the reply: "For strength." "Why do you sleep?" "For the same reason." And so it is with everything temporal.

If, however, you ask a good man: "Why do you love God?"—you will be answered: "I don't know—because he *is* God!"

"Why do you love truth?"

"For truth's sake."

"Why do you love justice?"

"For the sake of justice!"

"Why do you love goodness?"

"For goodness' sake!"

"And why do you live?"

"On my honor, I don't know—I like to live!" (241f.)

If it is true that God became man, it is also true that man became God . . . and so . . . you haven't got to borrow from God, for he is your own and therefore, whatever you get, you get from yourself. Before God, work that does not come from your [inmost] self is dead. . . . If a man's work is to live, it must come from the depths of him—not from alien sources outside himself—but from within. . . .

When God laughs at the soul and the soul laughs back at God, the persons of the Trinity are begotten. . . .

To get at the core of God at his greatest, one must first get into the core of himself at his least, for no one can know God who has not first known himself. Go to the depths of the soul, the secret place of the Most High, to the roots, to the heights; for all that God can do is focused there. (244-246)

A priest once said to Meister Eckhart: "I wish that your soul were in my body." To which he replied:

"You would really be foolish. That would get nowhere—it would accomplish as little as for your soul to be in my body. No soul can really do anything except through the body to which it is attached." (253)

Nicolas Berdyaev

Unground and Freedom

Boehme's immense importance lies in the fact that he introduced into the concept of God a dynamic principle opposed to the static concept of Greek philosophy and medieval Scholasticism—in other words, he saw in God an internal life, a tragic nature that belongs to all life. This view Boehme owed to the fact that he had, on the one hand, made the Bible his spiritual nourishment and meditated upon it free from the categories of Greek gods; and on the other hand, he had introduced into his contemplation of God the experience of evil in the life of the world: the opposing forces tearing at it, the battle between light and darkness, sweet and bitter, love and anger. Boehme was a new soul, who took his stand face to face with the problem of evil, but who could no longer bow humbly and be satisfied with the knowledge of being a sinner. Daring, he wanted to know the origin and the meaning of evil. To this extent he was a gnostic. He saw a dark principle in all the primary sources of existence, more deeply than he saw existence itself. He was compelled to admit such a principle in Deity itself, and even a positive sense in the very existence of the evil that troubled him so much. (xiif.)

According to Boehme, will—freedom—is the principle of all things. But Boehme holds that the Unground, the unfathomable will, resides in the depths of divinity and before divinity. The Unground is the divinity of apophatic theology, and is at the same time the abyss, the free nothingness which extends below God and beyond God. In God there is nature which is a principle different from Him. The first divinity, divine nothingness, is beyond good and evil, beyond light and darkness. The divine Unground exists in eternity before the birth of the Divine Trinity. God is engendered, is realized out of divine nothingness. This road, plunging into divine wisdom, is akin to that by which Meister Eckhardt distinguished between divinity and God. God as creator of the world and of man is correlative to creation. He surges from the depths of divinity, the inexpressible nothing. Such is the deepest and most secret idea of German mysticism.

Nothingness is deeper than and prior to something. Darkness

(which is not yet evil) is deeper than and prior to light, freedom is deeper than and prior to all nature. (xxf.)

Jacob Boehme

Six Theosophic Points

We have written this work . . . for the image of man, for those who are budding forth out of the animal image with a human image that belongs to God's kingdom, and who would fain live and grow in the human image, in the right man. Those who are often and much hindered by the contrarious life, and thus are involved in the mixed life, and travail in desire for the birth of the holy life: for them are these writings written. (3)

We see and find that every life is essential, and find moreover that it is based on will; for will is the driving of the essences.

It is thus, as if a hidden fire lay in the will, and the will continually uplifting itself towards the fire wished to awaken and kindle it.

For we understand that every will without the awakening of the fiery essences is an impotency, as it were dumb without life, wherein is no feeling, understanding nor substantiality. . . . The eternal Unground out of Nature is a will, like an eye wherein Nature is hidden; like a hidden fire that burns not, which exists and also exists not. . . .

For all is comprised in the will, and is an essence, which, in the eternal Unground, eternally takes its rise in itself, enters into itself, grasps itself in itself, and makes the centre in itself; but with that which is grasped passes out of itself, manifests itself in the brightness of the eye, and thus shines forth out of the essence in itself and from itself. It is its own, and yet also in comparison to Nature is as a nothing (understand, in comparison to palpable being, so to speak); though it is all, and all arises from thence. (5-8)

We now consider Desire, and find that it is a stern attraction, like an eternal elevation or motion. For it draws itself into itself, and makes itself pregnant, so that from the thin freedom where there is nothing a darkness is produced. For the desiring will becomes by the drawing-in thick and full, although there is nothing but darkness. (14)

. . . Anguish is as the centre where life and will eternally take their rise. For the will would be free from the great anguish, and yet cannot. It would flee, and yet is held by the sourness (astringency); and the greater the will for flight becomes, the greater becomes the bitter sting of the essences and plurality. . . .

Now, this other will in the Word of life has freedom in itself; and the anguishful will in the sharpness of Nature desires freedom, that freedom might be revealed in the anguish of the fierce wrathful mind.

Whence then also anguish arises, that the first will wishes to be free from the dark sourness (astringency), and freedom desires manifestation; for it cannot find itself in itself without sharpness or pain. . . .

Thus, the first will (which is called Father, and is itself freedom) desires Nature, and Nature with great longing desires freedom, that it may be released from the torment of anguish. And it receives freedom in its sharp fierceness in the imagination, at which it is terrified as a flash; for it is a terror of joy that it is released from the torment of anguish. (18)

. . . Fire is the life of all the principles,—understand, the cause of life, not the life itself. To the abyss it gives its pang, viz. the sting, so that death finds itself in a life; else the abyss were a stillness. It gives it its fierceness, which is the life, mobility and original condition of the abyss; else there were a still eternity and a nothing.

And to the light-world fire gives also its essence, else there were no feeling nor light therein, and all were only one. And yet beyond fire a Nothing, as an eye of wonders that knew not itself, in which were no understanding; but an eternal hiddenness, where no seeking or doing were possible. (40f.)

We are therefore highly to consider our life, what we would do and be at. We have evil and good in us. The one wherein we draw our will, its essence becomes active in us; and such a property we draw also from without into us. We have the two Mysteries, the divine and the devilish in us, of the two eternal worlds, and also of the outer world. What we make of ourselves, that we are; what we awaken in ourselves, that is moving in us. If we lead ourselves to good, then God's Spirit helps us; but if we lead ourselves to evil, then God's wrath and anger helps us. (87f.)

True Magic is not a being, but the desiring spirit of the being. It is a matrix without substance, but manifests itself in the substantial being.

Magic is spirit, and being is its body; and yet the two are but one, as body and soul is but one person.

Magic is the greatest secrecy, for it is above Nature, and makes Nature after the form of its will. (131)

By Magic is everything accomplished, both good and bad. In that which is good it is good, and in that which is evil it is evil.

It is impossible to express its depth, for it is from eternity a ground and support of all things. (134)

The unground is an eternal nothing, but makes an eternal beginning as a craving. For the nothing is a craving after something. But as there is nothing that can give anything, accordingly the craving itself is the giving of it, which yet also is a nothing, or merely a desirous seeking. And that is the eternal origin of Magic, which makes within itself where there is nothing; which makes something out of nothing, and that in itself only, though this craving is also a nothing, that is, merely a will. It has nothing, and there is nothing that can give it anything; neither has it any place where it can find or repose itself. . . .

. . . The will is a life without origin. The craving is certainly a cause of the will, but without knowledge or understanding. The will is the understanding of the craving.

Thus we give you in brief to consider of nature and the spirit of nature, what there has been from eternity without origin. And we find thus that the will, viz. the spirit, has no place for its rest; but the craving is its own place, and the will is a band to it, and yet is not held in check. . . .

We recognize, therefore, the eternal Will-spirit as God, and the moving life of the craving as Nature. For there is nothing prior, and either is without beginning, and each is a cause of the other, and an eternal bond.

Thus the Will-spirit is an eternal knowing of the unground, and the life of the craving an eternal being [body] of the will. (142-144)

If the natural life had no contrariety, and were without a limit, it would never inquire after its ground from which it arose; and hence the hidden God would remain unknown to the natural life. Moreover, were there no contrariety in life, there would be no sensibility, nor will, nor efficacy therein, also neither understanding nor science. For a thing that has only one will has no divisibility. If it find not a contrary will, which gives occasion to it exercising motion, it stands still. (167)

Blaise Pascal

Pensées

PASCAL'S PROFESSION OF FAITH

This year of Grace 1654,
Monday, November 23rd. . . .
From about half past ten at night, to
about half after midnight,
Fire.
God of Abraham, God of Isaac, God of Jacob,
Not of the philosophers and the wise. (2)

Whoso takes this survey of himself will be terrified at the thought that he is upheld in the material being, given him by nature, between these two abysses of the infinite and nothing, he will tremble at the sight of these marvels. . . .

For after all what is man in nature? A nothing in regard to the infinite, a whole in regard to nothing, a mean between nothing and the whole; infinitely removed from understanding either extreme. The end of things and their beginnings are invincibly hidden from him in impenetrable secrecy, he is equally incapable of seeing the nothing whence he was taken, and the infinite in which he is engulfed.

What shall he do then, but discern somewhat of the middle of things in an eternal despair of knowing either their beginning or their end? . . .

It is strange that they have wished to understand the origin of all that is, and thence to attain to the knowledge of the whole, with a presumption as infinite as their object. For there is no doubt that such a design cannot be formed without presumption or without a capacity as infinite as nature. . . .

Let us then know our limits; we are something, but we are not all. What existence we have conceals from us the knowledge of first principles which spring from the nothing, while the pettiness of that existence hides from us the sight of the infinite. . . .

Restricted in every way, this middle state between two extremes is common to all our weaknesses.

Our senses can perceive no extreme. Too much noise deafens us, excess of light blinds us, too great distance or nearness equally interfere with our vision, prolixity or brevity equally obscure a discourse, too much truth overwhelms us. . . .

In a word, all extremes are for us as though they were not; and we are not, in regard to them: they escape us, or we them.

This is our true state; this is what renders us incapable both of certain knowledge and of absolute ignorance. We sail on a vast expanse, ever uncertain, ever drifting, hurried from one to the other goal. If we think to attach ourselves firmly to any point, it totters and fails us; if we follow, it eludes our grasp, and flies us, vanishing for ever. Nothing stays for us. This is our natural condition, yet always the most contrary to our inclination; we burn with desire to find a steadfast place and an ultimate fixed basis whereon we may build a tower to reach the infinite. But our whole foundation breaks up, and earth opens to the abysses.

We may not then look for certainty or stability. Our reason is always deceived by changing shows, nothing can fix the finite between the two infinites, which at once enclose and fly from it. . . .

Were man to begin with the study of himself, he would see how incapable he is of proceeding further. How can a part know the whole? But he may perhaps aspire to know at least the parts with which he has proportionate relation. But the parts of the world are so linked and related, that I think it impossible to know one without another, or without the whole.

Man, for instance, is related to all that he knows. He needs place wherein to abide, time through which to exist, motion in order to live; he needs constituent elements, warmth and food to nourish him, air to breathe. He sees light, he feels bodies, he contracts an alliance with all that is. . . .

I hold it impossible to know one alone without all the others, that is to say impossible purely and absolutely.

Let us conceive then that this mixture of spirit and clay throws us out of proportion. . . .

Man is to himself the most marvellous object in Nature, for he cannot conceive what matter is, still less what is mind, and less than all how a material body should be united to a mind. This is the crown of all his difficulties, yet it is his very being. (20-26)

When I consider the short duration of my life, swallowed up in the eternity before and after, the small space which I fill, or even can see, engulfed in the infinite immensity of spaces whereof I know nothing, and which know nothing of me, I am terrified, and wonder that I am here rather than there, for there is no reason why here rather than there, or now rather than then. (28)

The nature of man is his whole nature, *omne animal.*

There is nothing we cannot make natural, nothing natural we cannot lose. . . .

It is dangerous to prove to man too plainly how nearly he is on a level with the brutes without showing him his greatness; it is also dangerous to show him his greatness too clearly apart from his vileness. It is still more dangerous to leave him in ignorance of both. But it is of great advantage to show him both. . . .

A thinking reed.—Not from space must I seek my dignity, but from the ruling of my thought. I should have no more if I possessed whole worlds. By space the Universe encompasses and swallows me as an atom, by thought I encompass it.

Man is but a reed, weakest in nature, but a reed which thinks. It needs not that the whole Universe should arm to crush him. A vapour, a drop of water is enough to kill him. But were the Universe to crush him, man would still be more noble than that which has slain him, because he knows that he dies, and that the Universe has the better of him. The Universe knows nothing of this. (46-48)

The Misery of Man.—We care nothing for the present. We anticipate the future as too slow in coming, as if we could make it move faster; or we call back the past, to stop its rapid flight. So imprudent are we that we wander through the times in which we have no part, unthinking of that which alone is ours; so frivolous are we that we dream of the days which are not, and pass by without reflection those which alone exist. For the present generally gives us pain; we conceal it from our sight because it afflicts us, and if it be pleasant we regret to see it vanish away. We endeavour to sustain the present by the future, and think of arranging things not in our power, for a time at which we have no certainty of arriving.

If we examine our thoughts, we shall find them always occupied with the past or the future. We scarcely think of the present, and if we do so, it is only that we may borrow light from it to direct the future. The present is never our end; the past and the present are our means, the future alone is our end. Thus we never live, but hope to live, and while we always lay ourselves out to be happy, it is inevitable that we can never be so. (74)

Man is full of wants, and cares only for those who can satisfy them all. "Such an one is a good mathematician," it is said. But I have nothing to do with mathematics, he would take me for a proposition. . . .

The last act is tragic, how pleasantly soever the play may have run through the others. At the end a little earth is flung on our head, and all is over for ever.

I feel that I might not have been, for the "I" consists in my thought; therefore I, who think, had not been had my mother been killed before I had life. So I am not a necessary being. (76f.)

Men are of necessity so mad, that not to be mad were madness in another form. (79)

Inconstancy.—Things have different qualities, and the soul different inclinations; for nothing is simple which presents itself to the soul, and the soul never presents itself simply to any subject. Hence it comes that men laugh and weep at the same thing. (81)

In one word Self has two qualities, it is unjust in its essence because it makes itself the centre of all, it is inconvenient to others, in that it would bring them into subjection, for each "I" is the enemy, and would fain be the tyrant of all others. . . .

Of Self-love.—The nature of self-love and of this human "I" is to love self only, and consider self only. But what can it do? It cannot prevent the object it loves from being full of faults and miseries; man would fain be great and sees that he is little, would fain be happy, and sees that he is miserable, would fain be perfect, and sees that he is full of imperfections, would fain be the object of the love and esteem of men, and sees that his faults merit only their aversion and contempt. The embarrassment wherein he finds himself produces in him the most unjust and criminal passion imaginable, for he conceives a mortal hatred against that truth which blames him and convinces him of his faults. Desiring to annihilate it, yet unable to destroy it in its essence, he destroys it as much as he can in his own knowledge, and in that of others; that is to say, he devotes all his care to the concealment of his faults, both from others and from himself, and he can neither bear that others should show them to him, nor that they should see them. (86)

The knowledge of God is very far from the love of him. (252)

The heart has its reasons, which reason knows not. (306)

Hasidism

Sayings of Rabbi Nachman of Bratzlav[6]

Prayer

Let everyone cry out to God and lift up his heart to Him, as if he were hanging by a hair and a tempest were raging to the very heart of heaven so that he did not know what to do, and he had almost no more time left to cry out. And in truth there is no counsel and no refuge for him save to remain alone and to lift up his eyes and his heart to God and to cry out to Him. One should do this at all times, for a man is in great danger in the world.

Within and Without

Man is afraid of things that cannot harm him, and he knows it, and he craves things that cannot be of help to him, and he knows it; but in truth the one thing man is afraid of is within himself, and the one thing he craves is within himself.

Thinking and Speaking

All thoughts of man are speaking movement, even when he does not know it.

The Aim of the World

The world was created only for the sake of the choice and the choosing one.

Man, the master of choice, should say: The whole world has been created only for my sake. Therefore, man shall take care at every time and in every place to redeem the world and fill its want.

The Evil Urge

The evil urge is like one who runs about among men, and his hand is closed and no one knows what is in it. And he goes up to each and asks, "What do you suppose I have in my hand?" And each imagines that just what he most desires is in that hand. And everybody runs after it. And then he opens his hand, and it is empty.

One can serve God with the evil urge if one directs his passion

[6] Martin Buber, *The Tales of Rabbi Nachman.*

and his fervor of desiring to God. And without the evil urge there is no perfect service.

Ascent

No limits are set to the ascent of man, and to each the highest stands open. Here your choice alone decides.

Will and Obstacle

There is no obstacle that one cannot overcome, for the obstacle is only there for the sake of the willing, and in reality there are no obstacles save in the spirit.

The Kingdom of God

Those who do not walk in loneliness will be bewildered when the Messiah comes and they are called; but we shall be like a man who has been asleep and whose spirit is tranquil and composed.

The Wandering of the Soul

God never does the same thing twice. (36-40)

The Tales of the Hasidim—

THE EARLY MASTERS[7]

Themselves

The Baal Shem said:

"We say: 'God of Abraham, God of Isaac, and God of Jacob,' and not: 'God of Abraham, Isaac, and Jacob,' for Isaac and Jacob did not base their work on the searching and service of Abraham; they themselves searched for the unity of the Maker and his service." (48)

The Limits of Advice

The disciples of the Baal Shem heard that a certain man had a great reputation for learning. Some of them wanted to go to him and find out what he had to teach. The master gave them permission to go, but first they asked him: "And how shall we be able to tell whether he is a true zaddik?"

The Baal Shem replied. "Ask him to advise you what to do to keep unholy thoughts from disturbing you in your prayers and studies. If he gives you advice, then you will know that he belongs to those who are of no account. For this is the service of men in the world to the very hour of their death; to struggle time after

[7] Martin Buber, *The Tales of the Hasidim. The Early Masters.*

time with the extraneous, and time after time to uplift and fit it into the nature of the Divine Name." (66)

To Say Torah and to Be Torah

Rabbi Leib, son of Sarah, the hidden zaddik who wandered over the earth, following the course of rivers, in order to redeem the souls of the living and the dead, said this: "I did not go to the maggid in order to hear Torah from him, but to see how he unlaces his felt shoes and laces them up again." (107)

Suffering and Prayer

Whenever Rabbi Levi Yitzhak came to that passage in the Haggadah of Passover which deals with the four sons, and in it read about the fourth son, about him who "knows not how to ask," he said: " 'The one who knows not how to ask,' that is myself, Levi Yitzhak of Berditchev. I do not know how to ask you, Lord of the world, and even if I did know, I could not bear to do it. How could I venture to ask you why everything happens as it does, why we are driven from one exile into another, why our foes are allowed to torment us so. But in the Haggadah, the father of him 'who knows not how to ask,' is told: 'It is for you to disclose it to him.' And the Haggadah refers to the Scriptures, in which it is written: 'And thou shalt tell thy son.' And, Lord of the world, am I not your son? I do not beg you to reveal to me the secret of your ways—I could not bear it! But show me one thing; show it to me more clearly and more deeply: show me what this, which is happening at this very moment, means to me, what it demands of me, what you, Lord of the world, are telling me by way of it. Ah, it is not why I suffer, that I wish to know, but only whether I suffer for your sake." (212f.)

The Query of Queries

Before his death, Rabbi Zusya said: "In the coming world, they will not ask me: 'Why were you not Moses?' They will ask me: 'Why were you not Zusya?' " (251)

The Way

Rabbi Baer of Radoshitz once said to his teacher, the rabbi of Lublin: "Show me one general way to the service of God." The zaddik replied: "It is impossible to tell men what way they should take. For one way to serve God is through the teachings, another through prayer, another through fasting, and still another through eating. Everyone should carefully observe what way his heart draws him to, and then choose this way with all his strength." (313)

THE LATER MASTERS[8]

Of Modern Inventions

"You can learn something from everything," the rabbi of Sadagora once said to his hasidim. "Everything can teach us something, and not only everything God has created. What man has made has also something to teach us."

"What can we learn from a train?" one hasid asked dubiously.

"That because of one second one can miss everything."

"And from the telegraph?"

"That every word is counted and charged."

"And the telephone?"

"That what we say here is heard there." (70)

Everyone Has His Place

Rabbi Abraham was asked:

"Our sages say: 'And there is not a thing that has not its place. And so man too has his own place. Then why do people sometimes feel so crowded?" He replied: "Because each wants to occupy the place of the other." (72)

How the Rabbi of Sasov Learned How to Love

Rabbi Moshe Leib told this story:

"How to love men is something I learned from a peasant. He was sitting in an inn along with other peasants, drinking. For a long time he was as silent as all the rest, but when he was moved by the wine, he asked one of the men seated beside him: 'Tell me, do you love me or don't you love me?' The other replied: 'I love you very much.' But the first peasant replied: 'You say that you love me, but you do not know what I need. If you really loved me, you would know.' The other had not a word to say to this, and the peasant who had put the question fell silent again.

"But I understood. To know the needs of men and to bear the burden of their sorrow—that is the true love of men." (86)

An Hour

Rabbi Moshe Leib said:

"A human being who has not a single hour for his own every day is no human being." (92)

The Spoon

Rabbi Elimelekh's servant once forgot a spoon for Rabbi Mendel who was a guest at Rabbi Elimelekh's table. Everyone ate ex-

[8] Martin Buber, *The Tales of the Hasidim. The Later Masters.*

cept Rabbi Mendel. The zaddik observed this and asked: "Why aren't you eating?"
"I have no spoon," said his guest.
"Look," said Rabbi Elimelekh, 'one must know enough to ask for a spoon, and a plate too, if need be!"
Rabbi Mendel took the word of his teacher to heart. From that day on his fortunes were on the mend. (125)

Acceptable Offering

Rabbi Uri said:
"It is written: 'And Abel brought, also he . . .' He brought his own 'he,' his own self. Only when a man offers himself as well, is his offering acceptable." (145)

In His Father's Footsteps

When Rabbi Noah, Rabbi Mordecai's son, assumed the succession after his father's death, his disciples noticed that there were a number of ways in which he conducted himself differently from his father, and asked him about this.
"I do just as my father did," he replied. "He did not imitate, and I do not imitate." (157)

Accepting the World

One of Rabbi Moshe's hasidim was very poor. He complained to the zaddik that his wretched circumstances were an obstacle to learning and praying.
"In this day and age," said Rabbi Moshe, "the greatest devotion, greater than learning and praying, consists in accepting the world exactly as it happens to be." (166)

Most Important

Soon after the death of Rabbi Moshe, Rabbi Mendel of Kotzk asked one of his disciples:
"What was most important to your teacher?"
The disciple thought and then replied:
"Whatever he happened to be doing at the moment." (173)

Give and Take

Rabbi Yitzhak Eisik said:
"The motto of life is 'Give and take.' Everyone must be both a giver and a receiver. He who is not both is as a barren tree." (220)

Two Pockets

Rabbi Bunam said to his disciples:
"Everyone must have two pockets, so that he can reach into the

one or the other, according to his needs. In his right pocket are to be the words: 'For my sake was the world created,' and in his left: 'I am earth and ashes.' " (249f.)

Master and Disciple

Rabbi Hanokh told this story:

"For a whole year I felt a longing to go to my master Rabbi Bunam and talk with him. But every time I entered the house, I felt I wasn't man enough. Once though, when I was walking across a field and weeping, I knew that I must run to the rabbi without delay. He asked: 'Why are you weeping?'

"I answered: 'I am after all alive in this world, a being created with all the senses and all the limbs, but I do not know what it is I was created for and what I am good for in this world.'

" 'Little fool,' he replied, 'that's the same question I have carried around with me all my life. You will come and eat the evening meal with me today.' " (251)

God's Dwelling

"Where is the dwelling of God?"

This was the question with which the rabbi of Kotzk surprised a number of learned men who happened to be visiting him.

They laughed at him: "What a thing to ask! Is not the whole world full of his glory!"

Then he answered his own question:

"God dwells wherever man lets him in." (277)

Holiness

It is written: "And ye shall be holy men unto Me."

The rabbi of Kotzk explained: "Ye shall be holy unto me, but as men, ye shall be humanly holy unto me." (281)

Comparing One to Another

Someone once told Rabbi Mendel that a certain person was greater than another whom he also mentioned by name. Rabbi Mendel replied: "If I am I because I am I, and you are you because you are you, then I am I, and you are you. But if I am I because you are you, and you are you because I am I, then I am not I, and you are not you." (283)

A Vain Search

Rabbi Hanokh told this story:

There was once a man who was very stupid. When he got up in the morning it was so hard for him to find his clothes that at night he almost hesitated to go to bed for thinking of the trouble he would have on waking. One evening he finally made a great effort, took paper and pencil and as he undressed noted down exactly where he put everything he had on. The next morning, very well pleased with himself, he took the slip of paper in hand and read: "cap"—there it was, he set it on his head; "pants"—there they lay, he got into them; and so it went until he was fully dressed.

"That's all very well, but now where am I myself?" he asked in great consternation. "Where in the world am I?" He looked and looked, but it was a vain search; he could not find himself. "And that is how it is with us," said the rabbi. (314)

Friedrich Schelling

Of Human Freedom

Idealism is the soul of philosophy; realism is its body; only the two together constitute a living whole. Realism can never furnish the first principles but it must be the basis and the instrument by which idealism realizes itself and takes on flesh and blood. If a philosophy lacks this vital basis, usually a sign that the ideal principle was but weak from the outset, it then loses itself in those systems whose attenuated concepts of *a-se-ity,* modality, etc., stand in the sharpest contrast to the vital power and fullness of reality. (30f.)

. . . The world as we now behold it, is all rule, order and form; but the unruly lies ever in the depths as though it might again break through, and order and form nowhere appear to have been original, but it seems as though what had initially been unruly had been brought to order. This is the incomprehensible basis of reality in things, the irreducible remainder which cannot be resolved into reason by the greatest exertion but always remains in the depths. Out of this which is unreasonable. reason in the true sense is born. (34)

In man there exists the whole power of the principle of darkness and, in him too, the whole force of light. . . . By reason of the fact that man takes his rise from the depths (that he is a creature) he contains a principle relatively independent of God. But just because this very principle is transfigured in light—without therefore ceasing to be basically dark—something higher, the *spirit,* arises in man. . . . Only in man, then, is the Word completely articulate, which in all other creatures was held back and left unfinished. But in the articulate word the spirit reveals itself, that is God as existing, in act. Now inasmuch as the soul is the living identity of both principles, it is spirit; and spirit is in God. . . . Selfhood, *as such,* is spirit; or man as an egocentric, particularized being (divorced from God) is spirit—the very relation [to God] constitutes personality. But by reason of the fact that selfhood is spirit, it is at the same time raised from the level of the creature to a higher level. It is will beholding itself in complete freedom, no longer the tool of the universal will operating in nature, but above and outside all nature. (38-40)

Creation is not an event but an act. There are no consequences of universal laws; but God, that is God's person, is the universal law, and all that happens because of God's personality—not on account of an abstract necessity, which in action would be unendurable for *us,* let alone for God. (75) . . . All existence must be conditioned in order that it may be actual, that is, personal, existence. God's existence, too, could not be personal if it were not conditioned, except that he has the conditioning factor *within* himself and not outside himself. . . . Man never gains control over the condition even though in evil he strives to do so; it is only loaned to him independent of him; hence his personality and selfhood can never be raised to complete actuality. This is the sadness which adheres to all finite life. . . . Activated selfhood is necessary for life's intensity; without it there would be complete death, goodness slumbering; for where there is no battle there is no life. The will of the depths is therefore only the awakening of life, not evil immediately and for itself. . . . Whoever has no material or force for evil in himself is also impotent for good. (79-81)

The time of merely historical faith is past, as soon as the possibility of immediate knowledge is given. (98)

The Philosophy of Revelation[9]

The philosopher might argue that the God who is mere idea in reason becomes real in feeling. . . . But what if one were to show that this so-called real God is a mere creature of our feeling,

9 From Emil L. Fackenheim, "Schelling's Philosophy of Religion." Selected and translated by Professor Fackenheim.

that every idea has merely psychological significance? (II, 3, 154)

The self might be satisfied with the purely ideal God, if he could remain in the state of contemplation. But this is impossible. The surrender of action cannot be carried out. Action is inevitable. . . . The former despair returns. For the discord is not overcome. (II, 1, 560)

Him he wants, the God who acts . . . who as an existing God can oppose the fact of the fall, the God who is the Lord of being. . . . The self cannot arrogate unto himself the task of finding Him. God Himself must meet him with his aid and succour. But the self may will Him, and hope to gain blessedness by His aid. (II, 1, 566)

The true content of Christianity is a history into which the divine enters. . . . The historical element is not accidental to the doctrine, but the doctrine itself. (II, 3, 195)

Ludwig Feuerbach

Basic Principles of the Philosophy of the Future

1. The task incumbent upon the modern era was the realization and humanization of God—the transformation and resolution of theology into anthropology.
2. The *religious* and *practical* way to achieve this humanization was Protestantism. The God who is Man, the human God: Christ—he alone is the God of Protestantism. Protestantism is no longer concerned—as is Catholicism—with the problem of what God in himself is, but only with *what he is for man.* For this very reason Protestantism no longer has any speculative or contemplative tendencies, as compared with Catholicism. It is no longer *theology,* but in its essence exclusively *christology, i.e., religious anthropology.* (269)
7. . . . Now then, if God is an object of man—which, of course, he necessarily and essentially is—the essence of this object merely expresses man's own essence. In this one object there is no distinction between what the object is *in itself* and what it is *for*

man. . . . Thus the very essence of God is characterized by the fact that he is an object to no other being but man, that he is a specifically human object, a mystery pertaining to man. But if God is exclusively an object to man, what does God's essence reveal to us? Nothing but the essence of man. (274f.)

10. God is pure spirit, pure being, pure act—*Actus purus*—, devoid of passions, independent of outside determining factors, devoid of sensuality, devoid of matter. Speculative philosophy is this *pure spirit,* this *pure act, actualized as an act of thinking—absolute being* (represented) as *absolute thinking.*

As at one time abstraction from everything sensual and material was the requisite condition of theology, it also was the requisite condition of speculative philosophy. . . . (278)

18. . . . Modern philosophy has proven only the *divinity of the mind*—has recognized as the divine, the absolute being, only the mind, specifically the abstract mind. . . . Consequently, the abstract and transcendent essence of God in itself could be realized and resolved *only in an abstract and transcendent manner.* In order to transform God into reason, reason itself had to assume the character of the abstract, divine being.

22. Just as the divine essence is nothing but the essence of man, freed from the restriction by nature, thus the essence of *absolute idealism* is nothing *but the essence of subjective idealism, freed from the—reasonable—restriction by subjectivity, i.e., of sensuality or object character altogether.* (302)

24. *The identity of thinking and being, central point of the philosophy of identity,* is nothing less than a *necessary result* and *development* of the *conception of God* as the being whose concept or essence contains Being . . . a (form of) Being *undifferentiated from thinking,* a Being which is *predicated* or determined only by reason, that is to say, only a *presumed, abstract* Being, in actuality *no* Being at all. Therefore, the identity of thinking and being expresses only the *identity of thinking with itself.* That means: absolute thinking *cannot get away from itself;* it *does not reach being outside of itself.* Although absolute philosophy has transformed for us *the other-worldliness of* theology into a *this-worldliness,* at the same time it has changed for us the *actuality of our real world into a beyond.*

26. A being which only thinks—*thinks in abstract terms*—has no idea of *being, existence, or reality. Being is the boundary of thinking; being as being is not an object for absolute philosophy,* at least *not for abstract absolute philosophy.* (309)

32. That which is real *in its reality* or *as something real* is real *as a sense object,* it is *the sensual. Truth, reality, and sensuality*

are identical. Only a sensual being is a *true,* a *real* being. Only through the *senses* is an *object* perceived *in its true meaning*—not through thinking *per se.* An *object inherent in or identical with thinking is only a thought.*

For an object, a real object, is given to me only in those instances in which I am confronted with a being that affects me, when my individual action—starting from the viewpoint of thinking—meets its limit, an obstacle, in the action of another being. In its origin the object concept is nothing but the conception of *another I*—thus in his childhood man conceives of all things as independent, arbitrary beings—. Therefore the concept of the *object* is altogether conveyed by means of the concept of the *Thou,* the *objective* I. An object, *i.e.,* another I, is presented not to my own I, but to the non-I in me—to use Fichte's terms, because only when I become transformed from an I into a Thou, only when I am acted upon, may there arise in me the conception of an agent existing outside of myself, *i.e.,* an objective one. But only through the senses can the I become a *non-I.* . . . The mystery of interaction is resolved only through sense perception. Only sensual beings can affect each other. I am I—for myself—and at the same time Thou—for something else. But this I am only as a sensual being. Abstract reasoning, however, isolates this being-by-itself, as substance, atom, God. With this it can only *arbitrarily* combine being-for-something-else, because the *prerequisite* of such a combination rests exclusively in sensuality, from which the mind, however, draws its abstractions. (321f.)

33. . . . Only in feeling, only in love, his "*This* (*one*)"—this person, this thing—*i.e.,* the individual, absolute worth, does the *finite* become the *infinite;* this and this alone constitutes the unending depth, divinity, and truth of love. In love alone does the God who counts the hairs on our heads attain truth and reality. The Christian God is in himself only an abstraction drawn of human love, only its image. But just because "This" has its absolute worth only in love, it is to love, alone, and not to abstract thinking, that the mystery of being is revealed. Love is passion, and passion alone is the criterion of existence. Only that IS which is the object of passion, be it an actual or potential one. As only through love, through feeling altogether, can I distinguish between being and non-being, only through love can I perceive an *object* as distinct from myself. (323)

35. If the *old* philosophy stated: that which is *not being thought of, does not exist,* the *new* philosophy, on the other hand, states the following: that which is not loved, that which *cannot be loved, does not exist.* (324)

63. If the *old philosophy* started out from the principle: *I am an*

abstract, exclusively a thinking being, my body is not a part of my essence, the new philosophy, on the other hand, postulates: *I am a real, a sensual being: my body is an integral part of my essence, yea, my body in its totality is my I, my very essence.* (325)

41. Not only *"external"* things are objects of the *senses. Man* is presented to *himself only through sensory perception; he is an object to himself as an object of his senses.* The *identity of subject and object*—which in man's *consciousness* is only an *abstract thought*—has *truth* and *reality* only in the *sensual perception of one person by another.* (329)

44. Time and space are *not mere phenomena*—they are *essential conditions, forms of reasoning power, laws of being, as well as of thinking.* (332)

47. The only means by which opposed or contradictory elements can be *combined* in one single being, in accordance with reality conditions, is—*time.*

50. *That which is real in its actuality and totality*—the *object* of the *new* philosophy—can likewise be the object only of a *real* and *total* being. Therefore, the new philosophy has as its *epistemological principle,* as its *subject, not the I, not the absolute, i.e.,* abstract mind, in short, *not reason in abstracto but rather the real and total being of man. Reality, the subject of reasoning power,* is *man* alone. It is *man* who thinks, not the I, nor reasoning power. The new philosophy bases itself on the *divine character, i.e., truth of the total man* . . . only *the human is true and real;* for the human alone is reasonable; man is the measure of reason.

51. The *identity* of *thinking* and *being* has meaning and truth only if *man* is conceived of as the *ground, the subject of this identity.* Only a *real being* can apprehend *real things;* only when thinking is not the *subject per se* but rather *predicated upon* a *real* being, only then does *thought not become isolated from being.* (339)

55. *Art, religion, philosophy or science* are but manifestations or phenomena of the *true essence of man.*

56. *Absolute philosophy of identity* has *completely upset* the *standpoint of truth.* The *natural perspective* of man, the perspective determined by his *differentiation between I* and *Thou, subject* and *object,* that is the *true and absolute perspective,* consequently also the *perspective of philosophy.*

57. . . . The new philosophy, by positing the essential and supreme object of the heart, *i.e.,* man, likewise as the essential and supreme object of the mind, succeeds in establishing a reasonable unity of head and heart, thinking and living. (344)

58. Truth does not lie in thinking, not in knowledge *per se. Truth is only the sum total of human life and essence.* (344)

59. The individual human being *by himself* does *not* contain the *essence of man within himself, either as a moral or as a thinking being.* The essence of man is contained only in the community, in the *unity of man with his fellow man*—a unity which, however, rests only on the *reality* of the *distinctness of I and Thou.*
60. *Aloneness* means *finitude* and *limitation, community* means *freedom* and *infinity.* Man *by himself* is man (in the usual sense of the word); man *together with* man—the *unity of I and Thou—is God.* (344)
61. In analogy to the *L'état c'est moi* of the absolutist monarch and to the *L'être c'est moi* of the absolutist God, the absolutist philosopher said, or at least thought, of himself—as a thinker, naturally, not as a man—: *la vérité c'est moi.* Instead, the humane philosopher says: *even in thinking, even as a philosopher, I am a man together with other men.* (345)
62. *True* dialectic is *not a monologue carried on by the solitary thinker with himself,* it is a *dialogue between I and Thou.* (345)
63. The *Trinity* was the *supreme mystery,* the *central point* of *absolutist philosophy* and *religion.* But, the mystery of the Trinity . . . is the mystery of *communal and social life*—the mystery of the *need of the I for the Thou*—the truth (of the fact) that no being, whether it be, or be called, man or God or mind or I, is *by itself and alone* a *true* and *pefect,* an *absolute* being; that *truth* and *perfection* are found only in the *community,* in the *union* of kindred beings. Therefore, the supreme and ultimate principle of philosophy is the *union between man and man.* All basic relationships—the fundamentals of the different sciences—are but *different modes and manifestations of this union.* (345)

Karl Marx

Alienated Labor

From political economy itself, in its own words, we have shown that the worker sinks to the level of a commodity, and to a most miserable commodity; that the misery of the worker increases with the power and volume of his production; that the necessary result of competition is the accumulation of capital in a few hands, and thus a restoration of monopoly in a more terrible form; and finally that the distinction between capitalist and landlord, and between agricultural laborer and industrial worker, must disappear and the whole of society divide into the two classes of property *owners* and propertyless *workers*. . . .

Let us not begin our explanation, as does the economist, from a legendary primordial condition. . . .

We shall begin from a *contemporary* economic fact. The worker becomes poorer the more wealth he produces and the more his production increases in power and extent. The worker becomes an ever cheaper commodity the more goods he creates. The *devaluation* of the human world increases in direct relation with the *increase in value* of the world of things. Labor does not only create goods; it also produces itself and the worker as a *commodity,* and indeed in the same proportion as it produces goods.

This fact simply implies that the object produced by labor, its product, now stands opposed to it as an *alien being,* as a *power independent* of the producer. The product of labor is labor which has been embodied in an object and turned into a physical thing; this product is an *objectification* of labor. The performance of work is at the same time its objectification. The performance of work appears in the sphere of political economy as a *vitiation* of the worker, objectification as a *loss* and as *servitude to the object,* and appropriation as *alienation.*

So much does the performance of work appear as vitiation that the worker is vitiated to the point of starvation. So much does objectification appear as loss of the object that the worker is deprived of the most essential things not only of life but also of work. Labor itself becomes an object which he can acquire only by the greatest effort and with unpredictable interruptions. So much does the appropriation of the object appear as alienation that the more objects the worker produces the fewer he can possess and the more he falls under the domination of his product, of capital.

All these consequences follow from the fact that the worker is related to the *product of his labor* as to an *alien* object. For it is clear on this presupposition that the more the worker expends himself in work the more powerful becomes the world of objects which he creates in face of himself, the poorer he becomes in his inner life, and the less he belongs to himself. It is just the same as in religion. The more of himself man attributes to God the less he has left in himself. The worker puts his life into the object, and his life then belongs no longer to himself but to the object. The greater his activity, therefore, the less he possesses. What is embodied in the product of his labor is no longer his own. The greater this product is, therefore, the more he is diminished. The *alienation* of the worker in his product means not only that his labor becomes an object, assumes an *external* existence, but that it exists independently, *outside himself,* and alien to him, and that it stands opposed to him as an autonomous power. The life which he has given to the object sets itself against him as an alien and hostile force. . . .

In both respects, therefore, the worker becomes a slave of the object; first, in that he receives an *object of work,* i.e., receives *work,* and secondly that he receives *means of subsistence.* Thus the object enables him to exist, first as a *worker* and secondly, as a *physical subject.* The culmination of this enslavement is that he can only maintain himself as a *physical subject* so far as he is a *worker,* and that it is only as a *physical subject* that he is a worker.

(The alienation of the worker in his object is expressed as follows in the laws of political economy: the more the worker produces the less he has to consume; the more value he creates the more worthless he becomes; the more refined his product the more crude and misshapen the worker; the more civilized the product the more barbarous the worker; the more powerful the work the more feeble the worker; the more the work manifests intelligence the more the worker declines in intelligence and becomes a slave of nature.) . . .

However, alienation appears not only in the result, but also in the *process,* of *production,* within *productive activity* itself. How could the worker stand in an alien relationship to the product of his activity if he did not alienate himself in the act of production itself? The product is indeed only the *résumé* of activity, of production. Consequently, if the product of labor is alienation, production itself must be active alienation—the alienation of activity and the activity of alienation. The alienation of the object of labor merely summarizes the alienation in the work activity itself.

What constitutes the alienation of labor? First, that the work is *external* to the worker, that it is not part of his nature; and that, consequently, he does not fulfill himself in his work but denies himself, has a feeling of misery rather than well being, does not develop freely his mental and physical energies but is physically exhausted and mentally debased. The worker therefore feels himself at home only during his leisure time, whereas at work he feels homeless. His work is not voluntary but imposed, *forced labor*. It is not the satisfaction of a need, but only a *means* for satisfying other needs. Its alien character is clearly shown by the fact that as soon as there is no physical or other compulsion it is avoided like the plague. External labor, labor in which man alienates himself, is a labor of self-sacrifice, of mortification. Finally, the external character of work for the worker is shown by the fact that it is not his own work but work for someone else, that in work he does not belong to himself but to another person.

Just as in religion the spontaneous activity of human fantasy, of the human brain and heart, reacts independently as an alien activity of gods or devils upon the individual, so the activity of the worker is not his own spontaneous activity. It is another's activity and a loss of his own spontaneity.

We arrive at the result that man (the worker) feels himself to be freely active only in his animal functions—eating, drinking and procreating, or at most also in his dwelling and in personal adornment—while in his human functions he is reduced to an animal. The animal becomes human and the human becomes animal.

Eating, drinking and procreating are of course also genuine human functions. But abstractly considered, apart from the environment of other human activities, and turned into final and sole ends, they are animal functions. . . .

This is the relationship of the worker to his own activity as something alien and not belonging to him, activity as suffering (passivity), strength as powerlessness, creation as emasculation, the *personal* physical and mental energy of the worker, his personal life (for what is life but activity?) as an activity which is directed against himself, independent of him and not belonging to him. This is *self-alienation* as against the above-mentioned alienation of the *thing*. . . .

The universality of man appears in practice in the universality which makes the whole of nature into his inorganic body: (1) as a direct means of life; and equally (2) as the material object and instrument of his life activity. Nature is the *inorganic body* of man; that is to say, nature excluding the human body itself. . . .

Since alienated labor: (1) alienates nature from man; and (2) alienates man from himself, from his own active function, his life activity; so it alienates him from the species. It makes *species life* into a means of individual life. In the first place it alienates species life and individual life, and secondly, it turns the latter, as an abstraction, into the purpose of the former, also in its abstract and alienated form.

For labor, *life activity, productive life*, now appear to man only as *means* for the satisfaction of a need, the need to maintain his physical existence. Productive life is, however, species life. It is life creating life. In the type of life activity resides the whole character of a species, its species-character; and free, conscious activity is the species-character of human beings. Life itself appears only as a *means of life*. . . .

Conscious life activity distinguishes man from the life activity of animals. Only for this reason is he a species-being. Or rather, he is only a self-conscious being, i.e. his own life is an object for him, because he is a species-being. Only for this reason is his activity free activity. Alienated labor reverses the relationship, in that man because he is a self-conscious being makes his life activity, his *being*, only a means for his *existence*. . . .

It is just in his work upon the objective world that man really proves himself as a *species-being*. This production is his active species life. By means of it nature appears as *his* work and his reality. The object of labor is, therefore, the *objectification of man's species life;* for he no longer reproduces himself merely intellectually, as in consciousness, but actively and in a real sense, and he sees his own reflection in a world which he has constructed. While, therefore, alienated labor takes away the object of production from man, it also takes away his *species life*, his real objectivity as a species-being, and changes his advantage over animals into a disadvantage in so far as his inorganic body, nature, is taken from him.

Just as alienated labor transforms free and self-directed activity into a means, so it transforms the species life of man into a means of physical existence.

Consciousness, which man has from his species, is transformed through alienation so that species life becomes only a means for him.

(3) Thus alienated labor turns the *species life of man*, and also nature as his mental species-property, into an *alien* being and into a *means* for his *individual existence*. It alienates from man his own body, external nature, his mental life and his *human* life.

(4) A direct consequence of the alienation of man from the product of his labor, from his life activity and from his species life is that *man* is *alienated* from other *men*. When man confronts himself he also confronts *other* men. What is true of man's relationship to his work, to the product of his work and to himself, is also true of his relationship to other men, to their labor and to the objects of their labor.

In general, the statement that man is alienated from his species life means that each man is alienated from others, and that each of the others is likewise alienated from human life.

Human alienation, and above all the relation of man to himself, is first realized and expressed in the relationship between each man and other men. Thus in the relationship of alienated labor every man regards other men according to the standards and relationships in which he finds himself placed as a worker. . . .

The *alien* being to whom labor and the product of labor belong, to whose service labor is devoted, and to whose enjoyment the product of labor goes, can only be *man* himself. If the product of labor does not belong to the worker, but confronts him as an alien power, this can only be because it belongs to *a man other than the worker*. If his activity is a torment to him it must be a source of enjoyment and pleasure to another. Not the gods, nor nature, but only man himself can be this alien power over men.

Consider the earlier statement that the relation of man to himself is first realized, objectified, through his relation to other men. If therefore he is related to the product of his labor, his objectified labor, as to an *alien*, hostile, powerful and independent object, he is related in such a way that another alien, hostile, powerful and independent man is the lord of this object. If he is related to his own activity as to unfree activity, then he is related to it as activity in the service, and under the domination, coercion and yoke, of another man.

Every self-alienation of man, from himself and from nature, appears in the relation which he postulates between other men and himself and nature. Thus religious self-alienation is necessarily exemplified in the relation between laity and priest, or, since it is here a question of the spiritual world, between the laity and a mediator. In the real world of practice this self-alienation can only be expressed in the real, practical relation of man to his fellow-men. The medium through which alienation occurs is itself a *practical* one. Through alienated labor, therefore, man not only produces his relation to the object and to the process of production as to alien and hostile men; he also produces the relation of other men to his production and his product, and the relation between himself and other men. Just as he creates his own production as a vitiation, a punishment, and his own product as a loss, as a product which does not belong to him, so he creates the domination of the non-producer over production and its product. As he alienates his own activity, so he bestows upon the stranger an activity which is not his own. . . .

Private property is therefore the product, the necessary result, of *alienated labor*, of the external relation of the worker to nature and to himself.

Private property is thus derived from the analysis of the concept of *alienated labor;* that is, alienated man, alienated labor, alienated life, and estranged man.

Only in the final stage of the development of private property is its secret revealed, namely, that it is on one hand the *product* of alienated labor, and on the other hand the *means* by which labor is alienated, the *realization of this alienation.* (93-106)

Herman Melville

Moby Dick

Though in many of its aspects this visible world seems formed in love, the invisible spheres were formed in fright. . . .

Is it that by its indefiniteness it shadows forth the heartless voids and immensities of the universe, and thus stabs us from behind with the thought of annihilation, when beholding the white depths of the milky way? Or is it, that as in essence whiteness is not so much a color as the visible absence of color, and at the same time the concrete of all colors; is it for these reasons that there is such a dumb blankness, full of meaning, in a wide landscape of snows—a colorless, all-color of atheism from which we shrink? . . . Like wilful travellers in Lapland, who refuse to wear colored and coloring glasses upon their eyes, so the wretched infidel gazes himself blind at the monumental white shroud that wraps all the prospect around him. (192)

There, then, he sat, holding up that imbecile candle in the heart of that almighty forlornness. There, then, he sat, the sign and symbol of a man without faith, hopelessly holding up hope in the midst of despair. (223)

As this appalling ocean surrounds the verdant land, so in the soul of man there lies one insular Tahiti, full of peace and joy, but encompassed by all the horrors of the half known life. God keep thee! Push not off from that isle, thou canst never return! (273)

All men live enveloped in whale-lines. All are born with halters round their necks; but it is only when caught in the swift, sudden turn of death, that mortals realize the silent, subtle, ever-present perils of life. And if you be a philosopher, though seated in the whale-boat, you would not at heart feel one whit more of terror, than though seated before your evening fire with a poker, and not a harpoon, by your side. (280)

. . . The awful lonesomeness is intolerable. The intense concentration of self in the middle of such a heartless immensity, my God! who can tell it? (411)

Seat thyself sultanically among the moons of Saturn, and take high abstracted man alone; and he seems a wonder, a grandeur, and a woe. But from the same point, take mankind in mass, and for the most part, they seem a mob of unnecessary duplicates, both contemporary and hereditary. (461)

Fyodor Dostoevsky

Notes from the Underground

But, goodness gracious me, what do I care for the laws of nature and arithmetic if for some reason or other I don't like those laws of twice-two? . . .

As though such a stone wall were really the same thing as peace of mind, and as though it really contained some word of comfort simply because a stone wall is merely the equivalent of twice-two-makes-four. (118)

You, gentlemen, have, so far as I know, drawn up your entire list of positive human values by taking the averages of statistical figures and relying on scientific and economic formulae. (126)

. . . I therefore bluntly declare that all these fine systems, all these theories which try to explain to man all his normal interests so that, in attempting to obtain them by every possible means, he should at once become good and honourable, are in my opinion nothing but mere exercises in logic. (128)

. . . Man has always and everywhere—whoever he may be—preferred to do as he chose, and not in the least as his reason or advantage dictated; and one may choose to do something even if it is against one's own advantage, and sometimes one *positively should* (that is my idea). One's own free and unfettered choice, one's own whims, however wild, one's own fancy, overwrought though it sometimes may be to the point of madness—that is that same most desirable good which we overlooked and which does not fit into any classification, and against which all theories and systems are continually wrecked. . . . All man wants is an absolutely *free* choice, however dear that freedom may cost him and wherever it may lead him to. (131)

But reason is only reason, and it can only satisfy the reasoning ability of man, whereas volition is a manifestation of the whole of life, I mean, of the whole of human life, including reason with all its concomitant head-scratchings. And although our life, thus manifested, very often turns out to be a sorry business, it is life none the less and not merely extractions of square roots. (133)

It is just his fantastic dreams, his most patent absurdities, that he will desire above all else for the sole purpose of proving to himself (as though that were so necessary) that men are still men and not keys of a piano on which the laws of nature are indeed playing any tune they like, but are in danger of going on playing until no one is able to desire anything except a mathematical table. . . . And if he has no other remedy, he will plan destruction and chaos, he will devise all sorts of sufferings, and in the end he will carry his point! . . . The whole meaning of human life can be summed up in the one statement that man only exists for the purpose of proving to himself every minute that he is a man and not an organ-stop! (136)

. . . Twice-two-makes-four is not life, gentlemen. It is the beginning of death. . . . And why are you so firmly, so solemnly, convinced that only the normal and positive, in short, only prosperity, is of benefit to man? . . . Perhaps suffering is just as good for him as prosperity? And man does love suffering very much sometimes. . . .

In the Crystal Palace it is unthinkable: suffering is doubt, it is negation, and what sort of Crystal Palace would it be if one were to have any doubts about it? And yet I am convinced that man will never renounce real suffering, that is to say, destruction and chaos. Suffering! Why, it's the sole cause of consciousness! . . . Yet I know that man loves it and will not exchange it for any satisfaction. Consciousness, for instance, is infinitely superior to twice-two. (139f.)

We have lost touch so much that occasionally we cannot help feeling a sort of disgust with "real life," and that is why we are so angry when people remind us of it. Why, we have gone so far that we look upon "real life" almost as a sort of burden, and we are all agreed that "life" as we find it in books is much better. . . .

We even find it hard to be men, men of *real* flesh and blood, *our own* flesh and blood. We are ashamed of it. We think it a disgrace. And we do our best to be some theoretical "average" men. We are stillborn, and for a long time we have been begotten not by living fathers, and that's just what we seem to like more and more. (239f.)

The Possessed

"If there is no God, then I am God." . . .

"If God exists, all is His will and from His will I cannot escape. If not, it's all my will and I am bound to show self-will." . . .

"Because all will has become mine. Can it be that no one in the whole planet, after making an end of God and believing in his own will, will dare to express his self-will on the most vital point?" . . . "I have no higher idea than disbelief in God. I have all the history of mankind on my side. Man has done nothing but invent God so as to go on living, and not kill himself; that's the whole of universal history up till now. I am the first one in the whole history of mankind who would not invent God." (253f.)

The Brothers Karamazov

. . . The absurd is only too necessary on earth. The world stands on absurdities, and perhaps nothing would have come to pass in it without them. We know what we know! . . . "I want to stick to the fact. I made up my mind long ago not to understand. If I try to understand anything, I shall be false to the fact and I have determined to stick to the fact." . . . Surely I haven't suffered, simply that I, my crimes and my sufferings, may manure the soil of the future harmony for somebody else. I want to see with my own eyes the hind lie down with the lion and the victim rise up and embrace his murderer. I want to be there when every one suddenly understands what it has all been for. . . . It's not worth the tears of that one tortured child who beat itself on the breast with its little fist and prayed in its stinking outhouse, with its unexpiated tears to "dear, kind God"! It's not worth it, because those tears are unatoned for. . . . I don't want harmony. From love for humanity I don't want it. I would rather be left with the unavenged suffering. I would rather remain with my unavenged suffering and unsatisfied indignation, *even if I were wrong*. (299-301)

Friedrich Nietzsche

Thus Spake Zarathustra

I tell you: one must still have chaos in one, to give birth to a dancing star. I tell you: ye have still chaos in you. . . .

Alas! There cometh the time when man will no longer give birth to any star. Alas! There cometh the time of the most despicable man, who can no longer despise himself.

"We have discovered happiness"—say the last men, and blink thereby. . . .

They have left the regions where it is hard to live; for they need warmth. One still loveth one's neighbour and rubbeth against him; for one needeth warmth. . . .

A little poison now and then: that maketh pleasant dreams. And much poison at last for a pleasant death. . . .

No shepherd, and one herd! Everyone wanteth the same; everyone is equal: he who hath other sentiments goeth voluntarily into the madhouse. (11f.)

What is the great dragon which the spirit is no longer inclined to call Lord and God? "Thou-shalt," is the great dragon called. But the spirit of the lion saith, "I will." . . .

All values have already been created, and all created values—do I represent. Verily, there shall be no "I will" any more. Thus speaketh the dragon. . . .

To create new values—that, even the lion cannot yet accomplish: but to create itself freedom for new creating—that can the might of the lion do.

To create itself freedom, and give a holy Nay even unto duty: for that, my brethren, there is need of the lion. . . .

Innocence is the child, and forgetfulness, a new beginning, a game, a self-rolling wheel, a first movement, a holy Yea.

Aye, for the game of creating, my brethren, there is needed a holy Yea unto life: *its own* will, willeth now the spirit; *his own* world winneth the world's outcast. (24f.)

Once on a time, Zarathustra also cast his fancy beyond man, like all backworldsmen. The work of a suffering and tortured God, did the world then seem to me. . . .

Good and evil, and joy and woe, and I and thou—coloured

vapours did they seem to me before creative eyes. The creator wished to look away from himself,—thereupon he created the world. . . .

Ah, ye brethren, that God whom I created was human work and human madness, like all the gods! . . .

Suffering was it, and impotence—that created all backworlds; and the short madness of happiness, which only the greatest sufferer experienceth.

Weariness, which seeketh to get to the ultimate with one leap, with a death-leap; a poor ignorant weariness, unwilling even to will any longer: that created all gods and backworlds. . . .

But that "other world" is well concealed from man, that dehumanised, inhuman world, which is a celestial naught; and the bowels of existence do not speak unto man, except as man. . . .

Yea, this ego, with its contradiction and perplexity, speaketh most uprightly of its being—this creating, willing, evaluing ego, which is the measure and value of things.

And this most upright existence, the ego—it speaketh of the body, and still implieth the body, even when it museth and raveth and fluttereth with broken wings. . . .

A new pride taught me mine ego, and that teach I unto men: no longer to thrust one's head into the sand of celestial things, but to carry it freely, a terrestrial head, which giveth meaning to the earth! (28-30)

Instruments and playthings are sense and spirit: behind them there is still the Self. The Self seeketh with the eyes of the senses, it hearkeneth also with the ears of the spirit. . . .

Behind thy thoughts and feelings, my brother, there is a mighty lord, an unknown sage—it is called Self; it dwelleth in thy body, it is thy body. (33)

No people could live without first valuing; if a people will maintain itself, however, it must not value as its neighbour valueth. . . .

A table of excellencies hangeth over every people. Lo! it is the table of their triumphs; lo! it is the voice of their Will to Power. . . .

Verily, my brother, if thou knewest but a people's need, its land, its sky, and its neighbour, then wouldst thou divine the law of its surmountings, and why it climbeth up that ladder to its hope. . . .

Values did man only assign to things in order to maintain himself—he created only the significance of things, a human significance! Therefore, calleth he himself "man," that is, the valuator.

Valuing is creating: hear it, ye creating ones! Valuation itself is the treasure and jewel of the valued things.

Through valuation only is there value; and without valuation the nut of existence would be hollow. Hear it, ye creating ones!

Change of values—that is, change of the creating ones. Always doth he destroy who hath to be a creator. (60f.)

"Will to Truth" do ye call it, ye wisest ones, that which impelleth you and maketh you ardent?

Will for the thinkableness of all being: thus do *I* call your will!

All being would ye *make* thinkable: for ye doubt with good reason whether it be already thinkable.

But it shall accommodate and bend itself to you! So willeth your will. Smooth shall it become and subject to the spirit, as its mirror and reflection. (122f.)

Ah, that ye would renounce all half-willing, and would decide for idleness as ye decide for action!

Ah, that ye understood my word: "Do ever what ye will—but first be such as *can will.*

Love ever your neighbour as yourselves—but first be such as *love themselves*—(190)

"This—is now *my* way,—where is yours?" Thus did I answer those who asked me "the way." For *the* way—it doth not exist! (217)

What thou doest can no one do to thee again. Lo, there is no requital. (221)

Part II

PHENOMENOLOGY AND ONTOLOGY

ONE OF THE ASPECTS of existentialism that makes it most difficult to characterize it as a single philosophical movement is phenomenology. Phenomenology is one of the streams of influence that has flowed into the thought of a number of important twentieth-century existentialists. Yet the leading phenomenologists were not themselves existentialists, and many existentialists are not, or are only very secondarily, phenomenologists. This makes it impossible to understand existentialism without phenomenology, but equally impossible to understand it by means of phenomenology alone, as some have tried to do.

Although the name of one of Hegel's best-known works is *The Phenomenology of the Mind*, it was Wilhelm Dilthey (1833-1911) who raised phenomenology to a separate method of knowing and a distinct approach to philosophy and the history of culture. Dilthey based his thought on the radical difference between the way of knowing proper to the "*Geisteswissenschaften*"—the human studies such as philosophy, the social sciences, and psychology—and that proper to "*Naturwissenschaften*"—the natural sciences. In the former the knower cannot be merely a detached scientific observer but must also participate himself, for it is through his participation that he discovers both the typical and the unique in the aspects of human life that he is studying. At the same time he must suspend the foregone conclusions and the search for causality that mark the natural scientist in favor of an open attempt to discover what offers itself. If Dilthey is something of a cultural relativist, it is from the standpoint of a broadly humanistic philosophy of life (*Lebensphilosophie*) that is willing to value the unique that reveals itself in every human phenomenon if approached with that openness which he calls "understanding" (*das Verstehen*).

While Dilthey had an important influence on such existentialists as the German philosopher Karl Jaspers (1883-) and the Israeli philosopher Martin Buber (1878-), the latter of whom studied with him, the man who raised phenomenology from an approach to philosophy to a systematic philosophy was the German philosopher Edmund Husserl (1859-1938). In his important mature work *Cartesian Meditations,* Husserl offers us an introduction to phenomenology which begins with Descartes' *cogito* only to go decisively beyond him in the recognition that one cannot divorce the "I think" from that which is thought. By the method of "parenthesizing" or phenomenological reduction, which he calls by the Greek *epoché,* Husserl replaces the detached subject and independent object of older philosophy by a field of knowing in which the phenomena are accented as pure phenomena without questioning their independent existence. From this he also obtains a "transcendental ego" which, as the subject of knowing, transcends all contents of knowing, including the psychophysical ego. The contents of knowing also have a transcendence, i.e., announce themselves as other than the subject, but one less immediately known. The existential status of the world arises "from me as the transcendental Ego," and the exploration of the field of transcendental experience becomes equivalent to the phenomenological knowledge of the world. Husserl also goes beyond Descartes in positing the reality of other I's, known by analogy, and in seeing human culture and society as a world of intersubjectivity within which man lives. For all this, Husserl remains an idealist who, if he does not discover universal ideas, like Plato, or universal orderings of knowledge, like Kant, does attain "eidetic" insight into universal essences in the necessary structure of experience.

It was inevitable that Husserl's existentialist successors should either emphasize the direct experiential quality of his thought as opposed to the idealist, like the French philosopher Maurice Merleau-Ponty (1907-1961), or break with the transcendental ego altogether while retaining the method of phenomenology and the reality of intersubjectivity, like the French philosopher, novelist and playwright Jean-Paul Sartre (1905-), or transform phenomenology from a method of knowledge into a "fundamental ontology," like the German philosopher Martin Heidegger (1889-). Both Sartre and Heidegger accept Husserl's motto "To the things themselves" as an obstacle to any attempt to find Being behind the phenomena. Only an existential analysis of the existent, the "ontic," will yield any knowledge of being. For Heidegger this analysis is posited on his special use of *Dasein*—the person's "being there" in the world, thrown into a situation apart from which neither subject nor consciousness have any meaning. But while Sartre rejects the transcendental ego in favor of an impersonal consciousness which is nothing other than an emptiness or absence in the presence of the solid being of existents, Heidegger moves toward a concept of Being—the "ontological"—that is linked more with person than consciousness—the person who becomes aware of himself as *there*, "thrown" in-the-world.

Karl Jaspers, under the influence of Kant, Kierkegaard, and Dilthey, but independent of Husserl, developed his own phenomenology of "limit situations," which had an important influence on Heidegger in *Being and Time*. Later Jaspers explicitly rejected "ontology"—the study of Being that both Sartre and the early Heidegger see as the proper issue of phenomenology—in favor of "the Encompassing," or "the Comprehensive"—a way of knowing that transcends the subject-object relation even more radically than phenomenology. Martin Buber shows how the phenomenology of Dilthey could lead into the knowing that is central to the "I-Thou" relation—a knowing which because it emphasizes the noncomparable uniqueness of what is known and the over-againstness of man and the world leads Buber to oppose Husserl's phenomenological reduction. Through the late development of his philosophical anthropology—the study of the problem of man—Buber has developed his own ontology of distance and relation which illuminates his insistence that "real living" is found not in the self but in the "between"—in "meeting."

Wilhelm Dilthey

Pattern and Meaning in History

Throughout history a living, active, creative and responsive soul is present at all times and places. . . .

Understanding is the rediscovery of the I in the Thou; the mind rediscovers itself at ever higher levels of connectedness; this sameness of the mind in the I and the Thou and in every subject of a community, in every system of culture and, finally, in the totality of mind and universal history, makes the working together of the different processes in the human studies possible. In these the knowing subject is one with its object, which is the same at all stages of its objectification. (67f.)

If we consider mankind only in terms of perception and knowledge it would be merely a physical fact for us and, as such, could only be explained in terms of the natural sciences. But, insofar as man experiences human states, gives expression to his experience and understands the expressions, mankind becomes the subject of the human studies. The interrelation of life, expression and understanding, embraces gestures, facial expressions and words by which men communicate with each other, permanent mental creations revealing the profundity of the creator to the man who can grasp it, and permanent objectifications of the mind in social structures in which human nature is surely and for ever manifest. . . . Only his actions, his formulated expressions of life and the effects of these on others, teach man about himself. Thus, he comes to know himself only by the circuitous route of understanding. . . . Briefly, it is through the process of understanding that life gains illumination about its depths and yet we understand ourselves and others only by putting what we have actually experienced into every kind of expression of our own and others' lives. So, mankind becomes the subject matter of the human studies only because the relation between experience, expression and understanding exists. (70f.)

Life is the fundamental fact which must form the starting point for philosophy. It is that which is known from within, that behind which we cannot go. Life cannot be brought before the judgement seat of reason. Life seen as a temporal succession of events which affect each other is historical life. It is only possible to grasp it through the reconstruction of the course of events in a memory which reproduces not the particular event but the system of connections and the stages of its development. What memory accomplishes when it surveys the course of a life is achieved in history by linking together the expressions of life which have become part of the objective mind, according to their temporal and dynamic relationships. This is history. . . . (73)

Life and experience of it are the ever freshly flowing sources of the understanding of the social-historical world; starting from life, understanding penetrates into ever new depths; only in reacting on life and society do the human studies achieve their highest significance and this is constantly growing. But the road to such effectiveness must pass through the objectivity of scientific knowledge. . . . We are today filled with the desire to develop this objectivity of the human studies with an open mind, critically and stringently. (81)

Life, from the point of view of value, thus appears as an infinite multiplicity of positive and negative existential values. It is like a chaos of chords and discords. Each is a structure of notes which fills a present but has no musical relation to the others. The category of purpose, or of good, which considers life as directed towards the future, presupposes that of value. The connectedness of life cannot be established from this category either, for the relations of purposes to each other are only those of possibility, choice and subordination. Only the category of meaning goes beyond mere co-existence or subordination of the parts of life. . . . A new aspect of life, conditioned by time but, being something new, transcending it, now becomes apparent. (104f.)

Every expression of life has a meaning insofar as it is a sign which expresses something that is part of life. Life does not mean anything other than itself. There is nothing in it which points to a meaning beyond it. . . .

. . . The concept of meaning arises, first of all, in relation to the process of understanding. It contains the relation of something outward, something given to the senses, to something inward, of which it is the expression. . . . Our understanding of life is only a constant approximation; that life reveals quite different sides to us according to the point of view from which we consider its course in time, is due to the nature of both understanding and life. . . . (107-109) Understanding and interpretation is the method used throughout the human studies and all functions unite in it. It contains all the truths of the human studies. Everywhere understanding opens up a world. . . . On the basis of experience and self-understanding and the constant interaction between them, understanding of other people and their expressions of life is developed. . . .

What is given are always expressions of life; occurring in the world of the senses they are always expressions of a mind which they help us to understand. I include here not only expressions of life which mean or signify something but also those which, without intending to signify anything make the mind of which they are expressions comprehensible to us. (116f.)

From this world of objective mind the self receives sustenance from earliest childhood. It is the medium in which the understanding of other people and their expressions takes place. For everything in which the mind has objectified itself contains something held in common by the I and the Thou. Every square planted with trees, every room in which seats are arranged, is intelligible to us from our infancy because human planning, arranging and valuing—common to us all—have assigned its place to every square and every object in the room. The child grows up within the order and customs of the family which it shares with the other members and its mother's orders are accepted in this context. Before it learns to talk it is already wholly immersed in that common medium. . . . In this objective mind the past is a permanently enduring present for us. Its realm extends from the style of life and the forms of social intercourse, to the system of purposes which society has created for itself, to custom, law, state, religion, art, science and philosophy. . . . The expression of life which the individual grasps is, as a rule, not simply an isolated expression but filled with a knowledge of what is held in common and of a relation to the mental content. (120f.)

. . . We must start from the reality of life; in life all the aspects of the mind are involved. Hegel construed metaphysically, we analyse the given. The contemporary analysis of human existence fills us all with a sense of fragility, of the power of dark instinct, of the suffering from obscurities and illusions, of the finitude of all that is life, even where the highest creations of communal life arise from it. Thus we cannot understand the objective mind through reason but must go back to the structural connections found in living individuals and, by extension, in communities. We cannot place the objective mind into the order of an ideal construction; we must, rather, start with its reality. (125f.)

Selections

Nowhere but in inner experience, in the facts of consciousness, did I find a firm anchorage for my thought, and I venture to believe that no reader will be able to escape the force of my argument on this point. All knowledge is knowledge of experience; but the original unity of all experience and its resulting validity are conditioned by the factors which mould the consciousness within which it arises, i.e., by the whole of our nature. This standpoint, which consistently realizes the impossibility of going behind these conditions, of seeing as it were without an eye or directing the gaze of knowledge behind the eye itself, I call the epistemological standpoint; modern knowledge can recognize no other. But then it further became apparent to me that from this standpoint the independence of the human studies finds a foundation such as the historical school required. For from this standpoint our view of the whole natural world turns out to be a mere shadow cast by a reality hidden from us, while it is only in the facts of consciousness given in inner experience that we possess reality as it is. The analysis of these facts lies at the centre of the human studies, and so, in accord with the standpoint of the historical school, in knowing the principles which govern the world of mind we remain within that world, and the human studies form an independent system by themselves. . . .

In the veins of the knowing subject constructed by Locke, Hume, and Kant runs no real blood, but the diluted fluid of reason in the sense of mere thought-activity. But I was led, by my concern as historian and psychologist with the whole man, to make this whole man, in the full diversity of his powers, this willing, feeling, thinking being, the foundation for explaining even knowledge and its concepts (such as those of the external world, time, substance, cause), however much it may seem that knowledge weaves these its concepts only from the material of perception, imagination, and thought. The method of the following exposition is therefore as follows: I bring every element in our present-day abstract scientific thinking into relation with the whole nature of man as revealed by experience, by linguistic and historical study, and I look for the connections between the one and the other. The result is to show that the most important elements in the way we picture and know reality, such as personal identity, the external world, individuals outside ourselves, their life in time and their interactions—all these can be explained in terms of this whole nature of man, in which volition, feeling, and cognition are only different sides of a single real life-process. It is not by the assumption of rigid *a priori* principles belonging to our cognitive faculty, but only by starting with the totality of our being and tracing the course of its development, that we can answer the questions which we all have to address to philosophy. (112-114)

. . . The individual in the world of mind is an intrinsic value, indeed the only intrinsic value that we can establish beyond doubt. Hence he concerns us not only as a case of human nature in general, but as an individual whole. (120)

It is the same living relationship too, in the first instance, which enables us to amplify tradition and exclude what is not authentic, whatever rational factors may also contribute. . . . Here is the mother earth from which even the most abstract operations in the human studies must continually draw their strength. Understanding here can never be transmuted into rational comprehension. It is vain to wish to make the hero or the genius comprehensible in terms of miscellaneous circumstances. The most proper approach to him is the most subjective. For the highest possibility of grasping what is powerful in him lies in the lived experience of his effects upon ourselves, in the enduring conditions to which our own life is subjected because of him. (129)

But if for these reasons no metaphysic can satisfy the demands for scientific proof, yet philosophy still retains a firm point in the relation between the subject and his world, by virtue of which each attitude of the subject brings to expression one side of the universe. Philosophy cannot comprehend the world in its essence by means of a metaphysical system, and set forth this knowledge in a way that is universally valid; but as in all serious poetry there is disclosed an aspect of life which has not been seen before, as poetry in this way reveals to us the various sides of life in ever new works, as we do not possess a comprehensive view of life in any work of art and yet approximate to it by means of them all: so in the typical outlooks of philosophy we meet a world such as it appears when a powerful philosophical personality makes one of the attitudes to it predominate over the others and subordinates the other categories to the categories native to the one attitude. Thus from all the enormous labour of the metaphysical mind there remains the historical consciousness, which repeats that labour in itself and so experiences in it the inscrutable depths of the world. The last word of the mind which has run through all the outlooks is not the relativity of them all, but the sovereignty of the mind in face of each one of them, and at the same time the positive consciousness of the way in which, in the various attitudes of the mind, the one reality of the world exists for us. (155f.)

Edmund Husserl

Cartesian Meditations

. . . This "phenomenological epoché" and "parenthesizing" of the Objective world . . . does not leave us confronting nothing. On the contrary we gain possession of something by it; and what we (or, to speak more precisely, what I, the one who is meditating) acquire by it is my pure living, with all the pure subjective processes making this up, and everything meant in them, *purely as* meant in them: the universe of "phenomena". . . . The concrete subjective processes, let us repeat, are indeed the things to which his attentive regard is directed: but the attentive Ego, qua philosophizing Ego, practices abstention with respect to what he intuits. Likewise everything *meant* in such accepting or positing processes of consciousness (the meant judgment, theory, value, end, or whatever it is) is still retained completely—but with the acceptance-modification, "mere phenomenon". . . . The world is for me absolutely nothing else but the world existing for and accepted by me in such a conscious *cogito*. . . .

Thus the being of the pure ego and his *cogitationes,* as a being that is prior in itself, is antecedent to the natural being of the world—the world of which I always speak, the one of which I *can* speak. Natural being is a realm whose existential status [*Seinsgeltung*] is secondary; it continually presupposes the realm of transcendental being. The fundamental phenomenological method of transcendental epoché, because it leads back to this realm, is called transcendental-phenomenological reduction. (20f.)

. . . There is no psychological Ego and there are no psychic phenomena in the sense proper to psychology, i.e., as components of psychophysical men. . . . This world, with all its Objects . . . derives its whole sense and its existential status, which it has for me, from me myself, *from me as the transcendental*

Ego, the Ego who comes to the fore only with transcendental-phenomenological epoché. (26)

If the Ego, as naturally immersed in the world, experiencingly and otherwise, is called *"interested" in the world,* then the phenomenologically altered—and, as so altered, continually maintained—attitude consists in a *splitting of the Ego:* in that the phenomenological Ego establishes himself as *"disinterested onlooker,"* above the naïvely interested Ego. That this takes place is then itself accessible by means of a new reflection, which, as transcendental, likewise demands the very same attitude of looking on *"disinterestedly"*—the Ego's sole remaining interest being to see and to describe adequately what he sees, purely as seen, as what is seen and seen in such and such a manner. . . . That signifies restriction to the pure data of transcendental reflection, which therefore must be taken precisely as they are given in simple evidence, purely "intuitively," and always kept free from all interpretations that read into them more than is genuinely seen. . . . Consequently I, the transcendental phenomenologist, have *objects* (singly or in universal complexes) as a theme for my universal descriptions: *solely as the intentional correlates of modes of consciousness of them.* . . . Or, stated more distinctly: I, the meditating phenomenologist, set myself the all-embracing task of *uncovering myself,* in my full concreteness—that is, with all the intentional correlates that are included therein. (35-38)

Consequently the world is a universal problem of egology, as is likewise the whole of conscious life, in its immanent temporality, when we direct our regard to the purely immanent. . . . Any "Objective" object, *any object whatever* (even an immanent one), points to *a structure, within the transcendental ego, that is governed by a rule.* (53)

That the being of the world "transcends" consciousness in this fashion (even with respect to the evidence in which the world presents itself), and that it necessarily remains transcendent, in no wise alters the fact that it is conscious life alone, wherein everything transcendent becomes constituted as something inseparable from consciousness, and which specifically, as world-consciousness, bears within itself inseparably the sense: world—and indeed: "this actually existing" world. (62)

Since, by his *own active generating,* the Ego constitutes himself as *identical substrate of Ego-properties,* he constitutes himself also as a "fixed and abiding" *personal Ego.* . . . Since the monadically concrete ego includes also the whole of actual and potential conscious life, it is clear that the problem of *explicating this monadic ego phenomenologically* (the problem of his constitution for himself) must include *all constitutional problems without exception.* Consequently the phenomenology of this *self-constitution* coincides with *phenomenology as a whole.* (67f.)

Thus removed from all factualness, it has become the pure "*eidos*" perception, whose "*ideal*" extension is made up of all ideally possible perceptions, as purely phantasiable processes. Analyses of perception are then "*essential*" or "*eidetic*" analyses . . . an *intuitive and apodictic consciousness of something universal.* The eidos itself is a beheld or beholdable universal, one that is pure, "unconditioned"—that is to say: according to its own intuitional sense, a universal not conditioned by any fact. It is *prior to all "concepts,"* in the sense of verbal significations; indeed, as pure concepts, these must be made to fit the eidos. . . . Eidetic phenomenology, accordingly, explores the universal Apriori without which neither I nor any transcendental Ego whatever is "imaginable"; or, since every eidetic universality has the value of an unbreakable law, eidetic phenomenology explores the all-embracing laws that prescribe for every factual statement about something transcendental the possible sense (as opposed to the absurdity or inconsistency) of that statement. . . . *Along with phenomenological reduction, eidetic intuition is the fundamental form of all particular transcendental methods.* . . . Both of them determine, through and through, the legitimate sense of a transcendental phenomenology. (70-72)

Every imaginable sense, every imaginable being, whether the latter is called immanent or transcendent, falls within the domain of transcendental subjectivity, as the subjectivity that constitutes sense and being. The attempt to conceive the universe of true being as something lying outside the universe of possible consciousness, possible knowledge, possible evidence, the two being related to one another merely externally by a rigid law, is nonsensical. They belong together essentially; and, as belonging together essentially, they are also concretely one, one in the only absolute concretion: transcendental subjectivity. . . . Genuine theory of knowledge is accordingly possible [*sinnvoll*] only as a transcendental-phenomenological theory, which, instead of operating with inconsistent inferences leading from a supposed immanency to a supposed transcendency (that of no matter what "thing in itself," which is alleged to be essentially unknowable), has to do exclusively with systematic clarification of the knowledge performance, a clarification in which this must become thoroughly understandable as an intentional performance. . . . *The proof of this idealism is therefore phenomenology itself.* (84-86)

First of all, my "transcendental clue" is the experienced Other, given to me in straightforward consciousness and as I immerse myself in examining the noematic-ontic content belonging to him (purely as correlate of my cogito, the particular structure of which is yet to be uncovered). . . . As "psychophysical" Objects, they are *"in" the world.* On the other hand, I experience them at the same time as *subjects for this world,* as experiencing it (this same world that I experience) and, in so doing, experiencing me too, even as I experience the world and others in it. (90f.)

Accordingly *the intrinsically first other* (the first "non-Ego") *is the other Ego.* And the other Ego makes constitutionally possible a new infinite domain of what is "other": an *Objective Nature* and a whole Objective world, to which all other Egos and I myself belong. . . . An *Ego-community,* which includes me, becomes constituted (in my sphere of ownness, naturally) as a community of Egos existing with each other and for each other—*ultimately a community of monads,* which, moreover, (in its communalized intentionality) constitutes the *one identical world. In this world* all Egos again present themselves, but *in an Objectivating apperception* with the sense *"men"* or "psychophysical men as worldly Objects". . . . I can recognize that the Objective world does not, in the proper sense, *transcend* that sphere or that sphere's own intersubjective essence, but rather inheres in it as an "immanent" transcendency. Stated more precisely: The Objective world as an *idea*—the ideal correlate of an intersubjective (intersubjectively communalized) experience, which ideally can be and is carried on as constantly harmonious—is essentially related to intersubjectivity (itself constituted as having the ideality of endless openness), whose component particular subjects are equipped with mutually corresponding and harmonious constitute systems. Consequently, *the constitution of the world essentially involves a "harmony" of the monads.* (107f.)

. . . *Ego* and *alter ego* are always and necessarily given *in an original "pairing".* . . . We find, more particularly, a living mutual awakening and an overlaying of each with the objective sense of the other . . . the limiting case being that of complete "likeness." As the result of this overlaying, there takes place in the paired data a mutual transfer of sense. (112f.)

But, since the other body there enters into a pairing association with my body here and, being given perceptually, becomes the core of an appresentation, the core of my experience of a coexisting ego, that ego, according to the whole sense-giving course of the association, must be appresented *as an ego now coexisting in the mode There,* "such as I should be if I were there." My own ego however, the ego given in constant self-perception, is actual now with the content belonging to his Here. Therefore an ego is *appresented*, as *other* than mine. . . . It is quite comprehensible that, *as a further consequence*, an "empathizing" of definite contents belonging to the *"higher psychic sphere"* arises. Such contents too are indicated somatically and in the conduct of the organism toward the outside world—for example: as the outward conduct of someone who is angry or cheerful, which I easily understand from my own conduct under similar circumstances. (119f.)

. . . Since every pairing association is reciprocal, every such understanding uncovers my own psychic life in its similarity and difference and, by bringing new features into prominence, makes it fruitful for new associations. . . .

The first thing constituted in the form of community, and the *foundation for all other intersubjectively common things*, is the *commonness of Nature*, along with that of the *Other's organism* and *his psychophysical Ego*, as paired with *my own psychophysical Ego*. (120)

If that body functions appresentatively, then, in union with it, the other Ego becomes an object of my consciousness—and primarily the other Ego with his organism, as given to him in the manner of appearance pertaining to his "absolute Here." (121)

The only conceivable manner in which others can have for me the sense and status of existent others, thus and so determined, consists in their being constituted *in me* as others . . . as monads, existing for themselves precisely as I exist for myself, yet existing also in communion, therefore (I emphasize the expression already used earlier) in *connexion with me* qua concrete ego, qua monad. . . . *Something that exists is in intentional communion with something else that exists.* It is an essentially *unique connectedness*, an actual community and precisely the one that makes transcendentally possible the being of a world, a world of men and things. . . . In the sense of *a community of men* and in that of *man*—who, even as solitary, has the sense: member of a community—there is implicit a *mutual being for one another*, which entails an *Objectivating equalization* of my existence with that of all others—consequently: I or anyone else, as a man among other men. If, with my understanding of someone else, I penetrate more deeply into him, into his horizon of ownness, I shall soon run into the fact that just as his animate bodily organism lies in my field of perception, so my animate organism lies in his field of perception and that, in general, he experiences me forthwith as an Other for him, just as I experience him as *my* Other. Likewise I shall find that, in the case of a plurality of Others, they are experienced also by one another as Others, and consequently that I can experience any given Other not only as himself an Other but also as related in turn to *his* Others and perhaps—with a mediatedness that may be conceived as reiterable—related at the same time to me. . . . Openly endless Nature itself then becomes a Nature that includes an open plurality of men (conceived more generally: animalia), distributed one knows not how in infinite space, as subjects of possible intercommunion. To this community there naturally corresponds, in transcendental concreteness, a similarly open community of monads, which we designate as *transcendental intersubjectivity.* We need hardly say that, as existing for me, it is constituted purely within me, the meditating ego, purely by virtue of sources belonging to my intentionality; nevertheless it is constituted thus *as* a community constituted also in every other monad (who, in turn, is constituted with the modification: "other") as the same community—only with a different subjective mode of appearance—and as necessarily bearing within itself the same Objective world. (128-130)

Our monadological results are *metaphysical,* if it be true that ultimate cognitions of being should be called metaphysical. On the other hand, what we have here is *anything but metaphysics in the customary sense:* a historically degenerate metaphysics, which by no means conforms to the sense with which metaphysics, as "first philosophy," was instituted originally. Phenomenology's purely intuitive, concrete, and also apodictic mode of demonstration excludes all "metaphysical adventure," all speculative excesses. (139)

For the first time, the problem of empathy has been given its true sense, and the true method for its solution has been furnished, by constitutional phenomenology. . . . It has never been recognized that the otherness of "someone else" becomes extended to the whole world, as its "Objectivity," giving it this sense in the first place. (147)

I must first explicate *my own as such, in order to understand that, within my own, what is not my own likewise receives existential sense*—and does so as something appresented analogically. . . . The *illusion* of a solipsism is dissolved, *even though* the proposition that everything existing for me must derive its existential sense exclusively from me myself, from my sphere of consciousness, retains its validity and fundamental importance. . . . *Monadology* . . . draws its content purely from phenomenological explication of the transcendental experience laid open by transcendental reduction, accordingly from the most originary evidence, wherein all conceivable evidences must be grounded.

. . . Phenomenological explication does nothing but *explicate the sense this world has for us all, prior to any philosophizing,* and obviously gets solely from our experience—*a sense which philosophy can uncover but never alter.* (150f.)

Science—as a system of *phenomenological* disciplines, which treat correlative themes and are ultimately grounded, not on an axiom, ego cogito, but on an *all-embracing self-investigation.* . . . Philosophical knowledge . . . is necessarily the path of universal self-knowledge—first of all monadic, and then intermonadic. . . . Positive science is a science lost in the world. I must lose the world by epoché, in order to regain it by a universal self-examination. (156f.)

Maurice Merleau-Ponty

What Is Phenomenology?

Phenomenology is the study of essences and accordingly its treatment of every problem is an attempt to define an essence, the essence of perception, or the essence of consciousness, for example. But phenomenology is also a philosophy which replaces essences in existence, and does not believe that man and the world can be understood save on the basis of their state of fact. It is a transcendental philosophy which suspends our spontaneous natural affirmations in order to understand them, but it is also a philosophy for which the world is always "already there" as an inalienable presence which precedes reflection. The whole effort of phenomenology is to recover this naive contact with the world and to give it, at last, a philosophical status. It is a philosophy intent upon being an "exact science," but it is also an account of space, time, and the world "as lived." . . .

It is a question of description, and not of explanation or analysis. That first command which Husserl gave to the new phenomenology, that it be a "descriptive psychology" or that it return "to the things themselves" is above all a disavowal of science. I am not the result of the intersection of a multiplicity of causal influences which determine my body and my "psychism." I cannot think of myself as a part of the world, the simple object of biology, psychology and sociology, nor can I shut myself out of the universe of science. Everything that I know of the world, even through science, I know on the basis of a view which is my own, or an experience of the world without which the symbols of science would be meaningless. The entire universe of science is constructed upon the world as lived, and if we wish to think about science itself rigorously, appreciating its meaning and scope exactly, we must first of all reawaken that experience of the world of which science is an inferior expression. Science has not and will never have the same sense of being that the world as perceived has, for the simple reason that it is a determination or explanation of that world.

I am not a "living being" or even a "man" or even a "consciousness" with all the characteristics which zoology, social anatomy or inductive psychology attributes to these products of nature or history. I am the absolute source. My existence does not come from my antecedents or my physical and social entourage, but rather goes toward them and sustains them. For it is I that make exist for myself (and hence "be" in the only sense that the word can have for me) that tradition which I chose to adopt or that horizon whose distance from me tends to disappear, since it would have no such property as distance were I not there to view it. Scientific views according to which I am an event in the world are always naive and hypocritical because, without mentioning the fact, they sustain themselves on that other view, that consciousness by which, initially, a world is disposed around me and begins to exist for me. To turn back to the things themselves is to return to that world prior to knowledge of which knowledge speaks, and with regard to which every scientific determination is abstractive, dependent and a sign; it is like the relationship of geography to the countryside where we first learned what a forest, a prairie or a river was. This movement is absolutely distinct from the idealist turning upon consciousness, and the demands of pure description exclude both the procedure of reflective analysis and that of scientific explanation. . . .

Perception is not a science of the world, nor even an act, a deliberate taking up of a position. It is the basis from which every act issues and it is presupposed by them. The world is not an object the law of whose constitution I possess. It is the natural milieu and the field of all my thoughts and of all my explicit perceptions. Truth does not "dwell" only in the "interior man" for there is no interior man. Man is before himself in the world and it is in the world that he knows himself. . . .

If the other person is in his own right, and not merely for me, and if we are for each other, and are not merely one and another for God, we must appear to one another. He must have an exterior and so must I. Beyond the *Pour Soi* perspective—my view of myself and his view of himself—there must be a *Pour Autrui* perspective—my view of him and his view of me. . . . I must be my exterior and he his body. This paradox and the dialectic of the Ego and the Alter-Ego are only possible if each is defined by his situation and not freed of all inherence. They are only possible if philosophy does not attain its completion in the return to the self, and if I discover by reflection not only my presence to myself but also . . . an internal weakness which prevents me from being absolutely individual, exposing me to the regard of others as a man among men or at least a consciousness among consciousnesses. . . .

The world that I distinguished from myself as a sum of things or of causally connected processes is re-discovered "in me" as the permanent horizon of all my thinking and as a dimension in relation to which I never cease to situate myself. The genuine Cogito does not define the existence of the subject by the thought that it has of existing. It does not convert the certitude of the world into certitude of the world as thought, nor does it replace the world by the signification world. On the contrary it recognizes my thought as an inalienable fact and it eliminates every type of idealism in discovering me as presence to a world. . . .

Here, reflection does not retreat from the world toward the unity of a consciousness upon which the world is founded. It withdraws in order to see the transcendences stand forth clearly. It distends the intentional ties which bind us to the world in order to make them appear. It alone is consciousness of the world because it reveals it as strange and paradoxical. . . . Precisely in order to see the world and to seize it as a paradox, it is necessary to disrupt our familiarity with it, and that disruption can teach us nothing save the unmotivated surging forth of the world. The greatest lesson of the reduction is the impossibility of a complete reduction. . . . Far from being, as one might think, the formula for an idealist philosophy, the phenomenological reduction is that of an existentialist philosophy: the "In-der-Welt-Sein" of Heidegger only appears on the basis of the phenomenological reduction. . . .

The fact that essences are instrumental in reflection does not mean that philosophy takes them as its object, but rather that our existence is too strictly caught up in the world to know itself as such at the moment when it is thrown forth upon the world, and that it needs the idea in order to recognize and conquer its state of fact. . . . It is the function of language to make essences exist in a separation, which is actually only apparent since they still repose on the antepredicative life of consciousness. . . . Seeking the essence of consciousness . . . means recovering my effective presence to myself. (65)

The eidetic reduction . . . is the resolution to make the world appear as it is prior to all turning upon ourselves. It is the ambition to make reflection equal to the nonreflective life of consciousness. . . . For if I can speak of "dreams" and of "reality," and pose for myself the question of the imaginary and the real, and if I can doubt the real, it is because that distinction is already made for me prior to the analysis, and because I have an experience of the real as well as of the imaginary. . . .

We must not wonder, then, if we really perceive a world. Rather, we must say that the world is that which we perceive. . . . To look for the essence of perception is to declare, not that perception is presumed to be truth, but that it is defined for us as access to truth. . . . The evidence of perception is not an adequate thought nor apodictic evidence. The world is not what I think, but that which I live. I open out upon the world. Unquestionably I communicate with it, but I do not take possession of it. It is inexhaustible. "There is a world," or rather, "there is the world": this is a constant theme of my life which I can never completely think through. . . .

Whether it is a case of something perceived, or a historical event or doctrine, "to understand" means to seize again the total intention. . . . Seizing the total intention means grasping the unique manner of existing which is expressed in the properties of the pebble, the glass or the piece of wax, in all the facts of a revolution, in all the thoughts of a philosopher. In each civilization the Idea must be found . . . the formula of a unique behavior with regard to others, nature, time and death. . . . In relation to them, no single word nor human gesture, however habitual or distracted, is without meaning. . . . The chance happenings compensate each other, and that dust of facts forms an agglomeration. There appears the outline of a way of facing the human situation, an event whose contours are defined and of which one can speak. . . .

The most important acquisition of phenomenology is undoubtedly to have joined extreme subjectivism and extreme objectivism in its notion of world or of rationality. Rationality is exactly measured out in the experiences in which it reveals itself. There is rationality, that is, perspectives overlap, perceptions confirm one another, and a meaning appears. But it cannot be set apart and transformed into either absolute Spirit or world in the realist sense. The phenomenological world is not pure being, but the meaning which appears at the intersection of my experiences and at the intersection of my experiences with those of others by the enmeshing of one with the other. Thus it is inseparable from the subjectivity and from the intersubjectivity which form their unity by taking up my past experiences in my present experiences and the experience of others in my own. . . . The phenomenological world is not a more primary being rendered explicit, but the foundation of being. Philosophy is not the reflection of a more original truth but the art of making a truth real. . . .

The world and reason are no problem. They are mysterious, but mystery defines them. There is no question of dissipating the mystery by some solution, for they are prior to solutions. Genuine philosophy is re-learning to see the world, and in this sense a story recounted can signify the world with as much "depth" as a treatise in philosophy. Our fate is in our own hands. We become responsible for our history by reflection, but also by a decision in which we commit our life. In each case the act is violent and is verified only in actual exercise. . . .

It is not accidental that phenomenology was a movement before being a doctrine or a system. It is as laborious as the work of Balzac, or of Proust or of Valéry or of Cézanne, because of the same type of attention and wonder, the same demands of consciousness, the same will to seize the meaning of the world or of history in its state of genesis. In this regard it fuses with modern thought. (59-70)

Jean-Paul Sartre

The Transcendence of the Ego

Phenomenology is a scientific, not a Critical, study of consciousness. Its essential way of proceeding is by intuition. Intuition, according to Husserl, puts us in the presence of *the thing.* We must recognize, therefore, that phenomenology is a science of *fact,* and that the problems it poses are problems *of fact;* which can be seen, moreover, from Husserl's designation of phenomenology as a *descriptive* science. Problems concerning the relations of the *I* to consciousness are therefore existential problems. . . .

Like Husserl, we are persuaded that our psychic and psycho-physical *me* is a transcendent object which must fall before the ἐποχή. But we raise the following question: is not this psychic and psycho-physical *me* enough? Need one double it with a transcendental *I*, a structure of absolute consciousness? (35f.)

. . . The phenomenological conception of consciousness renders the unifying and individualizing role of the *I* totally useless. It is consciousness, on the contrary, which makes possible the unity and the personality of my *I*. The transcendental *I*, therefore, has no *raison d'être*.

But in addition, this superfluous *I* would be a hindrance. If it existed it would tear consciousness from itself; it would divide consciousness; it would slide into every consciousness like an opaque blade. The transcendental *I* is the death of consciousness. . . . Consciousness is then no longer a spontaneity; it bears within itself the germ of opaqueness. But in addition we would be forced to abandon that original and profound view which makes of consciousness a *non-substantial* absolute. A pure consciousness is an absolute quite simply because it is consciousness of itself. It remains therefore a "phenomenon" in the very special sense in which "to be" and "to appear" are one. It is all lightness, all translucence. This it is which differentiates the *Cogito* of Husserl from the Cartesian *Cogito*. But if the *I* were a necessary structure of consciousness, this opaque *I* would at once be raised to the rank of an absolute. We would then be in the presence of a monad. And this, indeed, is unfortunately the orientation of the new thought of Husserl (see *Cartesianische Meditationen*). Consciousness is loaded down; consciousness has lost that character which rendered it the absolute existent *by virtue of non-existence*. It is heavy and *ponderable*. All the results of phenomenology begin to crumble if the *I* is not, by the same title as the world, a relative existent: that is to say, an object *for* consciousness. (40-42)

I quite recognize that Husserl grants to the *I* a special transcendence which is not the transcendence of the object, and which one could call a transcendence "from above." But by what right? And how account for this privileged treatment of the *I* if not by metaphysical and Critical preoccupations which have nothing to do with phenomenology? (50f.)

. . . The *I* never appears except on the occasion of a reflective act. . . . The transcendent *I* must fall before the stroke of phenomenological reduction. The *Cogito* affirms too much. The certain content of the pseudo-"Cogito" is not "*I have* consciousness of this chair," but "There is consciousness of this chair." This content is sufficient to constitute an infinite and absolute field of investigation for phenomenology. (53f.)

The Transcendental Field, purified of all egological structure, recovers its primary transparency. In a sense, it is a *nothing,* since all physical, psycho-physical, and psychic objects, all truths, all values are outside it; since my *me* has itself ceased to be any part of it. But this nothing is *all* since it is *consciousness of* all these objects. (93)

The ego is not the owner of consciousness; it is the object of consciousness. To be sure, we constitute spontaneously our states and actions as productions of the ego. But our states and actions are also objects. We never have a direct intuition of the spontaneity of an instantaneous consciousness as produced by the ego. That would be impossible. It is only on the level of meanings and psychological hypotheses that we can conceive such production—and this error is possible only because on this level the ego and the consciousness are indicated *emptily.* In this sense, if one understands the *I Think* so as to make of thought a production of the *I,* one has already constituted thought as passivity and as *state,* that is to say, as object. One has left the level of pure reflection, in which the ego undoubtedly appears, but appears *on the horizon* of a spontaneity. . . .

We may therefore formulate our thesis: transcendental consciousness is an impersonal spontaneity. It determines its existence at each instant, without our being able to conceive anything *before* it. Thus each instant of our conscious life reveals to us a creation *ex nihilo.* Not a new *arrangement,* but a new existence. (97-99)

Everything happens, therefore, as if consciousness constituted the ego as a false representation of itself, as if consciousness hypnotized itself before this ego which it has constituted, absorbing itself in the ego as if to make the ego its guardian and its law. It is thanks to the ego, indeed, that a distinction can be made between the possible and the real, between appearance and being, between the willed and the undergone.

But it can happen that consciousness suddenly produces itself on the pure reflective level. . . . Then consciousness, noting what could be called the fatality of its spontaneity, is suddenly anguished: it is this dread, absolute and without remedy, this fear of itself, which seems to us constitutive of pure consciousness.

. . . If "the natural attitude" appears wholly as an effort made by consciousness to escape from itself by projecting itself into the *me* and becoming absorbed there, and if this effort is never completely rewarded, and if a simple act of reflection suffices in order for conscious spontaneity to tear itself abruptly away from the *I* and be given as independent, then the ἐποχή is no longer a miracle, an intellectual method, an erudite procedure: it is an anxiety which is imposed on us and which we cannot avoid: it is both a pure event of transcendental origin and an ever possible accident of our daily life. (101-103)

. . . Nothing is more unjust than to call phenomenologists "idealists." On the contrary, for centuries we have not felt in philosophy so realistic a current. The phenomenologists have plunged man back into the world; they have given full measure to man's agonies and sufferings, and also to his rebellions. Unfortunately, as long as the *I* remains a structure of absolute consciousness, one will still be able to reproach phenomenology for being an escapist doctrine, for again pulling a part of man out of the world and, in that way, turning our attention from the real problems. (105)

Being and Nothingness

The appearance does not hide the essence, it reveals it; it is the essence. The essence of an existent is no longer a property sunk in the cavity of this existent; it is the manifest law which presides over the succession of its appearances, it is the principle of the series. . . . But essence, as the principle of the series, is definitely only the concatenation of appearances; that is, itself an appearance. This explains how it is possible to have an intuition of *essences* (the *Wesenschau* of Husserl, for example). The phenomenal being manifests itself; it manifests its essence as well as its existence, and it is nothing but the well connected series of its manifestations. . . . This new opposition, the "finite and the infinite," or better, "the infinite in the finite," replaces the dualism of being and appearance. It is altogether *within*, in that it manifests itself *in* that aspect; it shows itself as the structure of the appearance, which is at the same time the principle of the series. It is altogether outside, for the series itself will never appear nor can it appear. Thus the outside is opposed in a new way to the inside, and the being-which-does-not-appear, to the appearance. Similarly a certain "potency" returns to inhabit the phenomenon and confer on it its very transcendence—a potency to be developed in a series of real or possible appearances. . . . Since there is nothing behind the appearance, and since it indicates only itself (and the total series of appearances), it can not be *supported* by any being other than its own. The appearance can not be the thin film of nothingness which separates the being-of-the-subject from absolute-being. . . . The object does not *possess* being, and its existence is not a participation in being, nor any other kind of relation. It *is*. That is the only way to define its manner of being; the object does not hide being, but neither does it reveal being. . . .

The existent is a phenomenon; this means that it designates itself as an organized totality of qualities. It designates itself and not its being. . . . It is being-for-revealing (*être-pour-dévoiler*) and not revealed being (*être dévoilé*). What then is the meaning of the surpassing toward the ontological, of which Heidegger speaks? Certainly I can pass beyond this table or this chair toward its being and raise the question of the being-of-the-table or the being-of-the-chair. . . . But at that moment I turn my eyes away from the phenomenon of the table in order to concentrate on the phenomenon of being, which is no longer the condition of all revelation, but which is itself something revealed—an appearance which as such, needs in turn a being on the basis of which it can reveal itself. . . . The being of the phenomenal although coextensive with the phenomenon, can not be subject to the phenomenal condition—which is to exist only in so far as it reveals itself . . . —consequently it surpasses the knowledge which we have of it and provides the basis for such knowledge. . . . And since we have restricted reality to the phenomenon, we can say of the phenomenon that it *is* as it *appears*. Why not push the idea to its limit and say that the being of the appearance is its appearing? . . . And it is in fact just what Husserl and his followers are doing when after having effected the phenomenological reduction, they treat the noema as *unreal* and declare that its *esse* is *percipi*. . . . All consciousness, as Husserl has shown, is consciousness of something. This means that there is no consciousness which is not a *positing* of a transcendent object, or if you prefer, that consciousness has no "content." We must renounce those neutral "givens" which, according to the system of reference chosen, find their place either "in the world" or "in the psyche." A table is not *in* consciousness—not even in the capacity of a representation. A table is *in* space, beside the window, *etc*. The existence of the table in fact is a center of opacity for consciousness. . . . The first procedure of a philosophy ought to be to expel things from consciousness and to reestablish its true connection with the world, to know that consciousness is a positional consciousness of the world. All consciousness is positional in that it transcends itself in order to reach an object, and it exhausts itself in this same positing. All that there is of *intention* in my actual consciousness is directed toward the outside, toward the table. . . . If we wish to avoid an infinite regress, there must be an immediate, non-cognitive relation of the self to itself. . . . Every positional consciousness of an object is at the same time a non-positional consciousness of itself. . . . This self-consciousness we ought to consider not as a new consciousness, but as *the only mode of existence which is possible for a consciousness of something*. (xlviii-lvi)

Thus by abandoning the primacy of knowledge, we have discovered the *being* of the *knower* and encountered the absolute. . . . This is no longer the subject in Kant's meaning of the term, but it is subjectivity itself, the immanence of self in self. Henceforth we have escaped idealism. For the latter, being is measured by knowledge, which subjects it to the law of duality. There is only *known* being; it is a question of thought itself. Thought appears only through its own products; that is, we always apprehend it only as the signification of thoughts produced. . . . We, on the other hand, have apprehended a being which is not subject to knowledge and which founds knowledge, a thought which is definitely not given as a representation or a signification of expressed thoughts, but which is directly apprehended such as it is —and this mode of apprehension is not a phenomenon of knowledge but is the structure of being. We find ourselves at present on the ground of the phenomenology of Husserl although Husserl himself has not always been faithful to his first intuition. . . . The table is before knowledge and can not be identified with the knowledge which we have of it; otherwise it would be consciousness—*i.e.*, pure immanence—and it would disappear *as* table. (lviiif.)

The perceived being is before consciousness; consciousness can not reach it, and it can not enter into consciousness; and as the perceived being is cut off from consciousness, it exists cut off from its own existence. It would be no use to make of it an unreal in the manner of Husserl; even as unreal it must exist. . . . The transphenomenal being of consciousness can not provide a basis for the transphenomenal being of the phenomenon. Here we see the error of the phenomenalists: having justifiably reduced the object to the connected series of its appearances, they believed they had reduced its being to the succession of its modes of being. That is why they have explained it by concepts which can be applied only to the modes of being, for they are pointing out the relations between a plurality of already existing beings. . . . Transcendence in immanence does not bring us out of the subjective. It is true that things give themselves in profile; that is, simply by appearances. And it is true that each appearance refers to other appearances. But each of them is already in itself alone a *transcendent being,* not a subjective material of impressions—a *plenitude of being,* not a lack—a *presence,* not an absence. It is futile by a sleight of hand to attempt to found the *reality* of the object on the subjective plenitude of impressions and its *objectivity* on non-being; the objective will never come out of the subjective nor the transcendent from immanence, nor being from non-being.

But, we are told, Husserl defines consciousness precisely as a transcendence. In truth he does. This is what he posits. This is his essential discovery. But from the moment that he makes of the *noema* an *unreal,* a correlate of the *noesis,* a *noema* whose *esse* is *percipi,*[1] he is totally unfaithful to his principle. . . . To say that consciousness is consciousness of something means that for consciousness there is no being outside of that precise obligation to be a revealing intuition of something—*i.e.*, of a transcendent being. Not only does pure subjectivity, if initially given, fail to transcend itself to posit the objective; a "pure" subjectivity disappears. What can properly be called subjectivity is consciousness (of) consciousness. But this consciousness (of being) consciousness must be qualified in some way, and it can be qualified only as revealing intuition or it is nothing. Now a revealing intuition implies something revealed. . . . It is not a question of showing that the phenomena of inner sense imply the existence of objective spatial phenomena, but that consciousness implies in its being a non-conscious and transphenomenal being. . . . To say that consciousness is consciousness of something is to say that it must produce itself as a revealed-revelation of a being which is not it and which gives itself as already existing when consciousness reveals it. . . .

Thus we have left pure appearance and have arrived at full being. Consciousness is a being whose existence posits its essence, and inversely it is consciousness of a being, whose essence implies its existence; that is, in which appearance lays claim to *being.* Being is everywhere. . . . We must understand that this being is no other than the transphenomenal being of phenomena

[1] Translated into plain English: "But from the moment that he makes of the known an unreal, a correlate of the act of knowing, a known whose being consists entirely in its being perceived, . . ."—M.F.

and not a noumenal being which is hidden behind them. It is the being of this table, of this package of tobacco, of the lamp, more generally the being of the world which is implied by consciousness. It requires simply that the being of that which *appears* does not exist *only* in so far as it appears. The transphenomenal being of what exists *for consciousness* is itself in itself (*lui-même en soi*). . . . Consciousness is the revealed-revelation of existents, and existents appear before consciousness on the foundation of their being. . . . Consciousness can always pass beyond the existent, not toward its being, but toward the meaning of this being. A fundamental characteristic of its transcendence is to transcend the ontic toward the ontological. The meaning of the being of the existent in so far as it reveals itself to consciousness is the phenomenon of being. . . . This elucidation of the meaning of being is valid only for the being of the phenomenon. (lxi-lxv)

For being is the being of becoming and due to this fact it is beyond becoming. It is what it is. This means that by itself it can not even be what it is not. . . . It is full positivity. It knows no otherness; it never posits itself as *other-than-another-being*. It can support no connection with the other. It is itself indefinitely and it exhausts itself in being. . . . Consciousness absolutely can not derive being from anything, either from another being, or from a possibility, or from a necessary law. Uncreated, without reason for being, without any connection with another being, being-in-itself is *de trop* for eternity. (lxviii)

Martin Heidegger

Being and Time

. . . To work out the question of Being adequately, we must make an entity—the inquirer—transparent in his own Being. The very asking of this question is an entity's mode of *Being;* and as such it gets its essential character from what is inquired about —namely, Being. This entity which each of us is himself and which includes inquiring as one of the possibilities of its Being, we shall denote by the term "*Dasein*." * (27) . . . *understanding of being is itself a definite characteristic of Dasein's being.* Dasein is ontically distinctive in that it *is* ontological. . . . By "existentiality" we understand the state of Being that is constitutive for those entities that exist. But in the idea of such a constitutive state of Being, the idea of Being is already included. And thus even the possibility of carrying through the analytic of Dasein depends on working out beforehand the question about the meaning of Being in general. . . . Thus Dasein's understanding of Being pertains with equal primordiality both to an understanding of something like a "world," and to the understanding of the Being of those entities which become accessible within the world. . . . Therefore *fundamental ontology,* from which alone all other ontologies can take their rise, must be sought in the *existential analytic of Dasein.* (32-34)

. . . Whenever Dasein tacitly understands and interprets something like Being, it does so with *time* as its standpoint. Time must be brought to light—and genuinely conceived—as the horizon for all understanding of Being and for any way of interpreting it. (39) . . . The question of the meaning of Being must be carried through by explicating Dasein beforehand in its temporality and historicality. . . . Dasein simultaneously falls prey to the tradition of which it has more or less explicitly taken hold. . . . When tradition thus becomes master, it does so in such a way that what it "transmits" is made so inaccessible, proximally and for the most part, that it rather becomes concealed. (42f.)

With the question of the meaning of Being, our investigation comes up against the fundamental question of philosophy. This is one that must be treated *phenomenologically.* . . . The term "phenomenology" expresses a maxim which can be formulated as "To the things themselves!" It is opposed to all free-floating constructions and accidental findings; it is opposed to taking over any conceptions which only seem to have been demonstrated; it is opposed to those pseudo-questions which parade themselves as

* The word "Dasein" plays so important a role in this work and is already so familiar . . . that it seems simpler to leave it untranslated except in the . . . passages in which Heidegger himself breaks it up with a hyphen ("Da-sein") to show its etymological construction: literally "Being-there." Though in traditional German philosophy it may be used quite generally to stand for almost any kind of Being or "existence" which we can say that something *has* . . . , in everyday usage it tends to be used more narrowly to stand for the kind of Being that belongs to *persons.* Heidegger . . . often uses it to stand for any *person* who has such Being. . . .

"problems," often for generations at a time. . . . The expression *"phenomenon"* signifies *that which shows itself in itself,* the manifest. Accordingly the "phenomena" are the totality of what lies in the light of day or can be brought to the light—what the Greeks sometimes identified simply with entities. (49-51)

Thus "phenomenology" means to let that which shows itself be seen from itself in the very way in which it shows itself from itself. . . . "Phenomenology" neither designates the object of its researches, nor characterizes the subject-matter thus comprised. The word merely informs us of the *"how"* with which *what* is to be treated in this science gets exhibited and handled. To have a science "of" phenomena means to grasp its objects *in such a way* that everything about them which is up for discussion must be treated by exhibiting it directly and demonstrating it directly. . . . That which remains *hidden* in an egregious sense, or which relapses and gets *covered up* again, or which shows itself only *"in disguise,"* is not just this entity or that, but rather the *being* of entities. This Being can be covered up so extensively that it becomes forgotten and no question arises about it or about its meaning. Thus that which demands that it become a phenomenon, and which demands this in a distinctive sense and in terms of its ownmost content as a thing, is what phenomenology has taken into its grasp thematically as its object. . . . *Only as phenomenology, is ontology possible.* In the phenomenological conception of "phenomenon" what one has in mind as that which shows itself is the Being of entities, its meaning, its modifications and derivatives. . . . Least of all can the Being of entities ever be anything such that "behind it" stands something else "which does not appear." . . . And just because the phenomena are proximally and for the most part *not* given, there is need for phenomenology. Covered-up-ness is the counter-concept to "phenomenon." . . . Because phenomena, as understood phenomenologically, are never anything but what goes to make up Being, while Being is in every case the Being of some entity, we must first bring forward the entities themselves if it is our aim that Being should be laid bare; and we must do this in the right way. These entities must likewise show themselves with the kind of access which genuinely belongs to them. . . . With regard to its subject-matter, phenomenology is the science of the Being of entities—ontology. . . . Our investigation itself will show that the meaning of phenomenological description as a method lies in *interpretation.* . . . Being and the structure of Being lie beyond every entity and every possible character which an entity may possess. *Being is the* transcendens *pure and simple.* And the transcendence of Dasein's Being is distinctive in that it implies the possibility and the necessity of the most radical *individuation*. Every disclosure of Being as the *transcendens* is *transcendental* knowledge. *Phenomenological truth* (*the disclosedness of Being*) *is* veritas transcendentalis. . . . Philosophy is universal phenomenological ontology, and takes its departure from the hermeneutic of Dasein, which, as an analytic of *existence*, has made fast the guiding-line for all philosophical inquiry at the point where it *arises* and to which it *returns*. (58-62)

. . . If we are to Interpret this entity *ontologically*, the problematic of its Being must be developed from the existentiality of its existence. . . . It is particularly important that Dasein should not be Interpreted with the differentiated character of some definite way of existing, but that it should be uncovered in the undifferentiated character which it has proximally and for the most part. . . . We call this everyday undifferentiated character of Dasein "*averageness*." (69)

. . . Descartes, who is credited with providing the point of departure for modern philosophical inquiry by his discovery of the "*cogito sum*," . . . investigates the "*cogitare*" of the "*ego*," at least within certain limits. On the other hand, he leaves the "*sum*" completely undiscussed, even though it is regarded as no less primordial than the *cogito*. Our analytic raises the ontological question of the Being of the "*sum*." Not until the nature of this Being has been determined can we grasp the kind of Being which belongs to *cogitationes*. (71) . . . Over and above the attempt to determine the essence of "man" as an entity, the question of his Being has remained forgotten. This Being is rather conceived as something obvious or "self-evident" in the sense of *Being-present-at-hand* of other created Things. . . . But since even the *cogitationes* are either left ontologically undetermined, or get tacitly assumed as something "self-evidently" "given" whose "Being" is not to be questioned, the decisive ontological foundations of anthropological problematics remain undetermined. (75)

Taking up relationships towards the world is possible only *because* Dasein, as Being-in-the-world, is as it is. This state of Being does not arise just because some other entity is present-at-hand outside of Dasein and meets up with it. Such an entity can "meet up with" Dasein only in so far as it can, of its own accord, show itself within a *world*. (84) . . . If Being-in-the-world is a basic state of Dasein, and one in which Dasein operates not only in general but pre-eminently in the mode of everydayness, then it must also be something which has always been experienced ontically.*

* Ontological inquiry is concerned primarily with *Being;* ontical inquiry is concerned primarily with *entities* and the facts about them.

(86) . . . And furthermore, the perceiving of what is known is not a process of returning with one's booty to the "cabinet" of consciousness after one has gone out and grasped it; even in perceiving, retaining, and preserving, the Dasein which knows *remains outside,* and it does so *as Dasein. . . . A "commercium"* of the subject with a world does not get *created* for the first time by knowing, nor does it *arise* from some way in which the world acts upon a subject. Knowing is a mode of Dasein founded upon Being-in-the-world. Thus Being-in-the-world, as a basic state, must be Interpreted *beforehand.* . . . Even the forgetting of something, in which every relationship of Being towards what one formerly knew has seemingly been obliterated, must be conceived *as a modification of the primordial Being-in;* and this holds for every delusion and for every error. (89f.)

"Worldhood" is an ontological concept, and stands for the structure of one of the constitutive items of Being-in-the-world. But we know Being-in-the-world as a way in which Dasein's character is defined existentially. Thus worldhood itself is an *existentiale.* . . . Ontologically, "world" is not a way of characterizing those entities which Dasein essentially is *not;* it is rather a characteristic of Dasein itself. (92) . . . *Dasein, in its familiarity with significance, is the ontical condition for the possibility of discovering entities which are encountered in a world with involvement (readiness-to-hand) as their kind of being, and which can thus make themselves known as they are in themselves.* Dasein as such is always something of this sort; along with its Being, a context of the ready-to-hand is already essentially discovered: Dasein, in so far as it *is,* has always submitted itself already to a "world" which it encounters, and this *submission* belongs essentially to its Being. But in significance itself, with which Dasein is always familiar, there lurks the ontological condition which makes it possible for Dasein, as something which understands and interprets, to disclose such things as "significations"; upon these, in turn, is founded the Being of words and of language. (120f.) . . .

. . . Even the positive Interpretation of Dasein which we have so far given, already forbids us to start with the formal givenness of the "I," if our purpose is to answer the question of the "who" in a way which is phenomenally adequate. In clarifying Being-in-the-world we have shown that a bare subject without a world never "is" proximally, nor is it ever given. And so in the end an isolated "I" without Others is just as far from being proximally given. If, however, "the Others" already *are there with us* in Being-in-the-world, and if this is ascertained phenomenally, even this should not mislead us into supposing that the *ontological* structure of what is thus "given" is obvious, requiring no investigation. Our task is to make visible phenomenally the species to which this Dasein-with in closest everydayness belongs, and to Interpret it in a way which is ontologically appropriate. . . . *If the "I" is an essential characteristic of Dasein, then it is one which must be interpreted existentially.* In that case the "Who?" is to be answered only by exhibiting phenomenally a definite kind of Being which Dasein possesses. If in each case Dasein is its Self only in *existing*, then the constancy of the Self no less than the possibility of its "failure to stand by itself" requires that we formulate the question existentially and ontologically as the sole appropriate way of access to its problematic. (152f.)

A state-of-mind not only discloses Dasein in its thrownness and its submission to that world which is already disclosed with its own Being; it is itself the existential kind of Being in which Dasein constantly surrenders itself to the "world" and lets the "world" "matter" to it in such a way that somehow Dasein evades its very self. . . . A state-of-mind is a basic existential way in which Dasein is its "there." It not only characterizes Dasein ontologically, but, because of what it discloses, it is at the same time methodologically significant in principle for the existential analytic. Like any ontological Interpretation whatsoever, this analytic can only, so to speak, "listen in" to some previously disclosed entity as regards its Being. And it will attach itself to Dasein's distinctive and most far-reaching possibilities of disclosure, in order to get information about this entity from these. Phenomenological Interpretation must make it possible for Dasein itself to disclose things primordially; it must, as it were, let Dasein interpret itself. Such Interpretation takes part in this disclosure only in order to raise to a conceptual level the phenomenal content of what has been disclosed, and to do so existentially. (178f.)

Even where the issue is not only one of ontical experience, but also one of ontological understanding, the interpretation of Being takes its orientation in the first instance from the Being of entities within-the-world. Thereby the Being of what is proximally ready-to-hand gets passed over, and entities are first conceived as a context of Things which are present-at-hand. *"Being"* acquires the meaning of *"reality."* Substantiality becomes the basic characteristic of Being. . . . Like any other entity, *Dasein* too is *present-at-hand as real.* In this way *"Being in general"* acquires the meaning of *"reality."* Accordingly the concept of Reality has a peculiar priority in the ontological problematic. By this priority the route to a genuine existential analytic of Dasein gets diverted, and so too does our very view of the Being of what is proximally ready-to-hand within-the-world. (245)

Karl Jaspers

Limit-Situations[2]

The collisions of values which compel man not only to affirm but also to destroy values, represent only one occasion among many that make existence appear as much a process creating values as a process destroying them. This destruction of values and this limitation to their origination is experienced in infinitely manifold concrete situations. Such destruction and limitation at first do not appear to the individual as absolutely necessary; things it seems, could also be otherwise. True as this is for man in his activity, nevertheless he is involved, beyond all individual situations, in certain decisive, essential situations, which are an unavoidable condition of finite human existence. As long as his view is directed toward the objective in the dichotomy of subject and object, it does not reach beyond these ultimate situations. These situations, which at the limits of our existence are everywhere felt, experienced, conceived, we therefore call "limit-situations." Common to them is, that—always in the world split between subject and object, in the world of the objective—there is nothing fixed, no Absolute that cannot be doubted, no adequate foothold for every experience and every thought. Everything is in flux, in a restless movement of being questioned; everything is relative, finite, split into opposites; never the whole, the absolute, the essential.

We cannot bear the stark confrontation with the limit-situations; therefore, they almost never enter into our living experience in total clarity, yet actually we almost always have some support when facing them. Without such a support life would cease. In fact man is almost never desperate. Before he can even become desperate, he finds a hold; not everybody, only a very few live in limit-situations. We ask how do so many avoid these

2 From Jaspers' *Psychologie der Weltanschauungen.*

limit-situations or how do they get out of them. With that we hit upon the problem of the core of the various spiritual types of man. What kind of hold man has, how he has, seeks, finds, preserves it, that is the characteristic manifestation of his spiritual forces. To ask about the spiritual type is to ask where man finds his values. . . .

The quest for values meets resistance everywhere. These resisting elements are frequently experienced and understood as accidental, avoidable, surmountable; as such they are provisional in character and do not constitute an absolute limit. The resisting elements do mean misfortune and suffering to man, but as long as the quest for values remains dominant, they are subordinate and constitute merely relative obstacles. However, experience of the world has here also shown to man a way toward the Absolute: no matter how conscious he becomes of the sovereignty of the values and of their realization,—as soon as he wants to assure himself of totality, he finds everything attained and attainable embedded in the resisting elements and in the elements destructive of the course of the world. At the limit, experience seems to find everywhere absolute chance, death, guilt. In the conditions underlying the origination of values nothing, to man's eye, is guaranteed and necessary, but the ultimate is chance, and from his empirical point of view all objective existence of values is followed by total destruction.

The external situation—changing as it is and as unequally as it hits different people—is double-edged to all, furthering and hindering, unavoidably limiting, destructive, undependable, uncertain. The deeper the knowledge and vocation, the clearer becomes generally—what innumerable people live through and experience in individual cases, forgetting it quickly—the consciousness of the world's antinomic structure: with everything wanted something unwanted is linked in the actual realization (in the objective world); with all wanting is linked a non-wanting, a counterwanting (in the subjective world); we ourselves and the world are split in antinomies. This manifests itself in the unavoidable and essentially unchangeable misery of the objective world situation —no matter of what kind—and in the consciousness—again so different in its nature—of sinfulness, exhaustion, depravity, worthlessness, contemptibleness. . . .

Real opposites are antinomies, when conceived as something ultimate, which from the standpoint of valuing appears both essential and questionable, and when existence is conceived as ultimately split into opposites, so that all individual existence is real only when these opposite forces or appearances meet one another.

Kinds of antinomies: The actual—thinking, feeling, acting—man is standing as it were between two worlds: in front of him the realm of objects, in back of him the forces and predispositions of the subject. His situation is determined from both sides, in front of him the object, in back of him the subject, both infinite, both inexhaustible and impenetrable. On both sides lie decisive antinomies (229-233) [The five antinomies the subject faces in his existence are death, guilt, suffering, strife, and chance.]

The relation of man to his own death is different from that to all other transitoriness; only the non-existence of the world is at all a comparable idea. Man is able to experience every kind of transitoriness as a fact, toward which he can afterwards take a stand, while only the perishing of his own being or that of the world as such has for him a character of totality. Death in general or the death of others he can conceive of as a physical occurrence, as the non-existence of his fellow human beings, while he himself continues to exist; he can experience physical pain, anxiety, mortal dread of unavoidable death—and yet survive the danger: but he has no experience of death, always only of the relationship of the living to death; he can also circumvent all these experiences and die without noticing them.

Death is something inconceivable, something really unthinkable. What we imagine and think about it are only negations and secondary phenomena, never anything positive. This way we do not really "experience" the death of our fellow man. He leaves us and yet remains to us the same; he is and is not. Our general knowledge of death and our experienced relation to death are quite heterogeneous: We can know death in general, and at the same time there is something in us which instinctively does not believe it necessary or possible. . . . The question of the reaction to death that the individual experiences can come up only after man has faced death as a limit-situation. (261f.)

The limits are looked for, behind which there is no additional world and yet where not only nothingness need be. Man seeks clear consciousness of the possible orientation in the world by pointing out that Being itself never appears anywhere in the world or as the world, but only as fragmented being. With this presupposition of the consciousness of limit I am able to live with the world as with that about which pertinent, objective orientation is possible, and yet I need not surrender to the world, but I can live related to Being itself, which I cannot orient in the world.[3] (53)

[3] Jaspers, *Philosophie,* Vol. I.

The Perennial Scope of Philosophy

We call the being that is neither only subject nor only object, that is rather on both sides of the subject-object split, *das Umgreifende*, the Comprehensive. Although it cannot be an adequate object, it is of this, and with this in mind, that we speak when we philosophize. (14)

The Comprehensive is either the *Being in itself* that surrounds us or the *Being that we are*.

The Being that surrounds us, is called world and transcendence.

The Being that we are is called *Dasein*, "Being there," consciousness in general, spirit, existence. (17)

. . . Since the encounter between existence and transcendence is an encounter in the world, it is bound to the world from the standpoint of time. Because what is for us, must manifest itself within the temporality of the world, there is no direct knowledge of God and existence. The study of the world is our only road to knowledge, self-realization in the world is the only road to existential self-realization. If we are lost to the world, we are also lost to ourselves. (39)

Ontology: Ontology purports to be a doctrine of being itself as such and as a whole. In practice, however, it inevitably becomes a particular knowledge of something within being, not a knowledge of being itself. (143)

Reason and Existenz

Empirical existence and spirit produce forms of reality; consciousness as such is the form in which we envisage the Encompassing[4] as the condition of the universally valid and communicable. . . . The Encompassing which we are is not Being itself, but rather the genuine appearance in the Encompassing of Being itself.

This Being itself which we feel as indicated at the limits, and which therefore is the last thing we reach through questioning from our situation, is in itself the first. It is not made by us, is not interpretation, and is not an object. Rather it itself brings forth our questioning and permits it no rest. . . .

[4] "The Encompassing" is a variant translation of *das Umgreifende* and one that is preferable, in my opinion, to "the Comprehensive."—M.F.

The Encompassing which we are has its other limit in the question through which it is. Being itself is the Transcendence which shows itself to no investigative experience, not even indirectly. It is that which as the absolute Encompassing just as certainly "is" as it remains unseen and unknown. (59f.)

Reason, through the pre-eminence of thought, can bring all the modes of the Encompassing to light by continually transcending limits, without itself being an Encompassing like them. . . . Reason of itself is no source; but, as it is an encompassing bond, it is like a source in which all sources first come to light. It is the unrest which permits acquiescence in nothing; it forces a break with the immediacy of the unconscious in every mode of the Encompassing which we are. It pushes on continually. But it is also that which can effect the great peace, not the peace of a self-confident rational whole, but that of Being itself opened up to us through reason. (65)

The great poles of our being, which encounter one another in every mode of the Encompassing, are thus reason and Existenz. They are inseparable. Each disappears with the disappearance of the other. . . . Existenz only becomes clear through reason; reason only has content through Existenz. . . . Reason is oriented toward its Other, toward the content of the Existenz which supports it, which clarifies itself in reason, and which gives decisive impulses to reason. (67)

. . . The Encompassing can never be known as a particular something from which other things can be deduced. Every object of thought, be it ever so comprehensive, every conceived whole, every objectively conceived Encompassing, remains as an object merely an individual, for it has other objects outside it and also stands over against us. The Encompassing itself, whether it be the Encompassing which we are or Being in itself, escapes from every determinate objectivity. Insofar as we are that Encompassing, it can only be illuminated; insofar as it is thought of as Being in itself, it is apprehended by inquiry into its infinite appearance; insofar as it speaks as Transcendence it is heard by absolute, historical Existenz. (70)

. . . The authentic idea of the Encompassing disappears with every attempt to establish, isolate, and absolutize it. . . . No known being is Being itself. Every time I let Being itself slip into known being, Transcendence disappears and I become dark to myself. . . .

The purpose and therefore the meaning of a philosophical idea is not the cognition of an object, but rather an alteration of our consciousness of Being and of our inner attitude toward things.

Understanding the meaning of the Encompassing has the significance of creating a possibility. The philosopher therein says to himself: preserve the open space of the Encompassing! Do not lose yourself in what is merely known! Do not let yourself become separated from Transcendence! . . .

Man can seek the path of his truth in unfanatical absoluteness, in a decisiveness which remains open. (73-76)

Martin Buber

Pointing the Way

This is the glorious paradox of our existence that all comprehensibility of the world is only a footstool of its incomprehensibility. But this incomprehensibility has a new, a wonderful secret to bestow; it is like Adam's knowledge when he "knew" his wife Eve. What the most learned and ingenious combination of concepts denies, the humble and faithful beholding, grasping, knowing of any situation bestows. The world is not comprehensible, but it is embraceable: through the embracing of one of its beings. Each thing and being has a twofold nature: the passive, absorbable, usable, dissectible, comparable, combinable, rationalizable, and the other, the active, non-absorbable, unusable, undissectible, incomparable, noncombinable, nonrationalizable. This is the confronting, the shaping, the bestowing in things. He who truly experiences a thing so that it springs up to meet him and embraces him of itself has in that thing known the world. . . .

The loving man is one who grasps non-relatively each thing he grasps. He does not think of inserting the experienced thing into relations to other things; at the moment of experience nothing else exists, nothing save this beloved thing, filling out the world and indistinguishably coinciding with it. Where you with agile fingers draw out the qualities common to all things and distribute them in ready-made categories, the loving man's dream-powerful and primally-awake heart beholds the non-common. This, the unique, is the bestowing shape, the self of the thing, that cannot be detained within the pure circle of world comprehensibility. What you extract and combine is always only the passivity of things. But their activity, their effective reality, reveals itself only to the loving man who knows them. And thus he knows the world. In the features of the beloved, whose self he realizes, he discerns the enigmatic countenance of the universe. . . .

True science is a loving science. The man who pursues such science is confronted by the secret life of things which has confronted none before him; this life places itself in his hands, and he experiences it, and is filled with its happening to the rim of his existence. Then he interprets what he has experienced in simple and fruitful concepts, and celebrates the unique and incomparable that happened to him with reverent honesty. (27-29)

I and Thou

. . . The mankind of mere *It* that is imagined, postulated, and propagated . . . has nothing in common with a living mankind where *Thou* may truly be spoken. The noblest fiction is a fetish, the loftiest fictitious sentiment is depraved. Ideas are no more enthroned above our heads than resident in them; they wander amongst us and accost us. (13f.)

Certainly the world "dwells" in me as an image, just as I dwell in it as a thing. But it is not for that reason in me, just as I am not in it. The world and I are mutually included, the one in the other. This contradiction in thought, inherent in the situation of *It*, is resolved in the situation of *Thou*, which sets me free from the world in order to bind me up in solidarity of connexion with it.

I bear within me the sense of Self, that cannot be included in the world. The world bears within itself the sense of being, that cannot be included in the image. This sense of being, however, is not a "will" that can be thought, but simply the total status of the world as world, just as the sense of Self is not a "knowing subject" but simply the total status of the *I* as *I*. Here no further "reduction" is possible; he who does not honour the last unities frustrates their apprehensible but not comprehensible sense. (93f.)

Distance and Relation

. . . One can enter into relation only with being which has been set at a distance, more precisely, has become an independent opposite. And it is only for man that an independent opposite exists. . . . It is not possible to think of an existence over against a world which is not also an attitude to it as a world, and that means the outline of an attitude of relation. . . . Here and here alone a being has arisen from the whole, endowed and entitled to detach the whole from himself as a world and to make it an opposite to himself, instead of cutting out with his senses the part he needs from it, as all other beings do, and being content with that. . . .

. . . The great phenomena on the side of acts of distance are preponderantly universal, and those on the side of acts of relation preponderantly personal. . . . Man sets things which he uses at a distance, he gives them into an independence in which function gains duration, he reduces and empowers them to be the bearers of the function. In this way the first movement of the principle is satisfied, but the second is not. Man has a great desire to enter into personal relation with things and to imprint on them his relation to them. To use them, even to possess them, is not enough, they must become his in another way, by imparting to them . . . his relation to them. . . .

Art is neither the impression of natural objectivity nor the expression of spiritual subjectivity, but it is the work and witness of the relation between the *substantia humana* and the *substantia rerum*, it is the realm of "between" which has become a form. (97-100)

Maurice Friedman

Martin Buber: The Life of Dialogue

THEORY OF KNOWLEDGE

What takes place in the present is ordered through the abstracting function of I-It into the world of categories—of space and time, cause and effect. We usually think of these categories as reality itself, but they are actually merely the symbolic representation of what has become. . . . The contrast between the presentness of I-Thou and the pastness of I-It . . . provides us with a key to . . . the I-Thou relation with nature. . . . The reason that objects are It to us and not Thou is that they have already been enregistered in the subject-object world of the past. We think that we know the "real" objects although usually we know them only in directly and conceptually through the categories of I-It. Consequently, we find it difficult to understand Buber's meaning when he says in "Dialogue" that all things "say" something to us. Similarly, because we tend to associate "person" with the human body-mind individual abstracted from his relation to the Thou, we forget that he is only a "person" when he is actually or potentially in such a relation and that the term "personal" applies as much to the relationship itself as to the members of the relation. . . .

In the presentness of meeting . . . are included all those things which we see in their uniqueness and for their own selves, and not as already filtered through our mental categories for purposes of knowledge or use. In this presentness it is no longer true (as it obviously is in the "having become" world of active subject and passive object) that the existing beings over against us cannot in some sense move to meet us as we them. Because these existing beings are real, we can feel the impact of their active reality even though we cannot know them as they are in themselves or describe that impact apart from our relation to it. This "impact" is not that which can be objectively observed by any subject, for in objective observation the activity of the object is actually thought of as part of a causal order in which nothing is really active of itself. It is rather the "impact" of the relation in the present moment between the human I and that non-human existing being which has become real for him as "Thou." This impact makes manifest the only true uniqueness, for that inexhaustible difference between objects which we sometimes loosely call "uniqueness" is really nothing other than a product of our comparison of one object with another and is nothing that exists in the object in itself.

Though natural things may "say" something to us and in that sense have "personal" relations with us, they do not have the continuity, the independence, or the living consciousness and consciousness of self which make up the person. A tree can "say" something to me and become my Thou, but I cannot be a Thou for it. This same impossibility of reciprocity is found in the work of literature and art which becomes Thou for us, and this suggests by analogy that as the poem is the "word" of the poet, so the tree may be the "word" of Being over against us, Being which is more than human yet not less than personal. This does not mean, however, any monistic or mystical presupposition of unity between subject and object. Quite to the contrary, this view alone allows to non-human existing beings their true "otherness" as something more than the passive objects of our thought categories and the passive tools of our will to use. (168-171)

Part III

THE EXISTENTIAL SUBJECT

WITH THE existential subject we have reached the heartland of existentialism and the area where there is probably the maximum agreement among existentialists. Here each thinker places his stress upon becoming a real person, a "single one," an authentic human being. Here each thinker finds himself in opposition to those trends of the age that level, objectify, depersonalize, alienate, or divide the human person. Here each thinker understands man from within the situation of the active subject who may be world-historically nothing, but is, as Kierkegaard puts it, ethically and religiously everything. At the same time, it is inevitable that we glimpse here the beginnings of those basic distinctions, particularly as regard intersubjectivity and religion, that constitute the major issues between the existentialists.

There is a sense in which Søren Kierkegaard (1813-1855) was also a phenomenologist, for example in his elaboration of the forms of the "sickness unto death" (see Part VI). But what makes him the real founder of the philosophy of existence is his emphasis upon the existential subject. Kierkegaard opposes the "Single One" (the true individual) to "the crowd" (which he equates with untruth), but he sees this Single One as set in a direct relation with a transcendent God. Before this relationship can come into being, a man must have discovered his true inwardness, and it is with all the passion of this inwardness that Kierkegaard clings to the "absurd" and attacks the "system."

One of the most vivid and expressive presentations of the existential subject is the brilliant essay, "In Search of Goethe from Within" by José Ortega y Gasset (1883-1955). He shows not only the need of commitment and choice, as opposed to the perpetual adolescence of the uncommitted, but also that being a genuine subject has nothing to do with being subjective but represents, on the contrary, a definite and unique relation to what is not the self. Martin Heidegger's treatment of the existential subject, though lacking the religious counter-pole of Kierkegaard's, is like his in his contrast between the authentic self and *"das Man"*—the "One" or the "They" who is lost in the anonymity of what others think. Through resolute anticipation of one's death as one's non-relational, not-to-be-outstripped, ownmost reality, one is called back to authentic existence. With Sartre the existential subject becomes still more sharply and complexly defined, first, by his cutting off from the self every link with Being or transcendence that would serve as a guide to value decisions and second, through his fruitful, and sometimes tortured, dialectic between *pour-soi*—the subjectivity of the self when seen from within and "for itself"—and *en soi*—the self regarded objectively, whether by another or oneself, as "in itself," in the same sense that any definite object is. On this basis Sartre criticizes Heidegger's elevation of one's own death to the key to one's uniqueness since it is *en soi* and not *pour-soi*. For Jaspers the true self is found in what he calls *Existenz*—genuine existence—and in the relation to the Encompassing. For the Russian Orthodox philosopher Nicolas Berdyaev (1874-1948) it is found in "personality" which he sets in strongest possible contrast to the objectification of nature and society. The French Neo-Thomist thinker Jacques Maritain (1882-) has, as one would expect, a larger dose of the essential and the rational than the other existentialists, but also a very real concern with the distinction between the unique "person" and the mere "individual." Martin Buber finds the authentic self in the sharing of the I-Thou relation, in the "Single One" who is also responsible to the Thou. Existence for Buber is not "toward death," as it is for Heidegger, but toward the realization of one's unique direction—a direction apprehended ever anew in one's meeting with the concrete situation in which one finds oneself.

I have included in this part a selection from my book *Problematic Rebel: An Image of Modern Man* (1963). This selection grew out of an interpretation of the Czech-Jewish novelist Franz Kafka (1883-1924) and shows some implications of his thought for the existential subject that have not heretofore been stressed. Also it presents a significantly different view of the existential subject from any of the others in Part III.

Søren Kierkegaard

Point of View, "That Individual"

The crowd, in fact, is composed of individuals; it must therefore be in every man's power to become what he is, an individual. From becoming an individual no one, no one at all, is excluded, except he who excludes himself by becoming a crowd. (121)

Purity of Heart

The talk asks you, then, *whether you live in such a way that you are conscious of being an "individual."* . . . For in the outside world, the crowd is busy making a noise. The one makes a noise because he heads the crowd, the many because they are members of the crowd. But the all-knowing One, who in spite of anyone is able to observe it all, does not desire the crowd. He desires the individual; He will deal only with the individual, quite unconcerned as to whether the individual be of high or low station, whether he be distinguished or wretched.

Each man himself, as an individual, should render his account to God. No third person dares venture to intrude upon this accounting between God and the individual. Yet the talk, by putting its question, dares and ought to dare, to remind man, in a way never to be forgotten, that the most ruinous evasion of all is to be hidden in the crowd in an attempt to escape God's supervision of him as an individual, in an attempt to get away from hearing God's voice as an individual.

But in eternity each shall render account as an individual. That is, eternity will demand of him that he shall have lived as an individual. . . . For, after all, what is eternity's accounting other than that the voice of conscience is forever installed with its eternal right to be the exclusive voice? What is it other than that throughout eternity an infinite stillness reigns wherein the conscience may talk with the individual about what he, as an individual, of what he has done of Good or of evil, and about the fact that during his life he did not wish to be an individual? What is it other than that within eternity there is infinite space so that each person, as an individual, is apart with his conscience? . . . Here in the temporal order conscience is prepared to make each person into an individual. But here in the temporal order, in the unrest, in the noise, in the pressure of the mob, in the crowd, in the primeval forest of evasion, alas, it is true, the calamity still happens that someone completely stifles the voice of his conscience—his conscience, for he can never rid himself of it. It continues to belong to him, or more accurately, he continues to belong to it. (184-86)

Eternity scatters the crowd by giving each an infinite weight, by making him heavy—as an individual. For what in eternity is the highest blessing is also the deepest seriousness. What, there, is the most blessed comfort, is also the most appalling responsibility. (193)

He is not, therefore, eternally responsible for whether he reaches his goal within this world of time. But without exception, he is eternally responsible for the kind of means he uses. And when he will only use or only uses those means which are genuinely good, then, in the judgment of eternity, he is at the goal. If reaching the goal should be the excuse and the defense for the use of illicit or questionable means—alas, suppose he should die tomorrow. Then the clever one would be caught in his own folly. He had used illicit means, and he died before reaching the goal. For reaching the goal comes at the conclusion; but using the means comes at the beginning. Reaching the goal is like hitting the mark with his shot; but using the means is like taking aim. . . . He whose means are invariably just as important as the end, never comes too late. (202f.)

. . . In eternity there is not the remotest thought of any common plight. In eternity, the individual, yes, you, my listener, and I as individuals will each be asked solely about himself as an individual and about the individual details in his life. (212)

Concluding Unscientific Postscript

While objective thought is indifferent to the thinking subject and his existence, the subjective thinker is as an existing individual essentially interested in his own thinking, existing as he does in his thought. His thinking has therefore a different type of reflection, namely the reflection of inwardness, of possession, by virtue of which it belongs to the thinking subject and to no one else. While *objective thought* translates everything into *results*, and helps all mankind to cheat, by copying these off and reciting them by rote, *subjective thought* puts everything in process and omits the result; partly because this belongs to him who has the way, and partly because as an existing individual he is constantly in *process of coming to be,* which holds true of every human being who has not permitted himself to be deceived into becoming objective, inhumanly identifying himself with speculative philosophy in the abstract.

The reflection of inwardness gives to the subjective thinker a *double reflection.* In *thinking,* he thinks the *universal;* but as existing in this thought and as assimilating it in his inwardness, he becomes more and more subjectively *isolated.* (67f.)

An existing individual is constantly in process of becoming; the actual existing subjective thinker constantly reproduces this existential situation in his thoughts, and translates all his thinking into terms of process. (79) The systematic Idea is the identity of subject and object, the unity of thought and being. Existence, on the other hand, is their separation. It does not by any means follow that existence is thoughtless; but it has brought about, and brings about, a separation between subject and object, thought and being. . . . Being an individual man is a thing that has been abolished, and every speculative philosopher confuses himself with humanity at large; whereby he becomes something infinitely great, and at the same time nothing at all. . . . And when one finds that every cellar-dweller can play the game of being humanity, one learns at last, that being purely and simply a human being is a more significant thing than playing the society game in this fashion. (112f.) To be a particular individual is world-historically absolutely nothing, infinitely nothing—and yet, this is the only true and highest significance of a human being, so much higher as to make every other significance illusory. (134)

. . . If initially my human nature is merely an abstract something, it is at any rate the task which life sets me to become subjective; and in the same degree that I become subjective, the uncertainty of death comes more and more to interpenetrate my subjectivity dialectically. It thus becomes more and more important for me to think it in connection with every factor and phase of my life; for since the uncertainty is there in every moment, it can be overcome only by overcoming it in every moment. (149)

Not for a single moment is it forgotten that the subject is an existing individual, and that existence is a process of becoming, and that therefore the notion of the truth as identity of thought and being is a chimera of abstraction, in its truth only an expectation of the creature; not because the truth is not such an identity, but because the knower is an existing individual for whom the truth cannot be such an identity as long as he lives in time. . . . If an existing individual were really able to (transcend himself), the truth would be for him something final and complete; but where is the point at which he is outside himself? . . . All knowledge which does not *inwardly* relate itself to existence, in the reflection of inwardness, is, essentially viewed, accidental knowledge. . . . It means that knowledge has a relationship to the knower, who is essentially an existing individual, and that for this reason all essential knowledge is essentially related to existence. Only ethical and ethico-religious knowledge has an essential relationship to the existence of the knower. . . . The fact that the truth becomes a paradox is rooted precisely in its having a relationship to an existing subject. . . .

When the question of truth is raised in an objective manner, reflection is directed objectively to the truth, as an object to which the knower is related. Reflection is not focussed upon the relationship, however, but upon the question of whether it is the truth to which the knower is related. If only the object to which he is related is the truth, the subject is accounted to be in the truth. When the question of the truth is raised subjectively, reflection is directed subjectively to the nature of the individual's relationship; if only the mode of this relationship is in the truth, the individual is in the truth even if he should happen to be thus related to what is not true. (176-178)

The objective accent falls on WHAT is said, the subjective accent on HOW it is said. This distinction holds even in the aesthetic realm, and receives definite expression in the principle that what is in itself true may in the mouth of such and such a person become untrue. . . . In the ethico-religious sphere, accent is again on the "how." But this is not to be understood as referring to demeanor, expression, or the like; rather it refers to the relationship sustained by the existing individual, in his own existence, to the content of his utterance. Objectively the interest is focussed merely on the thought-content, subjectively on the inwardness. At its maximum this inward "how" is the passion of the infinite, and the passion of the infinite is the truth. But the passion of the infinite is precisely subjectivity, and thus subjectivity becomes the truth. . . . *An objective uncertainty held fast in an appropriation-process of the most passionate inwardness is the truth,* the highest truth attainable for an *existing* individual. (181f.)

All knowledge about reality is possibility. The only reality to which an existing individual may have a relation that is more than cognitive, is his own reality, the fact that he exists; this reality constitutes his absolute interest. Abstract thought requires him to become disinterested in order to acquire knowledge; the ethical demand is that he become infinitely interested in existing. . . . The real subject is not the cognitive subject, since in knowing he moves in the sphere of the possible; the real subject is the ethically existing subject. An abstract thinker exists to be sure, but this fact is rather a satire on him than otherwise. For an abstract thinker to try to prove his existence by the fact that he thinks, is a curious contradiction; for in the degree that he thinks abstractly he abstracts from his own existence. In so far his existence is revealed as a presupposition from which he seeks emancipation; but the act of abstraction nevertheless becomes a strange sort of proof for his existence, since if it succeeded entirely his existence would cease. (280f.)

The ethical is concerned with particular human beings, and with each and every one of them by himself. . . . The ethical lays hold of each individual and demands that he refrain from all contemplation, especially of humanity and the world; for the ethical, as being the internal, cannot be observed by an outsider. It can be realized only by the individual subject, who alone can know what it is that moves within him. This ethical reality is the only reality which does not become a mere possibility through being known, and which can be known only through being thought; for it is the individual's own reality. (284)

José Ortega y Gasset

In Search of Goethe from Within

Life is an operation which is done in a forward direction. One lives *toward* the future, because to live consists inexorably in *doing*, in each individual life *making* itself. (289)

If you ask your own self, strictly and peremptorily, Who am I? —not, What am I? but, Who is that *I* of whom I perpetually talk in my daily life—you will become aware of the incredible manner in which philosophy has always gone astray by giving the name of "I" to the most unlikely things but never to the thing you call "I" in your daily life. That I which is you, my dear friend, does not consist in your body, nor yet in your soul, your consciousness, or your character. You found yourself with a body, a soul, a character, as you found yourself with the capital which your parents left you, with the country in which you were born, and with the human society in which you move. Just as you are not your liver, be it sound or diseased, neither are you your memory, be it good or bad, nor your will, be it strong or weak, nor your intelligence, be it acute or dull. The I which you are, found itself with these physical or psychical *things* when it found itself alive. You are the person who has to live *with* them, *by means of* them, and perhaps you spend your life protesting against the soul with which you were endowed—of its lack of will, for example—as you protest against your bad stomach or of the cold climate of your country. The soul, then, remains as much *outside* the *I* which you are, as the landscape remains outside your body. Let us say, if you choose, that among the things with which you found yourself, your soul is the closest to you, but it is not you yourself. We must learn to free ourselves from the traditional idea which would have reality always consist in some *thing*, be it physical or mental. You are no *thing*, you are simply the person who has to live *with* things, *among* things, the person who has to live, not *any* life but a *particular* life. There is no abstract living. Life means the inexorable necessity of realizing the design for an existence which each one of us is. This design in which the I consists, is not an idea or plan ideated by the person involved, and freely chosen. It is anterior to (in the sense of independent from) all the ideas which his intellect forms, to all the decisions of his will. Our will is free *to realize or not to realize* this vital design which we ultimately are, but it cannot correct it, change it, abbreviate it, or substitute anything for it. We are indelibly that single programmatic personage who must be realized. The outside world or our own character makes that realization easier or more difficult. Life is essentially a drama, because it is a desperate struggle—with things and even with our character—to succeed in being in fact that which we are in design. . . .

We must get over the error which makes us think that a man's life takes place inside himself and that, consequently, it can be reduced to pure psychology. Would that our lives did take place inside ourselves! Then life would be the easiest thing imaginable: it would be to float in its own element. But life is as far as possible from a subjective phenomenon. It is the most objective of all realities. It is a man's *I* finding itself submerged in precisely what is not himself, in the pure *other* which is his environment. To live is to be outside oneself, to realize oneself.—The vital program which each one of us irremediably is, overpowers environment to lodge itself there. This unity of dramatic dynamism between the two elements, the I and the world—is life. . . .

Nothing can so properly be called *I* as that programmatic personage, because upon its peculiarity depends the value which all *our* things—our body, our soul, our character, our circumstances —finally assume in our life. They are ours through their favorable or unfavorable relation to the personage who has to be realized. For this reason, it cannot be said that two different men find themselves in the same situation. The disposition of things around them, which abstractly would seem to be identical, responds differently to the different inner destiny which is each of them. I am a certain absolutely individual pressure upon the world: the world is the no less definite and individual resistance to that pressure.

A man—that is, his soul, his gifts, his character, his body—is the sum of organs *by* which his life is lived; he is therefore equivalent to an actor bidden to represent the personage which is his real I. And here appears the most surprising thing in the drama of life: a man possesses a wide margin of freedom with respect to his I or destiny. He can refuse to realize it, he can be untrue to himself. Then his life lacks authenticity. If "vocation" is not taken to mean what it commonly does—merely a generic form of professional occupation, of the civil *curriculum*—but to mean an integral and individual program of existence, the simplest thing would be to say that our I is our vocation. Thus we can be true to our vocation to a greater or lesser degree, and consequently have a life that is authentic to a greater or lesser degree. . . .

The matter of the greatest interest is not the man's struggle with the world, with his external destiny, but his struggle with his vocation. How does he behave when faced with his inexorable vocation? Does he subscribe to it basically; or, on the contrary, is he a deserter from it, does he fill his existence with substitutes for what would have been his authentic life? Perhaps the most tragic thing about the human situation is that a man may try to supplant himself, that is, to falsify his life. . . .

When something is merely an object, it is merely an appearance for another and not a reality for itself. Life cannot be a mere object, because it consists precisely in its execution, in being actually lived, and hence being never concluded, never definitive. It does not allow itself to be contemplated from without: the eye must transport itself there and *make reality itself its point of view*. . . .

. . . Goethe . . . is the man in whom for the first time there dawned the consciousness that human life is man's struggle with his intimate and individual destiny—that is, that human life is made up of the problem of itself, that its substance consists not in something that already *is*—like the substance of the Greek philosopher and, more subtly but in the last analysis equally, that of the modern idealist philosopher—but in something which has to make itself, which, therefore, is not a *thing* but an absolute and problematical *task*. (293-296)

. . . Let there be no confounding the *ought to be* of morality, which inhabits man's intellectual region, with the vital imperative, the *has to be* of personal vocation, situated in the most profound and primary region of our being. All the things of the intellect and the will are secondary, are actually a reaction provoked by our basic being. If the human intellect functions, it is actually in order to solve the problems which the man's inner destiny sets it. . . . Man recognizes his I, his unique vocation, only through the liking or aversion aroused in him by each separate situation. Unhappiness, like the needle of a registering apparatus, tells him when his actual life realizes his vital program, his entelechy, and when it departs from it. . . . *Only his sufferings and his satisfactions instruct him concerning himself*. Who is this "himself" which is only discernible *a posteriori*, in its collision with what befalls it? Obviously it is our life-design, which, in the case of suffering, does not coincide with our actual life: the man is torn apart, is cut in two—the man who had to be and the man he came to be. Such a dislocation manifests itself in the form of grief, anxiety, ennui, depression, emptiness; coincidence, on the contrary, produces the prodigious phenomenon of happiness. (298f.)

. . . A vocation, although it is always individual, is obviously composed of numerous generic ingredients. However much of an individual you may be . . . you have to be a man, to be a German or a Frenchman, to be of one period or another, and each one of these designations brings in its train a whole repertory of definite destinies. However, all this is not properly destiny until it has been individually modulated. Destiny is never abstract and generic, although not all destinies have the same degree of concretion. . . . It would be a fundamental error to believe that a man's vocation coincides with his most indisputable gifts. . . . Sometimes a man's vocation does not run in the direction of his gifts, sometimes it runs contrary to them. There are cases—such as

Goethe's—in which the multiplicity of gifts troubles and disorients the vocation, or at least the man who is its axis. . . .

Life is our reaction to the basic insecurity which constitutes its substance. Hence it is an extremely serious matter for a man to find himself too much surrounded by apparent securities. A consciousness of security kills life. . . . A man can have but *one* authentic life, the life which his vocation demands of him. When his freedom induces him to deny his irrevocable *I* and arbitrarily substitute some other for it—arbitrarily, even though in accordance with the most respectable "reasons"—he leads a spectral, unsatisfied life between . . . "poetry and reality." . . . Once the idea that life is a symbol is accepted, one thing is as good as another. . . . But destiny is precisely the opposite of the "as good as" of symbolism! . . . If all that a man does is mere symbol, what is the definite reality which is symbolized in it, in what does his authentic task consist? . . . It is impossible that there should be a more complete reversal of the truth. Because living is precisely the inexorable necessity to make oneself determinate, to *enter into an exclusive destiny,* to accept it—that is, to resolve to *be it.* We *have,* whether we like it or not, to realize our "personage," our vocation, our vital program, our "entelechy" —there is no lack of names for the terrible reality which is our authentic I. (303-307)

The fact is that *there is no species aeternitatis.* And not fortuitously. What there *is,* is the real, *what composes destiny.* And the real is never *species, aspect, spectacle,* an object of contemplation. All that is precisely the unreal. It is our idea, not our being. Europe needs to cure itself of its "Idealism"—which is also the only way to overcome all materialism, positivism, utopism. Ideas are always too close to our whim, are obedient to it—they are always revocable. We have, no doubt, increasingly to live *with* ideas—but we must stop living *from* our ideas and learn to live *from* our inexorable, irrevocable destiny. Our destiny must determine our ideas, and not vice versa. Primitive man was lost in the world of things, there in the forest; we are lost in a world of ideas which show us existence as a cupboard full of equivalent possibilities, of things comparatively indifferent, of *Ziemlichgleichgültigkeiten.* (Our ideas—that is, culture. The present crisis is less a crisis of culture than of the position we have given to culture. We have set it before and above life, when it ought to be behind and below life—because it is a reaction to life. . . .)

Life consists in giving up the state of availability. Mere availability is the characteristic of youth faced with maturity. The youth, because he is not yet anything determinate and irrevocable, is everything potentially. Herein lies his charm and his insolence. Feeling that he is everything potentially he *supposes* that he is everything actually. The youth does not need to live on himself: he lives all other lives potentially—he is simultaneously Homer and Alexander, Newton, Kant, Napoleon, Don Juan. He has *inherited* all these lives. The youth is always a *patrician,* always the "young master." The growing insecurity of his existence proceeds to eliminate possibilities, matures him. . . . Serious economic difficulties begin, the struggle with the rest of mankind begins. The asperity, the bitterness, the hostility of our mundane environment appear. This first attack either forever annihilates our heroic resolve to be what we secretly are and gives birth to the philistine in us; or, on the other hand, in the collision with the *counter-I* which the universe is, our I is revealed to itself, resolves to be, to impose itself, to stamp its image on external destiny. But if at this period, instead of coming against the world's resistance for the first time, we find it giving way before us, roused to no waves by our passage, fulfilling our desires with magic docility, our I will fall voluptuously asleep; instead of being revealed to itself, it remains vague. Nothing so saps the profound resources of a life as finding life too easy. (308f.)

Note: Heidegger's admirable book, *Being and Time,* published in 1927, arrives at a definition of life not far from this. It would be impossible for me to say how close Heidegger's philosophy comes to that which has always inspired my writings—among other things, because Heidegger's work is not yet finished, nor, on the other hand, have my ideas been adequately developed *in print.* But I am obliged to say that I owe Heidegger very little. Of Heidegger's important concepts, but one or two at most have not been previously expressed in one of my books, sometimes thirteen years earlier. For example: the idea of life as uneasiness, preoccupation, and insecurity, and of culture as security and preoccupation with security. . . . The same is true of liberation from all "substantialism," from all that is "thing," in the idea of being—. . . . Life as the confrontation of the I and *its* environment, as a "dynamic dialogue between the individual and the world," in many passages. The structure of life as futurition is the most persistent *leitmotiv* of my writings. . . . Even the interpretation of truth as *aletheia,* in its etymological sense of "disclosure, unwrapping, removing a veil or covering," is to be found on page 80, with the additional circumstance that in this book cognition, under the names of "light" and "clarity" (which are now so much in evidence!), already appears as the imperative and mission enclosed "in the root of the *constitution of man.*" . . . Philosophy is consubstantial with human life, because human life has to go out into the "world," which . . . signifies not the sum of things but the "horizon" (*sic*) of totality *above* things and distinct from them. . . . The theme of our time consists in reducing pure reason to "vital reason." (312f.)

Martin Heidegger

Being and Time

We are ourselves the entities to be analysed. The Being of any such entity is *in each case mine*. . . . Accordingly those characteristics which can be exhibited in this entity are not "properties" present-at-hand of some entity which "looks" so and so and is itself present-at-hand; they are in each case possible ways for it to be, and no more than that. . . . Dasein has *in each case mineness,* one must always use a *personal* pronoun when one addresses it: "I am," "you are." . . . In each case Dasein *is* its possibility, and it "has" this possibility, but not just as a property, as something present-at-hand would. And because Dasein is in each case essentially its own possibility, it *can,* in its very Being, "choose" itself and win itself; it can also lose itself and never win itself; or only "seem" to do so. But only in so far as it is essentially something which can be *authentic*—that is, something of its own—can it have lost itself and not yet won itself. As modes of Being, *authenticity* and *inauthenticity* are both grounded in the fact that any Dasein whatsoever is characterized by mineness. (67f.)

Dasein understands its ownmost Being in the sense of a certain "factual Being-present-at-hand." And yet the "factuality" of the fact of one's own Dasein is at bottom quite different ontologically from the factual occurrence of some kind of mineral, for example. (82)

. . . This "I-here" does not mean a certain privileged point—that of an I-Thing—but it is to be understood as Being-in in terms of the "yonder" of the world that is ready-to-hand—the "yonder" which is the dwelling-place of Dasein as *concern.* (155) . . . But this distantiality which belongs to Being-with, is such that Dasein, as everyday Being-with-one-another, stands in *subjection* to Others. It itself *is* not; its Being has been taken away by the Others. Dasein's everyday possibilities of Being are for the Others to dispose of as they please. These Others, moreover, are not *definite* Others. On the contrary, any Other can represent them. What is decisive is just that inconspicuous domination by Others which has already been taken over unawares from Dasein as Being-with. One belongs to the Others oneself and enhances their power. "The

Others" whom one thus designates in order to cover up the fact of one's belonging to them essentially oneself, are those who proximally and for the most part *"are there"* in everyday Being-with-one-another. The "who" is not this one, not that one, not oneself, not some people, and not the sum of them all. The "who" is the neuter, *the "they"*. . . . This Being-with-one-another dissolves one's own Dasein completely into the kind of Being of "the Others," in such a way, indeed, that the Others, as distinguishable and explicit, vanish more and more. In this inconspicuousness and unascertainability, the real dictatorship of the "they" is unfolded. We take pleasure and enjoy ourselves as *they* take pleasure; we read, see, and judge about literature and art as *they* see and judge; likewise we shrink back from the "great mass" as *they* shrink back; we find "shocking" what *they* find shocking. The "they," which is nothing definite, and which all are, though not as the sum, prescribes the kind of Being of everydayness. . . . Every kind of priority gets noiselessly suppressed. Overnight, everything that is primordial gets glossed over as something that has long been well known. Everything gained by a struggle becomes just something to be manipulated. Every secret loses its force. This care of averageness reveals in turn an essential tendency of Dasein which we call the "levelling down" of all possibilities of Being. . . . It is insensitive to every difference of level and of genuineness and thus never gets to the "heart of the matter." By publicness everything gets obscured, and what has thus been covered up gets passed off as something familiar and accessible to everyone.

The "they" is there alongside everywhere, but in such a manner that it has always stolen away whenever Dasein presses for a decision. Yet because the "they" presents every judgment and decision as its own, it deprives the particular Dasein of its answerability. The "they" can, as it were, manage to have "them" constantly invoking it. It can be answerable for everything most easily, because it is not someone who needs to vouch for anything. It "was" always the "they" who did it, and yet it can be said it has been "no one." . . . Everyone is the other, and no one is himself. The *"they,"* which supplies the answer to the question of the *"who"* of everyday Dasein, is the *"nobody"* to whom every Dasein has already surrendered itself in Being-among-one-other. . . . The Self of everyday Dasein is the *they-self,* which we distinguish from the *authentic self*—that is, from the Self which has been taken hold of in its own way. As they-self, the particular Dasein has been *dispersed* into the "they," and must first find itself. . . . *Proximally,* it is not "I," in the sense of my own Self, that "am," but rather the Others, whose way is that of the "they." In terms of the "they," and as the "they," I am "given" proximally to "myself." Proximally Dasein is "they," and for the most part it remains so. If Dasein discovers the world in its own way and brings it close, if it discloses to itself its own authentic Being, then this discovery of the "world" and this disclosure of Dasein are always accomplished as a clearing-away of concealments and obscurities, as a breaking up of the disguises with which Dasein bars its own way. . . . From the kind of Being which belongs to the "they"—the kind which is closest—everyday Dasein draws its pre-ontological way of interpreting its Being. . . . It understands Dasein in terms of the world and comes across it as an entity within-the-world. . . . *Authentic being-one's-self* does not rest upon an exceptional condition of the subject, a condition that has been detached from the "they"; *it is rather an existentiell modification of the "they"—of the "they" as an essential existentiale*. But in that case there is ontologically a gap separating the selfsameness of the authentically existing Self from the identity of that "I" which maintains itself throughout its manifold Experiences. (164-168)

This entity carries in its ownmost Being the character of not being closed off. In the expression "there" we have in view this essential disclosedness. By reason of this disclosedness, this entity (Dasein), together with the Being-there of the world, is "there" for itself. . . . To say that it is "illuminated" means that *as* Being-in-the-world it is cleared in itself, not through any other entity, but in such a way that it *is* itself the clearing. . . . By its very nature, Dasein brings its "there" along with it. If it lacks its "there," it is not factically the entity which is essentially Dasein; indeed, it is not this entity at all. *Dasein is its disclosedness.* (171) . . . *Facticity is not the factuality of the factum brutum of something present-at-hand, but a characteristic of Dasein's Being—one which has been taken up into existence, even if proximally it has been thrust aside.*

. . . An entity of the character of Dasein is its "there" in such a way that, whether explicitly or not, it finds itself in its thrownness. In a state-of-mind Dasein is always brought before itself, and has always found itself, not in the sense of coming across itself by perceiving itself, but in the sense of finding itself in the mood that it has. . . . Ontologically mood is a primordial kind of Being for Dasein, in which Dasein is disclosed to itself *prior* to all cognition and volition, and *beyond* their range of disclosure. . . . Ontologically, we thus obtain as the *first* essential characteristic of states-of-mind that *they disclose Dasein in its thrown-*

ness, and—proximally and for the most part—in the manner of an evasive turning-away. . . . We have seen that the world, Dasein-with, and existence are *equiprimordially disclosed;* and state-of-mind is a basic existential species of their disclosedness, because this disclosedness itself is essentially Being-in-the-world. . . . Dasein's openness to the world is constituted existentially by the attunement of a state-of-mind. . . . *Existentially, a state-of-mind implies a disclosive submission to the world, out of which we can encounter something that matters to us.* Indeed *from the ontological point of view* we must as a general principle leave the discovery of the world to "bare mood." Pure beholding, even if it were to penetrate to the innermost core of the Being of something present-at-hand, could never discover anything like that which is threatening. . . . [We must] recognize the existentially positive character of the capacity for delusion. It is precisely when we see the "world" unsteadily and fitfully in accordance with our moods, that the ready-to-hand shows itself in its specific worldhood, which is never the same from day to day. . . . Any cognitive determining has its existential-ontological Constitution in the state-of-mind of Being-in-the-world. (174-177)

Only an entity for which in its Being this very Being is an issue, can be afraid. Fearing discloses this entity as endangered and abandoned to itself. Fear always reveals Dasein in the Being of its "there." (180) . . . State-of-mind is *one* of the existential structures in which the Being of the "there" maintains itself. Equiprimordial with it in constituting this Being is *understanding.* A state-of-mind always has its understanding, even if it merely keeps it suppressed. Understanding always has its mood. . . . The kind of Being which Dasein has, as potentiality-for-Being, lies existentially in understanding. Dasein is not something present-at-hand which possesses its competence for something by way of an extra; it is primarily Being-possible. . . . The Being-possible which is essential for Dasein, pertains to the ways of its solicitude for Others and of its concern with the "world," as we have characterized them; and in all these, and always, it pertains to Dasein's potentiality-for-Being towards itself, for the sake of itself. . . . Possibility as an *existentiale* is the most primordial and ultimate positive way in which Dasein is characterized ontologically. . . . Dasein is Being-possible which has been delivered over to itself—*thrown possibility* through and through. Dasein is the possibility of Being-free *for* its ownmost potentiality-for-Being. (182f.)

Understanding is the existential Being of Dasein's own poten-

tiality-for-Being; and it is so in such a way that this Being discloses in itself what its Being is capable of. (184) . . . The sight which is related primarily and on the whole to existence we call "*transparency*." We choose this term to designate "knowledge of the Self" in a sense which is well understood, so as to indicate that here it is not a matter of perceptually tracking down and inspecting a point called the "Self," but rather one of seizing upon the full disclosedness of Being-in-the-world *throughout all* the constitutive items which are essential to it, and doing so with understanding. In existing, entities sight "themselves" only in so far as they have become transparent to themselves with equal primordiality in those items which are constitutive for their existence: their Being-alongside the world and their Being-with Others. (187)

. . . Dasein is proximally and for the most part *alongside* the "world" of its concern. This "absorption in . . ." has mostly the character of Being-lost in the publicness of the "they." Dasein has, in the first instance, fallen away from itself as an authentic potentiality for Being its Self, and has fallen into the "world." "Fallenness" into the "world" means an absorption in Being-with-one-another, in so far as the latter is guided by idle talk, curiosity, and ambiguity. . . . Idle talk discloses to Dasein a Being towards its world, towards Others, and towards itself—a Being in which these are understood, but in a mode of groundless floating. Curiosity discloses everything and anything, yet in such a way that Being-in is everywhere and nowhere. Ambiguity hides nothing from Dasein's understanding, but only in order that Being-in-the-world should be suppressed in this uprooted "everywhere and nowhere." . . . If Dasein itself, in idle talk and in the way things have been publicly interpreted, presents to itself the possibility of losing itself in the "they" and falling into groundlessness, this tells us that Dasein prepares for itself a constant temptation towards falling. Being-in-the-world is in itself *tempting.* (220f.)

Accordingly *Dasein's "average everydayness"* can be defined as *"Being-in-the-world which is falling and disclosed, thrown and projecting, and for which its ownmost potentiality-for-Being is an issue, both in its Being-alongside the 'world' and in its Being-with others."* (225) . . . Anxiety throws Dasein back upon that which it is anxious about—its authentic potentiality-for-Being-in-the-world. Anxiety individualizes Dasein for its ownmost Being-in-the-world, which as something that understands, projects itself essentially upon possibilities. . . . Anxiety makes manifest in Dasein its Being towards its ownmost potentiality-for-Being—that is, for *Being-free-for* the freedom of choosing itself and taking hold of itself. Anxiety brings Dasein face to face with its *Being-free-for* the authenticity of its Being, and for this authenticity as a possibility which it always is. (232) . . . That kind of Being-in-the-world which is tranquillized and familiar is a mode of Dasein's uncanniness, not the reverse. *From an existential-ontological point of view, the "not-at-home" must be conceived as the more primordial phenomenon.* . . . But in anxiety there lies the possibility of a disclosure which is quite distinctive; for anxiety individualizes. This individualization brings Dasein back from its falling, and makes manifest to it that authenticity and inauthenticity are possibilities of its Being. (234f.)

If the "cogito sum" is to serve as the point of departure for the existential analytic of Dasein, then it needs to be turned around, and furthermore its content needs new ontologico-phenomenal confirmation. The "sum" is then asserted first, and indeed in the sense that "I am in a world." As such an entity, "I am" is the possibility of Being towards various ways of comporting myself—namely, *cogitationes*—as ways of Being alongside entities within-the-world. (254) . . . The most primordial, and indeed the most authentic, disclosedness in which Dasein, as a potentiality-for-Being, can be, is the *truth of existence.* (264) . . . *Because the kind of Being that is essential to truth is of the character of Dasein, all truth is relative to Dasein's Being.* . . . Even the "universal validity" of truth is rooted solely in the fact that Dasein can uncover entities in themselves and free them. (270) . . . The ideas of a "pure 'I'" and of a "consciousness in general" are so far from including the *a priori* character of "actual" subjectivity that the ontological characters of Dasein's facticity and its state of Being are either passed over or not seen at all. . . . Both the contention that there are "eternal truths" and the jumbling together of Dasein's phenomenally grounded "ideality" with an idealized absolute subject, belong to those residues of Christian theology within philosophical problematics which have not as yet been radically extruded. (272)

No one can take the other's dying away from him. . . . By its very essence, death is in every case mine, in so far as it "is" at all. And indeed death signifies a peculiar possibility-of-Being in which the very Being of one's own Dasein is an issue. In dying, it is shown that mineness and existence are ontologically constitutive for death. Dying is not an event; it is a phenomenon to be understood existentially. . . . But if "ending," as dying, is constitutive for Dasein's totality, then the Being of this wholeness itself must be conceived as an existential phenomenon of a Dasein which is in each case one's own. (284) . . . Death is a possibility-of-Being which Dasein itself has to take over in every case. With death, Dasein stands before itself in its ownmost potentiality-for-Being. This is a possibility in which the issue is nothing less than Dasein's Being-in-the-world. Its death is the possibility of no-longer-being-able-to-be-there. If Dasein stands before itself as this possibility, it has been *fully* assigned to its ownmost potentiality-for-Being. When it stands before itself in this way, all its relations to any other Dasein have been undone. This ownmost non-relational possibility is at the same time the uttermost one. . . . Anxiety in the face of death is anxiety "in the face of" that potentiality-for-Being which is one's ownmost, non-relational, and not to be outstripped. (294f.) . . . *The "they" does not permit us the courage for anxiety in the face of death.* . . . In thus falling and fleeing *in the face of* death, Dasein's everydayness attests that the very "they" itself already has the definite character of *Being-towards-death,* even when it is not explicitly engaged in "thinking about death." (298f.)

. . . To project itself on its ownmost potentiality-for-Being means to be able to understand itself in the Being of the entity so revealed—namely, to exist. Anticipation turns out to be the possibility of understanding one's *ownmost* and uttermost potentiality-for-Being—that is to say, the possibility of *authentic existence.* . . . Death is Dasein's *ownmost* possibility. Here it can become manifest to Dasein that in this distinctive possibility of its own self, it has been wrenched away from the "they." This means that in anticipation any Dasein can have wrenched itself away from the "they" already. . . . When, by anticipation, one becomes free *for* one's own death, one is liberated from one's lostness in those possibilities which may accidentally thrust themselves upon one; and one is liberated in such a way that for the first time one can authentically understand and choose among the factical possibilities lying ahead of that possibility which is not to be outstripped. Anticipation discloses to existence that its uttermost possibility lies in giving itself up, and thus it shatters all one's tenaciousness to whatever existence one has reached. . . . Holding death for true (death *is* just one's own) shows another kind of certainty, and is more primordial than any certainty which relates to entities encountered within-the-world, or to formal objects; for it is certain of Being-in-the-world. As such, holding death for true does not demand just *one* definite kind of behaviour in Dasein, but demands Dasein itself in the full authenticity of its existence. . . . In anticipating the definite certainty of death, Dasein opens itself to a constant *threat* arising out of its own "there." In this very threat Being-towards-the-end must maintain itself. . . . *The state-of-mind which can hold open the utter and constant threat to itself arising from Dasein's ownmost individualized Being, is anxiety.* In this state-of-mind, Dasein finds itself *face to face* with the "nothing" of the possible impossibility of its existence. . . . *Anticipation reveals to Dasein its lostness in the they-self, and brings it face to face with the possibility of Being itself, primarily unsupported by concernful solicitude, but of Being itself, rather, in an impassioned* FREEDOM TOWARDS DEATH—*a freedom which has been released from the illusions of the "they," and which is factical, certain of itself, and anxious.* (307-311)

With Dasein's lostness in the "they," that factical potentiality-for-Being which is closest to it (the tasks, rules, and standards, the urgency and extent, of concernful and solicitous Being-in-the-world) has already been decided upon. The "they" has always kept Dasein from taking hold of these possibilities of Being. The "they" even hides the manner in which it has tacitly relieved Dasein of the burden of explicitly *choosing* these possibilities. It remains indefinite who has "really" done the choosing. So Dasein makes no choices, gets carried along by the nobody, and thus ensnares itself in inauthenticity. This process can be reversed only if Dasein specifically brings itself back to itself from its lostness in the "they." But this bringing-back must have that kind of Being *by the neglect of which* Dasein has lost itself in inauthenticity. When Dasein thus brings itself back from the "they," the they-self is modified in an existentiell manner so that it becomes *authentic* Being-one's Self. This must be accomplished by *making up for not choosing.* But "making up" for not choosing signifies *choosing to make this choice*—deciding for a potentiality-for-Being, and making this decision from one's own Self. In choosing to make this choice, Dasein *makes possible*, first and foremost, its authentic potentiality-for-Being.

But because Dasein is *lost* in the "they," it must first *find* itself. In order to find *itself* at all, it must be "shown" to itself in its possible authenticity. In terms of its *possibility,* Dasein *is* already a potentiality-for-Being-its-Self, but it needs to have this potentially attested. . . . This potentiality is attested by that which, in Dasein's everyday interpretation of itself, is familiar to us as the "*voice of conscience.*" . . . The call of conscience has the character of an *appeal* to Dasein by calling it to its ownmost potentiality-for-Being-its-Self; and this is done by way of *summoning* it to its ownmost Being-guilty. (312-314)

When the they-self is appealed to, it gets called to the Self. But it does not get called to that Self which can become for itself an "object" on which to pass judgment, nor to that Self which inertly dissects its "inner life" with fussy curiosity, nor to that Self which one has in mind when one gazes "analytically" at psychical conditions and what lies behind them. The appeal to the Self in the they-self does not force it inwards upon itself, so that it can close itself off from the "external world." The call passes over everything like this and disperses it, so as to appeal solely to that Self which, notwithstanding, is in no other way than Being-in-the-world. (318) . . . The call comes *from* me and yet *from beyond me*. (320) . . . The call discourses in the uncanny mode of *keeping silent*. And it does this only because, in calling the one to whom the appeal is made, it does not call him into the public idle talk of the "they," but *calls* him *back* from this *into the reticence of his existent* potentiality-for-Being. . . . Conscience, in its basis and its essence, is *in each case mine*—not only in the sense that in each case the appeal is to one's ownmost potentiality-for-Being, but because the call comes from that entity which in each case I myself am. (322f.)

The Self, which as such has to lay the basis for itself, can *never* get that basis into its power. . . . *Dasein as such is guilty*, if our formally existential definition of "guilt" as "Being-the-basis of a nullity" is indeed correct. . . . Not only can entities whose Being is care load themselves with factical guilt, but they *are* guilty in the very basis of their Being; and this Being-guilty is what provides, above all, the ontological condition for Dasein's ability to come to owe anything in factically existing. This essential Being-guilty is, equiprimordially, the existential condition for the possibility of the "morally" good and for that of the "morally" evil—that is, for morality in general and for the possible forms which this may take factically. The primordial "Being-guilty" cannot be defined by morality, since morality already presupposes it for itself. . . . Only because Dasein is guilty in the basis of its Being, and closes itself off from itself as something thrown and falling, is conscience possible. . . . The appeal calls back by calling forth: it calls Dasein *forth* to the possibility of taking over, in existing, even that thrown entity which it is; it calls Dasein *back* to its thrownness so as to understand this thrownness as the null basis which it has to take up into existence. . . . The call of conscience, coming from Dasein itself, is directed towards that entity alone. But if so, the "summons to Being-guilty" signifies a calling-forth to that potentiality-for-Being which in each case I as Dasein am already. Dasein need not first load a "guilt" upon itself through its failures or omissions; it must only *be* "guilty" *authentically*—"guilty" in the way in which it is. Hearing the appeal correctly is thus tantamount to having an understanding of oneself in one's ownmost potentiality-for-Being—that is, to projecting oneself upon one's *ownmost* authentic potentiality for becoming guilty. When Dasein understandingly lets itself be called forth to this possibility, this includes its *becoming free* for the call—its readiness for the potentiality of getting appealed to. In understanding the call, Dasein is *in thrall to its ownmost possibility of existence.* It has chosen itself. (330-334)

This distinctive and authentic disclosedness, which is attested in Dasein itself by its conscience—*this reticent self-projection upon one's ownmost being-guilty, in which one is ready for anxiety*—we call *"resoluteness."* . . . The "world" which is ready-to-hand does not become another one "in its content," nor does the circle of Others get exchanged for a new one; but both one's Being towards the ready-to-hand understandingly and concernfully, and one's solicitous Being with Others, are now given a definite character in terms of their ownmost potentiality-for-Being-their-Selves. . . . Resoluteness, as *authentic being-one's-self,* does not detach Dasein from its world, nor does it isolate it so that it becomes a free-floating "I." And how should it, when resoluteness as authentic disclosedness, is *authentically* nothing else than *Being-in-the-world*? Resoluteness brings the Self right into its current concernful Being-alongside what is ready-to-hand, and pushes it into solicitous Being-with-Others. . . . Resoluteness, by its ontological essence, is always the resoluteness of some factical Dasein at a particular time. The essence of Dasein as an entity is its existence. (343-345) . . . When the call of conscience summons us to our potentiality-for-Being, it does not hold before us some empty ideal of existence, but *calls us forth into the situation.* . . . Resoluteness does not first take cognizance of a Situation and put that Situation before itself; it has put itself into that Situation already. . . . *Resoluteness, however, is only that authenticity which, in care, is the object of care, and which is possible as care—authenticity of care itself.* (347f.)

. . . It is only in the anticipation of death that resoluteness, as Dasein's *authentic* truth, has reached the *authentic certainty* which *belongs* to it. . . . *Temporality gets experienced in a phenomenally primordial way in Dasein's authentic being-a-whole, in the phenomenon of anticipatory resoluteness.* (350f.) . . . The call of conscience passes over its appeal all Dasein's "worldly" prestige and potentialities. Relentlessly it individualizes Dasein down to its potentiality-for-Being-guilty, and exacts of it that it should be this potentiality authentically. (354) . . . An ticipation makes it manifest that this entity has been thrown into the indefiniteness of its "limit-Situation"; when resolved upon the latter, Dasein gains its authentic potentiality-for-Being-a-whole. . . . The "nothing" with which anxiety brings us face to face, unveils the nullity by which Dasein, in its very *basis,* is defined; and this basis itself is as thrownness into death. . . . Anticipatory resoluteness is not a way of escape, fabricated for the "overcoming" of death; it is rather that understanding which follows the call of conscience and which frees for death the possibility of acquiring *power* over Dasein's *existence* and of basically dispersing all fugitive Self-concealments. (356f.)

. . . If the Self belongs to the essential attributes of Dasein, while Dasein's "Essence" lies in *existence,* then "I"-hood and Selfhood must be conceived *existentially.* (365) . . . *In saying "I," Dasein expresses itself as Being-in-the-world.* . . . The they-self keeps on saying "I" most loudly and most frequently because at bottom it *is not authentically* itself, and evades its authentic potentiality-for-Being. . . . Selfhood is to be discerned existentially only in one's authentic potentiality-for-Being-one's-Self—that is to say, in the authenticity of Dasein's Being *as care.* . . . *The constancy of the self,* in the double sense of steadiness and steadfastness, is the *authentic* counter-possibility to the non-Self-constancy which is characteristic of irresolute falling. Existentially, *"self-constancy"* signifies nothing other than anticipatory resoluteness. The ontological structure of such resoluteness reveals the existentiality of the Self's Selfhood. (368f.)

In resoluteness, the Present is not only brought back from distraction with the objects of one's closest concern, but it gets held in the future and in having been. That *present* which is held in authentic temporality and which thus is *authentic* itself, we call the *"moment of vision."* . . . The authentic coming-towards-itself of anticipatory resoluteness is at the same time a coming-back to one's ownmost Self, which has been thrown into its individualization. This ecstasis makes it possible for Dasein to be able to take over resolutely that entity which it already is. (387f.) . . . The forgetting which is constitutive for fear, bewilders Dasein and lets it drift back and forth between "worldly" possibilities which it has not seized upon. In contrast to this making-present which is not held on to, the Present of anxiety is *held on to* when one brings oneself back to one's ownmost thrownness. The existential meaning of anxiety is such that it cannot lose itself in something with which it might be concerned. . . . When fear assails us, it does so from what is within-the-world. Anxiety arises out of Being-in-the-world as thrown Being-towards-death. . . .

But anxiety can mount authentically only in a Dasein which is resolute. He who is resolute knows no fear; but he understands the possibility of anxiety as the possibility of the very mood which neither inhibits nor bewilders him. Anxiety liberates him *from* possibilities which "count for nothing," and lets him become free *for* those which are authentic. (394f.)

The resoluteness in which Dasein comes back to itself, discloses current factical possibilities of authentic existing, and discloses them *in terms of the heritage* which that resoluteness, as thrown, *takes over*. In one's coming back resolutely to one's thrownness, there is hidden a *handing down* to oneself of the possibilities that have come down to one, but not necessarily *as* having thus come down. If everything "good" is a heritage, and the character of "goodness" lies in making authentic existence possible, then the handing down of a heritage constitutes itself in resoluteness. The more authentically Dasein resolves—and this means that in anticipating death it understands itself unambiguously in terms of its ownmost distinctive possibility—the more unequivocally does it choose and find the possibility of its existence, and the less does it do so by accident. Only by the anticipation of death is every accidental and "provisional" possibility driven out. Only Being-free *for* death, gives Dasein its goal outright and pushes existence into its finitude. Once one has grasped the finitude of one's existence, it snatches one back from the endless multiplicity of possibilities which offer themselves as closest to one—those of comfortableness, shirking, and taking things lightly—and brings Dasein into the simplicity of its *fate*. This is how we designate Dasein's primordial historizing, which lies in authentic resoluteness and in which Dasein *hands* itself *down* to itself, free for death, in a possibility which it has inherited and yet has chosen. (435)

Resoluteness constitutes the *loyalty* of existence to its own Self. As resoluteness which is ready for *anxiety*, this loyalty is at the same time a possible way of revering the sole authority which a free existing can have—of revering the repeatable possibilities of existence. . . . In inauthentic historicality, on the other hand, the way in which fate has been primordially stretched along has been hidden. With the inconstancy of the they-self Dasein makes present its "today." In awaiting the next new thing, it has already forgotten the old one. The "they" evades choice. Blind for possibilities, it cannot repeat what has been, but only retains and receives the "actual" that is left over, the world-historical that has been, the leavings, and the information about them that is present-at-hand. (443)

. . . The temporality of resoluteness has, with relation to its Present, the character of a *moment of vision.* When such a moment makes the Situation authentically present, this making-present does not itself take the lead, but is *held* in that future which is in the process of having-been. One's existence in the moment of vision temporalizes itself as something that has been stretched along in a way which is fatefully whole in the sense of the authentic historical *constancy* of the Self. This kind of temporal existence has its time *for* what the Situation demands of it, and it has it "constantly." But resoluteness discloses the "there" in this way only as a Situation. So if he who is resolute encounters anything that has been disclosed, he can never do so in such a way as to lose his time on it irresolutely. (463)

Existence and Being

. . . Only in and from *Da-sein,* as a thing to which we have entry, can any approximation to the truth of Being evolve for historical man. . . . Every sort of "anthropology" and every sort of subjectivity (of man regarded as a subject) [is] abandoned, as was already the case in "Sein und Zeit." (323)

As certainly as we shall never comprehend absolutely the totality of what-is, it is equally certain that we find ourselves placed in the midst of what-is and that this is somehow revealed in totality. Ultimately there is an essential difference between comprehending the totality of what-is and finding ourselves in the midst of what-is-in-totality. The former is absolutely impossible. The latter is going on in existence all the time. . . . Even when, or rather, precisely when we are not absorbed in things or in our own selves, this "wholeness" comes over us—for example, in real boredom. Real boredom is still far off when this book or that play, this activity or that stretch of idleness merely bores us. Real boredom comes when "one is bored." This profound boredom, drifting hither and thither in the abysses of existence like a mute fog, draws all things, all men and oneself along with them, together in a queer kind of indifference. This boredom reveals what-is in totality.

There is another possibility of such revelation, and this is in the joy we feel in the presence of the being—not merely the person—of someone we love. . . . The affective state in which we find ourselves not only discloses, according to the mood we are in, what-is in totality, but this disclosure is at the same time far from being a mere chance occurrence and is the ground-phenomenon of our *Da-sein.* (333f.)

Jean-Paul Sartre

Existentialism

. . . Subjectivity must be the starting point. . . . (45) . . . If God does not exist, there is at least one being in whom existence precedes essence, a being who exists before he can be defined by any concept, and . . . this being is man, or, as Heidegger says, human reality. . . .

. . . First of all, man exists, turns up, appears on the scene, and, only afterwards, defines himself. If man, as the existentialist conceives him, is indefinable, it is because at first he is nothing. Only afterward will he be something, and he himself will have made what he will be. Thus, there is no human nature, since there is no God to conceive it. Not only is man what he conceives himself to be, but he is also only what he wills himself to be after this thrust toward existence. . . .

Man is nothing else but what he makes of himself. Such is the first principle of existentialism. It is also what is called subjectivity, the name we are labeled with when charges are brought against us. But what do we mean by this, if not that man has a greater dignity than a stone or table? For we mean that man first exists, that is, that man first of all is the being who hurls himself toward a future and who is conscious of imagining himself as being in the future. Man is at the start a plan which is aware of itself, rather than a patch of moss, a piece of garbage, or a cauliflower; nothing exists prior to this plan; there is nothing in heaven; man will be what he will have planned to be. Not what he will want to be. Because by the word "will" we generally mean a conscious decision, which is subsequent to what we have already made of ourselves. I may want to belong to a political party, write a book, get married; but all that is only a manifestation of an earlier, more spontaneous choice that is called "will." But if existence really does precede essence, man is responsible for what he is. Thus, existentialism's first move is to make every man aware of what he is and to make the full responsibility of his existence rest on him. And when we say that a man is responsible for himself, we do not only mean that he is responsible for his own individuality, but that he is responsible for all men. . . .

If . . . existence precedes essence, and if we grant that we exist and fashion our image at one and the same time, the image is valid for everybody and for our whole age. . . . If I want to marry, to have children; even if this marriage depends solely on my own circumstances or passion or wish, I am involving all humanity in monogamy and not merely myself. Therefore, I am responsible for myself and for everyone else. I am creating a certain image of man of my own choosing. In choosing myself, I choose man. . . . (18-21)

If existence really does precede essence, there is no explaining things away by reference to a fixed and given human nature. In other words, there is no determinism, man is free, man is freedom. On the other hand, if God does not exist, we find no values or commands to turn to which legitimize our conduct. So, in the bright realm of values, we have no excuse behind us, nor justification before us. We are alone, with no excuses. . . .

That is the idea I shall try to convey when I say that man is condemned to be free. Condemned, because he did not create himself, yet, in other respects is free; because, once thrown into the world, he is responsible for everything he does. The existentialist does not believe in the power of passion. He will never agree that a sweeping passion is a ravaging torrent which fatally leads a man to certain acts and is therefore an excuse. He thinks that man is responsible for his passion. . . . Therefore, he thinks that man, with no support and no aid, is condemned every moment to invent man. (27f.)

There can be no other truth to take off from than this: *I think; therefore, I exist.* There we have the absolute truth of consciousness becoming aware of itself. Every theory which takes man out of the moment in which he becomes aware of himself is, at its very beginning, a theory which confounds truth, for outside the Cartesian *cogito,* all views are only probable.

Secondly, this theory is the only one which gives man dignity, the only one which does not reduce him to an object. The effect of all materialism is to treat all men, including the one philosophizing, as objects, that is, as an ensemble of determined reactions in no way distinguished from the ensemble of qualities and phenomena which constitute a table or a chair or a stone. . . .

. . . If it is impossible to find in every man some universal essence which would be human nature, yet there does exist a universal human condition. It's not by chance that today's thinkers speak more readily of man's condition than of his nature. By condition they mean, more or less definitely, the *a priori* limits which outline man's fundamental situation in the universe. Historical situations vary; a man may be born a slave in a pagan society or a feudal lord or a proletarian. What does not vary is the necessity for him to exist in the world, to be at work there, to be there in the midst of other people, and to be mortal there. (43-45)

. . . Man is in an organized situation in which he himself is involved. Through his choice, he involves all mankind, and he can not avoid making a choice: either he will remain chaste, or he will marry without having children, or he will marry and have children; anyhow, whatever he may do, it is impossible for him not to take full responsibility for the way he handles this problem. Doubtless, he chooses without referring to pre-established values, but it is unfair to accuse him of caprice. (49)

He isn't ready-made at the start. In choosing his ethics, he makes himself, and force of circumstances is such that he can not abstain from choosing one. We define man only in relationship to involvement. It is therefore absurd to charge us with arbitrariness of choice. (51)

. . . To say that we invent values means nothing else but this: life has no meaning *a priori*. Before you come alive, life is nothing; it's up to you to give it a meaning, and value is nothing else but the meaning that you choose. In that way, there is a possibility of creating a human community. (58)

The Age of Reason

"A life," thought Mathieu, "is formed from the future just as bodies are compounded from the void." He bent his head; he thought of his own life. The future had made way into his heart, where everything was in process and suspense. The far-off days of childhood, the day when he had said: "I will be free," the day when he had said: "I will be famous," appeared to him even now with their individual future, like a small, circled individual sky above them all, and that future was himself, *himself* just as he was at present, weary and a little overripe, they had claims upon him across the passage of time past, they maintained their insistencies, and he was often visited by attacks of devastating remorse, because his casual, cynical present was the original future of those past days. It was he whom they had awaited for twenty years, it was he, this tired man, who was pestered by a remorseless child to realize his hopes; on him it depended whether these childish pledges should remain forever childish or whether they should become the first announcement of a destiny. His past was in continual process of retouching by the present; every day belied yet further those old dreams of fame, and every day had a fresh future; from one period of waiting to the next, from future to future, Mathieu's life was gliding—towards what? (234)

"Whatever happens, it is *by my agency* that everything must happen." Even if he let himself be carried off, in helplessness and in despair, even if he let himself be carried off like an old sack of coal, he would have chosen his own damnation; he was free, free in every way, free to behave like a fool or a machine, free to accept, free to refuse, free to equivocate; to marry, to give up the game, to drag this dead weight about with him for years to come. He could do what he liked, no one had the right to advise him, there would be for him no Good nor Evil unless he brought them into being. All around him things were gathered in a circle, expectant, impassive, and indicative of nothing. He was alone, enveloped in this monstrous silence, free and alone, without assistance and without excuse, condemned to decide without support from any quarter, condemned forever to be free. (275f.)

Being and Nothingness

. . . The human being . . . is at once a *facticity* and a *transcendence.* (56)

. . . Sincerity presents itself as a demand and consequently is not a state. Now what is the ideal to be attained in this case? It is necessary that a man be *for himself* only what he *is*. But is this not precisely the definition of the in-itself? . . . If man is what he is, bad faith is for ever impossible and candor ceases to be his ideal and becomes instead his being. But is man what he is? And more generally, how can he be what he is when he exists as consciousness of being? If candor or sincerity is a universal value, it is evident that the maxim "one must be what one is" does not serve solely as a regulating principle for judgments and concepts by which I express what I am. It posits not merely an ideal of knowing but an ideal of *being;* it proposes for us an absolute equivalence of being with itself as a prototype of being. In this sense it is necessary that we *make ourselves* what we are. But what are we then if we have the constant obligation to make ourselves what we are, if our mode of being is having the obligation to be what we are? (58f.)

. . . A consciousness which affects itself with sadness is sad precisely for this reason. But it is difficult to comprehend the nature of consciousness; the being-sad is not a ready-made being which I give to myself as I can give this book to my friend. I do not possess the property of *affecting myself with being.* If I make myself sad, I must continue to make myself sad from beginning to end. I can not treat my sadness as an impulse finally achieved and put it on file without recreating it, nor can I carry it in the manner of an inert body which continues its movement after the initial shock. There is no inertia in consciousness. If I make myself sad, it is because I *am* not sad—the being of the sadness escapes me by and in the very act by which I affect myself with it. The being-in-itself of sadness perpetually haunts my consciousness (of) being sad, but it is as a value which I can not realize; it stands as a regulative meaning of my sadness, not as its constitutive modality. . . .

. . . My consciousness appears originally to the Other as an absence. It is the object always present as the *meaning* of all my attitudes and all my conduct—and always absent, for it gives itself to the intuition of another as a perpetual question—still better, as a perpetual freedom. . . . Consciousness has to be its own being, it is never sustained by being; it sustains being in the heart of subjectivity, which means once again that it is inhabited by being but that it is not being: *consciousness is not what it is*. . . . Under these conditions what can be the significance of the ideal of sincerity except as a task impossible to achieve, of which the very meaning is in contradiction with the structure of my consciousness. To be sincere, we said, is to be what one is. . . . But we definitely establish that the original structure of "not being what one is" renders impossible in advance all movement toward being in itself or "being what one is." And this impossibility is not hidden from consciousness; on the contrary, it is the very stuff of consciousness; it is the embarrassing constraint which we constantly experience; it is our very incapacity to recognize ourselves, to constitute ourselves as being what we are. It is this necessity which means that, as soon as we posit ourselves as a certain being, by a legitimate judgment, based on inner experience or correctly deduced from *a priori* or empirical premises, then by that very positing we surpass this being—and that not toward another being but toward emptiness, toward *nothing*. . . .

Shall I determine the ensemble of purposes and motivations which have pushed me to do this or that action? But this is already to postulate a causal determinism which constitutes the flow of my states of consciousness as a succession of physical states. Shall I uncover in myself "drives," even though it be to affirm them in shame? But is this not deliberately to forget that these drives are realized with my consent, that they are not forces of nature but that I lend them their efficacy by a perpetually renewed decision concerning their value. Shall I pass judgment on my character, on my nature? Is this not to veil from myself at that moment what I know only too well, that I thus judge a past to which by definition my present is not subject? . . .

Let us take an example: A homosexual frequently has an intolerable feeling of guilt, and his whole existence is determined in relation to this feeling. One will readily foresee that he is in bad faith. In fact it frequently happens that this man, while recognizing his homosexual inclination, while avowing each and every particular misdeed which he has committed, refuses with all his strength to consider himself *"a paederast."* . . . His friend, who is his most severe critic, becomes irritated with this duplicity. The critic asks only one thing—and perhaps then he will show himself indulgent: that the guilty one recognize himself as guilty, that the homosexual declare frankly—whether humbly or boastfully matters little—"I am a paederast." We ask here: Who is in bad faith? The homosexual or the champion of sincerity?

The homosexual recognizes his faults, but he struggles with all his strength against the crushing view that his mistakes constitute for him a *destiny.* He does not wish to let himself be considered as a thing. He has an obscure but strong feeling that an homosexual is not an homosexual as this table is a table or as this red-haired man is red-haired. . . . But instead, he lays claim to "not being a paederast" in the sense in which this table *is not* an inkwell. He is in bad faith. . . . The critic demands of the guilty one that he constitute himself as a thing, precisely in order no longer to treat him as a thing. And this contradiction is constitutive of the demand of sincerity. . . . Who can not see that the sincere man constitutes himself as a thing in order to escape the condition of a thing by the same act of sincerity? The man who confesses that he is evil has exchanged his disturbing "freedom-for-evil" for an inanimate character of evil; he is evil, he clings to himself, he is what he is. But by the same stroke, he escapes from that *thing,* since it is he who contemplates it, since it depends on him to maintain it under his glance or to let it collapse in an infinity of particular acts. . . . Thus the essential structure of sincerity does not differ from that of bad faith since the sincere man constitutes himself as what he is *in order not to be it.* (61-65) . . . Consciousness conceals in its being a permanent risk of bad faith. The origin of this risk is the fact that the nature of consciousness simultaneously is to be what it is not and not to be what it is. (70)

. . . The consciousness which I have of the "I" never exhausts it, and consciousness is not what causes it to come into existence; the "I" is always given as *having been* there before consciousness

—and at the same time as possessing depths which have to be revealed gradually. Thus the Ego appears to consciousness as a transcendent-in-itself, as an existent in the human world, not as *of the nature* of consciousness. . . . Yet we need not conclude that the for-itself is a pure and simple "impersonal" contemplation. But the Ego is far from being the personalizing pole of a consciousness which without it would remain in the impersonal stage; on the contrary, it is consciousness in its fundamental selfness which under certain conditions allows the appearance of the Ego as the transcendent phenomenon of that selfness. . . . From its first arising, consciousness by the pure nihilating movement of reflection makes itself *personal;* for what confers personal existence on a being is not the possession of an Ego—which is only the *sign* of the personality—but it is the fact that the being exists for itself as a presence to itself. . . . Now this first reflective movement involves in addition a second or selfness. In selfness my possible is reflected on my consciousness and determines it as what it is. . . . What I seek in the face of the world is the coincidence with a for-itself which I am and which is consciousness *of* the world. . . . Without the world there is no selfness, no person; without selfness, without the person, there is no world. . . . The world (*is*) mine because it is haunted by possibles, and the consciousness of each of these is a possible self-consciousness which *I* am; it is these possibles as such which give the world its unity and its meaning as the world. (103f.)

. . . It is as the nihilation of the In-itself that the For-itself arises in the world, and it is by this absolute event that the Past as such is constituted as the original, nihilating relation between the For-itself and the In-itself. . . . If there is a *Before,* it is because the For-itself has arisen in the world, and it is from the standpoint of the For-itself that the past can be established. (138f.) . . . If the for-itself is to be the nothingness whereby "there is" being, then being can exist originally only as totality. Thus knowledge is the *world.* (181)

Thus the fundamental act of freedom is discovered; and it is this which gives meaning to the particular action which I can be brought to consider. This constantly renewed act is not distinct from my being; it is a choice of myself in the world and by the same token it is a discovery of the world. This enables us to avoid the perilous reef of the unconscious which psychoanalysis meets at the start. (461) . . . We choose the world, not in its contexture as in itself but in its meaning, by choosing ourselves. . . . The value of things, their instrumental role, their proximity and real distance (which have no relation to their spatial proximity and distance) do nothing more than to outline my image—that is, my choice. My clothing (a uniform or a lounge suit, a soft or a starched shirt) whether neglected or cared for, carefully chosen or ordinary, my furniture, the street on which I live, the city in which I reside, the books with which I surround myself, the recreation which I enjoy, everything which is mine (that is, finally, the world of which I am perpetually conscious, at least by way of a meaning implied by the object which I look at or use): all this informs me of my choice—that is, my being. . . .

Anguish, abandonment, responsibility, whether muted or full strength, constitute the *quality* of our consciousness in so far as this is pure and simple freedom. . . . In anguish we do not simply apprehend the fact that the possibles which we project are perpetually eaten away by our freedom-to-come; in addition we apprehend our choice—*i.e.*, ourselves—*as unjustifiable.* This means that we apprehend our choice as not deriving from any prior reality but rather as being about to serve as foundation for the ensemble of significations which constitute reality. . . . We project the future by our very being, but our existential freedom perpetually eats it away as we make known to ourselves what we are by means of the future but without getting a grip on this future which remains always possible without ever passing to the rank of the *real.* Thus we are perpetually *threatened* by the nihilation of our actual choice and perpetually threatened with choosing ourselves—and consequently with becoming—other than we are. (463-465)

Since human reality is act, it can be conceived only as being at its core a rupture with the given. It is the being which causes *there to be* a given by breaking with it and illuminating it in the light of the not-yet-existing. . . . The for-itself is free and can cause there to be a world because the for-itself is *the being which has to be what it was in the light of what it will be.* Therefore the freedom of the for-itself appears as its *being.* But since this freedom is neither a given nor a property, it can be only by choosing itself. The freedom of the for-itself is always *engaged;* there is no question here of a freedom which could be undetermined and which would pre-exist its choice. We shall never apprehend ourselves except as a choice in the making. But freedom is simply the fact that this choice is always unconditioned. . . . Human-reality can choose itself as it intends but is not able not to choose itself. It can not even refuse to be; suicide, in fact, is a choice and affirmation—of being. . . . The free project is fundamental, for it is my being. Neither ambition nor the passion to be loved nor the inferiority complex can be considered as fundamental projects. On the contrary, they of necessity must be understood in terms of a primary project which is recognized as the project which can no longer be interpreted in terms of any other and which is total. . . . The fundamental project which I am is a project concerning not my relations with this or that particular object in the world, but my total being-in-the-world; since the world itself is revealed only in the light of an end, this project posits for its end a certain type of relation to being which the for-itself wills to adopt. . . . Since I am free, I project my total possible, but I thereby posit that I am free and that I can always nihilate this first project and make it past. (478-480)

. . . The *situation,* the common product of the contingency of the in-itself and of freedom, is an ambiguous phenomenon in which it is impossible for the for-itself to distinguish the contribution of freedom from that of the brute existent. . . . Thus we begin to catch a glimpse of the paradox of freedom: there is freedom only in a *situation,* and there is a situation only through freedom. Human-reality everywhere encounters resistance and obstacles which it has not created, but these resistances and obstacles have meaning only in and through the free choice which human-reality is. (488f.)

Death reapprehends all this subjective which while it "lived" defended itself against exteriorization, and death deprives it of all subjective meaning in order to hand it over to any *objective* meaning which the Other is pleased to give to it. . . . Death can not therefore belong to the ontological structure of the for-itself. In so far as it is the triumph of the Other over me, it refers to a fact, fundamental to be sure, but totally contingent as we have seen, a fact which is the Other's existence. We should not know *this* death if the Other did not exist; it could not be revealed to us, nor could it be constituted as the metamorphosis of our being into a destiny; it would be in fact the simultaneous disappearance of the for-itself and of the world, of the subjective, and of the objective, of the meaningful and of all meanings. . . . To contemplate my life by considering it in terms of death would be to contemplate my subjectivity by adopting with regard to it the Other's point of view. We have seen that this is not possible.

Thus we must conclude in opposition to Heidegger that death, far from being my peculiar possibility, is *a contingent fact* which as such on principle escapes me and originally belongs to my facticity. I can neither discover my death nor wait for it nor adopt an attitude toward it, for it is that which is revealed as undiscoverable, that which disarms all waiting, that which slips into all attitudes (and particularly into those which are assumed with respect to death) so as to transform them into externalized and fixed conducts whose meaning is forever entrusted to others and not to ourselves. Death is a pure fact as is birth; it comes to us from outside and it transforms us into the outside. At bottom it is in no way distinguished from birth, and it is the identity of birth and death that we call facticity. . . . Death by being revealed to us as it really is frees us wholly from its so-called constraint. . . . Human reality would remain finite even if it were immortal, because it *makes* itself finite by choosing itself as human. . . . The very act of freedom is therefore the assumption and creation of finitude. If I make myself, I make myself finite and hence my life is unique. (544-546)

The situation can not be *subjective,* for it is neither the sum nor the unity of the *impressions* which things make on us. It is *the things themselves* and myself among things. . . . But neither can the situation be *objective* in the sense that it would be a pure given which the subject would establish without being in any way engaged in the system thus constituted. In fact the situation by the very meaning of the given (a meaning without which there *would not even be* any given) reflects to the for-itself its freedom. . . . It is the total facticity, the absolute contingency of the world, of my birth, of my place, of my past, of my environment, of the fact of my fellowman—and it is my freedom without limits as that which causes there to be for me a facticity. . . . Since the situation is illumined by ends which are themselves projected only in terms of the *being-there,* which they illuminated, it is presented as eminently *concrete.* . . . It must be understood as the *single countenance* which the world turns toward us as our unique and personal chance. . . . Among brute existents there can be no connection; it is freedom which founds the connections by grouping the existents into instrumental-complexes; and it is freedom which projects the *reason* for the connections—that is, its end. (548-551)

. . . The responsibility of the for-itself is overwhelming since he is the one by whom it happens that *there is* a world; since he is also the one who makes himself be, then whatever may be the situation in which he finds himself, the for-itself must wholly assume this situation with its peculiar coefficient of adversity, even though it be insupportable. He must assume the situation with the proud consciousness of being the author of it, for the very worst disadvantages or the worst threats which can endanger my person have meaning only in and through my project; and it is on the ground of the engagement which I am that they appear. It is therefore senseless to think of complaining since nothing foreign has decided what we feel, what we live, or what we are. . . . What happens to me happens through me, and I can neither affect myself with it nor revolt against it nor resign myself to it. Moreover everything which happens to me is *mine*. . . . The situation is *mine* because it is the image of my free choice of myself, and everything which it presents to me is *mine* in that this represents me and symbolizes me. . . .

. . . Each person is an absolute upsurge at an absolute date and is perfectly unthinkable at another date. . . . I am not distinct from this same epoch; I could not be transported to another epoch without contradiction. . . . "We have the war we deserve." Thus, totally free, undistinguishable from the period for which I have chosen to be the meaning, as profoundly responsible for the war as if I had myself declared it, unable to live without integrating it in *my* situation, engaging myself in it wholly and stamping it with my seal, I must be without remorse or regrets as I am without excuse; for from the instant of my upsurge into being, I carry the weight of the world by myself alone without anything or any person being able to lighten it. . . . The for-itself apprehends itself in anguish; as a being which is neither the foundation of its own being nor of the Other's being nor of the in-itselfs which form the world, but a being which is compelled to decide the meaning of being—within it and everywhere outside of it. The one who realizes in anguish his condition as *being* thrown into a responsibility which extends to his very abandonment has no longer either remorse or regret or excuse; he is no longer anything but a freedom which perfectly reveals itself and whose being resides in this very revelation. (553-556)

. . . Ontology and existential psychoanalysis (or the spontaneous and empirical application which men have always made of these disciplines) must reveal to the moral agent that he *is the being by whom values exist.* It is then that his freedom will become conscious of itself and will reveal itself in anguish as the unique source of value and the nothingness by which the *world exists.* (627)

Maurice Merleau-Ponty

Phenomenology of Perception

The tacit *cogito*, the presence of oneself to oneself, being no less than existence, is anterior to any philosophy, and knows itself only in those extreme situations in which it is under threat: for example, in the dread of death or of another's gaze upon me. What is believed to be thought about thought, as pure feeling of the self, cannot yet be thought and needs to be revealed. (404) . . . My existence as subjectivity is merely one with my existence as a body and with the existence of the world. . . . (408) . . . The alleged motive does not burden my decision; on the contrary my decision lends the motive its force. . . . In reality the deliberation follows the decision, and it is my secret decision which brings the motives to light, for it would be difficult to conceive what the force of a motive might be in the absence of a decision which it confirms or to which it runs counter. (435)

Our freedom does not destroy our situation, but gears itself to it: as long as we are alive, our situation is open, which implies both that it calls up specially favoured modes of resolution, and also that it is powerless to bring one into being by itself. (442) . . . To be a bourgeois or a worker is not only to be aware of being one or the other, it is to identify oneself as worker or bourgeois through an implicit or existential project which merges into our way of patterning the world and co-existing with other people. My decision draws together a spontaneous meaning of my life which it may confirm or repudiate, but not annul. (447) . . . It is true that I can at any moment interrupt my projects. But what *is* this power? It is the power to begin something else, for we never remain suspended in nothingness. . . . My actual freedom is not on the hither side of my being, but before me, in things. . . . Consciousness holds itself responsible for everything, and takes everything upon itself, but it has nothing of its own and makes its life in the world. . . .

Taken concretely freedom is always a meeting of the inner and the outer. . . . The choice which we make of our life is always based on a certain givenness. . . . All explanations of my conduct in terms of my past, my temperament and my environment are therefore true, provided that they be regarded not as separable contributions, but as moments of my total being, the significance of which I am entitled to make explicit in various ways, without its ever being possible to say whether I confer their meaning upon them or receive it from them. . . . The fact remains that I am free, not in spite of, or on the hither side of, these motivations, but by means of them. For this significant life, this certain significance of nature and history which I am, does not limit my access to the world, but on the contrary is my means of entering into communication with it. It is by being unrestrictedly and unreservedly what I am at present that I have a chance of moving forward; it is by living my time that I am able to understand other times, by plunging into the present and the world, by taking on deliberately what I am fortuitously, by willing what I will and doing what I do, that I can go further. (452-456)

Karl Jaspers

The Illumination of Existenz

Figuratively the moment can be conceived as extendable from the narrow circle of the present reality to the infinite circles of religious or metaphysical presence. In both extremes the present is experienced very vividly, but the wider the circles of the spirit are drawn, the stronger are the claims of the spirit against itself to be and to possess in the present even that which is most distant. Thus a tension arises between the demands of the immediate empirical situation and the impulse to realize the most distant. And the moment fails again and again through the power of the empirical present.[1] (116) [The moment can be captured only in the enthusiastic attitude.]

Contrary to life in the quiet of traditional customs, in which the antinomies of the world were not perceived, contrary to life in inner aloofness which, in spite of all superficial activity remains in the limited relative spheres, life in the enthusiastic attitude is

1 Jaspers. *Psychologie der Weltanschauungen.*

everywhere deeply agitated and at the same time strengthened, tested and invigorated in love and hate, in union and strife, in unconditional devotion. Contrary to a life either without solid substance or a life in which this substance is never affected, only the enthusiastic attitude means a life awake, a life in totality and authenticity. . . . Enthusiasm is becoming oneself in the act of devoting oneself. (119f.)

In the empirical sense the doubt about the reality of the "I am" is solved immediately by the thinking activity involved in doubting itself. That I doubt implies that I exist at this moment. Of course even here something more than thinking is needed: the permeation of existence by a vital feeling. If, under pathological conditions, this feeling is absent, I may come to the terrible conclusion that I am dead, that I am no longer at all, and that I must remain dead forever. The doubt about the "I am" in the existential sense, however, cannot be solved through any reasoning at all, but only through unconditioned actions, in which I am conscious of myself as a beginning and as a freely responsible agent. The formula "I am" then is not the expression of knowing, but a sign for the reality behind my appearance of which I become aware when in deciding freely I fulfill my *Existenz.* Whatever in the statement "I am" is thought of non-objectively, as eternal Being and therefore that which always vanishes in knowledge, appears to me as not yet finally decided, so that in existential thinking it is determined whether I am future or eternity, becoming or being. In appearance I exist only insofar as I become myself, in eternity only insofar as I reveal myself in appearance. I create myself in the phenomenal world yet I am not self-creator in eternity.

To become oneself by conquering oneself: As appearance I became myself only through conquering myself. I could conceive my being empirically as my personality, my being-like-that; to my real self I *am* not my character; I possess it and have a certain relation to it. Its given, and therefore blind being, I transform through struggle into a freely willed one; I develop myself in it and take it upon myself as my guilt. My true self places itself above my character—ascending from a purely formal independence in passive contemplation to active influence.

This position of "otherness" of my true self has the effect that no motive which becomes present to me as impulse through my character is compelling; that there is no one motive which in a fight would necessarily dominate through quantitative power, for its domination would be over myself. Rather without being a motive myself, I permit all motives to become effective and to recede, while I move beyond them, dominating them or yielding to them.

Even if I myself am in the motives, without conquest of the self, there can be no authentic "I" in the appearance. The "I" casts off its shells, which it finds untrue, in order to gain the deeper and authentic, infinite, true self. To become oneself while suffering defeat is the realization of authentic Being. . . .

Mythically expressed, Being is the sea of light which glides off the self and in which the whole I sinks and dissolves; being as authentic Being is the mutual reflection of the souls, which are manifest to one another in eternal presence. . . .

I myself am nothing if I only have empirical existence. To be oneself means the unity of the twofold: to live in independence and to have surrendered to the world and to Transcendence. Alone I am helpless, but having surrendered to the world and to Transcendence I as myself have vanished. As myself I am independent, but not sufficient to myself. . . .

The self is actually only real when it manifests itself objectively in the world. Just as I do not exist without the world, I am not myself without Transcendence. It is true that through my own decision I become the foundation and origin of my being, I create myself through rational perceptions and autonomous actions. But my phenomenal being, enlightened through this reasoning, becomes the origin of my authentic being only in such a manner that I myself have also been given to myself. Having been furnished with the empirical matter of my being through which I have built myself up, my origins are given to me as a present in which I freely meet myself. I confront Transcendence, which I do not encounter as phenomenon in the world but which speaks to me as potentiality out of everything there is and most decidedly out of my authentic being. The depth of myself has its measure in the Transcendence which I confront. . . .

Authentic being can be conscious of its immortality in the sense that Being and immortality are the same. The self has this consciousness without knowledge, without an adequate idea or objective guarantee, but to the degree that it is acting and deciding in the world in the presence of Transcendence. It is conscious of being dependent upon a Transcendence which has demanded the ultimate possible: a free authentic Being which becomes its own origin and realizes itself in the transitoriness of temporal existence. Therefore, the self, lacking foundation, is certain of itself only in relation to Transcendence, without which it glides into the abyss of nothingness. . . . I see Transcendence and become certain of my being. . . . Selfhood does not mean an isolated self; it means a self existing in existential communication. It ceases to mean a pure, replaceable consciousness and exists only as historically unique at this time and this place. It ceases to be an empirical fact; it exists only as freedom.[2] (46-49)

Within my freedom my guilt is each time a specific one and as such something which I try to shun. But because I am free, my guilt is an indeterminable and therefore immeasurable one, which becomes the ground for all specific guilt, insofar as the latter is unavoidable. . . .

We exist either in authentic activity or we do not exist, because passivity is equal to nothingness. I must will; for to will must be my ultimate if I want to exist authentically. However, the manner in which I will freely determines how Transcendence manifests itself to me . . . As I am, I am responsible for myself and yet only in being free do I discover who I am. . . .

Transcendence is not my freedom, but is present in it. (197, 199)

The Perennial Scope of Philosophy

The Comprehensive that I am is in every form a polarity of subject and object:

As *being-there* I am: inner world and environment,

as *consciousness* I am: consciousness and object,

as *mind* I am: the idea that is in me and the objective idea that comes to me from things,

as *existence* I am: existence and transcendence.

The Comprehensive that I am comprehends, as it were, the Comprehensive that Being is and at the same time is comprehended by it. This Being is called "world" in the first three polarities and then refers to the environment, the objectively intelligible, the idea. In the fourth polarity, it is called "transcendence." (20)

Reason and Existenz

Whether we call the Encompassing which we are our empirical existence, consciousness as such, or spirit, in no case can it be grasped as though it were something in the world which appeared before us. Rather it is that in which all other things appear to us. In general, we do not appropriately cognize it as an object; rather we become aware of it as a limit. (54)

The central point of philosophizing is first reached in the awareness of potential Existenz.

Existenz is the Encompassing, not in the sense of the vastness

[2] Jaspers, *Philosophie*, Vol. II.

of a horizon of all horizons, but rather in the sense of a fundamental origin, the condition of selfhood without which all the vastness of Being becomes a desert. Existenz, although never itself becoming an object or form, carries the meaning of every mode of the Encompassing.

While mere empirical existence, consciousness as such, and spirit all appear in the world and become scientifically investigable realities, Existenz is the object of no science. In spite of which, we find here the very axis about which everything in the world turns if it is to have any genuine meaning for us. . . . In all modes of the Encompassing, the self can become genuinely certain of itself only as Existenz. . . .

If we first contrast Existenz with consciousness as such, it becomes the hidden ground in me to which Transcendence is first revealed. The Encompassing which we are exists only in relation to something other than itself. . . . I am Existenz only as I know Transcendence as the power through which I genuinely am myself. The Other is either the being which is in the world for consciousness as such, or it is Transcendence for Existenz. This twofold Other first becomes clear through the inwardness of Existenz. Without Existenz the meaning of Transcendence is lost. It remains only something indifferent and not to be known, something supposed to be at the bottom of things, something excogitated, or, perhaps for our animal consciousness, something weird or terrifying plunging it into superstition and anxiety, a subject to be investigated psychologically and removed through a rational insight into the factual by consciousness as such. Only through Existenz can Transcendence become present without superstition, as the genuine reality which to itself never disappears. . . .

When Existenz understands itself, it is not like my understanding of another, nor the sort of understanding whose contents can be abstracted from the person understanding, nor a sort of looking at; rather it is an origin which itself first arises in its own self-clarification. It is not like sharing in something else, but is at once the understanding and the being of what is understood. It is not understanding through universals, but moves above such understanding in the medium of spirit to become an understanding without any generalization in the absolute present, in deed, in love, and in every form of absolute consciousness. It is the difference between the love of another, which I understand but yet never really understand, and my own love, which I understand because I am that love. Or, in other words, the difference between understanding other things by empathy as process or experience, and understanding myself as unique since I know myself before Transcendence.

When we compare Existenz with consciousness as such, spirit, or any other mode of the Encompassing, the same thing appears: without Existenz everything seems empty, hollowed out, without ground, fake, because everything has turned into endless masks, mere possibilities, or mere empirical existence. . . . The Being of the Encompassing which we are, which was either our empirical existence (the still indeterminate, comprehensive actuality), or consciousness as such (the site of all objective and intelligible validities for us), or spirit (the single whole of coherent movement of consciousness as it is activated by Ideas).

But for the source from which all these modes of the Encompassing receive animation and for which they speak, we touched upon Existenz, the dark ground of selfhood, the concealment out of which I come to encounter myself and for which Transcendence first becomes real. (60-64)

Nicolas Berdyaev

Slavery and Freedom

Personality is a break through, a breaking in upon this world; it is the introduction of something new. Personality is not nature, it does not belong to the objective hierarchy of nature, as a subordinate part of it. . . . Man is a personality not by nature but by spirit. By nature he is only an individual. . . . But personality is not a part of the universe, the universe is a part of personality, it is its quality. . . . Personality cannot be recognized as an object, as one of the objects in a line with other objects in the world, like a part of the world. . . . In that way man is looked at partially: but there is in that case no mystery of man, as personality, as an existential centre of the world. Personality is recognized only as a subject, in infinite subjectivity, in which is hidden the secret of existence. (21f.)

Personality is not a part of society, as it is not part of a race. The problem of man, that is to say, the problem of personality, is more primary than the problem of society. All the sociological doctrines about man are erroneous, they know only the superficial, objectified stratum in man. . . . But only an existential philosophy, and not a sociological philosophy, any more than a biological philosophy can construct the true doctrine of man as personality.

Personality is a subject, and not an object among other objects, and it has its roots in the inward scheme of existence, that is in the spiritual world, the world of freedom. Society on the other hand is an object. . . . The object is always evil, only the subject can be good. . . . Personality is the absolute existential centre. Personality determines itself from within, outside the whole object world, and only determination from within and arising out of freedom, is personality. Everything defined from without, everything determined, everything that is based upon the power of the object world is not personal, it is the impersonal in man. Everything determined in the human ego is past and has become impersonal.

But personality is the coming into being of the future, it consists of creative acts. Objectivization is impersonality, the ejection of man into the world of determinism. The existence of personality presupposes freedom. The mystery of freedom is the mystery of personality. . . . The worth of man is the personality within him. Human worth consists solely in personality. . . . God is the guarantee of the freedom of personality from the enslaving power of nature and society, of the Kingdom of Caesar and of the object world. . . . Personality is suffering. The struggle to achieve personality and its consolidation are a painful process. The self-realization of personality presupposes resistance, it demands a conflict with the enslaving power of the world, a refusal to conform to the world. Refusal of personality, acquiescence in dissolution in the surrounding world can lessen the suffering, and man easily goes that way. Acquiescence in slavery diminishes suffering, refusal increases it. Pain in the human world is the birth of personality, its fight for its own nature. . . .

Man, human personality is the supreme value, not the community, not collective realities which belong to the object world, such as society, nation, state, civilization, church. . . . Personalist philosophy must recognize that spirit does not generalize but individualizes, that it creates, not a world of ideal values, supra-human and common, but a world of personalities with their qualitative content, that it forms personalities. The triumph of the spiritual principle means, not the subordination of man to the universe, but the revelation of the universe in personality. . . . The realization of personality in man is this continuous transcending of self. Man desires to go out from the closed circle of subjectivity and this movement always takes place in two different and even opposite directions. Emergence from subjectivity proceeds by way of objectivization. This is the way which leads out into society with its forms of universal obligation, it is the way of science with its laws of universal obligation. On this path there takes place the alienation of human nature, its ejection into the object world: personality does not find itself. The other path is emergence from subjectivity through the process of transcendence. This is a passing over into the transsubjective and not to the objective. This path lies in the deeps of existence, on this path there take place the existential meeting with God, with other people, with the interior existence of the world. It is the path not of objective communication but of existential communion. Personality reaches full realization of itself only on this path. . . .

Personality is certainly not the soul as distinct from the body, which links man with the life of nature. Personality is the entire image of man in which the spiritual principle has the mastery over all the powers of man's soul and body. The unity of personality is created by the spirit. . . . Dualism exists, not between soul and body, but between spirit and nature, between freedom and necessity. Personality is the victory of the spirit over nature, of freedom over necessity. (26-31)

. . . Man is the point of intersection of two worlds, in him there takes place the conflict between spirit and nature, freedom and necessity, independence and dependence. . . . There are not two separate men, but one and the same man is both an individual and a personality. . . . Inward unity and integrality are inherent in personality; whereas the individual may be torn to pieces by the forces of the world. (36f.)

Personality is not part of the world, it is a correlative of the world, and a correlative of God also. Personality allows only of correlation, meeting, communion. And God as personality does not desire a man over whom He can rule, and who ought to praise Him, but man as personality who answers His call and with whom communion of love is possible. . . .

Consciousness arises in the relation between the ego and the non-ego, it denotes a going out from the ego, but at the same time it may be a hindrance to the going out of the I to the Thou as inward communion. It objectifies and may prevent the process of transcending. Consciousness is "unhappy consciousness." Consciousness is subject to law, which takes cognizance of the common but not of the individual. For this reason it is easy to fall a prey to illusion, through not having a true understanding of the relation between the personal and the suprapersonal. The very structure of consciousness readily produces slavery. But it is always necessary to keep in view the double rôle of consciousness, it both closes and opens out. . . .

Outside personality there is no absolute unity and totality in the world, to which personality would be subordinate: outside personality everything is partial, even the world itself is partial. . . . An existential centre, and a suffering destiny are to be found in subjectivity, not in objectivity. But all the higher hierarchical ranks to which they subordinate personality belong to the world of objectivization. Objectivization is always antipersonalistic, hostile to personality and signifies the estrangement of personality. And everything which is existential in the objectivized ranks of the world, in the nation, in mankind, in the cosmos, etc. belongs to the inward being of personality and is not subordinate to any hierarchical centre. The cosmos, mankind, nation, etc., are to be found in human personality as in an individualized universe or microcosm, and their falling away from it, their ejection into external reality among objects, is the result of the fall of man, of his subordination to impersonal reality, exteriorization, and alienation. . . .

Personality is I and Thou, another I. But the Thou to whom the I goes out and with whom it enters into communion is not an object, it is another I, it is personality. . . . There is something lacking in the humanity of the egocentric man. He loves abstractions which nourish his egoism. He does not love living concrete people. . . . Personalist ethics signify just that going out from the "common" which Kierkegaard and Shestov consider a break with ethics, which they identify with standards of universal obligation. The personalistic transvaluation of values regards as immoral everything which is defined exclusively by its relation to the "common"—to society, the nation, the state, an abstract idea, abstract goodness, moral and logical law—and not to concrete man and his existence. (40-43)

Personality is independent of the determination of society, it has its own world, it is an exception, it is unique and unrepeatable. And at the same time personality is social, in it there are traces of the collective unconscious. It is man's way out from isolation. It belongs to history, it realizes itself in society and in history. Personality is communal; it presupposes communion with others, and community with others. (46)

Personality is bound up with the consciousness of vocation. Every man ought to be conscious of that vocation, which is independent of the extent of his gifts. It is a vocation in an individually unrepeatable form to give an answer to the call of God and to put one's gifts to creative use. Personality which is conscious of itself listens to the inward voice and obeys that only. It is not submissive to outward voices. The greatest among men have always listened exclusively to the inward voice and have refused to conform so far as the world is concerned. Personality is connected also with asceticism and presupposes asceticism, that is to say spiritual exercise, the concentration of inward strength, the making of choice, the refusal to acquiesce in a mingling with impersonal forces, both within man and in the surrounding world. This certainly ought not to mean the acceptance of all the traditional forms of asceticism which belong to historical Christianity, in which there was much which was by no means Christian and which was even injurious to personality. Asceticism in its essence should mean the active exposition and the preservation of the forms of personality, of its image, active resistance to the power of the world, which desires to tear personality to pieces and to enslave it. (48f.)

Personality in man cannot be socialized. The socialization. of man is only partial and does not extend to the depth of personality, to its conscience, to its relation to the source of life. Socialization which is extended to the depth of existence, to spiritual life, is the triumph of *das Man*, and of social routine. It is the tyranny of the average and common over the personally individual. (58)

Jacques Maritain

Existence and the Existent

When a man is awake to the intuition of being he is awake at the same time to the intuition of subjectivity; he grasps, in a flash that will never be dimmed, the fact that *he is a self*, as Jean-Paul said. . . .

But the intuition of subjectivity is an existential intuition which surrenders no essence to us. We know *that which* we are by our phenomena, our operations, our flow of consciousness. The more we grow accustomed to the inner life, the better we decipher the astonishing and fluid multiplicity which is thus delivered to us; the more, also, we feel that it leaves us ignorant of the essence of our self. Subjectivity *as subjectivity* is inconceptualisable; is an unknowable abyss. It is unknowable by the mode of notion, concept, or representation, or by any mode of any science whatsoever—introspection, psychology, or philosophy. . . . Subjectivity is known or rather felt in virtue of a formless and diffuse knowledge which, in relation to reflective consciousness, we may call unconscious or pre-conscious knowledge. This is knowledge of the "concomitant" or spontaneous consciousness, which, without giving rise to a distinct act of thought, envelops in fact, *in actu exercito,* our inner world in so far as it is integrated into the vital activity of our spiritual faculties. Even for the most superficial persons, it is true that from the moment when they say *I,* the whole unfolding of their states of consciousness and their operations, their musings, memories, and acts, is subsumed by a virtual and ineffable knowledge, a vital and existential knowledge of the totality immanent in each of its parts, and immersed, without their troubling to become aware of it, in the diffuse glow, the unique freshness, the maternal connivance as it were, which emanates from subjectivity. Subjectivity is not known, it is felt as a propitious and enveloping night. (76-79)

. . . Many contemporary philosophers, while they talk of nothing but person and subjectivity, nevertheless radically misunderstand those words. They remain lightheartedly ignorant of the metaphysical problem of that *subsistence.* . . . They do not see that personality, metaphysically considered, being the subsistence of the spiritual soul communicated to the human composite, and enabling the latter to possess its existence, to perfect itself and to give itself freely, bears witness in us to the generosity or expansivity of being which, in an incarnate spirit, proceeds from the spirit and which constitutes, in the secret springs of our ontological structure, a source of dynamic unity and unification from within.

Because analysis wearies them, they are ignorant of what the proper life of the intelligence consists in, and in what the proper life of the will consists. They do not see that, because his *spirit* makes man cross the threshold of independence properly so-called, and of self-inwardness, the subjectivity of the person demands as its most intimate privilege communications proper to love and intelligence. They do not see that, even before the exercise of free choice, and in order to make free choice possible, the most deeply rooted need of the person is to communicate with *the other* by the union of the intelligence, and with *others* by the affective union. Their subjectivity is not a *self*, because it is wholly phenomenal. . . .

What reveals subjectivity to itself is not an irrational break (however profound and gratuitous it may be) in an irrational flow of moral and psychological phenomena, of dreams, automatisms, urges, and images surging upwards from the unconscious. Neither is it the anguish of forced choice. It is self-mastery for the purpose of self-giving. When a man has the obscure intuition of subjectivity, the reality, whose sudden invasion of his consciousness he experiences, is that of a secret totality, which contains both itself and its upsurge, and which superabounds in knowledge and in love. Only by love does it attain to its supreme level of existence—existence as self-giving.

This is what I mean: Self-knowledge as a mere psychological analysis of phenomena more or less superficial, a wandering through images and memories, is but an egotistic awareness, however valuable it may be. But when it becomes ontological, then knowledge of the Self is transfigured, implying intuition of Being and the discovery of the actual abyss of subjectivity. At the same time, it is the discovery of the basic generosity of existence. Subjectivity, this essentially dynamic, living and open centre, both receives and gives. It receives through the intellect, by superexisting in knowledge. It gives through the will, by superexisting in love; that is, by having within itself other beings as inner attractions directed towards them and giving oneself to them, and by spiritually existing in the manner of a gift. And "it is better to give than to receive." The spiritual existence of love is the supreme revelation of existence for the Self. The Self, being not only a material individual but also a spiritual personality, possesses itself and holds itself in hand in so far as it is spiritual and in so far as it is free. And to what purpose does it possess itself and dispose of itself, if not for what *is better*, in actual existence and absolutely speaking, or to give of itself? Thus it is that when a man has been really awakened to the sense of being or existence, and grasps intuitively the obscure, living depth of the Self and subjectivity, he discovers by the same token the basic generosity of existence and realises, by virtue of the inner dynamism of this intuition, that love is not a passing pleasure or emotion, but the very meaning of his being alive.

By love, finally, is shattered the impossibility of knowing another except as object. I have emphasised this impossibility above at length and noted that it directly concerns the senses and the intellect. To say that union in love makes the being we love another *ourself* for us is to say that it makes that being another subjectivity for us, another subjectivity that is ours. To the degree that we truly love (which is to say, not for ourselves but for the beloved; and when—which is not always the case—the intellect within us becomes passive as regards love, and, allowing its concepts to slumber, thereby renders love a formal means of knowledge), to this degree we acquire an obscure knowledge of the being we love, similar to that which we possess of ourselves; we know that being in his very subjectivity (at least in a certain measure) by this experience of union. Then he himself is, in a certain degree, cured of his solitude; he can, though still disquieted, rest for a moment in the nest of the knowledge that we possess of him as subject. (88-91)

Martin Buber

I and Thou

The *Thou* meets me through grace—it is not found by seeking. But my speaking of the primary word to it is an act of my being, is indeed *the* act of my being.

The *Thou* meets me. But I step into direct relation with it. Hence the relation means being chosen and choosing, suffering and action in one; just as any action of the whole being, which means the suspension of all partial actions and consequently of all sensations of actions grounded only in their particular limitation, is bound to resemble suffering.

The primary word *I-Thou* can be spoken only with the whole being. Concentration and fusion into the whole being can never take place through my agency, nor can it ever take place without me. I become through my relation to the *Thou;* as I become *I,* I say *Thou.*

All real living is meeting. . . .

. . . The real, filled present, exists only in so far as actual presentness, meeting, and relation exist. The present arises only in virtue of the fact that the *Thou* becomes present.

The *I* of the primary word *I-It,* that is, the *I* faced by no *Thou,* but surrounded by a multitude of "contents," has no present, only the past. Put in another way, in so far as man rests satisfied with the things that he experiences and uses, he lives in the past, and his moment has no present content. . . . (11f.)

The unlimited reign of causality in the world of *It,* of fundamental importance for the scientific ordering of nature, does not weigh heavily on man, who is not limited to the world of *It,* but can continually leave it for the world of relation. Here *I* and *Thou* freely confront one another in mutual effect that is neither connected with nor coloured by any causality. Here man is assured of the freedom both of his being and of Being. Only he who knows relation and knows about the presence of the *Thou* is capable of decision. He who decides is free, for he has approached the Face.

The fiery stuff of all my ability to will seethes tremendously, all that I might do circles around me, still without actuality in the world, flung together and seemingly inseparable, alluring glimpses of powers flicker from all the uttermost bounds: the universe is my temptation, and I achieve being in an instant, with both hands plunged deep in the fire, where the single deed is hidden, the deed which aims at me—now is the moment! Already the menace of the abyss is removed, the centreless Many no longer plays in the iridescent sameness of its pretensions; but only two alternatives are set side by side—the other, the vain idea, and the one, the charge laid on me. But now realisation begins in me. For it is not decision to do the one and leave the other a lifeless mass, deposited layer upon layer as dross in my soul. But he alone who directs the whole strength of the alternative into the doing of the charge, who lets the abundant passion of what is rejected invade the growth to reality of what is chosen—he alone who "serves God with the evil impulse" makes decision, decides the event. . . . If there were a devil it would not be one who decided against God, but one who, in eternity, came to no decision.

Causality does not weigh on the man to whom freedom is assured. He knows that his mortal life swings by nature between *Thou* and *It.* . . . He who forgets all that is caused and makes decision out of the depths, who rids himself of property and raiment and naked approaches the Face, is a free man, and destiny confronts him as the counterpart of his freedom. It is not his boundary, but his fulfilment; freedom and destiny are linked together in meaning. And in this meaning destiny, with eyes a moment ago so severe now filled with light, looks out like grace itself. . . . To all men indeed, even to the dullest, meeting—the present—has come somehow, naturally, impulsively, dimly: all men have somewhere been aware of the *Thou;* now the spirit gives them full assurance. (51-53)

The *I* of the primary word *I-It* makes its appearance as individuality and becomes conscious of itself as subject (of experiencing and using).

The *I* of the primary word *I-Thou* makes its appearance as person and becomes conscious of itself as subjectivity (without a dependent genitive).

Individuality makes its appearance by being differentiated from other individualities.

A person makes his appearance by entering into relation with other persons.

The one is the spiritual form of natural detachment, the other the spiritual form of natural solidarity of connexion. . . .

He who takes his stand in relation shares in a reality, that is, in a being that neither merely belongs to him nor merely lies outside him. All reality is an activity in which I share without being able to appropriate for myself. Where there is no sharing there is no reality. Where there is self-appropriation there is no reality. The more direct the contact with the *Thou*, the fuller is the sharing.

The *I* is real in virtue of its sharing in reality. The fuller its sharing the more real it becomes.

But the *I* that steps out of the relational event into separation and consciousness of separation, does not lose its reality. Its sharing is preserved in it in a living way. . . . This is the province of subjectivity in which the *I* is aware with a single awareness of its solidarity of connexion and of its separation. Genuine subjectivity can only be dynamically understood, as the swinging of the *I* in its lonely truth. Here, too, is the place where the desire is formed and heightened for ever higher, more unconditioned relation, for the full sharing in being. In subjectivity the spiritual substance of the person matures. . . .

The person looks on his Self, individuality is concerned with its My—my kind, my race, my creation, my genius.

No man is pure person and no man pure individuality. None is wholly real, and none wholly unreal. Every man lives in the twofold *I*. But there are men so defined by person that they may be called persons, and men so defined by individuality that they may be called individuals. True history is decided in the field between these two poles. . . . The stronger the *I* of the primary word *I-Thou* is in the twofold *I*, the more personal is the man.

According to his saying of *I*—according to what he means, when he says *I*—it can be decided where a man belongs and where his way leads. The word *I* is the true shibboleth of mankind.

How discordant the *I* of the individual! It may stir great compassion if it comes from lips compressed in the tragedy of concealed self-contradiction. It may rouse horror if it comes chaotically from lips that wildly, heedlessly, unsuspectingly, show forth the contradiction. If it comes idly and glibly it is painful or disagreeable.

He who speaks the separated *I*, with emphasis on the capital, lays bare the shame of the world-spirit which has been degraded to spirituality.

But how lovely and how fitting the sound of the lively and impressive *I* of Socrates! It is the *I* of endless dialogue, and the air of dialogue is wafted around it in all its journeys, before the judges and in the last hour in prison. This *I* lived continually in the relation with man which is bodied forth in dialogue. It never ceased to believe in the reality of men, and went out to meet them. So it took its stand with them in reality, and reality forsakes it no more. Its very loneliness can never be forsakenness, and if the world of man is silent it hears the voice of the daimonion say *Thou*.

How lovely and how legitimate the sound of the full *I* of Goethe! It is the *I* of pure intercourse with nature; nature gives herself to it and speaks unceasingly with it, revealing her mysteries to it but not betraying her mystery. . . . How powerful, even to being overpowering, and how legitimate, even to being self-evident, is the saying of *I* by Jesus! For it is the *I* of unconditional relation in which the man calls his *Thou* Father in such a way that he himself is simply Son, and nothing else but Son. (62-67)

Between Man and Man

. . . In spite of all similarities every living situation has, like a new-born child, a new face, that has never been before and will never come again. It demands of you a reaction which cannot be prepared beforehand. It demands nothing of what is past. It demands presence, responsibility; it demands you. I call a great character one who by his actions and attitudes satisfies the claim of situations out of deep readiness to respond with his whole life, and in such a way that the sum of his actions and attitudes expresses at the same time the unity of his being in its willingness to accept responsibility. . . .

All this does not mean that the great character is beyond the acceptance of norms. No responsible person remains a stranger to norms. But the command inherent in a genuine norm never becomes a maxim and the fulfilment of it never a habit. Any command that a great character takes to himself in the course of his development does not act in him as part of his consciousness or as material for building up his exercises, but remains latent in a basic layer of his substance until it reveals itself to him in a concrete way. What it has to tell him is revealed whenever a situation arises which demands of him a solution of which till then he had perhaps no idea. Even the most universal norm will at times be recognized only in a very special situation. I know of a man whose heart was struck by the lightning flash of "Thou shalt not steal" in the very moment when he was moved by a very different desire from that of stealing, and whose heart was so struck by it that he not only abandoned doing what he wanted to do, but with the whole force of his passion did the very opposite. Good and evil are not each other's opposites like right and left. The evil approaches us as a whirlwind, the good as a direction. There is a direction, a "yes," a command, hidden even in a prohibition, which is revealed to us in moments like these. In moments like these the command addresses us really in the second person, and the *Thou* in it is no one else but one's own self. Maxims command only the third person, the each and the none. (114)

Real existence, that is, real man in his relation to his being, is comprehensible only in connexion with the nature of the being to which he stands in relation. To exemplify what I mean I choose one of the most audacious and profound chapters of Heidegger's book, which treats of man's relation to his death. Here everything is perspective, what matters is how man looks to his end, whether he has the courage to anticipate the *whole* of his existence, which is made fully revealed only in death. But only when the subject of discussion is man's relation to his being is death to be limited to the end-point; if one is thinking of objective being itself, then death is also there in the present second as a force which wrestles with the force of life. The state of this struggle at a given time helps to determine man's whole nature at that moment, his existence at that moment, his attitude towards being at that moment; and if man looks now to his end, the manner of this looking cannot be separated from the reality of death's power in this very moment. In other words, man as existence, as comprehension of being that looks towards death, cannot be separated from man as a creature that begins to die when it begins to live, and that cannot possess life without death, or preserving power without destructive and disintegrative power.

Heidegger abstracts from the reality of human life the categories which originate and are valid in the relation of the individual to what is not himself, and applies them to "existence" in the narrower sense, that is, to the relation of the individual to his own being. (164f.)

Productivity and Existence[3]

. . . The dominant delusion of our time [is] that creativity is the criterion of human worth. . . . Only that can be a criterion from which genuine creativity arises: that is, the immediate. . . . The overvaluation of productivity that is afflicting our age has so thrived and its pan-technical glance has set up a senseless exclusiveness of its own that even genuinely creative men allow their organic skills to degenerate into an autonomous growth to satisfy the demand of the day. . . . They wear themselves out turning all experience to account as public communication; they renounce true necessity and give themselves over to the arbitrary. They poison experience, for already while it is taking place they are dominated by the will to produce. . . . They forfeit both life and art, and all that they gain is the applause of their production-mad contemporaries. . . . He who meets men with a double glance, an open one that invites his fellows to sincerity and the concealed one of the observer stemming from a conscious aim; he who in friendship and in love is cleft into two men, one who surrenders himself to his feelings and another who is already standing by to exploit them—this man cannot be delivered by any creative talent from the blight that he has brought upon himself and his work, for he has poisoned the springs of his life. (8-10)

Elements of the Interhuman

That there resides in every man the possibility of attaining authentic human existence in the special way peculiar to him can be grasped in the Aristotelian image of entelechy, innate self-realization; but one must note that it is an entelechy of the work of creation. It would be mistaken to speak here of individuation alone. Individuation is only the indispensable personal stamp of all realization of human existence. The self as such is not ultimately the essential, but the meaning of human existence given in creation again and again fulfills itself as self. The help that men give each other in becoming a self leads the life between men to its height. The dynamic glory of the being of man is first bodily present in the relation between two men each of whom in meaning the other also means the highest to which this person is called, and serves the self-realization of this human life as one true to

3 Martin Buber, *Pointing the Way.*

creation without wishing to impose on the other anything of his own realization. (111f.)

Good and Evil

It is a cruelly hazardous enterprise, this becoming a whole, becoming a form, of crystallization of the soul. Everything in the nature of inclinations, of indolence, of habits, of fondness for possibilities which has been swashbuckling within us, must be overcome, and overcome, not by elimination, by suppression, for genuine wholeness can never be achieved like that, never a wholeness where downtrodden appetites lurk in the corners. Rather must all these mobile or static forces, seized by the soul's rapture, plunge of their own accord, as it were, into the mightiness of decision and dissolve within it. Until the soul as form has such great power over the soul as matter, until chaos is subdued and shaped into cosmos, what an immense resistance! It is thus understandable enough that the occurrence—which at times, as we know to be the case with dreams encompassing a whole drama, lasts no longer than a minute—so frequently terminates in a persistent state of indecision. (129)

The Way of Man

HEART-SEARCHING

Whatever success and enjoyment he may achieve, whatever power he may attain and whatever deeds he may do, his life will remain way-less, so long as he does not face the Voice. . . . The decisive heart-searching is the beginning of the way in man's life; it is, again and again, the beginning of a human way. But heart-searching is decisive only if it leads to the way. For there is a sterile kind of heart-searching, which leads to nothing but self-torture, despair and still deeper enmeshment. . . .

There is a demonic question, a spurious question, which apes God's question, the question of Truth. Its characteristic is that it does not stop at: "Where art thou?" but continues: "From where you have got to, there is no way out." This is the wrong kind of heart-searching, which does not prompt man to turn, and put him on the way, but, by representing turning as hopeless, drives him to a point where it appears to have become entirely impossible and man can go on living only by demonic pride, the pride of perversity. (134-136)

THE PARTICULAR WAY

Every person born into this world represents something new, something that never existed before, something original and unique. . . . Every man's foremost task is the actualization of his unique, unprecedented and never-recurring potentialities, and not the repetition of something that another, and be it even the greatest, has already achieved. . . . The way by which a man can reach God is revealed to him only through the knowledge of his own being, the knowledge of his essential quality and inclination. "Everyone has in him something precious that is in no one else." But this precious something in a man is revealed to him only if he truly perceives his strongest feeling, his central wish, that in him which stirs his inmost being. (139f., 142)

NOT TO BE PREOCCUPIED WITH ONESELF

To begin with oneself, but not to end with oneself; to start from oneself, but not to aim at oneself; to comprehend oneself, but not to be preoccupied with oneself. . . . True, each is to know itself, purify itself, perfect itself, but not for its own sake—neither for the sake of its temporal happiness nor for that of its eternal bliss—but for the sake of the work which it is destined to perform upon the world. (163, 165f.)

Maurice Friedman

Problematic Rebel: An Image of Modern Man

. . . Each man has need of the personal confirmation that can come only when he knows his "calling"—his existence in the fullest sense of the term—as an answer to a call. No man is able simply to confirm himself. He may be able to do without the admiration of crowds, but he cannot do without that silent dialogue, often internalized within himself, through which he places his efforts within the context of a mutual contact with what is not himself. He needs to feel that his work is "true"—both as a genuine expression of the reality that he encounters in his life and as a genuine response to some situation or need that calls him. . . .

. . . Every man must risk himself to establish himself as the person that he is and risk failure in so doing. Paradoxically, this means that while the "calling" is in its original meaning an answer to a call, one may have to take the first step oneself and assert that one is called before the call comes. Everyone, no matter how great his training, experiences a moment of uneasy relation between his personal and professional self when he first steps forward as a "doctor," a "psychotherapist," a "minister," a "teacher," a "lawyer," or even a "husband," a "wife," a "father," or a "mother." At this moment the question, "What am I doing taking on this role?" may well produce an invisible inner panic that has nothing to do with competence or "self-confidence." This is the sense of incongruity that comes when one part of oneself is consciously "role-playing" while another part looks on and asks whether one can, in all good faith, identify oneself with this role. If the person who takes this venture can make it "stick," he will then be confirmed by others in his "calling" and soon will come to identify himself so much with his social role that his self-image will be unthinkable without it. The transition from not having a role in society to having one is soon forgotten, but it is instructive in the nature of the confirmation that the person is seeking. (365-369)

The man who makes the assertion that he is a doctor or minister "stick" does not necessarily thereby receive personal confirmation. It may happen, on the contrary, that the more successful he is in his social role, the less he feels confirmed as a person. This is bound to be the case when his social role remains "role-playing" and is never integrated in any thoroughgoing fashion with his existence as a person. This is particularly true of those whose social roles elevate them above the populace and make it necessary for them to pretend to attitudes, convictions, and ideals that they do not really hold. But it is also likely to be true of anyone who, in his desperate need for the confirmation of others, prefers to sacrifice his personal integrity rather than run the risk of not being established in a definite, socially approved role.

The man who enters the transition stage stands, therefore, in the tension point between personal and social confirmation. He cannot resolve this tension by renouncing social confirmation, for no man can live without it: everybody must play a social role, both as a means to economic livelihood and as the simplest prerequisite for any sort of relations with other people in the family and society. On the other hand, he cannot resolve the tension by sacrificing personal confirmation, for this suppression of a basic human need results in an anxiety that may be more and more difficult to handle as the gap between person and role widens. To stand in this tension, however, is to insist that one's confirmation in society also be in some significant sense a confirmation of oneself as a unique person who does not fit into any social category. (377f.)

The impossibility of identifying social and personal confirmation, on the one hand, and of separating them, on the other, is paradigmatic of the whole situation of the self. The self experiences the vertigo of being a free and directing consciousness, on the one hand, and an "eddy in the social current"—to use George Herbert Mead's phrase—on the other. . . . The anxious and at the same time reflective man . . . fights for his freedom and independence yet recognizes both the necessity of social binding and the extent to which he himself is not so much an individual as a social unit. . . . This paradox is . . . inseparable from the very existence of the self. . . . The harder a man tries to fight his way through this ambiguity, in fact, the deeper his confusion must be if he is both honest and aware.

The other border is between the social and the ultimate reality—what we might call "ontological reality" in order to distinguish it in some way from the social without erecting it into a separate metaphysical or theological realm. Here too the self experiences great confusion, this time from the side of the call. The call seems to come through the social, yet in such a way that it not only becomes indistinct but often highly dubious. It tempts one to believe, as a result, either that there really is no call or that it comes to one from some metaphysical, religious, or eternal realm quite outside the social. The problematic of the social, as a result, becomes essential to understanding both the self and the call. (382)

The need of the self for confirmation, the problematic of the calling and the call, the tension between personal and social confirmation, the impossibility of either separating or identifying social reality and the reality that speaks through the medium of the social—all these make impossible those simple contrasts between the self and the other, the "autonomous individual" and the "mass society," the "Single One" and the "crowd," the "insider" and the "outsider," the "beat" and the "square" with which the problematic of the Modern Rebel has been obscured and the real crisis of the person in our age ignored. . . . The person does not exist as a self-evident, self-sufficient reality any more than he can be subsumed under his social role or group category. The person in the modern world exists as pure paradox: responding with a calling of which he is never sure to a call which he can never clearly hear. . . . It cannot be a question of overthrowing the "authoritarian" in favor of the "humanistic," . . . but of discovering the human again and again in the very heart of the bewildering social hierarchy, personal meaning in the midst of the impersonal absurd. (459f.)

Part IV

INTERSUBJECTIVITY

WITH intersubjectivity we come to the most crucial and the most subtle area for the understanding of the convergence and divergence of existentialist thinkers. In Kierkegaard the relation between man and man tends to be secondary and inessential—an obstacle to becoming a single one and to having an absolute relation to the Absolute. The twentieth-century existentialists, in contrast, all recognize intersubjectivity in one form or another as essential to human existence. Yet, even here, a distinction must be made between such thinkers as Heidegger, Sartre, and Tillich, for whom the intersubjective tends to remain a dimension of the self, and such thinkers as Buber, Gabriel Marcel (1889-), Jaspers, and Camus, who in one way or another see the relations *between* man and man as central to human existence. Even between Heidegger and Sartre there are important differences, as Sartre's critique of Heidegger shows. Heidegger's intersubjectivity remains the vague we of his *"Mitsein"* or *"Mitdasein"*—a being with others which expresses itself in solicitude but not in that sharp conflict between one particular person and another which enters into intersubjectivity for Sartre. Buber criticizes Heidegger's "solicitude" as monological, and Heidegger's treatment of death as one's ownmost, ultimate, non-relational reality does, in fact, show that *Mitsein* is not as basic for him as *Dasein*. On the other hand, Sartre's emphasis on conflict and particularity never takes him beyond what Buber would call the "I-It" relation, in which I know the other only as a subject because I am aware of his looking at me as an object or because, as in lovemaking, I am trying to possess his freedom and make it subject to my own. This also leaves Sartre short of the more rationalistic notion of communication which is so central to the thinking of Karl Jaspers, as of the existence "for others" which Merleau-Ponty recognizes in his phenomenology. Camus, like Sartre, starts with the *cogito* yet he goes on to the dialogue between men in which men really come to exist, and sees both the interchange and the limitations of that dialogue as the key to real humanity. Gabriel Marcel, starting from a somewhat more traditional standpoint and showing a continuing influence of idealists such as the American Josiah Royce, arrives like Buber at a radical philosophy of I and Thou (*je et toi*), which he also, like Buber, understands as an approach to epistemology as well as to ethics and religion. He has not made this insight as central to his philosophy as Buber has, however, and his critique of Buber shows the extent to which Marcel has more of a sense of underlying ground or community making possible the I-Thou relation as opposed to Buber's less idealistic "over-againstness."

Søren Kierkegaard

Fear and Trembling

. . . The knight remembers everything, but precisely this remembrance is pain, and yet by the infinite resignation he is reconciled with existence. Love for that princess became for him the expression for an eternal love, assumed a religious character, was transfigured into a love for the Eternal Being, which did to be sure deny him the fulfilment of his love, yet reconciled him again by the eternal consciousness of its validity in the form of eternity, which no reality can take from him. Fools and young men prate about everything being possible for a man. That, however, is a great error. Spiritually speaking, everything is possible, but in the world of the finite there is much which is not possible. This impossible, however, the knight makes possible by expressing it spiritually, but he expresses it spiritually by waiving his claim to it. The wish which would carry him out into reality, but was wrecked upon the impossibility, is now bent inward, but it is not therefore lost, neither is it forgotten.

He keeps this love young, and along with him it increases in years and in beauty. On the other hand, he has no need of the intervention of the finite for the further growth of his love. From the instant he made the movement the princess is lost to him. He has no need of those erotic tinglings in the nerves at the sight of the beloved etc., nor does he need to be constantly taking leave of her in a finite sense, because he recollects her in an eternal sense, and he knows very well that the lovers who are so bent upon seeing "her" yet once again, to say farewell for the last time, are right in being bent upon it, are right in thinking that it is the last time, for they forget one another the soonest. He has comprehended the deep secret that also in loving another person one must be sufficient unto oneself. He no longer takes a finite interest in what the princess is doing, and precisely this is proof that he has made the movement infinitely. Here one may have an opportunity to see whether the movement on the part of a particular person is true or fictitious. There was one who also believed that he had made the movement; but lo, time passed, the princess did something else, she married—a prince, let us say—then his soul lost the elasticity of resignation. Thereby he knew that he had not made the movement rightly; for he who has made the act of resignation infinitely is sufficient unto himself. The knight does not annul his resignation, he preserves his love just as young as it was in its first moment, he never lets it go from him, precisely because he makes the movements infinitely. What the princess does, cannot disturb him, it is only the lower natures which find in other people the law for their actions, which find the premises for their actions outside themselves. If on the other hand the princess is like-minded, the beautiful consequence will be apparent. She will introduce herself into that order of knighthood into which one is not received by balloting, but of which everyone is a member who has courage to introduce himself, that order of knighthood which proves its immortality by the fact that it makes no distinction between man and woman. The two will preserve their love young and sound, she also will have triumphed over her pains, even though she does not, as it is said in the ballad, "lie every night beside her lord." These two will to all eternity remain in agreement with one another, with a well-timed *harmonia praestabilita,* so that if ever the moment were to come, the moment which does not, however, concern them finitely (for then they would be growing older), if ever the moment were to come which offered to give love its expression in time, then they will be capable of beginning precisely at the point where they would have begun if originally they had been united. He who understands this, be he man or woman, can never be deceived, for it is only the lower natures which imagine they were deceived. No girl who is not so proud really knows how to love; but if she is so proud, then the cunning and shrewdness of all the world cannot deceive her. (54-56)

Point of View, "That Individual"

For a "crowd" is the untruth. In a godly sense it is true, eternally, Christianly, as St. Paul says, that "only one attains the goal" —which is not meant in a comparative sense, for comparison takes others into account. It means that every man can be that one, God helping him therein—but only one attains the goal. And again this means that every man should be chary about having to do with "the others," and essentially should talk only with God and with himself—for only one attains the goal. And again this means that man, or to be a man, is akin to deity. . . . Only one attains the goal. Hence where there is a multitude, a crowd, or where decisive significance is attached to the fact that there is a multitude, *there* it is sure that no one is working, living, striving for the highest aim, but only for one or another earthly aim; since to work for the eternal decisive aim is possible only where there is one, and to be this one which all can be is to let God be the helper—the "crowd" is the untruth. . . .

. . . A crowd in its very concept is the untruth, by reason of the fact that it renders the individual completely impenitent and irresponsible, or at least weakens his sense of responsibility by reducing it to a fraction. . . . For "crowd" is an abstraction and has no hands: but each individual has ordinarily two hands. (112-115)

And to honour every man, absolutely every man, is the truth, and this is what it is to fear God and love one's "neighbour." But from an ethico-religious point of view, to recognize the "crowd" as the court of last resort is to deny God, and it cannot exactly mean to love the "neighbour." And the "neighbour" is the absolutely true expression for human equality. . . . The crowd, in fact, is composed of individuals; it must therefore be in every man's power to become what he is, an individual. From becoming an individual no one, no one at all, is excluded, except he who excludes himself by becoming a crowd. (120f.)

Concluding Unscientific Postscript

A double reflection is implicit in the very idea of communication. Communication assumes that the subject who exists in the isolation of his inwardness, and who desires through this inwardness to express the life of eternity, where sociality and fellowship is unthinkable, because the existential category of movement, and with it also all essential communication, is here unthinkable, since everyone must be assumed essentially to possess all, nevertheless wishes to impart himself; and hence desires at one and the same time to have his thinking in the inwardness of his subjective existence, and yet also to put himself into communication with others. This contradiction cannot possibly (except for thoughtlessness, for which indeed all things are possible) find expression in a direct form. That a subject who exists in this manner might wish to impart himself is not so difficult to understand. A lover, for example, whose inwardness is his love, may very well wish to communicate; but he will not wish to communicate himself directly, precisely because the inwardness of his love is for him essential. Essentially occupied constantly in acquiring and reacquiring the inwardness of love, he has no result, and is never finished. But he may nevertheless wish to communicate, although he can never use a direct form, because such a form presupposes results and finality. So, too, in the case of a God-relationship. Precisely because he himself is constantly in process of becoming inwardly or in inwardness, the religious individual can never use direct communication, the movement in him being the precise opposite of that presupposed in direct communication. Direct communication presupposes certainty; but certainty is impossible for anyone in process of becoming, and the semblance of certainty constitutes for such an individual a deception. Thus, to make use of an erotic relationship, if a loving maiden were to long for the wedding day on account of the assured certainty that it would give her; if she desired to install herself as wife in a legal security, exchanging maidenly longing for wifely yawning, her lover would have the right to complain of her unfaithfulness, and that although she loved no one else; because she had lost the Idea constitutive of the inwardness of love, and did not really love him. And it is this which characterizes all essential faithlessness in the erotic relationship; loving another is accidental. . . .

Ordinary communication between man and man is wholly immediate, because men in general exist immediately. When one man sets forth something and another acknowledges the same, word for word, it is taken for granted that they are in agreement, and that they have understood one another. Precisely because the speaker has not noticed the reduplication requisite to a thinking mode of existence, he also remains unaware of the double reflection involved in the process of communication. Hence he does not suspect that an agreement of this nature may be the grossest kind of misunderstanding. Nor does he suspect that, just as the subjective existing thinker has made himself free through the reduplication given his reflection, so the secret of all communication consists precisely in emancipating the recipient, and that for this reason he must not communicate himself directly; aye, that it is even irreligious to do so. This last holds true the more the subjective is of the essence of the matter, and hence applies first and foremost in the religious sphere. . . .

The subjective religious thinker, who in order to become such must have apprehended the doubleness characteristic of existence, readily perceives that a direct mode of communication is an attempt to defraud God, possibly depriving him of the worship of another human being in truth. He sees also that it is a fraud practised upon himself, as if he had ceased to be an existing individual; and an attempt to defraud the recipient of the communication, who possibly acquires a merely relative God-relationship; and moreover, that it is a fraud which brings him into contradiction with his entire thought. (68f.)

The communication of results is an unnatural form of intercourse between man and man, in so far as every man is a spiritual being, for whom the truth consists in nothing else than the self-activity of personal appropriation, which the communication of a result tends to prevent. Let a teacher in relation to the essential truth (for otherwise a direct relationship between teacher and pupil is quite in order) have, as we say, much inwardness of feeling, and be willing to publish his doctrines day in and day out; if he assumes the existence of a direct relationship between the learner and himself, his inwardness is not inwardness, but a direct outpouring of feeling; the respect for the learner which recognizes that he is in himself the inwardness of truth, is precisely the teacher's inwardness. (217)

Not even God, then, enters into a direct relationship with derivative spirits. . . . Much less can a human being sustain such a direct relationship to another *in the truth*. Nature, the totality of created things, is the work of God. And yet God is not there; but within the individual man there is a potentiality (man is potentially spirit) which is awakened in inwardness to become a God-relationship, and then it becomes possible to see God everywhere. . . . A direct relationship between one spiritual being and another, with respect to the essential truth, is unthinkable. If such a relationship is assumed, it means that one of the parties has ceased to be spirit. . . . Socrates was an ethical teacher, but he took cognizance of the non-existence of any direct relationship between teacher and pupil, because the truth is inwardness, and because this inwardness in each is precisely the road which leads them away from one another. (220f.)

. . . In the case of another person's reality he could have no knowledge about it until he conceived it in coming to know it, which means that he transformed it from a reality into a possibility. . . . This implies that there is no immediate relationship, ethically, between subject and subject. When I understand another person, his reality is for me a possibility, and in its aspect of possibility this conceived reality is related to me precisely as the thought of something I have not done is related to the doing of it. (284f.)

Every human being is gloriously constituted, but what ruins so many is, among other things, also the wretched tittle-tattle between man and man about that which should be suffered and matured in silence, this confession before men instead of before

God, this hearty communication between this man and that about what ought to be secret and exist only before God in secrecy, this impatient craving for intermediary consolation. No, in suffering the pain of his annihilation, the religious individual has learned that human indulgence profits nothing, and therefore refuses to listen to anything from that side; but he exists before God and exhausts the suffering of being human and at the same time existing before God. Therefore it cannot comfort him to know what the human crowd knows, man with man, what men know who have a shopkeeper's notion of what it means to be a man, and facile gossipy notion at seventeenth hand of what it means to exist before God. (437)

Martin Heidegger

Being and Time

The world of Dasein is a *with-world*. Being-in is *Being-with* Others. Their Being-in-themselves within-the-world is *Dasein-with*.

When Others are encountered, it is not the case that one's subject is *proximally* present-at-hand and that the rest of the subjects, which are likewise occurrents, get discriminated beforehand and then apprehended; nor are they encountered by a primary act of looking at oneself in such a way that the opposite pole of a distinction first gets ascertained. . . . Even if Others become themes for study, as it were, in their own Dasein, they are not encountered as person-Things present-at-hand: we meet them "at work," that is, primarily in their Being-in-the-world. . . . Being-with is an existential characteristic of Dasein even when factically no Other is present-at-hand or perceived. Even Dasein's Being-alone is Being-with in the world. The Other can *be missing* only *in* and *for* a Being-with. Being-alone is a deficient mode of Being-with; its very possibility is the proof of this. . . . Concern is a character-of-Being which Being-with cannot have as its own, even though Being-with, like concern, is a *Being towards* entities encountered within-the-world. . . . These entities are not objects of concern, but rather of *solicitude*. . . . Dasein maintains itself proximally and for the most part in the deficient modes of solicitude. Being for, against, or without one another, passing one another by, not "mattering" to one another—these are possible ways of solicitude. And it is precisely these last-named deficient and Indifferent modes that characterize everyday, average Being-with-one-another. . . . Ontologically there is an essential distinction between the "indifferent" way in which Things at random occur together and the way in which entities who are with one another do not "matter" to one another.

With regard to its positive modes, solicitude has two extreme possibilities. It can, as it were, take away "care" from the Other and put itself in his position in concern: it can *leap in* for him. This kind of solicitude takes over for the Other that with which he is to concern himself. The Other is thus thrown out of his own position; he steps back so that afterwards, when the matter has been attended to, he can either take it over as something finished and at his disposal, or disburden himself of it completely. In such solicitude the Other can become one who is dominated and dependent, even if this domination is a tacit one and remains hidden from him. . . . In contrast to this, there is also the possibility of a kind of solicitude which does not so much leap in for the Other as *leap ahead* of him in his existentiell potentiality-for-Being, not in order to take away his "care" but rather to give it back to him authentically as such for the first time. This kind of solicitude pertains essentially to authentic care—that is, to the existence of the Other, not to a *"what"* with which he is concerned; it helps the Other to become transparent to himself *in* his care and to become *free for* it. . . .

. . . When they devote themselves to the same affair in common, their doing so is determined by the manner in which their Dasein, each in its own way, has been taken hold of. They thus become *authentically* bound together, and this makes possible the right kind of objectivity, which frees the Other in his freedom for himself. . . . As Being-with, Dasein "is" essentially for the sake of Others. . . . Even if the particular factical Dasein does *not* turn to Others, and supposes that it has no need of them or manages to get along without them, it *is* in the way of Being-with. . . . The structure of the world's worldhood is such that Others are not proximally present-at-hand as free-floating subjects along with other Things, but show themselves in the world in their special environmental Being, and do so in terms of what is ready-to-hand in that world. . . .

. . . Because Dasein's Being is Being-with, its understanding of Being already implies the understanding of Others. . . . Knowing oneself is grounded in Being-with, which understands primordially. It operates proximally in accordance with the kind of Being which is closest to us—Being-in-the-world as Being-with. . . . Solicitous concern is understood in terms of what we are concerned with, and along with our understanding of it. Thus in concernful solicitude the Other is proximally disclosed. . . . Even the explicit disclosure of the Other in solicitude grows only out of one's primarily Being with him in each case. . . . Not only is Being towards Others an autonomous, irreducible relationship of Being: this relationship, as Being-with, is one which, with Dasein's Being, already is. Of course it is indisputable that a lively mutual acquaintanceship on the basis of Being-with, often depends upon how far one's own Dasein has understood itself at the time; but this means that it depends only upon how far one's essential Being with Others has made itself transparent and has not disguised itself. And that is possible only if Dasein, as Being-in-the-world, already is with Others. "Empathy" does not first constitute Being-with; only on the basis of Being-with does "empathy" become possible. (155-162)

. . . Ambiguity is always tossing to curiosity that which it seeks; and it gives idle talk the semblance of having everything decided in it. But this kind of Being of the disclosedness of Being-in-the-world dominates also Being-with-one-another as such. The Other is proximally "there" in terms of what "they" have heard about him, what "they" say in their talk about him, and what "they" know about him. Into primordial Being-with-one-another, idle talk first slips itself in between. Everyone keeps his eye on the Other first and next, watching how he will comport himself and what he will say in reply. Being-with-one-another in the "they" is by no means an indifferent side-by-side-ness in which everything has been settled, but rather an intent, ambiguous watching of one another, a secret and reciprocal listening-in. Under the mask of "for-one-another," an "against-one-another" is in play. (219)

. . . Because Being-in-the-world is essentially care, Being-alongside the ready-to-hand could be taken in our previous analyses as *concern,* and Being with the Dasein-with of Others as we encounter it within-the-world could be taken as *solicitude*. . . . So neither does "care" stand primarily and exclusively for an isolated attitude of the "I" towards itself. If one were to construct the expression "care for oneself," following the analogy of "concern" and "solicitude," this would be a tautology. (237)

. . . Evasive concealment in the face of death dominates

everydayness so stubbornly that, in Being with one another, the "neighbours" often still keep talking the "dying person" into the belief that he will escape death and soon return to the tranquillized everydayness of the world of his concern. Such "solicitude" is meant to "console" him. It insists upon bringing him back into Dasein, while in addition it helps him to keep his ownmost non-relational possibility-of-Being completely concealed. In this manner the "they" provides a *constant tranquillization about death.* At bottom, however, this is a tranquillization not only for him who is "dying" but just as much for those who "console" him. And even in the case of a demise, the public is still not to have its own tranquillity upset by such an event, or be disturbed in the carefreeness with which it concerns itself. Indeed the dying of Others is seen often enough as a social inconvenience, if not even a downright tactlessness, against which the public is to be guarded. (298)

The ownmost possibility is *non-relational.* Anticipation allows Dasein to understand that that potentiality-for-being in which its ownmost Being is an issue, must be taken over by Dasein alone. Death does not just "belong" to one's own Dasein in an undifferentiated way; death *lays claim* to it as an *individual* Dasein. The non-relational character of death, as understood in anticipation, individualizes Dasein down to itself. This individualizing is a way in which the "there" is disclosed for existence. It makes manifest that all Being-alongside the things with which we concern ourselves, and all Being-with Others, will fail us when our ownmost potentiality-for-Being is the issue. Dasein can be *authentically itself* only if it makes this possible for itself of its own accord. But if concern and solicitude fail us, this does not signify at all that these ways of Dasein have been cut off from its authentically Being-its-Self. As structures essential to Dasein's constitution, these have a share in conditioning the possibility of any existence whatsoever. Dasein is authentically itself only to the extent that, *as* concernful Being-alongside and solicitous Being-with, it projects itself upon its ownmost potentially-for-Being rather than upon the possibility of the they-self. The entity which anticipates its non-relational possibility, is thus forced by that very anticipation into the possibility of taking over from itself its ownmost Being, and doing so of its own accord. . . . As the non-relational possibility, death individualizes—but only in such a manner that, as the possibility which is not to be outstripped, it makes Dasein, as Being-with, have some understanding of the potentiality-for-Being of Others. (308f.)

. . . Dasein, as a Being-with which understands, can *listen* to Others. Losing itself in the publicness and the idle talk of the "they," it *fails to hear* its own Self in listening to the they-self. If Dasein is to be able to get brought back from this lostness of failing to hear itself, and if this is to be done through itself, then it must first be able to find itself—to find itself as something which has failed to hear itself, and which fails to hear in that it *listens away* to the "they." This listening-away must get broken off; in other words, the possibility of another kind of hearing which will interrupt it, must be given by Dasein itself. (315f.) . . . When the call is understood with an existentiell kind of hearing, such understanding is more authentic the more non-relationally Dasein hears and understands *its* own Being-appealed-to, and the less the meaning of the call gets perverted by what one says or by what is fitting and accepted. (325) . . . The idea of "Guilty!" must be sufficiently *formalized* so that those ordinary phenomena of "guilt" which are related to our concernful Being with Others, will *drop out.* (328)

Wanting to have a conscience is . . . the most primordial existentiell presupposition for the possibility of factically coming to owe something. In understanding the call, Dasein lets its ownmost Self *take action in itself* in terms of that potentiality-for-Being which it has chosen. Only so can it *be* answerable. Factically, however, any taking-action is necessarily "conscienceless," not only because it may fail to avoid some factical moral indebtedness, but because, on the null basis of its null projection, it has, in Being with Others, already become guilty towards them. Thus one's wanting-to-have-a-conscience becomes the taking-over of that essential consciencelessness within which alone the existentiell possibility of *Being* "good" subsists. (334)

In the light of the "for-the-sake-of-which" of one's self-chosen potentiality-for-Being, resolute Dasein frees itself for its world. Dasein's resoluteness towards itself is what first makes it possible to let the Others who are with it "be" in their ownmost potentiality-for-Being, and to co-disclose this potentiality in the solicitude which leaps forth and liberates. When Dasein is resolute, it can become the "conscience" of Others. Only by authentically Being-their-Selves in resoluteness can people authentically be with one another—not by ambiguous and jealous stipulations and talkative fraternizing in the "they" and in what "they" want to undertake. (344f.)

. . . If fateful Dasein, as Being-in-the-world, exists essentially in Being-with Others, its historizing is a co-historizing and is determinative for it as *destiny.* This is how we designate the historizing of the community, of a people. Destiny is not something that puts itself together out of individual fates, any more than

Being-with-one-another can be conceived as the occurring together of several Subjects. Our fates have already been guided in advance, in our Being with one another in the same world and in our resoluteness for definite possibilities. Only in communicating and in struggling does the power of destiny become free. Dasein's fateful destiny in and with its "generation" goes to make up the full authentic historizing of Dasein. (436)

Letter on Humanism

To take care of or care for a "thing" or a "person" in their essence means to love or like* them.

Such liking means in a more primary sense to endow with essence. For *Mögen* is the true essence of *Vermögen,* which not merely can achieve one thing or another but can let something "realize itself" true to its origin† and as it comes towards us, that is, to let it *be*. (57)

Man . . . is not merely a living creature possessing among other faculties that of language. Language is rather the house of Being and man ec-sists dwelling therein as he guards the truth of Being to which he belongs. (79)

Existence and Being

The ability to speak and the ability to hear are equally fundamental. We are a conversation—and that means: we can hear from one another. We are a conversation, that always means at the same time: we are a *single* conversation. But the unity of a conversation consists in the fact that in the essential word there is always manifest that one and the same thing on which we agree, and on the basis of which we are united and so are essentially ourselves. Conversation and its unity support our existence. (278)

Only now can we appreciate in its entirety what is meant by: "Since we have been a conversation. . . ." Since the gods have led us into conversation, since time has been time, ever since then

* Heidegger uses as equivalent for "like" German *Mögen,* which has the same root as English "may," "might (v.)," and "might (n.)." Etymologically therefore, the meaning implied here is not only that of "liking" but also that of "possibility," "potential," "permission," and "power"—as still evident in the derivatives *Macht* (might, power) and *Vermögen* (might, power, potential).—Trans.

† The German word used here is *Her-kunft* which ordinarily means "origin" but in this hyphenated spelling evokes the original meaning of "coming towards."—Trans.

the basis of our existence has been a conversation. The proposi tion that language is the supreme event of human existence has through it acquired its meaning and foundation. (280)

Jean-Paul Sartre

Existentialism

. . . One discovers in the *cogito* not only himself, but others as well.

The philosophies of Descartes and Kant to the contrary, through the *I think* we reach our own self in the presence of others, and the others are just as real to us as our own self. Thus, the man who becomes aware of himself through the *cogito* also perceives all others, and he perceives them as the condition of his own existence. He realizes that he can not be anything (in the sense that we say that someone is witty or nasty or jealous) unless others recognize it as such. In order to get any truth about myself, I must have contact with another person. The other is indispensable to my own existence, as well as to my knowledge about myself. This being so, in discovering my inner being I discover the other person at the same time, like a freedom placed in front of me which thinks and wills only for or against me. Hence, let us at once announce the discovery of a world which we shall call inter-subjectivity; this is the world in which man decides what he is and what others are. (44f.)

No Exit

INEZ: Obviously there aren't any physical torments—you agree, don't you? And yet we're in hell. And no one else will come here. We'll stay in this room together, the three of us, for ever and ever. . . . Each of us will act as torturer of the two others.

GARCIN [*gently*]: No, I shall never be your torturer. I wish neither of you any harm, and I've no concern with you. None at all. So the solution's easy enough; each of us stays put in his or her corner and takes no notice of the others. (17f.)

GARCIN: . . . We'll look at the floor and each must try to forget the others are there.

[*A longish silence.* GARCIN *sits down. The women return hesitantly to their places. Suddenly* INEZ *swings round on him.*]

INEZ: To forget about the others? How utterly absurd! I *feel* you there, in every pore. Your silence clamors in my ears. You can nail up your mouth, cut your tongue out—but you can't prevent your *being there.* Can you stop your thoughts? I hear them ticking away like a clock, tick-tock, tick-tock, and I'm certain you hear mine. It's all very well skulking on your sofa, but you're everywhere, and every sound comes to me soiled, because you've intercepted it on its way. Why, you've even stolen my face; you know it and I don't! (23)

GARCIN: Alone, none of us can save himself or herself; we're linked together inextricably. (29)

GARCIN: . . . We're chasing after each other, round and round in a vicious circle, like the horses on a roundabout. (31)

INEZ: . . . For thirty years you dreamt you were a hero, and condoned a thousand petty lapses—because a hero, of course, can do no wrong. An easy method, obviously. Then a day came when you were up against it, the red light of real danger—and you took the train to Mexico.

GARCIN: I "dreamt," you say. It was no dream. When I chose the hardest path, I made my choice deliberately. A man is what he wills himself to be.

INEZ: Prove it. Prove it was no dream. It's what one does, and nothing else, that shows the stuff one's made of.

GARCIN: I died too soon. I wasn't allowed time to—to do my deeds.

INEZ: One always dies too soon—or too late. And yet one's whole life is complete at that moment, with a line drawn neatly under it, ready for the summing up. You are—your life, and nothing else.

GARCIN: What a poisonous woman you are! With an answer for everything.

INEZ: Now then! Don't lose heart. It shouldn't be so hard, convincing me. Pull yourself together, man, rake up some arguments. [GARCIN *shrugs his shoulders.*] Ah, wasn't I right when I said you were vulnerable? Now you're going to pay the price, and what a price! You're a coward, Garcin, because I wish it. I wish it—do you hear?—I wish it. And yet, just look at me, see how weak I am, a mere breath on the air, a gaze observing you, a formless thought that thinks you. [*He walks towards her, opening his hands.*] Ah, they're open now, those big hands, those coarse, man's hands! But what do you hope to do? You can't throttle thoughts with hands. So you've no choice, you must convince me, and you're at my mercy. . . .

GARCIN: So this is hell. I'd never have believed it. You remember all we were told about the torture-chambers, the fire and brimstone, the "burning marl." Old wives' tales! There's no need for red-hot pokers. Hell is—other people! (44-47)

The Reprieve

. . . I have never known what I *am*? My vices, my virtues, are under my nose, but I can't see them, nor stand far enough back to view myself as a whole. I seem to be a sort of flabby mass in which words are engulfed; no sooner do I name myself than what is named is merged in him who names, and one gets no farther. I have often wanted to hate myself and, as you know, had good reasons for so doing. But my attempted hatred of myself was absorbed into my insubstantiality and was nothing but a recollection. I could not love myself either—I am sure, though I have never tried to. But I was eternally compelled to *be myself;* I was my own burden, but never burdensome enough, Mathieu. For one instant, on that June evening when I elected to confess to you, I thought I had encountered myself in your bewildered eyes. You *saw* me, in your eyes I was solid and predictable; my acts and moods were the actual consequences of a definite entity. And through me you knew that entity. I described it to you in my words, I revealed to you facts unknown to you, which had helped you to visualize it. And yet you saw it, I merely saw you seeing it. For one instant you were the heaven-sent mediator between me and myself, you perceived that compact and solid entity which I was and wanted to be in just as simple and ordinary a way as I perceived you. For, after all, I exist, I *am,* though I have no sense of being; and it is an exquisite torment to discover in oneself such utterly unfounded certainty, such unsubstantiated pride. I then understood that one could not reach oneself except through another's judgment, another's hatred. And also through another's love perhaps. . . .

Sometimes I wanted to see you again, sometimes I dreamed of murdering you. But one fine day I realized our relations were strictly mutual. Without me, you would be that same insubstantial entity that I am for myself. It is by my agency that you can at times get an occasional and doubtless rather exasperating glimpse of yourself—as you really are: a rather limited rationalist, superficially self-confident, but fundamentally without convictions, well disposed to everything within the compass of your reason, blind and disingenuous towards anything else; rational by self-interest, naturally sentimental, by no means sensual; in brief, a cautious, moderate intellectual, an excellent middle-class product. If it be true that I cannot get at myself without your intercession, you need mine if you want to know yourself. . . .

You must have experienced, in the subway, in the foyer of a theater, or in a train the sudden and irksome sense that you were being looked at from behind. You turn around, but the observer has buried his nose in a book; you can't discover *who* was looking at you. You turn back, but you are sure that the unknown eyes are again upon you, there's a faint tingling all over your back, like a sudden twitch of all your tissues. Well, that is what I felt for the first time, on September 26, at three o'clock in the afternoon, in the hotel garden. No one was there, you understand, Mathieu, no one at all. But the look was there. Try to understand completely: I did not see it, as one sees a passing profile, a forehead, or a pair of eyes; for its essential character is to be *beyond perception.* But I became more compact and concentrated, I was both transparent and opaque, I existed *in the presence* of a look. Since then I have been continually under observation, even in my solitary room; sometimes, the consciousness of transfixion by that sword-blade, of that eye upon me while asleep, awoke me with a start. I have, in fact, almost entirely lost the capacity for sleep. Ah, Mathieu, what a discovery! *I was seen,* I struggled to know myself, I seemed to be slipping out of my extremities, I claimed your kindly intercession, and all the time I was seen, the inexorable look, an invisible steel blade, was on me. And you too, skeptic and scoffer as you are, *you are seen.* But you don't know it. I can easily describe that look: it is nothing; it is a purely negative entity: imagine a pitch-dark night. It's the night that looks at you, but it's a dazzling night, in fullest splendor; the night behind the day. I am flooded with black light; it is all over my hands and eyes and heart, and I can't see it. Believe me, I first loathed this incessant violation of myself; as you know, I used to long to become invisible, to go and leave no trace, on earth or in men's hearts. What anguish to discover that look as a universal medium from which I can't escape! But what a relief as well! I know at last that I am. I adapt for my own use, and to your disgust, your prophet's foolish wicked words: "I think, therefore I am," which used to trouble me so sorely, for the more I thought, the less I seemed to be; and I say: "I am seen, therefore I am." I need no longer bear the responsibility of my turbid and disintegrating self: he who sees me causes me to be; I am as he sees me. . . .

At last I am transmuted into myself. Hated, despised, sustained, a presence supports me to continue thus forever. I am infinite and infinitely guilty. But *I am,* Mathieu, I am. Before God and before men, I *am. Ecce homo.* (313-315)

Being and Nothingness

. . . The objective fact of the being-in-itself of the consciousness of the Other is posited in order to disappear in negativity and in freedom: consciousness of the Other is as not-being; its being-in-itself "here and now" is not-to-be. . . . *Consciousness of the Other is what it is not.* (62)

There is no privilege for *my* self: my empirical Ego and the Other's empirical Ego appear in the world at the same time. The general meaning of "Others" is necessary to the constitution of each one of these "Egos." Thus each object far from being constituted as for Kant, by a simple relation to the *subject,* appears in my concrete experience as polyvalent; it is given originally as possessing systems of reference to an indefinite plurality of consciousnesses. . . . The meaning of "the Other" can not come from the experience nor from a reasoning by analogy effected on the occasion of the experience; on the contrary, it is in the light of the concept of *the Other* that the experience is interpreted. . . . Actually the Other is *never* that empirical person who is encountered in my experience; he is the transcendental subject to whom this person by nature refers. Thus the true problem is that of the connection of transcendental subjects who are beyond experience. . . . Even if outside the empirical Ego there is *nothing other* than the consciousness of that Ego—that is, a transcendental field without a subject—the fact remains that my affirmation of the Other demands and requires the existence beyond the world of a similar transcendental field. Consequently the only way to escape solipsism would be here again to prove that my transcendental consciousness is in its very being, affected by the extra-mundane existence of other consciousnesses of the same type. Because Husserl has reduced being to a series of meanings, the only connection which he has been able to establish between my being and that of the Other is a connection of *knowledge.* Therefore Husserl can not escape solipsism any more than Kant could. (233-235) . . .

The empirical image which may best symbolize Heidegger's intuition is not that of a conflict but rather a *crew.* The original relation of the Other and my consciousness is not the *you* and *me;* it is the *we.* (246) . . . The ontological co-existence which appears as the structure of "being-in-the-world" can in no way serve as a foundation to an ontic being-with, such as, for example, the co-existence which appears in my friendship with Pierre or in the couple which Annie and I make. . . . Heidegger's *transcendence* is a concept in bad faith. . . . Heidegger does not escape idealism; his flight outside the self, as an *a priori* structure of his being, isolates him as surely as the Kantian reflection on the *a priori* conditions of our experience. In fact what human-reality rediscovers at the inaccessible limit of this flight outside itself is still the self: the flight outside the self is a flight toward the self, and the world appears as the pure distance between the self and the self. . . . Human-reality at the very heart of its ekstases remains alone. . . . Because the Other's existence has the nature of a contingent and irreducible fact. We *encounter* the Other; we do not constitute him. And if this fact still appears to us in the form of a necessity, yet it does not belong with those "conditions of the possibility of our experience" or—if you prefer—with ontological necessity. . . . If the Other is to be capable of being given to us, it is by means of a direct apprehension which leaves to the encounter its character as facticity. (248-250)

. . . Each Other finds his being in the Other. (252) . . . Thus this relation which I call "being-seen-by-another," far from being merely one of the relations signified by the word *man*, represents an irreducible fact which can not be deduced either from the essence of the Other-as-object, or from my being-as-subject. . . . My apprehension of the Other in the world as *probably being* a man refers to my permanent possibility of *being-seen-by-him;* that is, to the permanent possibility that a subject who sees me may be substituted for the object seen by me. "Being-seen-by-the-Other" is the *truth* of "seeing-the-Other." (257) . . . Beyond any knowledge which I can have, I am this self which another knows. And this self which I am—this I am in a world which the Other has made alien to me. . . . Thus I am my *Ego* for the Other in the midst of a world which flows toward the Other. . . . The Other's freedom is revealed to me across the uneasy indetermination of the being which I am for him. . . . For the Other *I am seated* as this inkwell *is on* the table; for the Other, *I am leaning over* the keyhole as this tree *is bent* by the wind. Thus for the Other I have stripped myself of my transcendence. . . . The alienation of myself, which is the act of being-looked-at, involves the alienation of the world which I organize. (261-263) . . . Being-seen constitutes me as a defenseless being for a freedom which is not my freedom. (267)

The Other is present to me without any intermediary as a transcendence *which is not mine.* But this presence is not reciprocal. . . . Thus this pure subject which by definition I am unable to know—*i.e.*, to posit as object—is always *there* out of reach and without distance whenever I try to grasp myself as object. In experiencing the look, in experiencing myself as an unrevealed objectness, I experience the inapprehensible subjectivity of the Other directly and with my being. . . . At the same time I experience the Other's infinite freedom. It is for and by means of a freedom and only for and by means of it that my possibles can be limited and fixed. (270) . . . Just as my consciousness apprehended by the *cogito* bears indubitable witness of itself and of its own existence, so certain particular consciousnesses—for example, "shame-consciousness"—bear indubitable witness to the *cogito* both of themselves and of the existence of the Other. (273)

. . . Being-for-others is not an ontological structure of the For-itself. We can not think of deriving being-for-others from a being-for-itself as one would derive a consequence from a principle, nor conversely can we think of deriving being-for-itself from being-for-others. . . . What the *cogito* reveals to us here is just factual necessity: it is found—and this is indisputable—that our being along with its being-for-itself is also for-others. . . . Selfness is reinforced by arising as a negation of another selfness. . . . Consciousness must freely disengage itself from the Other and wrench itself away by choosing itself as a nothingness which is simply Other than the Other and thereby must be reunited in "itself." This very detachment, which is the being of the For-itself, causes there to be an Other. (282f.) . . .

In view of this presence of the Other-as-subject to me in and through my assumed object-ness, we can see that my making an object out of the Other must be the second moment in my relation to him. . . . If there is an Other who puts me out of play by positing my transcendence as purely contemplated, this is because I wrench myself away from the Other by assuming my limit. The consciousness (of) this wrenching away of the consciousness of (being) the same in relation to the Other is the consciousness (of) my free spontaneity. By this very wrenching away which puts the Other in possession of my limit, I am already putting the Other out of play. . . . The new negation, although it has the other negation for its motivation, in turn disguises it. The Other appears to me as a degraded presence. . . . By one and the same stroke I have regained my being-for-itself through my consciousness (of) myself as a perpetual center of infinite possibilities, and I have transformed the Other's possibilities into dead-possibilities by affecting them all with the character of *"not-lived-by-me"*—that is as *simply given*. . . .

. . . Shame is only the original feeling of having my being *outside*, engaged in another being and as such without any defense, illuminated by the absolute light which emanates from a pure subject. (287f.) . . . In pride I recognize the Other as the subject through whom my being gets its object-state. . . . There are two authentic attitudes: that by which I recognize the Other as the subject through whom I get my object-ness—this is shame; and that by which I apprehend myself as the free object by which the Other gets his being-other—this is arrogance or the affirmation of my freedom confronting the Other-as-object. But pride—or vanity—is a feeling without equilibrium, and it is in bad faith. In vanity I attempt in my capacity as Object to act upon the Other. (290)

The difference of principle between the Other-as-object and the Other-as-subject stems solely from this fact: that the Other-as-subject can in no way be known nor even conceived as such. (293) . . . Thus the Other-as-object is an explosive instrument which I handle with care because I foresee around him the permanent possibility that *they* are going to make it explode and that with this explosion I shall suddenly experience the flight of the world away from me and the alienation of my being. Therefore my constant concern is to contain the Other within his objectivity, and my relations with the Other-as-object are essentially made up of ruses designed to make him remain an object. But one look on the part of the Other is sufficient to make all these schemes collapse and to make me experience once more the transfiguration of the Other. Thus I am referred from transfiguration to degradation and from degradation to transfiguration without ever being able either to get a total view of the ensemble of these two modes of being on the part of the Other—for each of them is self-sufficient and refers only to itself—or to hold firmly to either one of them—for each has its own instability and collapses in order for the other to rise from its ruins. (297)

. . . The upsurge of the Other touches the for-itself in its very heart. By the Other and for the Other the pursuing flight is fixed in in-itself. . . . My concrete relations with the Other are wholly governed by my attitudes with respect to the object which I am for the Other. And as the Other's existence reveals to me the being which I am without my being able either to appropriate that being or even to conceive it, this existence will motivate two opposed attitudes: First—The Other *looks* at me and as such he holds the secret of my being, he knows what I *am*. Thus the profound meaning of my being is outside of me, imprisoned in an absence. The Other has the advantage over me. Therefore in so far as I am fleeing the in-itself which I am without founding it, I can attempt to deny that being which is conferred on me from outside; that is, I can turn back upon the Other so as to make an object out of him in turn since the Other's object-ness destroys my object-ness for him. But on the other hand, in so far as the Other as freedom is the foundation of my being-in-itself, I can seek to recover that freedom and to possess it without removing from it its character as freedom. . . .

Everything which may be said of me in my relations with the Other applies to him as well. While I attempt to free myself from the hold of the Other, the Other is trying to free himself from mine; while I seek to enslave the Other, the Other seeks to enslave me. . . . Conflict is the original meaning of being-for-others. . . . We experience our inapprehensible being-for-others in the form of a *possession.* I am possessed by the Other; the Other's look fashions my body in its nakedness, causes it to be born, sculptures it, produces it as it *is,* sees it as I shall never see it. . . . By virtue of consciousness the Other is for me simultaneously the one who has stolen my being from me and the one who causes "there to be" a being which is my being. . . . Thus my project of recovering myself is fundamentally a project of absorbing the Other. . . . I do not thereby cease to assert the Other—that is, to deny concerning myself that I am the Other. . . .

. . . Precisely because I exist by means of the Other's freedom, I have no security; I am in danger in this freedom. It moulds my being and *makes me be,* it confers values upon me and removes them from me; and my being receives from it a perpetual passive escape from self. Irresponsible and beyond reach, this protean freedom in which I have engaged myself can in turn engage me in a thousand different ways of being. My project of recovering my being can be realized only if I get hold of this freedom and reduce it to being a freedom subject to my freedom. . . . Thus the lover does not desire to possess the beloved as one possesses a thing; he wants to possess a freedom as freedom. . . . He is and consents to be an *object.* But on the other hand, he wants to be the object in which the Other's freedom consents to lose itself, the object in which the Other consents to find his being and his *raison d'être* as his second facticity. . . . Thus to want to be loved is to infect the Other with one's own facticity; it is to wish to compel him to recreate you perpetually as the condition of a freedom which submits itself and which is engaged; it is to wish both that freedom found fact and that fact have pre-eminence over freedom. (362-368)

Whereas before being loved we were uneasy about that unjustified, unjustifiable protuberance which was our existence, whereas we felt ourselves *"de trop,"* we now feel that our existence is taken up and willed even in its tiniest details by an absolute freedom which at the same time our existence conditions and which we ourselves will with our freedom. . . . It is the Other's freedom which founds our essence. If we could manage to interiorize the whole system, we should be our own foundation. Such then is the real goal of the lover in so far as his love is an enterprise—*i.e.*, a project of himself. This project is going to provoke a conflict. The beloved in fact apprehends the lover as one Other-as-object among others; that is, he perceives the lover on the ground of the world, transcends him, and utilizes him. The beloved is a *look.* He can not therefore employ his transcendence to fix an ultimate limit to his surpassings, nor can he employ his freedom to captivate itself. The beloved can not will to love. Therefore the lover must seduce the beloved, and his love can in no way be distinguished from the enterprise of seduction. (371)

. . . It suffices that the lovers should be *looked at* together by a third person in order for each one to experience not only his own objectivation but that of the other as well. Immediately the Other is no longer for me the absolute transcendence which founds me in my being; he is a transcendence-transcended, not by me but by another. . . . Even if nobody sees us, we exist for *all* consciousnesses and we are conscious of existing for all. The result is that love as a fundamental mode of being-for-others holds in its being-for-others the seed of its own destruction. . . . The Other's awakening is always possible; at any moment he can make me appear as an object—hence the lover's perpetual insecurity. Love is an absolute which is perpetually *made relative* by others. One would have to be alone in the world with the beloved in order for love to preserve its character as an absolute axis of reference—hence the lover's perpetual shame (or pride—which here amounts to the same thing).

Thus it is useless for me to have tried to lose myself in objectivity; my passion will have availed me nothing. The Other has referred me to my own unjustifiable subjectivity—either by himself or through others. This result can provoke a total despair and a new attempt to realize the identification of the Other and myself. Its ideal will then be the opposite of that which we have just described; instead of projecting the absorbing of the Other while preserving in him his otherness, I shall project causing myself to be absorbed by the Other and losing myself in his subjectivity in order to get rid of my own. This enterprise will be expressed concretely by the *masochistic* attitude. . . . Masochism is characterized as a species of vertigo, vertigo before the abyss of the Other's subjectivity. . . . The more he tries to taste his objectivity, the more he will be submerged by the consciousness of his subjectivity—hence his anguish. . . . In seeking to apprehend his own objectivity he finds the Other's objectivity, which in spite of himself frees his own subjectivity. . . .

. . . To look at the Other's look is to posit oneself in one's own freedom and to attempt on the ground of this freedom to confront the Other's freedom. The meaning of the conflict thus sought would be to bring out into the open the struggle of two freedoms confronted as freedoms. But this intention must be immediately disappointed, for by the sole fact that I assert myself in my freedom confronting the Other, I make the Other a transcendence-transcended—that is, an object. . . . I can choose myself as looking at the Other's look and can build my subjectivity upon the collapse of the subjectivity of the Other. It is this attitude which we shall call *indifference toward others*. . . . Blindness as concerns the Other concurrently causes the disappearance of every lived apprehension of my *objectivity*. Nevertheless the Other as freedom and my objectivity as my alienated-self *are there*, unperceived, not thematized, but given in my very comprehension of the world and of my being in the world. . . .

My original attempt to get hold of the Other's free subjectivity through his objectivity-for-me is *sexual desire*. (376-382) We do not desire the body as a purely material object; a purely material object is not *in situation*. Thus this organic totality which is immediately present to desire is desirable only in so far as it reveals not only life but also an appropriate consciousness. (386) . . . Consciousness is clogged, so to speak, by sexual desire; it seems that one is invaded by facticity, that one ceases to flee it and that one slides toward a *passive* consent to the desire. At other moments it seems that facticity invades consciousness in its very flight and renders consciousness opaque to itself. It is like a yeasty tumescence of *fact*. . . .

. . . Desire is not only the revelation of the Other's body but the revelation of my own body. And this, not in so far as this body *is an instrument* or a *point of view*, but in so far as it is pure facticity. . . . The For-itself *is not* this contingency; it continues to exist but it experiences the vertigo of its own body. Or, if you prefer, this vertigo is precisely its way of existing its body. . . . The Other's body is originally a body in situation; flesh on the contrary, appears as the *pure contingency of presence*. Ordinarily it is hidden by cosmetics, clothing, *etc.;* in particular it is hidden by *movements*. Nothing is less "in the flesh" than a dancer even though she is nude. Desire is an attempt to strip the body of its movements as of its clothing and to make it exist as pure flesh; it is an attempt to *incarnate* the Other's body. . . .

In caressing the Other I cause her flesh to be born beneath my caress, under my fingers. The caress is the ensemble of those rituals which *incarnate* the Other. . . . But the caress reveals the flesh by stripping the body of its action, by cutting it off from the possibilities which surround it; the caress is designed to uncover the web of inertia beneath the action—*i.e.*, the pure "being-there" —which sustains it. . . . I make her enjoy my flesh through her flesh in order to compel her to feel herself flesh. And so possession truly appears as a *double reciprocal incarnation*. Thus in desire there is an attempt at the incarnation of consciousness (this is what we called earlier the clogging of consciousness, a troubled consciousness, *etc.*) in order to realize the incarnation of the Other. (388-391)

Since I can grasp the Other only in his objective facticity, the problem is to ensnare his freedom within this facticity. . . . This is the true meaning of the word *possession*. It is certain that I want to possess the Other's body, but I want to possess it in so far as it is itself a "possessed"; that is, in so far as the Other's consciousness is identified with his body. . . . It is necessary that I drag him onto the level of pure facticity; he must be reduced for himself to being only flesh. Thus I shall be reassured as to the permanent possibilities of a transcendence which can at any instant transcend me on all sides. . . . It is my flesh alone which knows how to find the road to the Other's flesh, and I lay my flesh next to her flesh so as to awaken her to the meaning of flesh. In the caress when I slowly lay my inert hand against the Other's flank, I am making that flank feel my flesh, and this can be achieved only if it renders itself inert. The shiver of pleasure which it feels is precisely the awakening of its consciousness as flesh. . . . It is not by chance that desire while aiming at the body as a whole attains it especially through masses of flesh which are very little differentiated, grossly nerveless, hardly capable of spontaneous movement, through breasts, buttocks, thighs, stomach: these form a sort of image of pure facticity. This is why also the true caress is the contact of two bodies in their mostly fleshy parts, the contact of stomachs and breasts; the caressing hand is too delicate, too much like a perfected instrument. But the full pressing together of the flesh of two people against one another is the true goal of desire.

Nevertheless desire is itself doomed to failure . . . Consider especially the penetration of the female by the male. This does, to be sure, conform to that radical incarnation which desire wishes to be. (We may in fact observe the organic passivity of sex in coitus. It is the whole body which advances and withdraws, which *carries* sex forward or withdraws it. Hands help to introduce the penis; the penis itself appears as an instrument which one manages, which one makes penetrate, which one withdraws, which one utilizes. And similarly the opening and the lubrication of the vagina can not be obtained voluntarily.) Yet coitus remains a perfectly contingent modality of our sexual life. It is as much a pure contingency as sexual pleasure proper. . . . But pleasure is the death and the failure of desire. It is the death of desire because it is not only its fulfillment but its limit and its end. This, moreover, is only an organic contingency: it *happens that* the incarnation is manifested by erection and that the erection ceases with ejaculation. But in addition pleasure closes the sluice to desire because it motivates the appearance of a reflective consciousness of pleasure, whose object becomes a reflective enjoyment; that is, it is *attention to the incarnation of the For-itself which is reflected-on* and by the same token it is forgetful of the Other's incarnation. . . . Immediately there is a rupture of contact and desire misses its goal. It happens very often that this failure of desire motivates a passage to masochism; that is, consciousness apprehending itself in its facticity demands to be apprehended and transcended as body-for-the-Other by means of the Other's consciousness. In this case the Other-as-object collapses, the Other-as-look appears, and my consciousness is a consciousness swooning in its flesh beneath the Other's look. . . .

. . . By the very fact that I now attempt to seize the Other's body, to pull it toward me, to grab hold of it, to bite it, my own body ceases to be flesh and becomes again the synthetic instrument *which I am.* And by the same token the Other ceases to be an incarnation; she becomes once more an instrument in the midst of the world which I apprehend in terms of its situation. . . . This situation brings about the rupture of that reciprocity of incarnation which was precisely the unique goal of desire. . . . Sadism is a refusal to be incarnated and a flight from all facticity and at the same time an effort to get hold of the Other's facticity. . . . But whereas the For-itself in desire loses itself in its own flesh in order to reveal to the Other that he too is flesh, the sadist refuses his own flesh at the same time that he uses instruments to reveal by force the Other's flesh to him. . . . The object of sadism is immediate appropriation. . . . It *wants* the non-reciprocity of sexual relations, it enjoys being a free appropriating power confronting a freedom captured by flesh. (394-399)

Love does not demand the abolition of the Other's freedom but rather his enslavement as freedom; that is, freedom's self-enslavement. Similarly the sadist does not seek to suppress the freedom of the one whom he tortures but to force this freedom freely to identify itself with the tortured flesh. This is why the moment of pleasure for the torturer is that in which the victim betrays or humiliates himself. . . . As soon as I seek to *take* the Other's body, which through my incarnation I have induced to incarnate itself, I break the reciprocity of incarnation, I surpass my body toward its own possibilities, and I orient myself in the direction of sadism. Thus sadism and masochism are the two reefs on which desire may founder—whether I surpass my troubled disturbance toward an appropriation of the Other's flesh or, intoxicated with my own trouble, pay attention only to my flesh and ask nothing of the Other except that he should be the look which aids me in realizing my flesh. It is because of this inconstancy on the part of desire and its perpetual oscillation between these two perils that "normal" sexuality is commonly designated as "sadistic-masochistic." . . . What the sadist seeks to appropriate is in actuality the transcendent freedom of the victim. But this freedom remains on principle out of reach. And the more the sadist persists in treating the other as an instrument, the more this freedom escapes him. . . . The sadist discovers his error when his victim *looks* at him; that is, when the sadist experiences the absolute alienation of his being in the Other's freedom. (403-405)

Just as Love finds its failure within itself and just as Desire arises from the death of Love in order to collapse in turn and give way to Love, so all the patterns of conduct toward the Other-as-object include within themselves an implicit and veiled reference to an Other-as-subject, and this reference is their death. Upon the death of a particular conduct toward the Other-as-object arises a new attitude which aims at getting hold of the Other-as-subject, and this in turn reveals its instability and collapses to give way to the opposite conduct. . . . At whatever moment a person is considered, he is in one or the other of these attitudes—unsatisfied by the one as by the other. . . . To borrow an expression from Jean Wahl, we are—in relation to the Other—sometimes in a state of *trans-descendence* (when we apprehend him as an object and integrate him with the world), and sometimes in a state of *trans-ascendence* (when we experience him as a transcendence which transcends us). But neither of these two states is sufficient in itself, and we shall never place ourselves concretely on a plane of equality; that is, on the plane where the recognition of the Other's freedom would involve the Other's recognition of our freedom. . . . The Other is on principle inapprehensible; he flees me when I seek him and possesses me when I flee him. . . . From the moment that I exist I establish a factual limit to the Other's freedom. I *am* this limit, and each of my projects traces the outline of this limit around the Other. . . . To train the child by persuasion and gentleness is no less to compel him. Thus respect for the Other's freedom is an empty word. (408f.)

. . . The "we" is not an inter-subjective consciousness nor a new being which surpasses and encircles its parts as a synthetic whole in the manner of the collective consciousness of the sociologists. The "we" is experienced by a particular consciousness. . . . The being-for-others precedes and founds the *being-with-others*. (414) . . . The experience of the We-subject is a pure psychological, subjective event in a single consciousness; it corresponds to an inner modification of the structure of this consciousness but does not appear on the foundation of a concrete ontological relation with others and does not realize any *Mitsein*. It is a question only of a way of feeling myself in the midst of others. (425) . . . The *Mitsein* by itself would be *impossible* without a preliminary recognition of what the Other is. . . . The very nature of the We-subject implies that it is made up of only fleeting experiences without metaphysical bearing. (428f.)

Maurice Merleau-Ponty

The Phenomenology of Perception

In the experience of dialogue, there is constituted between the other person and myself a common ground; my thought and his are interwoven into a single fabric, my words and those of my interlocutor are called forth by the state of the discussion, and they are inserted into a shared operation of which neither of us is the creator. We have here a dual being, where the other is for me no longer a mere bit of behaviour in my transcendental field, nor I in his; we are collaborators for each other in consummate reciprocity. Our perspectives merge into each other, and we co-exist through a common world. . . . It is only retrospectively, when I have withdrawn from the dialogue and am recalling it that I am able to reintegrate it into my life and make of it an episode in my private history, and that the other recedes into his absence, or, in so far as he remains present for me, is felt as a threat. (354f.) . . . Once the other is posited, once the other's gaze fixed upon me has, by inserting me into his field, stripped me of part of my being, it will readily be understood that I can recover it only by establishing relations with him, by bringing about his clear recognition of me, and that my freedom requires the same freedom for others. (357)

. . . The nation and class are neither versions of fate which hold the individual in subjection from the outside nor values which he posits from within. They are modes of co-existence which are a call upon him. . . . The problem of the existential modality of the social is here at one with all problems of transcendence. Whether we are concerned with my body, the natural world, the past, birth or death, the question is always how I can be open to phenomena which transcend me, and which nevertheless exist only to the extent that I take them up and live them; *how the presence to myself . . . which establishes my own limits and conditions every alien presence . . . at the same time . . . throws me outside myself.* Both idealism and realism, the former by making the external world immanent in me, the latter by subjecting me to a causal action, falsify the motivational relations existing between the external and internal worlds, and make this relationship unintelligible. (363f.)

It is true that the other person will never exist for us as we exist ourselves; he is always a lesser figure, and we never feel in him as we do in ourselves the thrust of time-creation. But two temporalities are not mutually exclusive as are two consciousnesses, because each one arrives at self-knowledge only by projecting itself into the present where both can be joined together. (433) . . . The present mediates between the For Oneself and the For Others, between individuality and generality. True reflection presents me to myself not as idle and inaccessible subjectivity, but as identical with my presence in the world and to others, as I am now realizing it: I am all that I see, I am an intersubjective field, not despite my body and historical situation, but, on the contrary, by being this body and this situation, and through them, all the rest. (452)

Karl Jaspers

Communication

The beloved is always an individual. Individuality is another expression for the absolutely concrete. The conceptual category of individuality is fulfilled only in the movement of love. The individual, otherwise indifferent, exists as unique only for the loving person and to all others is only an incidental particularity, one individual among many. . . . In love the individual is grasped as an infinity, which can never become the object of thought or knowledge. Between human beings love is also what is ambiguously called perfect understanding.* (124) . . . Revealing oneself is a process which goes on in the individual and at the same time in communication. Laying oneself open, doubting oneself, giving oneself up completely and essentially is possible to man in isolation and, in love, also through communication. (421)

In contrast to the isolation of the objects touching one another but having no inner relations, mutual understanding between one consciousness and another is still not the expression of authentic communication, as the orientation of both is toward a universally understandable object. In this communication each consciousness can be replaced by another. The limit is reached where this replaceability becomes fundamentally impossible, because one self in its authentic being enters into relation with another. Thereby existential communication between individuals becomes possible as ever unique, incomprehensible, and to any other persons non-communicable. It originates in freedom, a freedom which realizes itself only in existential communication.† (55)

The relationships which are real for psychology and sociology are the object of scientific research; true communication, in which I know my self only by creating it with the other self, has no empirical existence; its illumination is the task of philosophy.‡ (51)

Though in every communication I experience a specific satisfaction, it is never absolute. For when I become conscious of the

* *Psychologie der Weltanschauungen.*
† *Philosophie,* Vol. I.
‡ *Philosophie,* Vol. II.

particularity of my communication and thereby reach its limits, I become dissatisfied. I was engaged only in a certain direction, as mere existence, as a replaceable individual, as function of an ideal whole, as this character, not as myself.

Therefore, the dissatisfaction with communication is an origin for the breakthrough to *Existenz* and for a philosophizing which tries to illuminate it. (55)

In existential communication I feel responsible not only for myself but also for the other, as if he were I and I were he. I feel the beginning of existential communication only when the other meets me in the same way. Through my actions alone I do not reach existential communication; the action of the other has to meet mine. I have to enter into the tormenting relation of eternal discontent at the moment when the other makes himself an object to me, instead of meeting me. If the other does not become himself in his action, neither do I. Neither the submission nor the domination of the other permits me to become myself. Only in mutual recognition do both of us become ourselves. Only together can we achieve what each of us wants to achieve. . . .

If communication fails, it becomes my guilt. Communication evidently cannot be accomplished only through the effort of the well-intentioned understanding. I also must commit myself; for I become myself only in communication. It never succeeds, when I keep myself in reserve, treating relative and partial communications as already ultimate possibilities. The consciousness of being a decisive factor for myself and the other drives me to utmost readiness for communication. . . .

To be is not only being empirically together but to be together as *Existenz*. Yet this togetherness of *Existenz* is in time not as something permanent but as process and risk. . . .

In the existential communication in which I feel myself touched, the other is only this specific other: his uniqueness is the appearance of his essence. Existential communication can neither be simulated nor imitated but is ever plainly unique. It exists between two selves who are unique, not representative, and therefore not replaceable. The self has its certitude in this absolutely historical, externally unrecognizable communication. In it alone one self exists for the other in mutual creation. In an historical decision it has resolved itself as isolated existence in order to seize authentic being in communication. . . .

True communication excludes other possibilities. I cannot reach all human beings. I destroy communication by trying to establish it with as many as possible. If I try to do justice to everybody I meet, I fill my existence with superficialities and, because of an imaginary universal possibility, I deny myself the unique historical possibility with its limitation. (57f., 60)

In communication I am revealed to myself together with the other. However, this is at the same time only the realization of myself as self. . . . He who wills to be incommunicative (to wear a mask, to build up protective devices) only seemingly enters into communication and does not risk himself, because he confuses his being-like-that with his eternal being and wants to save it. . . . For in becoming manifest I am losing myself (as empirical existence), in order to find myself (as potential *Existenz*). . . .

This process of realizing oneself does not develop in isolated *Existenz* but only in communication with the other. . . . This communication is not blind love, indifferent to its object, but a contending love which is clear-sighted. It challenges, complicates, demands, and draws the other potential *Existenz* out of its potentiality. . . . Nothing that is felt to be relevant may remain unanswered in communication. . . . Communication is a fight for the truth of *Existenz* and not for something of universal validity. . . .

Without the media of relevant this-worldly conditions, the love between *Existenzen* cannot be sustained in direct communication. . . .

Without the objects of the world, existential communication has no means to become visible; without communication the objects of the world become meaningless and empty. (64-69)

Love is not yet communication but its source, which illuminates itself through love. The harmony of belonging together, unrealizable in the world, makes perceptible an absolute that from now on is a condition of communication and makes possible in it the loving struggle of unrelenting truthfulness. . . .

I and Thou, separate in existence, are united in Transcendence, there not meeting and not missing each other. Here they encounter each other in the development of struggling communication which manifests and confirms itself in danger. . . .

But without existential communication all love is subject to doubt. Although communication does not originate love, there is still no love which is not confirmed in communication. If communication breaks off definitively, love ceases because it was delusion. If it was real, however, communication cannot cease, it can only transform itself. (71-73)

Nobody can win blessing alone. There is no truth through which alone I could reach the object aimed at. I participate in what the others are and am responsible for what exists beside me, because I can speak to it and enter into active relation to it; I am as potential *Existenz* to other *Existenzen.* Therefore, I reach the goal of my existence only if I comprehend what is around me. I become myself only when the world, with which I can enter into potential communication, has come to itself with me. Freedom is bound to the freedom of the others; authentic Being has its measure in the authentic being of those closest to me and finally of all.* (226)

Reason and Existenz

. . . To be genuinely true, truth must be communicable.

We represent this original phenomenon of our humanity thus: we are what we are only through the community of mutually conscious understandings. There can be no man who is a man for himself alone, as a mere individual. (77)

. . . Both what man is and what is for him are in some sense bound up with communication. The Encompassing which we are is, in every form, communication; the Encompassing which is Being itself exists for us only insofar as it achieves communicability by becoming speech or becoming utterable. . . .

Truth therefore cannot be separated from communicability. It only appears in time as a reality-through-communication. Abstracted from communication, truth hardens into an unreality. The movement of communication is at one and the same time the preservation of, and the search for, the truth.

In general then, it applies to my being, my authenticity, and my grasp of the truth that, not only factually am I not for myself alone, but I cannot even become myself alone without emerging out of my being with others. (79f.)

Community through communication is found, to be sure, already among the merely living existences; it is in consciousness as such, and it is in spirit. However, on the level of mere vitality, it can remain instinctive sympathies or interests limited to certain purposes. In consciousness as such, it can remain an unconcerned agreement upon what is correct or valid; in spirit, a deceptive consciousness of totality which however suddenly breaks off fellowship. (85)

The communication of Existenz is accomplished through membership in the spirit, through the universality of consciousness as such, through proving itself in empirical existence, but also by breaking through these, passing beyond them in the loving struggle of those who will to become themselves. In contrast to the

* *Philosophie,* Vol. III.

communication of identical and indifferently replaceable points of consciousness as such, this existential communication is between irreplaceable individuals. In contrast to the struggle for existence over power, superiority, and annihilation, here the struggle over the content of Existenz is without the will to power in the same sense; it is a struggle where every advance of the individual comes only if the other advances too, and every destruction of the other is my own. In contrast to spiritual community, where there is security in the comprehensive Idea, it does not overlook the crack in Being for us, and it is open for Transcendence. It expresses the inevitability of struggle in temporal existence and the inability of truth to be completed by unceasingly pushing the movement of communication forward as the authentic appearance of truth. To be self and to be true are nothing else than to be in communication unconditionally. Here in the depths, to preserve oneself would be precisely to lose oneself.

Existenz, then, only becomes apparent and thereby real if it comes to itself through, and at the same time with, another Existenz. What is authentically human in the community of reason and Existenz is not, as before in physical life, simply present in a plurality of naturally generated examples, which then find one another and bind themselves together. Rather communication seems to produce for the first time that which is communicating: independent natures which come to consciousness of themselves, however, as though they were not touched by the contingencies of empirical existence, but had been bound together eternally. . . .

Now, in existential communication, reason is what penetrates everything. Existenz as the ground bears in its depths the organ which is present in all modes of the Encompassing, which is the universal bond as well as the unrest which disturbs every fixation. Reason, having its substance in Existenz, arises from the authentic communication of one nature with another, and it arises in such a fashion that empirical existence, consciousness as such, and spirit are, so to speak, the body of its appearance. . . .

Communication remains original and unrestricted only where reason is dependably present, a reason which as a source can not be objectified nor directly perceived in any argumentation. It is truth itself, the total will-to-communicate. . . . In existential and rational communication, it is the existing man who speaks decisively—the man who is not merely living vitality, nor merely an abstract understanding, but who is himself in all of these. . . . Existenz finds itself in a realm of mind which can not be closed, of Existenz open before Transcendence. . . .

The dissatisfaction with every particular mode of communication leads to a will to total communication, a will which can only be one and which is the authentically driving and binding force in all the modes of communication. . . .

From this situation of Existenz in time, it follows first that, if truth is bound up with communication, truth itself can only *become*—that in its depths, it is not dogmatic but communicative. Out of the consciousness of a becoming truth, first springs the possibility of a radical openness of the will to communicate in actuality—a will, however, that can never fulfill itself except in an historical moment which, precisely as such, becomes incommunicable.

There follows secondly, in being wrecked by the multiplicity of truth, a self-recovery of the unlimited will to communicate in an attitude which just as resolutely envisages failure in the whole while it nevertheless holds to its path, not knowing where it leads.

It follows thirdly that, if truth in communication can never be definitively won and established—truth like communication seeing itself, so to speak, disappear before Transcendence, change before Being—nevertheless, its resolute actualization brings forth also the deepest openness for Transcendence. . . .

It would be a truth which would arise for the first time in communication, which would become actual only in and through it; it would be a truth which is neither already here to be transmitted to another, nor which presents us with a methodically attainable end in which it could be valid without communication. . . .

The openness in the will-to-communicate is a double one: first, openness to the knowability of what is not yet known. Since that which is not communicable is as though it were not at all, openness strives to bring every possibility into the medium of communication so that it might attain being for us. Secondly, this openness must be ready to encounter the substance of every being that really communicates with me as another who I am not, but in solidarity with whom I can without limit will to become myself. This loving search of men reaches no termination. . . . The unlimited will-to-communicate, then, never means simply to submit oneself to the other as such, but rather to know that other, to hear him, to will to reckon with him even unto the necessity of a transformation of oneself.

Since it is impossible for man to have Transcendence in time as a knowable object, identical for everybody like something in the world, every mode of the One Truth as absolute in the world can in fact only be historical: unconditional for this Existenz but, precisely for this reason, not universally valid. . . . The total will-to-communicate trusts the truth of others which is not its own, but which, as truth, must contain a possibility of communication. (91-101)

The Perennial Scope of Philosophy

Reason demands boundless *communication,* it is itself the total will to communicate. Because, in time, we cannot have objective possession of a truth that is the eternal truth, and because being-there is possible only with other being-there, and existence can come into its own only with other existence, communication is the form in which truth is revealed in time.

The great seductions are: through belief in God to withdraw from men; through supposed knowledge of the absolute truth to justify one's isolation; through supposed possession of being itself to fall into a state of complacency that is in truth lovelessness. And to these may be added the assertion that every man is a self-contained monad, that no one can emerge from himself, that communication is a delusion.

In opposition to these stands philosophical faith, which may also be called faith in communication. For it upholds these two propositions: Truth is what joins us together; and, truth has its origin in communication. The only reality with which man can reliably and in self-understanding ally himself in the world, is his fellow man. At all the levels of communication among men, companions in fate lovingly find the road to the truth. This road is lost to the man who shuts himself off from others in stubborn self-will, who lives in a shell of solitude. (48f.)

Philosophical faith is inseparable from complete openness to communication. For authentic truth arises only where faiths meet in the presence of the Comprehensive. . . .

Men are not as they are; they themselves remain question and task: all total judgments concerning them say more than we can know.

Communication in every form is so much a part of man as man in the very depth of his being, that it must always remain possible and one can never know how far it will go. . . .

In our present distress, we understand that communication is the fundamental task before us. (173f.)

Gabriel Marcel

Metaphysical Journal

August 23, 1918

. . . Yet this *I* seems always to be posited as being in confrontation with a *thou,* for whom in turn I myself am a *thou.* And it is in function of this dialogue and in relation to it that a *he* or *it* can be defined, that is, an independent world or at least a world that is—doubtless by a fiction—treated as independent. . . . I glimpse a sort of slow transition from pure dialectics to love, in the measure in which the *thou* becomes *thou* more and more profoundly. For it begins so to speak by being essentially a *him* with the form of a *thou* . . . he participates more and more in the absolute which is *unrelatedness* and we cease more and more to be "somebody" and "somebody else." We become simply "us." . . . For me, the being I love is a *third person* in the least possible degree. Moreover, that being discovers me to myself, since the efficacy of his or her presence is such that I am less and less *him* for myself—my interior defences fall at the same time as the barriers that separate me from somebody else. (146f.)

Being and Having

. . . The problem of the reality of other selves . . . can be stated in such a way as to exclude in advance any solution which can be accepted or even understood; that is, by centring my reality on my consciousness of myself. If we begin, like Descartes, by assuming that my essence is self-consciousness, there is no longer a way out.

November 11th

Not only do we have a right to assert that others exist, but I should be inclined to contend that existence can be attributed only to others, and in virtue of their otherness, and that I cannot think of myself as existing except in so far as I conceive of myself as not being the others: and so as other than them. I would go so far as to say that it is of the essence of the Other that he exists. I cannot think of him as other without thinking of him as existing.

Doubt only arises when his otherness is, so to say, expunged from my mind.

I would go so far as to ask if the *cogito* (whose incurable ambiguity can never be too clearly exposed) does not really mean: "when I think, I am standing back from myself, I am raising myself up before myself as other, and I therefore appear as existent." Such a conception as this is radically opposed to the idealism which defines the self as self-consciousness. Would it be absurd to say that the self in so far as it is self-consciousness is only *subexistent*? It only exists in so far as it treats itself as being for another, with reference to another; and therefore in so far as it recognises that it eludes itself. . . .

When I treat another as a Thou and no longer as a He, does this difference of treatment qualify me alone and my attitude to this other, or can I say that by treating him as a Thou I pierce more deeply into him and apprehend his being or his essence more directly? . . . If by "piercing more deeply" or "apprehending his essence more directly," we mean reaching a more exact knowledge, a knowledge that is in some sense more objective, then we must certainly reply "No." In this respect, if we cling to a mode of objective definition, it will always be in our power to say that the Thou is an illusion. But notice that the term *essence* is itself extremely ambiguous; by essence we can understand either a nature or a freedom. It is perhaps of my essence *qua* freedom to be able to conform myself *or not* to my essence *qua* nature. *It may be of my essence to be able not to be what I am;* in plain words, to be able to betray myself. Essence *qua* nature is not what I reach in the Thou. In fact if I treat the Thou as a He, I reduce the other to being only nature; an animated object which works in some ways and not in others. If, on the contrary, I treat the other as Thou, I treat him and apprehend him *qua* freedom. I apprehend him *qua* freedom because he *is* also freedom, and is not only nature. What is more, I help him, in a sense, to be freed, I collaborate with his freedom. The formula sounds paradoxical and self-contradictory, but love is always proving it true. . . . The other, in so far as he is other, only exists for me in so far as I am open to him, in so far as he is a Thou. But I am only open to him in so far as I cease to form a circle with myself, inside which I somehow place the other, or rather his idea; for inside this circle the other becomes the idea of the other, and the idea of the other is no longer the other *qua* other, but the other *qua* related to me; and in this condition he is uprooted and taken to bits, or at least in process of being taken to bits. (104-107)

There is probably no fundamental difference between being

conscious of something and manifesting it to others (*i.e.*, making them conscious of it). The *other* is already there when I am conscious for myself, and expression is, I suppose, only possible because this is so. (149f.)

Reflection and Mystery

He is lifted out of that stifling here-and-nowness in which, if I may be allowed a homely comparison, his ego was sticking to him as an adhesive plaster sticks to a small cut. He is lifted right out of the here and now, and, what is very strange surely, this unknown person whom he has just met accompanies him on this sort of magic voyage. They are together in what we must call an elsewhere, an elsewhere, however, which has a mysteriously intimate character. Let us say, if you like, that they are linked to each other by a shared secret. I shall have to come back, no doubt, to the notion of the secret as a mainspring of intersubjectivity. . . . It is in the sort of case where I discover that a stranger has recognized the deep, individual quality of somebody whom I myself have tenderly loved and who retains a place in my heart, that true intersubjectivity arises. (218f.)

Let us take an example. Two or three years ago, I ran into an old schoolfellow whom I had not seen for a good forty years; I remembered him as a boy with red cheeks and bright eyes; I rediscovered him as an old gentleman with a flaccid face, whose eyes were quite expressionless. There was nothing in the quality of these two appearances, nor in my feelings about them, that could confirm that they were two appearances of the same person. . . .

This example is rather an instructive one, for it enables us to emphasize the contrast, where identity is concerned, between the realm of the He, She, or It on the one hand and that of the Thou on the other. There was nothing within me that, when I saw my old comrade, cried out joyously: "So it is you, so it is really you again. . . ." Life, in such a case as this, has eroded something away; yet on the other hand I have an indefeasible certitude—some would say a mystical certitude—that if beyond the gulf of death I were to re-encounter those whom I have really loved (those, that is, who have been linked in the most intimate possible intersubjective fashion to what I am) I should recognize them instantaneously and as if by a flash of lightning, and it would be just as if no separation had ever taken place. (230f.)

We could say that the man sitting beside us was in the same room as ourselves, but that he was not really *present* there, that his *presence* did not make itself felt. . . . What we have with this person, who is in the room, but somehow not really present to us, is communication without communion: unreal communication, in a word. He understands what I say to him, but he does not understand *me;* I may even have the extremely disagreeable feeling that my own words, as he repeats them to me, as he reflects them back at me, have become unrecognizable. By a very singular phenomenon indeed, this stranger interposes himself between me and my own reality, he makes me in some sense also a stranger to myself; I am not really myself while I am with him.

The opposite phenomenon, however, can also take place. When somebody's presence does really make itself felt, it can refresh my inner being; it reveals me to myself, it makes me more fully myself than I should be if I were not exposed to its impact. . . .

. . . This very fact that charm, which is the expression of a presence, works in some conditions and not in others, for some people and not for others, underlines the non-objective character of the notion of presence. *Non-objective* does not, however, in our present context, really in the least mean *merely subjective,* in the privative interpretation of that phrase; it does not mean being more or less of the nature of an intermittent hallucination. Instead of subjectivity, we should think of intersubjectivity. . . . The communion in which presences become manifest to each other, and the transmission of purely objective messages, do not belong to the same realm of being. . . . The very act by which we incline ourselves towards a presence is essentially different from that through which we grasp at an object; in the case of a presence, the very possibility of grasping at, of seizing, is excluded in principle. . . . A presence is something which can only be gathered to oneself or shut out from oneself, be welcomed or rebuffed. . . . In so far as a presence, as such, lies beyond the grasp of any possible prehension, one might say that it also in some sense lies beyond the grasp of any possible *com*prehension. A presence can, in the last analysis, only be invoked or evoked. (252-256)

Faith and Reality

We must fully realize that this being whom I love is not only a *Thou;* in the first place he is an object which comes within my view, and towards whom I can effect all the operations whose possibility is included in my condition of physical agent. He is a *that,* and it is precisely to that extent that he is a thing; in so far, on the other hand, as he is a *Thou,* he is freed from the nature of things, and nothing that I can say about things can concern him, can concern the *Thou.* (172)

I and Thou

By a striking coincidence, I discovered the particular reality of the "Thou" at approximately the same time Buber was writing his book. His name was quite unknown to me, moreover, as were the names of Ferdinand Ebner and Franz Rosenzweig, who appear to have preceded us on this path. Thus, we are faced with one of those cases of spiritual convergence which always merit attention. . . . At a time when a philosophy which concentrated more and more exclusively upon the world of the "it," the denotable, upon the *Eswelt,* was leading into technocratic developments increasingly perilous for the integrity of man and even for his physical existence—the current atomic threat representing merely the paroxysm of this trend—it was surely inevitable that here and there were men moved to bring clearly and methodically to consciousness a counterpoise, that is, a consideration of the "Thou."

Having underscored this convergence of the thought of Buber and my own investigations as these appeared in my *Journal Métaphysique,* I feel bound to stress the fact that the Jewish thinker went much further than I in elucidating this structural aspect of the fundamental human situation. . . .

The *Thou* is he to whom I address myself: perhaps we would not be wrong in saying that he is essentially in the dative case, and that I denature him by putting him in the accusative case. Note well that this word "dative" is certainly to be taken literally: it is a question of a gift, an offering, and thereby an act. . . .

In addition, it does not seem accurate to say: in the beginning was the relation. In the beginning, rather, is a certain felt unity which becomes progressively articulated so as to make room for an ensemble involving interrelated terms. It seems to me that on this point Bradley saw more clearly [than Buber]. . . . In the presence of human beings, there is created among them, let us not say even a field of forces, but a creative milieu, in which each finds possibilities of renewal.

Albert Camus

The Rebel

In order to exist, man must rebel, but rebellion must respect the limit it discovers in itself—a limit where minds meet and, in meeting, begin to exist. (22)

. . . The mutual recognition of a common destiny and the communication of men between themselves are always valid. Rebellion proclaimed them and undertook to serve them. In the same way it defined, in contradiction to nihilism, a rule of conduct that has no need to await the end of history to explain its actions and which is, nevertheless, not formal. Contrary to Jacobin morality, it made allowances for everything that escapes from rules and laws. It opened the way to a morality which, far from obeying abstract principles, discovers them only in the heat of battle and in the incessant movement of contradiction. Nothing justifies the assertion that these principles have existed eternally; it is of no use to declare that they will one day exist. But they do exist, in the very period in which we exist. With us, and throughout all history, they deny servitude, falsehood, and terror.

There is, in fact, nothing in common between a master and a slave; it is impossible to speak and communicate with a person who has been reduced to servitude. Instead of the implicit and untrammeled dialogue through which we come to recognize our similarity and consecrate our destiny, servitude gives sway to the most terrible of silences. If injustice is bad for the rebel, it is not because it contradicts an eternal idea of justice, but because it perpetuates the silent hostility that separates the oppressor from the oppressed. It kills the small part of existence that can be realized on this earth through the mutual understanding of men. In the same way, since the man who lies shuts himself off from other men, falsehood is therefore proscribed and, on a slightly lower level, murder and violence, which impose definitive silence. The mutual understanding and communication discovered by rebellion can survive only in the free exchange of conversation. Every ambiguity, every misunderstanding, leads to death; clear language and simple words are the only salvation from this death.*

* It is worth noting that the language peculiar to totalitarian doctrines is always a scholastic or administrative language.

The climax of every tragedy lies in the deafness of its heroes. Plato is right and not Moses and Nietzsche. Dialogue on the level of mankind is less costly than the gospel preached by totalitarian regimes in the form of a monologue dictated from the top of a lonely mountain. On the stage as in reality, the monologue precedes death. Every rebel, solely by the movement that sets him in opposition to the oppressor, therefore pleads for life, undertakes to struggle against servitude, falsehood, and terror, and affirms, in a flash, that these three afflictions are the cause of silence between men, that they obscure them from one another and prevent them from rediscovering themselves in the only value that can save them from nihilism—the long complicity of men at grips with their destiny. (283f.)

Rebellion, at the same time that it suggests a nature common to all men, brings to light the measure and the limit which are the very principle of this nature. (294)

Each tells the other that he is not God; this is the end of romanticism. (306)

Neither Victims Nor Executioners

Today no one speaks any more (except those who repeat themselves) because history seems to be in the grip of blind and deaf forces which will heed neither cries of warning, nor advice, nor entreaties. The years we have just gone through have killed something in us. And that something is simply the old confidence man had in himself, which led him to believe that he could always elicit human reactions from another man if he spoke to him in the language of a common humanity. We have seen men lie, degrade, kill, deport, torture—and each time it was not possible to persuade them not to do these things because they were sure of themselves and because one cannot appeal to an abstraction, *i.e.*, the representative of an ideology.

Mankind's long dialogue has just come to an end. And naturally a man with whom one cannot reason is a man to be feared. The result is that—besides those who have not spoken out because they thought it useless—a vast conspiracy of silence has spread all about us, a conspiracy accepted by those who are frightened and who rationalize their fears in order to hide them from themselves, a conspiracy fostered by those whose interest it is to do so. . . .

We live in terror because persuasion is no longer possible; because man has been wholly submerged in History; because he can no longer tap that part of his nature, as real as the historical part, which he recaptures in contemplating the beauty of nature and of human faces; because we live in a world of abstractions, of bureaus and machines, of absolute ideas and of crude messianism. We suffocate among people who think they are absolutely right, whether in their machines or in their ideas. And for all who can live only in an atmosphere of human dialogue . . . this silence is the end of the world. (5f.) . . . What strikes me, in the midst of polemics, threats and outbursts of violence, is the fundamental good will of every one. (8)

Not the language of the heart but merely that of clear thinking is what we need today. (12)

There is no suffering, no torture anywhere in the world which does not affect our everyday lives. . . . Today, tragedy is collective. (15)

Yes, it is fear and silence and the spiritual isolation they cause that must be fought today. And it is dialogue and the universal intercommunication of men that must be defended. Slavery, injustice and lies destroy this intercourse and forbid this dialogue; and so we must reject them. . . . There is no reason why some of us should not take on the job of keeping alive, through the apocalyptic historical vista that stretches before us, a modest thoughtfulness which, without pretending to solve everything, will constantly be prepared to give some human meaning to everyday life. (22f.)

Martin Buber

I and Thou

. . . Love itself cannot persist in direct relation. It endures, but in interchange of actual and potential being. The human being who was even now single and unconditioned, not something lying to hand, only present, not able to be experienced, only able to be fulfilled, has now become again a *He* or a *She*, a sum of qualities, a given quantity with a certain shape. Now I may take out from him again the colour of his hair or of his speech or of his goodness. But so long as I can do this he is no more my *Thou* and cannot yet be my *Thou* again. (17)

In the beginning is relation—as category of being, readiness, grasping form, mould for the soul; it is the *a priori* of relation, *the inborn Thou.*

The inborn *Thou* is realised in the lived relations with that which meets it. (27)

Institutions are "outside," where all sorts of aims are pursued, where a man works, negotiates, bears influence, undertakes, concurs, organises, conducts business, officiates, preaches. . . .

Feelings are "within," where life is lived and man recovers from institutions. Here the spectrum of the emotions dances before the interested glance. . . .

But the separated *It* of institutions is an animated clod without soul, and the separated *I* of feelings an uneasily fluttering soul-bird. Neither of them knows man: institutions know only the specimen, feelings only the "object"; neither knows the person, or mutual life. Neither of them knows the present: even the most up-to-date institutions know only the lifeless past that is over and done with, and even the most lasting feelings know only the flitting moment that has not yet come properly into being. Neither of them has access to real life. Institutions yield no public life, and feelings no personal life. (43f.)

From your own glance, day by day, into the eyes which look out in estrangement of your "neighbour" who nevertheless does need you, to the melancholy of holy men who time and again vainly offered the great gift—everything tells you that full mutuality is not inherent in men's life together. It is a grace, for which one must always be ready and which one never gains as an assured possession.

Yet there are some *I-Thou* relationships which in their nature may not unfold to full mutuality if they are to persist in that nature. . . . In order to help the realisation of the best potentialities in the pupil's life, the teacher must really *mean* him as the definite person he is in his potentiality and his actuality; more precisely, he must not know him as a mere sum of qualities, strivings and inhibitions, he must be aware of him as a whole being and affirm him in this wholeness. But he can only do this if he meets him again and again as his partner in a bipolar situation. And in order that his effect upon him may be a unified and significant one he must also live this situation, again and again, in all its moments not merely from his own end but also from that of his partner: he must practise the kind of realisation which I call inclusion (*Umfassung*).

But however much depends upon his awakening the *I-Thou* relationship in the pupil as well—and however much depends upon the pupil, too, meaning and affirming him as the particular person he is—the special educative relation could not persist if the pupil for his part practised "inclusion," that is, if he lived the teacher's part in the common situation. Whether the *I-Thou* relationship now comes to an end or assumes the quite different character of a friendship, it is plain that the specifically educative relation as such is denied full mutuality. (131f.)

Between Man and Man

DIALOGUE

The realms of the life of dialogue and the life of monologue do not coincide with the realms of dialogue and monologue. . . .

I know three kinds. There is genuine dialogue—no matter whether spoken or silent—where each of the participants really has in mind the other or others in their present and particular being and turns to them with the intention of establishing a living mutual relation between himself and them. There is technical dialogue, which is prompted solely by the need of objective understanding. And there is monologue disguised as dialogue, in which two or more men, meeting in space, speak each with himself in strangely tortuous and circuitous ways and yet imagine they have escaped the torment of being thrown back on their own resources. . . .

. . . Real dialogue is . . . continually hidden in all kinds of odd corners and, occasionally in an unseemly way, breaks surface surprisingly and inopportunely—certainly still oftener it is arrogantly tolerated than downright scandalizing—as in the tone of a railway guard's voice, in the glance of an old newspaper vendor, in the smile of the chimney-sweeper. . . .

A *debate* in which the thoughts are not expressed in the way in which they existed in the mind but in the speaking are so pointed that they may strike home in the sharpest way, and moreover without the men that are spoken to being regarded in any way present as persons; a *conversation* characterized by the need neither to communicate something, nor to learn something, nor to influence someone, nor to come into connexion with someone, but solely by the desire to have one's own self-reliance confirmed by marking the impression that is made, or if it has become unsteady to have it strengthened; a *friendly chat* in which each regards himself as absolute and legitimate and the other as relativized and questionable; a *lovers' talk* in which both partners alike enjoy their own glorious soul and their precious experience—what an underworld of faceless spectres of dialogue!

The life of dialogue is not one in which you have much to do with men, but one in which you really have to do with those with whom you have to do. It is not the solitary man who lives the life of monologue, but he who is incapable of making real in the context of being the community in which, in the context of his destiny, he moves. . . . He who is living the life of monologue is never aware of the other as something that is absolutely not himself and at the same time something with which he nevertheless communicates. . . .

This must not be confused with the contrast between "egoism" and "altruism" conceived by some moralists. I know people who are absorbed in "social activity" and have never spoken from being to being with a fellow-man. I know others who have no personal relation except to their enemies, but stand in such a relation to them that it is the enemies' fault if the relation does not flourish into one of dialogue.

Nor is dialogic to be identified with love. I know no one in any time who has succeeded in loving every man he met. Even Jesus obviously loved of "sinners" only the loose, lovable sinners, sinners against the Law; not those who were settled and loyal to their inheritance and sinned against him and his message. Yet to the latter as to the former he stood in a direct relation. Dialogic is not to be identified with love. But love without dialogic, without real outgoing to the other, reaching to the other, and companying with the other, the love remaining with itself—this is called Lucifer.

Certainly in order to be able to go out to the other you must have the starting place, you must have been, you must be, with yourself. Dialogue between mere individuals is only a sketch, only in dialogue between persons is the sketch filled in. But by what could a man from being an individual so really become a person as by the strict and sweet experiences of dialogue which teach him the boundless contents of the boundary?

What is said here is the real contrary of the cry, heard at times in twilight ages, for universal unreserve. He who can be unreserved with each passer-by has no substance to lose; but he who cannot stand in a direct relation to each one who meets him has a fulness which is futile. . . .

The basic movement of the life of dialogue is the turning towards the other. . . .

The basic movement of the life of monologue is not turning away as opposed to turning towards; it is "reflexion."

When I was eleven years of age, spending the summer on my grandparents' estate, I used, as often as I could do it unobserved, to steal into the stable and gently stroke the neck of my darling, a broad dapple-grey horse. It was not a casual delight but a great, certainly friendly, but also deeply stirring happening. If I am to explain it now, beginning from the still very fresh memory of my hand, I must say that what I experienced in touch with the animal was the Other, the immense otherness of the Other, which, however, did not remain strange like the otherness of the ox and the ram, but rather let me draw near and touch it. When I stroked the mighty mane, sometimes marvellously smooth-combed, at other times just as astonishingly wild, and felt the life beneath my hand, it was as though the element of vitality itself bordered on my skin, something that was not I, was certainly not akin to me, palpably the Other, not just another, really the Other itself; and yet it let me approach, confided itself to me, placed itself elementally in the relation of *Thou* and *Thou* with me. The horse, even when I had not begun by pouring oats for him into the manger, very gently raised his massive head, ears flicking, then snorted quietly, as a conspirator gives a signal meant to be recognizable only by his fellow-conspirator; and I was approved. But once—I do not know what came over the child, at any rate it was childlike enough—it struck me about the stroking, what fun it gave me, and suddenly I became conscious of my hand. The game went on as before, but something had changed, it was no longer the same thing. And the next day, after giving him a rich feed, when I stroked my friend's head he did not raise his head. A few years later, when I thought back to the incident, I no longer supposed that the animal had noticed my defection. But at the time I considered myself judged.

Reflexion is something different from egoism and even from "egotism". . . . I term it reflexion when a man withdraws from accepting with his essential being another person in his particularity . . . and lets the other exist only as his own experience, only as a "part of myself." For then dialogue becomes a fiction, the mysterious intercourse between two human worlds only a game, and in the rejection of the real life confronting him the essence of all reality begins to disintegrate. (19-24)

The Eros of dialogue has the simplicity of fulness; the Eros of monologue is manifold. Many years I have wandered through the land of men, and have not yet reached an end of studying the varieties of the "erotic man" (as the vassal of the broken-winged one at times describes himself). There a lover stamps around and is in love only with his passion. There one is wearing his differentiated feelings like medal-ribbons. There one is enjoying the adventures of his own fascinating effect. There one is gazing enraptured at the spectacle of his own supposed surrender. There one is collecting excitement. There one is displaying his "power." There one is preening himself with borrowed vitality. There one is delighting to exist simultaneously as himself and as an idol very unlike himself. There one is warming himself at the blaze of what has fallen to his lot. There one is experimenting. And so on and on—all the manifold monologists with their mirrors, in the apartment of the most intimate dialogue! (29f.)

THE QUESTION TO THE SINGLE ONE

Our relations to creatures incessantly threaten to get incapsulated. . . . Here the monastic forms of life in the world, the loneliness in the midst of life into which we turn as into hostelries, help us to prevent the connexion between the conditioned bonds and the one unconditioned bond from slackening. This too, if we do not wish to see our participation in the Present Being dying off, is an imperative interchange, the systole to the diastole of the soul; and the loneliness must know the quality of strictness, of a monastery's strictness, in order to do its work. But it must never wish to tear us away from creatures, never refuse to dismiss us to them. By that it would act contrary to its own law and would close us, instead of enabling us, as is its office, to keep open the gates of finitude. (54f.)

He who "has entered on marriage," who has entered into marriage, has been in earnest, in the intention of the sacrament, with the fact that the other *is;* with the fact that I cannot legitimately share in the Present Being without sharing in the being of the other; with the fact that I cannot answer the lifelong address of God to me without answering at the same time for the other; with the fact that I cannot be answerable without being at the same time answerable for the other as one who is entrusted to me. But thereby a man has decisively entered into relation with otherness; and the basic structure of otherness, in many ways uncanny but never quite unholy or incapable of being hallowed, in which I and the others who meet me in my life are inwoven, is the body politic. It is to this, into this, that marriage intends to lead us. . . .

This person is other, essentially other than myself, and this otherness of his is what I mean, because I mean him; I confirm it; I wish his otherness to exist, because I wish his particular being to exist. That is the basic principle of marriage and from this basis it leads, if it is real marriage, to insight into the right and the legitimacy of otherness and to that vital acknowledgement of many-faced otherness—even in the contradiction and conflict with it—from which dealings with the body politic receive their religious ethos. That the men with whom I am bound up in the body politic and with whom I have directly or indirectly to do, are essentially other than myself, that this one or that one does not have merely a different mind, or way of thinking or feeling, or a different conviction or attitude, but has also a different perception of the world, a different recognition and order of meaning, a different touch from the regions of existence, a different faith, a different soil: to affirm all this, to affirm it in the way of a creature, in the midst of the hard situations of conflict, without relaxing their real seriousness, is the way by which we may officiate as helpers in this wide realm entrusted to us as well, and from which alone we are from time to time permitted to touch in our doubts, in humility and upright investigation, on the other's "truth" or "untruth," "justice" or "injustice." But to this we are led by marriage, if it is real, with a power for which there is scarcely a substitute, by its steady experiencing of the life-substance of the other as other, and still more by its crises and the overcoming of them which rises out of the organic depths. (60-62)

The man who is living with the body politic is not bundled, but bound. . . . At the place where he stands, whether lifted up or unnoticed he does what he can, with the powers he possesses, whether compressed predominance or the word which fades, to make the crowd no longer a crowd. . . . Even if he has to speak to the crowd he seeks the person, for a people can find and find again its truth only through persons, through persons standing their test. (64f.)

Our age is intent on escaping from the demanding "ever anew" of . . . responsibility by a flight into a protective "once-for-all." The last generation's intoxication with freedom has been followed by the present generation's craze for bondage; the untruth of intoxication has been followed by the untruth of hysteria. He alone is true to the one Present Being who knows he is bound to his place—and just there free for his proper responsibility. Only those who are bound and free in this way can still produce what can truly be called community. (70)

EDUCATION

A reversal of the single instinct takes place, which does not eliminate it but reverses its system of direction. Such a reversal can be effected by the elemental experience with which the real process of education begins and on which it is based. I call it *experiencing the other side*. [italics added]

A man belabours another, who remains quite still. Then let us assume that the striker suddenly receives in his soul the blow which he strikes: the same blow; that he receives it as the other who remains still. For the space of a moment he experiences the situation from the other side. Reality imposes itself on him. What will he do? Either he will overwhelm the voice of the soul, or his impulse will be reversed.

A man caresses a woman, who lets herself be caressed. Then let us assume that he feels the contact from two sides—with the palm of his hand still, and also with the woman's skin. The twofold nature of the gesture, as one that takes place between two persons, thrills through the depth of enjoyment in his heart and stirs it. If he does not deafen his heart he will have—not to renounce the enjoyment but—to love.

I do not in the least mean that the man who has had such an experience would from then on have this two-sided sensation in every such meeting—that would perhaps destroy his instinct. But the one extreme experience makes the other person present to him for all time. A transfusion has taken place after which a mere elaboration of subjectivity is never again possible or tolerable to him. . . .

It would be wrong to identify what is meant here with the familiar but not very significant term "empathy." Empathy means, if anything, to glide with one's own feeling into the dynamic structure of an object, a pillar or a crystal or the branch of a tree, or even of an animal or a man, and as it were to trace it from within, understanding the formation and motoriality of the object with the perceptions of one's own muscles; it means to "transpose" oneself over there and in there. Thus it means the exclusion of one's own concreteness, the extinguishing of the actual situation of life, the absorption in pure aestheticism of the reality in which one participates. Inclusion is the opposite of this. It is the extension of one's own concreteness, the fulfilment of the actual situation of life, the complete presence of the reality in which one participates.

. . . This one person, without forfeiting anything of the felt reality of his activity, at the same time lives through the common event from the standpoint of the other.

A relation between persons that is characterized in more or less degree by the element of inclusion may be termed a dialogical relation.

A dialogical relation will show itself also in genuine conversation, but it is not composed of this. Not only is the shared silence of two such persons a dialogue, but also their dialogical life continues, even when they are separated in space, as the continual potential presence of the one to the other, as an unexpressed intercourse. . . .

Trust, trust in the world, because this human being exists—

that is the most inward achievement of the relation in education. Because this human being exists, meaninglessness, however hard pressed you are by it, cannot be the real truth. Because this human being exists, in the darkness the light lies hidden, in fear salvation, and in the callousness of one's fellow-men the great Love.

Because this human being exists: therefore he must be really there, really facing the child, not merely there in spirit. He may not let himself be represented by a phantom: the death of the phantom would be a catastrophe for the child's pristine soul. He need possess none of the perfections which the child may dream he possesses; but he must be really there. In order to be and to remain truly present to the child he must have gathered the child's presence into his own store as one of the bearers of his communion with the world, one of the focuses of his responsibilities for the world. Of course he cannot be continually concerned with the child, either in thought or in deed, nor ought he to be. But if he has really gathered the child into his life then that subterranean dialogic, that steady potential presence of the one to the other is established and endures. When there is reality *between* them, there is mutuality. (96-98)

WHAT IS MAN?

Heidegger is right to say that all understanding of indebtedness must go back to a primal guilt. He is right to say that we are able to discover a primal guilt. But we are not able to do this by isolating a part of life, the part where the existence is related to itself and to its own being, but by becoming aware of the whole life without reduction, the life in which the individual, in fact, is essentially related to something other than himself. . . . If I stand up to them, concern myself with them, meet them in a real way, that is, with the truth of my whole life, then and only then am I "really" there: I am there if I am *there,* and where this "there" is, is always determined less by myself than by the presence of this being which changes its form and its appearance. If I am not really there I am guilty. When I answer the call of present being—"Where art thou?"—with "Here am I," but am not really there, that is, not with the truth of my whole life, then I am guilty. Original guilt consists in remaining with oneself. If a form and appearance of present being move past me, and I was not really there, then out of the distance, out of its disappearance, comes a second cry, as soft and secret as though it came from myself: "Where were you?" *That* is the cry of conscience. It is not my existence which calls to me, but the being which is not I. . . .

Human life possesses absolute meaning through transcending

in practice its own conditioned nature, that is, through man's seeing that which he confronts, and with which he can enter into a real relation of being to being, as not less real than himself, and through taking it not less seriously than himself. Human life touches on absoluteness in virtue of its dialogical character, for in spite of his uniqueness man can never find, when he plunges to the depth of his life, a being that is whole in itself and as such touches on the absolute. Man can become whole not in virtue of a relation to himself but only in virtue of a relation to another self. This other self may be just as limited and conditioned as he is; in being together the unlimited and the unconditioned is experienced. . . .

Heidegger's "existence" is monological. And monologue may certainly disguise itself ingeniously for a while as dialogue, one unknown layer after the other of the human self may certainly answer the inner address, so that man makes ever fresh discoveries and can suppose that he is really experiencing a "calling" and a "hearing"; but the hour of stark, final solitude comes when the dumbness of being becomes insuperable and the ontological categories no longer want to be applied to reality. When the man who has become solitary can no longer say "Thou" to the "dead" known God, everything depends on whether he can still say it to the living unknown God by saying "thou" with all his being to another living and known man. If he can no longer do this either, then there certainly remains for him the sublime illusion of detached thought that he is a self-contained self; as man he is lost. The man of "real" existence in Heidegger's sense, the man of "self-being," who in Heidegger's view is the goal of life, is not the man who really lives with man, but the man who can no longer really live with man, the man who now knows a real life only in communication with himself. But that is only a semblance of real life, an exalted and unblessed game of the spirit. This modern man and this modern game have found their expression in Heidegger's philosophy. Heidegger isolates from the wholeness of life the realm in which man is related to himself, since he absolutizes the temporally conditioned situation of the radically solitary man, and wants to derive the essence of human existence from the experience of a nightmare. . . .

"Resolution," he says, "in fact makes the self into a being with what is to hand, taking care each time, and urges it into a life of solicitude with others." Further, "Real life together is the first thing to arise out of the real self-being of resolution." Thus it looks as though Heidegger fully knew and acknowledged that a relation to others is essential. But this is not actually the case.

For the relation of solicitude which is all he considers cannot *as such* be an essential relation, since it does not set a man's life in direct relation with the life of another, but only one man's solicitous help in relation with another man's lack and need of it. Such a relation can share in essential life only when it derives its significance from being the effect of a relation which is essential in itself—such as that between mother and child; of course it can lead to such a relation, as when genuine friendship or love arises between the solicitous person and the object of his solicitude. In its essence solicitude does not come from mere co-existence with others, as Heidegger thinks, but from essential, direct, whole relations between man and man.

In *mere* solicitude man remains essentially with himself, even if he is moved with extreme pity; in action and help he inclines towards the other, but the barriers of his own being are not thereby breached; he makes his assistance, not his self, accessible to the other; nor does he expect any real mutuality, in fact he probably shuns it; he "is concerned with the other," but he is not anxious for the other to be concerned with him. In an essential relation, on the other hand . . . one life [opens] to another—not steadily, but so to speak attaining its extreme reality only from point to point, yet also able to acquire a form in the continuity of life; the other becomes present not merely in the imagination or feeling, but in the depths of one's substance, so that one experiences the mystery of the other being in the mystery of one's own. The two participate in one another's lives in very fact, not psychically, but ontically. . . . Certainly, in the course of their life many will be given the opportunity of it which they do not fulfil in their existence; they acquire relations which they do not make real, that is, which they do not use to open themselves to another; they squander the most precious, irreplaceable and irrecoverable material; they pass their life by. But then this very void penetrates the existence and permeates its deepest layer. . . .

What Feuerbach pointed out, that the individual does not have the essence of man in himself, that man's essence is contained in the unity of man with man, has entirely failed to enter Heidegger's philosophy. For him the individual has the essence of man in himself and brings it to existence by becoming a "resolved" self. Heidegger's self is *a closed system.* (166-171)

. . . Only the man who has become a Single One, a self, a real person, is able to have a complete relation of his life to the other self, a relation which is not beneath but above the problematic of the relations between man and man, and which comprises, withstands and overcomes all this problematic situation. A *great* relation exists only between real persons. It can be strong as death, because it is stronger than solitude, because it breaches the barriers of a lofty solitude, subdues its strict law, and throws a bridge from self-being to self-being across the abyss of dread of the universe. It is true that the child says *Thou* before it learns to say *I;* but on the height of personal existence one must be truly able to say *I* in order to know the mystery of the *Thou* in its whole truth. . . .

The person who is the object of my mere solicitude is not a *Thou* but a *He* or a *She*. The nameless, faceless crowd in which I am entangled is not a *We* but the "one." [1] But as there is a *Thou* so there is a *We*. . . . By *We* I mean a community of several independent persons, who have reached a self and self-responsibility, the community resting on the basis of this self and self-responsibility, and being made possible by them. The special character of the *We* is shown in the essential relation existing, or arising temporarily, between its members; that is, in the holding sway within the *We* of an ontic directness which is the decisive presupposition of the *I-Thou* relation. The *We* includes the *Thou* potentially. Only men who are capable of truly saying *Thou* to one another can truly say *We* with one another. . . . A man is truly saved from the "one" not by separation but only by being bound up in genuine communion. (175-177)

Man in a collective is not man with man. Here the person is not freed from his isolation, by communing with living beings, which thenceforth lives with him; the "whole," with its claim on the wholeness of every man, aims logically and successfully at reducing, neutralizing, devaluating, and desecrating every bond with living beings. That tender surface of personal life which longs for contact with other life is progressively deadened or desensitized. Man's isolation is not overcome here, but overpowered and numbed. Knowledge of it is suppressed, but the actual condition of solitude has its insuperable effect in the depths, and rises secretly to a cruelty which will become manifest with the scattering of the illusion. . . . Only when the individual knows the other in all his otherness as himself, as man, and from there breaks through to the other, has he broken through his solitude in a strict and transforming meeting.

It is obvious that such an event can only take place if the person is stirred up as a person. In individualism the person, in consequence of his merely imaginary mastery of his basic situation, is

[1] This is, R. G. Smith's translation of Heidegger's "*das Man*" which is translated in *Being and Time* as "the they."—M.F.

attacked by the ravages of the fictitious, however much he thinks, or strives to think, that he is asserting himself as a person in being. In collectivism the person surrenders himself when he renounces the directness of personal decision and responsibility. In both cases the person is incapable of breaking through to the other: there is genuine relation only between genuine persons. . . .

The fundamental fact of human existence is neither the individual as such nor the aggregate as such. Each, considered by itself, is a mighty abstraction. The individual is a fact of existence in so far as he steps into a living relation with other individuals. The aggregate is a fact of existence in so far as it is built up of living units of relation. The fundamental fact of human existence is man with man. . . .

I call this sphere, which is established with the existence of man as man but which is conceptually still uncomprehended, the sphere of "between". . . . "Between" is not an auxiliary construction, but the real place and bearer of what happens between men; it has received no specific attention because, in distinction from the individual soul and its context, it does not exhibit a smooth continuity, but is ever and again re-constituted in accordance with men's meetings with one another; hence what is experienced has been annexed naturally to the continuous elements, the soul and its world. . . . In the deadly crush of an air-raid shelter the glances of two strangers suddenly meet for a second in astonishing and unrelated mutuality; when the All Clear sounds it is forgotten; and yet it did happen, in a realm which existed only for that moment. . . . The dialogical situation can be adequately grasped only in an ontological way. But it is not to be grasped on the basis of the ontic of personal existence, or of that of two personal existences, but of that which has its being between them, and transcends both. In the most powerful moments of dialogic, where in truth "deep calls unto deep," it becomes unmistakably clear that it is not the wand of the individual or of the social, but of a third which draws the circle round the happening. On the far side of the subjective, on this side of the objective, on the narrow ridge, where *I* and *Thou* meet, there is the realm of "between." (201-204)

Distance and Relation

The basis of man's life with man is twofold, and it is one—the wish of every man to be confirmed as what he is, even as what he can become, by men; and the innate capacity in man to confirm his fellow-men in this way. That this capacity lies so immeasurably fallow constitutes the real weakness and questionableness of the human race: actual humanity exists only where this capacity unfolds. . . . Men need, and it is granted to them, to confirm one another in their individual being by means of genuine meetings. But beyond this they need, and it is granted to them, to see the truth, which the soul gains by its struggle, light up to the others, the brothers, in a different way, and even so be confirmed.

The realisation of the principle in the sphere between men reaches its height in an event which may be called "making present." . . . It rests on a capacity possessed to some extent by everyone, which may be described as "imagining" the real: . . . "Imagining" the real means that I imagine to myself what another man is at this very moment wishing, feeling, perceiving, thinking, and not as a detached content but in his very reality, that is, as a living process in this man. . . . This "making present" increases until it is a paradox in the soul when I and the other are embraced by a common living situation, and (let us say) the pain which I inflict upon him surges up in myself, revealing the abyss of the contradictoriness of life between man and man. . . .

". . . Becoming a self with me" . . . is ontologically complete only when the other knows that he is made present by me in his self and when this knowledge induces the process of his inmost self-becoming. For the inmost growth of the self is not accomplished, as people like to suppose to-day, in man's relation to himself, but in the relation between the one and the other, between men, that is, pre-eminently in the mutuality of the making present —in the making present of another self and in the knowledge that one is made present in his own self by the other—together with the mutuality of acceptance, of affirmation and confirmation. . . .

. . . Sent forth from the natural domain of species into the hazard of the solitary category, surrounded by the air of a chaos which came into being with him, secretly and bashfully he watches for a Yes which allows him to be and which can come to him only from one human person to another. It is from one man to another that the heavenly bread of self-being is passed. (102-104)

Elements of the Interhuman

THE SOCIAL AND THE INTERHUMAN

It is well known that some existentialists assert that the basic factor between men is that one is an object for the other. But so far as this is actually the case, the specific reality of the interhuman, the fact of the contact, has been largely eliminated. . . . We have in common with all existing beings that we can be made objects of observation. But it is my privilege as man that by the hidden activity of my being I can establish an impassable barrier to objectification. Only in partnership can my being be perceived as an existing whole. . . .

. . . By the sphere of the interhuman I mean solely actual happenings between men, whether wholly mutual or tending to grow into mutual relations. For the participation of both partners is in principle indispensable. The sphere of the interhuman is one in which a person is confronted by the other. We call its unfolding the dialogical.

In accordance with this, it is basically erroneous to try to understand the interhuman phenomena as psychological. When two men converse together, the psychological is certainly an important part of the situation, as each listens and each prepares to speak. Yet this is only the hidden accompaniment to the conversation itself, the phonetic event fraught with meaning, whose meaning is to be found neither in one of the two partners, nor in both together, but only in their dialogue itself, in this "between" which they live together.

BEING AND SEEMING

The essential problem of the sphere of the interhuman is the duality of being and seeming. . . .

We may distinguish between two different types of human existence. The one proceeds from what one really is, the other from what one wishes to seem. In general, the two are found mixed together. . . . The one who lives from his being looks at the other just as one looks at someone with whom he has personal dealings. His look is "spontaneous," "without reserve"; of course he is not uninfluenced by the desire to make himself understood by the other, but he is uninfluenced by any thought of the idea of himself which he can or should awaken in the person whom he is looking at. His opposite is different. . . . With the help of the capacity, in greater or lesser degree peculiar to man, to make a definite element of his being appear in his look, he produces a look which is meant to have, and often enough does have, the effect of a spontaneous utterance—not only the utterance of a psychical event moment, but also, as it were, the reflection of a personal life of such-and-such a kind. . . .

Whatever the meaning of the word "truth" may be in other realms, in the interhuman realm it means that men communicate themselves to one another as what they are. It does not depend on one saying to the other everything that occurs to him, but only on his letting no *seeming* creep in between himself and the other. It does not depend on one letting himself go before another, but on his granting to the man to whom he communicates himself a share in his being. This is a question of the authenticity of the interhuman, and where this is not to be found, neither is the human element itself authentic. . . .

It is no light thing to be confirmed in one's being by others, and seeming deceptively offers itself as a help in this. To yield to seeming is man's essential cowardice, to resist it is his essential courage. But this is not an inexorable state of affairs which is as it is and must so remain. One can struggle to come to oneself—that is, to come to confidence in being. One struggles, now more successfully, now less, but never in vain, even when one thinks he is defeated. One must at times pay dearly for life lived from the being; but it is never too dear. Yet is there not bad being, do weeds not grow everywhere? I have never known a young person who seemed to me irretrievably bad. Later indeed it becomes more and more difficult to penetrate the increasingly tough layer which has settled down on a man's being. Thus there arises the false perspective of the seemingly fixed "nature" which cannot be overcome. It is false; the foreground is deceitful; man as man can be redeemed. . . .

PERSONAL MAKING PRESENT

By far the greater part of what is today called conversation among men would be more properly and precisely described as speechifying. In general, people do not really speak to one another, but each, although turned to the other, really speaks to a fictitious court of appeal whose life consists of nothing but listening to him. Chekhov has given poetic expression to this state of affairs in *The Cherry Orchard*, where the only use the members of a family make of their being together is to talk past one another. But it is Sartre who has raised to a principle of existence what in Chekhov still appears as the deficiency of a person who is shut up in himself. Sartre regards the walls between the partners in a conversation as simply impassable. For him it is inevitable human destiny that a man has directly to do only with himself and his own affairs. The inner existence of the other is his own concern, not mine; there is no direct relation with the other, nor can there be. This is perhaps the clearest expression of the wretched fatalism of modern man, which regards degeneration as the unchangeable nature of Homo sapiens and the misfortune of having run into a blind alley as his primal fate, and which brands every thought of a break-through as reactionary romanticism. He who really knows how far our generation has lost the way of true freedom, of free giving between *I* and *Thou,* must himself, by virtue of the demand implicit in every great knowledge of this kind, practice directness—even if he were the only man on earth who did it—and not depart from it until scoffers are struck with fear and hear in his voice the voice of their own suppressed longing.

The chief presupposition for the rise of genuine dialogue is that each should regard his partner as the very one he is. I become aware of him, aware that he is different, essentially different from myself, in the definite, unique way which is peculiar to him, and I accept whom I thus see, so that in full earnestness I can direct what I say to him as the person he is. . . .

To be aware of a man . . . means in particular to perceive his wholeness as a person determined by the spirit; it means to perceive the dynamic center which stamps his every utterance, action, and attitude with the recognizable sign of uniqueness. Such an awareness is impossible, however, if and so long as the other is the separated object of my contemplation or even observation, for this wholeness and its center do not let themselves be known to contemplation or observation. It is only possible when I step into an elemental relation with the other—that is, when he becomes present to me. Hence I designate awareness in this special sense as "personal making present."

The perception of one's fellow man as a whole, as a unity, and as unique—even if his wholeness, unity, and uniqueness are only partly developed, as is usually the case—is opposed in our time by almost everything that is commonly understood as specifically modern. In our time there predominates an analytical, reductive, and deriving look between man and man. This look is analytical, or rather pseudoanalytical, since it treats the whole being as put together and therefore able to be taken apart—not only the so-called unconscious which is accessible to relative objectification, but also the psychic stream itself, which can never, in fact, be grasped as an object. This look is a reductive one, because it tries to contract the manifold person, who is nourished by the microcosmic richness of the possible, to some schematically surveyable and recurrent structures. And this look is a deriving one, because it supposes it can grasp what a man has become, or even is becoming, in genetic formulae, and it thinks that even the dynamic central principle of the individual in this becoming can be represented by a general concept. An effort is being made today radically to destroy the mystery between man and man. The personal life, the ever-near mystery, once the source of the stillest enthusiasms, is leveled down. . . .

. . . "Imagining the real" . . . is not a looking at the other, but a bold swinging, demanding the most intensive stirring of one's being, into the life of the other. This is the nature of all genuine imagining, only that here the realm of my action is not the all-possible, but the particular real person who confronts me, whom I can attempt to make present to myself just in this way, and not otherwise, in his wholeness, unity, and uniqueness, and with his dynamic center which realizes all these things ever anew.

Let it be said again that all this can only take place in a living partnership—that is, when I stand in a common situation with the other and expose myself vitally to his share in the situation as really his share. It is true that my basic attitude can remain unanswered, and the dialogue can die in seed. But if mutuality stirs, then the interhuman blossoms into genuine dialogue.

IMPOSITION AND UNFOLDING

There are two basic ways of affecting men in their views and their attitude to life. In the first a man tries to impose himself, his opinion and his attitude, on the other in such a way that the latter feels the psychical result of the action to be his own insight which has only been freed by the influence. In the second basic way of affecting others, a man wishes to find and to further in the soul of the other the disposition toward what he has recognized in himself as the right. Because it is the right, it must also be alive in the microcosm of the other, as one possibility. The other need only be opened out in this potentiality of his; moreover, this opening out takes place not essentially by teaching but by meeting, by existential communication between someone that is in actual being and someone that is in a process of becoming. The first way has been most powerfully developed in the realm of propaganda, the second in that of education. . . . Wherever men have dealings with one another, one or the other attitude is to be found in more or less degree. (106-111)

Guilt and Guilt Feelings

Each man stands in an objective relationship to others; the totality of this relationship constitutes his life as one that factually participates in the being of the world. It is this relationship, in fact, that first makes it at all possible for him to expand his environment (*Umwelt*) into a world (*Welt*). It is his share in the human order of being, the share for which he bears responsibility. An objective relationship in which two men stand to one another can rise, by means of the existential participation of the two, to a personal relation; it can be merely tolerated; it can be neglected; it can be injured. Injuring a relationship means that at this place the human order of being is injured. (120)

What Is Common to All

The genuine We is to be recognized in its objective existence, through the fact that in whatever of its parts it is regarded, an essential relation between person and person, between I and Thou, is always evident as actually or potentially existing. For the word always arises only between an I and a Thou, and the element from which the We receives its life is speech, the communal speaking that begins in the midst of speaking to one another.

Speech in its ontological sense was at all times present wherever men regarded one another in the mutuality of I and Thou; wherever one showed the other something in the world in such a way that from then on he began really to perceive it; wherever one gave another a sign in such a way that he could recognize the designated situation as he had not been able to before; wherever one communicated to the other his own experience in such a way that it penetrated the other's circle of experience and supplemented it as from within, so that from now on his perceptions were set within a world as they had not been before. All this flowing ever again into a great stream of reciprocal sharing of knowledge—thus came to be and thus is the living We, the genuine We, which, where it fulfills itself, embraces the dead who once took part in colloquy and now take part in it through what they have handed down to posterity. . . .

Man has always had his experiences as I, his experiences with others, and with himself; but it is as We, ever again as We, that he has constructed and developed a world out of his experiences. . . .

Man has always thought his thoughts as I, and as I he has transplanted his ideas into the firmament of the spirit, but as We he has ever raised them into being itself, in just that mode of existence that I call "the between" or "between-ness." That is the mode of existence between persons communicating with one another, which we cannot coordinate with either the psychic or the physical realms. . . .

The flight from the common cosmos into a special sphere that is understood as the true being is, in all its stages, from the elemental sayings of the ancient Eastern teachings to the arbitrariness of the modern counsel to intoxication, a flight from the existential claim on the person who must verify himself in We. It is flight from the authentic spokenness of speech in whose realm a response is demanded, and response is responsibility.

The fleeing man acts as if speech were nothing but the temptation to falsehood and convention, and it can, indeed, become temptation; but it is also our great pledge of truth.

For the typical man of today the flight from responsible personal existence has singularly polarized. Since he is not willing to answer for the genuineness of his existence, he flees either into the general collective which takes from him his responsibility or into the attitude of a self who has to account to no one but himself and finds the great general indulgence in the security of being identical with the Self of being. Even if this attitude is turned into a deepened contemplation of existing being, it remains a flight from the leaping fire.

The clearest mark of this kind of man is that he cannot really listen to the voice of another; in all his hearing, as in all his seeing, he mixes observation. The other is not the man over against him whose claim stands over against his own in equal right; the other is only his object. But he who existentially knows no Thou will never succeed in knowing a We.

In our age, in which the true meaning of every word is encompassed by delusion and falsehood and the original intention of the human glance is stifled by tenacious mistrust, it is of decisive importance to find again the genuineness of speech and existence as We. This is no longer a matter which concerns the small circles that have been so important in the essential history of man; this is a matter of leavening the human race in all places with genuine We-ness. Man will not persist in existence if he does not learn anew to persist in it as a genuine We. (376-378)

Part V

ATHEIST, HUMANIST, AND RELIGIOUS EXISTENTIALISM

NOTHING has so impeded the popular understanding of the complexity of existentialism as Jean-Paul Sartre's essay *Existentialism is a Humanism.* In the first place, Sartre presumes to speak for all existentialists in a way that reinforces the tendency to identify existentialism with the best-known literary figure in it. In the second place, his facile definition of existentialism as "existence precedes essence" is not only not true, in that form of most existentialists but is not even true for Sartre himself, who does hold certain things *a priori* essential, such as not being in bad faith with oneself. In the third place, Sartre's still more facile distinction between the atheist existentialists, among whom he includes Heidegger and himself, and the religious existentialists, among whom he includes Jaspers and Marcel, grossly oversimplifies and distorts the actual situation among the existentialists. Heidegger has rejected Sartre's identification of their thought with all explicitness and trenchancy, and has insisted that his ontology begins neither with atheism nor subjectivity. Unfortunately these unqualified denials have not had much effect till now on the English-speaking readers who continue to read Sartre's *Existentialism* but have had no access, until recently, to Heidegger's "Letter on Humanism"—a selection of which we include here.

Jaspers can only be called a "religious" existentialist in a carefully qualified way since his religion is more of a "philosophical faith," to use his own term, closer to Kant than to Kierkegaard. Still more important is the fact that the distinction atheist-theist obscures real differences and similarities of attitude which are far more important, even in terms of religion. Camus never ceased to speak of himself as an atheist yet the latter Camus is closer in attitude to the theist Buber than he is to the atheist Sartre, which Camus himself confirmed by saying that he would not mind being called religious in Buber's sense. Heidegger, on the other hand, classifies himself as neither atheist nor theist.

One of the most important questions to the student of Heidegger is the development from his early thought of *Being and Time* to the later thought from which all the selections in this part are taken. As Heidegger's early thought represents a progression from phenomenology to "fundamental ontology," so his later thought represents a progression from "fundamental ontology" to metaphysics. Metaphysics to Heidegger begins by asking why there is anything instead of nothing, and ends with a mystical Nothingness and a wonder in the face of it reminiscent of Jacob Boehme's *Ungrund.* Heidegger's renunciation of the title "fundamental ontology" is meant more as a clarification of the purpose of his early thought than as a rejection of it. Nonetheless, the reader of his earlier and later thought may well conclude that while his goal—reaching the truth of Being—has not changed, his way to that goal is different. In *Being and Time* Heidegger was exclusively occupied with an existential analysis of *Dasein* (even the projected parts which he did not write seem to have that goal) whereas in his later thought he proceeds more directly to Being or Nothingness as such, even though it is a Being which he carefully guards from any confusion with the static or ideal Absolutes of the traditional metaphysicians.

Nietzsche, Sartre, Heidegger, and Buber all speak of the "death of God," but to each it means something essentially different—to Nietzsche the loss of a base for values that makes way for the will to power which creates new values and leads to the superman; for Sartre the necessity of inventing one's own values and choosing oneself as an image of man for all men; for Heidegger a void that cannot be filled by any superman but the occasion, nonetheless, for a new succession of divine images arising out of man's clarifying thought about being; for Buber the "eclipse of God" which comes when God answers man's turning away—the predominance of the "I-It" relation—by seeming to be absent himself.

Rainer Maria Rilke (1875-1926) and Franz Kafka (1883-1924) are two figures who clearly belong in this series yet defy any clear division into non-religious or religious. "Kafka and God have nothing to do with each other," one Kafka scholar assured me. Since so many of Kafka's aphorisms are of a distinctly religious nature, I could only assume that this scholar was guarding against the mistaken theological interpretations of Kafka by going to the opposite extreme. Kafka, however, has a unique position in regard to religion, and there is no need whatsoever to falsify it by forcing it into the strait jacket of an "either-or." Paul Tillich has said that existentialism provides the questions, the religious traditions or essentialism, the answer. This is only partially true, however. An essential difference between the so-called religious existentialists, which makes them quite as varied as the non-religious, is that some of them understand the "answers" in as thoroughly existentialist terms as the questions while others follow an existentialist analysis of the human condition or the situation of modern man with an apppeal to traditional theology as the only valid response to that situation. Although here too one cannot draw any clear lines, we must distinguish, in fact, between religious existentialists, such as Martin Buber, Franz Rosenzweig (1886-1929), Nicolas Berdyaev, Ferdinand Ebner, and Gabriel Marcel, and existentialist theologians such as Paul Tillich (1886-) and Jacques Maritain. To this latter group belong three important figures whom we have not included in this anthology just because they are essentially theologians—Emil Brunner, Rudolph Bultmann, and Reinhold Niebuhr. No one, so far as I can see, has made this distinction (Will Herberg lumps Maritain, Tillich, Buber, and Berdyaev together as *Four Existentialist Theologians*), yet it is one that is essential to understanding the relation of religion to existentialism.

Paul Tillich is of particular interest in this connection. Not only has he incorporated his existentialist analyses into his systematic theology, but he has also attempted to use his existential approach as a specific proof of the superiority of Protestant Christianity to all other forms of religion (see selections from *Dynamics of Faith*, p. 97f.). The contrast between Tillich and Buber is particularly illuminating because of the close resemblance of these thinkers on a number of points. Tillich accepts Buber's "I-Thou" relation with God but ultimately wants to go beyond it to "the God beyond God," the "ground of Being" which he sees as superior to both mysticism and theism. Tillich's failure to recognize a third alternative to theism and supertheism, namely God as "the Absolute Person," the eternal Thou who *is* not a person but becomes one only in relation with us—may be explained in part by his leaning toward the *Ungrund* of Boehme, Schelling, and Heidegger. But in part it seems to be as well the theologian's desire for a *gnosis*—a knowledge which will give a more secure foundation to faith than that existential trust that knows meeting and presence but knows no continuity and security.

The foregoing observations explain the order of the thinkers in Part V—the shadings from atheist to humanist to religious to theological existentialism. What one finds in this ordering are no clear lines of distinctions between categories but a gradual moving from Nietzsche, Sartre, and Albert Camus (1913-1960), who represent the most explicit atheism; through Heidegger and Rilke, both of whom have something of an immanentistic religion of the illuminating of Being in existence; to Jaspers, with his teaching of the ciphers and utter transcendence of God; to Kierkegaard, for whom God's transcendence necessitates rather than excludes a personal relation with him; to the Catholic existentialist Ferdinand Ebner (1882-1931), who, under the influence of Kierkegaard, advances to the I-Thou relationship with God; to Franz Kafka, Martin Buber, and Franz Rosenzweig—three Jewish existentialists each in a quite different sense—; to the Catholic philosopher Gabriel Marcel, the Russian Orthodox philosopher Nicolas Berdyaev, the Protestant theologian Paul Tillich, and the Catholic philosopher and theologian Jacques Maritain. Ferdinand Ebner is here introduced to the English-speaking reader for the first time. His largely aphoristic and unsystematic thinking had a strong impact on Emil Brunner and many other theologians, and he shares with Buber, Rosenzweig, and Marcel the credit for recognizing the central importance of the "I-Thou" relationship with God. That he does not see, like these others, the I-Thou relationship with God as inseparable from that with man is made clear by Buber's comment on Ebner that we have included. The implications of this protest against the separation of these two relationships is brought out from the opposite side by Buber's critique of Jaspers' teaching of the "cipher-script" in which Jaspers sees the full communication between man and man as crippled, rather than completed, if man says Thou to God. Buber's critique proceeds from within existentialism; Maritain makes a suggestive distinction between "existential existentialism" and "philosophical existentialism," though his critique is largely from without.

Is the starting point of existentialism the "death of God," as Sartre claims? Our answer must be both No and Yes. No, if this means, as it does for Sartre, that existentialism draws the logical consequences of an atheistic position. The majority of existentialists are not atheists, and there is nothing in existentialism *per se* that necessitates atheism—which, in its negative way is as much of a metaphysical and essentialist position as that of any theologian. But Yes, if it means the recognition of the crisis that has brought modern man face to face with the absence of a meaningful direction of existence, with the "absurd," or with "the eclipse of God." It is to this crisis that I point in the selections in this part from my *Problematic Rebel.* What I say there concerning "the dialogue with the absurd" and "the Modern Job" is of significance for this question. Through these concepts I am suggesting a position that cannot be classified either as atheist or theist, non-religious or religious, one that I believe to be faithful to such different thinkers as Camus, Kafka, and Buber without overlooking their differences or distorting any one of the three in the direction of any other.

Friedrich Nietzsche

Thus Spake Zarathustra

"And what doeth the saint in the forest?" asked Zarathustra.

The saint answered: "I make hymns and sing them; and in making hymns I laugh and weep and mumble: thus do I praise God.

With singing, weeping, laughing, and mumbling do I praise the God who is my God. But what dost thou bring us as a gift?"

When Zarathustra had heard these words, he bowed to the saint and said: "What should I have to give thee! Let me rather hurry hence lest I take aught away from thee!"—And thus they parted from one another, the old man and Zarathustra, laughing like schoolboys.

When Zarathustra was alone, however, he said to his heart: "Could it be possible! This old saint in the forest hath not yet heard of it, that *God is dead!*" (5f.)

But that I may reveal my heart entirely unto you, my friends: *if* there were gods, how could I endure it to be no God! *Therefore* there are no gods. (91)

He was also indistinct. How he raged at us, this wrath-snorter, because we understood him badly! But why did he not speak more clearly?

And if the fault lay in our ears, why did he give us ears that heard him badly? If there was dirt in our ears, well! who put it in them?

Too much miscarried with him, this potter who had not learned thoroughly! That he took revenge on his pots and creations, however, because they turned out badly—that was a sin against *good taste.*

There is also good taste in piety: *this* at last said: "Away with *such* a God! Better to have no God, better to set up destiny on one's own account, better to be a fool, better to be God oneself!" (291f.)

"I know thee well," said he, with a brazen voice, "*thou art the murderer of God!* Let me go.

"Thou couldst not *endure* him who beheld *thee,*—whoever beheld thee through and through, thou ugliest man. Thou tookest revenge on this witness!" (294)

"But he—*had* to die: he looked with eyes which beheld *everything,*—he beheld men's depths and dregs, all his hidden ignominy and ugliness.

His pity knew no modesty: he crept into my dirtiest corners. This most prying, over-intrusive, over-pitiful one had to die.

He ever beheld *me:* on such a witness I would have revenge—or not live myself." (297)

Jean-Paul Sartre

Existentialism

. . . Man is constantly outside of himself; in projecting himself, in losing himself outside of himself, he makes for man's existing; and, on the other hand, it is by pursuing transcendent goals that he is able to exist; man, being this state of passing-beyond, and seizing upon things only as they bear upon this passing-beyond, is at the heart, at the center of this passing-beyond. There is no universe other than a human universe, the universe of human subjectivity. This connection between transcendency, as a constituent element of man—not in the sense that God is transcendent, but in the sense of passing beyond—and subjectivity, in the sense that man is not closed in on himself but is always present in a human universe, is what we call existentialist humanism. Humanism, because we remind man that there is no law-maker other than himself, and that in his forlornness he will decide by himself; because we point out that man will fulfill himself as man, not in turning toward himself, but in seeking outside of himself a goal which is just this liberation, just this particular fulfillment. . . .

Existentialism is nothing else than an attempt to draw all the consequences of a coherent atheistic position. . . . Existentialism isn't so atheistic that it wears itself out showing that God doesn't exist. Rather, it declares that even if God did exist, that would change nothing. (59-61)

The existentialist . . . thinks it very distressing that God does not exist, because all possibility of finding values in a heaven of ideas disappears along with Him; there can no longer be an *a priori* Good, since there is no infinite and perfect consciousness to think it. Nowhere is it written that the Good exists, that we must be honest, that we must not lie; because the fact is we are on a plane where there are only men. Dostoevsky said, "If God didn't exist, everything would be possible." That is the very starting point of existentialism. Indeed, everything is permissible if God does not exist, and as a result man is forlorn, because neither within him nor without does he find anything to cling to. He can't start making excuses for himself. (26f.)

. . . I'm quite vexed that that's the way it is; but if I've discarded God the Father, there has to be someone to invent values. (58)

Being and Nothingness

A clear view of the phenomenon of being has often been obscured by a very common prejudice which we shall call "creationism." Since people supposed that God had given being to the world, being always appeared tainted with a certain passivity. But a creation *ex nihilo* can not explain the coming to pass of being; for if being is conceived in a subjectivity, even a divine subjectivity, it remains a mode of intra-subjective being. Such subjectivity can not have even the *representation* of an objectivity, and consequently it can not even be affected with the *will* to create the objective. Furthermore being, if it is suddenly placed outside the subjective by the fulguration of which Leibniz speaks, can only affirm itself as distinct from and opposed to its creator; otherwise it dissolves in him. The theory of perpetual creation, by removing from being what the Germans call *Selbständigkeit*, makes it disappear in the divine subjectivity. If being exists as over against God, it is its own support; it does not preserve the least trace of divine creation. In a word, even if it had been created, being-in-itself would be *inexplicable* in terms of creation; for it assumes its being beyond the creation. (lxvi)

. . . My being-for-others is haunted by the indication of an absolute-being which would be itself as other and other as itself and which by freely giving to itself its being-itself as other and its being-other as itself, would be the very being of the ontological proof—that is, God. This ideal can not be realized without my surmounting the original contingency of my relations to the Other. (365)

Each human reality is at the same time a direct project to

metamorphose its own For-itself into an In-itself-For-itself and a project of the appropriation of the world as a totality of being-in-itself, in the form of a fundamental quality. Every human reality is a passion in that it projects losing itself so as to found being and by the same stroke to constitute the In-itself which escapes contingency by being its own foundation, the *Ens causa sui*, which religions call God. Thus the passion of man is the reverse of that of Christ, for man loses himself as man in order that God may be born. But the idea of God is contradictory and we lose ourselves in vain. Man is a useless passion. (615)

The Flies

ZEUS: Once freedom lights its beacon in a man's heart, the gods are powerless against him. It's a matter between man and man, and it is for other men, and for them only, to let him go his gait, or to throttle him. . . .

ORESTES: What do I care for Zeus? Justice is a matter between men, and I need no god to teach me it. (104f.)

ZEUS: Orestes, I created you, and I created all things. Now see! [*The walls of the temple draw apart, revealing the firmament, spangled with wheeling stars.* ZEUS *is standing in the background. His voice becomes huge—amplified by loud-speakers —but his form is shadowy.*] See those planets wheeling on their appointed ways, never swerving, never clashing. It was I who ordained their courses, according to the law of justice. Hear the music of the spheres, that vast, mineral hymn of praise, sounding and resounding to the limits of the firmament. [*Sounds of music.*] It is my work that living things increase and multiply, each according to his kind. I have ordained that man shall always beget man, and dog give birth to dog. It is my work that the tides with their innumerable tongues creep up to lap the sand and draw back at the appointed hour. I make the plants grow, and my breath fans round the earth the yellow clouds of pollen. You are not in your own home, intruder; you are a foreign body in the world, like a splinter in flesh, or a poacher in his lordship's forest. For the world is good; I made it according to my will, and I am Goodness. . . . The Good is everywhere, it is the coolness of the wellspring, the pith of the reed, the grain of flint, the weight of stone. Yes, you will find it even in the heart of fire and light; even your own body plays you false, for it abides perforce by my law. Good is everywhere, in you and about you; sweeping through you like a scythe, crushing you like a mountain. Like an ocean it buoys you up and rocks you to and fro, and it enabled the success of your evil plan, for it was in the brightness of the torches, the temper of your blade, the strength of your right arm. And that of which you are so vain, the Evil that you think is your creation, what is it but a reflection in a mocking mirror, a phantom thing that would have no being but for Goodness. No, Orestes, return to your saner self; the universe refutes you, you are a mite in the scheme of things. Return to Nature, Nature's thankless son. Know your sin, abhor it, and tear it from you as one tears out a rotten, noisome tooth. Or else—beware lest the very seas shrink back at your approach, springs dry up when you pass by, stones and rocks roll from your path, and the earth crumbles under your feet.

ORESTES: Let it crumble! Let the rocks revile me, and flowers wilt at my coming. Your whole universe is not enough to prove me wrong. You are the king of gods, king of stones and stars, king of the waves of the sea. But you are not the king of man.

ZEUS: Impudent spawn! So I am not your king? Who, then, made you?

ORESTES: You. But you blundered; you should not have made me free. . . . I *am* my freedom. No sooner had you created me than I ceased to be yours. . . . Yesterday, when I was with Electra, I felt at one with Nature, this Nature of your making. It sang the praises of the Good—*your* Good—in siren tones, and lavished intimations. To lull me into gentleness, the fierce light mellowed and grew tender as a lover's eyes. And, to teach me the forgiveness of offenses, the sky grew bland as a pardoner's face. Obedient to your will, my youth rose up before me and pleaded with me like a girl who fears her lover will forsake her. That was the last time, the last, I saw my youth. Suddenly, out of the blue, freedom crashed down on me and swept me off my feet. Nature sprang back, my youth went with the wind, and I knew myself alone, utterly alone in the midst of this well-meaning little universe of yours. I was like a man who's lost his shadow. And there was nothing left in heaven, no right or wrong, nor anyone to give me orders. . . .

. . . Outside nature, against nature, without excuse, beyond remedy, except what remedy I find within myself. But I shall not return under your law; I am doomed to have no other law but mine. Nor shall I come back to nature, the nature you found good; in it are a thousand beaten paths all leading up to you—but I must blaze my trail. For I, Zeus, am a man, and every man must find out his own way. Nature abhors man, and you too, god of gods, abhor mankind. . . . You are God and I am free; each of us is alone, and our anguish is akin. . . . Human life begins on the far side of despair.

[*A short silence.*]

ZEUS: Well, Orestes, all this was foreknown. In the fullness of time a man was to come, to announce my decline. And you're that man, it seems. (119-123)

The Devil and the Good Lord

GOETZ: I alone. I supplicated, I demanded a sign, I sent messages to Heaven, no reply. Heaven ignored my very name. Each minute I wondered what I could BE in the eyes of God. Now I know the answer: nothing. God does not see me, God does not hear me, God does not know me. You see this emptiness over our heads? That is God. You see this gap in the door? It is God. You see that hole in the ground? That is God again. Silence is God. Absence is God. God is the loneliness of man. There was no one but myself; I alone decided on Evil; and I alone invented Good. It was I who cheated, I who worked miracles, I who accused myself today, I alone who can absolve myself; I, man. If God exists, man is nothing; if man exists. . . . Heinrich, I am going to tell you a colossal joke: God doesn't exist. [HEINRICH *throws himself upon* GOETZ *and strikes him. Under the rain of blows,* GOETZ *laughs and shouts.*] He doesn't exist. Joy, tears of joy. Halleluiah! Fool! Don't strike me! I have delivered us. No more Heaven, no more Hell; nothing but earth. . . . No way, now, of escaping men. Farewell monsters, farewell saints. Farewell pride. There is nothing left but mankind.

HEINRICH: Mankind will not accept you, bastard.

GOETZ: Bah! I'll manage somehow. [*Pause.*] Heinrich, I haven't lost my case: for lack of a judge, it was not heard. [*Pause.*] I am beginning again. . . .

HILDA: Did you win your case?

GOETZ: There was no trial: I tell you, God is dead. [*He takes her in his arms.*] We have no witness now, I alone can see your hair and your brow. How REAL you have become since He no longer exists. Look at me, don't stop looking at me for one moment: the world has been struck blind; if you turned away your head, I should be afraid of annihilation. [*He laughs.*] (141-143)

Albert Camus

The Myth of Sisyphus

. . . In a universe suddenly divested of illusions and lights, man feels an alien, a stranger. His exile is without remedy since he is deprived of the memory of a lost home or the hope of a promised land. This divorce between man and his life, the actor and his setting, is properly the feeling of absurdity. (5)

. . . Man stands face to face with the irrational. He feels within him his longing for happiness and for reason. The absurd is born of this confrontation between the human need and the unreasonable silence of the world. (21)

If there is an absurd, it is in man's universe. The moment the notion transforms itself into eternity's springboard, it ceases to be linked to human lucidity. . . . To an absurd mind reason is useless and there is nothing beyond reason. (26f.)

The theme of the irrational, as it is conceived by the existentials, is reason becoming confused and escaping by negating itself. The absurd is lucid reason noting its limits. . . . The leap does not represent an extreme danger as Kierkegaard would like it to do. The danger, on the contrary, lies in the subtle instant that precedes the leap. Being able to remain on that dizzying crest —that is integrity and the rest is subterfuge. . . . I don't know whether this world has a meaning that transcends it. But I know that I do not know that meaning and that it is impossible for me just now to know it. What can a meaning outside my condition mean to me? I can understand only in human terms. What I touch, what resists me—that is what I understand. And these two certainties—my appetite for the absolute and for unity and the impossibility of reducing this world to a rational and reasonable principle—I also know that I cannot reconcile them. What other truth can I admit without lying, without bringing in a hope I lack and which means nothing within the limits of my condition? (36-38)

Knowing whether or not one can live *without appeal* is all that interests me. I do not want to get out of my depth. (45)

To become god is merely to be free on this earth, not to serve an immortal being. Above all, of course, it is drawing all the inferences from that painful independence. If God exists, all depends on him and we can do nothing against his will. If he does not exist, everything depends on us. (79f.)

. . . A tremendous remark rings out: "Despite so many ordeals, my advanced age and the nobility of my soul make me conclude that all is well." Sophocles' Oedipus, like Dostoevsky's Kirilov, thus gives the recipe for the absurd victory. . . . "I conclude that all is well," says Oedipus, and that remark is sacred. It echoes in the wild and limited universe of man. It teaches that all is not, has not been, exhausted. It drives out of this world a god who had come into it with dissatisfaction and a preference for futile sufferings. It makes of fate a human matter, which must be settled among men.

All Sisyphus' silent joy is contained therein. His fate belongs to him. His rock is his thing. Likewise, the absurd man, when he contemplates his torment, silences all the idols. In the universe suddenly restored to its silence, the myriad wondering little voices of the earth rise up. Unconscious, secret calls, invitations from all the faces, they are the necessary reverse and price of victory. There is no sun without shadow, and it is essential to know the night. The absurd man says yes and his effort will henceforth be unceasing. If there is a personal fate, there is no higher destiny, or at least there is but one which he concludes is inevitable and despicable. For the rest, he knows himself to be the master of his days. . . .

The Land Surveyor's last attempt is to recapture God through what negates him, to recognize him, not according to our categories of goodness and beauty, but behind the empty and hideous aspects of his indifference, of his injustice, and of his hatred. That stranger who asks the Castle to adopt him is at the end of his voyage a little more exiled because this time he is unfaithful to himself, forsaking morality, logic, and intellectual truths in order to try to enter, endowed solely with his mad hope, the desert of divine grace. . . .

It is strange in any case that works of related inspiration like those of Kafka, Kierkegaard, or Chestov—those, in short, of existential novelists and philosophers completely oriented toward the Absurd and its consequences—should in the long run lead to that tremendous cry of hope.

They embrace the God that consumes them. It is through humility that hope enters in. For the absurd of this existence assures them a little more of supernatural reality. If the course of this life leads to God, there is an outcome after all. . . . Kafka refuses his god moral nobility, evidence, virtue, coherence, but only the better to fall into his arms. The absurd is recognized, accepted, and man is resigned to it, but from then on we know that it has ceased to be the absurd. Within the limits of the human condition, what greater hope than the hope that allows an escape from that condition? As I see once more, existential thought in this regard (and contrary to current opinion) is steeped in a vast hope. The very hope which at the time of early Christianity and the spreading of the good news inflamed the ancient world. But in that leap that characterizes all existential thought, in that insistence, in that surveying of a divinity devoid of surface, how can one fail to see the mark of a lucidity that repudiates itself? (99f.)

The Rebel

The rebel is a man who is on the point of accepting or rejecting the sacred and determined on laying claim to a human situation in which all the answers are human—in other words, formulated in reasonable terms. From this moment every question, every word, is an act of rebellion while in the sacred world every word is an act of grace. It would be possible to demonstrate in this manner that only two possible worlds can exist for the human mind: the sacred (or, to speak in Christian terms, the world of grace) and the world of rebellion. . . . Nowadays whole societies have wanted to discard the sacred. We live in an unsacrosanct moment in history. Insurrection is certainly not the sum total of human experience. But history today, with all its storm and strife, compels us to say that rebellion is one of the essential dimensions of man. It is our historic reality. Unless we choose to ignore reality, we must find our values in it. Is it possible to find a rule of conduct outside the realm of religion and its absolute values? That is the question raised by rebellion. (21)

. . . The metaphysical rebel . . . attacks a shattered world in order to demand unity from it. He opposes the principle of justice which he finds in himself to the principle of injustice which he sees being applied in the world. . . . Metaphysical rebellion is a claim, motivated by the concept of a complete unity, against the suffering of life and death and a protest against the human condition both for its incompleteness, thanks to death, and its wastefulness, thanks to evil. If a mass death sentence defines the human condition, then rebellion, in one sense, is its contemporary. At the same time that he rejects his mortality, the rebel refuses to recognize the power that compels him to live in this condition. The metaphysical rebel is therefore not definitely an atheist, as one might think him, but he is inevitably a blasphemer.

Quite simply, he blasphemes primarily in the name of order, denouncing God as the father of death and as the supreme outrage. . . . If the metaphysical rebel ranges himself against a power whose existence he simultaneously affirms, he only admits the existence of this power at the very instant that he calls it into question. Then he involves this superior being in the same humiliating adventure as mankind's, its ineffectual power being the equivalent of our ineffectual condition. He subjects it to our power of refusal, bends it to the unbending part of human nature, forcibly integrates it into an existence that we render absurd, and finally drags it from its refuge outside time and involves it in history, very far from the eternal stability that it can find only in the unanimous submission of all men. Thus rebellion affirms that, on its own level, any concept of superior existence is contradictory, to say the least.

And so the history of metaphysical rebellion cannot be confused with that of atheism. . . . The rebel defies more than he denies. Originally, at least, he does not suppress God; he merely talks to Him as an equal. But it is not a polite dialogue. It is a polemic animated by the desire to conquer. The slave begins by demanding justice and ends by wanting to wear a crown. He must dominate in his turn. His insurrection against his condition becomes an unlimited campaign against the heavens for the purpose of bringing back a captive king who will first be dethroned and finally condemned to death. Human rebellion ends in metaphysical revolution. It progresses from appearances to acts, from the dandy to the revolutionary. When the throne of God is overturned, the rebel realizes that it is now his own responsibility to create the justice, order, and unity that he sought in vain within his own condition, and in this way to justify the fall of God. (23-25)

Human insurrection, in its exalted and tragic forms, is only, and can only be, a prolonged protest against death, a violent accusation against the universal death penalty. In every case that we have come across, the protest is always directed at everything in creation which is dissonant, opaque, or promises the solution of continuity. Essentially, then, we are dealing with a perpetual demand for unity. The rejection of death, the desire for immortality and for clarity, are the mainsprings of all these extravagances, whether sublime or puerile. Is it only a cowardly and personal refusal to die? No, for many of these rebels have paid the ultimate price in order to live up to their own demands. The rebel does not and for clarity, are the mainsprings of all these extravagances, implied by death. If nothing lasts, then nothing is justified; everything that dies is deprived of meaning. To fight against death amounts to claiming that life has a meaning, to fighting for order and for unity. . . .

Even if God existed, Ivan would never surrender to Him in the face of the injustice done to man. But a longer contemplation of this injustice, a more bitter approach, transformed the "even if you exist" into "you do not deserve to exist," therefore "you do not exist." The victims have found in their own innocence the justification for the final crime. Convinced of their condemnation and without hope of immortality, they decided to murder God. (100-103)

The Plague

"Do you believe in God, doctor?"

Again the question was put in an ordinary tone. But this time Rieux took longer to find his answer.

"No—but what does that really mean? I'm fumbling in the dark, struggling to make something out. But I've long ceased finding that original."

"Isn't that it—the gulf between Paneloux and you?"

"I doubt it. Paneloux is a man of learning, a scholar. He hasn't come in contact with death; that's why he can speak with such assurance of the truth—with a capital T. But every country priest who visits his parishioners and has heard a man gasping for breath on his deathbed thinks as I do. He'd try to relieve human suffering before trying to point out its excellence." . . .

"Why do you yourself show such devotion, considering you don't believe in God? . . ."

His face still in shadow, Rieux said that he'd already answered: that if he believed in an all-powerful God he would cease curing the sick and leave that to Him. But no one in the world believed in a God of that sort; no, not even Paneloux, who believed that he believed in such a God. And this was proved by the fact that no one ever threw himself on Providence completely. Anyhow, in this respect Rieux believed himself to be on the right road—in fighting against creation as he found it. . . .

". . . Since the order of the world is shaped by death, mightn't it be better for God if we refuse to believe in Him and struggle with all our might against death, without raising our eyes toward the heaven where He sits in silence."

Tarrou nodded.

"Yes. But your victories will never be lasting; that's all."

Rieux's face darkened.

"Yes, I know that. But it's no reason for giving up the struggle."

"No reason, I agree. Only, I now can picture what this plague must mean for you."

"Yes. A never ending defeat." (116-118)

Martin Heidegger

Being and Time

Something like "Being" has been disclosed in the understanding-of-Being which belongs to existent Dasein as a way in which it understands. Being has been disclosed in a preliminary way, though nonconceptually; and this makes it possible for Dasein as existent Being-in-the-world to comport itself *towards entities*—towards those which it encounters within-the-world as well as towards itself as existent. *How is this disclosive understanding of Being at all possible for Dasein?* . . . Is there a way which leads from primordial *time* to the meaning of *Being*? Does *time* itself manifest itself as the horizon of *Being*? (488)

The Way Back into the Ground of Metaphysics

. . . This attempt is called, in *Being and Time* (page 13) "fundamental ontology" [*Fundamentalontologie*]. Yet this title, like any title, is soon seen to be inappropriate. From the point of view of metaphysics, to be sure, it says something that is correct; but precisely for that reason it is misleading, for what matters is success in the transition from metaphysics to recalling the truth of Being. As long as this thinking calls itself "fundamental ontology" it blocks and obscures its own way with this title. For what the title "fundamental ontology" suggests is, of course, that the attempt to recall the truth of Being—and not, like all ontology, the truth of beings—is itself (seeing that it is called "fundamental ontology") still a kind of ontology. In fact, the attempt to recall the truth of Being sets out on the way back into the ground of metaphysics, and with its first step it immediately leaves the realm of all ontology. On the other hand, every philosophy which revolves around an indirect or direct conception of "transcendence" remains of necessity essentially an ontology, whether it achieves a new foundation of ontology or whether it assures us that it repudiates ontology as a conceptual freezing of experience. (219)

Of the Nature of the Ground

. . . Man, as the existing transcendence which swings beyond into possibilities, *is a being of distance*. Only through new distances which man in his transcendence creates for himself towards all-that-is, there arises in him the true proximity to things. And only this ability to listen into the distance evokes for *Dasein* as Self the answer of *Dasein*-with in whose presence it can surrender its ego in order to gain its true Self. (53)

Introduction to Metaphysics

. . . A faith that does not perpetually expose itself to the possibility of unfaith is no faith but merely a convenience. (6)

. . . Being-there signifies: care of the ecstatically manifested being of the essent as such, not only of human being. Being-there is "in every case mine"; this means neither "posited through me" nor "apportioned to an individual ego." Being-there is *itself* by virtue of its essential relation to being in general. That is the meaning of the sentence that occurs frequently in *Sein und Zeit:* Being-there implies awareness of being. (24)

. . . The darkening of the world, the flight of the gods, the destruction of the earth, the transformation of men into a mass, the hatred and suspicion of everything free and creative, have assumed such proportions throughout the earth that such childish categories as pessimism and optimism have long since become absurd. (31)

. . . "Ontology" signifies the endeavor to make being manifest itself, and to do so by way of the question "how does it stand with being?" (and not only with the essent as such). (34)

Only the tired latecomers with their supercilious wit imagine that they can dispose of the historical power of appearance by declaring it to be "subjective," hence very dubious. The Greeks experienced it differently. They were perpetually compelled to wrest being from appearance and preserve it against appearance. (The essence of being is un-concealment.)

. . . In the Sophists and in Plato . . . appearance was declared to be mere appearance and thus degraded. At the same time being, as *idea*, was exalted to a suprasensory realm. A chasm, *chōrismos*, was created between the merely apparent essent here below and real being somewhere on high. In that chasm Christianity settled down, at the same time reinterpreting the lower as the created and the higher as the creator. These refashioned weapons it turned against antiquity (as paganism) and so disfigured it. Nietzsche was right in saying that Christianity is Platonism for the people. (89f.)

. . . The man who holds to being as it opens round him and whose attitude toward the essent is determined by his adherence to being, must take three paths. If he is to take over being-there in the radiance of being, he must bring being to stand, he must endure it in appearance and against appearance, and he must wrest both appearance and being from the abyss of nonbeing. (93)

. . . The *deinon* as the overpowering (*dikē*) and the *deinon* as the violent (*technē*) confront one another, though not as two given things. In this confrontation *technē* bursts forth against *dikē*, which in turn, as Fug, the commanding order, disposes (*verfügt*) of all *technē*. The reciprocal confrontation *is*. It is only insofar as the strangest thing of all, being-human, is actualized, insofar as man is present as history. . . . Man is forced into such a being-there, hurled into the affliction (Not)* of such being, because the overpowering as such, in order to appear in its power, *requires* a place, a scene of disclosure. The essence of being-human opens up to us only when understood through this need compelled by being itself. The being-there of historical man means: to be posited as the breach into which the preponderant power of being bursts in its appearing, in order that this breach itself should shatter against being. . . . The being-there of the historical man is the breach through which the being embodied in the essent can open. (135-137)

The question of how it stands with being proves to be the question of how it stands with our being-there in history, the question of whether we *stand* in history or merely stagger. From a metaphysical point of view, we *are staggering*. We move about in all directions amid the essent, and no longer know how it stands with being. Least of all do we know that we no longer know. (169)

* The dictionary meanings of the German word "Not" are need, want, anguish, distress, affliction, peril, necesity. Insofar as one meaning can be disengaged from the whole, Heidegger's primary meaning is "need," because he has used this word "Not" as a translation for *chre* in the sixth fragment of Parmenides. But the word as used in German speech and poetry carries the primary implication of distress, trouble, affliction.

Existence and Being

ON THE ESSENCE OF TRUTH

. . . Absolute mystery, mystery as such (the dissimulation of the dissimulated), pervades the whole of man's *Da-sein*. (313)

He is the more mistaken the more exclusively he takes himself as the measure of all things.

WHAT IS METAPHYSICS?

For Nothing is anterior to it. As we said, Nothing is "at one with" what-is as this slips away in totality. . . .

Only in the clear night of dread's Nothingness is what-is as such revealed in all its original overtness (*Offenheit*): that it "is" and is not Nothing. . . .

The essence of Nothing as original nihilation lies in this: that it alone brings *Dasein* face to face with what-is as such. (338f.)

The permeation of *Da-sein* by nihilating modes of behaviour points to the perpetual, ever-dissimulated manifestness of Nothing, which only dread reveals in all its originality. Here, of course, we have the reason why original dread is generally repressed in *Da-sein*. Dread is there, but sleeping. All *Da-sein* quivers with its breathing: the pulsation is slightest in beings that are timorous, and is imperceptible in the "Yea, yea!" and "Nay, nay!" of busy people; it is readiest in the reserved, and surest of all in the courageous. But this last pulsation only occurs for the sake of that for which it expends itself, so as to safeguard the supreme greatness of *Da-sein*.

The dread felt by the courageous cannot be contrasted with the joy or even the comfortable enjoyment of a peaceable life. It stands—on the hither side of all such contrasts—in secret union with the serenity and gentleness of creative longing. (342f.)

Only because Nothing is revealed in the very basis of our *Da-sein* is it possible for the utter strangeness of what-is to dawn on us. Only when the strangeness of what-is forces itself upon us does it awaken and invite our wonder. Only because of wonder, that is to say, the revelation of Nothing, does the "Why?" spring to our lips. Only because this "Why?" is possible as such can we seek for reasons and proofs in a definite way. Only because we can ask and prove are we fated to become enquirers in this life.

The enquiry into Nothing puts us, the enquirers, ourselves in question. It is a metaphysical one. . . . That is why metaphysics belongs to the nature of man. It is neither a department of scholastic philosophy nor a field of chance ideas. Metaphysics is the ground-phenomenon of *Da-sein*. . . . In so far as we exist, we are already there. (347f.)

. . . We should . . . equip ourselves and make ready for one thing only: to experience in Nothing the vastness of that which gives every being the warrant to be. That is Being itself. Without Being, whose unfathomable and unmanifest essence is vouchsafed us by Nothing in essential dread, everything that "is" would remain in Beinglessness (*Sein-losigkeit*). . . .

An experience of Being as sometimes "other" than everything that "is" comes to us in dread, provided that we do not, from dread of dread, i.e. in sheer timidity, shut our ears to the soundless voice which attunes us to the horrors of the abyss. . . .

Readiness for dread is to say "Yes!" to the inwardness of things, to fulfil the highest demand which alone touches man to the quick. Man alone of all beings, when addressed by the voice of Being, experiences the marvel of all marvels: that what-is *is*. Therefore the being that is called in its very essence to the truth of Being is always attuned in an essential sense. The clear courage for essential dread guarantees that most mysterious of all possibilities: the experience of Being. For hard by essential dread, in the terror of the abyss, there dwells awe (*Scheu*). Awe clears and enfolds that region of human being within which man endures, as at home, in the enduring. . . . Being is not a product of thinking. It is more likely that essential thinking is an occurrence of Being. (353-356)

The need is: to preserve the truth of Being no matter what may happen to man and everything that "is." Freed from all constraint, because born of the abyss of freedom, this sacrifice is the expense of our human being for the preservation of the truth of Being in respect of what-is. In sacrifice there is expressed that hidden *thanking* which alone does homage to the grace wherewith Being has endowed the nature of man, in order that he may take over in his relationship to Being the guardianship of Being. Original thanking is the echo of Being's favour wherein it clears a space for itself and causes the unique occurrence: that what-is is. This echo is man's answer to the Word of the soundless voice of Being. The speechless answer of his thanking through sacrifice is the source of the human word, which is the prime cause of language as the enunciation of the Word in words. Were there not an occasional thanking in the heart of historical man he could never attain the thinking— . . . which originally thinks the thought of Being. But how else could humanity attain to original thanking unless Being's favour preserved for man, through his open relationship to this favour, the splendid poverty in which the freedom of sacrifice hides its own treasure? Sacrifice is a valediction to everything that "is" on the road to the preservation of the favour of Being. Sacrifice can be made ready and can be served by doing and working in the midst of what-is, but never consummated there. Its consummation comes from the inwardness out of which historical man by his actions—essential thinking is also an act—dedicates the *Da-sein* he has won for himself to the preservation of the dignity of Being. This inwardness is the calm that allows nothing to assail man's hidden readiness for the valedictory nature of all sacrifice. Sacrifice is rooted in the nature of the event through which Being claims man for the truth of Being. Therefore it is that sacrifice brooks no calculation, for calculation always miscalculates sacrifice in terms of the expedient and the inexpedient, no matter whether the aims are set high or low. Such calculation distorts the nature of sacrifice. The search for a purpose dulls the clarity of the awe, the spirit of sacrifice ready prepared for dread, which takes upon itself kinship with the imperishable.

The thought of Being seeks no hold in what-is. Essential thinking looks to the slow signs of the incalculable and sees in this the unforeseeable coming of the ineluctable. Such thinking is mindful of the truth of Being and thus helps the Being of truth to make a place for itself in man's history. This help effects no results because it has no need of effect. Essential thinking helps as the simple inwardness of existence, insofar as this inwardness, although unable to exercise such thinking or only having theoretical knowledge of it, kindles its own kind.

Obedient to the voice of Being, thought seeks the Word through which the truth of Being may be expressed. Only when the language of historical man is born of the Word does it ring true. But if it does ring true, then the testimony of the soundless voice of hidden springs lures it ever on. The thought of Being guards the Word and fulfils its function in such guardianship, namely care for the use of language. . . . The thinker utters Being. The poet names what is holy. . . .

One of the essential theatres of speechlessness is dread in the sense of the terror into which the abyss of Nothing plunges us. Nothing, conceived as the pure "Other" than what-is, is the veil of Being. In Being all that comes to pass in what-is is perfected from everlasting. (358-360)

Letter on Humanism

If man is to regain once more . . . proximity with Being, then he must learn first of all to exist in the nameless. He must recognize the seduction of public existence as well as the impotence of individual existence. Man must, before speaking himself, let himself again be spoken to by Being at the risk of having little to say or of rarely saying anything when Being thus engages him. Only thus will the preciousness of its essence be restored to the word and, to man, the house where he can dwell in the truth of Being. (60f.)

Metaphysics pays no heed to the simple essential fact that man realizes himself in his nature (*west in seinem Wesen*) only when he is spoken to by Being. Only through thus being spoken to by Being "has" he found that wherein his essence abides. It is only through such abiding that he "has language" as the abode which the ec-static preserves for his nature. Standing in the clearing where Being comes to light—that is what I call the ec-sistence of man. . . .

It is also for this reason that ec-sistence as such can never be thought of as one particular species among other species of living creatures—if we presume that man is destined to contemplate the nature of his Being and not merely to record the natural and social history of his make-up and activities. Thus even that which is considered *animalitas* in man—as we compare him to the "animal"—is rooted in the nature of ec-sistence. . . .

The body of man is essentially different from an animal organism. The errors of biologism are not yet corrected if we superpose a soul upon man's body, a mind upon his soul, the existentialistic upon his mind. . . . (66f.)

Sartre states the axiom of existentialism in the following manner: "Existence precedes essence." He uses the terms *existentia* and *essentia* here in the sense of metaphysics, which has maintained since Plato that *essentia* precedes *existentia*. Sartre turns this statement around. However, the reversal of a metaphysical statement is still a metaphysical statement and, like metaphysics itself, remains oblivious of the truth of Being. (72)

Man in his own nature essentially realizes himself in Being by standing ec-statically *within* the truth of Being. . . .

Man was "thrown" . . . by Being itself into Its truth in order that, thus ec-sisting, he may guard Its truth and that, in the light of Being, that-which-is may appear as that which it is. Whether it appears and in what way; whether and how God and the gods, history and nature enter into the clearing where Being comes to light; whether they appear or disappear, does not depend on man's decision. The arrival of that-which-is is destined by Being. Man, however, is faced with the question whether he finds his nature in correspondence with this destining. For according to it he has to be ec-sistent and to guard the truth of Being. Man is the shepherd of Being. . . .

"Being" is not God nor is it a supreme cause. Being is more remote than all-that-is and yet is closer to man than that-which-is, whether it be a rock, animal, piece of art, machine, angel or God. Being is that which is closest. Yet what is close remains most remote to man. Primarily man clings always and only to that-which-is. When thought presents that-which-is as that-which-is, it refers, of course, to Being. In fact, however, it is precisely always concerned only with that-which-is as such and never with Being as such. . . .

What, however, is the relationship of Being to ec-sistence—provided that one may ask such a question at all? Being Itself is the relationship in as much as It holds ec-sistence—in its existentialistic, that is, ec-static essence—and gathers it about Itself as the place of the truth of Being in the midst of that-which-is. (74-77)

Can such thought—if labels are to be heeded at all—still be termed "humanism"? Not at all if humanism thinks metaphysically. Not at all if it is existentialism and represents the statement made by Sartre: "Précisément nous sommes sur un plan où il y a seulement des hommes." (*L'Existentialisme est un humanisme*, p. 36.) In the spirit of *Sein und Zeit* we should rather say: précisément nous sommes sur un plan où il y a principalement l'Etre. But what is this *plan* and what its origin? L'Etre et le plan are one and the same. (79f.)

The home for such historical dwelling is proximity to Being.

In such proximity, if at all, it may be decided whether and in what manner God and the gods withhold themselves and night prevails; whether and in what manner the day of holiness dawns; whether and in what manner, in the dawn of holiness, a manifestation of God and the gods may renew itself. The holy however, which is but the essential habitat of divinity and merely provides the dimension for the gods and God, begins to shine only when, after much preparation, Being has cleared and illumined itself and has been experienced in Its truth. Only thus, out of Being, can be overcome the homelessness to wander in which has been the lot not only of man but also of man's nature. (85f.)

What Marx, on the basis of Hegel's philosophy, recognized in an essential and important sense as man's alienation, has its roots in the homelessness of modern man. . . . Since Marx, in his awareness of this alienation, attains an essential dimension of history, the Marxist conception of history is superior to all others. (87)

Man is not the master of that-which-is. Man is the shepherd of Being. . . . Man is the neighbor of Being. . . . In *Sein und Zeit* (p. 38) I have stated that all philosophical inquiry "strikes back into existence." But existence here is not the reality of the *ego cogito*. Nor is it the reality of subjects working with and for each other and thereby finding themselves. "Ec-sistence," in fundamental contrast to all *existentia* and "existence," is ec-static dwelling in proximity to Being. It means the guardianship of, the care for Being. (90f.)

When ultimately "god" is proclaimed as "the highest value," the essence of God is devalued. Here and elsewhere any thinking in terms of values is the greatest possible blasphemy against Being. Thus opposition to values does not mean that one beats the drum for the worthlessness and insignificance of that-which-is. It means rather that one confronts thought with the clearing where the truth of Being comes to light instead of subjectifying that-which-is into a mere object. . . .

Man is never primarily this side of the world as a "subject," whether in the sense of an "I" or a "we." Nor is he primarily and exclusively a subject and always in relationship to an object so that his nature is to be seen in a subject-object relationship. Man, in his nature, ec-sists rather primarily into the openness of Being, and it is this openness which illumines and clears the "between" where it is possible for a subject-object "relationship" to "be." . . .

The existentialistic definition of the nature of man, therefore, reaches no conclusion as yet concerning "God's existence" or the possibility or impossibility of the gods. Consequently, it would be not only rash but also fundamentally wrong to claim that any definition of the nature of man concerning its relationship to the truth of Being is atheistic. . . . Some people overlook the fact that, in 1929, I stated on page 28 of my essay entitled *Vom Wesen des Grundes* that "The ontological interpretation of *Dasein* as Being-in-the-world represents neither a positive nor a negative decision with regard to the possibility of Being-towards-God. However, the elucidation of transcendence helped us to gain first of all a *sufficient comprehension of Dasein* which enables us now to investigate the ontological aspect of the relationship between *Dasein* and God." . . .

Only out of the truth of Being can we think the essence of the holy; only out of the holy can we think the essence of divinity. And only in the light of the essence of divinity can we think or say what the word "God" is to denote. Or should not we be able above all to hear and comprehend these words carefully, if as human, that is, as ec-sisting beings, we are to be permitted the experience of the relationship of God to man? How can we of this historical era possibly ask in all seriousness and graveness whether God is approaching or withdrawing, if our thinking fails to penetrate first of all into the one and only dimension where this question can be asked? This dimension, however, is that of the holy which, even as dimension, remains closed unless the openness of Being has been cleared and in its illumination is close to man. What is perhaps most remarkable about our era is that the dimension of the holy (*des Heilen*) is closed. This alone is perhaps what is unholy. (*Unheil*).*

But such thinking which points towards the truth of Being as something deserving of thought has by no means taken the side of theism. It can no more be theistic than atheistic. Not because of any attitude of indifference but rather because it observes the limits set it by that which offers itself as matter for thought, namely, by the truth of Being. Insofar as such thinking acquiesces in its task, it directs man, at this moment in world history, into the primary dimension of his historical sojourn. By uttering thus the truth of Being, thought has entrusted itself to something more essential than any values and anything-that-is. (99-102)

All the same, thought never creates the house of Being. Thought rather leads the historical ec-sistence, that is, the *humanitas* of the *homo humanus* into the realm where what is whole and holy (*das Heile*) rises. (112)

Only insofar as man, ec-sisting into the truth of Being, belongs to Being, can Being Itself give those directions which must become laws and rules for man. (114)

The Time of the World Image

A . . . phenomenon of our times is its increasing godlessness. This expression does not mean the mere repudiation of the gods, that is, vulgar atheism. Increasing godlessness is a two-faced phenomenon. On the one hand, the world image becomes Christian-

* *Des Heilen* is a genitive of *das Heile* (the whole, the intact) but, in this context, one is reminded of the origin it shares with *Heil* (salvation, holy, good-fortune). Heidegger here telescopes all these meanings and also makes us see in the word *Unheil* the meaning of "unholy" in addition to its current meaning of misfortune.—Trans.

ized insofar as the ground of the world is regarded as the infinite, the unconditioned and absolute. On the other hand, Christendom interprets Christianity in terms of a world view (the Christian world view), as it modernizes itself. Increasing godlessness means a state of indecision about the god and the gods. Christendom is largely responsible for its advent. Yet increasing godlessness is so far from excluding religiousness that, precisely through it, man's relationship to the gods has been transformed into religious experience. When such has come to pass the gods have fled, and the vacuum they leave behind is being filled with historical and psychological research into the mythos. (70)

Nietzsche's Statement "God Is Dead"

[To Nietzsche] God is the designation for the realm of ideas and ideals. This realm of the transcendent has been considered since Plato, or more precisely, following the late Greek and Christian interpretations of Platonic philosophy, as the true and truly real world. Compared to it the world of the senses is but the here and now, a transitory world and therefore but appearance and unreality. The here and now is the vale of tears as distinguished from the mount of eternal blessedness in the hereafter. . . . Nietzsche's statement "God is dead" means that the transcendent world is without effective power. It is not life-giving. Metaphysics, by which Nietzsche means occidental philosophy understood as Platonism, has come to an end. If God as ground of the transcendent and end of all that is real is dead; if the transcendent world of ideas has lost its binding and, above all, its evocative and constructive force, then there remains nothing to which man can turn for support and guidance. (199f.)

. . . Nietzsche understands nihilism as a historical phenomenon. He interprets it as the devaluation of values hitherto of the highest order. God, the transcendent world as the truly existing world which determines all, ideals and ideas, ends and grounds which determine all-that-is and human existence in particular—all this is posited in terms of highest values. What we even now understand by this is: the true, the good, and the beautiful. The true is that which truly is. The good is that on which everything depends. The beautiful is the order and unity of that-which-is in its entirety. These ultimate values, however, begin to devaluate as soon as the conviction spreads that the ideal world cannot and will never be effected within the real world. (205)

God is not yet a living God if we continue our attempts to master the real without first taking reality seriously and questioning it, without considering whether man has ripened far enough into the nature towards which he is drawn out of Being so that he can endure this destiny because of his nature rather than with the delusive help of mere expedients. . . . Man can never put himself in the place of God, because the nature of man never attains the realm of God's nature. On the contrary, indeed, something which is much more uncanny, compared to this impossibility, may come to pass—something whose nature we have hardly begun to reflect upon. In metaphysical terms, God's place is the effectual causing and maintaining of that-which-is as something created. God's place may remain vacant. In its stead another, metaphysically corresponding, place may open up—coinciding neither with the realm of God nor that of man but to which man may gain an eminent relationship. The superman does not and never will usurp the place of God. The place towards which the will of the superman is directed is rather a different realm with a different grounding for that-which-is in its different Being. This different Being of that-which-is has meanwhile—and this indicates the beginning of modern metaphysics—become subjectivity. (234-236)

The hardest blow against God is not that God is considered to be inconceivable or that God's existence has been shown as being incapable of proof, but that the god considered as real is being raised to the highest value. (240)

One might think of metaphysics as the history of the truth of that-which-is which has come about as such through Being's very destining. Essentially metaphysics would be the unthought, because unknown, secret of Being itself. . . .

What this era forces thought to think about is not some thickly veiled underlying meaning but something that is obvious and close: the closest and most obvious in fact which we have been perpetually overlooking because it is merely such. By overlooking it we are—without being aware of it—perpetually decimating the Being of that-which-is. In order to pay heed and learn to pay heed to it we may first of all consider what Nietzsche's Madman said about the death of God and how he said it. Perhaps we will not miss then quite so readily [what is stated at the beginning of the passage explicated, namely] that the Madman "was crying incessantly: I am seeking God! I am seeking God!" . . . Was this perhaps a thinker crying *de profundis*? And what about our thought's ear? Is it still unable to hear the cry? It will fail to hear it as long as it delays thinking. Thinking only begins upon our realization that reason—glorified for so many centuries—is its most stubborn adversary. (244-246)

Rainer Maria Rilke

Letters to a Young Poet

EIGHT

Borgeby gård, Flädie, Sweden,
August 12th, 1904

I want to talk to you again a while, dear Mr. Kappus, although I can say almost nothing that is helpful, hardly anything useful. You have had many and great sadnesses, which passed. And you say that even this passing was hard for you and put you out of sorts. But, please, consider whether these great sadnesses have not rather gone right through the center of yourself? Whether much in you has not altered, whether you have not somewhere, at some point of your being, undergone a change while you were sad? Only those sadnesses are dangerous and bad which one carries about among people in order to drown them out; like sicknesses that are superficially and foolishly treated they simply withdraw and after a little pause break out again the more dreadfully; and accumulate within one and are life, are unlived, spurned, lost life, of which one may die. Were it possible for us to see further than our knowledge reaches, and yet a little way beyond the outworks of our divining, perhaps we would endure our sadnesses with greater confidence than our joys. For they are the moments when something new has entered into us, something unknown; our feelings grow mute in shy perplexity, everything in us withdraws, a stillness comes, and the new, which no one knows, stands in the midst of it and is silent.

I believe that almost all our sadnesses are moments of tension that we find paralyzing because we no longer hear our surprised feelings living. Because we are alone with the alien thing that has entered into our self; because everything intimate and accustomed is for an instant taken away; because we stand in the middle of a transition where we cannot remain standing. For this reason the sadness too passes: the new thing in us, the added thing, has entered into our heart, has gone into its inmost chamber and is not even there any more,—is already in our blood. And we do not learn what it was. We could easily be made to believe that nothing has happened, and yet we have changed, as a house changes into which a guest has entered. We cannot say who has come, perhaps we shall never know, but many signs indicate that the future enters into us in this way in order to transform itself in us long before it happens. And this is why it is so important to be lonely and attentive when one is sad: because the apparently uneventful and stark moment at which our future sets foot in us is so much closer to life than that other noisy and fortuitous point of time at which it happens to us as if from outside. The more still, more patient and more open we are when we are sad, so much the deeper and so much the more unswervingly does the new go into us, so much the better do we make it ours, so much the more will it be *our* destiny, and when on some later day it "happens" (that is, steps forth out of us to others), we shall feel in our inmost selves akin and near to it. And that is necessary. It is necessary—and toward this our development will move gradually—that nothing strange should befall us, but only that which has long belonged to us. We have already had to rethink so many of our concepts of motion, we will also gradually learn to realize that that which we call destiny goes forth from within people, not from without into them. Only because so many have not absorbed their destinies and transmuted them within themselves while they were living in them, have they not recognized what has gone forth out of them; it was so strange to them that, in their bewildered fright, they thought it must only just then have entered into them, for they swear never before to have found anything like it in themselves. As people were long mistaken about the motion of the sun, so they are even yet mistaken about the motion of that which is to come. The future stands firm, dear Mr. Kappus, but we move in infinite space.

How should it not be difficult for us?

And to speak of solitude again, it becomes always clearer that this is at bottom not something that one can take or leave. We *are* solitary. We may delude ourselves and act as though this were not so. That is all. But how much better it is to realize that we are so, yes, even to begin by assuming it. We shall indeed turn dizzy then; for all points upon which our eye has been accustomed to rest are taken from us, there is nothing near any more and everything far is infinitely far. A person removed from his own room, almost without preparation and transition, and set upon the height of a great mountain range, would feel something of the sort: an unparalleled insecurity, an abandonment to something inexpressible would almost annihilate him. He would think himself falling or hurled out into space, or exploded into a thousand pieces: what a monstrous lie his brain would have to invent to catch up with and explain the state of his senses! So for him who becomes solitary all distances, all measures change; of these changes many take place suddenly, and then, as with the man on the mountaintop, extraordinary imaginings and singular sensations arise that seem to grow out beyond all bearing. But it is necessary for us to experience *that* too. We must assume our existence as *broadly* as we in any way can; everything, even the unheard-of, must be possible in it. That is at bottom the only courage that is demanded of us: to have courage for the most strange, the most singular and the most inexplicable that we may encounter. That mankind has in this sense been cowardly has done life endless harm; the experiences that are called "visions," the whole so-called "spirit-world," death, all those things that are so closely akin to us, have by daily parrying been so crowded out of life that the senses with which we could have grasped them are atrophied. To say nothing of God. But fear of the inexplicable has not alone impoverished the existence of the individual; the relationship between one human being and another has also been cramped by it, as though it had been lifted out of the riverbed of endless possibilities and set down in a fallow spot on the bank, to which nothing happens. For it is not inertia alone that is responsible for human relationships repeating themselves from case to case, indescribably monotonous and unrenewed; it is shyness before any sort of new, unforeseeable experience with which one does not think oneself able to cope. But only someone who is ready for everything, who excludes nothing, not even the most enigmatical, will live the relation to another as something alive and will himself draw exhaustively from his own existence. For if we think of this existence of the individual as a larger or smaller room, it appears evident that most people learn to know only a corner of their room, a place by the window, a strip of floor on which they walk up and down. Thus they have a certain security. And yet that dangerous insecurity is so much more human which drives the prisoners in Poe's stories to feel out the shapes of their horrible dungeons and not be strangers to the unspeakable terror of their abode. We, however, are not prisoners. No traps or snares are set about us, and there is nothing which should intimidate or worry us. We are set down in life as in the element to which we best correspond, and over and above this we have through thousands of years of accommodation become so like this life, that when we hold still we are, through a happy mimicry, scarcely to be distinguished from all that surrounds us. We have no reason to mistrust our world, for it is not against us. Has it terrors, they are *our* terrors; has it abysses, those abysses belong to us; are dangers at hand, we must try to love them. And if only we arrange our life according to that principle which counsels us that we must always hold to the difficult, then that which now still seems to us the most alien will become what we most trust and find most faithful. How should we be able to forget those ancient myths that are at the beginning of all peoples, the myths about dragons that at the last moment turn into princesses; perhaps all the dragons of our lives are princesses who are only waiting to see us once beautiful and brave. Perhaps everything terrible is in its deepest being something helpless that wants help from us.

So you must not be frightened, dear Mr. Kappus, if a sadness rises up before you larger than any you have ever seen; if a restiveness, like light and cloud-shadows, passes over your hands and over all you do. You must think that something is happening with you, that life has not forgotten you, that it holds you in its hand; it will not let you fall. Why do you want to shut out of your life any agitation, any pain, any melancholy, since you really do not know what these states are working upon you? Why do you want to persecute yourself with the question whence all this may be coming and whither it is bound? Since you know that you are in the midst of transitions and wished for nothing so much as to change. If there is anything morbid in your processes, just remember that sickness is the means by which an organism frees itself of foreign matter; so one must just help it to be sick, to have its whole sickness and break out with it, for that is its progress. In you, dear Mr. Kappus, so much is now happening; you must be patient as a sick man and confident as a convalescent; for perhaps you are both. And more: you are the doctor too, who has to watch over himself. But there are in every illness many days when the doctor can do nothing but wait. And this it is that you, insofar as you are your own doctor, must now above all do.

Do not observe yourself too much. Do not draw too hasty conclusions from what happens to you; let it simply happen to you. Otherwise you will too easily look with reproach (that is, morally) upon your past, which naturally has its share in all that you are now meeting. But that part of the errors, desires and longings of your boyhood which is working in you is not what you remember and condemn. The unusual conditions of a lonely and helpless childhood are so difficult, so complicated, open to so many influences and at the same time so disengaged from all real connections with life that, where a vice enters into it, one may not without more ado simply call it vice. One must be so careful with names anyway; it is so often on the *name* of a misdeed that a life goes to pieces, not the nameless and personal action itself, which was perhaps a perfectly definite necessity of that life and would have been absorbed by it without effort. And the expenditure of energy seems to you so great only because you overvalue victory; it is not the victory that is the "great thing" you think to have done, although you are right in your feeling; the great thing is that there was already something there which you could put in the place of that delusion, something true and real. Without this even your victory would have been but a moral reaction, without wide significance, but thus it has become a segment of your life. Your life, dear Mr. Kappus, of which I think with so many wishes. Do you remember how that life yearned out of its childhood for the "great"? I see that it is now going on beyond the great to long for greater. For this reason it will not cease to be difficult, but for this reason too it will not cease to grow.

And if there is one thing more that I must say to you, it is this: Do not believe that he who seeks to comfort you lives untroubled among the simple and quiet words that sometimes do you good. His life has much difficulty and sadness and remains far behind yours. Were it otherwise he would never have been able to find those words.

Yours:
RAINER MARIA RILKE
(63-72)

Duino Elegies

I

Yes, the Springs had need of you. Many a star
was waiting for you to espy it. Many a wave
would rise on the past towards you; or, else, perhaps,
as you went by an open window, a violin
would be giving itself to someone. All this was a trust.
But were you equal to it? Were you not always
distracted by expectation, as though all this
were announcing someone to love? . . .
Voices, voices. Hear, O my heart, as only
saints have heard: heard till the giant-call
lifted them off the ground; yet they went impossibly
on with their kneeling, in undistracted attention:
so inherently hearers. Not that you could endure
the voice of God—far from it. (23, 25)

VIII

With all its eyes the creature-world beholds
the open. But our eyes, as though reversed,

encircle it on every side, like traps
set round its unobstructed path to freedom. . . .
. . . Free from death.
We only see death; the free animal
has its decease perpetually behind it
and God in front, and when it moves, it moves
into eternity, like running springs.
We've never, no, not for a single day,
pure space before us, such as that which flowers
endlessly open into: always world,
and never nowhere without no: that pure,
unsuperintended element one breathes,
endlessly knows, and never craves. A child
sometimes gets quietly lost there, to be always
jogged back again. Or someone dies and *is* it. . . .
Always facing Creation, we perceive there
only a mirroring of the free and open,
dimmed by our breath. Or that a dumb brute's calmly
raising its head to look us through and through.
That's what Destiny means: being opposite,[1]
and nothing else, and always opposite.

Did consciousness such as we have exist
in the sure animal that moves towards us
upon a different course, the brute would drag us
round in its wake. But its own being for it
is infinite, inapprehensible,
unintrospective, pure, like its outward gaze.
Where we see Future, it sees Everything,
itself in Everything, for ever healed. . . .
And we, spectators always, everywhere,
looking at, never out of, everything!
It fills us. We arrange it. It decays.
We re-arrange it, and decay ourselves.

Who's turned us round like this, so that we always,
do what we may, retain the attitude
of someone who's departing? Just as he,
on the last hill, that shows him all his valley
for the last time, will turn and stop and linger,
we live our lives, for ever taking leave. (67-71)

IX

Why, when this span of life might be fleeted away
as laurel, a little darker than all
the surrounding green, with tiny waves on the border
of every leaf (like the smile of a wind):—oh, why

[1] *Gegenüber*—literally, "over against" or "face to face."—M.F.

have to be human, and, shunning Destiny,
long for Destiny? . . .
Not because happiness really
exists, that premature profit of imminent loss.
Not out of curiosity, not just to practise the heart,
that could still be there in laurel. . . .
But because being here amounts to so much, because all
this Here and Now, so fleeting, seems to require us and strangely
concerns us. Us the most fleeting of all. Just once,
everything, only for once. Once and no more. And we, too,
once. And never again. But this
having been once, though only once,
having been once on earth—can it ever be cancelled?

And so we keep pressing on and trying to perform it,
trying to contain it within our simple hands,
in the more and more crowded gaze, in the speechless heart.
Trying to become it. To give it to whom? We'd rather
hold on to it all for ever. . . . Alas, but the other relation,—
what can be taken across? Not the art of seeing, learnt here
so slowly, and nothing that's happened here. Nothing at all.
Sufferings, then. Above all, the hardness of life,
the long experience of love; in fact,
purely untellable things. But later,
under the stars, what then? the more deeply untellable stars?
For the wanderer doesn't bring from the mountain slope
a handful of earth to the valley, untellable earth, but only
some word he has won, a pure word, the yellow and blue
gentian. Are we, perhaps, here just for saying: House,
Bridge, Fountain, Gate, Jug, Olive tree, Window,—
possibly: Pillar, Tower? . . . . but for saying, remember,
oh, for such saying as never the things themselves
hoped so intensely to be. Is not the secret purpose
of this sly earth, in urging a pair of lovers,
just to make everything leap with ecstasy in them?
Threshold: how much it can mean
to two lovers, that they should be wearing their own
worn threshold a little, they too, after the many before,
before the many to come, ... as a matter of course!

Here is the time for the Tellable, *here* is its home.
Speak and proclaim. More than ever
the things we can live with are falling away, and their place
being oustingly taken up by an imageless act.
Act under crusts, that will readily split as soon
as the doing within outgrows them and takes a new outline.
Between the hammers lives on
our heart, as between the teeth

the tongue, which, nevertheless,
remains the bestower of praise.

Praise the world to the Angel, not the untellable: you
can't impress him with the splendour you've felt; in the cosmos
where he more feelingly feels you're only a tyro. So show him
some simple thing, remoulded by age after age,
till it lives in our hands and eyes as a part of ourselves.
Tell him *things*. He'll stand more astonished; as you did
beside the roper in Rome or the potter in Egypt.
Show him how happy a thing can be, how guileless and ours;
how even the moaning of grief purely determines on form,
serves as a thing, or dies into a thing,—to escape
to a bliss beyond the fiddle. These things that live on departure
understand when you praise them: fleeting, they look for
rescue through something in us, the most fleeting of all.
Want us to change them entirely, within our invisible hearts,
into—oh, endlessly—into ourselves! Whosoever we are.

Earth, isn't this what you want: an invisible
re-arising in us? Is it not your dream
to be one day invisible? Earth! invisible!
What is your urgent command, if not transformation?
Earth, you darling, I will! Oh, believe me, you need
your Springs no longer to win me: a single one,
just one, is already more than my blood can endure.
I've now been unspeakably yours for ages and ages.
You were always right, and your holiest inspiration's
Death, that friendly Death.
Look, I am living. On what? Neither childhood nor future
are growing less. . . . . Supernumerous existence
wells up in my heart. (73-77)

The Book of Hours

You, neighbor God, if sometimes in the night
I rouse you with loud knocking, I do so
only because I seldom hear you breathe;
I know: you are alone.
And should you need a drink, no one is there
to reach it to you, groping in the dark.
Always I hearken. Give but a small sign.
I am quite near.

Between us there is but a narrow wall,
and by sheer chance; for it would take
merely a call from your lips or from mine

to break it down,
and that without a sound.

The wall is builded of your images.

They stand before you hiding you like names,
And when the light within me blazes high
that in my inmost soul I know you by,
the radiance is squandered on their frames.

And then my senses, which too soon grow lame,
exiled from you, must go their homeless ways. (13)

What will you do, God, when I die?
When I, your pitcher, broken, lie?
When I, your drink, go stale or dry?
I am your garb, the trade you ply,
you lose your meaning, losing me.

Homeless without me, you will be
robbed of your welcome, warm and sweet.
I am your sandals: your tired feet
will wander bare for want of me.

Your mighty cloak will fall away.
Your glance that on my cheek was laid
and pillowed warm, will seek, dismayed,
the comfort that I offered once—
to lie, as sunset colors fade
in the cold lap of alien stones.

What will you do, God? I am afraid. (29)

Karl Jaspers

Metaphysics[2]

Existenz, rising from doubtful existence, confronts Transcendence in defiance and devotion. . . . (69) The unrelenting conse-

[2] *Philosophie*, Vol. III.

quence of truthfulness becomes itself the real relation to Transcendence.

However, if contrary to compelling empirical facts and judicious reason, something is declared to be true in the name of a godhead, especially if, contrary to the injustice contained in all existence, a factual although hidden justice is positively maintained, then, as in the Book of Job, the will to truthfulness quarrels with this representation of the godhead. The passionate striving for truth in its freedom is conscious of being in agreement with its God. In dialectical movement the godhead is apprehended as paradoxical. Trusting in the godhead to which he devotes himself in his will to truth, Job lives with the certitude that the godhead that he defies will also be the godhead that will vindicate his rights. . . .

Only the godhead that out of my freedom permits me to become myself allows me to overcome defiance through selfhood; yet not through a miraculous supernatural act, but through my binding myself in my existence to the One to which I remain bound historically and absolutely. With it alone I become myself through giving myself up to it. Giving oneself up occurs in the world, without the mediation of which there is no way leading to Transcendence. For Transcendence requires that I give myself up in the actuality of existence. (74f.)

To the extent that in life I unconditionally comprehend the One, I can believe the one God. That I as *Existenz* in the historical actuality of my life transcend toward the One, is a condition of transcending toward the one godhead. That after this last leap I live with the certitude of the one God, is conversely the origin of my considering the One as unconditional in my world. There is only as much Transcendence for me as the One is present in the continuity of my existence. In this way, through the presence of the One, the one God is in my existence invariably my God. Only as the exclusive One is He close.[3] I do not possess Him in the community of all men. The closeness of the One is a function of my transcending; but even the most certain presence is objectively merely a potentiality, a reaching down to me, simply the way in which He can be One for me. This closeness does not invalidate the different gods which I encounter in the belief of others. Yet, when I look at this world, the One is to me remote and inaccessible. When the one godhead becomes perceptible in the unity of *Existenz*, it either enters into the non-transferable, incommunica-

[3] The reference to the divine as impersonal one time and personal another is Jaspers' own inconsistency and not that of the translation.—M.F.

ble closeness of this historical moment, or it becomes abstract, unattainable, remote. Transcendence never becomes identical with me and in utter closeness it keeps an absolute distance. Its nearness is like presence. . . . Whether close or remote, the one godhead is plainly unknown. It exists as limit and is absolute only as the One. . . .

What is certain is what I experience and do: the factual community with others, the factual inner activity in the attitude toward myself, my actions in the external world. What God is I shall never know; I become certain of Him through that which I am.

Although Transcendence is not universal, it does not remain the absolutely incommunicable transcendence of the isolated individual but becomes a source of deepest existential communication. (121-123)

Transcendence of the one godhead: The rationally compelling God leads into unavoidable absurdities, which I must overcome to become aware of Him. In existential relation his is the hand responding to me whenever I am truly myself.

. . . Through our awareness of his Being, this God can teach us to bear our mortality. . . . The agony caused by the awareness that in this world all I love and I myself must die, this agony is acknowledged and comprehended without delusion. The strength to achieve this is possible in the presence of the one eternal God Who exists, though inaccessible and hidden. (125)

Existenz never conceives of divine help as granting or preventing something as a result of prayer. The divine reveals itself in the cipher and still remains hidden. The cipher in which it reveals itself most directly and most decisively is my own action. But prayer, as certainty of absolute consciousness in its transcendent relation, is in its actual historical uniqueness incommunicable, non-objectifiable existential presence—as soaring up to the One. . . .

But its proximity, which seems to come to me from another world, must not make me forget its remoteness, through which the world in its discord is what it is.

The One, sublime and ultimate refuge, may become an existential danger unless it is seized out of the full tension of potential *Existenz*. . . . Having to abandon the union with my Transcendence in existence, I find the way back to defiance, to potential revolt and darkness, and to the particulars—this course must be repeated as long as I am in temporal existence. (127)

Not abstract thought, but the cipher in the historical particularity of the present, mediates Being. It is not a metaphysical hypothesis, from which I infer and compute what Being could be, which reveals Being to me, but the living cipher, beyond which I do not think, because Being is shining in it. . . . Experience of Transcendence is the fainter the more universal it becomes; conversely, it is the more decisive the more it rises to the peak of something fulfilling itself only here and now. (131)

Immanent Transcendence is that immanence which is at the same time always vanishing; it is Transcendence which in the world only speaks as cipher. . . . The cipher constitutes that kind of reality which brings Transcendence into presence, without transforming it into an object and *Existenz* into a subject. (137)

What speaks as cipher depends on the *Existenz* which listens. Potentially it speaks everywhere, but it is not received everywhere. Apprehension of the cipher depends on the free choice of the one reading it. In it I convince myself that my being is what it is because I so will—although I plainly produce nothing therein but receive what I choose. (155)

Ontology must be dissolved in order that the individual may return to concrete authentic *Existenz.* If one takes the road to authenticity, Transcendence becomes perceptible to him in the cipher-script which permeates his whole existence. . . . In ontology man necessarily perceives existence as an individualization of the universal. . . . In reading the cipher-script one looks, in contrast, from the unique *Existenz* into unique and universal Transcendence through the inner activity of the one reading it. . . .

The cipher is the essence of the limit beyond which man cannot go. It is the language of Transcendence in which Transcendence is close to man but not as itself. Because our world as cipher cannot be read completely, because, speaking mythologically, the cipher of the devil is as visible as the cipher of the godhead, because the world is not a direct revelation but only a language—which without becoming universally valid is historically perceptible to *Existenz* only and even then not conclusively decipherable—therefore, Transcendence presents itself as hidden. It is remote because in itself it is inaccessible. It is also the other and completely and incomparably different. It comes into this world as a foreign power, out of its remote being, and speaks to *Existenz;* it approaches *Existenz* only as cipher.

The tension of the relationship to this hidden Transcendence is the life of *Existenz,* in which truth is sought, experienced, seen in the questions and answers of fate and yet it still remains veiled as long as temporal existence lasts. The tension is the authentic manifestation of selfhood, but also its torment. To escape torment man wants to draw the godhead close to himself, to relax the tension, to know what is, and to what he may cling and surrender himself. He regards as absolute Being what as cipher is potential truth.

If man turns to the godhead in prayer, it is to him a Thou with which he wants to enter into communication out of his solitude. The godhead becomes for him a personal image of father, helper, lawgiver, and judge. . . . Only in the image of a person is God really near.

Though this mythical idea of a personal image can become present as cipher for a moment, nevertheless authentic consciousness of Transcendence refuses to conceive God as simply a person. I shrink back immediately from the impulse to make the godhead my Thou, because I feel that I am offending Transcendence. In the mere idea I become involved in delusion. For personality is the mode of being-a-self which according to its nature cannot be alone; it lives in relation to something besides itself: persons and nature. The godhead would be in need of us, men, for communication. In the idea of a personal God Transcendence would be reduced to existence. . . . Finally, communication with the godhead has the tendency to hinder communication among men. For it produces blind communities without developing the selfhood of the individual. Communication from self to self as truly present reality in which Transcendence may speak is paralyzed if Transcendence is brought too close and is degraded, by being directly related to as a Thou.

It is difficult to reduce the personal God to a cipher. God as Transcendence remains remote. He becomes closer to me for a moment in this cipher which I myself as a human being create. . . . But the abyss of Transcendence is too deep. This cipher is not a relaxation of the tension. It is fulfilling and questionable at the same time; it is and is not. The love which I turn toward the personal godhead may be called love only metaphorically. It becomes real love only in the world, in relation to the individual human being, and it develops into enthusiasm for the beauty of existence. Love without the world is love of nothing, a groundless bliss. Love of Transcendence is real only as loving transfiguration of the world. . . .

Speculation, true as play in the reading of the cipher-script, becomes false when it regards as Being that Transcendence which lies beyond any determinable thought, thereby converting it into an object. . . . Then everything becomes godhead, or the godhead becomes the world. The denial of the world and the denial of God are two poles which belong to each other, whereas cipher-script neither resolves Transcendence when it becomes immanent nor makes it a frozen possession, but permits it to remain historical as Transcendence present for *Existenz*. . . .

Man must not become nothing before the idol of himself, whatever image he is making of himself, before mankind, or before a godhead which has become a personal image. He shall defend his right against all these and other images; he shall defend his right also against the godhead which becomes present as cipher, his right which the transcendent godhead out of its remoteness gives and confirms: God wills as Transcendence that I shall be myself. (163-168)

The reality of Transcendence cannot be established empirically or by rationally compelling conclusion. Transcendence is reached in transcending, but is neither observed nor thought out. (199)

Cipher is existence which has to be recognized, in which I find myself and can truly become only what I am. (206)

As the godhead remains hidden, there is firm support only between *Existenzen* holding each other by the hand.

For *Existenz* the temporality of this world is itself a cipher though not an unambiguous one. . . . Ciphers are true only if they sustain themselves in the cipher of shipwreck which . . . becomes serious in existential limit-situations. (218)

The cipher of immortality becomes clear not when I *will* to but when I dare to shipwreck. . . . Yet it remains true that whatever is essential perishes in appearance and that only the way in which such perishing is experienced reveals the depth which permits us to look to the ground of Being. To make eternal therefore would be: to construct a world with a will to permanence but with the consciousness, readiness, daring, and knowledge of possible perishing in which eternity manifests itself in temporality. (223-225)

The non-being of all being accessible to us, which reveals itself in shipwreck, is the Being of Transcendence. . . . For shipwreck is the comprehensive foundation of all cipher-being. Seeing the cipher as reality of Being originates only in the experience of shipwreck. From this experience all ciphers not rejected receive their ultimate confirmation. . . .

The uninterpretable as ultimate cipher . . . remains open, therefore its silence. It may become absolute emptiness as well as final fulfillment. . . .

The leap from anguish to peace is the most enormous man can accomplish. *Existenz* succeeds because its ground is beyond itself; man's faith links him indeterminably to Transcendence.

Only he who makes the leap from anguish to peace is able to

see world-reality without reservation. Mere anguish and mere peace conceal reality. . . . That man can at once see reality, be real himself, and can still live without perishing in anguish, binds him in most decisive closeness to reality; but this is an ever ongoing relationship in which neither anguish nor calm are the ultimate and no reality is ever final. Because, in order to see reality, it is necessary to experience even the most extreme anguish as one's own, only this anguish renders possible the most difficult and the most incomprehensible leap to peace in which reality remains unconcealed. . . .

It is sufficient that Being is. Knowledge of the godhead becomes superstition; but truth is where shipwrecked *Existenz* is able to translate the equivocal language of Transcendence into the most natural certitude that there is ultimate Being.

Only in this peace is, for a fleeting moment, the vision of perfection without delusion possible. Real proximity to the world originates where the cipher of perishing is read. *Existenz* accepts the world completely only when the shipwreck of *Existenz* is also absorbed by the transparence of everything. . . . Love of existence can now untiringly create reality, and the world becomes inexpressibly beautiful in its abundance founded on Transcendence. But the world in its terribleness remains even then a question which in temporal existence will never be answered decisively once and for all, even though the individual may be able to endure it consciously and to find tranquillity. (234-236)

The Perennial Scope of Philosophy

If that which authentically is, is not an object, that is, not an object for a subject, then it is beyond cognition, which denotes object knowledge of something. . . .

If authentic being *is not experience* as subject for a focal point of consciousness observing it, then it also evades all psychological knowledge. . . .

If authentic being is not the *thought structure* of the categories, not logos, it also evades logical knowledge. . . .

The authentic being, that is neither object nor subject, but that is manifested in the whole of the subject-object dichotomy, and that must fill the categories in order to give them purpose and meaning, we have called the Comprehensive.

The question of authentic being must therefore find its answer through elucidation of the modes of the Comprehensive—of world and transcendence—of being-there, consciousness, mind, existence. But in so far as all these modes are rooted in one, the ultimate answer is that authentic being is transcendence (or God). (31f.)

God is: Transcendence beyond the world or before the world is called God. There is the profoundest difference whether I regard the universe as being in itself and nature as God, or whether I regard the universe as not grounded in itself and find the foundation of the world and myself in something outside the world. . . .

. . . In every case, the presence of gaps in the world structure, the failure of all attempts to conceive of the world as self-contained, the abortion of human planning, the futility of human designs and realizations, the impossibility of fulfilling man himself brings us to the edge of the abyss, where we experience nothingness or God.

But never do we gain a scientifically cogent proof. A proved God is no God. Accordingly: only he who starts from God, can seek him. A certainty of the existence of God, however rudimentary and intangible it may be, is a premise, not a result of philosophical activity. (34-36)

First, recognition of the absolute transcendence of God in relation to the world: the *deus absconditus* recedes into the distance when I seek to fathom him, he is infinitely near in the absolute historicity of the unique situation—and the situation is always unique.

Secondly, the experience of the world as the language of God: the world has no independent existence, in it is manifested the speech of God, a speech that has always many meanings and that can become historically unequivocal for existence only in the evanescent moment.

For such faith our being in time is an encounter of existence and transcendence—of the eternal that we are, as beings that are both created and self-given—and of the eternal in itself. The world is the meeting point of that which is eternal and that which manifests itself in time. (39)

Søren Kierkegaard

Fear and Trembling

In our time nobody is content to stop with faith but wants to go further. . . . In those old days it was different, then faith was a task for a whole lifetime, because it was assumed that dexterity in faith is not acquired in a few days or weeks. When the tried oldster drew near to his last hour, having fought the good fight and kept the faith, his heart was still young enough not to have forgotten that fear and trembling which chastened the youth, which the man indeed held in check, but which no man quite outgrows. (23)

If there were no eternal consciousness in a man, if at the foundation of all there lay only a wildly seething power which writhing with obscure passions produced everything that is great and everything that is insignificant, if a bottomless void never satiated lay hidden beneath all—what then would life be but despair? . . .

Everyone shall be remembered, but each became great in proportion to his *expectation.* One became great by expecting the possible, another by expecting the eternal, but he who expected the impossible became greater than all. . . . He who strove with the world became great by overcoming the world, and he who strove with himself became great by overcoming himself, but he who strove with God became greater than all. (30f.)

The ethical expression for what Abraham did is, that he would murder Isaac; the religious expression is, that he would sacrifice Isaac; but precisely in this contradiction consists the dread. (41)

I am unable to make the movements of faith, I cannot shut my eyes and plunge confidently into the absurd, for me that is an impossibility . . . but I do not boast of it. I am convinced that God is love, this thought has for me a primitive lyrical validity. When it is present to me, I am unspeakably blissful, when it is absent, I long for it more vehemently than does the lover for his object; but I do not believe, this courage I lack. For me the love of God is, both in a direct and in an inverse sense, incommensurable with the whole of reality. I am not cowardly enough to whimper and complain, but neither am I deceitful enough to deny that faith is something much higher. I can well endure living in my way, I am joyful and content, but my joy is not that of faith, and in comparison with that it is unhappy. I do not trouble God with my petty sorrows, the particular does not trouble me, I gaze only at my love, and I keep its virginal flame pure and clear. Faith is convinced that God is concerned about the least things. I am content in this life with being married to the left hand, faith is humble enough to demand the right hand—for that this is humility I do not deny and shall never deny. . . .

Abraham believed that God would not require Isaac of him, whereas he was willing nevertheless to sacrifice him if it was required. He believed by virtue of the absurd; for there could be no question of human calculation, and it was indeed the absurd that God who required it of him should the next instant recall the requirement. . . . That sorrow can derange a man's mind, that we see, and it is sad enough. That there is such a thing as strength of will which is able to haul up so exceedingly close to the wind that it saves a man's reason, even though he remains a little queer, that too one sees. I have no intention of disparaging this; but to be able to lose one's reason, and therefore the whole of finiteness of which reason is the broker, and then by virtue of the absurd to gain precisely the same finiteness—that appalls my soul, . . . it is the only prodigy. . . .

. . . Our age is not willing to stop with faith, with its miracle of turning water into wine, it goes further, it turns wine into water. . . .

. . . I make the movements of infinity, whereas faith does the opposite: after having made the movements of infinity, it makes those of finiteness. . . .

The knights of the infinite resignation are easily recognized: their gait is gliding and assured. Those on the other hand who carry the jewel of faith are likely to be delusive, because their outward appearance bears a striking resemblance to that which both the infinite resignation and faith profoundly despise . . . to Philistinism. . . .

One can discover nothing of that aloof and superior nature whereby one recognizes the knight of the infinite. He takes delight in everything, and whenever one sees him taking part in a particular pleasure, he does it with the persistence which is the mark of the earthly man whose soul is absorbed in such things. . . . And yet, and yet—actually I could become furious over it, for envy if for no other reason—this man has made and every instant is making the movements of infinity. With infinite resignation he has drained the cup of life's profound sadness, he knows the bliss of the infinite, he senses the pain of renouncing everything, the dearest things he possesses in the world, and yet finiteness tastes to him just as good as to one who never knew anything higher, for his continuance in the finite did not bear a trace of the cowed and fearful spirit produced by the process of training; and yet he has this sense of security in enjoying it, as though the finite life were the surest thing of all. And yet, and yet the whole earthly form he exhibits is a new creation by virtue of the absurd. He resigned everything infinitely, and then he grasped everything again by virtue of the absurd. He constantly makes the movements of infinity, but he does this with such correctness and assurance that he constantly gets the finite out of it, and there is not a second when one has a notion of anything else. (44-51)

A purely human courage is required to renounce the whole of the temporal to gain the eternal. . . . But a paradoxical and humble courage is required to grasp the whole of the temporal by virtue of the absurd, and this is the courage of faith. (59)

. . . What a tremendous paradox faith is, a paradox which is capable of transforming a murder into a holy act well-pleasing to God, a paradox which gives Isaac back to Abraham, which no thought can master, because faith begins precisely there where thinking leaves off. . . .

The ethical as such is the universal, and as the universal it applies to everyone, which may be expressed from another point of view by saying that it applies every instant. It reposes immanently in itself, it has nothing without itself which is its *telos*, but is itself *telos* for everything outside it, and when this has been incorporated by the ethical it can go no further. Conceived immediately as physical and psychical, the particular individual is the individual who has his *telos* in the universal, and his ethical task is to express himself constantly in it, to abolish his particularity in order to become the universal. . . .

Faith is precisely this paradox, that the individual as the particular is higher than the universal, is justified over against it, is not subordinate but superior—yet in such a way . . . that it is the particular individual who . . . as the particular is superior to the universal, for the fact that the individual as the particular stands in an absolute relation to the absolute. This position cannot be mediated, for all mediation comes about precisely by virtue of the universal; it is and remains to all eternity a paradox, inaccessible to thought. . . .

Now the story of Abraham contains such a teleological suspension of the ethical. . . . He acts by virtue of the absurd, for it is precisely absurd that he as the particular is higher than the universal. . . . Abraham is therefore at no instant a tragic hero but something quite different, either a murderer or a believer. The middle term which saves the tragic hero, Abraham has not. (64-67)

Even if a man were born in humble circumstances, I would require of him nevertheless that he should not be so inhuman toward himself as not to be able to think of the King's castle except at a remote distance, dreaming vaguely of its greatness and wanting at the same time to exalt it and also to abolish it by the fact that he exalted it meanly. I require of him that he should be man enough to step forward confidently and worthily even in that place. He should not be unmanly enough to desire impudently to offend everybody by rushing straight from the street into the King's hall. By that he loses more than the King. On the contrary, he should find joy in observing every rule of propriety with a glad and confident enthusiasm which will make him frank and fearless. This is only a symbol, for the difference here remarked upon is only a very imperfect expression for spiritual distance. I require of every man that he should not think so inhumanly of himself as not to dare to enter those palaces where not merely the memory of the elect abides but where the elect themselves abide. He should not press forward impudently and impute to them kinship with himself; on the contrary, he should be blissful every time he bows before them, but he should be frank and confident and always be something more than a charwoman, for if he will not be more, he will never gain entrance. And what will help him is precisely the dread and distress by which the great are tried, for otherwise, if he has a bit of pith in him, they will merely arouse his justified envy.[4] (74f.)

. . . To him who follows the narrow way of faith no one can give counsel, him no one can understand. Faith is a miracle, and yet no man is excluded from it; for that in which all human life is unified is passion, and faith is a passion. (77)

The paradox of faith is this, that the individual is higher than the universal, that the individual . . . determines his relation to the universal by his relation to the absolute, not his relation to the absolute by his relation to the universal. The paradox can also be expressed by saying that there is an absolute duty toward God; for in this relationship of duty the individual as an individual stands related absolutely to the absolute. . . . From this, however, it does not follow that the ethical is to be abolished, but it acquires an entirely different expression, the paradoxical expression—that, for example, love to God may cause the knight of faith

[4] This passage may have had an important influence on Franz Kafka's novel *The Castle*.—M.F.

to give his love to his neighbor the opposite expression to that which, ethically speaking, is required by duty. . . . The paradox of faith has lost the intermediate term, i.e. the universal. On the one side it has the expression for the extremest egoism (doing the dreadful thing it does for one's own sake); on the other side the expression for the most absolute self-sacrifice (doing it for God's sake). . . . Faith is this paradox, and the individual absolutely cannot make himself intelligible to anybody.

The one knight of faith can render no aid to the other. Either the individual becomes a knight of faith by assuming the burden of the paradox, or he never becomes one. In these regions partnership is unthinkable. Every more precise explication of what is to be understood by Isaac the individual can give only to himself. . . . Hence even if a man were cowardly and paltry enough to wish to become a knight of faith on the responsibility of an outsider, he will never become one; for only the individual becomes a knight of faith as the particular individual. (80-82)

The tragic hero renounces himself in order to express the universal, the knight of faith renounces the universal in order to become the individual. As has been said, everything depends upon how one is placed. He who believes that it is easy enough to be the individual can always be sure that he is not a knight of faith, for vagabonds and roving geniuses are not men of faith. The knight of faith knows, on the other hand, that it is glorious to belong to the universal. He knows that it is beautiful and salutary to be the individual who translates himself into the universal, who edits as it were a pure and elegant edition of himself, as free from errors as possible and which everyone can read. He knows that it is refreshing to become intelligible to oneself in the universal so that he understands it and so that every individual who understands him understands through him in turn the universal, and both rejoice in the security of the universal. He knows that it is beautiful to be born as the individual who has the universal as his home, his friendly abiding-place, which at once welcomes him with open arms when he would tarry in it. But he knows also that higher than this there winds a solitary path, narrow and steep; he knows that it is terrible to be born outside the universal, to walk without meeting a single traveller. . . .

The knight of faith knows that to give up oneself for the universal inspires enthusiasm, and that it requires courage, but he also knows that security is to be found in this, precisely because it is for the universal. . . . This is the terrible thing. He who does not see it can always be sure that he is no knight of faith, but he who sees it will not deny that even the most tried of tragic heroes walks with a dancing step compared with the knight of faith, who comes slowly creeping forward. And if he has perceived this and assured himself that he has not courage to understand it, he will at least have a presentiment of the marvellous glory this knight attains in the fact that he becomes God's intimate acquaintance, the Lord's friend, and (to speak quite humanly) that he says "Thou" to God in heaven, whereas even the tragic hero only addresses Him in the third person.

The knight of faith has only himself alone, and this constitutes the dreadfulness of the situation. . . . The hero does the deed and finds repose in the universal, the knight of faith is kept in constant tension. . . .

The true knight of faith is a witness, never a teacher, and therein lies his deep humanity, which is worth a good deal more than this silly participation in others' weal and woe which is honored by the name of sympathy, whereas in fact it is nothing but vanity. He who would only be a witness thereby avows that no man, not even the lowliest, needs another man's sympathy or should be abased that another may be exalted. But since he did not win what he won at a cheap price, neither does he sell it out at a cheap price, he is not petty enough to take men's admiration and give them in return his silent contempt, he knows that what is truly great is equally accessible to all. (86-91)

Silence is the snare of the demon, and the more one keeps silent, the more terrifying the demon becomes; but silence is also the mutual understanding between the Deity and the individual. (97)

. . . When the individual by his guilt has gone outside the universal he can return to it only by virtue of having come as the individual into an absolute relationship with the absolute. . . . Sin is not the first immediacy, sin is a later immediacy. By sin the individual is already higher (in the direction of the demoniacal paradox) than the universal, because it is a contradiction on the part of the universal to impose itself upon a man who lacks the *conditio sine qua non.*

The conclusions of passion are the only reliable ones, that is, the only convincing conclusions. Fortunately existence . . . excludes no man, not even the lowliest, it fools no one, for in the world of spirit only he is fooled who fools himself. (108f.)

. . . From the start the genius is disoriented in relation to the it be that in despair at his limitation (which in his eyes transforms his omnipotence into impotence) he seeks a demoniacal reassurance and therefore will not admit such limitation either before God or men, or whether he reassures himself religiously by love to the Deity. Here are implied psychological topics to which, it seems to me, one might gladly sacrifice a whole life. (116)

. . . Is not the thing most needed an honest seriousness which dauntlessly and incorruptibly points to the tasks, an honest seriousness which lovingly watches over the tasks, which does not frighten men into being over hasty in getting the highest tasks accomplished, but keeps the tasks young and beautiful and charming to look upon and yet difficult withal and appealing to noble minds. For the enthusiasm of noble natures is aroused only by difficulties. Whatever the one generation may learn from the other, that which is genuinely human no generation learns from the foregoing. In this respect every generation begins primitively, has no different task from that of every previous generation, nor does it get further, except in so far as the preceding generation shirked its task and deluded itself. This authentically human factor is passion, in which also the one generation perfectly understands the other and understands itself. Thus no generation has learned from another to love, no generation begins at any other point than at the beginning, no generation has a shorter task assigned to it than had the preceding generation. . . .

But the highest passion in a man is faith, and here no generation begins at any other point than did the preceding generation, every generation begins all over again, the subsequent generation gets no further than the foregoing—in so far as this remained faithful to its task and did not leave it in the lurch. . . . The task is always sufficient for a human life. . . .

Faith is the highest passion in a man. There are perhaps many in every generation who do not even reach it, but no one gets further. . . . But for the man also who does not so much as reach faith life has tasks enough, and if one loves them sincerely, life will by no means be wasted, even though it never is comparable to the life of those who sensed and grasped the highest. But he who reached faith (it makes no difference whether he be a man of distinguished talents or a simple man) does not remain standing at faith. . . . Nevertheless he does not get further, does not reach anything different. . . . (130f)

Concluding Unscientific Postscript

Let us take as an example the knowledge of God. Objectively, reflection is directed to the problem of whether this object is the true God; subjectively, reflection is directed to the question whether the individual is related to a something *in such a manner* that his relationship is in truth a God-relationship. . . . God is a subject, and therefore exists only for subjectivity in inwardness. (178)

Without risk there is no faith. Faith is precisely the contradiction between the infinite passion of the individual's inwardness and the objective uncertainty. If I am capable of grasping God objectively, I do not believe, but precisely because I cannot do this I must believe. If I wish to preserve myself in faith I must constantly be intent upon holding fast the objective uncertainty, so as to remain out upon the deep, over seventy thousand fathoms of water, still preserving my faith. (182)

What now is the absurd? The absurd is—that the eternal truth has come into being in time, that God has come into being, has been born, has grown up, and so forth, precisely like any other individual human being, quite indistinguishable from other individuals. (188)

. . . No anonymous author can more cunningly conceal himself, no practitioner of the maieutic art can more carefully withdraw himself from the direct relationship, than God. He is in the creation, and present everywhere in it, but directly He is not there; and only when the individual turns to his inner self, and hence only in the inwardness of self-activity, does he have his attention aroused, and is enabled to see God. . . . Nature is, indeed, the work of God, but only the handiwork is directly present, not God. (218)

The eternal happiness of the individual is decided in time through the relationship to something historical, which is furthermore of such a character as to include in its composition that which by virtue of its essence cannot become historical, and must therefore become such by virtue of an absurdity. (345)

. . . In making the absolute venture he becomes another individual . . . a gulf which the understanding cannot bridge either forward or backward. (379)

. . . The individual can do absolutely nothing of himself, but is as nothing before God; for here again the negative is the mark by which the God-relationship is recognized, and self-annihilation is the essential form for the God-relationship. And this self-annihilation must not receive an external expression, for then we have the monastic movement, and the relationship becomes after all a worldly one; and the individual must not allow himself to imagine that it can be done once for all, for this is aesthetics. And even if it could be done at a stroke, because the individual is an existing individual, he will again encounter suffering in the repetition. (412)

The monastic movement is an attempt to be superhuman, an enthusiastic, perhaps even a devout attempt to resemble God. But herein lies the profound suffering of true religiosity, the deepest thinkable, namely, to stand related to God in an absolutely decisive manner, and to be unable to find any decisive external expression for this. (440)

. . . Whoever desires to know, in absolute inwardness, that he is one of the elect, is *eo ipso* lacking in inwardness, since his life is on a comparative basis. It is this comparative and relativising tendency which often enough seeks with unconscious self-deception an easy indulgence, under the form of a mutual heart-felt outpouring of feeling. . . . The religiosity of hidden inwardness does not permit the individual to regard himself as better than any other human being; nor does it permit him to be distinguished by the God-relationship in any other way than every human being can be, much less more distinguished than others. But he also knows that if there is a third party present as a witness (with his knowledge, that is, for otherwise it is the same as if there were no witness) to the fact that he humbles himself before God, then he does not humble himself before God. (456)

. . . Rather let us mock God, out and out, as has been done before in the world—this is always preferable to the disparaging air of importance with which one would prove God's existence. For to prove the existence of one who is present is the most shameless affront, since it is an attempt to make him ridiculous. . . . How could it occur to anybody to prove that he exists, unless one had permitted oneself to ignore him, and now makes the thing all the worse by proving his existence before his very nose? . . . One proves God's existence by worship . . . not by proofs. (485)

Speculative philosophy (in so far as it does not desire to do away with all religiousness in order to introduce us *en masse* into the promised land of pure being) must consistently hold the opinion that religiousness A is higher than B, since it is the religiousness of immanence. . . . The edifying element in the sphere of religiousness A is essentially that of immanence, it is the annihilation by which the individual puts himself out of the way in order to find God, since precisely the individual himself is the hindrance. . . . In religiousness B the edifying is a something outside the individual, the individual does not find edification by finding the God-relationship within himself, but relates himself to something outside himself to find edification. The paradox consists in the fact that this apparently aesthetic relationship (the individual being related to something outside himself) is nevertheless the right relationship; for in immanence God is neither a something (He being all and infinitely all), nor is He outside the individual, since edification consists precisely in the fact that He is in the individual. The paradoxical edification corresponds therefore to the determination of God in time as the individual man; for if such be the case, the individual is related to something outside himself. The fact that it is not possible to think this, is precisely the paradox. . . . The qualitative dialectic enjoins that one is not to fool *in abstracto* with that which is the highest, and hence want to dabble at it, but must comprehend *in concreto* one's essential task and essentially express it. (496-499)

. . . As the eternal came into the world at a moment of time, the existing individual does not in the course of time come into relation with the eternal and think about it (this is A), but *in time* it comes into relation with the eternal *in time;* so that the relation is within time, and this relationship conflicts equally with all thinking, whether one reflect upon the individual or upon the Deity. . . . *Speculative philosophy* discounts existence; in its eyes the fact of existing amounts to having existed (the past), existence is a transitory factor resolved into the pure being of the eternal. Speculative philosophy as the abstract can never be contemporary with existence as existing but can only see it in retrospect. . . . Precisely the thought that the eternal *is* at a definite moment of time, is an expression for the fact that existence is abandoned by the concealed immanence of the eternal. In the religiousness A the eternal is *ubique et nusquam,* but concealed by the actuality of existence; in the paradoxical religiousness the eternal is at a definite place, and precisely this is the breach with immanence. (506)

. . . To require the greatest possible subjective passion, to the point of hating father and mother, and then to put this together with an historical knowledge, which at its maximum can only be an approximation—that is the contradiction. . . . (510)

. . . Understanding applies only in case the possibility is higher than the actuality, whereas here, on the contrary, the actuality is the highest, the paradox; for Christianity as a thought-project is not difficult to understand; the difficulty, the paradox, is that it is real. (514)

Purity of Heart

Father in Heaven! What is a man without Thee! What is all that he knows, vast accumulation though it be, but a chipped fragment if he does not know Thee! What is all his striving, could it even encompass the world, but a half-finished work if he does not know

Thee: Thee the One, who art one thing and who art all! So may Thou give to the intellect, wisdom to comprehend that one thing; to the heart, sincerity to receive this understanding; to the will, purity that wills only one thing. In prosperity may Thou grant perseverance to will one thing; amid distractions, collectedness to will one thing; in suffering, patience to will one thing. Oh, Thou that giveth both the beginning and the completion, may Thou early, at the dawn of day, give to the young man the resolution to will one thing. As the day wanes, may Thou give to the old man a renewed remembrance of his first resolution, that the first may be like the last, the last like the first, in possession of a life that has willed only one thing. Alas, but this has indeed not come to pass. Something has come in between. The separation of sin lies in between. Each day, and day after day something is being placed in between: delay, blockage, interruption, delusion, corruption. . . . Oh, Thou that givest both the beginning and the completion, give Thou victory in the day of need so that what neither a man's burning wish nor his determined resolution may attain to, may be granted unto him in the sorrowing of repentance: to will only one thing. (218f.)

Ferdinand Ebner

The Word and Spiritual Realities

Assuming that human existence in its core is in general a spiritual one, i.e., one that does not exhaust its meaning in its natural affirmation in the process of world happening . . . , it is fundamentally established on a relation to something spiritual outside it through which and in which it exists. . . . Society in the human sense is not the presupposition of speech but rather has as the presupposition of its continuance the word laid in man. If we now . . . call this spiritual in man "I," that outside him, in relation to which he exists, "Thou," then we must consider that this I and this Thou are given to us in their "inwardness" through and in the word; not, however, as "empty" words in which no relation to a reality dwells—as which, indeed, they already appear in their abstract, substantive and substantialized use—, rather as the word that "reduplicates" its "content" and reality-content in the concreteness and actuality of being spoken in the situation created through speaking. (12f.)

I-solitude is not original in the I, but the event of a spiritual act in it, a deed of the I, namely its shutting itself off from the Thou. The I and the Thou are the spiritual realities of life. The I exists only in its relation to the Thou and not outside it. . . .

All mathematical thinking is rooted in the I-solitude of human spirit and lives in it. . . .

The most important, which throws light on the final essence of the word, is that man's relation to God takes the form of this I-Thou relationship. It is the basic and primal form of the relation to God, that just because it is and shall be a "personal" one it can be no other than the relation of the I to the Thou. In the last ground of our spiritual life God is the true Thou of the true I in man. Man's I "concretizes" itself in his relation to God. . . .

The spiritual life of man is bound up with speech in the closest and most indissoluble manner and rests like the latter on the relation of the I to the Thou. (15-18)

No man can have an "objective," standpointless, and perspectiveless relation to the spiritual in other men.

The I has no absolute existence, for it exists only in relationship to the Thou. To its objective being-given-in-the-word corresponds the "subjective" perseverance in love; so that the word and love belong together in their spiritual ground. . . .

God created man in speaking to him. He created him through the word, in which was life. . . . . In the spirituality of his origin in God, man was not the "first" person but the "second" person—the first was and is God. . . .

It cannot be a question of objectively proving the "existence of God"—no proof touches the real existence of God, for it is conducted in the I-solitude of human life and thought, therefore apart from the realities of spiritual life.

To believe in the name of God means to believe in God as the addressed being, as the "addressed person," as precisely the Thou of the I in man; in other words: in his personal existence. . . .

We all live by the grace of God and there is no man who in his innermost being does not know about God, believe in God. (24-29)

Because God exists personally, his relation to man is also a personal one, and we mean nothing else than this when we speak of the Grace of God which corresponds to man's humble trust in him, the trust of the I in the Thou that comes to meet it. . . .

If the I had an absolute existence, i.e., one independent of its relation to the Thou, then God would have no other than a merely ideal existence. . . .

The "word" is the light through which the consciousness which man shares with the animals is illuminated into self-consciousness. (32-34)

That God has created man to a personal being, i.e., to a personal relation to him, does not lie in the necessity of his existence as God and personality, but in his "free will." (37)

The meaning of the word is the relationship of the spiritual in man to the spiritual outside him. . . .

Man becomes clear about himself, understands the need of his existence and himself in this need only in "dialogue with God."

The I of the insane man lacks the Thou—and that is already "symptom"; even though the talk in and for itself appears entirely rational. The genius also often speaks past man. He does not speak directly to the concrete Thou, overlooks it or even despises it. When a genius becomes mad it is not through his genius, but because it has left him in a fix so that he now no longer finds in himself the means of becoming master of his spiritual illness—and man becomes spiritually ill in no other way than through the Thou-lessness of the I. That, however, is the difference between the genius and the madman, the former has at least a relation to an ideal Thou, the latter only speaks to a fictitious Thou. . . .

There is no truth in a thought that is absolutely independent of the relation of the word to the Thou that it, ideally or concretely, addresses. "Objective" truth exists only in the abstract levels of being—and of thought—and it too is in the end no truth "in itself." It is the relation to the right Thou that makes the thought born of words into an "objective" truth. . . . The I that cannot find its Thou moves in sheer displaced thoughts—and half-truths.

No man can understand another in his relation to God—otherwise it is no real relation to God. . . . In the truth of the relation to God in other men . . . I can always only believe. We can only understand that which is given to us with mathematical precision or as something developing out of itself. (43-49)

The word mediates spiritually between man and man—in the last ground, however, between him and God, between him and the spiritual ground of his existence unto which the understanding does not reach. (54f.)

He who understands the meaning of a poem has a creative share in it. . . .

The "metaphysical" is nothing other than the aesthetic transported into the sphere of thought. . . .

Substance is no necessity of being but of thought. (59-61)

The inwardness of the musical is I-Less—like the mystical "experience of God." In the musical intuition man is not aware of the I-solitude of his existence, but he also knows nothing in it of the existence of the Thou. (68f.)

It is above all the spoken word that enters into the ear of man that has the power of moving his feelings and shaking up his spirit. (74)

The aesthetic fulfillment of life and experience is only a seeming fulfillment, dream and not reality. (76)

The Logos of the Gospel of John is quite correctly translated by Word, verbum. And this "word" is by no means merely a symbol for an inborn Son of God, but may and must be understood literally. . . .

Originally in an expression and a form of the placement of the spiritual in man, the I in its *eo ipso* personal relation to the Thou—hence an expression of the relation to God—, the reason only becomes factual and impersonal, speculative and creative of ideas when the I closes itself off from its relation to the Thou. . . . Man shall not, speculating metaphysically, make reason into an impersonal factor in the world process—that would be anthropomorphism. . . .

The "irrationality" of the insane is the spiritual expression of the closing off from before the word: but that is the closedness of the I before the Thou. The insane man literally "says nothing." Insanity is, as it were, the completion of the I-solitude, the Thoulessness of the I, in which this latter naturally runs aground; a condition of the spirit in which the word that begets the spiritual life and also love . . . no longer reach the man. (78-81)

Man takes nothing else with him out of this life into eternity than what he has made in this life out of the relation of his I to the Thou, in which his spiritual life consists. . . . In love is the mercy and forgiveness of our sins. But he who goes over without it and without belief from this life into eternity, for him the word becomes eternal judgment. . . .

In its I-solitude science sets in the place of the love that creates and expresses the relation of the I to the Thou the objective validity of thought as the bond between man and man. . . .

The psychic first arises when the I shuts itself off from the Thou, and only then does man become an "object of psychology." (95-97)

The problem of the word, because it is identical with self-consciousness, is truly the Archimedean point of philosophy. (111)

The idea is not the spiritual bond between man and man, between the I and the Thou and also not between man and God, but in the best case only between the individual and "mankind." . . . There dwells in the right word the power to break through the Chinese wall. All human misfortune in the world rests on the fact that men so seldom know how to speak the right word. If they knew it they would be spared the misery and horror of war. There is no human suffering that cannot be dispelled by the right word. . . . The word that love speaks is eternal. (115f.)

The I-solitude of all scientific-mathematic thinking has as a consequence that the Word stands in diametrical opposition to the mathematical formula. The mathematical formula in its abstractness relates to the substantial as its concrete content. But the substance, at base, is the absolute I-less reality whose subjective expression would be the madness of the final mathematical knowledge. In that this, in its word-and-love-lessness, completes the closedness of the I before the Thou, it removes that I itself and consciousness in general. (141)

Man is not concerned about the salvation of his soul, which belongs always to the sphere of the "psychological" in which the I relates to itself, not yet stepping forth out of its I-solitude . . . Man knows the sins of his existence—and he never recognizes them without horror over himself, without anxiety; his concern, however, is his relation to God and its realization in faith and in love. The salvation of his soul he lays, trusting unshakably in grace, in the hand of Him who is the spiritual ground of his existence. (147f.)

The truth of the concretely spoken word demands belief in the other as the personal decision for him. (151)

Only in that the I is directed to a relation to the Thou—and not to the concretely experienced "resistance of matter" and also not to a logical proof, tiresome to conduct and, if successful, still only understood by a few—have we the guarantee that this world that we experience is real and not merely dreamt and a "projection of the I." . . . But we in no way directly believe in the reality of the world, for it can never be object and content of belief; it is the positive relation of I to Thou, it is our faith in God, that mediates to us the reality of this world. . . . The more the I closes itself off from the Thou. . . , the more it makes the world unreal and into its "projection"; if not in the praxis of its inner life, for that leads directly to madness, at least in the "theory" of metaphysical speculations. (154f.)

The more personally inward my relation to a personality is, so much the less can it occur to me to come to an objective, "third person" understanding about him with a third person. For that means nothing else than to depersonalize his personality and to surrender my personal relation to him. (169f.)

The I is something becoming, the Thou something being, which means ultimately: the I is something human, the Thou something divine. God is the concretion of the Thou. . . .

God is not enthroned in a metaphysical distance unreachable by man. He is not the God of the Dead but of the living, he is near us in life. God is near in each and above all in the man who stands next to us, in the neighbor. . . . He who has done it to the least of my brothers, has done it to me, says the Gospel. . . . The demand of Christianity is that man found his relation to other men on his relation to God and bring the latter to expression in the former. Only in the fulfillment of the divine command of love does he find the true Thou of his true I. He finds it in God and in other men and he finds God in other men. He loves man because he loves God. (178-181)

The object of love is not beauty and the idea—these we shall know—and not the good—this we shall do; not nature and art, not wisdom and science, but the Thou. And since God is the true Thou of the I in man, therefore he is the only object of the true love.

Love was before the "law" and above it. When it went astray and died in man, when the I closed itself off from the Thou, there came the law. . . . No one is spiritually lost, so long as a spark of love is still in him, so long as love is still able to reach him. . . . It is love and not law which creates the true community of men, the community of the spiritual life that has no other basis than the relation to God. The kingdom of love is also the kingdom of God . . . the kingdom of God is not in man in the inner aloneness of his existence, in the aloneness of his I, but in that the I opens to the Thou in love and in the Word—and then it is "among us" as the community of our spiritual life. Although man stands before God just as the "Single One," still he cannot pray without praying in the spiritual community with all men. Man does not pray and speak to God for himself alone but for all men. (183f.)

The human and the divine are never and in no manner to be simply identified. The deep-meaning of the mystic is a self-deception that rests on the perspectivelessness of the mystical sinking in oneself. The I is and remains human and is not divine and the spiritual in man is also in its deepest grounds never anything else than the I that God has created. . . . Only in this "concrete" I is the irremovable standpoint with that only right perspective given that makes the identification of the I with the Thou, the human with the divine absolutely impossible. . . .

God is no spiritual content of feeling . . . God is experienced in no feeling be it ever so deep and "all-embracing." . . .

Only in so far as it is grasped as the relation of the I . . . to God can the right and true relation between man and man in its authentic humanity be established. . . .

If one takes the truth that God is in man, making possible his spiritual life, out of the sphere of personality and removes it into the objective, impersonal perspective-losing spheres of theological-metaphysical speculation, it ceases to be a truth and becomes the object and prey of philosophical hair-splitting and dialectical subtlety. (186-192)

The more spiritual a man is, so much the more he suffers from his sexuality so long as it has not yet been neutralized through the "rebirth" of his existence in the spirit. (197)

Man's will to affirm himself in the world must be broken. . . . He must surrender his natural good opinion of himself and with it remove from under his feet the natural ground and floor of human existence. (214f.)

The Christian ethic is by no means an "altruism," which always has only the alter ego in mind, even when put on the same level with the I in its I-solitude, and never can do what the spirit of Christianity demands and can do: to bring the I in man to its true life in the spirit, to set it in relation to a Thou. (220f.)

The man who has found the true Thou of his I, the meaning of his existence in God, no longer asks about the meaning of life. He knows his existence as laid in the hand of God and, despite all need, all suffering and misfortune, all the breaking up of his life in the world, he demands no other meaning for it than he clearly and simply grasps in his relationship with God. (228f.)

A man who inwardly grasps the problem of life as wholly his problem—and not poetically-philosophically as that of man always meant only ideally, as the problem of "mankind"—a man who takes on himself entirely the difficulty and burden of this problem, must be able to believe in God, in the "Thou coming to meet him"—or he becomes insane. Christianity demands of man that he be serious concerning the life of the generation, not an idea whose realization gradually succeeds in this life . . . but entirely a matter and situation of the individual himself in reference to himself. (238f.)

What came over and still comes over Europe, two foresaw, two who saw the salvation of man in the spirit of Christianity: Kierkegaard and Dostoevsky. (243)

Franz Kafka

Parables and Paradoxes

We were fashioned to live in Paradise, and Paradise was destined to serve us. Our destiny has been altered; that this has also happened with the destiny of Paradise is not stated. (29)

He is a free and secure citizen of the world, for he is fettered to a chain which is long enough to give him the freedom of all earthly space, and yet only so long that nothing can drag him past the frontiers of the world. But simultaneously he is a free and secure citizen of Heaven as well, for he is also fettered by a similarly designed heavenly chain. So that if he heads, say, for the earth, his heavenly collar throttles him, and if heads for Heaven, his earthly one does the same. And yet all the possibilities are his, and he feels it; more, he actually refuses to account for the deadlock by an error in the original fettering. (31)

Reflections on Sin, Pain, Hope, and the True Way

1

The true way goes over a rope which is not stretched at any great height but just above the ground. It seems more designed to make people stumble than to be walked upon. (253)

3

There are two cardinal sins from which all the others spring: impatience and laziness. Because of impatience we were driven out of Paradise, because of laziness we cannot return. Perhaps, however, there is only one cardinal sin: impatience. Because of inpatience we were driven out, because of impatience we cannot return. (153f.)

10

A first sign of nascent knowledge is the desire for death. This life seems unendurable, any other unattainable. One is no longer ashamed of wishing to die; one prays to be conducted from the old cell that one hates into a new one that one has yet to hate. There is in this a vestige of faith that during the change the Master may chance to walk along the corridor, contemplate the prisoner, and say: "You must not lock up this one again. He is to come to me." (256)

17

Leopards break into the temple and drink the sacrificial chalices dry; this occurs repeatedly, again and again: finally it can be reckoned upon beforehand and becomes a part of the ceremony. (258)

19

You are the problem. No scholar to be found far and wide. (258)

21

Grasp your great good fortune that the ground on which you stand cannot be greater than the two feet that cover it. (258)

23

There are countless places of refuge, there is only one place of salvation; but the possibilities of salvation, again, are as numerous as all the places of refuge. (259)

29

The crows maintain that a single crow could destroy the heavens. Doubtless that is so, but it proves nothing against the heavens, for the heavens signify simply: The impossibility of crows. (261)

35

A man was astonished how easily he went the eternal way; he happened to be rushing backwards along it. (262)

38

Only our concept of Time makes it possible for us to speak of the Day of Judgment by that name; in reality it is a summary court in perpetual session. (263)

44

The word "*sein*" signifies in German both things: to be, and to belong to Him. (264)

48

Man cannot live without an enduring trust in something indestructible in himself. Yet while doing that he may all his life be unaware of that indestructible thing and of his trust in it. One of the possible ways in which this permanent unawareness may be expressed is to have faith in a personal God. (266)

50

In the fight between you and the world back the world. (266)

52

There is only a spiritual world; what we call the physical world is the evil in the spiritual one, and what we call evil is only a necessary moment in our endless development.

In a light that is fierce and strong one can see the world dissolve. To weak eyes it becomes solid, to weaker eyes it shows fists, before still weaker eyes it feels ashamed and smites down him who dares to look at it. (267)

60

The fact that there is only a spiritual world robs us of hope and gives us certainty. (269)

71

Test yourself on humanity. It makes the doubtful doubt, the believer believe. (273)

84

Death confronts us not unlike the historical battle scene that hangs on the wall of the classroom. It is our task to obscure or quite obliterate the picture by our deeds while we are still in this world. (277)

90

Two tasks on the threshold of life: To narrow your circle more and more, and constantly to make certain that you have not hidden yourself somewhere outside it. (280)

99

You can hold back from the suffering of the world, you have free permission to do so and it is in accordance with your nature, but perhaps this very holding back is the one suffering that you could have avoided. (283)

101

Humility provides every one, even the lonely and despairing, with the firmest relation to his fellow-men, a relation, too, that is instantaneous, though only if the humility is complete and permanent. It can do this because it is the true language of prayer, at once worship and firmest union. Our relation to our fellowmen is that of prayer, our relation to ourselves, that of effort; from prayer we draw the strength for effort. (284)

You do not need to leave your room. Remain sitting at your table and listen. Do not even listen, simply wait. Do not even wait, be quite still and solitary. The world will freely offer itself to you to be unmasked, it has no choice, it will roll in ecstasy at your feet. (286)

Conversations with Kafka[5]

"I am no protestant. I wish to accept everything and bear it patiently." . . .

". . . Only those fear to be put to the proof who have a bad conscience. They are the ones who do not fulfil the tasks of the present. Yet who knows precisely what his task is? No one. So that every one of us has a bad conscience. . . ." (50)

"In such a godless time one must be gay. It is a duty . . . sorrow has no prospects. And all that matters is prospects, hope, going forward. There is danger only in the narrow, restricted moment. Behind it lies the abyss. If one overcomes it, everything is different. Only the moment counts. It determines life." (57)

"Bloy writes that the tragic guilt of the Jews is that they did not recognize the Messiah." "Perhaps that is really so," said Kafka. "Perhaps they really did not recognize him. But what a cruel God it is who makes it possible for his creatures not to recognize him. After all, a father always makes himself known to his children, when they cannot think or speak properly." (70)

"What is sin? . . . We know the word & the practice, but the sense and the knowledge of sin have been lost. Perhaps that is itself damnation, God-forsakenness, meaninglessness." (73)

"The only really difficult and insoluble problems are those which we cannot formulate, because they have the difficulties of life itself as their content." (76)

"Whoever has faith cannot define it, and whoever has none can only give a definition which lies under the shadow of grace withheld. The man of faith cannot speak and the man of no faith ought not to speak. . . . I try to be a true attendant upon grace. Perhaps it will come—perhaps it will not come. Perhaps this quiet yet unquiet waiting is the harbinger of grace, or perhaps it is grace itself. I do not know. But that does not disturb me. In the meantime I—have made friends with my ignorance." . . .

[5] By Gustav Janouch.

"God can only be comprehended personally. Each man has his own life and his own God. His protector and judge. Priests and rituals are only crutches for the crippled life of the soul." "Truth is what every man needs in order to live, but can obtain or purchase from no one. Each man must reproduce it for himself from within, otherwise he must perish. Life without truth is not possible. Truth is perhaps life itself." . . . "A game with truth is always a game with life." . . . "A lie is often an expression of the fear that one may be crushed by the truth. It is a projection of one's own littleness, of the sin of which one is afraid." . . .

"Man voluntarily limits his own self, surrenders his highest and most real property, his own person, in order to find salvation. By outward restraint he tries to achieve inner freedom. That is the meaning of self-submission to the Law." "But if a man does not know the Law," I said, "how will he achieve freedom?" "He will have the law beaten into him. If he does not know the Law, he will be harried and whipped into knowledge." "So you mean that sooner or later every man must arrive at true knowledge." "I did not quite say that. I did not speak of knowledge, but of freedom as a goal. The knowledge is only a way . . ." "To fulfilment? Then life is only a task, a commission." Kafka made a helpless gesture. "That is just it. Man cannot see beyond himself. He is in the dark." . . .

"The Jewish people . . . is the chosen race of a personal God which can never sink to the mean level of an anonymous and therefore soulless mass, as long as it can hold fast to the fulfilment of the Law. Mankind can only become a grey, formless, and therefore nameless, mass through a fall from the Law which gives it form. But in that case there is no above and below any more; life is levelled out into mere existence; there is no struggle, no drama, only the Jewry." . . . "Sin is turning away from one's own vocation, misunderstanding, impatience, and sloth—that is sin." (92-97)

"Life has so many possibilities, and each one only mirrors the inescapable impossibility of one's own existence." . . . "I have said yes to everything. In that way suffering becomes an enchantment, and death—it is only an ingredient in the sweetness of life." (100f.)

Dearest Father

From outside one will always triumphantly impress theories upon the world, then fall straight into the ditch one has dug, but only from inside will one keep oneself and the world quiet and true. (66f.)

The thornbush is the old obstacle in the road. It must catch fire if you want to go further.

Evil is whatever distracts.

Evil knows of the Good, but Good does not know of Evil.

Knowledge of oneself is something only Evil has.

One means that Evil has is the dialogue.

Anyone who believes cannot experience miracles. By day one does not see any stars. . . .

Only he who is a party can really judge, but as a party he cannot judge. Hence it follows that there is no possibility of judgment in the world, only a glimmer of it. (75f.)

Believing means liberating the indestructible element in oneself, or, more accurately, being indestructible, or, more accurately, being. . . .

Evil is the starry sky of the Good. . . .

The Bible is a sanctum; the world, sputum.

Not everyone can see the truth, but he can be it. . . .

He who seeks does not find, but he who does not seek will be found. (78-80)

Suffering is the positive element in this world, indeed it is the only link between this world and the positive. . . .

. . . This world is our going astray. (90)

I should welcome eternity, and when I do find it I am sad. I should feel myself perfect by virtue of eternity—and feel myself depressed? . . .

In saying this do you express a commandment that is within yourself?

That is what I mean. . . . I believe . . . it is a continual commandment, but that I hear it only occasionally. . . . I hear it, as it were, even when I do not hear it, in such a way that, although it is not audible itself, it muffles or embitters the voice bidding me do the other thing: that is to say, the voice that makes me ill at ease with eternity.

And do you hear the other voice in a similar way when the commandment of eternity is speaking?

Yes, then too, indeed sometimes I believe I hear nothing but the other voice and everything else seems to be only a dream and it is as though I were just letting the dream go on talking at random. (92)

. . . Eternity is not temporality at a standstill. What is oppressive about the concept of the eternal is the justification, incomprehensible to us, that time must undergo in eternity and the logical conclusion of that, the justification of ourselves as we are. . . .

. . . If I wish to fight against this world, I must fight against its decisively characteristic element, that is, against its transience. (94f.)

Your will is free means: it was free when it wanted the desert, it is free since it can choose the path that leads to crossing the desert, it is free since it can choose the pace, but it is also unfree since you must go through the desert, unfree since every path in labyrinthine manner touches every foot of the desert's surface. (97f.)

It is not inertia, ill will, awkwardness—even if there is something of all this in it, because "vermin is born of the void"—that cause me to fail, or not even to get near failing: family life, friendship, marriage, profession, literature. It is not that, but the lack of ground underfoot, of air, of the commandment. . . . I have brought nothing with me of what life requires, so far as I know, but only the universal human weakness. With this—in this respect it is gigantic strength—I have vigorously absorbed the negative element of the age in which I live, an age that is, of course, very close to me, which I have no right ever to fight against, but as it were a right to represent. The slight amount of the positive, and also of the extreme negative, which capsizes into the positive, are something in which I have had no hereditary share. I have not been guided into life by the hand of Christianity—admittedly now slack and failing—as Kierkegaard was, and have not caught the hem of the Jewish prayer shawl—now flying away from us—as the Zionists have. I am an end or a beginning. (99f.)

We see every human being living his life (or dying his death). This achievement would not be possible without an inner justification: no human being can live an unjustified life. . . .

The evolution of mankind—a growth of death-force.

Our salvation is death, but not this one.

Every human being is here asked two questions of creed: first as to the credibility of this life, secondly as to the credibility of his goal. (100f.)

Diaries, 1914-1923

October 18, 1921. Eternal childhood. Life calls again.

It is entirely conceivable that life's splendor forever lies in wait about each one of us in all its fulness, but veiled from view, deep down, invisible, far off. It is there, though, not hostile, not reluctant, not deaf. If you summon it by the right word, by its right name, it will come. This is the essence of magic which does not create but summons. (195)

Martin Buber

I and Thou

Spirit is not in the *I*, but between *I* and *Thou*. It is not like the blood that circulates in you, but like the air in which you breathe. Man lives in the spirit, if he is able to respond to his *Thou*. He each relation and consummated in none. It is consummated only in virtue of his power to enter into relation is he able to live in the spirit. (39)

Every particular *Thou* is a glimpse through to the eternal *Thou;* by means of every particular *Thou* the primary word addresses the eternal *Thou*. . . . The inborn *Thou* is realised in each relation and consummated in none. It is consummated only in the direct relation with the *Thou* that by its nature cannot become *It*. . . .

. . . All God's names are hallowed, for in them He is not merely spoken about, but also spoken to. (75)

Men do not find God if they stay in the world. They do not find Him if they leave the world. He who goes out with his whole being to meet his *Thou* and carries to it all being that is in the world, finds Him who cannot be sought.

Of course God is the "wholly Other"; but He is also the wholly Same, the wholly Present. Of course He is the *Mysterium Tremendum* that appears and overthrows; but He is also the mystery of the self-evident, nearer to me than my *I*.

If you explore the life of things and of conditioned being you come to the unfathomable, if you deny the life of things and of conditioned being you stand before nothingness, if you hallow this life you meet the living God. . . .

God cannot be inferred in anything—in nature, say, as its author, or in history as its master, or in the subject as the self that is thought in it. Something else is not "given" and God then elicited from it; but God is the Being that is directly, most nearly, and lastingly, over against us, that may properly only be addressed, not expressed. . . .

You know always in your heart that you need God more than everything; but do you not know too that God needs you—in the fulness of His eternity needs you? How would man be, how would you be, if God did not need him, did not need you? You need God, in order to be—and God needs you, for the very meaning of your life. In instruction and in poems men are at pains to say more, and they say too much—what turgid and presumptuous talk that is about the "God who becomes"; but we know unshakably in our hearts that there is a becoming of the God that is. The world is not divine sport, it is divine destiny. There is divine meaning in the life of the world, of man, of human persons, of you and of me.

Creation happens to us, burns itself into us, recasts us in burning—we tremble and are faint, we submit. We take part in creation, meet the Creator, reach out to Him, helpers and companions. (79-82)

I know nothing of a "world" and a "life in the world" that might separate a man from God. What is thus described is actually life with an alienated world of *It,* which experiences and uses. He who truly goes out to meet the world goes out also to God. (95)

The relation with man is the real simile of the relation with God; in it true address receives true response; except that in God's response everything, the universe, is made manifest as language. (103)

Life cannot be divided between a real relation with God and an unreal relation of *I* and *It* with the world—you cannot both truly pray to God and profit by the world. He who knows the world as something by which he is to profit knows God also in the same way. His prayer is a procedure of exoneration heard by the ear of the void. He—not the "atheist," who addresses the Nameless out of the night and yearning of his garret-window—is the godless man. (107)

The meaning that has been received can be proved true by each man only in the singleness of his being and the singleness of his life. As no prescription can lead us to the meeting, so none leads from it. As only acceptance of the Presence is necessary for the approach to the meeting, so in a new sense is it so when we emerge from it. As we reach the meeting with the simple *Thou* on our lips, so with the *Thou* on our lips we leave it and return to the world. . . .

This is the eternal revelation that is present here and now. I know of no revelation and believe in none whose primal phenomenon is not precisely this. . . . (111)

Meeting with God does not come to man in order that he may concern himself with God, but in order that he may confirm that there is meaning in the world. All revelation is summons and sending. (115)

Degeneration of the religions means degeneration of prayer in them. Their power to enter into relation is buried under increasing objectification, it becomes increasingly difficult for them to say *Thou* with the whole undivided being, and finally, in order to be able to say it, man must come out of the false security into the venture of the infinite—out of the community, that is now overarched only by the temple dome and not also by the firmament, into the final solitude. (118)

. . . God [is] the absolute Person, i.e. the Person who cannot be limited. It is as the absolute Person that God enters into direct relation with us. The contradiction yields to deeper insight.

As a Person God gives personal life, he makes us as persons become capable of meeting with him and with one another. But no limitation can come upon him as the absolute Person, either from us or from our relations with one another; in fact we can dedicate to him not merely our persons but also our relations to one another. The man who turns to him therefore need not turn away from any other *I-Thou* relation; but he properly brings them to him, and lets them be fulfilled "in the face of God." . . .

God's speech to men penetrates what happens in the life of each one of us, and all that happens in the world around us, biographical and historical, and makes it for you and me into instruction, message, demand. Happening upon happening, situation upon situation, are enabled and empowered by the personal speech of God to demand of the human person that he take his stand and make his decision. Often enough we think there is nothing to hear, but long before we have ourselves put wax in our ears.

The existence of mutuality between God and man cannot be proved, just as God's existence cannot be proved. Yet he who dares to speak of it, bears witness, and calls to witness him to whom he speaks. (136f.)

Between Man and Man

DIALOGUE

Real faith is not a *what* at all, it is said into my very life; it is no experience that can be remembered independently of the situation, it remains the address of that moment and cannot be isolated, it remains the question of a questioner and will have its answer. . . . Faith stands in the stream of "happening but once" which is spanned by knowledge. . . . Lived life is tested and fulfilled in the stream alone. . . .

The true name of concrete reality is the creation which is entrusted to me and to every man. In it the signs of address are given to us.

A Conversion

In my earlier years the "religious" was for me the exception. There were hours that were taken out of the course of things. From somewhere or other the firm crust of everyday was pierced. Then the reliable permanence of appearances broke down; the attack which took place burst its law asunder. "Religious experience" was the experience of an otherness which did not fit into the context of life. It could begin with something customary, with consideration of some familiar object, but which then became unexpectedly mysterious and uncanny, finally lighting a way into the lightning-pierced darkness of the mystery itself. But also, without any intermediate stage, time could be torn apart —first the firm world's structure then the still firmer self-assurance flew apart and you were delivered to fulness. The "religious" lifted you out. Over there now lay the accustomed existence with its affairs, but here illumination and ecstasy and rapture held without time or sequence. Thus your own being encompassed a life here and a life beyond, and there was no bond but the actual moment of the transition.

The illegitimacy of such a division of the temporal life, which is streaming to death and eternity and which only in fulfilling its temporality can be fulfilled in face of these, was brought home to me by an everyday event, an event of judgment, judging with that sentence from closed lips and an unmoved glance such as the ongoing course of things loves to pronounce.

What happened was no more than that one forenoon, after a morning of "religious" enthusiasm, I had a visit from an unknown young man, without being there in spirit. I certainly did not fail to let the meeting be friendly, I did not treat him any more remissly than all his contemporaries who were in the habit of seeking me out about this time of day as an oracle that is ready to listen to reason. I conversed attentively and openly with him—only I omitted to guess the questions which he did not put. Later, not long after, I learned from one of his friends—he himself was no longer alive—the essential content of these questions; I learned that he had come to me not casually, but borne by destiny, not for a chat but for a decision. He had come to me, he had come in this hour. What do we expect when we are in despair and yet go to a man? Surely a presence by means of which we are told that nevertheless there is meaning.

Since then I have given up the "religious" which is nothing but the exception, extraction, exaltation, ecstasy; or it has given me up. I possess nothing but the everyday out of which I am never taken. The mystery is no longer disclosed, it has escaped or it has made its dwelling here where everything happens as it happens. I know no fulness but each mortal hour's fulness of claim and responsibility. Though far from being equal to it, yet I know that in the claim I am claimed and may respond in responsibility, and know who speaks and demands a response.

I do not know much more. If that is religion then it is just *everything,* simply all that is lived in its possibility of dialogue. . . . You are not swallowed up in a fulness without obligation, you are willed for the life of communion. . . .

Who Speaks?

In the signs of life which happens to us we are addressed. Who speaks?

It would not avail us to give for reply the word "God," if we do not give it out of that decisive hour of personal existence when we had to forget everything we imagined we knew of God, when we dared to keep nothing handed down or learned or self-contrived, no shred of knowledge, and were plunged into the night. . . .

The word of him who wishes to speak with men without speaking with God is not fulfilled; but the word of him who wishes to speak with God without speaking with men goes astray. . . . True address from God directs man into the place of lived speech, where the voices of the creatures grope past one another, and in their very missing of one another succeed in reaching the eternal partner. (12-15)

THE QUESTION TO THE SINGLE ONE

"In order to come to love," says Kierkegaard about his renunciation of Regina Olsen, "I had to remove the object." That is sublimely to misunderstand God. Creation is not a hurdle on the road to God, it is the road itself. We are created along with one another and directed to a life with one another. Creatures are placed in my way so that I, their fellow-creature, by means of them and with them find the way to God. A God reached by their exclusion would not be the God of all lives in whom all life is fulfilled. A God in whom only the parallel lines of single approaches intersect is more akin to the "God of the philosophers" than to the "God of Abraham and Isaac and Jacob." God wants us to come to him by means of the Reginas he has created and not by renunciation of them. . . . The real God lets no shorter line reach him than each man's longest, which is the line embracing the world that is accessible to this man. (52)

Religion as a specification misses its mark. God is not an object beside objects and hence cannot be reached by renunciation of objects. God, indeed, is not the cosmos, but far less is he Being *minus* cosmos. He is not to be found by subtraction and not to be loved by reduction. (58)

Certainly the relation of faith is no book of rules which can be looked up to discover what is to be done now, in this very hour. I experience what God desires of me for this hour—so far as I do experience it—not earlier than *in* the hour. But even then it is not given me to experience it except by answering before God for this hour as *my* hour. . . . Only one thing matters, that as the situation is presented to me I expose myself to it as to the word's manifestation to me, to the very ground where hearing passes into being, and that I perceive what is to be perceived and answer it. . . . God tenders me the situation to which I have to answer; but I have not to expect that he should tender me anything of my answer. . . .

I say, therefore, that the Single One, that is, the man living in responsibility, can make even his political decisions properly only from that ground of his being at which he is aware of the event as divine speech to him; and if he lets the awareness of this ground be strangled by his group he is refusing to give God an actual reply. (68-70)

Eclipse of God

. . . The crucial religious experiences of man do not take place in a sphere in which creative energy operates without contradiction, but in a sphere in which evil and good, despair and hope, the power of destruction and the power of rebirth, dwell side by side. The divine force which man actually encounters in life does not hover above the demonic, but penetrates it. To confine God to a producing function is to remove Him from the world in which we live—a world filled with burning contradictions, and with yearning for salvation. (21)

It is not necessary to know something about God in order really to believe in Him: many true believers know how to talk *to* God but not *about* Him. If one dares to turn toward the unknown God, to go to meet Him, to call to Him, Reality is present. He who refuses to limit God to the transcendent has a fuller conception of Him than he who does so limit Him. But he who confines God within the immanent means something other than Him. (28)

Even if the believer has in mind an unlimited and nameless absolute which cannot be conceived in a personal form, if he really thinks of it as existing Being which stands over against him, his belief has existential reality. Conversely, even if he thinks of the absolute as limited within personal form, if he reflects on it as on an object, he is philosophizing. . . . The religious relationship, no matter what different forms and constellations it takes, is in its essence nothing other than the unfolding of the existence that is lent to us. The philosophical attitude is the product of a consciousness which conceives of itself as autonomous and strives to become so. (31f.)

The religious essence in every religion can be found in its highest certainty. That is the certainty that the meaning of existence is open and accessible in the actual lived concrete, not above the struggle with reality but in it.

That meaning is open and accessible in the actual lived concrete does not mean it is to be won and possessed through any type of analytical or synthetic investigation or through any type of reflection upon the lived concrete. Meaning is to be experienced in living action and suffering itself, in the unreduced immediacy of the moment. Of course, he who aims at the experiencing of experience will necessarily miss the meaning, for he destroys the spontaneity of the mystery. Only he reaches the meaning who stands firm, without holding back or reservation, before the whole might of reality and answers it in a living way. He is ready to confirm with his life the meaning which he has attained. . . .

All religious reality begins with what Biblical religion calls the "fear of God." It comes when our existence between birth and death becomes incomprehensible and uncanny, when all security is shattered through the mystery. . . . Through this dark gate (which is only a gate and not, as some theologians believe, a dwelling) the believing man steps forth into the everyday which is henceforth hallowed as the place in which he has to live with the mystery. He steps forth directed and assigned to the concrete, contextual situations of his existence. . . . He will not remove himself from the concrete situation as it actually is; he will, instead, enter into it, even if in the form of fighting against it. Whether field of work or field of battle, he accepts the place in which he is placed. He knows no floating of the spirit above concrete reality; to him even the sublimest spirituality is an illusion if it is not bound to the situation. (35-38)

God can never become an object for me; I can attain no other relation to Him than that of the I to its eternal Thou, that of the Thou to its eternal I. But if man is no longer able to attain this relation, if God is silent toward him and he toward God, then something has taken place, not in human subjectivity but in Being itself. It would be worthier not to explain it to oneself in sensational and incompetent sayings, such as that of the "death" of God, but to endure it as it is and at the same time to move existentially toward a new happening, toward that event in which the word between heaven and earth will again be heard. Thus the perseverance of the "religious need," to which Sartre objects and which he thinks contradicts the silence of the transcendent, instead points directly to the situation in which man becomes aware of this silence as such.

Still more questionable is Sartre's demand, reminiscent of Ludwig Feuerbach, that man should recover for himself the creative freedom which he ascribed to God and that he should affirm himself as the being through whom a world exists. That ordering of known phenomena which we call the world is, indeed, the composite work of a thousand human generations, but it has come into being through the fact that manifold being, which is not our work, meets us, who are, likewise, together with our subjectivity, not our work. Nor is this meeting, out of which arises the whole of the phenomena which we order into the "world," our work. All that being is *established*, we are established, our meeting with it is established, and in this way the becoming of a world, which takes place through us, is established. . . . He who sets in the place of it the postulate of the "recovery of freedom" turns aside from true human existence, which means being sent and being commissioned.

"If I have done away with God the father (*si j'ai supprimé Dieu le père*)," Sartre says literally, "someone is needed to invent values (*pour inventer les valeurs*). . . . Life has no meaning *a priori* . . . it is up to you to give it a meaning, and value is nothing else than this meaning which you choose." That is almost exactly what Nietzsche said, and it has not become any truer since then. One can believe in and accept a meaning or value, one can set it as a guiding light over one's life if one has discovered it, not if one has invented it. It can be for me an illuminating meaning, a direction-giving value only if it has been revealed to me in my meeting with Being, not if I have freely chosen it for myself from among the existing possibilities. (68-70)

This is not the place for a critical discussion of Heidegger's theory of being. I shall only confess that for me a concept of being that means anything other than the inherent fact of all existing being, namely, that it exists, remains insurmountably empty. . . . " 'Being'—that is not God and it is not a ground of the world. Being is more than all that exists and is, nonetheless, nearer than any existing thing, be it . . . an angel or God. Being is the nearest thing." If by the last sentence, . . . something other is meant than that I myself am, and not indeed as the subject of a *cogito*, but as my total person, then the concept of being loses for me the character of genuine conceivability that obviously it eminently possesses for Heidegger. . . .

Being turned toward us, descended to us, showed itself to us, spoke to us in the immanence. The Coming One came of his own will out of the mystery of his withdrawnness; we did not cause him to come. . . . God does not let Himself be conjured, but He also will not compel. He is of Himself, and He allows that which exists to be of itself. Both of these facts distinguish divine from demonic powers. It may not be, indeed, unimportant to God whether man gives himself or denies himself to Him. Through this giving or denying, man, the whole man with the decision of his whole being, may have an immeasurable part in the actual revelation or hiddenness of the divine. But there is no place between heaven and earth for an influence of concept-clarifying thought. He whose appearance can be effected or co-effected through such a modern magical influence clearly has only the name in common with Him whom we men, basically in agreement despite all the differences in our religious teachings, address as God. To talk of a reappearance of this conjured god of thought is inadmissible. (73-76)

Of the two who have taken up Nietzsche's expression of the death of God, one, Sartre, has brought it and himself *ad absurdum* through his postulate of the free invention of meaning and value. The other, Heidegger, creates a concept of a rebirth of God out of the thought of truth which falls into the enticing nets of historical time. The path of this existentialism seems to vanish. (78)

It is indeed legitimate to speak of the person of God within the religious relation and in its language; but in so doing we are making no statement about the Absolute which reduces it to the personal. . . . In our human mode of existence the only reciprocal relation with us that exists is a personal one. . . .

Even when the individual calls an absolute criterion handed down by religious tradition his own, it must be reforged in the fire of the truth of his personal essential relation to the Absolute if it is to win true validity. But always it is the religious which bestows, the ethical which receives. (96-98)

. . . Man, while created by God, was established by Him in an independence which has since remained undiminished. In this independence he stands over against God. So man takes part with full freedom and spontaneity in the dialogue between the two which forms the essence of existence. (105)

In our age the I-It relation, gigantically swollen, has usurped, practically uncontested, the mastery and the rule. The I of this relation, an I that possesses all, makes all, succeeds with all, this I that is unable to say Thou, unable to meet a being essentially, is the lord of the hour. This selfhood that has become omnipotent, with all the It around it, can naturally acknowledge neither God nor any genuine absolute which manifests itself to men as of non-human origin. It steps in between and shuts off from us the light of heaven. (129)

Good and Evil

. . . The humanly right is ever the service of the single person who realises the right uniqueness purposed for him in his creation. . . . Every ethos has its origin in a revelation, whether or not it is still aware of and obedient to it; and every revelation is revelation of human service to the goal of creation, in which service man authenticates himself. Without authentication, that is, without setting off upon and keeping to the One direction, as far as he is able, *quantum satis,* man certainly has what he calls life, even the life of the soul, even the life of the spirit, in all freedom and fruitfulness, all standing and status—existence there is none for him without it. (142f.)

Hasidism and Modern Man

. . . The crisis of Western man . . . was already recognized by Kierkegaard a hundred years ago as an unprecedented shaking of the foundations of man as man. But it is only in our generation that we have seriously begun to occupy ourselves with the fact that in this crisis something begins to be decided that is bound up in the closest manner with a decision about ourselves. . . . We must take the injured wholeness of man upon us as a life burden in order to press beyond all that is merely symptomatic, and grasp the true sickness through which those motifs receive the force to work as they have worked. Those who, instead of this, contemplate the cruel problematic as a subject of unsurpassable interest, who know how to describe and even perhaps to praise it, contribute, at times with the highest gifts, to the massive decisionlessness whose true name is the decision for nothing.

An especially threatening trait of the crisis is the secularized form of the radical separation between the sacred and the profane. The sacred has become in many cases a concept empty of reality, now of merely historical and ethnological significance. But its character of detachment has found an heir. One no longer knows the holy face to face; but one believes that one knows and cherishes its heir, the "spiritual," without, of course, allowing it the right to determine life in any way. The spirit is hedged in and its claim on personal existence is warded off through a comprehensive apparatus; one can now enjoy it without having to fear awkward consequences. One has ideas, one just has them and displays them to one's own satisfaction and occasionally also to that of others. One seems to take them with grim seriousness; but that must be the end of it. One enthrones them on golden thrones to which their limbs are chained. No false piety has ever attained this concentrated degree of inauthenticity. . . .

Over against all this behavior of present-day man, Hasidism sets the simple truth that the wretchedness of our world is grounded in its resistance to the entrance of the holy into lived life. The spirit was not spun in the brain; it has been from all eternity, and life can receive it into human reality. A life that does not seek to realize what the living person, in the ground of his self-awareness, understands or glimpses as the right is not merely unworthy of the spirit; it is also unworthy of life. (38-40)

Man cannot approach the divine by reaching beyond the human; he can approach Him through becoming human. To become human is what he, this individual man, has been created for. This, so it seems to me, is the eternal core of Hasidic life and of Hasidic teaching. (42f.)

The Way of Man

HERE WHERE ONE STANDS

Most of us achieve only at rare moments a clear realization of the fact that they have never tasted the fulfilment of existence, that their life does not participate in true, fulfilled existence, that, as it were, it passes true existence by. . . .

The environment which I feel to be the natural one, the situation which has been assigned to me as my fate, the things that happen to me day after day, the things that claim me day after day—these contain my essential task and such fulfilment of existence as is open to me. . . . If we think only in terms of momentary purposes, without developing a genuine relationship to the beings and things in whose life we ought to take part, as they in ours, then we shall ourselves be debarred from true, fulfilled existence. It is my conviction that this doctrine is essentially true. The highest culture of the soul remains basically arid and barren unless, day by day, waters of life pour forth into the soul from those little encounters to which we give their due; the most formidable power is intrinsically powerlessness unless it maintains a secret covenant with these contacts, both humble and helpful, with strange, and yet near, being. (172-174)

"God dwells wherever man lets him in."

This is the ultimate purpose: to let God in. But we can let him in only where we really stand, where we live, where we live a true life. If we maintain holy intercourse with the little world entrusted to us, if we help the holy spiritual substance to accomplish itself in that section of Creation in which we are living, then we are establishing, in this our place, a dwelling for the Divine Presence. (176)

The History of the Dialogical Principle

In February 1919 Rosenzweig's *Star of Redemption* was completed. But in the same winter and in the spring following Ferdinand Ebner, a Catholic folk school teacher in the Austrian province, heavily afflicted by sickness and depressions, wrote his "pneumatological fragments" which he then collected in the book *The Word and Spiritual Realities* (1921). Ebner proceeds from the experience of the "solitude of the I" (*Icheinsamkeit*) in that existential sense that it has won in our time; it is for him "nothing original," but the result of the "closing off from the Thou." . . . He acknowledges himself, in direct reference to Kierkegaard, as one who was not able to find the Thou in man. Already in 1917 he had described the danger of going under spiritually in consciousness of this "impossibility." He finds salvation in the thought: "There is only one single Thou and that is even God." To be sure, he also postulates, as does Kierkegaard: "Man shall love not only God but also men." But where it is a question of the authenticity of existence, every other Thou disappears for him before that of God. If we ask here, as with Kierkegaard, about what is finally valid, we stand again before the self-relating individuals who look at the world, to be sure, but are in the last instance acosmic, who love men, to be sure, but are in the last instance ananthropic. (291f.)

Karl Jaspers' concept of "communication" and his teaching of the cipher-script . . . form together the exemplary conclusion of a phase of development in which "free" philosophy takes possession of the new discovery by reducing it. I say reducing because the connection of transcendence with the concrete is treated by it as arbitrary, the advance to the boundlessness of the Thou is in effect annulled. . . . We have recognized that just the same Thou that goes from man to man is that Thou which descends from the divine to us and ascends from us to the divine. It was and is a question of this which is in common to these two relationships otherwise so utterly uncommon. That Biblical union of the love of God and the love of man in the double command directs our gaze to the transparence of the finite Thou, but also to the grace of the infinite which appears where and as it will. Now, however, our saying Thou to the Godhead is censured as illegitimate. . . .

God may be everything [to Jaspers] but just not a person, and for the reason, indeed, that personality is *per definitionem* "the mode of being that by its nature cannot be alone." As though such a definition must also hold true in the paradox of the absolute Person, when the Absolute, in so far as it can be thought of at all, can only appear to thought as a *complexio oppositorum!* . . . The praying man who humbly ventures to turn in personal immediacy to the super-existent as present to him, just thereby degrades it [holds Jaspers] and just thereby cripples in himself the ability to communicate with his fellow-men. Within the unfolding of what seems to be the same [dialogical] idea, here the opposite pole becomes manifest to our insight. (299-302)

Franz Rosenzweig

The New Thinking

I really believe that a philosophy, to be adequate, must rise out of thinking that is done from the personal standpoint of the thinker. To achieve being objective, the thinker must proceed boldly from his own subjective situation. (179)

Philosophy has always inquired into the "essence" of things. This is the concern that marks it off from the unphilosophical thinking of sound common sense, which never bothers to ask what a thing "actually" is. Common sense is content to know that a chair is a chair, and is unconcerned with the possibility that it may, actually, be something quite different. It is just this possibility that philosophy pursues in its inquiry into the essence of things. Philosophy refuses to accept the world as world, God as God, man as man! . . . This very point, where traditional philosophy comes to the end of its way of thinking, is the beginning of philosophy based on experience. . . .

Our assumption that one of these essences could be closer, the other remoter from us, rests on a confusion between the *essence* and the *reality* of God, world, and man—a confusion closely related to the misapplication of meaningless words "immanent" and "transcendent." Between God, world, and man there can indeed be nearness and distance, approach and withdrawal, but these do not take shape as permanent qualities in the sense that God, for instance, must be a transcendent being. So far as their essence is concerned, God, the world, and man are all equally transcendent in regard to each other. (190-193)

Philosophy's claim that the self is omnipresent in all knowledge distorts the content of this consciousness. . . . What the new philosophy, the new thinking, actually does is to employ the method of sound common sense as a method of scientific thinking. . . . Common sense waits, goes on living; it has no fixed idea; it knows: all in due time! . . .

The new thinking, like the age-old thinking of sound common sense, knows that it cannot have cognition independent of time—though heretofore one of philosophy's boasts has been that is able to do this very thing. . . . A deed is a deed only while it is still in the offing. Once done, it is merely something that has happened, quite indistinguishable from anything else that has happened.

Thus the tenses of reality cannot be interchanged. . . .

If in the "deepest core" the other were identical with myself, as Schopenhauer asserts, I could not love him, for I should be merely loving myself. If God were "within me," or if he were "only my loftier self" then this would be no more than an unnecessarily obscure formulation of an otherwise clear relationship. Above all, this God would hardly have anything to tell me since I know anyhow what my loftier self wishes to tell me. And if there were such a thing as a "godly" man, a theory proclaimed by some German professor fresh from the impact of Rabindranath Tagore's robe, this man would find himself barred from the path to God that is open to every truly human man. . . .

To require time means that we cannot anticipate, that we must wait for everything, that what is ours depends on what is another's. . . . The difference between the old and the new, the "logical" and the "grammatical" thinking, does not lie in the fact that one is silent while the other is audible, but in the fact that the latter needs another person, and takes time seriously—actually, these two things are identical. . . . "Speaking" means speaking to some one and thinking for some one. And this some one is always a quite definite some one, and he has not merely ears, like "all the world," but also a mouth. . . .

. . . Theological concerns have assisted the new thinking in coming to the fore. But this does not mean that the new thinking itself is theological, at least not in the sense in which the term has been used up to now, either with respect to the end or the means. . . . Theological problems must be translated into human terms, and human problems brought into the pale of theology. . . . God did not, after all, create religion; he created the world. And when he reveals himself, that world not only persists all around us but is more created than ever. . . . Revelation is always present, and if it occurred in the past, then it was in that past which is the beginning of the history of mankind: it is the revelation granted to Adam. . . . The new thinking is Jewish or Christian thinking only because and to the extent that these renew the "revelation granted to Adam." . . . There is no temple built so close to him as to give man reassurance in its closeness, and none is so far from him as to make it too difficult for man's hand to reach. There is no direction from which it would not be possible for him to come, and none from which he must come. . . .

In the Star of Redemption the picture of Judaism and Christianity is determined above all by the quest for an eternity that *exists*. (196-203)

The experience of factuality . . . precedes all facts of real experience. . . . Truth must be truth for some one. . . . "The" truth must be converted into "our" truth. Thus truth ceases to be what "is" true and becomes a verity that wants to be verified, realized in active life. This becomes the fundamental concept of this new theory of knowledge. This theory replaces the old theories of non-contradiction and objects, and introduces a dynamic for the old static concept of objectivity. Regarded from this new plane, hopelessly static truths like those of mathematics, which the old theory of knowledge took as its point of departure without really ever getting beyond that point, are on the limits (the inferior limits), just as rest is a limit case of motion. The higher and the highest truths can be conceived as truths only via the new thinking, which does not necessitate their being altered to fiction, postulates, or human desiderata. From those most unimportant truths, such as "two times two are four," on which people are apt to agree without making more than a minimum use of their brains (a little less for the multiplication table through ten, a little more for the theory of relativity), the way leads over those truths for which man is willing to pay, on to those that he cannot verify save at the cost of his life, and finally to those that cannot be verified until generations upon generations have given up their lives to that end. (205f.)

. . . The remote God is none other than the near, the unknown God none other than the revealed, the Creator none other than the Redeemer. . . . This is the thought which was discovered over and over in the sphere of revelation, which inside and outside that sphere was forgotten over and over throughout the centuries, from Paul and Marcion to Harnack and Barth. . . . We just cannot do otherwise, for he is so very close to us. (279)

It is not nearness or remoteness that matters. What matters is that, near or remote, whatever is uttered, is uttered before God with the "Thou" of the refrain of our poem, a "Thou" that never turns away.

The paradox of God's being simultaneously near and remote is essentially expressed in the fact that he has a name. Whatever has a name can be talked about, can be talked to, according to whether it is absent or present. God is never absent. Hence there is no theoretical concept of God; there is of the false gods, but not of the one, the true. God alone has a name that is also a concept; his concept is also his name. . . . Everything created has a double function: first, it is simply there, it has being, its own being, and its own purpose. But it is also there for the sake of *something* else, in the final analysis, for the sake of *everything* else. Insofar as it is itself and its own purpose, it experiences the near God; insofar as it is related to something else, it experiences the remote God. For the remote God is the God of the world, which is always a whole, a whole made up of totally different parts, while the near God is the God of the heart, the heart which is never as much itself, and nothing but itself, as when it suffers. (281)

A rabbinical legend tells of a river in a far-off country, a river so devout that it does not flow on the Sabbath. If, instead of the Main, it were this river that flowed through Frankfort, all the Frankfort Jews would doubtless practice the strictest observance of the Sabbath. God does not give signs like these. Apparently, he fears the inevitable result: the most enslaved, the timid, and the meager of soul would then be the most devout. It appears that God desires for his own only the free. . . .

All that God ever reveals in revelation is—revelation. Or, to express it differently, he reveals nothing but himself to man. The relation of this accusative and dative to each other is the one and only content of revelation. Whatever does not follow directly from this covenant between God and man, whatever cannot prove its direct bearing on this covenant, cannot be a part of it. The problem has not been *solved* for the visionary who beheld the vision; it has been *dissolved*. (284f.)

Understanding the Sick and the Healthy

The terms of life are not "essential" but "real"; they concern not "essence" but "fact." . . . Common sense puts its faith in the strength of reality. The philosopher, suspicious, retreats from the flow of reality into the protected circle of his wonder; slowly he submerges to the depths, to the region of the essences. Nothing can disturb him there. He is safe. Why should he concern himself with the crowd of "non-essences." And reality, is, so to speak, "unessential." (30)

. . . The man who proposes and the woman who replies . . . cling to the unchangeable. What is the unchangeable? Unbiassed reflection reveals once more that it is only a name. In this instance, it is the names of the respective lovers. And appropriately enough, the first relief from tension in the enchanted game of love usually comes when the lovers call each other by their first names. This act stands as a solitary pledge that the yesterdays of the two individuals will be incorporated in their todays. . . . And common sense in action is concerned that the name, not the "essence," remain. (35-37)

The lover merely applied the question "What actually is it?" to a human being. The answer he received resulted in the immediate disappearance of two very concrete individuals—the questioner himself and his beloved. No matter whether the answer is "the peak of creation" or "an insect crawling in the dust," the concrete individual is replaced by a ghost. The ghost may be of heaven or hell; it may be devil or angel—but a man cannot live with these rarified essences; and the question concerning the "essence" of man cannot yield more substantial results. (40)

Reality, matter, nature, are all terms denoting "essence" and are just as unacceptable as "spirit" or "idea." All claim to "be" either reality itself or the "essence" of reality. All abstract from life. All neglect the fact of names. Consequently all these *isms* fail to conciliate thought and action, which is, after all, the one thing desired. They fail precisely because they are *isms*, whether "idealisms" or "realisms." (45)

"Something" is a simple word. . . . To dive from this board is neither impossible nor difficult. A man destroys any possibility of acquiring knowledge of the world unless he begins with the commonplace that the world is something rather than nothing, something—not I, not God, not everything. It does not matter whether this course is taken consciously as a thinking person might take it, or unconsciously in the process of living. Man takes his first step towards an answer as part of the continuing process of life and of thought. . . .

The world is something. That is to say, it is not nothing; neither is it everything. There are other entities. This preliminary knowledge presupposes that the other entities, namely God and I, are at every moment accessible to the world, reach the world. Mention of the world requires the very next instant mention of man and God. The world is something only because it enters the stream to which it and everything else belongs. . . .

To utter a word is to affix a seal as a witness of man's presence. The word is not part of the world; it is the seal of man. . . . Each word, as soon as it comes into existence, requires the strength of continuation and the capacity to traverse the river of time so that it may finally become the ultimate word. The word of man, an initial word whenever it is uttered by man, joins that which was ultimate from the first, the word of God. . . .

It is man's privilege to give new names. It is his duty to use the old ones, a duty which he must perform, though unwillingly. His obligation to pass on the old names, to appropriate them and translate them into names he himself designates—this creates the continuity of mankind. Mankind is always absent. Present is a man, this fellow or that one. The thing, however, is tied to all of mankind by language and by its inherent law of transmission and translation. . . .

There is no one for whom the word of God is not meant, whose presence is not implied by it; the word of man implies the presence of the speaker and someone to whom his speech is addressed—and so also with the word of God. . . .

Language stamps the sign of God and man upon all the things of this world. That a thing is considered something by the world gives it its continuity. The thing is not an appearance, an illusion; it is something. The thing does not gain in definition by being isolated and made stagnant; certainty of being "something" is not achieved by plumbing the depths of such an entity, but rather by opening the floodgates and permitting the stream of which it is part to inundate it. Our patient found himself incapable of purchasing a slab of butter because he could no longer avail himself of his God-given right, his privilege as a man, of conferring names. He had lost faith in the continuity of names and of other things; he had renounced his human privilege. And it was because he did not believe in the divine quality of language that he became uncertain of the names which he and others assigned to things. This necessarily followed from his insistence that the word "be" the thing, that his word be the word of others. We have learned that this is something that must be foregone. The thing is and as such immediately acquires a name. Its name bears it into the flow of things, and hence the question concerning the essence of things becomes meaningless. . . .

The world is real only insofar as it enters into this process, a process which brings all of it within the context of the human word and God's sentence. The world as such does not exist. To speak of the world is to speak of a world which is ours and God's. . . . We are certain that our names are the names of things and that the name we bestow will be confirmed by God. And thus each day we solve the ultimate question, frankly confronting each thing as we encounter it; we look for nothing beyond, do not try to walk suspiciously around the object; nor do we peer into its depths, but accept it rather as it is, as it hastens towards us. And then we leave it behind and wait for whatever is to come tomorrow. (58-62)

To escape the power of the past, to transcend the law which constitutes causation, the moment must, at each instant, be reborn. This continuous renewal and resumption of the present is a contribution of the future. The future is the inexhaustible well from which moments are drawn; every instant new-born moments rise and replace the moments disappearing into the past. At each moment the future presents to man the gift of being present to himself. And so man may use his moments freely and then deposit them in the vast receptacle of the past. In the enduring process of receiving and using his moments he is man, master of the present, of his present—for it is truly his, if it is present. It is indeed born anew each instant, and each instant it dies. . . .

Through his surname, man belongs to the past; all that coerces him is contained in that name. Fate has a hold on him, and his surname is the gate by which fate enters—the gate cannot be entirely closed—enters and bears down on him. His other name is his proper name. His parents chose it, and in choosing it drew a line of demarcation beyond which fate cannot trespass. A man's proper name serves as a declaration that this is to be a new human being; it lays claim to the present by confronting man with a future. It always bears with it dreams and desires. . . . His double name reminds him that he can only be a child of man if he does not refuse to be a child of the world and God as well. These latter powers exert their reality by speaking through the mouth of his environment. . . .

And does the man who calls him by his proper name wish to free him? Scarcely ever; perhaps he even attempts to make his life conform to a certain attitude; and yet he does liberate him, though not intending to; he summons him to live his particular and unique present. The future, alive with dreams and desires, speaks through his mouth. Through the voice of many callers, a single voice calls. Each call summons to the future. Who is the caller? . . .

And you, have you not always had the courage to live when you simply proceeded on your way, with the past at your heels, and the light of a dawning tomorrow already touching your brow? (69-71)

He is in possession of the moment and so he has everything. Thus he is enabled to fulfill the commandment given to him because the command is for the moment and always only for the moment. The person which he confronts represents the whole world and the very next instant may represent eternity. But the notion of development deprives him of the privilege of being human—a privilege which is also a duty. Evolution takes the place of man. . . .

If God is to be *something,* he can be neither mind nor nature; nor can he be everything. . . . God cannot be spoken of unless, at the very same moment, a bridge is constructed to man and the world. . . . He bears a name for our sake, so that we may call Him. It is for our sake that He permits Himself to be named and called by that name, since it is only by jointly calling upon Him that we become a "We." . . .

Man should remain human; he should not be converted into a thing, a part of the world, prey to its organization. And the world's law and order should be neither rescinded nor sentimentalized. Man ought to be able to abide by the world's constitution, judge by its laws, measure according to its standards, and yet remain human. He should feel no necessity to withdraw from the world's order because of his humanity. He should not despair and leave unfilled his obligation to judge, to designate, to name those things which the world parades before him. Yet how could he act, were he not sure that his actions and the world-process, his sentiments and its order, interrelate and agree? . . .

Truth waits for him; it stands before his eyes, it is "in thy heart and in thy mouth," within grasping distance; "that thou mayst do it." In the same way as he has achieved certainty concerning the reality of the world and has found the courage to live his life, he must also have faith in Him who brought him into existence. . . . The proper time then is the present—today. To avail himself of today, man must, for better or worse, put his trust in God. (77-81)

A man who asks cannot be disregarded; one must turn away one's eyes to reject his entreaties. As long as one meets him face-to-face, his request must be granted. As long as man is face-to-face with other men, he is protected from violence, if he does not lose his courage and with it the power to ask.

To ask, to pray, is the most human of acts. Even man's silence may entreat; and mute nature acquires speech when it supplicates—as in the case of the silent eyes of an animal. Prayer awakens the man in man. . . . He no sooner offers thanks than he must pray again for that which he requires next—his thanks are universal in intent, his prayer remains for the particular. Thus the cycle of events continues; and connecting prayer and thanksgiving, man and world, is He to whom they are addressed. (86)

Only the holidays merge to form the yearly cycle. Only through the feast days is the everlastingness of the stream experienced; here one sees the stream forever returning on itself. Only here does life become eternal. Then weariness, and anxiety, and disappointment depart; the course of the river has been mapped, the river whose end and beginning are one. But weakness, anxiety, and disappointment exist on the work days; though life gains new strength from the holidays, it does so only to gain further frailties, anxieties and disappointments. The road stretches out before us, but it does not lead, as on feast days, to an ever-young eternity; it is an endless road, an infinite one, extending towards its ultimate end. Life moves towards death.

We have wrestled with the fear to live, with the desire to step outside of the current; now we may discover that reason's illness was merely an attempt to elude death. Man, chilled in the full current of life, sees, like that famous Indian prince, death waiting for him. So he steps outside of life. If living means dying, he prefers not to live. He chooses death in life. He escapes from the inevitability of death into the paralysis of artificial death. We have released him from his paralysis, but we are unable to prevent his death; no physician can do that. By teaching him to live again, we have taught him to move towards death; we have taught him to live, though each step he takes brings him closer to death. . . .

It is so difficult to realize that all verification lies ahead, that death is the ultimate verification of life, that to live means to die. . . . Health is on good terms with Death. It knows that when the Grim Reaper comes he will remove his stone mask and catch the flickering torch from the anxious and weary and disappointed hands of Brother Life; it knows that he will dash it on the ground and extinguish it, but it also knows that only then the full brilliance of the nocturnal sky will brightly glow. It knows that it will be accepted into the open arms of Death. Life's eloquent lips are put to silence and the eternally Taciturn One will speak: "Do you finally recognize me? I am your brother." (89-91)

The Star of Redemption

Speech is truly the creator's morning gift to mankind, and yet at the same time it is the common property of all the children of men, in which each has his particular share and, finally, it is the seal of humanity in man. . . . The miraculous gift of speech was created for man and upon man at creation. Man did not make speech for himself, nor did it come to be for him gradually: at the instant of becoming man, man opened his mouth; at the instant of opening his mouth, he became a human being. (II 29, 222)

It is precisely the thought of creation which first tears the world out of its elemental self-containedness and unmovedness into the current of the universal, which opens outward its eyes hitherto turned inward, which renders its mystery revealed. . . . The creator is at the same time the revealer. Creation is a prediction which is not fulfilled except in the miraculous sign of revelation. . . . The keystone of the somber arch of creation turns into the cornerstone of the bright house of revelation. For the soul, revelation means the experience of a present which, while it rests on the presence of the past, nevertheless does not make its home in it but walks in the light of the divine countenance. . . . God is now present, present like the moment, like any moment, and therewith he proceeds to become a "matter of fact," somthing which as creator he had not yet truly been and which even now he only begins to become. (II 40, 60, 89, 95f.)

Only the love of a lover is such a continually renewed self-sacrifice; in love it is only he who gives himself away. . . . Revelation knows of no "all-loving" father; God's love is ever wholly of the moment and the point to which it is directed, and it attains, point by point, and suffuses the universe in the infinity of time, step by step. . . . His love roams the world with an ever-fresh drive. It is always and wholly of "today," but all the dead past and future will one day be devoured in the victorious to-day. This love is the eternal victory over death. (II 96-99)

The trusting faith of the beloved affirms the momentary love of the lover and consolidates it, too, into something enduring. That is requited love: the faith of the beloved in the lover. By its trust, the faith of the soul attests the love of God and confers upon it an enduring existence. . . . Only in the discovery of a "Thou" is it possible to hear an actual "I," an "I" that is not self-evident but emphatic and underlined. . . . Law operates with times, with a future, with duration: the commandment knows only the moment. . . . Thus the commandment is purely the present. . . . God's "I" remains the key-word, traversing revelation like a single sustained organ note; it resists any translation into "He"; it is an "I" and an "I" it must remain. Only an "I," not a "He," can pronounce the imperative of love, which may never be anything other than "love me." . . . God, the manifest God, only attains being when and as the (human) soul confesses before God's countenance, thereby acknowledging and attesting God's being: "if you acknowledge me, then I am." . . . The historicity of the marvel of creation is not its content—this is and remains its presentness—but rather its reason and its proof. . . . The imperative belongs to revelation as the indicative belongs to creation; only it (the imperative) does not leave the circle of I and Thou. . . . The he-she-it of the third person has sounded for the last time; it was but the base and soil out of which "I and Thou" grew forth. (II 107, 112, 115f., 121, 123, 126)

. . . The I and Thou of human discourse is without more ado also the I and Thou between God and man. The distinction between immanence and transcendence disappears in speech. The Song of Songs is an "authentic," i.e., a "worldly" love lyric; precisely for this reason, not in spite of it, it is a genuinely "spiritual" song of the love of God for man. . . . The person loved only by God is locked against the whole world and locks himself up. This is the element in all mysticism which not only appears unwholesome to every natural feeling but is in fact, objectively speaking, calamitous. . . . Only a man whose answer grows into a word, whose waiting for God grows into walking before him, can be a real, a full human being. (II 143f., 154, 156)

"We" is the pronoun of totality derived from the dual. Unlike "I" and its companion-piece "Thou," whose singularity can only be expanded, the totality of "We" can only be contracted, not expanded. Thus the final stanza of the hymn of redemption begins with this "We." . . . All the voices have now become discrete, each one singing the words in the mode peculiar to its own soul, yet all the modes accommodate themselves to the same rhythm and unite into a single harmony. . . . In the redemption of the world through man, of man by the world, God redeems himself. Man and world disappear in the redemption, but God perfects himself. . . . Man is to love his neighbor like himself. . . . "Like thyself"—not, therefore, "thyself." You remain "Thou" and are to remain "Thou." But your neighbor is not to remain a "He" and in fact, for you, a mere "it"; rather, he is like "Thee," like your "Thou," a "Thou" like you, an "I"—a soul. . . . Redemption originates with God, and man knows neither the day nor the hour (of it). He knows only that he is to love, ever to love his neighborhood and his neighbor. (II 192-194, 196, 198)

The "We" is eternal; before this, eternity's triumphant shout, death plunges into the void. Life itself becomes immortal in the eternal hymn of redemption. . . . Revelation is the guarantee of the world's assumption into eternity. (II 213, 221)

. . . Man must recognize that he is tempted from time to time for the sake of his freedom. He must learn to believe in his freedom. He must believe that his freedom, though it may be circumscribed everywhere else, is without confines in the face of God. . . . There is no act of brotherly love which plunges into the void. Precisely because it has been done blindly, the deed must appear somewhere, anywhere, in a place quite beyond calculation. Had it been done with open eyes, like a purposeful act, then, admittedly, it would be possible for it to drown without a trace. . . . Perhaps it is not too much to say that all the actual effects of love are side-effects. (III 9, 12f.)

Gabriel Marcel

Metaphysical Journal

July 23, 1918

. . . While an empirical *"thou"* can be converted into a *"him,"* God is the absolute "thou" who can never become a *"him."* The meaning of prayer. Scientific knowledge only speaks of the real in the third person. (137)

December 14th, 1918

. . . The very clear relation between the fact that there is no meaning in saying that God *exists*, and the impossibility of attributing characteristics to him, of converting him into a *he* or *it*.

December 18th, 1918

What is preoccupying me this morning is how to understand how God can surpass me infinitely without becoming a *he* or *it* for me. . . . The being to whom I address myself is someone of whom I can speak (and consequently on whom I can reflect). This possibility implies a double limitation of both him and me; it supposes that I can treat him as someone who is not there, that I can set him aside; and also, as far as *I* am concerned, that the bond between us is not absolute (I cannot really discuss the being I love absolutely with a third party). . . . In reality the being I love has not got qualities for me; I grasp him as a whole, that is why he is refractory to predication. . . . Nothing is more false than to identify the *thou* with a bounded and circumscribed content. Participation in divine life can only be grasped as participation in an infinite. . . . To pray is actively to refuse to think God as order, it is to think him as really God, as pure *Thou*. (157-160)

February 25th, 1919

. . . At the moment of my invocation . . . something more than an idea comes into play. Yet the invocation, if I may so put it, must have an ontological foundation. I cannot *really* invoke "anybody"; I can only "pretend to" do so. In other words it appears as if invocation can only be efficacious where there is community. In a deep sense that it is difficult to define we must be already together. (171)

October 15th, 1919

. . . In last analysis the *thou* is essentially that which I can invoke rather than that which I judge to be capable of answering me. . . . My soul is always a *thou* for God; for God it is always confounded with the subject who invokes him. And this can only occur for a subject in the measure in which the subject, through love, imitates what must be called the divine attitude. The more this *me* is an object of study, something described, something whose development is traced, the less it is a soul. Between the idea of soul and the idea of prayer, there is thus an intimate relation. (200)

December 17th, 1919

. . . To think that the world can be an object for God is to *deny God* as God. . . . To think an object . . . is to think that for which I do not matter. . . . Do I not lift myself to the idea of the living God for whom I am *thou* from the idea of a world for which I do not matter? . . . But, for this relation between me and God to be living and enriching, we are concerned with whether we must not renounce grasping God as being in some way above the universe . . . this elevation of the soul to God *above* all that happens is transitory and is only a preliminary step and a preamble so to speak of religious life. . . . I only really lift myself up to God from the moment at which I think that an infinity of other beings also matter for him, or at which I wish they should so matter with all my strength. (229f.)

November 30th, 1920

. . . If God is essentially a *thou*, for whom I exist, for whom I matter and who perhaps is only for me inasmuch as he wills to be, it is easy to understand that he is capable of not being for my neighbour. (n. The ideal substitutions of subject for subject which make objective knowledge possible are strictly impossible here.) Hence we see why no demonstration of the existence of God is possible. There is no logical transition by which we can mount up to God from a starting point which is not God. (261f.)

February 2nd, 1922

. . . There must be no question of enclosing God within the circle of his relations with me. (281)

March 5th, 1923

. . . I am obliged to admit that it is absurd to speak of *the* "thou" and thus to consider as a substantive what at bottom is the very negation of all substantiality. In reality, once I have singled it out, I objectivise a particular aspect of the experience of intimacy. From the core of the *us* I subtract the element that is *not-me* and call it *thou*. This element has an automatic tendency to take on the character of the *him*. And it is only in the measure in which I succeed in re-living this experience of intimacy after the event that I am able to resist this temptation. (303)

May 24, 1923

. . . As soon as we adopt a polemical attitude regarding the object of religion, the object of religion changes its nature. (313)

Being and Having

We can find no salvation for mind or soul unless we see the difference between our being and our life. . . . Since I *am* not my life, my life must have been given to me; in a sense unfathomable to man, I am previous to it; *I am* comes before *I live*. Second, my being is something which is in jeopardy from the moment my life begins, and must be saved; my being is a stake, and therein perhaps lies the whole meaning of life. And from this second point of view, I am not *before* but *beyond* my life. This is the only possible way to explain the ordeal of human life (and if it is not an ordeal, I do not see what else it can be). (199)

. . . Where the *whole* of a person is involved, no one can put himself *in my place*. And faith, when it is most real and most like itself (for we must of course not consider its degraded or mechanical expressions here) is most sure to issue from the whole being of a man and to *involve* him. (210)

The Philosophy of Existentialism

Faithfulness . . . refers invariably to a presence, or to something which can be maintained within us and before us as a presence, but which, *ipso facto,* can be just as well ignored, forgotten and obliterated: . . . Presence is mystery in the exact measure in which it is presence. . . . Fidelity is the active perpetuation of presence (35f.). . . . Presence involves a reciprocity which is excluded from any relation of subject to object or of subject to subject-object. (40)

. . . Existentialism stands to-day at a parting of the ways: it is, in the last analysis, obliged either to deny or to transcend itself. It denies itself quite simply when it falls to the level of infra-dialectical materialism. It transcends itself, or it tends to transcend itself, when it opens itself out to the experience of the suprahuman, an experience which can hardly be ours in a genuine and lasting way this side of death, but of which the reality is attested by mystics, and of which the possibility is warranted by any philosophy which refuses to be immured in the postulate of absolute immanence or to subscribe in advance to the denial of the beyond and of the unique and veritable transcendence. Not that there is anything in this which, in our itinerant condition, we can invest like a capital; this absolute life can be apprehended by us only in flashes and by virtue of a hidden initiative which can be nothing other than grace. I am, of course, thinking of the extravagantly dogmatic negativism which is common to Sartre, to Heidegger and even to Jaspers. (88)

My claim that I am free to respond or to refuse my response can always be questioned; for are there not indigent and ungrateful natures who are deprived of the gift of responding? Just as there are others who are incapable of trust, that is to say of faith, and who are therefore unable to recognise that life is a gift and that all things are given to them? . . . The question arises in this form only in a world where the individual is totally insulated. . . . In such a world, short of an especial grace, he is indeed doomed to see himself, like the man of Heidegger and of Sartre, as the victim of some cosmic catastrophe, flung into an alien universe to which he is bound by nothing. (102)

Faith and Reality

If I believe in something, it means that I place myself at the disposal of something, or again that I pledge myself fundamentally, and this pledge affects not only *what I have* but also *what I am*. In a modern philosophical vocabulary, this could be expressed by saying that to belief is attached an existential index which, in principle, is completely lacking to conviction. . . . If I *believe in*, I *rally to;* with that sort of interior gathering of oneself which the act of rallying implies. From this point of view one might say that the strongest belief, or more exactly the most living belief, is that which absorbs most fully all the powers of your being. . . .

. . . It is not certain that there is any real opposition between the personal and the suprapersonal. I should be much more inclined to admit that the personal is authentically itself only by reason of whatever is in it which smashes the frame in which it is always in danger of allowing itself to be imprisoned as *ego* pure and simple. In any case, I shall be able to open a credit only to what presents itself to me as incapable of being reduced to the condition which is that of *things*. The distinguishing mark of things lies, in fact, in being unable ever to provide me with anything which can be made to resemble an answer. . . . One cannot have confidence except in a "*toi*," in a reality which is capable of functioning as "*toi*," of being invoked, of being something to which one can have recourse. (87-89)

Prayer is possible only when intersubjectivity is recognized, where it is operative. . . . The intersubjective can only be acknowledged freely, and that implies further that it is always within our power to deny it. (119)

. . . When it is a question of the *transcendent Being*, to whom I am compelled to open an absolute, that is to say an unconditional, credit; . . . the more unconditional my faith is, the more genuine it will be. (153)

What we have to find out is whether one can radically separate faith in a God conceived in His sanctity from any affirmation which bears on the destiny of the intersubjective unity which is formed by beings who love one another and who live in and by one another. What is really important, in fact, is the destiny of that living link, and not that of an entity which is isolated and closed in on itself. That is what we more or less explicitly mean when we assert our faith in personal immortality. . . . Human love itself is nothing, it lies to itself, if it is not charged with infinite possibilities. . . . If human love is centered on itself, if it sinks into a mutually shared narcissism, it turns into idolatry and pronounces its own death sentence. (173-175)

. . . Each one of us is in a position to recognize that his own essence is a *gift*—that it is not a *datum;* that he himself is a gift, and that he has no existence at all through himself. On the other hand, however, it is on the basis of that gift that freedom can grow or expand—that freedom which coincides with the trial in the course of which each man will have to make his own decision. This trial implies a decisive option. I can put my meaning to you by saying that the physical possibility of suicide which is engraved in our nature of incarnate beings is nothing but the expression of another much more profound and more hidden possibility, the possibility of a spiritual denial of self or, what comes to the same thing, of an impious and demoniac affirmation of self which amounts to a radical rejection of being. There is a sense in which that rejection is the final falsehood and absurdity; for it can exist only *through* someone who is; but as it becomes embodied it develops into perverted being. (194)

The history of modern philosophy . . . seems to supply abundant illustrations of the progressive replacement of *atheism,* in the grammatically privative sense of the word, by an *anti-theism* whose mainspring is the will that God should not be. . . . If a man has experienced the presence of God, not only has he no need of proofs, he may even go so far as to consider the idea of a demonstration as a slur on what is for him a sacred evidence. Now, from the point of view of a philosophy of existence, it is this sort of testimony which is the central and irreducible datum. . . .

. . . From the point of view I have adopted, anguish is not and cannot be the last word. I should be so bold as to say, on the contrary, that the last word must be with love and joy; and this I say from my innermost heart. If we want to satisfy ourselves of the truth of this, we must emphasize the intelligible aspect of faith; and in doing so, we shall be obliged to diverge very considerably from the views both of the Danish philosopher and even perhaps of the writer in whom we may well be inclined to see his precursor—I mean Pascal. . . . (197-199)

. . . All authentic sin is sin against the light; in other words, against the universal. At root, it is the act of shutting oneself in on oneself or of taking one's own self as a centre. (203)

. . . From the moment when we open ourselves to these infiltrations of the invisible, we cease to be the unskilled and yet pretentious soloists we perhaps were at the start, and gradually become members, wide-eyed and brotherly, of an orchestra in which those whom we so inaptly call the dead are quite certainly much closer to Him of whom we should not perhaps say that He conducts the symphony, but that He *is* the symphony in its profound and intelligible unity; a unity in which we can hope to be included only by degrees, through individual trials, the sum total of which, though it cannot be foreseen by each of us, is inseparable from his own vocation. (210)

Nicolas Berdyaev

Freedom and the Spirit

Spirit is freedom unconstrained by the outward and the objective, where what is deep and inward determines all. To be in the spirit is to be in oneself. So far as the spirit is concerned the constraint of the natural world is only the reflection of inward processes. The religious pathos of freedom is the pathos of spirituality; to win true freedom is to enter into the spiritual world. (117) . . . It is the freedom of the spirit from which all nature springs. Freedom does not raise us up towards nature, but towards the idea of the divine, and towards the void which is prior to being. It is rooted in non-being. Free activity is original and entirely irrational, for all rational conceptions of it involve its identification with the phenomena of nature. . . . It is in freedom that the inward activity of all life is made perceptible. The experience of freedom is known to every being possessing a spiritual life. . . . The original phenomena of action and creation in their essentially dynamic character are given in the life of the spirit, and it is only in their secondary aspect that we catch a glimpse of them in the natural and determined world of external causality. (124f.)

Christ . . . wants us to accept Him freely, He desires the unforced love of man, and He can never compel anyone for He always has regard for our freedom. God can only accept the free. God expects the free love of man and man expects freedom from God, that is to say, the divine truth which will make him free. . . . True liberty is that which God demands from us and not that which we demand from God. It is upon this deep foundation that man's freedom is based; it is latent in the deepest recesses of his being. Truth gives us the highest kind of freedom but freedom is necessary for the acceptance of this truth. Truth can neither constrain nor compel, and it cannot give freedom to man through violence . . . Freedom cannot be the result of constraint even were this constraint divine. . . . The freedom of the spirit is not only the freedom of God, it is also that of man. Human freedom is not only freedom in God, but also freedom in relation to God. Man must be free in respect of God, the world, and his own nature. Freedom in the acceptance of Truth cannot be won from Truth itself, for it is prior to it. Freedom is not identical with goodness and perfection of life. (126f.)

Man bears upon him the mark of the divine image, he is the divine idea, the divine plan, without, however, being divine by nature, for had he been so he would not have been free. The freedom of man presupposes the possibility of his divinization as well as the possibility of the destruction of the divine idea and image. (131)

In human nature the divine idea and image have been obscured in the primal void of initial non-being, from which God called man to life by the act of creation. But human nature remains capable of enlightenment and there remains within it an ardent longing for the divine which makes both revelation and salvation possible. Evil has not finally possessed man's nature for it is a dual nature belonging to two worlds, and even after the Fall man did not completely break with God, Who continues to have dealings with him and to impart to him His regenerative powers. Man does not belong exclusively to the realm of non-being; he maintains a link with the Being whose activity is still directed towards him. (170)

Redemption is a dual process in which both God and man share; yet it is but one process, not two. Without human nature and the exercise of human freedom it would be impossible. (177)

Man's creative action, which is a continuation of the creation of the universe, is not arbitrary in character nor is it a revolt; rather it is the submission and surrender to God of all the forces of his spirit. Man in his creative love for God does not only invoke Him on behalf of his human needs, expecting salvation from Him: he also offers Him all the superabundance of his forces and all his fathomless liberty with absolute disinterestedness. If man does not bring his creative gift to God, if he does not participate actively in building the Kingdom of God, if he shows himself to be a slave, if he buries his talents in the earth, then the creation of the world will receive a check and the fulness of the divine-human life conceived by God will not be realized. (212f.)

The Promethean principle is the eternal principle without which man could not exist. In his separation from God man was obliged to exalt himself by the affirmation of the Promethean principle, without which he would have remained in a state of confusion, and could not even have been revealed. Man had to free himself from this submission to the gods of nature. . . . The image of man could only be manifested through the medium of this heroic and titanic principle of rebellion against the gods. It is the cosmic struggle in the sufferings of which man is born. (226)

The Destiny of Man

The Divine Nothing or the Absolute of the negative theology cannot be the Creator of the world. This has been made clear by German speculative mysticism. It is the burden of Eckehardt's doctrine of the *Gottheit* and of Boehme's conception of the *Ungrund.* Out of the Divine Nothing, the *Gottheit* or the *Ungrund,* the Holy Trinity, God the Creator is born. The creation of the world by God the Creator is a secondary act. From this point of view it may be said that freedom is not created by God: it is rooted in the Nothing, in the *Ungrund* from all eternity. Freedom is not determined by God; it is part of the nothing out of which God created the world. The opposition between God the Creator and freedom is secondary: in the primeval mystery of the Divine Nothing this opposition is transcended, for both God and freedom are manifested out of the *Ungrund.* God the Creator cannot be held responsible for freedom which gave rise to evil. Man is the child of God and the child of freedom—of nothing, of non-being, *το μηον*. Meonic freedom consented to God's act of creation; non-being freely accepted being. But through it man fell away from the work of God, evil and pain came into the world, and being was mixed with non-being. This is the real tragedy both of the world and of God. God longs for His "other," His friend; He wants him to answer the call to enter the fullness of the divine life and participate in God's creative work of conquering non-being. God does not answer His own call: the answer is from freedom which is independent of Him. God the Creator is all-powerful over being, over the created world, but He has no power over non-being, over the uncreated freedom which is impenetrable to Him. In the first act of creation God appears as the Maker of the world. But that act cannot avert the possibility of evil contained in meonic freedom. The myth of the Fall tells of this powerlessness of the creator to avert the evil resulting from freedom which He has not created. Then comes God's second act in relation to the world and to man. God appears not in the aspect of Creator but of Redeemer and Saviour, in the aspect of the suffering God who takes upon Himself the sins of the world. God in the aspect of God-the-Son descends into the abyss, into the *Ungrund,* into the depths of freedom out of which springs evil as well as every kind of good. . . .

God creates out of nothing the world and man and expects from them an answer to His call—an answer from the depths of freedom. At first the answer was consent to creation, then it was rebellion and hostility towards God, a return to original non-being. All rebellion against God is a return to non-being which assumes the form of false, illusory being, and is a victory of non-being over the divine light. And it is only then that the nothing which is not evil becomes evil. Then comes God's second act: He descends into non-being, into the abyss of freedom that has degenerated into evil; He manifests Himself not in power but in sacrifice. The Divine sacrifice, the Divine self-crucifixion must conquer evil meonic freedom by enlightening it from within without forcing it, without depriving the created world of freedom. . . . Man's "nature" is created by God, but his "freedom" is not created, not determined by any being and is prior to all being. Being springs from freedom and not freedom from being. (25-27)

The element of freedom does not come from God the Father, for it is prior to being. The tragedy in God is connected with freedom: God the Creator has absolute power over being, but not over freedom. Fathomless freedom springing from non-being entered the created world, consenting to the act of creation. God the Creator has done everything to bring light into that freedom, in harmony with His great conception of creation. But without destroying freedom He could not conquer the potency of evil contained in it. This is why there is tragedy and evil in the world; all tragedy is connected with freedom. And we can only reconcile ourselves to the tragedy of the world because God suffers in it too.

God shares His creatures' destiny. He sacrifices Himself for the world and for man whom He loves and yearns for. . . .

Three principles are active in the world: Providence, i.e. the supercosmic God; freedom, i.e. the human spirit; and fate or destiny, i.e. nature, the solidified, hardened outcome of the dark meonic freedom. The interaction between these three principles constitutes the complexity of the cosmic and the human life. . . . God created man in His own image and likeness, i.e. made him a creator too, calling him to free spontaneous activity and not to formal obedience to His power. Free creativeness is the creature's answer to the great call of its Creator. Man's creative work is the fulfilment of the Creator's secret will. But creativeness by its very nature is creation out of nothing, i.e. out of meonic freedom which is prior to the world itself. This element of freedom springing from the pre-existential abyss is present in every creative act of man, in artistic conception and inspiration. (29-32)

Through dividedness, pain and suffering man ascends to wholeness, unattainable for consciousness, to regeneration and bliss in God. Through the experience of evil he reaches the highest good. . . . There are three stages in the development of the spirit: the original paradisaical wholeness, pre-conscious wholeness which has not had the experience of thought and of freedom; division, reflection, valuation, freedom of choice; and, finally, superconscious wholeness and completeness that comes after freedom, reflection and valuation. (39)

The Beginning and the End

There is in this world no objective order of which there could be, in the commonly accepted phraseology, ontological, metaphysical and noumenal knowledge. There is no eternal and unchangeable "natural" order side by side with which the theologians recognize a "supernatural" order as a supplement to the "natural." The "natural" order to which only a relative and temporary stability belongs is simply a concatenation of phenomena which are open to scientific explanation. It is always an empirical, not a metaphysical order. Spirit can upset and change the "natural" order. . . . Spirit is not an epiphenomenon of the material world, the material world is an epiphenomenon of spirit. . . .

The most important task which the mind has to face is that of ceasing to objectify God, to give up thinking of him in naturalistic terms after the analogy of the things of this world and their relation with one another. God is a mystery but he is a mystery with which it is possible to enter into communion. There is nothing of God in the dull and prosaic normality of the objective world order. It is only in a disruptive act which breaks through the commonplace normality that he is to be found.

A supremacy over being belongs to freedom: and to spirit there belongs a supremacy over the whole of congealed nature. But freedom too is a mystery, it is not open to rationalization. The mysterious nature of freedom is expressed in the fact that while it creates a new and better life, it gives rise at the same time to evil, in other words, it possesses a capacity for self-destruction. . . .

. . . Freedom is not a teleological philosophy. Subordination to an end, for the sake of which man is compelled to come to terms with the most unfitting and improper means, is opposed to the freedom of man. What is important is not the aim, but the creative energy, the nobility of human beings who are creating life. And again what is important is radiation out of the depth, which illumines the life of men. (154-156)

Freedom involves the freedom of evil as well. Without the freedom of evil, good would not be free, it would be determined and imposed by force. At the same time, however, the freedom of evil gives rise to the necessity of servitude. Slavery itself can be the child of freedom, and there would be no freedom if it did not carry with it this possibility of giving rise to slavery; there would be but the servitude of good. But the servitude of the good is an evil thing, and the freedom of evil can be a greater good than the good which is a result of compulsion. It is a paradox to which no solution can be found within the confines of the history of the objective world, and it exerts a pull towards the end. (247)

The primary mystery is the mystery of the birth of God in man (who includes the world in himself) and the birth of man in God. In our imperfect language this means that there is in God a need for a responsive creative act on the part of man. Man is not merely a sinner; the consciousness of sin is but an experience which moves him as he treads his path; man is also a creator. The human tragedy from which there is no escape, the dialectic of freedom, necessity and grace finds its solution within the orbit of the divine Mystery, within the Deity, which lies deeper than the drama between Creator and creature. (254)

The Divine and the Human

Revelation is the fact of the Spirit in me, in the subject; it is spiritual experience, spiritual life. The intellectualist interpretation of revelation which finds its expression in dogmatics is precisely its objectivization, its adjustment to the average level of normal thought. But the events of the Spirit described in Holy Scripture, the manifestations of the Spirit in the lives of the apostles and saints were not of an intellectual character, the entire spiritual nature of man came into operation in them. . . .

The religious phenomenon has two sides; it is the disclosure of God in man and of man in God. The yearning of man for God comes to light in it and the yearning of God for man. Traditional rational theology denies this yearning of God for man from the fear of introducing affective passionate life into God. For the rational concept of perfection does not admit of yearning and need in the notion of completeness; it prefers the perfection of a stone. In that case the relations between God and man cease to be a drama of two which is capable of resolution in a third. Revelation is a creative act of the Spirit; it has both a theogonic and an anthropogonic character. (14f.)

The revelation of the Spirit . . . will be a divine-human revelation. The separation and opposition of the divine and the human will be overcome in the Spirit, although the distinction between them will be preserved. . . . Just as one cannot break the bond between the divine and the human, and affirm one of these principles in the abstract, so we must not make a break between the transcendent and the immanent, and affirm either of them in the abstract. Real life is in the inter-relation between the one and the other. The transcendent becomes immanent and without its immanence it is abstract and lifeless. It is merely objectivization at its limit. And equally the immanent must not be thought of without the transcendent. Life in the immanent postulates a process of transcendence. Pure immanentism which denies the transcendent is continuance in a circle which has no outlet. When the human is looked upon as the divine, and the identity of the two is affirmed, authentic life comes to an end and its dramatic character exists no longer. When the transcendent is thought of exclusively as immanent and there is no transcendent mystery and remoteness, the immanent is deprived of life and content. . . .

In the religion of the Spirit, the religion of freedom, everything will appear in a new light. There will be no authority and no retribution; the nightmare of a legalistic conception of Christianity and of an everlasting hell, will finally disappear. It will have as its basis not judgment at a tribunal and retribution, but creative development and transfiguration, assimilation to God. A new anthropology will be revealed and the religious meaning of human creativeness will be recognized. It will be understood that freedom is its primary basis. The idea of God will be purified from servile sociomorphism. The idea of God as sufficient unto Himself and as a potentate who wields power, still includes relics of an idolatry which is not yet overcome. It is only the conception of God as suffering, and yearning for the Other, and as sacrificed, which subdues atheism and the fight against God. There is a paradox in the knowledge of God which must be courageously faced and put into words, thus: the affirmation of God by my whole being means that God exists; human freedom creates God, and this means that God is; my creating of God is a divine-human act of creation. (183-185)

. . . The objectivization of Spirit, its alienation from itself, its projection into the external, is the chief hindrance to a new outpouring of the Holy Spirit in the world. (190)

It is only the path of evil which is fated. The path of good is constructed upon the freedom of man, who shares in the creation of the world. . . . The positive end, the end which decides things, must depend upon man as well, not only upon God. Fate can be overcome by freedom. . . . Spirit is freedom. Free community can only be the result of a movement which is both spiritual and social, and in which the spiritual and the social cease to be separate and opposed. . . . That which happened individually in the God-Man ought to happen in God-manhood, and that will be the third revelation of the Spirit. It is impossible to reconcile oneself to the idea that the creative vital impulse, the moments of luminous joy, of creative love and liberation, which have been experienced in ecstasy, will all disappear for ever, come to nothing and leave no trace. At the end of revelation there is infinity, not the sinister infinity which knows no end, but the good infinity which is eternity. (192f.)

. . . Existential time, which has its roots in eternity, remains, and it is in existential time that the end of things takes place. . . . From the philosophical point of view the end of the world and history is above all the triumph over objectivization, that is to say triumph over the world of alienation, necessity, impersonality, and hostility. It is the formation of a world of objects which is the source of all the misfortunes of man. The object is alien and intolerable to me.* (197f.)

* Sartre, whose philosophy is fashionable nowadays, a gifted man, and very characteristic of our time, is in fact the slave of objectivity, the world of things, the world of phenomena, which has no reality in itself. It is a profound truth that reality depends upon the creative activity of man. But Sartre would think that behind the apparent there is nothing, there is no mystery. See his book, *L'Etre et le Néant,* and mine, *Solitude and Society.*

The greatest religious and moral truth to which man must grow, is that we cannot be saved individually. My salvation presupposes the salvation of others also, the salvation of my neighbour, it presupposes universal salvation, the salvation of the whole world, the transfiguration of the world. The very idea of salvation arises from the oppressed condition of man; and it is associated with a forensic conception of Christianity. This ought to be replaced by the idea of creative transformation and enlightenment, by the idea of perfecting all life. "Behold I make all things new." It is not only God Who makes all things new, it is man too. The period of the end is not only a period of destruction, but also a period of divine-human creativeness, a new life and a new world. (201f.)

Paul Tillich

Existence and the Christ

The existential question, namely, man himself in the conflicts of his existential situation, is not the source for the revelatory answer formulated by theology. One cannot derive the divine self-manifestation from an analysis of the human predicament. God speaks to the human situation, against it, and for it. Theological supranaturalism, as represented, for example, by contemporary neo-orthodox theology, is right in asserting the inability of man to reach God under his own power. Man is the question, not the answer. It is equally wrong to derive the question implied in human existence from the revelatory answer. This is impossible because the revelatory answer is meaningless if there is no question to which it is the answer. Man cannot receive an answer to a question he has not asked. . . . The question, asked by man, is man himself. He asks it, whether or not he is vocal about it. He cannot avoid asking it, because his very being is the question of his existence. In asking it, he is alone with himself. He asks "out of the depth," and this depth is he himself. (13)

The material of the existential question is taken from the whole of human experience and its manifold ways of expression. This refers to past and present, to popular language and great literature, to art and philosophy, to science and psychology. It refers to myth and liturgy, to religious traditions, and to present experiences. All this, as far as it reflects man's existential predicament, is the material without the help of which the existential question cannot be formulated. The choice of the material, as well as the formulation of the question, is the task of the systematic theologian.

In order to do so, he must participate in the human predicament, not only actually—as he always does—but also in conscious identification. He must participate in man's finitude, which is also his own, and in its anxiety as though he had never received the revelatory answer of "eternity." He must participate in man's estrangement, which is also his own, and show the anxiety of guilt as though he had never received the revelatory answer of "forgiveness." The theologian does not rest on the theological answer which he announces. He can give it in a convincing way only if he participates with his whole being in the situation of the question, namely, the human predicament. . . . The question implied in human finitude is directed toward the answer: the eternal. The question implied in human estrangement is directed toward the answer: forgiveness. . . . The substance of the answers—the revelatory experience—is independent of the questions. But the form of the theological answer is *not* independent of the form of the existential question. . . . The answer can prejudice the question to such a degree that the seriousness of the existential predicament is lost. Or the question can prejudice the answer to such a degree that the revelatory character of the answer is lost. (15f.)

. . . A cognitive attitude in which the element of involvement is dominant is called "existential." The converse is also true. Since the element of involvement is so dominant, the most striking existentialist analyses have been made by novelists, poets, and painters. But even they could escape irrelevant subjectivity only by submitting themselves to detached and objective observation. As a result, the material brought out by the detached methods of therapeutic psychology are used in existentialist literature and art. Involvement and detachment are poles, not conflicting alternatives; there is no existentialist analysis without non-existential detachment. (26)

Man has freedom in contrast to all other creatures. They have analogies to freedom but not freedom itself. But man is finite, excluded from the infinity to which he belongs. One can say that nature is finite necessity, God is infinite freedom, man is finite freedom. It is finite freedom which makes possible the transition from essence to existence.

Man is free, in so far as he has language. With his language, he has universals which liberate him from bondage to the concrete situation to which even the highest animals are subjected. Man is free, in so far as he is able to ask questions about the world he encounters, including himself, and to penetrate into deeper and deeper levels of reality. Man is free, in so far as he can receive unconditional moral and logical imperatives which indicate that he can transcend the conditions which determine every finite being. Man is free, in so far as he has the power of deliberating and deciding, thus cutting through the mechanisms of stimulus and response. Man is free, in so far as he can play and build imaginary structures above the real structures to which he, like all beings, is bound. Man is free, in so far as he has the faculty of creating worlds above the given world, of creating the world of technical tools and products, the world of artistic expressions, the world of theoretical structures and practical organizations. Finally, man is free, in so far as he has the power of contradicting himself and his essential nature. Man is free even from his freedom; that is, he can surrender his humanity.

God is his own destiny. This means that he transcends the polarity of freedom and destiny. In man freedom and destiny limit each other, for he has finite freedom. This is true of every act of human freedom; it is true also of the final quality of human freedom, namely, the power of surrendering his freedom. Even the freedom of self-contradiction is limited by destiny. As finite freedom, it is possible only within the context of the universal transition from essence to existence. There is no individual Fall. In the Genesis story the two sexes and nature, represented by the serpent, work together. The transition from essence to existence is possible because finite freedom works within the frame of a universal destiny. . . . Only he who is the image of God has the power of separating himself from God. His greatness and his weakness are identical. Even God could not remove the one without removing the other. And if man had not received this possibility, he would have been a thing among things, unable to serve the divine glory, either in salvation or in condemnation. (31-33)

Creation and the Fall coincide in so far as there is no point in time and space in which created goodness was actualized and had existence. (44)

. . . One should speak of condemnation as removal from the eternal. This seems to be implied in the term "eternal death," which certainly cannot mean everlasting death, since death has no duration. The experience of separation from one's eternity is the state of despair. It points beyond the limits of temporality and to the situation of being bound to the divine life without being united with it in the central act of personal love. Neither experience nor language allows us to say more about it. For the negative can be experienced and spoken of only in union with the positive. Both for time and for eternity, one must say that even in the state of separation God is creatively working in us—even if his creativity takes the way of destruction. Man is never cut off from the ground of being, not even in the state of condemnation. (78)

Dynamics of Faith

Man is able to understand in an immediate personal and central act the meaning of the ultimate, the unconditional, the absolute, the infinite. This alone makes faith a human potentiality. . . . The term "ultimate concern" unites the subjective and the objective side of the act of faith. . . . In terms like ultimate, unconditional, infinite, absolute, the difference between subjectivity and objectivity is overcome. The ultimate of the act of faith and the ultimate that is meant in the act of faith are one and the same. (9-11)

Faith as the state of ultimate concern claims the whole man and cannot be restricted to the subjectivity of mere feeling. It claims truth for its concern and commitment to it. (39)

God as the ultimate in man's ultimate concern is more certain than any other certainty, even that of oneself. God as symbolized in a divine figure is a matter of daring faith, of courage and risk. (47)

The criterion of the truth of faith . . . is that it implies an element of self-negation. That symbol is most adequate which expresses not only the ultimate but also its own lack of ultimacy. Christianity expresses itself in such a symbol in contrast to all other religions, namely, in the Cross of the Christ. Jesus could not have been the Christ without sacrificing himself as Jesus to himself as the Christ. Any acceptance of Jesus as the Christ which is not the acceptance of Jesus the crucified is a form of idolatry. The ultimate concern of the Christian is not Jesus, but the Christ Jesus who is manifest as the crucified. The event which has created this symbol has given the criterion by which the truth of Christianity, as well as of any other religion, must be judged. . . . The fact that this criterion is identical with the Protestant principle and has become reality in the Cross of the Christ constitutes the superiority of Protestant Christianity. (97f.)

Out of the element of participation follows the certainty of faith; out of the element of separation follows the doubt in faith. And each is essential for the nature of faith. . . . Neither faith nor doubt can be eliminated from man as man. . . . Living faith includes the doubt about itself, the courage to take this doubt into itself, and the risk of courage. (100-102)

The ultimate concern gives depth, direction and unity to all other concerns and, with them, to the whole personality. A personal life which has these qualities is integrated, and the power of a personality's integration is his faith. . . . If a uniting center is absent, the infinite variety of the encountered world, as well as of the inner movements of the human mind, is able to produce or complete disintegration of the personality. There can be no other uniting center than the ultimate concern of the mind. (105, 107)

. . . Faith is not a phenomenon beside others, but the central phenomenon in man's personal life, manifest and hidden at the same time. It is religious and transcends religion, it is universal and concrete, it is infinitely variable and always the same. . . . It is the triumph of the dynamics of faith that any denial of faith is itself an expression of faith, of an ultimate concern. (126f.)

Systematic Theology

VOLUME I

If we speak, as we must, of the ego-thou relation between God and man, the thou embraces the ego and consequently the entire relation. If it were otherwise, if the ego-thou relation with God was proper rather than symbolic, the ego could withdraw from the relation. But there is no place to which man can withdraw from the divine thou, because it includes the ego and is nearer to the ego than the ego to itself. Ultimately, it is an insult to the divine holiness to talk about God as we do of objects whose existence or nonexistence can be discussed. It is an insult to the divine holiness to treat God as a partner with whom one collaborates or as a superior power whom one influences by rites and prayers. The holiness of God makes it impossible to draw him into the context of the ego-world and the subject-object correlation. He himself is the ground and meaning of this correlation, not an element within it. The holiness of God requires that in relation to him we leave behind the totality of finite relations and enter into a relation which, in the categorical sense of the word, is not a relation at all. We can bring all our relations into the sphere of the holy; we can consecrate the finite, including its internal and external relations, through the experience of the holy; but to do so we must first transcend all these relations. Theology, which by its nature is always in the danger of drawing God into the cognitive relation of the subject-object structure of being, should strongly point to the holiness of God and his unapproachable character in judgment of itself. (271f.)

. . . The ego-thou relation, although it is the central and most dynamic relation, is not the only one, for God is being-itself. In appellations like "Almighty God" the irresistible power of God's creativity is felt; in "Eternal God" the unchangeable ground of all life is indicated. . . . Contemplating the mystery of the divine ground, considering the infinity of the divine life, intuiting the marvel of the divine creativity, adoring the inexhaustible meaning of the divine self-manifestation—all these experiences are related to God without involving an explicit ego-thou relation. (289)

The Courage to Be

Acceptance by something which is less than personal could never overcome personal self-rejection. . . . Even if one is personally accepted it needs a self-transcending courage to accept this acceptance, it needs the courage of confidence. For being accepted does not mean that guilt is denied. . . . The ultimate power of self-affirmation can only be the power of being-itself. Everything less than this, one's own or anybody else's finite power of being, cannot overcome the radical, infinite threat of nonbeing which is experienced in the despair of self-condemnation. . . . The courage of confidence is conditioned not by anything finite but solely by that which is unconditional itself and which we experience as unconditional in a person-to-person encounter. (166f.)

The faith which makes the courage of despair possible is the acceptance of the power of being, even in the grip of nonbeing. Even in the despair about meaning being affirms itself through us. The act of accepting meaninglessness is in itself a meaningful act. It is an act of faith. . . . The vitality that can stand the abyss of meaninglessness is aware of a hidden meaning within the destruction of meaning. . . .

The theologians who speak so strongly and with such self-certainty about the divine-human encounter should be aware of a situation in which this encounter is prevented by radical doubt and nothing is left but absolute faith. . . . The courage to be in its radical form is a key to an idea of God which transcends both mysticism and the person-to-person encounter. (176-178)

Nonbeing, (that in God which makes his self-affirmation dynamic) opens up the divine self-seclusion and reveals him as power and love. Nonbeing makes God a living God. . . . Courage participates in the self-affirmation of being-itself, it participates in the power of being which prevails against nonbeing. . . . There are no valid arguments for the "existence" of God, but there are acts of courage in which we affirm the power of being, whether we know it or not. . . . The content of absolute faith is the "God above God." Absolute faith and its consequence, the courage that takes the radical doubt, the doubt about God, into itself, transcends the theistic idea of God. (180-182)

The God of theological theism is a being beside others and as such a part of the whole of reality. . . . He is seen as a self which has a world, as an ego which is related to a thou, as a cause which is separated from its effect, as having a definite space and an endless time. He is a being, not being-itself. As such he is bound to the subject-object structure of reality, he is an object for us as subjects. At the same time we are objects for him as a subject. And this is decisive for the necessity of transcending theological theism. For God as a subject makes me into an object which is nothing more than an object. He deprives me of my subjectivity because he is all-powerful and all-knowing. I revolt and try to make *him* into an object, but the revolt fails and becomes desperate. God appears as the invincible tyrant, the being in contrast with whom all other beings are without freedom and subjectivity. . . . This is the God Nietzsche said had to be killed because nobody can tolerate being made into a mere object of absolute knowledge and absolute control. This is the deepest root of atheism. . . . It is also the deepest root of the Existentialist despair and the widespread anxiety of meaninglessness in our period.

Theism in all its forms is transcended in the experience we have called absolute faith. It is the accepting of the acceptance without somebody or something that accepts. It is the power of being-itself that accepts and gives the courage to be. . . . Only if the God of theism is transcended can the anxiety of doubt and meaninglessness be taken into the courage to be. The God above God is the object of all mystical longing, but mysticism also must be transcended in order to reach him. Mysticism does not take seriously the concrete and the doubt concerning the concrete. It plunges directly into the ground of being and meaning, and leaves the concrete, the world of finite values and meanings, behind. Therefore it does not solve the problem of meaninglessness. In terms of the present religious situation this means that Eastern mysticism is not the solution of the problems of Western Existentialism. . . .

The God above the God of theism is present, although hidden, in every divine-human encounter. Biblical religion as well as Protestant theology are aware of the paradoxical character of this encounter. They are aware that if God encounters man God is neither object nor subject and is therefore above the scheme into which theism has forced him. They are aware that personalism with respect to God is balanced by a transpersonal presence of the divine. They are aware that forgiveness can be accepted only if the power of acceptance is effective in man—biblically speaking, if the power of grace is effective in man. They are aware of the paradoxical character of every prayer, of speaking to somebody to whom you cannot speak because he is not "somebody," of asking somebody of whom you cannot ask anything because he gives or gives not before you ask, of saying "thou" to somebody who is nearer to the I than the I is to itself. Each of these paradoxes drives the religious consciousness toward a God above the God of theism. . . .

Absolute faith, or the state of being grasped by the God beyond God, is not a state which appears beside other states of the mind. It never is something separated and definite, an event which could be isolated and described. It is always a movement in, with, and under other states of the mind. It is the situation on the boundary of man's possibilities. It *is* this boundary. Therefore it is both the courage of despair and the courage in and above every courage. It is not a place where one can live, it is without the safety of words and concepts, it is without a name, a church, a cult, a theology. But it is moving in the depth of all of them. It is the power of being, in which they participate and of which they are fragmentary expressions. (184-189)

Biblical Religion and the Search for Ultimate Reality

Man can experience the holy in and through everything, but, as the holy, it cannot be less than he is; it cannot be a-personal. Nothing that is less than we, nothing that encounters less than the center of our personality, can be of ultimate concern for us. . . . The personal encounter in religious experience is as real as the encounter of subject and object in the cognitive experience or the encounter of vision and meaning in the artistic experience. In this sense religious personalism expresses reality, namely, reality within the religious encounter. (24f.)

It is the unconditional character of the biblical God that makes the relation to him radically personal. For only that which concerns us in the center of our personal existence concerns us unconditionally. The God who is unconditional in power, demand, and promise is the God who makes us completely personal and who, consequently, is completely personal in our encounter with him. (27)

His Word is an event created by the divine Spirit in the human spirit. It is both driving power and infinite meaning. The Word of God is God's creative self-manifestation and not a conversation between two beings. Therefore, the Word is one of the aspects of God himself; it is God manifesting himself to himself. . . . The Word is an element in ultimate reality; it is the power of being, expressing itself in many forms. (78f.)

In every true prayer God is both he to whom we pray and he who prays through us. For it is the divine Spirit who creates the right prayer. At this point the ontological structure which makes God an object of us as subjects is infinitely transcended. God stands in the divine-human reciprocity, but only as he who transcends it and comprises both sides of the reciprocity. He reacts, but he reacts to that which is his own act working through our finite freedom. He never can become a mere object. This is the limit of the symbols of reciprocity. This makes the ontological question necessary. . . . The God who is *a* being is transcended by the God who is Being itself, the ground and abyss of every being. And the God who is *a* person is transcended by the God who is the Personal-Itself, the ground and abyss of every person. In statements like these, religion and ontology meet. . . .

This means that *being* and *person* are not contradictory concepts. Being includes personal being; it does not deny it. The ground of being is the ground of personal being, not its negation. . . .

Religiously speaking, this means that our encounter with the God who is a person includes the encounter with the God who is the ground of everything personal and as such not *a* person. . . . The I-thou character of the relation never darkens the transpersonal power and mystery of the divine. . . .

There is no saving ontology, but the ontological question is implied in the question of salvation. To ask the ontological question is a necessary task. *Against* Pascal I say: The God of Abraham, Isaac, and Jacob and the God of the philosophers is the same God. He is a person and the negation of himself as a person.

Faith comprises both itself and the doubt of itself. . . . To live serenely and courageously in these tensions and to discover finally their ultimate unity in the depths of our own souls and in the depth of the divine life is the task and the dignity of human thought. (81-85)

Jacques Maritain

Existence and the Existent

. . . There are two fundamentally different ways of interpreting the word existentialism. One way is to affirm the primacy of existence, but as implying and preserving essences or natures and as manifesting the supreme victory of the intellect and of intelligibility. This is what I consider to be authentic existentialism. The other way is to affirm the primacy of existence, but as destroying or abolishing essences or natures and as manifesting the supreme defeat of the intellect and of intelligibility. This is what I consider to be apocryphal existentialism, the current kind which "no longer signifies anything at all." I should think so! For if you abolish essence, or that which *esse* posits, by that very act you abolish existence, or *esse*. Those two notions are correlative and inseparable. An existentialism of this sort is self-destroying. (13)

An existence without essence, a subject without essence; from the very beginning we dwell in the unthinkable. Thereupon—and this absence of *fair play* is in my view the blackest stain on the philosophy in question*—there is substituted for the original

* I am quite aware that the notion of essence, like every other notion contained in the lexicon of metaphysics, has been re-cast in an entirely phenomenological perspective. Precisely because of this, if we are to call things by their right names, we are obliged to say that in the phenomenological existentialism that originates with Heidegger there is a radical *bad faith* which consists in appropriating to itself all the notions that we owe to the great metaphysicians of being, and which possess meaning only for the realistic intellect whose quest is the extra-mental mystery that surrounds what is. Those notions were appropriated for the purpose of exploiting them in the universe of phenomenological thought, the universe of the "appearance which *is* essence" (*L'Etre et le Néant,* p. 12), where, in reality, they cease to possess meaning, but where, since the aim is to remain a metaphysi-

affirmation, for the frank affirmation that existence is devoid of essence or excludes essence, the more elaborate and ambiguous affirmation that existence (Heidegger *dixit*) precedes essence.[6] I say ambiguous, because it could signify something true (namely that act precedes potency, that my essence owes to my existence its very presence in the world, and that it owes its intelligibility to Existence in pure act), whereas in reality it signifies something totally different (namely that existence actuates nothing, that I exist but I am nothing, that man exists but there is no human nature).

In the same way, the notion of "project" is an ambiguous substitute for the notion of essence or quiddity, and that of situation is an ambiguous substitute for the notion of an objective conditioning resulting from the causes and natures interacting in the world. . . .

. . . If the existentialist thinks that it is very embarrassing that God should not exist; if he declares—thus displaying evidence of metaphysical perspicacity—that there is no human nature because there is no God to conceive it, and that, God once abolished, nothing in the world is intelligible; nevertheless, his point of departure, and the aim of the shrewd energy that informs his whole undertaking, is to provide this nauseating human vibrio, which persists in increasing and multiplying, with the means to get along in a world without God, and to shift for itself under atheism. (15-18)

Subjectivity marks the frontier which separates the world of philosophy from the world of religion. This is what Kierkegaard felt so deeply in his polemic against Hegel. Philosophy runs against an insurmountable barrier in attempting to deal with subjectivity, because while philosophy of course knows subjects, it knows them only as objects. Philosophy is registered whole and

---

cian, they will continue to be used and corrupted in such a way that they may endlessly yield antinatural meanings. This sort of transcendental embezzlement could not but end in a tainted metaphysical system: phenomenology, under its existentialist aspect, is no more than a scholasticism corrupted at its root. Incidentally, this is what constitutes its undeniable historic interest. The metaphysics of being and scholasticism, though it be only in this corrupt form, is back in the main stream of modern philosophy, or rather, it makes plain to modern philosophy that a certain cycle has been completed. We may henceforth look forward to the birth of a new cycle in philosophy, both for good and for ill; and this corrupt scholasticism may perhaps be manuring the soil for a new germination of authentic metaphysics, at least wherever the earth shall have been vigorously enough ploughed.

[6] Maritain obviously has not read Heidegger's "Letter on Humanism" in which he explicitly rejects this formulation of Sartre's.—M.F.

entire in the relation of intelligence to object; whereas religion enters into the relation of subject to subject.

Religion is essentially that which no philosophy can be: a relation of person to person with all the risk, the mystery, the dread, the confidence, the delight, and the torment that lie in such a relationship. And this very relationship of subject to subject demands that into the knowledge of uncreated subjectivity which the created subjectivity possesses there shall be transferred something of that which the latter is as *subjectivity,* i.e., as that uncreated subjectivity is in the mystery of its personal life. Whence all religion comports an element of revelation. Therefore in the true faith it is the First Truth in Person which makes known to man the mystery of the divine subjectivity. (79f.)

If God exists, then not I, but He is the centre; and this time not in relation to a certain particular perspective, like that in which each created subjectivity is the centre of the universe it knows, but speaking absolutely, and as transcendent subjectivity to which all subjectivities are referred. At such time I can know both that I am without importance and that my destiny is of the highest importance. I can know this without falling into pride, know it without being false to my uniqueness. Because, loving the divine Subject more than myself, it is for Him that I love myself, it is to do as He wishes that I wish above all else to accomplish my destiny; and because, unimportant as I am in the world, I am important to Him; not only I, but all the other subjectivities whose lovableness is revealed in Him and for Him and which are henceforward, together with me, a *we,* called to rejoice in His life. . . .

I am known to God. He knows all of me, me as subject. I am present to Him in my subjectivity itself; He has no need to objectise me in order to know me. Then, and in this unique instance, man is known not as object but as subject in all the depth and all the recesses of subjectivity. Only God knows me in this wise; to Him alone am I uncovered. I am not uncovered to myself. The more I know of my subjectivity, the more it remains obscure to me. If I were not known to God, no one would know me. No one would know me in my truth, in my own existence. No one would know me—*me*—as subject. . . .

Finally, to know that I am known as subject in all the dimensions of my being is not only to know that my truth is known, and that in this knowledge justice is done me; it is also to know that I am *understood.* Even though God condemn me, I know that He understands me. (82-85)

. . . The posture of *saving my all,* was that of *existential existentialism* lived and exercised (*in actu exercito*). In this very fact lay the grandeur of its testimony, the power of its shattering strength, and the value of its intuitions. The existentialism of Kierkegaard, of Kafka, of Chestov, of Fondane, was an essentially religious irruption and claim, an agony of faith, the cry of the subjectivity towards its God. It was at the same time a revelation of the person and of his anguish in the face of the nothingness which is non-being *in* the existent, the "crack *in* the existent."

But because of the historic circumstances in which it was born, and particularly because of Hegel and the implacable fascination of his totalitarianism of the reason, it was the misfortune of this existentialism to arise and develop *within philosophy*. As it arose and developed it was inseparable from the philosophy with which it was in merciless conflict, held and gripped by the very philosophy it was seeking to strike to the heart—the principle of noncontradiction. Existential existentialism was thus like a man struggling in the coils of a gigantic reptile. By an astounding mistake, and as the effect of an inevitable illusion, this protest of a faith, caught in a Babylonian captivity, came forth into the world dressed in the livery of Babylon. It was a religious protest *in the guise of a philosophy*—a philosophy directed against the professionals of philosophy; and this was, of course, most comforting. But also (and here an entire tragedy was involved), it was a philosophy *against philosophy*. . . .

Philosophical or *academic existentialism* was bound to come: existentialism as designed (*in actu signato*), as a machine for making ideas, as an apparatus for the fabrication of theses. And indeed the blame should be put on existential existentialism which, except in the case of Kafka, had mistaken itself for a philosophy. The philosophical (I dare not say, *sapiential*) posture was naturally and inevitably to replace the *imprecatory* posture, and with it the agony and the anguish, of the man of faith. . . . It turns out that this seeking the kingdom of God by way of violence and revolt of the soul has had no other result than to debauch reason. The great existential existentialism, once it had been absorbed into the body of its enemy, succeeded only in bringing about, in philosophy itself, a philosophical destruction of the intellect, which is likely to yield profits for some years: a philosophical art of ideological proliferations of the absurd, cleverly barricaded behind Freudian analyses and phenomenological parentheses, and a complete philosophical liquidation of the basic realities and radical claims of the person and subjectivity.

Everything that was essentially linked with the supreme combat for the salvation of the self, or the imprecatory tension and posture of faith, has inevitably disappeared. The soul has been evacuated. The cry sent up to God, the frenzy or the despair born of excess of hope, the expectancy of miracle, the sense of sacrifice and the sense of sin, the spiritual agony, the eternal dignity of the existent, the grandeur of its liberty raised up on the ruins of its nature, all have necessarily been evacuated. Job has been evacuated: only the dunghill has been kept. The nothingness *in* the existent has been replaced by the nothingness *of* the existent. . . .

I am aware that there are other forms of philosophical existentialism, and that there is, in particular, a Christian existentialism which challenges atheistic existentialism with a perspicacity all the keener and a pugnacity all the more lively for the fact that theirs is a family quarrel. In the order of a genuine phenomenology (where moral and psychological analysis is really an approach to ontological problems and where the very purity of an unprejudiced investigation allows philosophy to plumb human experience and to isolate its real meanings and values) this Christian existentialism is past master, and it contributes very valuable discoveries. Nevertheless, I do not believe that it can ever develop into a metaphysic properly so called, any more than any other philosophy which refuses to admit the intellectual intuition of being. It cannot father a metaphysics that is comprehensive, articulated, founded upon reason, and capable of exercising the functions of wisdom as well as of knowledge. For the same reason I do not believe that in the evolution of philosophical thought, it will ever succeed in becoming more than a side issue, nor will it successfully resist the historic impetus which at the present time gives to atheistic existentialism (and will in the future give to new systems issuing in like fashion out of the central positions of the long tradition that goes back to Descartes) an ephemeral but vast power over men's minds. To arrest that trend the springs would have to be purified all the way back to their original source. It would be necessary to overcome acquired habits and critical negligence accumulated in the course of three centuries, and to break with the errors common to existentialist irrationalism, idealism, empirical nominalism, and classical rationalism. (131-136)

. . . Atheistic existentialism itself remains dependent upon theology, though an inverted theology. For it, as for Marxism, atheism is a *point of departure* accepted in advance. These two antagonistic philosophies, the one rationalist, the other irrationalist, both develop in the light of an *a-theo-logy* of which they are the *ancillae*. From this it follows that all the avenues of being are closed to them, because they are too liable to lead in the direction of the transcendent Being. However great their hostility to idealism, those philosophies *cannot* set themselves up as philosophies of being. Moreover, the very name of existentialism is, as regards atheistic existentialism, a name usurped. Neither being nor existence: such philosophies are in reality philosophies of action, either of *praxis* and the transforming action of the world, or of moral creation *a nihilo* and liberty for liberty's sake. (141)

Maurice Friedman

Problematic Rebel: An Image of Modern Man

The "death of God" does not mean that modern man does not "believe" in God, any more than it means that God himself has actually died. Whether or not one holds with Sartre that God never existed at all or with Buber that God is in "eclipse" and that it is we, the "slayers of God," who dwell in the darkness, the "death of God" means the awareness of a basic crisis in modern history —the crisis that comes when man no longer knows what it means to be human and becomes aware that he does not know this. This is not just a question of the relativization of "values" and the absence of universally accepted mores. It is the absence of an image of meaningful human existence, the absence of the ground that enabled Greek, Biblical, and Renaissance man to move with some sureness even in the midst of tragedy. (52)

Kafka's unique contribution to the problematic of modern man is his probing of the paradox of existence as a person in the modern world. Kafka offers us an image of modern man confronting a transcendent reality which can neither be dismissed as unreal nor rationalized as anything less than absurd. Kafka's hero is neither able to affirm meaning *despite* what confronts him, as do Nietzsche's Zarathustra, Sartre's Orestes, and Camus' Sisyphus, nor to fix meaning *in* what confronts him, as do Plato's philosopher or Kierkegaard's "knight of faith." Unable to believe any longer in an objective absolute or order through which his personal destiny is determined or in a Biblical God who calls him, he nonetheless knows himself as a person face to face with reality which transcends him. This reality demands from him response and punishes a failure to respond even while it offers neither confirmation nor meaning in return for response nor any guidance as to which response is "right" and which "wrong." (392)

Kafka abjures the path of the metaphysicians and the theologians, who are able to speak of God or the Absolute as if they have some knowledge of ultimate reality as it is in itself, apart from their relation to it. It also means, however, that he abjures the negative metaphysics of a Nietzsche, a Sartre, or a Jung who, because they cannot believe in any absolute simply independent of man, deny it altogether or remove it into the immanence of the human psyche. Instead, Kafka as artist stands where his hero stands—as a man face to face with a reality that he cannot avoid facing yet can see only from the ground on which he, the concrete, existing person, stands. (420)

If the Modern Promethean is marked by the either-or which holds that man must destroy the reality that faces him in order to recover his alienated freedom, the Modern Job is marked by the "both-and" which faithfully affirms what confronts him as the "given" of his own existence and at the same time does not submit to it but opposes and contends with it. The choice of the Modern Promethean is between submission and rebellion, that of the Modern Job between this very either-or, in which submission and rebellion are the two sides of the same coin, and that other rebellion which holds the tension between the affirmation of oneself and the faithful confronting of what faces one. (398)

At the heart of Job's contending lies the question of trust in existence—he begins not by cursing God but by cursing the day of his birth. It is not his belief in God that is undermined but his trust in existence: if he affirms his relationship with God throughout yet refuses to give up his demand for justice, it is because his trust in existence is at stake. It is this same problem of trust in existence that is at the center of the struggle of the Problematic Rebel—[Captain] Ahab, Ivan [Karamazov] and [Kafka's] K. In Ahab and Ivan, however, the trust has broken. Finding it impossible to hold together human values and the absurd, they have "turned their ticket in." K. has not. He insists on the reality of the goal even while he suspects that "the true way" is only a "wavering," more a "stumbling block" than a way forward. Similarly [Camus'] Rieux, even while he accepts the never-ending struggle with the plague as the inescapable human condition, also affirms that some meaning may emerge from that struggle. Standing one's ground before what confronts one rather than giving way before it or trying to escape it mark the Modern Job as much as they do the original one. The question of trust in existence which is at the heart of Job's dialogue with God is equally at the heart of K.'s and Rieux's dialogue with the absurd.

To the Modern Job, unlike the Modern Promethean, it need not matter whether this rebellion be expressed in terms of the "atheism" of a Camus or the "theism" of a Buber. The basic attitude is essentially the same. In both, dialogue and rebellion are inseparably coupled. "The dialogical leads inevitably to Job's question to God," writes Martin Buber. "My God will not allow to become silent in the mouth of his creature the complaint about the great injustice in the world, and when in an unchanged world his creature yet finds peace because God has again granted him his nearness, . . . that is a peace that is compatible with the fight for justice in the world." *

* From "Responsa," "Theology, Mysticism, Metaphysics," Chap. VI, trans. Maurice Friedman, in *The Philosophy of Martin Buber*, edited by Paul Arthur Schilpp and Maurice Friedman, *loc. cit.* That the Modern Job really means an essential affinity of spirit between these two men and not just an external resemblance is borne out by statements that each has made about the other. "Camus acknowledges a profound respect for Buber," writes R. W. B. Lewis on the basis of a remark made by Camus to him, "and Camus is even willing to say that for himself 'the sacred' is just that presence felt in the silence during a moment of genuine awareness. . . . Only in what Buber calls a condition of being aware is even a transitory moment of communion accomplished." (R. W. B. Lewis, *The Picaresque Saint* [Philadelphia and New York: J. B. Lippincott, 1959], p. 103. Cf. p. 302, footnotes 32 and 33 to Chap. III.) In a letter to me of Nov. 9, 1961, Buber points, by implication, to what we might characterize as the distinction between the atheism of a Modern Promethean like Sartre and that of a Modern Job like Camus: "I would not call Camus an atheist. He was one of the men who are destroying the old images. You know how I feel about them." The reference Buber is making is to the conclusion to his essay, "Religion and Philosophy": "The religious reality of the meeting with the Meeter, who shines through all forms and is Himself formless, knows no image of Him, nothing comprehensible as object. It knows only the presence of the Present One. Symbols of Him, whether images or ideas, always exist first when and insofar as Thou becomes He, and that means It. . . . They always quickly desire to be more than they are, more than signs and pointers toward Him. It finally happens ever again that they swell themselves up and obstruct the way to Him, and He removes Himself from them. Then comes round the hour of the philosopher, who rejects both the image and the God which it symbolizes and opposes to it the pure idea, which he even at times understands as the negation of all metaphysical ideas. This critical 'atheism' (*Atheoi* is the name which the Greeks gave to those who denied the traditional gods) is the prayer which is spoken in the third person in the form of speech about an idea. It is the prayer of the philosopher to the again unknown God. It is well suited to arouse religious men and to impel them to set forth right across the God-deprived

The Modern Promethean still harbors a touch of nineteenth-century romanticism—the grand gesture with which Ahab defies Moby Dick, Ivan's Inquisitor judges Christ, or Sartre's Orestes denies the power of Zeus. The Modern Job stands the other side of romanticism. The Modern Job begins with the world of Kafka's Castle, which cannot be captured by any direct assaults; with the Nazi occupation of France—Camus' model for *The Plague;* with the scientific extermination of six million Jews and a million gypsies. He is "the Job of the gas chambers" in the name of whom Martin Buber contrasts the Greek tragic hero who is overcome before "faceless fate" with those who "contend . . . with God." * . . . This dialogue implies both trust and contending, but it does not mean *either* denial *or* affirmation on principle. We stand our ground and meet what comes with open-eyed trust—in each new situation that confronts us affirming where we can affirm and withstanding where we have to withstand. (463f.)

In the face of this situation, meaning is not accessible either through the ancient Prometheanism that extends man's realm in an ordered cosmos or through the Renaissance Prometheanism that makes man a little world that reflects the great. Still less is it accessible through the Modern Prometheanism that defies what is over against man while striving at the same time to control, subdue, or destroy it, as Ahab strives to destroy Moby Dick. Today, meaning can be found, if at all, only through the attitude of the man who is willing to *live* with the absurd, to remain open to the mystery which he can never hope to pin down. In the world of "the plague" no room is left for the self-deifying postures of a Faust, an Ahab, or a Zarathustra. Nor is there room for that anthropomorphic approach to the absurd which led the early Camus to a stoic rebellion against a world that will never again assume the appearance of rationality longed for by the lucidity of subjective consciousness from Descartes to Sartre. Camus' call to face the absurd in *The Myth of Sisyphus* still represents the defiant protest of the Modern Promethean rather than the open contending of the Modern Job. Camus' very definition of the reality we confront as absurd depends upon his *expectation* of rationality:

---

reality to a new meeting. On their way they destroy the images which manifestly no longer do justice to God. The spirit moves them which moved the philosopher." (Martin Buber, *Eclipse of God. Studies in the Relation between Religion and Philosophy,* trans. Maurice S. Friedman et al. [New York: Harper Torchbooks, 1957], pp. 45f.) (441-443)

* Martin Buber, *At the Turning. Three Addresses on Judaism* (New York: Farrar, Straus & Young, 1952), "The Dialogue between Heaven and Earth," pp. 61f.

> A horde of irrationals has sprung up and surrounds man until his ultimate end. In his recovered and now studied lucidity, the feeling of the absurd becomes clear and definite. . . . This world in itself is not reasonable, that is all that can be said. But what is absurd is the confrontation of this irrational and the wild longing for clarity whose call echoes in the human heart. . . . Man stands face to face with the irrational. He feels within him his longing for happiness and for reason. The absurd is born of this confrontation between the human need and the unreasonable silence of the world.*

When we speak of dialogue with the absurd, it is not, therefore, the absurd of the early Camus that we mean—the product of a disappointed expectation born of a nostalgia for lucidity more characteristic of modern rationalism than of man as man. We mean, rather, the affirmation of a concrete reality that we can meet yet cannot comprehend as it is in itself apart from that meeting. This latter meaning of the absurd—the meaning Camus himself arrived at in *The Plague*—offers us a realistic approach to the "world" of modern science. The dialogue with the absurd means here an open-minded and courageous standing one's ground before a world which man cannot image and to which he can ascribe no independent, objective meaning. (468f.)

[In Sartre] the Modern Promethean reveals himself—the man who chooses as an image of man for all men the denial of all meaning transcending the self or arising from the self's meeting with being in favor of a "meaning" which man himself "invents."

Albert Camus, in contrast, portrays a number of genuinely different images of man, to each of which he lends validity, yet commits himself in *The Plague* to one image above all others—that of the dialogical rebel Doctor Rieux. If we compare Doctor Rieux with Matthieu Delarue, the hero of Sartre's novel *The Age of Reason,* we are impelled to a contrast between the man who is responsible only to himself and his own freedom and for that reason is unable to act (Delarue) and the man who is responsible to and for the situation in which he finds himself (Rieux). The former means futile suffering with no commitment except to the abstract ideal of not being committed. The latter means suffering *and* action through commitment to the concrete demands of the hour. This commitment is not a limitation of human freedom within a specific mode of conduct. It is, rather, the most practical possible assertion of freedom by a man who knows that only through commitment in the present will there be real freedom in the future. It is not a prescription for others that chooses the image of man

* *The Myth of Sisyphus*, pp. 16, 21.

for them, as Sartre would have it. It is a witness to an attitude that may be meaningful for any Problematic Rebel in his own personal encounter with "the plague"—the attitude of the Modern Job. (479f.)

Part VI

EXISTENTIALISM AND PSYCHOTHERAPY

THE ISSUES that have become clear in the previous Parts of *The Worlds of Existentialism* are illuminated and concretized through our selections on existentialism and psychotherapy in Part VI. I have chosen this one field in which to bring out the implications of existentialism because it is today that field in which existentialism is being most actively, if not always most lucidly, applied. The full significance of existentialism and psychotherapy can only be discovered, however, through beginning with the existentialist thinkers themselves—Kierkegaard, Tillich, Sartre, Merleau-Ponty, Buber, Jaspers—to see what they have said about psychology and psychotherapy, and then turning to psychiatrists and psychotherapists who, in one way or another, show a marked influence by these thinkers—Viktor von Weizsäcker, Ludwig Binswanger, Medard Boss, Rollo May, Leslie H. Farber, Viktor Frankl, Silvano Arieti, Carl Rogers, and Hans Trüb. Erwin Straus, at once philosopher and psychologist, is included for his application of Husserlian phenomenology to psychiatry, the philosopher Helen Merrell Lynd for her essentially existential treatment of shame, and the psychopathologist Kurt Goldstein for his existential approach to immediacy. I have concluded with two selections of my own, the second of which—"Existential Psychotherapy and the Image of Man"—raises issues which should serve as a transition to the conclusion.

"Existential psychotherapy," like existentialism itself, is a temper uniting divergent schools of thought, rather than an essentially unified approach. "Below the level of those who regard existential therapy with interest as a new fad and those who approach it with hostile questions about technique," said Rollo May in opening the first Conference on Existential Psychotherapy, "are those who approach it with an 'ontological hunger,' those who ask the ultimate questions about man, neurosis, health, and fulfillment." May himself recognizes that it would be premature to speak of existential psychotherapy as a school. Although in America there are groups such as the Council on Existential Psychology and Psychiatry which hold periodic conferences on existential psychotherapy, the papers of which are printed in the *Review of Existential Psychology and Psychiatry,* the actual members of the Council and the papers contributed to the *Review* represent a broad spectrum of approaches from various more traditional schools, informed though they are by a common concern.

The selections from psychologists and psychiatrists in Part VI illustrate this same variety of background. Rollo May identifies himself with the Harry Stack Sullivan school, Viktor von Weizsäcker was an important figure in German psychosomatic medicine as well as a noted psychiatrist. The Swiss psychotherapist Hans Trüb was a Jungian analyst for ten years, but broke from his personal and doctrinal dependence on Jung under the impact of his friendship with Martin Buber; Leslie Farber is former Chairman of the Washington School of Psychiatry (Sullivanian) and present chairman of the Council on Existential Psychology and Psychiatry; the American psychologist Carl Rogers is noted through his school of "client-centered" therapy; Silvano Arieti belongs to the Sullivan school. Only four of the psychiatrists included here are explicitly existential psychotherapists—all four European: the Viennese neuropsychiatrist Viktor Frankl, founder of "Logotherapy," the Swiss psychiatrists Ludwig Binswanger, founder of "Existential Analysis," Medard Boss, who calls his thought "Daseinanalysis," and Hans Trüb, who designates his therapy as "anthropological." Boss is strongly under the influence of Heidegger; May of Kierkegaard and Heidegger; Trüb, Rogers, and Farber of both Buber and Kierkegaard. Binswanger attempts to combine Heidegger's phenomenological ontology and Buber's philosophy of dialogue, and he is also influenced, as are many others (Tillich, Heidegger, Sartre, May, Farber, and Rogers) by Kierkegaard's categories of *Angst* (dread) and "sickness unto death" (the despairing will not to be oneself or the defiant will to be oneself).

The insights of these existential philosophers are applied in very different ways to psychotherapy, as in the uses that Tillich, Binswanger, Boss, and May make of Heidegger or the uses that Binswanger, Farber, Arieti, Rogers, and Trüb make of Buber. These are sometimes differences in the field in which the application is made (neurosis, schizophrenia, etc.), sometimes implicit or explicit issues (as in the critique of Boss's anxiety-free goal by Basescu, de Rosis, and Elkin; Binswanger's and May's affirmation of suicide as possible freedom or seriousness and Farber's rejection of it as willfulness; and Boss's critique of Binswanger's Heideggerian "world-design" as subjectivistic and un-Heideggerian!). Even when there is much more common understanding, there are often real issues, as is vividly illustrated in the "Dialogue between Martin Buber and Carl Rogers." Does the "I-Thou" relationship in psychotherapy mean full or limited mutuality between therapist and patient? Is the relationship the means to the end of the patient's becoming or is the "between" of reality and value in itself? Is there a significant difference between "acceptance" and "confirmation"? Is man by nature good, bad, or polar?

Since a number of the psychotherapists represented here identify themselves with the Harry Stack Sullivan school of interpersonal psychiatry, it is well to caution against the identification of Sullivan's interpersonal relations and the I-Thou relationship. Arieti tends to use these interchangeably while Farber has pointed in his writing to the difference between the two. The "social" includes the I-It relation as well as the I-Thou: many interpersonal relations are really characterized by one person's treating the other as an object to be known and used. Most interpersonal relations are, in fact, a mixture of I-Thou and I-It and some almost purely I-It. Sullivan includes something of the "interhuman" in his treatment of the interpersonal but he does not single it out as a separate, qualitatively different and essentially significant dimension. This same distinction applies to the "togetherness" of which Boss talks following Heidegger's definition of *Dasein* as *Mitsein.* Here too the social nature of I-Thou is confused with the social nature of I-It, the reality of direct dialogue with the indirect togetherness of ordinary social relations.[1]

In opposition to the tendency to identify existentialism and existential psychotherapy with "self-actualization" Viktor Frankl points to the life-task that calls one into unique, meaningful existence. Many psychotherapists who have gone beyond Freud find the goal of therapy in a vaguely conceived notion of self-realization. This critique (which Frankl applies to such varied thinkers as Kurt Goldstein, Karen Horney, Erich Fromm, Abraham Maslow, and Carl Rogers) is complemented by Helen Merrell Lynd who points out, in opposition to Horney, Fromm, and Sullivan, that one's true self is not an already given reality but a life-long task.

The proportion of Part VI that is devoted to phenomenology is considerably less than that in *Existence,* which includes, in addi-

[1] *Cf.*, Maurice Friedman, *Martin Buber: The Life of Dialogue* (New York: Harper Torchbooks, 1960), Chapter XIX—"Buber's Theory of Knowledge" and Chapter XXI—"Psychotherapy."

tion to Straus and Binswanger, excellent phenomenological studies by Eugene Minkowski, V. E. von Gebsattel, and Roland Kuhn. The reason for this weighting in our anthology is that phenomenology, while an indispensable ingredient in much existentialism, is not in itself existentialism. Still less is it *per se* existential psychotherapy. The chief emphases in Part VI, therefore, are existentialist insights, on the one hand, and their application to psychotherapy, on the other. At the same time, there are extensive selections from Straus and Binswanger. These raise the issue of the extent to which existential psychotherapy can remain a theoretical analysis without a decisive modification in practice. Putting it another way, is the *existential* part of existential psychotherapy found in phenomenological analysis of the patient's world-design or in the therapist-patient relationship, or in both?

Søren Kierkegaard

The Concept of Dread

. . . Dread is the dizziness of freedom which occurs when the spirit would posit the synthesis, and freedom then gazes down into its own possibility, grasping at finiteness to sustain itself. In this dizziness freedom succumbs. Further than this psychology cannot go and will not. That very instant everything is changed, and when freedom rises again it sees that it is guilty. Between these two instants lies the leap, which no science has explained or can explain. He who becomes guilty in dread becomes as ambiguously guilty as it is possible to be. Dread is a womanish debility in which freedom swoons. . . . In dread there is the egoistic infinity of possibility, which does not tempt like a definite choice, but alarms (*ængster*) and fascinates with its sweet anxiety (*Beængstelse*).

In the later individual dread is more reflective. This may be expressed by saying that the nothing which is the object of dread becomes, as it were, more and more a something. . . . The nothing of dread is a complex of presentiments which reflect themselves in themselves, coming nearer and nearer to the individual, notwithstanding that in dread they signify again essentially nothing, not, however, be it noted, a nothing with which the individual has nothing to do, but a nothing in lively communication with the ignorance of innocence. This reflectiveness is a predisposition which, before the individual becomes guilty, signifies essentially nothing, whereas when by the qualitative leap he becomes guilty it is the presupposition in which the individual goes beyond himself because sin presupposes itself, not of course before it is posited (that would be a predestination), but presupposes itself when it is posited. (55f.)

If one does not first make clear to oneself what "self" means, there is not much use in saying of sin that it is selfishness. But "self" signifies precisely the contradiction of positing the general as the particular (*Enkelte*). Only when the concept of the particular individual (*Enkelte*) is given can there be any question of the selfish. But although there have lived countless millions of such "selves," no science can state what the self is, without stating it in perfectly general terms. . . . The real "self" is first posited by the qualitative leap. In the situation preceding this there can be no question of such a thing. Therefore when one would explain sin by selfishness, one becomes involved in confusions, since on the contrary it is true that by sin and in sin selfishness comes into being. (70f.)

. . . Nature's security is due to the fact that time has no significance for it. Only in the instant does history begin. . . . The instant is that ambiguous moment in which time and eternity touch one another, thereby positing *the temporal,* where time is constantly intersecting eternity and eternity constantly permeating time. (80)

The possible corresponds precisely to the future. For freedom the possible is the future; and for time the future is the possible. Corresponding to both of these in the individual life is dread. . . . Dread is the psychological state which precedes sin, comes as near as possible to it, and is as provocative as possible of dread, but without explaining sin, which breaks forth first in the qualitative leap.

The instant sin is posited, the temporal is sin. (82)

In the state of innocence freedom was not posited as freedom, its possibility appears in the dread of the individuality. In the demoniacal the situation is reversed. Freedom is posited as unfreedom, for freedom is lost. The possibility of freedom is in turn dread. The difference is absolute; for the possibility of freedom manifests itself here in relation to unfreedom, which is exactly the opposite of innocence, which is a determinant oriented towards freedom.

The demoniacal is unfreedom which would shut itself off. This, however, is an impossibility; it always maintains a relationship, and even when this has apparently disappeared it is nevertheless there, and dread manifests itself at once in the instant of contact with the good. . . . The demoniacal is *shut-upness* [*det Indesluttede,* or *Indesluttedhed*] *unfreely revealed.* These two traits denote, as they should, the same thing; for the shut-up is precisely the mute, and if it has to express itself, this must come about against its will when the freedom lying prone in unfreedom revolts upon coming into communication with freedom outside and now betrays unfreedom in such a way that it is the individual who betrays himself against his will in dread. (109f.)

He who is educated by dread is educated by possibility, and only the man who is educated by possibility is educated in accordance with his infinity. Possibility is therefore the heaviest of all categories. . . . When such a person, therefore, goes out from the school of possibility, and knows more thoroughly than a child knows the alphabet that he can demand of life absolutely nothing, and that terror, perdition, annihilation, dwell next door to every man, and has learned the profitable lesson that every dread which alarms [*ængste*] may the next instant become a fact, he will then interpret reality differently, he will extol reality, and even when it rests upon him heavily he will remember that after all it is far, far lighter than the possibility was. (139f.)

Sickness unto Death

The Despair which is Conscious of being Despair, as also it is Conscious of being a Self wherein there is after all something Eternal, and then is either in despair at not willing to be itself, or in despair at willing to be itself. (180)

This form of despair is: despair at not willing to be oneself; or still lower, despair at not willing to be a self; or lowest of all, despair at willing to be another than himself, wishing for a new self. Properly speaking, immediacy has no self, it does not recognize itself, so neither can it recognize itself again, it terminates therefore preferably in the romantic. When immediacy despairs it possesses not even enough self to wish or to dream that it had become what it did not become. The immediate man helps himself in a different way: he wishes to be another. Of this one may easily convince oneself by observing immediate men. At the moment of despair no wish is so natural to them as the wish that they had become or might become another. In any case one can never forbear to smile at such a despairer, who, humanly speaking, although he is in despair, is so very innocent. Commonly such a despairer is infinitely comic. Think of a self (and next to God there is nothing so eternal as a self), and then that this self gets the notion of asking whether it might not let itself become or be made into another . . . than itself. And yet such a despairer, whose only wish is this most crazy of all transformations, loves to think that this change might be accomplished as easily as changing a coat. For the immediate man does not recognize his self, he recognizes himself only by his dress, he recognizes (and here again appears the infinitely comic trait) he recognizes that he has a self only by externals. There is no more ludicrous confusion, for a self is just infinitely different from externals. (186f.)

This despair is one quality deeper than the foregoing and is a sort which rarely is met with in the world. That blind door behind which there was nothing is in this case a real door, a door carefully locked to be sure, and behind it sits as it were the self and watches itself, employed in filling up time with not willing to be itself, and yet is self enough to love itself. This is what is called *introversion.* (196)

If the despairing *self* is *active*, it really is related to itself only as experimenting with whatsoever it be that it undertakes, however great it may be, however astonishing, however persistently carried out. It acknowledges no power over it, hence in the last resort it lacks seriousness and is able only to conjure up a show of seriousness when the self bestows upon its experiments its utmost attention. . . . It is so far from being true that the self succeeds more and more in becoming itself, that in fact it merely becomes more and more manifest that it is a hypothetical self. The self is its own lord and master, so it is said, absolutely its own lord, and precisely this is despair, but it also is what it regards as its pleasure and enjoyment. However, by closer inspection one easily ascertains that this ruler is a king without a country, he rules really over nothing; his condition, his dominion, is subjected to the dialectic that every instant revolution is legitimate. For in the last resort this depends arbitrarily upon the self. . . .

. . . In spite of or in defiance of the whole of . . . existence he wills to be himself with it, to take it along, almost defying his torment. For to hope in the possibility of help, not to speak of help by virtue of the absurd, that for God all things are possible—no, that he will not do. And as for seeking help from any other—no, that he will not do for all the world; rather than seek help he would prefer to be himself—with all the tortures of hell, if so it must be. . . .

But the more consciousness there is in such a sufferer who in despair is determined to be himself, all the more does despair too potentiate itself and become demoniac. (202-205)

This despair does not will to be itself with Stoic doting upon itself, nor with self-deification, willing in this way, doubtless mendaciously, yet in a certain sense in terms of its perfection; no, with hatred for existence it wills to be itself, to be itself in terms of its misery; it does not even in defiance or defiantly will to be itself, but to be itself in spite; it does not even will in defiance to tear itself free from the Power which posited it, it wills to obtrude upon this Power in spite, to hold on to it out of malice. And that is natural, a malignant objection must above all take care to hold on to that against which it is an objection. Revolting against the whole of existence, it thinks it has hold of a proof against it, against its goodness. This proof the despairer thinks he himself is, and that is what he wills to be, therefore he wills to be himself, himself with his torment, in order with this torment to protest against the whole of existence. (207)

Paul Tillich

The Courage to Be

Courage is self-affirmation "in-spite-of," that is in spite of that which tends to prevent the self from affirming itself. (32)

. . . Anxiety is the existential awareness of nonbeing. (35)

The fear of death determines the element of anxiety in every fear. Anxiety, if not modified by the fear of an object, anxiety in its nakedness, is always the anxiety of ultimate nonbeing. Immediately seen, anxiety is the painful feeling of not being able to deal with the threat of a special situation. But a more exact analysis shows that in the anxiety about any special situation anxiety about the human situation as such is implied. It is the anxiety of not being able to preserve one's own being which underlies every fear and is the frightening element in it. In the moment, therefore, in which "naked anxiety" lays hold of the mind, the previous objects of fear cease to be definite objects. They appear as what they always were in part, symptoms of man's basic anxiety. As such they are beyond the reach of even the most courageous attack upon them.

. . . The basic anxiety, the anxiety of a finite being about the threat of nonbeing, cannot be eliminated. It belongs to existence itself. (38f.)

. . . I suggest that we distinguish three types of anxiety according to the three directions in which nonbeing threatens being. Nonbeing threatens man's ontic self-affirmation, relatively in terms of fate, absolutely in terms of death. It threatens man's spiritual self-affirmation, relatively in terms of emptiness, absolutely in terms of meaninglessness. It threatens man's moral self-affirmation, relatively in terms of guilt, absolutely in terms of condemnation. The awareness of this threefold threat is anxiety appearing in three forms, that of fate and death (briefly, the anxiety of death), that of emptiness and loss of meaning (briefly, the anxiety of meaninglessness), that of guilt and condemnation (briefly, the anxiety of condemnation). In all three forms anxiety is existential in the sense that it belongs to existence as such and not to an abnormal state of mind as in neurotic (and psychotic) anxiety. . . .

THE ANXIETY OF FATE AND DEATH

The term "fate" for this whole group of anxieties stresses . . . their contingent character, their unpredictability, the impossibility of showing their meaning and purpose. . . . Yet it is not causal necessity that makes fate a matter of anxiety but the lack of ultimate necessity, the irrationality, the impenetrable darkness of fate. . . . Fate would not produce inescapable anxiety without death behind it. And death stands behind fate and its contingencies not only in the last moment when one is thrown out of existence but in every moment within existence. . . .

THE ANXIETY OF EMPTINESS AND MEANINGLESSNESS

The anxiety of meaninglessness is anxiety about the loss of an ultimate concern, of a meaning which gives meaning to all meanings. This anxiety is aroused by the loss of a spiritual center, of an answer, however symbolic and indirect, to the question of the meaning of existence. . . . The anxiety of emptiness is aroused by the threat of nonbeing to the special contents of the spiritual life. (41-47)

Ontic and spiritual self-affirmation must be distinguished but they cannot be separated. Man's being includes his relation to meanings. He is human only by understanding and shaping reality, both his world and himself, according to meanings and values. . . .

THE ANXIETY OF GUILT AND CONDEMNATION

Man's being, ontic as well as spiritual, is not only given to him but also demanded of him. He is responsible for it; literally, he is required to answer, if he is asked, what he has made of himself. He who asks him is his judge, namely he himself, who, at the same time, stands against him. This situation produces the anxiety which, in relative terms, is the anxiety of guilt; in absolute terms, the anxiety of self-rejection or condemnation. Man is essentially "finite freedom"; freedom not in the sense of indeterminacy but in the sense of being able to determine himself through decisions in the center of his being. Man, as finite freedom, is free within the contingencies of his finitude. But within these limits he is asked to make of himself what he is supposed to become. . . . A profound ambiguity between good and evil permeates everything he does, because it permeates his personal being as such. . . . In both anomism and legalism the anxiety of guilt lies in the background and breaks again and again into the open, producing the extreme situation of moral despair.

THE MEANING OF DESPAIR

The pain of despair is that a being is aware of itself as unable to affirm itself because of the power of nonbeing. Consequently it wants to surrender this awareness and its presupposition, the being which is aware. It wants to get rid of itself—and it cannot. Despair appears in the form of reduplication, as the desperate attempt to escape despair. (50-55)

Courage does not remove anxiety. Since anxiety is existential, it cannot be removed. But courage takes the anxiety of nonbeing into itself. . . . This analysis gives the key to understanding pathological anxiety. He who does not succeed in taking his anxiety courageously upon himself can succeed in avoiding the extreme situation of despair by escaping into neurosis. He still affirms himself but on a limited scale. *Neurosis is the way of avoiding nonbeing by avoiding being.* In the neurotic state self-affirmation is not lacking; it can indeed be very strong and emphasized. But the self which is affirmed is a reduced one. Some or many of its potentialities are not admitted to actualization, because actualization of being implies the acceptance of nonbeing and its anxiety. He who is not capable of a powerful self-affirmation in spite of the anxiety of nonbeing is forced into a weak, reduced self-affirmation. He affirms something which is less than his essential or potential being. He surrenders a part of his potentialities in order to save what is left. (66)

Pathological anxiety about fate and death impels toward a security which is comparable to the security of a prison. He who lives in this prison is unable to leave the security given to him by his self-imposed limitations. . . . The same structure can be observed in the pathological forms of the anxiety of guilt and condemnation. . . . The anxiety of becoming guilty, the horror of feeling condemned, are so strong that they make responsible decisions and any kind of moral action almost impossible. . . . The consciousness of guilt is misplaced. The moralistic self-defense of the neurotic makes him see guilt where there is no guilt or where one is guilty only in a very indirect way. Yet the awareness of real guilt and the self-condemnation which is identical with man's existential self-estrangement are repressed, because the courage which could take them into itself is lacking.

Neurotic anxiety builds a narrow castle of certitude which can be defended and is defended with the utmost tenacity. Man's power of asking is prevented from becoming actual in this sphere, and if there is a danger of its becoming actualized by questions asked from the outside he reacts with a fanatical rejection. . . . Pathological anxiety leads to self-affirmation on a limited, fixed, and unrealistic basis and to a compulsory defense of this basis. Pathological anxiety, in relation to the anxiety of fate and death, produces an unrealistic security; in relation to the anxiety of guilt and condemnation, an unrealistic perfection; in relation to the anxiety of doubt and meaninglessness, an unrealistic certitude. Pathological anxiety, once established, is an object of medical healing. (75-77)

Vitality, power of life, is correlated to the kind of life to which it gives power. The power of man's life cannot be seen separately from what the medieval philosophers called "intentionality," the relation to meanings. Man's vitality is as great as his intentionality; they are interdependent. . . . Vitality is the power of creating beyond oneself without losing oneself. The more power of creating beyond itself a being has the more vitality it has. (81)

Existence and the Christ

. . . The basic structure of finite being is the polarity of self and world. Only in man is this polarity fulfilled. Only man has a completely centered self and a structured universe to which he belongs and at which he is able to look at the same time. All other beings within our experience are only partly centered and consequently bound to their environment. Man also has environment, but he has it as a part of his world. He can and does transcend it with every word he speaks. He is free to make his world into an object which he beholds, and he is free to make himself into an object upon which he looks. In this situation of finite freedom he can lose himself and his world, and the loss of one necessarily includes the loss of the other. . . .

Self-loss as the first and basic mark of evil is the loss of one's determining center; it is the disintegration of the centered self by disruptive drives which cannot be brought into unity. So long as they are centered, these drives constitute the person as a whole. If they move against one another, they split the person. The further the disruption goes, the more the being of man as man is threatened. Man's centered self may break up, and, with the loss of self, man loses his world.

Self-loss is the loss of one's determining center, the disintegration of the unity of the person. This is manifest in moral conflicts and in psychopathological disruptions, independently or interdependently. The horrifying experience of "falling to pieces" gets hold of the person. To the degree in which this happens, one's world also falls to pieces. It ceases to be a world, in the sense of a meaningful whole. Things no longer speak to man; they lose their power to enter into a meaningful encounter with man, because man himself has lost this power. In extreme cases the complete unreality of one's world is felt; nothing is left except the awareness of one's own empty self. Such experiences are extreme, but extreme situations reveal possibilities in the ordinary situation. Possibilities of disruption are always present in man as a fully centered being. He cannot take his centeredness for granted. It is a form but not an empty one. It is actual only in unity with its content. The form of centeredness gives to the self the center which it needs to be what it is. There is no empty self, no pure subjectivity. Under the control of *hubris* and concupiscence, the self can approach the state of disintegration. The attempt of the finite self to be the center of everything gradually has the effect of its ceasing to be the center of anything. Both self and world are threatened. Man becomes a limited self, in dependence on a limited environment. He has lost his world; he has only his environment.

This fact includes the basic criticism of the environmental theories of man. They assert a view of man's essential nature which actually describes man's existential estrangement *from* his essential nature. Man essentially has a world because he has a fully centered self. He is able to transcend every given environment in the direction of his world. Only the loss of his world subjects him to the bondage of an environment which is not really *his* environment, namely, the result of a creative encounter with his world represented by a part of it. Man's true environment is the universe, and every special environment is qualified as a section of the universe. Only in estrangement can man be described as a mere object of environmental impact. (60-62)

Existentialism and Psychotherapy

Neurotic anxiety is misplaced compulsory anxiety, and not the basic anxiety about everything being finite. Basic anxiety is anxiety about being bound to the law of coming from nothing and going to nothing. Neurotic guilt is misplaced compulsory guilt feeling and not the existential experience of being guilty of a definite concrete act which expresses the general estrangement of our existence, an act for which responsibility cannot be denied, in spite of the element of destiny in it. Neurotic emptiness is a compulsory flight from meaning, even from that remnant of meaning which makes the experience of meaninglessness possible. It is the expression of an unreflective and unsophisticated understanding of men and life if these neurotic phenomena are confused with the universal structures of existence which make neurotic phenomena possible. . . .

For Freud, the "superego" is the name for the consciousness of norms. But the material of the superego is taken from the "id." It has no standing in itself, no objective validity. It has only the power of psychological oppressiveness. The reason for this construction is that Freud did not distinguish the essential structure of man's being, from which forms and principles are derived, and their existential distortion in the images of the superego. Certainly, there are images of destructive power in most human beings; but they are not identical with man's essential nature.

Essential norms, if obeyed, fulfill and give the joy of fulfillment because they represent our own essential being against our existential distortion. (14f.)

The Theological Significance of Existentialism and Psychoanalysis

. . . Both existentialism and depth psychology are interested in the description of man's existential predicament—in time and space, in finitude and estrangement—in contrast to man's essential nature. . . . The focus in both existentialism and depth psychology is man's estranged existence, the characteristics and symptoms of this estrangement, and the conditions of existence in time and space. . . .

However, there is a basic difference between them. Existentialism as philosophy speaks of the universal human situation, which refers to everybody, healthy or sick. Depth psychology points to the ways in which people try to escape the situation by fleeing into neurosis and falling into psychosis. . . .

These three considerations of human nature are present in all genuine theological thinking: essential goodness, existential estrangement, and the possibility of something, a "third," beyond essence and existence, through which the cleavage is overcome and healed. Now, in philosophical terms, this means that man's essential and existential nature points to his teleological nature (derived from *telos,* aim, that for which and towards which his life drives). . . .

Freud, in this respect, was unclear, namely, he was not able to distinguish man's essential and existential nature. This is a basic theological criticism, not of any special result of his thinking, but of his doctrine of man and the central intuition he has of man. His thought about libido makes this deficiency very obvious.

Man, according to him, has infinite libido which never can be satisfied and which therefore produces the desire to get rid of oneself, the desire he has called the death instinct. And this is not only true of the individual, it is also true of man's relation to culture as a whole. His dismay about culture shows that he is very consistent in his negative judgments about man as existentially distorted. Now if you see man only from the point of view of existence and not from the point of view of essence, only from the point of view of estrangement and not from the point of view of essential goodness, then this consequence is unavoidable. . . .

Freud's description of libido is to be viewed theologically as the description of man in his existential self-estrangement. . . . Freud does not know any other man, and this is the basic criticism that theology would weigh against him on this point. . . . His pessimism about the nature of man and his optimism about the possibilities of healing were never reconciled in him or in his followers. . . . But Freud, theologically speaking, saw more about human nature than all his followers who, when they lost the existentialist element in Freud, went more to an essentialist and optimistic view of man. (117-121)

The existential structures cannot be healed by the most refined techniques. They are objects of salvation. The analyst can be an instrument of salvation as every friend, every parent, every child can be an instrument of salvation. But as analyst he cannot bring salvation by means of his medical methods, for this requires the healing of the center of the personality. (123)

Jean-Paul Sartre

Being and Nothingness

By the distinction between the "id" and the "ego," Freud has cut the psychic whole into two. I *am* the ego but I *am not* the *id*. I hold no privileged position in relation to my unconscious psyche. . . . I stand in relation to *my* "id," in the position of the Other. . . . Psychoanalysis substitutes for the notion of bad faith, the idea of a lie without a liar. . . . It replaces the duality of the deceiver and the deceived, the essential condition of the lie, by that of the "id" and the "ego." It introduces into my subjectivity the deepest intersubjective structure of the *Mit-sein*. . . . How could the censor discern the impulses needing to be repressed without being conscious of discerning them? How can we conceive of a knowledge which is ignorant of itself? . . . The resistance of the patient implies on the level of the censor an awareness of the thing repressed as such, a comprehension of the end toward which the questions of the psychoanalyst are leading, and an act of synthetic connection by which it compares the *truth* of the repressed complex to the psychoanalytic hypothesis which aims at it. These various operations in their turn imply that the censor is conscious (of) itself. But what type of self-consciousness can the censor have? It must be the consciousness (of) being conscious of the drive to be repressed, but precisely *in order not to be conscious of it.* What does this mean if not that the censor is in bad faith? Psychoanalysis has not gained anything for us since in order to overcome bad faith, it has established between the unconscious and consciousness an autonomous consciousness in bad faith. . . .

. . . A Viennese psychiatrist, Steckel, . . . departs from the psychoanalytical tradition and writes in *La femme frigide:* "Every time that I have been able to carry my investigations far enough, I have established that the crux of the psychosis was conscious." In addition the cases which he reports in his work bear witness to a pathological bad faith which the Freudian doctrine can not account for. . . . Admissions which Steckel was able to draw out inform us that pathologically frigid women apply themselves to becoming distracted in advance from the pleasure which they dread; many for example at the time of the sexual act, turn their thoughts away toward their daily occupations, make up their household accounts. Will anyone speak of an unconscious here? Yet if the frigid woman thus distracts her consciousness from the pleasure which she experiences, it is by no means cynically and in full agreement with herself; it is *in order to prove to herself* that she is frigid. We have in fact to deal with a phenomenon of bad faith since the efforts taken in order not to be present to the experienced pleasure imply the recognition that the pleasure is experienced; they imply it *in order to deny it.* (50-54)

The *principle* of this [existential] psychoanalysis is that man is a totality and not a collection. Consequently he expresses himself as a whole in even his most insignificant and his most superficial behavior. In other words there is not a taste, a mannerism, or an human act which is not *revealing.* The *goal* of psychoanalysis is to *decipher* the empirical behavior patterns of man; that is to bring out in the open the revelations which each one of them contains and to fix them conceptually. Its *point of departure* is *experience;* its pillar of support is the fundamental, pre-ontological comprehension which man has of the human person. . . . Its *method* is comparative. Since each example of human conduct symbolizes in its own manner the fundamental choice which must be brought to light, and since at the same time each one disguises this choice under its occasional character and its historical opportunity, only the comparison of these acts of conduct can effect the emergence of the unique revelation which they all express in a different way. . . .

Existential psychoanalysis recognizes nothing *before* the original upsurge of human freedom; empirical psychoanalysis holds that the original affectivity of the individual is virgin wax *before* its history. . . . Empirical psychoanalysis seeks to determine the *complex,* the very name of which indicates the polyvalence of all the meanings which are referred back to it. Existential psychoanalysis seeks to determine the *original choice.* . . . Existential psychoanalysis rejects the hypothesis of the unconscious; it makes the psychic act coextensive with consciousness. But if the fundamental project is fully experienced by the subject and hence wholly conscious, that certainly does not mean that it must by the same token be *known* by him; quite the contrary. . . . All is there, luminous; reflection is in full possession of it, apprehends all. But this "mystery in broad daylight" is due to the fact that this possession is deprived of the means which would ordinarily permit *analysis* and *conceptualization.* It grasps everything, all at once, without shading, without relief, without connections of grandeur—not that these shades, these values, these reliefs exist somewhere and are hidden from it, but rather because they must be established by another human attitude and because they can exist only *by means of* and *for* knowledge. Reflection, unable to serve as the basis for existential psychoanalysis, will then simply furnish us with the brute materials toward which the psychoanalyst must take an objective attitude. Thus only will he be able to *know* what he *already understands*. . . . What always escapes these methods of investigation is the project as it is for itself, the complex in its own being. This project-for-itself can be experienced only as a living possession. . . .

. . . The choice to which existential psychoanalysis will lead us, precisely because it is a choice, accounts for its original contingency. . . . Each result then will be at once fully contingent and legitimately irreducible. Moreover it will always remain *particular;* that is, we will not achieve as the ultimate goal of our investigation and the foundation of all behavior an abstract, general term, libido for example, which would be differentiated and made concrete first in complexes and then in detailed acts of conduct, due to the action of external facts and the history of the subject. On the contrary, it will be a choice which remains unique and which is from the start absolute concreteness. Details of behavior can express or *particularize* this choice, but they can not make it more concrete than it already is. . . . A particular partial behavior is or expresses the original choice of this human reality since for human reality there is no difference between existing and choosing for itself. . . .

The environment can act on the subject only to the exact extent that he comprehends it; that is, transforms it into a situation. Hence no objective description of this environment could be of any use to us. From the start the environment conceived as a situation refers to the for-itself which is choosing, just as the for-itself refers to the environment by the very fact that the for-itself is in the world. By renouncing all mechanical causation, we renounce at the same time all *general* interpretation of the symbolization confronted. . . . The psychoanalyst will have to rediscover at each step a symbol functioning in the particular case which he is considering. If each being is a totality, it is not conceivable that there can exist elementary symbolic relationships (*e.g.;* the faeces = gold, or a pincushion = the breast) which preserve a constant meaning in all cases; that is, which remain unaltered when they pass from one meaningful ensemble to another ensemble. Furthermore the psychoanalyst will never lose sight of the fact that the choice is living and consequently can be revoked by the subject who is being studied. . . . Our concern here is to understand what is individual and often even instantaneous. The method which has served for one subject will not necessarily be suitable to use for another subject or for the same subject at a later period. . . . Existential psychoanalysis is a method destined to bring to light, in a strictly objective form, the subjective choice by which each living person makes himself a person; that is, makes known to himself what he is. (568-574)

. . . Human reality, far from being capable of being described as *libido* or will to power, is a *choice of being*. . . . Ontology alone in fact can take its place on the plane of transcendence and from a single viewpoint apprehend being-in-the-world with its two terms because ontology alone has its place originally in the perspective of the *cogito*. . . . The ideas of facticity and situation will enable us to understand the existential symbolism of things. . . . We can apprehend quality only as a symbol of a being which totally escapes us, even though it is totally there before us; in short, we can only make revealed being function as a symbol of being-in-itself. This means that a new structure of the "there is" is constituted which is the meaningful level although this level is revealed in the absolute unity of one and the same fundamental project. This structure we shall call the metaphysical purport of all intuitive revelation of being; and this is precisely what we ought to achieve and disclose by psychoanalysis. . . . It is impossible to derive the value of the psychic symbolism of "slimy" from the brute quality of the *this* and equally impossible to project the meaning of the *this* in terms of a *knowledge* of psychic attitudes. How then are we to conceive of this immense and universal symbolism which is translated by our repulsion, our hates, our sympathies, our attractions toward objects whose materiality must on principle remain non-meaningful? (602-605)

The horror of the slimy is the horrible fear that time might become slimy, that facticity might progress continually and insensibly and absorb the For-itself which *exists it*. It is the fear not of death, not of the pure In-itself, not of nothingness, but of a particular type of being, which does not actually exist any more than the In-itself-For-itself and which is only *represented* by the slimy. It is an ideal being which I reject with all my strength and which haunts me as *value* haunts my being, an ideal being in which the foundationless In-itself has priority over the For-itself. . . . What we say concerning the slimy is valid for all the objects which surround the child. The simple revelation of their matter extends his horizon to the extreme limits of being and bestows upon him at the same stroke a collection of clues for deciphering the being of all human facts. . . . The gluey, the sticky, the hazy, *etc.*, holes in the sand and in the earth, caves, the light, the night, *etc.*—all reveal to him modes of pre-psychic and pre-sexual being which he will spend the rest of his life explaining. . . .

. . . It is only through another—through the words which the mother uses to designate the child's body—that he learns that his anus is a *hole*. It is therefore the objective nature of the hole perceived in the world which is going to illuminate for him the objective structure and the meaning of the anal zone and which will give a transcendent meaning to the erogenous sensations which hitherto he was limited to merely "existing." In itself then the *hole* is the symbol of a mode of being which existential psychoanalysis must elucidate. . . . The hole is originally presented as a nothingness "to be filled" with my own flesh; the child can not restrain himself from putting his finger or his whole arm into the hole. It presents itself to me as the empty image of myself. I have only to crawl into it in order to make myself exist in the world which awaits me. . . . To plug up a hole means originally to make a sacrifice of my body in order that the plenitude of being may exist; that is, to subject the passion of the For-itself so as to shape, to perfect, and to preserve the totality of the In-itself. . . . It is only from this standpoint that we can pass on to sexuality. The obscenity of the feminine sex is that of everything which "gapes open." It is *an appeal to being* as all holes are. In herself woman appeals to a strange flesh which is to transform her into a fullness of being by penetration and dissolution. Conversely woman senses her condition as an appeal precisely because she is "in the form of a hole." Beyond any doubt her sex is a mouth and a voracious mouth which devours the penis—a fact which can easily lead to the idea of castration. The amorous act is the castration of the man; but this is above all because sex is a hole. We have to do here with a *pre-sexual* contribution which will become one of the components of sexuality as an empirical, complex, human attitude but which far from deriving its origin from the sexed being has nothing in common with basic sexuality. Nevertheless the experience with the hole, when the infant sees the reality, includes the ontological presentiment of sexual experience in general; it is with his flesh that the child stops up the hole and the hole, before all sexual specification, is an obscene expectation, an appeal to the flesh. . . .

. . . What chiefly interests the psychoanalyst is to determine the free project of the unique person in terms of the individual relation which unites him to these various symbols of being. I can love slimy contacts, have a horror of holes, *etc.* That does not mean that for me the slimy, the greasy, a hole, *etc.*, have lost their general ontological meaning, but on the contrary that *because* of this meaning, I determine myself in this manner in relation to them. If the slimy is indeed the symbol of a being in which the for-itself is swallowed up by the in-itself, what kind of a person am I if in encountering others, I love the slimy? (611-614)

Maurice Merleau-Ponty

The Phenomenology of Perception

By taking up a present, I draw together and transform my past, altering its significance, freeing and detaching myself from it. But I do so only by committing myself somewhere else. Psychoanalytical treatment does not bring about its cure by producing direct awareness of the past, but in the first place by binding the subject to his doctor through new existential relationships. It is not a matter of giving scientific assent to the psychoanalytical interpretation, and discovering a notional significance for the past; it is a matter of reliving this or that as significant, and this the patient succeeds in doing only by seeing his past in the perspective of his co-existence with the doctor. (455)

Martin Buber

I and Thou

—If a man does not represent the *a priori* of relation in his living with the world, if he does not work out and realise the inborn *Thou* on what meets it, then it strikes inwards. It develops on the unnatural, impossible object of the *I,* that is, it develops where there is no place at all for it to develop. Thus confrontation of what is over against him takes place within himself, and this cannot be relation, or presence, or streaming interaction, but only self-contradiction. . . . Here is the verge of life, flight of an unfulfilled life to the senseless semblance of fulfilment, and its groping in a maze and losing itself ever more profoundly. (69f.)

Another no less illuminating example of the normative limitation of mutuality is presented to us in the relation between a genuine psychotherapist and his patient. If he is satisfied to "analyse" him, i.e. to bring to light unknown factors from his microcosm, and to set to some conscious work in life the energies which have been transformed by such an emergence, then he may be successful in some repair work. At best he may help a soul which is diffused and poor in structure to collect and order itself to some extent. But the real matter, the regeneration of an atrophied personal centre, will not be achieved. This can only be done by one who grasps the buried latent unity of the suffering soul with the great glance of the doctor: and this can only be attained in the person-to-person attitude of a partner, not by the consideration and examination of an object. In order that he may coherently further the liberation and actualisation of that unity in a new accord of the person with the world, the psychotherapist, like the educator, must stand again and again not merely at his own pole in the bipolar relation, but also with the strength of present realisation at the other pole, and experience the effect of his own action. But again, the specific "healing" relation would come to an end the moment the patient thought of, and succeeded in, practising "inclusion" and experiencing the event from the doctor's pole as well. Healing, like educating, is only possible to the one who lives over against the other, and yet is detached. (132f.)

Between Man and Man

WHAT IS MAN?

The spirit *as a happening,* the spirit I have indicated in the child and the peasant, proves to us that it is not inherent in spirit, as Scheler contends, to arise by repression and sublimation of the instincts. Scheler, as is well-known, takes these psychological categories from Sigmund Freud's ideas, among whose greatest services is that he has formed them. But though these categories have general validity, the central position which Freud gives them, their dominating significance for the whole structure of personal and communal life, and especially for the origin and development of the spirit, is not based on the general life of man but only on the situation and qualities of the typical man of to-day. But this man is sick, both in his relation to others and in his very soul. The central significance of repression and sublimation in Freud's system derives from analysis of a pathological condition and is valid for this condition. The categories are psychological, their dominating power is pathopsychological. It can, indeed, be shown that nevertheless their significance is valid not only for our time but also for others akin to it, that is, for times of a pathological condition similar to our own, times like our own when a crisis is arising. But I know no such deep-reaching and comprehensive crisis in history as ours, and that indicates the extent of the significance of those categories. If I were to express our crisis in a formula I should like to call it the crisis of confidence. We have seen how epochs of security of human existence in the cosmos alternate with epochs of insecurity; but in the latter there still reigns for the most part a *social* certainty, one is borne along by a small organic community living in real togetherness. Being able to have confidence within this community compensates for cosmic insecurity; there is connexion and certainty. Where confidence reigns man must often, indeed, adapt his wishes to the commands of his community; but he must not repress them to such an extent that the repression acquires a dominating significance for his life. They often coalesce with the needs of the community, which are expressed by its commands. This coalescence, indeed, can really take place only where everything really lives with everything within the community, where, that is to say, there reigns not an enjoined and imagined but a genuine and elementary confidence. Only if the organic community disintegrates from within and mistrust becomes life's basic note does the repression acquire its dominating importance. The unaffectedness of wishing is stifled by mistrust, everything around is hostile or can become hostile, agreement between one's own and the other's desire ceases, for there is no true coalescence or reconciliation with what is necessary to a sustaining community, and the dulled wishes creep hopelessly into the recesses of the soul. But now the ways of the spirit are also changed. Hitherto it was the characteristic of its origin to flash forth from the clouds as the concentrated manifestation of the wholeness of man. Now there is no longer a human wholeness with the force and the courage to manifest itself. For spirit to arise the energy of the repressed instincts must mostly first be "sublimated," the traces of its origin cling to the spirit and it can mostly assert itself against the instincts only by convulsive alienation. The divorce between spirit and instincts is here, as often, the consequence of the divorce between man and man. (196f.)

The Origin and Meaning of Hasidism

. . . The relation of a soul to its organic life depends on the degree of its wholeness and unity. The more dissociated the soul, the more it is at the mercy of its sicknesses and attacks, the more concentrated it is, the more it is able to master them. It is not as if it conquered the body; rather through its unity it ever again saves and protects the unity of the body. This power rules suddenly and unmistakably where in a dispersed soul in an elemental moment it accomplishes a crystallization and unification; there takes place rapidly and visibly there what otherwise only grows in vegetative darkness, the "healing." Through nothing else can this process be effected so simply and directly as through the psychosynthetic appearance of a whole, united soul laying hold of the dispersed soul, agitating it on all sides, and demanding the event of crystallization. It does not "suggest"; it fashions in the fellow-soul by which it is called, a ground and center, and the more genuinely and fully, the more it is concerned that the appealing soul that calls it does not remain dependent on it: the helper establishes ground and center not in order that he might install his own image in the soul that is to be rebuilt, but in order that it might look through him, as through a glass, into being and now discover being in itself and let it be empowered as the core of living unity. Only the greatest . . . have performed this task adequately. They stand in the ranks of God's helpers. (142f.)

The Way of Man

BEGINNING WITH ONESELF

Manifestations of conflict are usually explained either by the motives of which the quarrelling parties are conscious as the occasion of their quarrel, and by the objective situations and processes which underlie these motives and in which both parties are involved; or, proceeding analytically, we try to explore the unconscious complexes to which these motives relate like mere symptoms of an illness to the organic disturbances themselves. Hasidic teaching coincides with this conception in that it, too, derives the problematics of external from that of internal life. But it differs in two essential points, one fundamental and one practical, the latter of which is even more important than the former.

The fundamental difference is that hasidic teaching is not concerned with the exploration of particular psychical complications, but envisages man as a whole. This is, however, by no means a quantitative difference. For the hasidic conception springs from the realization that the isolation of elements and partial processes from the whole hinders the comprehension of the whole, and that real transformation, real restoration, at first of the single person and subsequently of the relationship between him and his fellow-men, can only be achieved by the comprehension of the whole as a whole. (Putting it paradoxically: the search for the centre of gravity shifts it and thereby frustrates the whole attempt at overcoming the problematics involved.) This is not to say that there is no need to consider all the phenomena of the soul; but no one of them should be made so much the centre of attention as if everything else could be derived from it; rather, they should all be made starting-points—not singly but in their vital connection.

The practical difference is that in Hasidism man is not treated as an object of examination but is called upon to "straighten himself out." At first, a man should himself realize that conflict-situations between himself and others are nothing but the effects of conflict-situations in his own soul; then he should try to overcome this inner conflict, so that afterwards he may go out to his fellow-men and enter into new, transformed relationships with them.

Man naturally tries to avoid this decisive reversal—extremely repugnant to him in his accustomed relationship to the world—by referring him who thus appeals to him, or his own soul, if it is his soul that makes the appeal, to the fact that every conflict involves two parties and that, if he is expected to turn his attention from the external to his own internal conflict, his opponent should be expected to do the same. But just this perspective, in which a man sees himself only as an individual contrasted with other individuals, and not as a genuine person, whose transformation helps towards the transformation of the world, contains the fundamental error which hasidic teaching denounces. The essential thing is to begin with oneself, and at this moment a man has nothing in the world to care about than this beginning. Any other attitude would distract him from what he is about to begin, weaken his initiative, and thus frustrate the entire bold undertaking. . . .

The origin of all conflict between me and my fellow-men is that I do not say what I mean, and that I do not do what I say. For this confuses and poisons, again and again and in increasing measure, the situation between myself and the other man, and I, in my internal disintegration, am no longer able to master it but, contrary to all my illusions, have become its slave. By our contradiction, our lie, we foster conflict-situations and give them power over us until they enslave us. From here, there is no way out but by the crucial realization: Everything depends on myself, and the crucial decision: I will straighten myself out.

But in order that a man may be capable of this great feat, he must first find his way from the casual, accessory elements of his existence to his own self; he must find his own self, not the trivial ego of the egotistic individual, but the deeper self of the person living in a relationship to the world. (155-159)

Guilt and Guilt Feelings

To the valid scientific realm of psychotherapy belong the "inner" reactions of the individual to his passive and active life experience, the psychic elaboration of the biographical events, whether it takes place in conscious or in unconscious processes. The relationship of the patient to a man with whom he stands in a contact that strongly affects his own life is for the psychologist only important as such in so far as its effects on the psyche of the patient can serve the understanding of his illness. The relationship itself in its reciprocal reality, the significant actuality of what is happening and has happened between the two men, transcends his task as it transcends his method. He limits himself to those of its inner connections that his work of exploring the mind of the patient makes accessible to him. And yet, if he wishes to satisfy not merely what he owes to the laws of his discipline and their application, but also what he owes to the existence and the need of man, he may—in fact, he must—go beyond that realm where an existing person merely relates to himself. He must cast his glance again and again to where existing person relates to existing person. . . . Within a comprehensive service to knowledge and help, he must himself encounter guilt as something of an ontic character whose place is not the soul but being. . . . He must be ready even to step out of the established rules of his school. But a "doctor of souls" who really is one—that is, who does not merely carry on the work of healing but enters into it at times as a partner—is precisely one who dares. . . .

Almost everyone who seriously concerns himself with the problem of guilt proceeds to derive the guilt feelings that are met with in analysis from hidden elements, to trace them back to such elements, to unmask them as such. One seeks the powerful repressions in the unconscious as those that hide behind the phenomena of illness, but not also the live connection the image of which has remained in the living memory, time and again admonishing, attacking, tormenting, and, after each submersion in the river of no-longer-thinking-about-that, returning and taking up its work anew.

A man stands before us who, through acting or failing to act, has burdened himself with a guilt or has taken part in a community guilt, and now, after years or decades, is again and again visited by the memory of his guilt. Nothing of the genesis of his illness is concealed from him if he is only willing no longer to conceal from himself the guilt character of that active or passive occurrence. What takes possession of him ever again has nothing to do with any parental or social reprimand, and if he does not have to fear an earthly retribution and does not believe in a heavenly one, no court, no punishing power exists that can make him anxious. Here there rules the one penetrating insight—the one insight capable of penetrating into the impossibility of recovering the original point of departure and the irreparability of what has been done, and that means the real insight into the irreversibility of lived time, a fact that shows itself unmistakably in the starkest of all human perspectives, that concerning one's own death. From no standpoint is time so perceived as a torrent as from the vision of the self in guilt. Swept along in this torrent, the bearer of guilt is visited by the shudder of identity with himself. I, he comes to know, I, who have become another, am the same. . . .

The psychologist who sees what is here to be seen must be struck by the idea that guilt does not exist because a taboo exists to which one fails to give obedience, but rather that taboo and the placing of taboo have been made possible only through the fact that the leaders of early communities knew and made use of a primal fact of man as man—the fact that man can become guilty and know it.

Existential guilt—that is, guilt that a person has taken on himself as a person and in a personal situation—cannot be comprehended through such categories of analytical science as "repression" and "becoming-conscious." The bearer of guilt of whom I speak remembers it again and again by himself and in sufficient measure. Not seldom, certainly, he attempts to evade it—not the remembered fact, however, but its depths as existential guilt—until the truth of this depth overwhelms him and time is now perceived by him as a torrent. . . .

The doctor who confronts the effects on the guilty man of an existential guilt must proceed in all seriousness from the situation in which the act of guilt has taken place. Existential guilt occurs when someone injures an order of the human world whose foundations he knows and recognizes as those of his own existence and of all common human existence. The doctor who confronts such a guilt in the living memory of his patient must enter into that situation; he must lay his hand in the wound of the order and learn: this concerns you. . . .

. . . What I call existential guilt is only an intensification of what is found in some measure wherever an authentic guilt feeling burns, and the authentic guilt feeling is very often inextricably mingled with the problematic, the "neurotic," the "groundless." The therapist's methods, naturally, do not willingly concern themselves with the authentic guilt feeling which, in general, is of a strictly personal character and does not easily allow itself to be imprisoned in general propositions. It lies essentially nearer to the doctrine and practice to occupy itself with the effects of repressed childhood wishes or youthful lusts gone astray, than with the inner consequences of a man's betrayal of his friend or his cause. And for the patient it is a great relief to be diverted from his authentic guilt feeling to an unambiguous neurotic one that, favored within this category by the school of his doctor, allows itself to be discovered in the microcosmos of his dreams or in the stream of his free associations. To all this the genuine doctor of souls stands opposed with the postulative awareness that he should act here as at once bound and unbound. He does not, of course, desist from any of his methods, which have, in fact, become adaptable. But where, as here, he becomes aware of a reality between man and man, between man and the world, a reality inaccessible to any of the psychological categories, he recognizes the limits that are set here for his methods and recognizes that the goal of healing has been transformed in this case because the context of the sickness, the place of the sickness in being, has been transformed. If the therapist recognizes this, then all that he is obliged to do becomes more difficult, much more difficult—and all becomes more real, radically real. . . .

The unconscious is still far less concerned than the conscious about whether the essence of this man thrives. Essence—by this I mean that for which a person is peculiarly intended, what he is called to become. The conscious, with its planning and its weighing, concerns itself with it only occasionally; the unconscious, with its wishes and contradictions, hardly ever. Those are great moments of existence when a man discovers his essence or rediscovers it on a higher plane; when he decides and decides anew to become what he is and, as one who is becoming this, to establish a genuine relation to the world; when he heroically maintains his discovery and decision against his everyday consciousness and against his unconscious. . . .

The psychotherapist is no pastor of souls and no substitute for one. It is never his task to mediate a salvation; his task is always only to further a healing. But it is not merely incumbent upon him to interest himself in that need of the patient that has become symptomatically manifest in his sickness. . . . That need is also confided to him that first allows itself to be recognized in the immediacy of the partnership between the patient . . . and the doctor. . . . If he may now surrender himself to a more direct vision, it can still only be one that realizes its individual norms in each of its insights—norms that cannot be translated into general propositions. In this sphere of action, too, even though it seems left to his independent direction, the man of the intellectual profession learns that a true work is an affair of a listening obedience.

But in order that the therapist be able to do this, he must recognize just one thing steadfastly and recognize it ever again: there exists real guilt, fundamentally different from all the anxiety-induced bugbears that are generated in the cavern of the unconscious.

When the therapist recognizes an existential guilt of his patient, he cannot . . . show him the way to the world, which the latter must rather seek and find as his own personal law. The doctor can only conduct him to the point from which he can glimpse his personal way or at least its beginning. But in order that the doctor shall be able to do this, he must also know about the general nature of the way, common to all great acts of conscience. . . .

. . . Among all living beings known to us man alone is able to set at a distance not only his environment, but also himself. As a result, he becomes for himself a detached object about which he can not only "reflect," but which he can, from time to time, confirm as well as condemn. . . . The table of shalts and shalt-nots under which this man has grown up and lives determines only the conceptions which prevail in the realm of the conscience, but not its existence itself, which is grounded in just that distancing and distinguishing—primal qualities of the human race. The more or less hidden criteria that the conscience employs in its acceptances and rejections only rarely fully coincide with a standard received from the society or community. Connected with that is the fact that the guilt feeling can hardly ever be wholly traced to a transgression against a taboo of a family or of society. The totality of the order that a man knows to be injured or injurable by him transcends to some degree the totality of the parental and social taboos that bind him. The depth of the guilt feeling is not seldom connected with just that part of the guilt that cannot be ascribed to the taboo-offense, hence with the existential guilt. . . .

. . . The primeval concept of conscience, if only it is understood as a dynamic one rather than as a static, judging one, is more realistic than the modern structural concept of the superego. . . . If we now wish to speak of actions in the sphere of conscience in this high and strict sense, we do not mean thereby the well-known synthesis out of the internalization of censure, torment, and punishment that one customarily regards as the proper factual content of conscience—that pressuring and oppressing influence of an inner high court on an "ego" that is more or less subject to it. . . . What concerns us here is . . . that possible moment when the whole person who has become awake and unafraid ascends from the anguishing lowland of the conscience to its heights and independently masters the material delivered to him by it.

From this position a man can undertake the threefold action to which I have referred: first, to illuminate the darkness that still weaves itself about the guilt despite all previous action of the conscience—not to illuminate it with spotlights but with a broad and enduring wave of light; second, to persevere, no matter how high he may have ascended in his present life above that station of guilt—to persevere in that newly won humble knowledge of the identity of the present person with the person of that time; and third, in his place and according to his capacity, in the given historical and biographical situations, to restore the order-of-being injured by him through the relation of an active devotion to the world—for the wounds of the order-of-being can be healed in infinitely many other places than those at which they were inflicted.

In order that this may succeed in that measure that is at all attainable by this man, he must gather the forces and elements of his being and ever again protect the unity that is thus won from the cleavage and contradiction that threaten it. For, to quote myself, one cannot do evil with his whole soul, one can do good only with the whole soul. What one must wrest from himself, first, is not yet the good; only when he has first attained his own self does the good thrive through him. (114-122)

The bearer of existential guilt remains in the realm of conscious existence. This guilt is not one that allows itself to be repressed into the unconscious. It remains in the chamber of memory, out of which it can at any moment penetrate unexpectedly into that of consciousness, without it being possible for any barriers to be erected against this invasion. The memory receives all experiences and actions without the assistance of man. It may, however, retain the ingredients of what is remembered in such a manner that what ascends into the actual remembering does not enter it in its original character. The existential guilt, therefore, does not enter it as such. Only when the human person himself overcomes his inner resistance can he attain to self-illumination. (128)

Pointing the Way

HEALING THROUGH MEETING

. . . In certain cases, a therapist is terrified by what he is doing because he begins to suspect that, at least in such cases, but finally, perhaps, in all, something entirely other is demanded of him. Something incompatible with the economics of his profession, dangerously threatening, indeed, to his regulated practice of it. What is demanded of him is that he draw the particular case out of the correct methodological objectification and himself step forth out of the role of professional superiority, achieved and guaranteed by long training and practice, into the elementary situation between one who calls and one who is called. The abyss does not call to his confidently functioning security of action, but to the abyss, that is to the self of the doctor, that selfhood that is hidden under the structures erected through training and practice, that is itself encompassed by chaos, itself familiar with demons, but is graced with the humble power of wrestling and overcoming, and is ready to wrestle and overcome thus ever anew. Through his hearing of this call there erupts in the most exposed of the intellectual professions the crisis of its paradox. The psychotherapist, just when and because he is a doctor, will return from the crisis to his habitual method, but as a changed person in a changed situation. He returns to it as one to whom the necessity of genuine personal meetings in the abyss of human existence between the one in need of help and the helper has been revealed. He returns to a modified methodic in which, on the basis of the experiences gained in such meetings, the unexpected, which contradicts the prevailing theories and demands his ever-renewed personal involvement, also finds its place. . . .

. . . If one recognizes the ontic, in fact, suprapersonal ontic character of guilt, if one recognizes, therefore, that guilt is not hidden away inside the human person, but that the human person stands, in the most real way, in the guilt that envelops him then it also becomes clear that to understand the suppression of the knowledge of guilt as a merely psychological phenomenon will not suffice. It hinders the guilty man, in fact, from accomplishing the reconciliation whose ontic nature has, to be sure, been rather obscured by some discussions of moral philosophy and moral theology. . . . Reconciliation cannot take place merely in relation to the man towards whom one has become guilty (and who is perhaps dead), but in relation to all and each, according to the path of his individual life, according to his surroundings and his circumstances. . . .

In a decisive hour, together with the patient entrusted to and trusting in him, he has left the closed room of psychological treatment in which the analyst rules by means of his systematic and methodological superiority and has stepped forth with him into the air of the world where self is exposed to self. There, in the closed room where one probed and treated the isolated psyche according to the inclination of the self-encapsulated patient, the patient was referred to ever-deeper levels of his inwardness as to his proper world; here outside, in the immediacy of one human standing over against another, the encapsulation must and can be broken through, and a transformed, healed relationship must and can be opened to the person who is sick in his relations to otherness—to the world of the other which he cannot remove into his soul. A soul is never sick alone, but always a between-ness also, a situation between it and another existing being. The psychotherapist who has passed through the crisis may now dare to touch on this. (94-97)

Karl Jaspers

Reason and Anti-Reason in Our Age

There are in the world today independent psychotherapists who love man and want to help him. They work as individuals using their own personal methods. They also use psychoanalytical methods but without becoming their slaves. They do not organise and make a matter of mechanical technique what must always remain a matter of personal communication between individuals. They will permit the so-called training analysis for those who ask for it of their own free will but will not demand it for scientific or dogmatic reasons and they will refuse to admit it as the condition which a psychoanalytical doctor must fulfil before he can be registered.

But in one of the trends developing within the psychoanalytical movement, which appears to be steadily increasing, something quite different is happening. Just as Marxism owes its influence not to the particular insights it has contributed to scientific knowledge but to its totalitarian approach and unscientific character, so it is with this type of psychoanalysis. Psychoanalysis as a faith is made possible by basic scientific errors, a few of which I shall briefly describe.* First, to understand the meaning of something is not to explain its cause. The understanding of the meaning of something takes place in mutual communication: causality is foreign to this process and means recognising something as different and distant. Understanding does not have an effect on things, but leaves the road open to freedom. Causal explanation enables one to intervene to some extent in the process of events, to steer it towards certain desired ends. But if I confuse the possibility of the understanding of meaning, in the realm of freedom, and causal explanation I am violating freedom; for then, I am treating it as an object, as if it were a perceptible object, which is to degrade it. In addition I shall miss causal possibilities which really exist.

Secondly, the character of therapeutical effects is questionable. It is known that all kinds of psychotherapeutical processes have been successful in the hands of effective personalities throughout the ages. But psychoanalytical treatment has had as many successes and failures as other methods. The satisfaction which some patients derive from a detailed analysis of themselves and of their whole life-history can scarcely be called a cure. (21f.)

* The reference to the soul in contrast to the earlier isolated observation of physical phenomena is, in general, a great gain. . . . Many important discoveries have been made in the sphere of psychoanalysis. I have attempted to discuss these matters both critically and positively in theoretical psychology and in practice, in my *Allgemeine Psychopathologie*, 5th edition 1948, especially pp. 251-374, 563-598, and 661-686. In my book *Man in the Modern Age* (1931), I drew parallels between Marxism, psychoanalysis and the theory of race, as veiling in very different ways our true picture of man, and at the same time I pressed for a methodical development of genuine particular knowledge in these spheres.

Freedom turned into an object is no longer freedom at all. . . . Psychoanalysis and being psychoanalysed becomes the real life and the deepest satisfaction of those who believe in it. It is the materialisation of a belief in the flux of endless symbolic metamorphoses and descents into hell. This belief, though apparently in a constant movement of criticism, resists all criticism of its principles. It refuses to listen. But it is able to indulge in the infinite material of possible meanings and symbolic fixations. The development of the movement into an orthodox faith which began with Freud's sentence of excommunication on unfaithful disciples, is a trend inherent in the nature of the method. . . . The unconditional requirement of the so-called training analysis is the first step in this direction. (24f.)

Helen Merrell Lynd

On Shame and the Search for Identity

To some extent everyone experiences a loss of early trust, which may leave a nostalgia for familiar images unmarred by change. But the extent to which some form of early trust continues for a person, and the way in which it is transmuted into more mature and understanding confidence, determine in important ways his future sense of identity. . . .

Separate, discrete acts or incidents, including those seemingly most trivial, have importance because in this moment of *self*-consciousness, the self stands revealed. . . . The shameful situation frequently takes one by surprise. But one is overtaken by shame because one's whole life has been a preparation for putting one in this situation. (49)

Identifications with other persons in situations that make them feel ashamed lead . . . to the confrontation of the human condition and the possibilities and the tragic limitations of man's lot. This confrontation may be the beginning of the realization of shame as revelation—of oneself, of one's society, and of the world—and of the transcending of shame. . . . Apprehension that one's own life may be cut off from others, empty, void of significance, is a terrifying thing; but fear that this same isolation is true for others, and that the world itself may hold no meaning is infinitely worse. Experience of shame may call into question, not only one's own adequacy and the validity of the codes of one's immediate society, but the meaning of the universe itself. (56f.)

. . . The anguish of the experience of shame is not so much the fear that isolation or alienation will be the *penalty* for the shameful act as that the experience of shame is itself isolating, alienating, incommunicable. (67)

Protection against isolation and the difficulty of communicating such experiences as shame may take the form of impersonalization and dehumanization. If I cannot communicate with others, then I will at least not risk openness; I will deny the possibility of openness; I will protect myself against it. . . . If experiences of shame can be fully faced, if we allow ourselves to realize their import, they can inform the self, and become a revelation of oneself, of one's society, and of the human situation. (70f.)

The kind of perception human beings have of their bodies, the image they hold of them, is peculiarly involved in shame. . . . The body image is in part a social phenomenon. One's body image helps to shape one's image of the world, and one's image of the world affects the image one has of one's own body. . . . The "castration complex" is only one expression of the fear of dismemberment and the desire for integrity of all parts of the body. The loss of the sense of integrity of one's body and of intimacy with it results in a sense of depersonalization, loss of one's own identity, which is a symptom of mental disease. (136f.)

An interpretation of personality that includes purpose opens the way to understanding other people as persons, and to friendship, mutual discovery, and love in personal relations. . . . Freud's description of persons as objects that administer pleasure or pain tends to make a psychological necessity of what Marx accounted a defect of capitalism. Freud's view that almost every intimate personal relation leaves a sediment of aversion and hostility is closely allied, not only to Schopenhauer, whom he quotes, but to Proust, who believed that intimacy breeds contempt. . . . Fromm dissociates himself from Freud's view of other persons as objects or instruments of pleasure. But his use of "symbiotic" relations always in an invidious sense (turning the root meaning of symbiosis, living together in intimate association, into the derived meaning, parasitism) and his view that one must have a generalized love of everyone in order to love any one person can lead to a minimizing of the possibilities of mutual love between one person and another. (153)

If we take seriously the possibility of relating to other persons as persons, then seeing them primarily as need-satisfying objects, or in terms of their particular status or role relations to oneself, or as approving or disapproving audience is as limited as seeing personality primarily in terms of release of tension, return to quiescence, and self-preservation. . . . For some psychoanalysts the person is the patient in his office; other persons in the environment of the patient—family, friends, professional associates—are so many objects who foster or interfere with the patient's well-being. But there is some denial of human dignity with the loss of a perspective in which each person matters. (155)

The possibility of personal self-realization in and through relations with others and of a society in which alienation is overcome suggests Rousseau's, Hegel's, and Marx's vision of the good life in which self-realization and relations with other persons in one's social group will be not antithetical but mutually enhancing. . . .

The ability to enter into relations of intimacy and mutuality opens the way to experiences in which the self expands beyond its own limitations in depth of feeling, understanding, and insight. One's own identity may be, not weakened, but strengthened by the meaning one has for others in one's group and by respect for these other persons as distinct individuals. . . . This experience involves the risks of trusting oneself to other persons instead of regarding them in object, status, role, or audience relations. (159)

No profession has ever occupied a position or assumed a responsibility entirely comparable to that of psychoanalysis. The psychoanalyst has been compared to a surgeon. But because of the kind of intimate relation he has and encourages with his patient, his own character and his personal values enter into his therapeutic methods in a way and to an extent that is not true for the surgeon. He has been compared to a priest. But the priest by the nature of his assumptions does not do the kind of detailed probing over a period of years that the analyst does; and, to many persons who seek psychoanalysis today, to speak with the voice of Science is more than to speak with the voice of God. This particular combination of intimacy and impersonal authority is, I think, without precedent. It gives to the analyst enormous power. The persons who come to him are vulnerable, and the process of analysis tends, at least in its initial stages, to increase their vulnerability. Both because of the methods they use and the content of their therapy, there is probably no group of persons today—with the exception of priests and some practitioners of "mental healing"—in a position to exercise as much power over persons with whom they come into professional contact as psychoanalysts. . . .

There would seem to be two situations in which the kind of opening of oneself that is an essential of the analytic treatment is possible: one where the relation is one of mutuality, and there is in trust and love the opening of two persons to each other; the other where the person to whom one opens oneself is the surrogate of God or of some higher power. The analyst is in neither of these situations; he is likely to stand first on one foot, then on the other, and few analysts seem to me to have confronted the full complexity of this problem. (196)

. . . What is this real, spontaneous self independent of romanticism and of all authority—or at least of all irrational authority—that we are exhorted to realize? If the psychology of the market place, of achievement, and of success are to be repudiated, what is the reality that we must accept and adjust to if we are to avoid the unrealities of sentimentality and insubstantial idealism? The difficulties of self-realization in the midst of these conflicts may be more profound than Fromm sometimes seems to recognize. . . .

. . . Admonitions to be one's spontaneous, real self and at the same time to accept reality minimize the difficulties of the problems involved. Learning when to yield to a recalcitrant reality and when to try to change it is a main problem of life, one that must constantly be resolved afresh. The question is not whether to adjust to or to rebel against reality, but, rather, how to discriminate between those realities that must be recognized as unalterable and those that we should continue to try to change however unyielding they may appear. Our whole life is spent in an attempt to discover when our refusal to bow to limitations is romantic escape from actualities and when it is courage and rational faith. . . .

So, too, our whole life is an attempt to discover when our spontaneity is whimsical, sentimental irresponsibility and when it is a valid expression of our deepest desires and values. Horney, Fromm, and even Sullivan at times, seem to assume that there is an already existent real or true or spontaneous self which can be evoked into active existence almost at will. There is a tacit assumption that somehow we know the dictates of the real self, and that we should live in terms of these rather than of a romanticized self-image or of the pseudo-self of others' expectations. But, like understanding of "reality," such a real self is something to be discovered and created, not a given, but a lifelong endeavor. (202f.)

Psychologists and psychoanalysts, if not social scientists, have given more encouragement to the adjustment of individuals to the realities of a given society than to personal differentiation and deviation from them. They frequently fail to give explicit recognition to the distinction between normal or healthy in terms of whatever are the generally accepted norms of the society and in terms of what is humanly desirable. If the psychoanalyst or the social scientist does not rigorously examine his own values in relation to those of society, he almost inevitably tends to accept tacitly the dominant values of the society as the norm of behavior, and to measure mental health and illness by these. Scientific objectivity, then, becomes indistinguishable from acceptance of social determinants. (212)

Openness to relatedness with other persons and the search for self-identity are not two problems but one dialectical process; as one finds more relatedness to other persons one discovers more of oneself; as the sense of one's own identity becomes clearer and more firmly rooted one can more completely go out to others. It is not a loss of oneself, an "impoverishment," but a way of finding more of oneself when one means most to others whom one has chosen. Nor must complete finding of oneself, as Fromm and others sometimes seem to imply, precede finding oneself in and through other persons. Identity is never wholly realized. Love is never perfect. Strength to apprehend love that is beyond anxiety, beyond the need to use other persons for one's own security, beyond desire for power over others is never complete, but may grow throughout life. Like identity and mutuality with others it is a lifetime process of discovery. (241)

If . . . one can sufficiently risk uncovering oneself and sufficiently trust another person, to seek means of communicating shame, the risking of exposure can be in itself an experience of release, expansion, self-revelation, a coming forward of belief in oneself, and entering into the mind and feeling of another person. (249)

Kurt Goldstein

Human Nature in the Light of Psychopathology

FOREWORD—1963

All adequate human behavior presupposes concrete performance and abstract attitude. While an action is always performed by the person himself in a concrete way, the influence of the abstract attitude behind it can originate either in the same person or in another. But human life cannot be wholly understood through these attitudes alone. To grasp the fullness of life, one must consider another area of human experience. I have called this the "sphere of immediacy." While concrete-abstract behavior guarantees order and security, the sphere of immediacy makes unity possible between the world and ourselves, particularly in our relationship to other human beings.

It is not easy to describe this sphere. To enter it, we must try to disregard somewhat the "natural science" attitude which, since it does not comprise the totality of human nature, appears "unnatural" in this sphere. We achieve this immediacy only by surrendering ourselves to the world with which we come in contact. When we do this, the words we use to describe our experiences may appear strange and reminiscent of the language of poets. Such words reveal a new world not normally observed in our practical or scientific behavior. More properly, we intentionally repress this world because its influence may disturb the stability and security of the subject-object world of our culture. Yet these experiences of immediacy are related to the same world in which we otherwise live. They represent its deepest character. We are here involved in our totality, while in the subject-object world we experience only isolated parts of ourselves and the world—a point of view which may be preferable for special purposes.

In my book *The Organism* (re-issued by Beacon Press, 1963) I discuss the importance of adequate order between us and the world for the attainment of true knowledge. I must stress here that the impulse to *seek* for knowledge originates fundamentally in the sphere of immediacy. Through it, human life acquires its dynamic character. In this sphere is not only the source of all creativity, the development of friendship, love and religion, but also those possibilities for failure, sorrow and anxiety which are part of our life. While being in the sphere of immediacy may involve danger, we deliberately take this risk, since only thus can we realize ourselves fully (see my paper "On Emotions," *J. Psychol.*, 1951, *31*, p. 37).

The sphere of immediacy is already present in the first year of life (see my paper "The Smiling of the Infant and the Problem of Understanding the Other," *J. Psychol.*, 1957, *44*, p. 175). Within it the adequate relationship between mother and infant originates. Later it is especially significant for our understanding of what goes on in the "other." How deeply our life is rooted in the sphere of immediacy is shown by our reaction to any discrepancy between it and the subject-object sphere, which disturbs their unity or, more accurately, their harmony. If, for instance, on meeting a beloved friend we smilingly approach him in expectation of happiness and are deceived in this expectation, we may not simply have a sense of error, i.e., a failure in the concrete-abstract sphere; rather, we feel the ensuing shock as something dangerous which touches the core of our nature. Our well-being and possibilities for self-realization are endangered, our very existence and that of the world. For they are all based upon the experience of real unity with the other; they are experiences in the sphere of immediacy. (x-xiii)

Viktor von Weizsäcker

The Unity of Perception and Movement

The essential element in the crisis of the I is not only the transition from one order to another, but also the forfeiture of continuity or identity by the subject. It is the subject which is annihilated in the schism or leap if the transformation does not ensue once a compulsion to complete the impossible has been erected. After the leap, the ego would, so to speak, not land. We first notice the subject properly when it threatens to disappear in the crisis. . . . The subject is not a permanent possession: to possess it, one must continually earn it. . . . The unity of the subject does not come to be except in its perpetual restoration in spite of instability and crisis. The ephemeral character of the subject is a persuasive explanation for the fact that there is so much fear of subjectivity. . . . The re-erection of the subject which follows every crisis proves not its unreliability but its strength and resilience. . . . (176-178) The subject is composed of one-time occurrences and has to perpetuate itself over and beyond these. (181)

Now I can find no better designations for the structure of the crisis than those which language has fashioned for the dialectic of *freedom and necessity*. . . . Experience is supposed to teach that reinforcement of the will expands the limits of capacity. In that case, to be able would really mean to want to be able, but an even greater challenge would come up against that border at which even the will to do can no longer compel ability to do. . . . The solution of the problematic of hysteric paralysis could then also be found in the fact that the patient *could* if he only *would*. . . . The origin of action is decision, and this is as much a struggle between "having to do" and "wanting to do" as between necessity and freedom. . . . The mutual arrangement of these categories should be represented not by means of an ontic category such as space, time or causality, but through the social order of I and Thou, he and it, etc. (190-192)

It is the I which suddenly finds itself to be something else in another world. Waking and dreaming, enjoyment and reflection, melancholy and joy, feeling and objectivity, even eating and craftsmanship, lying down and dancing, composing and performing are all so different from one another that one may describe the one as infinitely strange in relation to the other. (194)

Doctor and Patient

I—THE DOCTOR AND THE PATIENT

To understand someone and to understand something are two incomparable cases. Because my understanding, as it were, slips over into the other, we will call this understanding someone a *transjective* in order to have a *terminus technicus*. (79)

The understanding of someone cannot be objective because and so far as this someone himself has an I just as I myself do, and because exactly that which is as much a subject as I am cannot "become" an object, and yet one can still understand *him* (not it!). (82)

We are, after all, attempting to find and designate the understanding of the doctor, since we did not turn to the theoretical but to the biographical truth, where the beginning does not concern itself with knowledge but with questions.

We have now found a method of medical anthropology; it is a biographical one. The investigation of medical knowledge does not follow the critical path here: it does not consider the logical or known theoretical presumptions of knowledge (as in Kant); it is also not the genetic method (as Kant called it) which considers the psychological or mechanical or organic mode of origin of knowledge; medical knowledge is neither critically nor genetically investigated. This is not it (psychology) and it is also not found in an "empathetic" or "understanding" psychology. Psychology is related to the medical task in exactly the same way as surgery, pathology, anatomy, clinical physiology; a means, not the thing itself. . . .

This beginning is a biographical scene and is at first a conversation. We also know the correct direction of this conversation; it must move toward something concrete and the first medical action must consist of a question. The beginning, then, is not knowledge, but questions. Nevertheless, the problem of the "I" is not lost but transformed. The first happening is not that I must recognize the I but that I must speak with him. In this case, the I is no longer an I; it becomes Thou for me. As we have already noted, the I is the subject for all objects and therefore can never "become" the object itself, not even for me. But it can still become "for me," only not "something" but "Thou." (86-88)

III—HISTORY OF ILLNESS

Which is now the way to attain actual experience? One such way is the comradeship along the way between the doctor and the patient, and in their study is revealed that which one can never describe objectively, that which remains much more a becoming. . . . But it doesn't speak about the sickness, it doesn't speak about the natural life history of this specific case, but about the most intensive, uttermost, real and actual truths of the life of this person or the death of this person. It is not the description of the sickness which happened objectively—not nosography—, but it is the perplexity of life itself in the patient; this life itself can still only be the life of *this real human being.* (136f.)

All individual observations and causal judgments belong in another classification of knowledge than the experience of need engenders. This is true for the scientific system of medicine as well as the psychoanalytic one; they both create different classifications and thereby necessarily different images of the reality of the suffering human being. But how can they then come in contact with this reality? Exactly through contact and only through sheer contact; sensory contact with nature in space and time, psychic contact with the person in perceptions and actions alone legitimatizes their insights. This *contact in experience* is thus the *via regia* to the real world, and through it and *only* through it do those sciences participate in the actual history of the patient, in the real human being. At the instant when the judging mind disengages itself from the moment of the experiencing contact, when he merely imagines the person in space as a spatial structure, in time as a process that is running down, only thinks of him as a soul, as an I or as a character—in that instant a false theory of man is generated. He is then thought of as a being of size, surface area, weight, function, desire, consciousness, characteristics and capabilities of all sorts. All these modes of knowledge which are built around the *being* in order to form a judgment about him have at once become false judgments, false images. . . .

In this way, a person is between body and mind, *through* both, in neither; everywhere one is through the other, never does one exist alone. Here, then, a doctrine of experience arises whose "beginning" must be a *perpetual* one in the contact of hand and eye, of ear and soul; a doctrine of the comradeship of the way between doctor and patient, which is not against or in spite of technique and rationalization but through and with these. (145f.)

It is not the objective and rational position of the doctor which makes his effectiveness possible; rather this position exists as a necessary condition of a bond affirmed *de facto*. If this ceases to be, then the objectivity is questionable and good for nothing. . . . Such a doctor is no longer objective toward the patient as he does not consider his sickness as an object but considers his I, therefore that which ontologically is not and cannot become an object, but just a subject. . . .

Right through psychotherapeutically and non-psychotherapeutically oriented doctors, right through the expectation of the patient, yes, right through each one of us goes the difference between objective and comprehensive therapy. . . . It always seems to me to be of the utmost importance that in a comprehensive therapy the doctor lets himself be changed by the patient; that he lets the profusion of excitations that emanate from the patient have an effect upon him; that he does not hem himself in within the system of diagnosis and the systematically isolated illness; that he not only responds with the objective sense of sight but also with hearing, which brings I and Thou closer together, that he be passively receptive with all psychic organs; not only receptive and then reactive, but a real melting away of one's own person through conscious experience and only then again giving in to those first, natural reactions to race, sex, political and social formation (which are included in every consulting hour from the first moment), in short, to all those sympathies and antipathies which taste of the nuances of psychic affinity. Only through this conscious dominion of a *relationship* over the psychic process, in this long and from-case-to-case-ever-newly-offered chain of sacrifices and new involvements of the personality can the doctor be educated in that which enables him to encompass the resistances and to set the projected goal beyond the circumscribed area of objective therapy. . . .

Causes, categories, fundamental thinking, in short, intellectual thinking and objectivity denote isolation, limitation, abstraction, distorted configurations of reality and thereby damage to love—the immediate danger of a false representation and of neurosis. . . .

Sickness is a chance to learn a bit about love and about that second way of knowing, and neither would be possible with a pure, objective treatment. Such an interpretation I would choose to call neither philosophical nor psychological nor biological but *anthropological*. Only anthropologically can we determine the actual effective value of a medical method, the active principle of a therapy. (167-172)

Every need is then an I-related condition; the person who acts from the equilibrium of his undisturbed center does not need to look after himself. The need first forces self-observation and is perhaps the birth of self-consciousness. Thus, in every need there lies a narcissistic aspect. But just because the need cuts short the unconscious giving oneself to the outside, to the world, the Thou, to everything not-I and painfully compels a relationship with oneself, just because of this one can also say: this primary phenomenon of need is not only one of I-for-myself but just as much the essential two-ness: it is a separation from others, from the world, from one's neighbor. Yes, we can say further, it is a separation from *the* closest one, the one who seems the closest, from I myself. It separates in me myself from my I. The need that arises from pain, when a limb is forcibly separated from me, the need that arises from vertigo when my I is separated from the spatial world, the need that arises from weakness when one is separated from one's everyday life—these are all separation manifestations in me and they all call to the other for help. So these are perceptions of the two-ness of our existence. And to that extent one can say that the need phenomena are facts of the relationship between man and man, and the self-perception is only a variant of the laws of the indissoluble community. This is shown, to be sure, by that very variant which as a need puts in question the relationship between man and man and just thereby calls it forth to another level. (176f.)

Cases and Problems

. . . A phenomenon that must make us mistrustful of many psychoses . . . is the quality of self-assessment. Its self-deification and self-degradation lack moderation. . . . The cause is hard to fathom; it lies at the bottom of the psychosis as the self-determined loneliness. The mentally ill person has no Thou for his I. . . . The struggle of the so-called mentally ill for his own worth and existence is only soluble through some kind of synthesis of his self-evaluation with the evaluation of his social environment. This synthesis would move towards integration, towards the finding of reality if the conflicting images of his value could be understood as mere reflections of each other, that is, as merely the reverse sides of the *same* truth. Truth is now an integration of opposing images; finding truth is only possible on the path of meeting, contact and union, thus through that which is called "communication" in the philosophy of Karl Jaspers, with whom I could agree if he did not demand communication as an occupation of philosophy but of human existence in general. From this insight, I believe, one can understand the important difficulties that have led to sterility in the diagnosis of schizophrenia. That sensory perception in which the patient sees himself as in bed and at the same time as standing next to the bed, is a delusion of a double doubling that is unavoidable after this person has lost binding with a Thou, trust and security in the We. This delusion of a double is nothing more than the hallucinated restoration of a two-ness, after one has reached the unbearable loneliness. It is a representation of a misplaced synthesis of I and Thou; the cleavage of the I represents—for a moment—the relationship of the I to the Thou which has become unattainable. It is a substitute for the latter. (188f.)

Within and Beyond Medicine

The meeting and intercourse of the doctor and patient is a prototype of every discernible and for us only through transformation discernible reality. . . . Here the world-view loses its classical-scientific and also its physical stability. The reality of man is here rather a continual interchange between the I and the environment, an ever-renewed meeting of the I with the environment, a flowing interaction between the I and the environment. . . . The reciprocity of relationships is without a doubt until now the least explored part of medical anthropology. . . . Interaction, reciprocity and solidarity would be, then, three basic concepts of an anthropology. (142, 146f.)

AFTER FREUD

When one arrives at the very ground of events, then the explanations always cease; things are as they are; that is why they are so. . . . But one thing is still noteworthy: the relationship of man to man plays a powerful role, and in this relationship first arises much of that which one calls ability, character, disposition and heredity. This pathology must to an entirely unusual extent be not only individual, but also social. (258)

Erwin Straus

The Primary World of Senses

THE HERE AND NOW

The Here and Now are neither universal nor objective. Every Here is my Here and every Now my Now. Only within the self-world relation can they reveal themselves as this relation's articulated delimitations. Here and Now are neither determinable from within the world alone nor the self alone. A Here or a Now can exist only for me in my world, but both are particular delimitations of the totality of my self-world relation. . . . The fleetingness of the temporal . . . belongs to the essence of the Now. . . . In the Now, I experience my self-world relation and my self as that which becomes. By clinging to its content in every transition, by allowing all contents to exist in the full arbitrariness of a Now, the Now indicates each moment as only a moment of *one* totality relation, as its particular delimitation. (250)

I do not experience myself *in addition* to the world . . . sensory experience unfolds in two directions: toward world and toward self. Sensing is sympathetic experiencing; i.e., in sensing I experience changes of my permanent relation to the world which outlast and unite all individual, particular moments. I, as a sensing being, am a finite, becoming subject, a part of the world toward whose manifold there-points I am directed from the standpoint of my Here in separating and uniting, in taking-in and ejecting. As a sensing being I am *in* the world: As a part of it and yet opposite it, directed toward it and meeting it in its counter-direction. (352) . . . The subject attains to himself only *in* sensing. As a sensing subject, he has a Here and a Now; a Here which is of equal dignity to the There. For that reason, it can move itself toward a There, it is in communication with the *other*. Individual sensations of touch and vision do not, of course, produce this communication. Because I *am* in communication, a particular given here and now can determine me. (356)

DISTANCE AND COMMUNITY

The phenomenal world of distance cannot be derived from the objective world. Distance is a primal phenomenon. Distance is not sensed; sensing unfolds into distance. There is no distance without a sensing and mobile subject; there is no sentience without distance. . . . Distance is . . . relative to a becoming, desiring being. It is *his* reach which determines the articulation of distance into the far and the near. . . . The articulation of distances depends on my state of being, on my Here and my Now. (384f.) . . . Direction would not be possible without distance, and spatio-temporal unity would not be possible without openness into the future. But since direction is equally essential and indispensable both to sensing and moving, . . . distance must be the spatio-temporal form of sensing. (392) The generality and universality of distance is thought of in such a way as to be co-ordinated with each individual subject, that is, as the form of a process of becoming which is open to the future and which itself is not yet fully determined. (395)

In order to have knowledge of sensing and moving human beings, . . . I must think of them as being in this primary, original relation of co-existing. Reflective knowledge can detach them from this relation to the individual observer only with the provision that it recognizes the spatio-temporal form of sympathetic experience, i.e., distance as such. (394) . . . Community, mutual understanding, and communication are connections between living beings founded on the relation of the together-with and the towards-each-other, which do not eliminate the monadic autonomy of the partners, their duality or plurality. . . . Communion demands distance which continues even during the most perfect forms of togetherness, of nearness, of the "we." . . . Communion exists for us as creatures. Because we as living, corporeal beings find ourselves opposite to the world and yet encompassed by the world as creatures and parts, we can meet other beings which . . . prove themselves partners. The encompassing *other* which becomes visible to us in seeing, makes possible the communion between us; it mediates between Me and You. (178) . . . All communication, lingual included, is based in the being-with-another of mobility, of meeting and fleeing in a common surrounding world. . . . In primal and basic communication I am not a knower and the other is not the object of my knowledge. He is not a thing singled out from a neutral background as an object of special interest. I discover the other, my fellow man or fellow creature, as a partner in my waking motor intentions, as a being which can come near me or withdraw from me. (289)

PSYCHOSIS AS A DEFORMITY OF DISTANCE AND MOVEMENT

As long as he remains passive, the world with all its rich content presses in upon the subject. But when he himself turns actively toward the world, then the apparitions disappear. . . . Psychotic hallucinations are . . . shaped in accordance with a fundamental change in communication. . . . Of the many manifestations of psychosis, the phenomenon of depersonalization might be chosen to illustrate our conception of the mode of communication of sensing. Here the most familiar surroundings exist merely as a world of pure perception; it is as though all sympathetic communication has been suspended. The patient, for example, knows that he has walked this particular street a thousand times and that that particular building is his own house, but this knowledge is of no help to him. . . .

Depressive patients not infrequently report the impression of floating while walking; they speak of the ground beneath them losing its firmness, that it rocks beneath their feet, or that they are standing on a slant and have the uneasy feeling that they are sliding off and falling down. . . . The ground is firm only for him who has a firm stance upon it, who has a firm hold upon himself and who can, in a well-defined manner, limit himself as over and against his world. (217-19)

The melancholic knows what it means to lose contact with the landscape. We have the landscape by developing in and with it. The depressive, frozen in unmoving time, is alienated from the landscape, he looks at the world, as it were, in a bird's eye view; he sees it from above like a map; he hovers over the ground. . . . The depressive is filled with an agonizing yearning for the small and the common, a yearning even after bodily pain which might restore to him the feeling of this world. Loss of home, loss of the landscape: This is what we clinically term depersonalization. (328)

In vertigo, the perception of space is changed even before the fall. The spatial continuum seems rent asunder. Nothing links the Here to the There. Indeed, there exists no real Here and There any more. Depth, and also height and breadth, become the absolute Other. And even thus is that place transformed where the vertiginous man stands. It is no longer a fixed Here. In vertigo, a man loses his stance, he cannot go forward or backward, he cannot proceed further, and he cannot stop. . . . The limitless or boundless is that which, without any reflection on his part, appears to the phobic when he confronts spaciousness. In this limitlessness, there are no more fixed and defined locations; no Here, from which a path leads to There. There is no longer a path, and at the same time the possibility of self-movement is suspended. (263)

Ludwig Binswanger

Freud's Conception of Man in the Light of Anthropology

Freud's idea of *homo natura* is a scientific *construct* that is only feasible if it based on a *destruction* of man's experiential knowledge of himself—a destruction, that is, of anthropological experience. . . . Man is not only mechanical necessity and organization, not merely world or in-the-world. His existence is understandable only as being-in-the-world, as the projection and disclosure *of* world—as Heidegger has so powerfully demonstrated. To this extent, his existence already embodies the principle of the possibility of separating necessity and freedom, "closed" form and "open" change, the unity of the formal structure and its abandonment and change into new formal structure. . . .

When this *my* or *our*, this *I* or *he* or *we* are bracketed out, the result is that psychology becomes "impersonal" and "objective," while losing, at the same time, the scientific character of a genuine psychology and becoming, instead, natural science. . . . In place of a reciprocal, "personal" communication within a we-relationship, we find a one-sided, i.e., irreversible, relationship between doctor and patient, and an even more impersonal relationship between researcher and object of research. Experience, participation, and confrontation between human beings in the present moment gives way to the "perfect tense" of theoretical investigation. (166, 169f.)

Heidegger's Analytic of Existence and Its Meaning for Psychiatry

In thus indicating the basic structure of the Dasein as being-in-the-world, Heidegger places in the psychiatrist's hands a key by means of which he can, free of the prejudice of any scientific *theory,* ascertain and describe the *phenomena* he investigates in their full phenomenal content and intrinsic context. . . . Only by referring intentionality back to the Dasein as transcendence or being-in-the-world and only, therefore, with the inclusion of the transcendental ego in the actual Dasein, was the ("objective-transcendental") question posed as to the *what-ness* of the beings that we ourselves are. . . .

In practice, whenever the psychiatrist himself tries to look beyond the limitations of his science and seeks to know the ontological grounds of his understanding and treatment of those placed in his care, it is Heidegger's analytic of existence that can broaden his horizon. For it offers the possibility of understanding man as both a creature of nature, and a socially determined or historical being—and this by means of *one* ontological insight, which thus obviates the separation of body, mind, and spirit. Man as a creature of nature is revealed in the thrownness of the Dasein, its "that-it-is," its *facticity.* . . . The Dasein, although it exists essentially for its own sake (*umwillen seiner*) has nevertheless not itself laid the ground of its *being.* And also, as a creature "come into existence," it is and remains, *thrown,* determined, i.e., enclosed, possessed and compelled by beings in general. Consequently it is not "completely free" in its world-design either. The "powerlessness" of the Dasein here shows itself in that certain of its possibilities of being-in-the-world are *withdrawn* because of commitment to and by beings, because of its facticity. But it is also just this withdrawal which lends the Dasein its *power:* for it is this that first brings *before* the Dasein the "real," graspable possibilities of world-design. . . . The thrownness of the Dasein, its facticity, is the transcendental horizon of all that scientific systematic psychiatry delimits as reality under the name of organism, body (and heredity, climate, milieu, etc.), and also for all that which is delimited, investigated and researched as psychic *determinateness:* namely, as mood and ill humor, as craziness, compulsive or insane "possessedness," as addiction, instinctuality, as confusion, phantasy determination, as, in general, unconsciousness. Now, whereas the science of psychiatry not only observes and establishes connections *between* these two spheres, but also erects the theoretical bridge of the psychophysical—*Daseinsanalyse* . . . shows that it is the scientific dichotomization of man's ontological wholeness that gives rise to this postulate in the first place. It shows that this dichotomization results from projecting the whole of human being upon the screen of that which is merely objectively present [*vorhanden*]. It also indicates the general world-design of science as stemming from one and the same Dasein, from, namely, the Dasein's ontological potentiality of scientific being-in-the-world. Here, too, it is true to say that what lends the world-design its (limited) scientific power is obtained only through its powerlessness to understand the being of human existence [Dasein] as a whole. . . . Thus what in psychiatry is irreversibly separated into discrete realities of fields of study, namely, the finite human Dasein, is presented here in its basic structural unity. . . . The Dasein can thus never get "behind" its thrownness and can only project those possibilities into which it is thrown. Only, therefore, as surrendered over to its *that*, as thrown, does the Dasein *exist* within the ground of its power-to-be. The self of existence, although it has to lay its own ground, can therefore never have power over this ground. As a being, it has to be "as it is and can be." . . . That human beings *can* become "neurotic" at all is *also* a sign of the thrownness of the Dasein and a sign of its potentiality of fallenness—a sign, in short, of its finitude, its transcendental limitedness or unfreedom.

Only he who scorns these limits, who—in Kierkegaard's terms—is at odds with the fundamental conditions of existence, can become "neurotic," whereas only he who "knows" of the unfreedom of finite human existence and who obtains "power" over his existence within this very powerlessness is unneurotic or "free." The *sole task* of "psychotherapy" lies in assisting man toward this "power." It is only the *ways* to this goal that are *various*. . . . What is *essentially* involved is not just the attitude of the "medical man" toward his scientific object. What is involved is his *relation* . . . to the patient, a relation rooted equally in "care" and love. It is of the *essence* of being a psychiatrist, *therefore*, that he reaches beyond all factual knowledge and the abilities that go with it, and that he reaches beyond *scientific* knowledge found in the fields of psychology, psychopathology, and psychotherapy. . . . The psychiatrist in his being summons and lays claim to the whole man. . . . Being a psychiatrist also claims the existence of the psychiatrist. For where meeting and mutual understanding furnish the grounds and basis for everything that can be viewed as symptoms or even as disease and health per se, and where, therefore, there can be nothing human upon which—*in a psychiatric sense*—judgment cannot be passed, then hobby, science, philosophy, art, and religion must be capable of being projected and understood from the perspective of personal existence as ontological potentialities and conceptual projects. (206f., 212-214, 218-220)

Basic Forms and Knowledge of Human Existence

In contrast to a purely objective or objectifying psychology, which can but set walls of theory around love, existential knowledge has its authentic ground and basis in the loving being-together [*liebenden Miteinandersein*] of I and Thou. Questions involving objectivities obscure this loving being-together and resign themselves to a mere detour of the phenomenon. Questions, however, as to human being receive their proper directives from this being itself. For it is out of the undivided fullness of being of the Each-other [*des Einander*] that I and Thou first emerge to attain their "selfhood" *in* each other. But it is also true that the mere act of *taking* "the other" *at something*—his word, his weak point, etc.,—this "handling" of a person, or traffic of one person with another or others in social life, politics (great or small), in legal or business contexts: this *taking-at* is also understandable only when it is revealed as a "constriction" of or "fall" from being-together [*Mit-einander-Seins*] into mere being-with [*Mit-Sein*] of one person and another. This is especially true in regard to the being-unto-itself of the self-sufficient ego. In our times psychology proceeds from the absolutized individual ego, thus "fallen," and its powers, dispositions, events, processes, activities, tendencies, functions or acts, and from there orients itself as to its method and structure. But this merely indicates that it has taken the directives of its search from the impersonal objectivity of a conception of "social life" patterned after nature, and the concepts of thing, property, function and energy found in the natural sciences. At best, it takes its cue from the idealism of a one-sidedly constituted *intentionality*. (21)

We are the highest spatial principle since you are not without my being there. It is only *because* you and I *are* already "in" the We—as belonging together—that I *belong* there where you are, that I can be *there where* you are, that there, where you are, can a place "for me" "arise." . . .

Love cannot be ontologically understood as something which binds together two self-subsisting individuals, or which permits two subjects . . . [or] existences to share (communicate) each other's one-sidedly constituted world. It can be understood only as the Dasein's being open to its *oneness* or, if one prefers, its *wholeness* in the primal form of the We. Apart from this basic existential form amorousness may very well be possible, but not either the Communio or the "meeting" of love. (29f.)

. . . The There of love and the selfhood of the Dasein as love does not mean a disclosedness of the There for my self . . . but for *our*-selves . . . the selfhood of love does not amount to a selfhood of the *I*, but of the We. The There of the Dasein as love is not disclosedness by which Dasein (as mine) is there "for itself," but, rather, "disclosedness" by which Dasein (as We) is there for *our-self*, for *you and me*, for *each*,—and this, again, not as the sense of the being-there [Da-sein] of the world (of Care), but as the being-there [Da-sein] of the "world" of Each-Other. (34)

The temporality of love—in contrast to all those forms of concern—"arises" not out of the finitude of the Dasein as mine, but out of the "eternity" as ours, out of the "eternal We." (37)

Buber's comparison between object (= standstill) and essentiality (= duration), between past and present, lies in the same direction as our comparison between time ("life") and love as eternal duration. But, at the same time, his distinction corresponds to the Heideggerean separation of the inauthentic present in the sense of the temporality of fallenness into the world of concern (satisfaction with the "fleeting" and "transient" things which man *knows* and *makes use of*), and authentic temporality in the sense of the resolute retrieving of self from this fallenness in the *instant* which brings with it existence "in the situation." . . .

However much we may learn from Jaspers, his instant still remains within the historical-ethical sphere of "existential processes"; it is to be "grasped" only in the philosophical consciousness ("as a phenomenon of eternal being"). Though genuine love may have a certain relation to such an existential process, ontologically its nature is precisely *not* such a process. Love is neither historicity, nor ethical being, nor philosophical attitude. In *one* word, it does not claim the Dasein philosophically as existence or selfhood, but completely "naively" as We. (47f.)

. . . This making-present has no other sense than that of *each of us* making room for the other, I for you and you for me, which means that it makes room for the There of the Dasein in the "deepest sense" of unique *belonging* to each other, for the *homeland* [Heimat] of "I and Thou," the dual *We*. (57)

This "spatiality" has, now, its own mode of *meeting* (in regard to this expression, cf. Martin Buber, *I and Thou*) quite different from the mode of the meeting of "people" concerning themselves with the surrounding world and *sharing that* world with each other. The meeting of lovers as lovers spatializes precisely the "space" of loving being-together, and is only another expression of the *making room* of love, namely, the *disclosure* of the *We-space*, the spatiality of each-other, I and Thou. In the context of the *with-world* [*Mitwelt*] this meeting can—"in" a look, a greeting, a word, a handshake, a deed, a disposition, "phantasy" or "idea"—"come into view," flash forth in the phenomenon, or be "lived through." These are all expressions for the fact that in and with this meeting a new "world" opens up or is disclosed, the "world" of the loving We. This meeting, if it be truly a *loving* meeting, cannot be repeated in the wordly-temporal sense of "again" or "once more." . . . But it would be false to think that loving meeting can flash forth, i.e. *be*, only "in the moment" of a *particular* meeting in the surrounding with-world. The "Mysterium of love" is understood only when one sees that the meeting of lovers as lovers—in which I and Thou are born as we-both, in which the world of our love opens itself and we there stand transformed and under a new "law"—, that this particular meeting would not be possible in the first place were not the Dasein in its ground already a loving meeting. We are therefore not speaking, here, of *empirical* preconditions of this moment in the sense, say of "unconscious impulses" which "may" (but not necessarily) precede the becoming conscious of love, nor are we speaking of those "conditioning factors" of love whose intricacies Freud's genius sought out and described. What is involved is, rather, a component of the Dasein's ontological structure. This element is not to be understood in terms of the Dasein's concernful *being-with* in relation to others; phenomenologically and ontologically, it is more primary. That is, it is not an existentially derivative element. Only if Dasein already has the character of meeting, only when "I and Thou" are already part of its ontological structure, is love between Me and You at all possible. . . .

To say that the Dasein is in itself already loving meeting is to say that this meeting *is* not only in the encounters of the surrounding with-world and in the meetings with a particular individual Thou, but that it already *is* [ontologically prior—trans.] as a "going forward" toward the "awaited" and as yet unspecified Thou, as a being drawn toward "Thou," and as a search "for the Thine." . . . In the "meeting" of lovers we must distinguish the following: 1. Their meeting *within-the-world* as beings *concerned-with* [*als Besorgende*], i.e., the with-worldly meeting which arises out of the surrounding world which is the object of concern and out of the spatiality of Care. Such a meeting "does not yet have anything to do" with love. 2. Their meeting *as lovers,* i.e. as the spatiality of the being-together of love [*liebenden Miteinander*], making room for the "plenum" of the loving We. This alone shall be spoken of as *meeting* or loving meeting. (82-86)

It is precisely because we are in the world as loving and *not only* as caring that, loving, we can permeate the Care world; it is, moreover, on these grounds that world—environment as well as with-world—is at all *possible,* not only as a ready-to-hand, "objective" and with-worldly being, but also as the Thou of love, as loving meeting. (98)

Just as, loving, I can only say *I* as a member of a We, i.e., "with reference to" or "in addressing" You, so it is that something can come from my heart only "in reference to" You and as "directed towards" You. Indeed, only *because* of this can I *say* the loving *I* at all. When something comes from the heart or goes right to the heart it is an exclusively I-Thou phenomenon. It is otherwise when we *take* something to heart or experience something which *touches* the heart. We must distinguish between two different concepts of "heart." One sense coincides with the homeland of love, the "I and Thou"; the other overflows in the world of the "emotional."

You . . . can show me your self-sufficiency positively only if You—as second person—at the same time *give* yourself, in *first person,* to me and *receive* me; just as I can show you my self-sufficiency positively only if I—as your second person—at the same time *give* myself to you and *receive* you. The selfhood of this I and Thou is thus grounded not in the Dasein as mine or thine, but in the Dasein as *ours,* i.e., in the being of the Dasein as *We.* Here selfhood issues only from the We. (126)

Without the possibility of loneliness, you could not be your-*self* in the sense of the selfhood of love. You would be either an "unself-sufficient" second person, my mere alter ego within a common (mystical or orgiastic) ego-state, or even a "third person," an "other" exhaustible in his finite "role" as a being "standing over against me." "Opposite me" . . . all these psychological actualities would not be at all possible were not love in itself—that is ontologically and phenomenologically—already this "rhythmic" dialectical movement of dualness and loneliness in the We. . . . The more of me I give you, the more I have my self, and the more you give me of you, the more you have your self. Loneliness, therefore, does not signify my-turning-away-from-you or even my-secluding-myself-from-you; on the contrary, it signifies *my-revealing* or *becoming-transparent* in giving-myself-to-*you* and being-received-*by-you*. (132f.)

The origins of this my self-abasement through you are already there when you avoid limiting yourself through me, through "my immanent separateness," and allow me to exist only as *your own experience*, as an element of "thine-ness." (166) . . . The spoken dialogue of the loving We is, like all forms of love, solely "governed" and articulated by the "sincerity of the heart." This sincerity or openness is, however, not thematic, but is, rather, the "native" ["*heimatliche*"] atmosphere of loving dialogue. It is this atmosphere alone which is decisive as to the nearness and remoteness of the loving We. (213) . . . Taking-part does not "bring about" the I-Thou relationship or the With-another; it is, rather, being-with-another, the We, which is the ground of taking-part. . . . Taking-part is no "one-sided" act of "empathy," putting oneself in the other's place, of fellow-feeling—for if it were it would be mere sym-pathy with a human or animate creature. It is, rather, a "two-sided" receiving and giving based on a "mutual" loving readiness for what the future has to offer. (234f.)

Extravagance [Verstiegenheit]

. . . Only where the *communio* of love and the *communicatio* of friendship is missing and where mere intercourse and traffic with "others" and with one's self has taken over the exclusive direction of our existence, only there can height and depth, nearness and distance, present and future, have so much importance that human existence can *go too far*, can attain to an *end* and a *now* from which there is neither retreat nor progress. In such a case, we speak of conversion into Extravagance. . . . Robbed of *communio* and *communicatio*, the Dasein can no longer widen. revise, or examine its "experiential horizon" and remains rooted to a "narrow minded," i.e., sharply limited, standpoint. . . . Even schizophrenic insanity can, in my opinion, be understood . . . only if it is taken initially as an *existential mode* of Extravagance. . . . The disproportion evidenced in the manic pattern of life is spoken of daseinsanalytically as *flightiness*. It signifies the impossibility of obtaining a genuine foothold on the "ladder" of human problems and, in this respect, thus *also* signifies the impossibility of authentic decision, action, and maturation. Detached from loving *communio* and authentic *communicatio*, all too far and hastily driven *forward* and *carried upward*, the manic hovers in fraudulent heights in which he cannot take a stand or make a "self-sufficient" decision. Love and friendship have, in these *airy* heights, lost their power. Human intercourse is reduced to the level of psychiatric treatment. . . .

. . . Extravagance signifies therefore, the *"absolutizing"* of a single *decision*. Again, such "absolutizing" is only possible where the Dasein is "despairingly" exiled from the home and eternalness of love and friendship, where, therefore, it no longer knows or senses the "relativity" of the "above" and "below" seen against the background of an unquestioning *trust* in Being, an unproblematic ontological security. It stands isolated from this security, and from intercourse or traffic with others, and is thus barred from the challenge and correction which can only be derived from such intercourse. . . . Consequently, rescue from the Extravagant position becomes possible only by means of "outside help," as is true of a mountain-climber who has climbed too far out upon a precipice. . . .

The neurotic, too, can be "rescued" from the Extravagance and confinedness of his existence (for example, in cases of phobia) only by outside help, in the sense of collaboration and communication with someone else. . . . What we call psychotherapy is basically no more than an attempt to bring the patient to a point where he can "see" the manner in which the totality of human existence or "being-in-the-world" is structured and to see at which of its junctures he has overreached himself. That is: the goal of psychotherapy is to bring the patient safely back "down to earth" from his Extravagance. Only from this point is any new *departure* and *ascent* possible. (343-349)

Introduction to Schizophrenie

The inconsistency of experience undergoes an apparently new ordering, the apparent taking of a stance amid the disorder of experiential inconsistency. . . . The Dasein now stakes everything on "maintaining" this stance, on—in other words—pursuing this ideal "through thick and thin." The ideal is Extravagant in that it is completely inappropriate to the total life-situation and does not, therefore, represent a genuine means. On the contrary, it sets up an insurmountable and impenetrable wall in the path of existence. The Dasein can no longer find its way back out of this Extravagance and instead becomes more and more deeply enmeshed in it. The effect of this is even more catastrophic in that the formation of Extravagant ideals represents only one aspect of the alternative, while the other embraces everything that contradicts this ideal. . . . Giving up the Extravagant ideal means the bottomless *anxiety* of succumbing to the other side of the alternative. . . .

Now, the complete submersion of the Dasein in the particular pair of alternatives also means that the existence can, in general, temporalize itself only in the mode of "deficiency"—in the mode, namely, that we have come to know as *fallenness* to the world, or, in short, as "*mundanization*" [*Verweltlichung*]. This is manifested most clearly in the "concealment" involved in the phenomenon of "protecting" shame . . . (modesty, *pudeur, Scham*) by means of the deficient mode of public shame (stemming from one's own reflection thrown upon others—*Schande, la honte*). But the same thing (mundanization) is also manifested in the deficiency of those modes in which we encounter *conscience, regret,* genuine *humor* and, above all, *love* in our patients. We almost always find that the authentic *dual* existential mode of the Dasein is present in the mode of deficiency. . . . If, now, the Dasein "senses the enemy" everywhere, if in every event and act it not only suspects, but sees hostile intentions, the reason lies not in an alteration of the Dasein's sense of reality or meaning, its perception or psychic functioning, nor does the reason lie in a "physiognomic" alteration of the world and "sympathetic relationships" in Erwin Straus's sense. All these alterations are, rather, secondary and tertiary consequences of the resignation of the Dasein in the form of its self-withdrawal from its own decisional frame of reference.

It should be clear now that the content of the psychosis (in this case the sadistic orgies of the enemies) also represents nothing primary. It merely indicates to us the mode in which the Dasein fills "with phantasy" the experiential gaps or vacua which its retreat from the antinomic tension has left. . . . The decisive element lies, as has been said, in the particular, individual nature of the *resignation* or final capitulation of the Dasein, culminating in the withdrawal from the Dasein's decisional frame of reference —in other words, the Dasein's surrendering of itself to the will of "alien" forces or "alien" persons. In the place of an antinomic tension (arising from the inconsistency of experience) between two irreconcilable alternatives, what emerges now is a more "one-sided" and thus more consistent, "incorrigible," "unproblematic" experience in the sense of a psychotic experiential model according to which all new experience is fashioned. (254f., 257, 264)

The Case of Lola Voss

In the case of Lola, we could observe in an extreme degree the phenomenon of what we call mundanization [*Verweltlichung*], a process in which the Dasein is abandoning itself in its actual, free potentiality of being-itself, and is giving itself over to a specific world-design. In all these cases, the Dasein can no longer freely allow the world to be, but is, rather, increasingly surrendered over to one particular world-design, possessed by it, overwhelmed by it. . . . Far from widening or deepening the ability of being-oneself, the Extravagant [*verstiegene*] ideal restricts the possibilities of being-oneself, so much so that the existence is only able to be itself within quite specific, ever narrower limits; outside these limits it becomes more and more dependent and bonded, that is, squeezed in the vise of a single world-design or world-model. This is what we called "thrown-ness," absorption of the existence by "world." . . . Becoming overwhelmed in this sense finds its extreme expression in the phenomenon of delusion. . . . Just as Ellen West pursued the ideal of slenderness, of having an ethereal body, Jürg Zünd, that of societal security, so Lola was after the ideal of security of existence in general. And as Ellen foundered ("went to the bottom spiritually") due to the overwhelming "claims" of her body or those of her environment, so Lola foundered through the "claims" of the disturbing world at large. While Ellen sought cover against getting fat by fasting, Nadja against becoming "conspicuous" by hiding, and Jürg tried to be "inconspicuous" by wearing a protective overcoat, appearing harmless, and mixing with upper-class company, so Lola sought cover from the world, which disturbed her security and peace of mind, by the continuous interrogation of "fate." Thus, everything unfamiliar or threatening was to be kept away or removed. All these are attempts to maintain and defend the thoroughly unfree (because once and for all determined) "ideal" self against anything contradictory. . . . In Lola's case, however, despair is not only, as in the other cases, despair at having to be in the world in a particular way and no other; it is despair at being-in-the-world at all. . . .

When it retreats from the world of fellowmen, from its coexistors, the Dasein also forgoes itself, or rather forgoes itself as a self. This only applies to complete schizophrenic autism. . . . By existential weakness we mean that a person does not stand autonomously in his world, that he blocks himself off from the ground of his existence, that he does not take his existence upon himself but trusts himself to alien powers, that he makes alien powers "responsible" for his fate instead of himself. All this applies in an extreme degree to the case of Lola Voss. . . . While Jürg Zünd's existence was completely possessed by the coexistence of the others, by the preponderance of public opinion and judgment, Lola's existence is possessed by and exposed to a very different, still more anonymous, still less tangible superpower that seduces existence time and again, reassures it temporarily, alienates it more and more from itself, and completely prevails upon it. . . . The decisive part is played by a superior, uncanny, even dreadful *it,* confronted with which the Dasein feels completely forlorn, abandoned by the others (and even more so by the thou), and left to its own devices. . . .

Being "delivered to," "possessed by," "having surrendered," "thrownness"—all these expressions imply, in terms of time, the bare inauthentic present; "bare" insofar as this present is not temporalized out of the future and the past into a genuine present. The bare present, in contrast to the actual moment, can only mean a nondwelling [*Unverweilen*], a lack of location. Where, as in the case of Lola, existence has surrendered in so large a measure to the Overpowering, it remains totally closed to itself. It may again and again be at rest for a moment, only to be "driven about," disturbed, harassed anew. . . . Inasmuch as continuity is tantamount to freedom, to existence, or to formation of an authentic self [*Selbstigung*] and hence also tantamount to communication (without which authentic existence is not possible), negation of continuity means unfreedom, being-possessed by the overpowering Sudden and, at the same time, lack of independence and of communication. Indeed, existence as it is "thrown" into uncanniness is destined to be isolated. . . . Existence escapes its actual task and its actual meaning, but it does not escape anxiety. What it gains through mundanization—displacement of its own responsibility and guilt onto an outside "fate"—has to be paid for with the loss of freedom and compulsive entanglement in the net of external circumstances and occurrences. . . . Since what Kierkegaard called "the Profound in existence"—that nonfreedom makes a prisoner of itself—is valid for all human existence, schizophrenia merely represents a particularly intensive and peculiarly constituted variation of that change of freedom into non-freedom or, as we express it, of existence into world. . . . Freedom consists in the commitment of the Dasein to its thrownness as such, non-freedom in denying it autocratically and violating it on the basis of an Extravagant ideal. Such wrong-doing to existence is most cruelly punished in schizophrenic existence. . . . What we are facing here is not a moral guilt—which would be far more harmless—but the lack of existence as such, due to Extravagance. Extravagance, however, is man's ignoring of the fact that he has not himself laid the ground of his existence, but is a finite being, whose ground is beyond his control. . . .

Like the genuine phobias, delusions can only be understood in terms of existential anxiety (and by no means through the "affect of anxiety"). "World" now no longer means a totality of conditions which the existence has taken in its stride, but a condition definitely determined by the being as something frightful, a condition of hostility, of something which is, once and for all, hostile or threatening. It is a world-design which is no longer carried by nor bears any traces of *love* and *trust*, or of the closeness to humans and things which results from these feelings. . . . Where the existence is no longer in a position to design the world freely, it also suffers the loss of the self. (284-286, 288, 290-292, 294f., 300)

Existential Analysis and Psychotherapy

A psychotherapy on existential-analytic bases thus proceeds *not* merely by showing the patient where, when and to what extent he has failed to realize the fullness of his humanity, but it tries to make him *experience* this as radically as possible. . . .

. . . The existential analyst . . . will always stand on the same plane with his patients—the plane of common existence. He will therefore not degrade the patient to an object toward which he is subject, but he will see in him an existential partner. He will therefore not consider the bond between the two partners to be as that of two electric batteries—a "psychic contact"—but as an *encounter* on what Martin Buber calls the "sharp edge of existence," [2] an existence which *essentially* "is in the world," not merely as a self but also as a being-together with one another—

[2] The authorized and more accurate translation of this phrase is "the narrow ridge." [*Cf.* Maurice Friedman, *Martin Buber: The Life of Dialogue* (New York: Harper Torchbooks, 1960), Chapter I—"The Narrow Ridge."] Martin Buber also prefers "meeting" to "encounter" as the translation of his central concept "*Begegnung*." I have followed this usage in all the translations made especially for this book, of writers influenced by Buber (Binswanger, Trüb, and others).—M.F.

relatedness and love. Also what has, since *Freud,* been called transference is, in the existential-analytic sense, a kind of encounter. For encounter is a being-with-others in *genuine presence,* that is to say, in the present which is altogether continuous with the *past* and bears within it the possibilities of a *future.* (20f.)

. . . The existential analyst, insofar as he is a psychotherapist, not only is in possession of existential-analytic and psychotherapeutic competence, but . . . he must dare to risk committing his own existence in the struggle for the freedom of his partner's. (23)

Medard Boss

Psychoanalysis and Daseinsanalysis

The term *Daseinsanalyse* was orginally introduced by Ludwig Binswanger to characterize his method for investigating psychopathological phenomena and to distinguish this method from Heidegger's ontological analyses, *Daseinsanalytik.* (Although Heidegger provided the starting point for Binswanger's work, the latter has recently stated that he misunderstood Heidegger, adding that he hopes the misunderstanding will be a fruitful one. See L. Binswanger, "Daseinsanalyse und Psychotherapie," in *Acta Psychotherapeutica et Psychosomatica,* Vol. 8, No. 4, 1960, p. 258.)

For clarity I have decided to use "Daseinsanalysis" and its derivative forms "Daseinsanalytic" and "Daseinsanalyst" to designate Boss's approach exclusively. This decision has been facilitated by the fact that Binswanger's method has already been referred to in American publications as "existential analysis." See, for example, *Existence,* edited by Rollo May, Ernest Angel, and Henri F. Ellenberger (New York, 1958), which contains two case histories of Binswanger. (Ludwig Lefebre—trans.)

. . . Heidegger opposes the idea that man never has access to particular beings themselves, that he perceives them only through specific "designs" or projects, as if the meaningful connections of which "world" consists were a network with which the human subject overlays a merely extant material. There, too, and in sharp contradistinction to Sartre's school of existentialism as well as to Ludwig Binswanger's subjectivistic revision of the "Daseins-analytic" approach, Heidegger expressly mentions man's *immediate* ability to understand himself and what he encounters (i.e., things and other human beings) in the unity of the "there," in the world-openness of his horizons. . . .

. . . Each of man's concrete ways of handling something or of his becoming aware of something is inherently and essentially luminating and world-disclosing. (50f.)

Every individual human *Dasein* participates with all others essentially—and from the beginning—in the luminous world-openness, each in its own way, according to its possibilities for world-disclosing relationships. This world-openness, this *"Da,"* may, therefore, almost be compared with the brightness of a day, where all the sun's rays participate in being-with—and illuminating—the same things of the world. The fact that human existence is in every case "my" existence does *not* exclude "being-with" others of my own kind. On the contrary, it is of the essence of *Dasein* to "be with." The "world" of man's being-in-the-world is ever and primordially one which I share with others. The world of *Dasein* is essentially *Mitwelt.* For we never exist primarily as different subjects who only secondarily enter into interpersonal relations with one another and exchange ideas about the objects all of us perceive. Instead, as any direct observation shows, we are all out there in the world together, primarily and from the beginning, with the same things shining forth in the common light of all our existences. . . . No psychopathological symptom will ever be fully and adequately understood unless it is conceived of as a disturbance in the texture of the social relationships of which a given human existence fundamentally consists, and that all psychiatric diagnoses are basically only sociological statements.*

The Daseinsanalytic Reasons for Dropping the Assumption of an Unconscious. One of the immeasurable advantages of the Daseinsanalytic understanding of man lies in its making superfluous the assumption of an unconscious. Analysis of *Dasein* makes us realize that we have no basis for conjecturing the existence of subjective images which mirror an independent, external reality,

* See M. Boss, "Why Does Man Behave Socially After All?" *Proceedings of the Third World Congress of Psychiatry,* Montreal, 1961, pp. 228-233. (55 f.)

nor for assuming processes (occurring in some intrapsychic locality) which fabricate ideas and thoughts which correspond more or less to this external reality. . . . Instead, analysis of *Dasein* enables us to become aware that the things and fellow men which an individual encounters, appear to him—within the meaning-disclosing light of his *Dasein*—immediately (and without any subjective processes being involved) as what they are, according to the world-openness of his existence. Because it is the essence of *Dasein* to light up, illuminate, disclose, and perceive, we always find *Dasein* primordially *with* what it encounters. . . . Existing in this fashion, man depends on what he encounters as much as the encountered depends on the disclosing nature of man for its appearance.

From this point of view, one can understand without difficulty that a thing discloses itself even more fully and with greater reality if it appears in "condensation," i.e., if it has several meanings (which may even contradict each other), than if it is unequivocal. Though a thing may show itself in a manner which cannot be defined sharply by concepts, it may yet disclose more of itself than when it reveals only those features which can be forced into an unequivocal definition based on its utilitarian and calculable characteristics, in positivistic fashion. We also have good reason not to limit epithets such as "real" and "correct" to those perceptual phenomena which easily fit within the frame of reference of watch time and three-dimensional space, homogeneously extended. For we have seen . . . that both are "derived," insofar as they are specific manners in which original temporality and spatiality may be conceptualized. Altogether Daseinsanalysis can grant an immediate and autonomous reality to all kinds of phenomena which, in Freud's view, would be degraded from the start to incorrect deceptions of the unconscious. Daseinsanalysis can do this because it has not prejudged a whole host of phenomena according to an arbitrary decision as to the nature of the world and reality. Daseinsanalysis makes it unnecessary to go beyond immediate experience. It can elucidate without difficulty, on the basis of immediate experience alone, all those psychic phenomena that forced Freud to invent the unconscious. (93f.)

Transference is always a genuine relationship between the analysand and the analyst. In each being-together, the partners disclose themselves to each other as human beings; that is to say, each as basically the same kind of being as the other. No secondary "object cathexes," no "transfer of libido" from a "primarily narcissistic ego" to the "love object," no transfer of an affect from a former love object to a present-day partner, are necessary for such disclosure, because it is of the primary nature of *Dasein* to disclose being, including human being. This means that no interpersonal relationship whatsoever necessitates a "transfer of affect." (123)

On the contrary, Daseinsanalysis regards every analysand-analyst relationship as a genuine relationship *sui generis*. It is genuine despite the fact that the patient is carrying it out in a limited fashion owing to his mental distortions. It could not be otherwise. The analysand-analyst relationship, like any other, is grounded in the primary being-with of one man and another, which is part of *Dasein's* primary world-disclosure. The patient's "transference love" is not, therefore, "really" love of someone else—the father, for instance. It is love of the analyst himself, no matter how immature and distorted it may appear because of the limitations of perception imposed on the patient by his earlier relationship to his real father. (125)

In contrast to Freud's opinion, the Daseinsanalyst knows beforehand that so-called transference does not "transfer" anything. He also knows that cures are not effected by months of "working through," during which the supposed meaning of the patient's relationship to the analyst and of his acting-out are drilled into him. The Daseinsanalyst admits "transference love or hate" as the genuine interpersonal relationship to the analyst as which the analysand experiences them. The fact that the analysand behaves in an infantile manner, and therefore misjudges the actual situation to a large extent (because of his emotional immaturity, which in turn is due to faulty training in his youth), does not detract from the genuineness of his present feelings. The analysand begins to love the analyst as soon as he becomes aware that he has found someone—possibly for the first time in his life—who really understands him and who accepts him even though he is stunted by his neurosis. He loves him all the more because the analyst permits him to unfold more fully his real and essential being within a safe, interpersonal relationship on the "playground of the transference." As we have said before, all genuine love of one person for another is based on the possibility which the loved one offers to the lover for a fuller unfolding of his own being by being-in-the-world with him. On the other hand, the patient will hate his analyst as long as he is still (because of his childhood experiences) open only to a child-father or child-mother relationship which limits his perception of adults to frustrating experiences. He will hate him even more—and with good reason—if the analyst, because of his own so-called countertransference (i.e., his own neurotically restricted emotional attitude toward the patient) actually behaves like one of the formerly hated parents. (239f.)

The discovery that man is essentially one in whose meaning

disclosing relationships the phenomena of our world make their appearance, develops in the Daseinsanalytic therapist a basic respect for the intrinsic value and essential content of everything that shines forth and comes into its being in the light of a *Dasein*. Because he has realized that the meaning and context of everything that comes his way shows itself directly to him, he has no need to destroy what he actually sees and hears from the analysand and to replace it with assumed forces supposedly underlying the patient's behavior and perception. Daseinsanalysis thus enables the practitioner to dispense with the tedious intellectual acrobatics required by psychoanalytic theory. He is free to discard the psychoanalytic libido theory as well as the labored psychoanalytic interpretations of symbols, both of them obstacles to an immediate understanding between physician and patient. . . .

The psychotherapist becomes less prejudiced. He can devote himself fully to the analysand in the "evenly-hovering attention" that Freud always demanded. He does not approach the patient from the point of view of a scientific theory (which, by the way, cannot supply the therapist with a conscious motive for his undertaking); nor is his attention distracted by the observation of assumed anonymous forces within the patient. Instead, the analyst's behavior rests on the insight that, being human, he is called upon to disclose both things and men. This knowledge increases his sensitivity to all the obstacles which generally reduce the potential relationships of a patient to a few rigid and unauthentic modes of behavior. Such sensitivity in turn enables the Daseinsanalyst to carry out an "analysis of resistance," wherein the patient is tirelessly confronted with the limitations of his life and wherein these limitations are incessantly questioned, so that the possibility of a richer existence is implied. As a rule, neurotically reduced people regard their wretched interpersonal relations as the only ones possible. They do not know that greater freedom is available. If their restrictions are repeatedly questioned, previously non-admitted possibilities of behavior regularly appear, along with perception of the things and fellow human beings who belong to these world-disclosing possibilities. The analyst practicing in this fashion will not try to persuade patients that much of what they feel and mean is only a cloak for opposite wishes and tendencies. He will thus avoid giving the impression of devaluating their experience, thereby confusing them and arousing unnecessary anxiety. However, the Daseinsanalyst's respect for phenomena should not be confused with an exclusive concern with those phenomena of which the patient is already fully aware. He knows that the patient's being includes, apart from overtly admitted and accepted modes of behavior, a great many other modes of being, some of which the patient is trying hard not to become aware of, and many of which contrast with the overtly expressed modes. He also knows that these possibilities for relating have to be acknowledged by the patient as his own before he can get well. Nevertheless, all of the patient's modes of behavior—those openly carried out and those so far warded off—are considered autonomous by the therapist; he must treat all as valid. He must never try to deny the reality of a phenomenon. . . .

He is able to accept all the ways in which his analysands begin to relate. He has no need to put new obstacles, arising from his personal censorship based on theoretical prejudices, in the patient's way. The Daseinsanalyst's conscience is clear when he consistently refrains from declaring that one kind of behavior (for instance, instinctual reactions) is more real or fundamental than another. Such impartiality is of great practical importance. It eliminates the danger of so-called unbreakable transference. This therapeutic difficulty often arises when the analyst attempts to reduce (by means of interpretation) a new mode of behavior on the part of the patient to an earlier relationship in the patient's life, a relationship considered primary and causal *because* it took place earlier. If this budding possibility of relating is not permitted to unfold in its own fashion, it remains fixated on the embryonic level of the transference relationship. It is unlikely that this will happen if the patient's feelings are regarded as actually directed toward the analyst and thus accepted in their full reality, even though the patient's perception of the analyst is still distorted and restricted because of earlier experiences. The Daseinsanalyst's attitude toward patients' feelings in the transference situation is characteristic of his attitude toward all happenings during the analytic cure. What belongs to the creatural realm, for example, is permitted to be just that. The realm of the divine is similarly granted its authenticity; it is not regarded as a product of sublimation of infantile, libidinous strivings and thereby degraded to unreality.

Daseinsanalysis admits all phenomena on their own terms. Hence the therapist avoids a second danger—that of "curing" the patient's initial symptoms then inducing a new neurosis best called "psychoanalytis." This syndrome (by no means rare) leads its sufferers to ritualistic thinking and talking in psychoanalytic terms and symbols. Circles and sects are formed of similarly afflicted persons. While many such adherents may lose old symptoms, the neurotic nature of their new conduct is easy to detect. Instead of staying close to the immediately observable appearances of the world, they disregard them and speculate about what is "behind" them, unaware that their observations do not support their deductions. Instead of dwelling in openness toward the things and people they encounter, they "interpret" these same phenomena, human and material. Generally such people cling rigidly to their theoretical convictions and take great pains to avoid people with different ideas. Their symptoms indicate their inability to penetrate beyond the concepts and interpretations of psychoanalytic theory; they have failed to arrive at an open and immediate world-relation. Their fear of being contaminated by other ideas betrays their neurotically restricted mode of living, where genuine freedom and openness is always experienced as a threat. (233-236)

. . . In the strict sense of the term, no event in the life history of a person can ever be the "cause" of neurotic symptoms. Personal experiences merely initiate inhibitions against fully carrying out all possible interpersonal and interworldly relationships. (248)

The healing factor in psychoanalysis can never consist in . . . "living out," but consists, rather, in an increasing appropriation of all of one's life-possibilities as *possibilities*. Unless a human being has become aware of and acknowledged as his own all his possibilities of relating to what he encounters (whether they please him or his fellow men or not), no true self-knowledge, no authentic responsibility, is possible. The actual carrying out of these possibilities in one's relations toward partners outside the analytic situation, however, is—as must be made very clear to analysands—a completely different question, and must be in accord with the most productive unfolding of a patient's whole existence, including the welfare of those whom he encounters. (254)

. . . The analyst must realize that there can be no psychoanalysis without an existential bond between the analyst and the analysand. Analysis without countertransference is an illusion in a double sense. An emotional relationship with the analysand can never be avoided by the analyst; it can only be denied by him. (The objectifying attitude of indifference is itself a mode of emotional relating.) Second, "countertransference" is not transference at all, but a genuine emotional interhuman relationship between the analyst and his patient, distorted as it may be.

The adequate human relation between the analyst and his patient, wrongly called countertransference, presupposes in turn that the analyst himself has matured into the freedom of selfless concern for his patients. This includes full awareness of the true meaning of every permissive and frustrating action he undertakes in regard to the analysand's genuine maturing. It also includes a free relation of the analyst toward his own sensuality and his egotism. It means that the analyst has all his own sensual and egotistical tendencies at his free disposal and can keep them from interfering secretly or openly with his genuine concern and selfless love for the patient. (258f.)

Man's existential guilt consists in his failing to carry out the mandate to fulfill all his possibilities. Man is aware of existential guilt when he hears the never-ending call of his conscience. This essential, inevitable being-in-debt is *guilt,* and not merely a subjective *feeling* of guilt. It precedes all psychologically understandable feelings of guilt, no matter what neurotic guise these may appear in. Because of existential being-in-debt (experienced as guilt), even the most skillfully conducted psychoanalysis cannot free man of guilt. Actually, not a single analysand could be found in the whole world who has been transformed into a really guiltless person by psychoanalytic treatment. The most—and the worst—an analysis can accomplish in this regard is to deafen a patient to his pangs of conscience, and this is not to his advantage. The ideally new man, liberated from guilt by psychoanalysis, is an antiquated myth: charming and beautiful but, alas, incapable of realization.

Psychoanalysis, however, can accomplish something else. It can elucidate the past, present, and future of a patient's life to the point where he becomes thoroughly aware of his existential being-in-debt. This in turn enables him to acknowledge his debt, to say "yes" to it and take it upon himself. He becomes aware of his possibilities for living through listening to the call of his conscience; he can take them over responsibly, stand by himself, and thus make them part of himself.

Once a person has been freed for his essential and existential being-in-debt, he no longer experiences *neurotic* feelings of guilt. These latter did not originate in himself, but derive from a foreign and crippling mentality which his educators forced upon him. He had fallen prey to modes of life which were alien to him, but he could not shake them off. Such neurotic feelings of guilt continually increase existential guilt as well, since they result in a steadily increasing debt in regard to a fulfillment of one's own existence. As a result, the call of conscience becomes increasingly persistent. But the patient, caught in acquired moralistic concepts, misunderstands this voice as a demand to follow ever more rigidly a mode of living essentially foreign to himself. A vicious circle results. Only analysis can break its spell. (270f.)

If, through years of earnest effort beyond the scope of the

previous psychological theories, the Daseinsanalyst gains insight into the world-disclosing essence of man, he will . . . help many a patient beyond the relief of symptoms to participation in a human freedom and openness, the dimensions of which vastly transcend the conceptions of a "psyche," a "subjectivity," or a "personality." (282f.)

"Daseinsanalysis" and Psychotherapy

Up to now modern psychologists believed that their therapeutic approaches had found a sound basis in terms of their various psychodynamic theories about the human psyche. . . . Yet all these modern anthropologic theories can't possibly warrant an adequate understanding of the psychotherapeutic processes. For none of them answers what ought to be the first and foremost questions: what would have to be the nature of such a "Psyche," such a psychic apparatus, such a human I or Self or total personality in order that something like a mere perception of an object and of a human being, or even something like object relations and interpersonal and social relations, be at all possible? . . . Yet all these phenomena are central factors for a true healing.

The eminent importance of the "Daseinsanalysis" in the sense of Martin Heidegger's fundamental ontology for psychology and psychotherapy lies in the fact that it helps overcome just these shortcomings of the basic anthropologic concepts of our psychological thinking, shortcomings which until now actually kept us groping in the dark. The "Daseinsanalysis" is able to do so because its concept of man's basic nature is nothing more or less than an explicit articulation of that understanding of man which has always guided our therapeutic actions, independent of all secondary theories, although secretly only and without our awareness. Therefore, the daseinsanalytic understanding of man helps us comprehend directly and fundamentally why therapists *can* demand of their patients what they have in fact been asking all along, and why they even *must* demand it if they want to cure at all. In all their endeavors psychotherapists rely on the peculiar ability of man to exist in a variety of instinctual, feeling, thinking and acting relationships to the things and in social and interpersonal patterns of behavior towards the fellowmen of his world. The therapist tacitly counts on this human ability when he asks of his patient—and tries to help him achieve it by this or that psychotherapeutic method—that he knowingly and responsibly seize and adopt all his potentialities of relationships so that they no longer remain frozen in unconscious neurotic mental or physical symptoms because of early childhood inhibitions and repressions. . . .

. . . Daseinsanalysis had to learn again to see man unbiased, in the manner in which he directly reveals himself, and, in so doing, it made a very simple but all the more significant discovery about the fundamental nature of man. It found that man exists only *in* his relations and *as* his relations to the objects and fellowmen of his world. In order to exist in such manner, however, man must intrinsically possess a fundamental understanding of the fact that something *is* and can *be* at all. Man's special manner of being-in-the-world can therefore only be compared to the shining of a light, in the brightness of which the presence of all that is can occur, in which all things can appear and reveal themselves in their own, proper nature. . . . The intrinsic ability of the human "dasein" to be open to the world in this way does not just discover things which can be located somewhere in space and time. It also opens up ways for the direct and immediate understanding of beings, who, as human beings, not only are altogether different from the things, but who, according to their manner of being as "dasein," are in this world in the same way as I am. Because of this being-together-in-the-world the . . . world is always that which I share with others, the world of "dasein" is world-of-togetherness ("Mitwelt"). . . . (81-85)

This insight teaches us that there is a being-together which is of such intrinsic and essential nature that no man can in fact perceive another even in the distance, without being already—through the mere art of perceiving—involved in the other's particular world-relatedness in some specific way. Thus, from the very first encounter between the therapist and patient the therapist is already together with his patient in the patient's way of existing, just as the patient already partakes in the therapist's manner of living, no matter whether, either on the part of the therapist or the patient, their being-together manifests itself for some time only in aloof observation, indifference or even intense resistance. . . .

. . . Only in the primordial being-together as it was brought to light by Heidegger's "Daseinsanalysis" we are able now to recognize the very foundation of all psychotherapeutic possibilities. Owing to this basic structure of man's existence, the most seriously ill schizophrenic patient, for instance, partakes in some way or other as human being in the wholesome mode of living of his psychotherapist; hence, such a patient's fundamental possibility of being cured by the adequate being-together of a psychotherapeutic situation through which he may recollect his true self again. . . . The daseinsanalytic way of thinking . . . helps us understand such central phenomena as "psychic projection" and "transference" . . . with full justice to reality out of the primary intrinsic being-together of all men in the same world. (87-89)

Anxiety, Guilt, and Psychotherapeutic Liberation

Anxieties may . . . appear much earlier in a life history than feelings of guilt, late forms of human guilt phenomena may resemble early ones ever so much, but man's ability-to-feel-oneself-guilty as such is and remains in every guilt phenomenon an autochthonous being-guilty, with its own autonomous origin and essential nature. If the ability-to-be-guilty as such were not an entirely primal feature of man's very nature, no father would ever have been able to instill an awareness of guilt into a defiant son, no priest in a guilty believer, no capitalist boss in a slack employee, no people's commissar in a comrade who has not fulfilled his production quota. Thus not one single psychoanalysis either—against all the expectations bound up with the adoption of the naturalistic theories—has ever succeeded the other way round in making a patient feel really and fundamentally *free* of guilt. At best the various psychotherapies . . . succeed in modifying the different contents of the guilt feelings of patients. . . . (181)

. . . If one keeps oneself really exposed to the full and undissembled essence of anxiety, it is precisely anxiety that opens to man that dimension of freedom into which alone the experiences of love and trust can unfold at all. . . .

Since "guilt," "Schuld" as indebtedness, is what is missing and lacking, the nature of the human guilt can be understood only from the standpoint of the fullness and fulfillment of human existence. (186)

. . . Man's basic nature reveals itself to our immediate perception as that being that our world *needs* as the realm of lucidity necessary for the coming forth, the being-able-to-appear-and-to-be of its phenomena. However, it is just the allowing-oneself thus to-be-claimed and needed, and nothing else, which in his innermost recesses is what man owes to that which is and has to be. Thus all human feelings of guilt in general are rooted in *this* state of owing. *This* state of owing is, if you will, man's existential indebtedness and guiltiness. Consequently there is not a single phenomenon of the human conscience which would not have to and could not be understood basically as a summons and a monition to discharge the human duty to be a custodian and guardian of everything that has to appear, to be and to unfold in the light of any given human existence. . . . Man is, by the very terms of his being, guilty and remains in debt to his death. His entire being is not fulfilled until he has accepted and carried out all the possibilities of relationships to the phenomena continually hurled upon him by his future and until he has allowed the emergence of the world which seeks appearance in the light of his existence. Man's future, however, at best has reached him fully and in a genuinely human way in the moment of his dying. . . .

If he freely assumes his being-guilty, his being indebted, over against his given existential possibilities, if he decides in this sense in favor of having-a-conscience and accordingly *wanting*-to-let-himself-be-used and engaged as the luminating world-openness, then he no longer feels the essential being-indebted and being guilty of human existence as a *burden* of guilt and an *oppression* by indebtedness. The burden and oppression are overcome in the joyous readiness to place himself without reservation at the disposal of all phenomena as the light and clearing into which they can appear and unfold, and as their custodian.

These insights into the nature of human anxiety and guilt can now also become the supporting basis of the psychotherapeutic liberation of sick people from the fetters of their psychotherapeutic symptoms. . . . The highest aim of all psychotherapy is and remains the opening up of our patients to an ability-to-love-and-trust which permits all oppression by anxiety and guilt to be surmounted as mere misunderstandings. Such trust can and may be fitly called the most mature form of human openness. However, our mentally disturbed patients can attain to it only in the way in which human maturing in general is possible. Normally this happens first of all by way of the physical, concrete experience of a sufficient, imperturbable bestowal of maternal love. Our patients would not be ill if they had not come off the losers in this primary experience. However, this business of coming off the loser and so becoming ill never depends solely on what the mothers were in a position to give in the way of loving support and strength but just as much on the highly variable need for love in the children, which sometimes is insatiably strong. In psychotherapy the important thing is to let the patients first make up for the missing but at bottom indispensable experience of the protective and unshakable bestowal of care and love suited to the individual nature of the patients. . . . Genuine psychotherapeutic eros, in other words, has to distinguish itself by an otherwise never practiced selflessness, self-restraint and reverence before the partner's individuality and uniqueness. These qualities must not be shaken and perturbed either by cooperative, or by indifferent or by hostile behavior on the part of the patient. (188-192)

The greater the indebtedness and guiltiness become the more

tormenting become his neurotic guilt feelings, which again drive him into still more guilty behavior. This gives rise to a vicious circle which not seldom leads to a short-circuit in the form of insanity or suicide, for the future of a person so entangled stares him in the face with increasingly horrible meaninglessness and emptiness.

A psychotherapy based on these insights into the fundamental constitution of man is often enough in a position to break such a vicious circle. It can happen that patients free themselves out of that entanglement of their neurotic guilt feelings, realize their genuine existential indebtedness, and accept it willingly. Then they experience their life really as an anxiety-free, fortunate and meaningful state of being-summoned to belong immediately to the luminating world-openness. (194)

Comments on the Paper by Medard Boss

SABERT BASESCU
New York City

Dr. Boss asks if man is incapable of coming to terms with anxiety and answers that all psychotherapeutic efforts are doomed to failure if he is. But one of the main contributions of Existential therapy has been to clarify the task of the psychotherapeutic process in reducing pathological anxiety so that existential anxiety can be directly confronted. . . . Love does not eliminate anxiety, but rather freedom from pathological anxiety makes love possible. . . . There seems to be a plea in this paper for a return to the Garden of Eden before man ate the fruit of self knowledge—a state of unconscious communion with nature in which there is no self and therefore no anxiety. But this seems to be a way of saying that man would not experience anxiety if he were not characterized by what makes him distinctly human—namely, his self awareness.

LOUIS DE ROSIS
New York City

. . . The person who has developed neurotically . . . is . . . confronted with a double task. One task is that of separating from his eccentric form of integration and the other is the arduous one of engaging himself in the freedom in which the I-Thou relationship, heretofore not available to him, can now begin to occur. It is in the interstices of these double processes that anxiety, as well as guilt, are generated. (197-199)

HENRY ELKIN
New York City

. . . Boss remains Freud's disciple only on the score of the therapist's relation to the patient. A certain kind of objectivity and detachment (for want of less equivocal terms) are necessary, to be sure, for any good therapist. But in both Freud and Boss these qualities are founded on a "selflessness" by which the therapist relates to the patient as the living embodiment of an impersonal, supra-personal scientific or philosophic truth. Is then not the real self of the therapist largely concealed, unrelated to the patient? At any rate, the therapist acquires an aura of masterful imperturbability, an ineffable superiority over the tormented and needy patient. A "loving acceptance" in this human—or inhuman—context is quite different from that in a truly interpersonal, "I-Thou" relationship.

Boss, however, would look on this patient, I fear—because he devalues hatred—with that kind of imperturbable, inwardly dissociated, charitably tolerant "loving acceptance" which makes the small child regard his mother as an infinitely superior, serenely majestic Great Mother-Goddess. This brings to the patient, or child, a tremendous feeling of relief that he is not forthrightly rejected or annihilated. But does *he* feel accepted—*he*, his real self that was expressed in hatred? This "therapeutic" experience establishes, perhaps conclusively, what he has always apprehended, that his real self is too monstrously wicked to be acceptable, or too contemptuously weak to be worthy of respect.

In this enviable situation the therapist's warm, loving reassurance gives rise to that elemental splitting of the psyche which remains the structural core of the human psychological problem. Whereas the patient's more conscious mind is soothed by the therapist's loving responses, the deeper portion of his mind, ego, or self, remains tormented by loneliness, frustrated hatred, and a guilt which is all the more intensified by the therapist's expressions of goodwill and acceptance. . . . The "cured" patient, like the socially collectivized mass-man, lives thereafter always threatened by an underlying despair. But is there also a surrender of deep-rooted egocentricity, or autism? Far from it. The repressed destructive hatred of the now perhaps irrevocably autistic deeper self is transmuted by the collectivization, the "merging in love" of this self, into warm feelings of "love"—the inherently grasping, rapacious power and control-seeking love of the possessive mother or the seductive child. . . .

. . . Boss asserts that to view man as an individual finite being is to fall into a naive "error based on misunderstanding." He insists that the human individual is like a drop of water in the sea of infinite being. Is this an existential viewpoint? Modern existentialism, beginning with Kierkegaard, arose to uphold the supreme value of "the single one," the human person against the onslaught of impersonal forces that derived from modern, secular rationalism. Boss, however, though fighting the same opponent, is seeking to deliver up the person to a more dangerous foe, to Nature as conceived by minds that operate along similarly impersonal lines but, in their focus on greater immediacy of experience, are closer to schizophrenia. (204-206)

Rollo May

Existential Bases of Psychotherapy

. . . What are the essential characteristics which constitute this patient as an existing person, which constitute this self as a self? I wish to propose six characteristics, which I shall call principles, that I find in my work as a psychotherapist. They can as well be called *ontological characteristics*. . . . Neurosis is not to be seen as a deviation from our particular theories of what a person should be. *Is not neurosis, rather, precisely the method the individual uses to preserve his own center, his own existence*? His symptoms are ways of shrinking the range of his world . . . in order that the centeredness of his existence may be protected from threat, a way of blocking off aspects of the environment so that he may then be adequate to the remainder. . . .

. . . Every existing person *has the character of self-affirmation, the need to preserve its centeredness*. The particular name we give this self-affirmation in human beings is "courage." Paul Tillich's emphasis on the "courage to be" is very important, cogent, and fertile for psychotherapy at this point. He insists that in man, being is never given automatically, as it is in plants and animals, but depends upon the individual's courage, and without courage one loses being. This makes courage itself a necessary ontological corollary. By this token, I as a therapist place great importance upon expressions of the patients which have to do with willing, decisions, choice. . . .

Our third principle is . . . *all existing persons have the need and possibility of going out from their centeredness to participate in other beings.* This always involves risk; if the organism goes out too far, it loses its own centeredness, its identity—a phenomenon which can easily be seen in the biological world. If the neurotic is so afraid of loss of his own conflicted center that he refuses to go out and holds back in rigidity and lives in narrowed reactions and shrunken world space, his growth and development are blocked. This is the pattern in neurotic repressions and inhibitions, the common neurotic forms in Freud's day. But it may well be in our day of conformity and the outerdirected man, that the most common neurotic pattern takes the opposite form, namely, the dispersing of one's self in participation and identification with others until one's own being is emptied.

At this point we see the rightful emphasis of Martin Buber in one sense and Harry Stack Sullivan in another, that the human being cannot be understood as a self if participation is omitted. . . .

Our fourth principle is: *the subjective side of centeredness is awareness. . . . The uniquely human form of awareness is self-consciousness.* Awareness and consciousness should not be identified. . . .

Consciousness . . . is not simply my awareness of threat from the world but *my capacity to know myself as the one being threatened, my experience of myself as the subject who has a world.* Consciousness, to use Kurt Goldstein's terms, is man's capacity to transcend the immediate concrete situation, to live in terms of the possible; and it underlies the human capacity to use abstractions and universals, to have language and symbols. This capacity for consciousness underlies the wide range of possibility which man has in relating to his world, and it constitutes the foundation of psychological freedom. Thus, human freedom has its ontological base and I believe must be assumed in all psychotherapy. . . .

. . . Given self-consciousness, sex becomes a new gestalt, as is demonstrated in therapy all the time. Sexual impulses are always, then, conditioned by the *person* of the partner; what we think of the other male or female, in reality or fantasy or even repressed fantasy, can never be ruled out. The fact that the subjective person of the other to whom we relate sexually makes least difference in *neurotic* sexuality, say in patterns of compulsive sex or prostitution, only proves our point the more firmly, for such requires precisely the blocking off, the checking out, the distorting of self-consciousness. Thus, when we talk of sexuality in terms of sexual objects, as Kinsey does, we may garner interesting and useful statistics; but we simply are not talking about human sexuality. . . .

. . . *What we are dealing with in neurosis are those characteristics and functions that are distinctively human.* It is these that have gone awry in disturbed patients. The condition for these functions is self-consciousness—which accounts for what Freud rightly discovered, that the neurotic pattern is characterized by repression and blocking off of consciousness.

It is the task of the therapist, therefore, not only to help the patient become aware, but even more significantly, to help him *transmute this awareness into consciousness.* Awareness is his knowing that something is threatening from outside in his world —a condition that may, as in paranoids and their neurotic equivalents, be correlated with a good deal of acting-out behavior. But self-consciousness puts this awareness on a quite different level; it is the patient's seeing that *he is the one who is threatened,* that he is the being who stands in this world which threatens, that he is the subject who *has* a world. And this gives him the possibility of *in-sight,* of "inward sight," of seeing the world and his problems in relation to himself. And thus it gives him the possibility of doing something about them. . . .

We now come to the sixth and last characteristic of the existing person: *anxiety.* Anxiety is the state of the human being in the struggle against that which would destroy his being. It is, in Tillich's phrase, the state of a being in conflict with nonbeing, a conflict which Freud mythologically pictured in his powerful and important symbol of the death instinct. One wing of this struggle will always be against something outside one's self; but even more portentous and significant for psychotherapy is the inner side of the battle, . . . namely, the conflict within the person as he confronts the choice of whether and how far he will stand against his own being, his own potentialities. . . .

. . . *Consciousness itself implies always the possibility of turning against one's self, denying one's self.* The tragic nature of human existence inheres in the fact that consciousness itself involves the possibility and temptation at every instant to kill itself. . . .

The Context of Psychotherapy

The critical battles between approaches to psychology and psychoanalysis in our culture in the next decades, as always, will be on the battle ground of the image of man. That is to say, the conception of man which underlies the empirical research. The error Binswanger attacked is no more clearly illustrated than in the assumption so prominent in America that somehow scientific research is the one thing that has no presuppositions. It is as though one could stand outside one's own skin and perch on some Archimedes point, and have a way of surveying experience that does not itself depend upon the assumptions that one makes about the nature of man, or the nature of whatever one is studying. . . . The existential approach assumes that we must ask the question of the nature of the man as man. . . .

. . . The patient, like all other beings, is always in process of relationship. Concretely, that is, he *has the need and possibility of going out from centeredness* to participate in other beings. He is now struggling with the possibility of participating with the therapist. Now, this going out always involves risk; if the organism goes out too far, it loses its centeredness, its identity; but if the organism does not go out at all, growth is blocked, development is impossible, and shrinking of the organism (ultimately to death) is the result.

We note immediately that the neurotic problems which Freud described are pictures of people who were so afraid of losing their own conflicted center that they refused or were unable to go out. They held back rigidly, and lived in narrowed reactions and shrunken psychological world space. This is the typical picture of neurotic inhibitions. . . .

From the ontological approach that I have suggested, we see that sickness is precisely the method that the individual uses to preserve his being. The symptoms are methods of shrinking the range of his world in order that the centeredness of his life may be protected from threat. Sickness is a way of blocking off aspects of the environment so that the patient may then be adequate to the remainder of his world. We cannot assume in the usual oversimplified way that the patient automatically wants to get well; we must assume, rather, that he cannot permit himself to give up his neurosis, to get well, until other conditions in his existence and his relation to his world are changed. This indicates immediately the inadequacy of the concept that neurosis is a failure of adjustment. Neurosis is precisely the opposite; it is a method of adjustment, and the trouble is that it is all too successful; it is a method of adjustment to a curtailed world. Neurosis is a creative activity which has within it the creative potential of the individual that must in one way or another be shifted to the constructive side of life in a process of his overcoming his problems. Neurosis is a creative way of adjusting to a world, and it has within it the constructive potentialities which we hope to call forth in psychotherapy. . . .

. . . Unconscious experience can be understood only on the basis of our concept of consciousness. We must posit that the patient comes as a unity, no matter how clearly we can see that various neurotic symptoms have been blocked off and thereby have a compulsive effect upon him. The "unconscious" is the experiences that the person cannot permit himself to actualize. The questions in understanding unconscious phenomena are, "How does the individual reject or accept his possibilities for being conscious of himself and his world?" "How is it possible that he should shut out something which on another level he knows, and even also on this level *knows that he knows*?" The thing that continually surprises patients in psychoanalysis, and even sometimes surprises the analyst, is that when a buried memory or experience which has been subjected to radical repression into unconsciousness erupts into consciousness, the patient will maintain that he has the strange experience of having known it all the time. (290-295)

The symbol of suicide, the capacity to confront death, is placed in a central position in the existential approach in psychology and psychiatry. These things are not negations, though they are a tragic aspect of life. The capacity to confront death is a prerequisite to growth, a prerequisite to self-discovery and self-consciousness. I would take the orgasm as a psychophysical symbol. It is the experience of the capacity to abandon oneself, to give up present security in favor of wider experience. It is not by accident that this experience often appears symbolically as a partial death and rebirth. . . .

. . . Cutting through our rationalizations . . . implies not only taking responsibility for "what I did yesterday," but responsibility for, "what I shall do and feel and think tomorrow." This attitude implies another corollary, namely, aloneness. At the point where I am aware that I am this being, this one who is acting, I am at a point where nobody else can stand. No matter what the extenuating circumstances, this is *my* hatred and *my* destructiveness; and at this point a man relates to himself in a state of aloneness. I am the only one who can take that responsibility.

This tragic consciousness also implies (and this is the most difficult point of all) that a person recognizes the fact that he never can love completely the people to whom he is devoted, and there will always remain some elements of destructiveness. (The emphases that Freud made here are of great importance.) By the same token, we can never know absolutely whether a decision we now make is really the right decision, but, nevertheless, we must make the decision anyway. This risk inheres in self-consciousness. I think it involves the giving up of childhood omnipotence; we are no longer God, to put it symbolically. But we must act as though we were; we must act as though our decisions were right. This is the reaching out into the future that makes all of life a risk and makes all experience precarious. . . .

. . . Anxiety and guilt are never wholly negative phenomena. . . . I think a great deal of our error lies in a tendency to reassure anxiety, to dilute it, and to do the same with guilt feeling. I believe, rather, that the function of therapy is to give people a context in which they are able to confront and experience anxiety and guilt constructively—a context which is a human world, as well as a real world, of a person's own existence in relation to the therapist. . . .

Neurotic anxiety is anxiety which is inappropriate to the threat of a situation. Secondly, it involves repression into unconsciousness. Thirdly, it is expressed in symptom formation. Fourthly, it has destructive rather than constructive effects upon the organism. . . . Normal guilt, in contrast to neurotic, is guilt that is appropriate to the situation. . . . Secondly, there [is] no repression into unconsciousness. . . . Thirdly, conscious or normal guilt does not involve symptom formation. . . . Now, normal guilt is associated with admitting that one can know only partially, and involves admitting that what one says always does partial violence to the truth. We can only partially understand each other; this is normal guilt. It helps us to do the best we can in presenting our thoughts to each other, and it also gives us a humility as we communicate that makes us more open to each other and more sensitive. Therefore, fourthly, normal guilt has a constructive effect.

In New York these days, there are discussions about whether we shouldn't say "shame" rather than "guilt." I think that waters it down, and I do not agree that the best word is shame; I think it is guilt. Shame has with respect to guilt somewhat the same relation as fear does to anxiety. . . . I think shame can be understood in relation to a specific incident, say, if I were compulsive and mispronounced a word, I might blush. But we cannot understand that blush of mine unless we are able to relate it to some underlying stratum in me, which then will be the problem of guilt that shows itself in neurotic guilt, probably, in that illustration.

I think that normal guilt must be dealt with existentially, which means that all aspects of experience must be considered. Not only is it reparation in respect to fellow man (the term reparation is too much associated with Buber's mystical Jewish tradition), but

I would say rather, an openness. That is, normal guilt can be expressed conceptually by one's being a fellow man, by being open, humble, by loving—if one may use the term in that sense. Normal guilt must be involved in all aspects of experience, and it can only be lived out. . . .

To be able to sit in a real relationship with another human being who is going through profound anxiety, or guilt, or the experience of imminent tragedy taxes the best of the humanity in all of us. This is why we emphasize the importance of the "encounter" rather than "relationship." I think the term relationship psychologizes it. Encounter is what really happens; it is something much more than a relationship. In this encounter I have to be able, to some extent, to experience what the patient is experiencing. My job as a therapist is to be open to his world. . . .

Our chief concern in therapy is with the potentiality of the organism. The goal of therapy is to help the patient actualize his potentialities. The joy of the process of actualizing becomes more important than the pleasure of discharged energy—though that itself, in its own context, obviously has pleasurable aspects too. The goal is not the absence of anxiety, but rather the changing of neurotic anxiety into normal anxiety, and the development of the capacity to tolerate normal anxiety. The patient after therapy may well bear more anxiety than he had before, but it will be conscious anxiety and he will be able to use it constructively. Nor is the goal the absence of guilt feeling, but rather the transformation of neurotic guilt into normal guilt, together with the development of the capacity to use this normal guilt creatively. (299-304)

Some Comments on Existential Psychotherapy

There is considerable danger that psychoanalysis in its orthodox form, as well as other forms of psychotherapy and adjustment psychology, will become new representations of the fragmentation of man, that they will exemplify the loss of the individual's vitality and significance rather than the reverse, that the new techniques will assist in standardizing and giving cultural sanction to man's alienation from himself rather than solving it. This tendency seems to me to be present in its most outspoken form in the "behavior therapies," such as operant conditioning, in which the aim is to change external behavior without reference to the inner meaning of that behavior. The existential psychotherapy movement is precisely the movement which protests against this tendency to identify psychotherapy with any particular forms of adjustment or technical change solely; that is, it protests against the tendency to identify psychotherapy with technical reason.* It stands for basing psychotherapy on an understanding of what makes man the *human* being; it is concerned with those characteristics which constitute the self as self, on the assumption that those are the particular characteristics which have gone awry in neurosis; it stands for defining neurosis in terms of what destroys man's capacity to fulfill his own being. . . . Existential psychotherapy is the movement which, standing on one side on the scientific analysis owed chiefly to the genius of Freud, brings back also into the picture the understanding of man on the deeper, ontological level—man as the being who is human.

Knowing another human being, like loving him, involves a dialectical participation with and in the other, a *Mitsein*, a kind of union in its broadest sense. This is what Binswanger calls the "dual mode." One must have a readiness to love the other person, broadly speaking, if one is to be able to understand him. I do not mean to identify love and therapy: it is certainly possible for a therapist to be too identified with the patient; he is still the "Other being" in the relationship, and an element of objectivity is necessary on the part of the therapist. I mean, rather, to emphasize that the openness to the other person which requires at least the possibility of loving him is necessary if we are to be able to grasp him as a human being. . . . This is what makes the concept of "encounter" important in existential therapy. The therapist understandably will be often tempted to abstract himself from the encounter for the sake of his own comfort, performing this abstraction by thinking of the other as just a "patient," or by focussing on certain mechanisms of behavior. But if such a technical view is used predominantly in relating to the other person, the therapist has defended himself from anxiety at the price not only of the isolation of himself from the other but also at the price of the radical distortion of reality. The therapist does not then really *see* the other person. The other is a patient, to be sure, but a patient only within the context of his being first of all a person. I do not mean to disparage technique and the study of it in its rightful place when I point out that technique, like data about the patient, must be subordinated to the reality of the two persons existing together in the consulting room.

It is no doubt true that for any human being the possibility of acceptance by and trust in another human being is a necessary

*This term is explained in *Existence: A New Dimension in Psychiatry and Psychology*, Rollo May, Henri Ellenberger, and Ernest Angel, Eds., New York: Basic Books, 1958, Chapter I.

condition for the "I-am" experience. But the awareness of one's own being occurs basically on the level of grasping and being conscious of one's self; it is an experience of *Dasein,* realized in the realm of self-consciousness. And though the social realm is a necessary condition of the experience, the experience itself is not to be explained *essentially* in social categories. The acceptance by another person, such as the therapist, shows the patient that he no longer need fight his main battle on the front of whether anyone else, or the world, can accept him; the acceptance *frees* him to confront the question of the experiencing of his own being. This point needs to be emphasized because of the common error in many circles of assuming that the experiencing of one's own being will take place automatically if only one is accepted by someone else. This is the basic error in the superficial forms of "relationship therapy." The attitude of "If-I-love-and-accept-you, you-have-all-you-need," is in life and in therapy an attitude which may well minister to increased passivity and lack of responsibility for one's own existence. The crucial question is what the individual (in this sense the patient) himself, in his own awareness of and responsibility for his existence, does with the fact that he can be accepted. . . . *Being* is a category which cannot be reduced to introjection of social and ethical norms. It is, to use Nietzsche's phrase, "beyond good and evil." To the extent that my sense of existence is authentic, it is precisely *not* what others have told me I should be; it is how I *relate* to the fact of their telling me this or that; it is the one Archimedes point I have to stand on from which to judge what parents and other authorities demand.

When a person denies his potentialities, or fails to fulfill them, his situation can be described by the word *guilt.* The existential therapists do not mean this in any moralistic sense, or any failure to fulfill society's requirements. They rather refer to the locking up of essential potentialities within one's self. Any essential potentiality carries with it a need for its actualization; and unhealth is the condition of the persistent denial of such potentialities. (Note that I say "denial," not "lack of expression"; we are all in the situation of being unable over considerable periods of time to "express" some potentialities; my point is that the lack of expression must be come to terms with, on a level of consciousness.) The locking up of essential potentialities, we have said, is the situation of guilt; *therefore* one has *guilt feelings.* Guilt feelings, that is to say, are derivative from guilt, and not vice versa. Certainly patients, and all of us, have many *neurotic* guilt feelings, and it is the task of the therapist to help the patient transmute these to the normal guilt from which they stem, and of which they are a distortion. I believe neurotic guilt and neurotic guilt feelings, are the end result of un-confronted and denied normal guilt . . . . In a case given in his book, *Psychoanalysis and Daseinsanalysis,* Medard Boss puts this point in these words: If we "forget being"—by failing to bring ourselves to our entire being, by failing to be authentic, by slipping into the conformist anonymity of *das Man* —then we have in fact missed our being and to that extent experience guilt. "If you lock up potentialities, you are guilty against (or *indebted to,* as the German word may be translated) what is given you in your origin, your 'Core.' In this existential condition of being indebted and being guilty are founded all guilt feelings, Boss holds, in whatever thousand and one concrete forms and malformations they may appear in actuality. . . ."

The above is one form of existential (or "ontological") guilt, namely, that arising from forfeiting one's own potentialities. There are other forms as well. Another, for example, is existential guilt against one's fellows, arising from the fact that since each of us is an individual, he necessarily perceives his fellow men through his own limited and biased eyes. This means that he always to some extent does violence to the true situation of his fellow, and always to some extent fails fully to understand and meet the other's needs. This is not a question of moral failure or slackness—though it can be greatly increased by lack of moral sensitivity. It is rather an inescapable result of the fact that each of us is a separate individuality and has no choice but to look at the world through our own eyes. This guilt, rooted in our existential structure, is one of the most potent sources of a sound humility and an unsentimental attitude of forgiveness toward one's fellow men. . . . The existential guilt is universal in the sense that it characterizes every human being in whom self-consciousness has developed; it is not given by the culture; but the *content* of the guilt is given by the culture, and would largely vary from culture to culture. Just as neurotic anxiety is the end-product of unfaced normal ontological anxiety, so neurotic guilt is the end-result of unconfronted existential (or as some would say "ontological") guilt.

One of the distinctive characteristics of existential therapists is their emphasis upon the *future*. Having placed *time* in the center of the psychological picture, they propose that the future, in contrast to present and past, is the dominant mode of time for the human beings. This is not to omit the past and present, as is sometimes erroneously charged of this approach; rather it is to hold that the only way we know the past is in a living human being, who, in this particular instant of the present, is projecting himself into some future, be it only the sentence that he is at the moment in the process of uttering. Personality can be understood only as we see it on a trajectory toward its future; a man can understand himself only as he projects himself in some way into the future, only as he is in the process of *becoming*. (Eugene Minkowski has pointed out that the inability to conceive of and live in the future is the fundamental condition of depresssions and other forms of pyschological unhealth.*) This is a corollary of the fact that the person is always becoming, always emerging into the future. The self is to be seen in the light of its potentiality: "a self, every instant it exists," Kierkegaard wrote, "is in process of becoming, for the self . . . is only that which it is to become."

This significance of the future time dimension has an interesting application to the problem of bringing into awareness repressed memories. The recovering of past memories is never simply a question of going over the past *ad infinitum,* as every analyst has found out to his fatigue and regret; it rather depends upon the patient's growing capacity to orient to the future. The patient cannot let himself recall the significant events of his past and reexperience them until he is ready to make some orientation to the future on the basis of these memories. In this sense, the recall of the past depends upon our decision with regard to the future.

The discussion of the dynamisms of social adjustment, such as "introjection," "identification," and so forth, is oversimplified and inadequate when it omits the central fact of all, namely the person's capacity to be aware that he is the one responding to the social expectation, the one choosing or not choosing to guide himself according to a certain model. This is the distinction between rote social conformity on one hand, and the freedom, originality, and creativity of genuine social response on the other. The latter is the unique mark of the human being acting in the light of what Kurt Goldstein calls "the possible."

Consciousness (by which I mean consciousness of my self as the experiencing one, which is to be distinguished from mere "awareness") implies self-transcendence. The one has no reality without the other. . . . All of the peculiarly neurotic phenomena, such as the split of unconsciousness from consciousness, repression, blocking off of bodily awareness, self-deceit by way of symptoms, misperception and distortion of perceptions of others, ad infinitum, are distortions of the fundamental capacity of the human being to relate to himself and his world, as subject and object at the same time.

Existential analysis is a way of understanding human exist-

* *Ibid.,* Chapter IV.

ence, and its representatives believe that one of the chief (if not *the* chief) blocks to the understanding of human beings in Western culture is the over-emphasis on technique. This over-emphasis goes along with the tendency to see the human being as an object to be calculated, managed, "analyzed." Our Western tendency has been to believe that understanding follows *technique;* if we get the right technique, we can penetrate the riddle of the patient, or, as it is said popularly with amazing perspicacity, we can "get the other person's number." The existential approach holds the exact opposite, namely, that *technique follows understanding.* This, of course, is a far cry from the kinds of modern psychology which hold that our understanding must be defined in terms of the technique we employ, and therefore the psychologist lets himself see only what his technique can disclose. The central task and responsibility of the therapist is to seek to understand the patient as a being, and as being-in-his-world, and to create a situation in the consulting room in which the patient can himself understand and experience these forms of being. All technical problems are subordinate to this understanding.

What distinguishes existential therapy is not what the therapist would specifically do, say, in meeting anxiety or confronting resistance or in other specific incidents in therapy, but rather the *context* of the therapy. How an existential therapist might interpret a given dream, or an outburst of temper on the part of the patient, might not differ from what a classical psychoanalyst might say, if each event were taken in isolation. But the *context* of existential therapy would be distinct: it would focus on the questions of how this dream throws light on this particular patient's existence in his world, what it says about *where* he is at the moment and what he is moving toward, what latent orientation toward some decision is contained in the dream, and so forth. Existential therapists are particularly concerned, as I see them, with responding to elements of *will* and *decision* in the patient's utterances.* When the patient says "Maybe I can," or "Possibly I could do that," I always make sure he knows that I have heard him. Existential technique is also characterized by flexibility and versatility, varying from patient to patient and from one phase of treatment to another with the same patient.

The existential approach does not deny the significance and usefulness of psychological dynamisms, such as transference, re-

* One significant study of existential therapists in contrast to orthodox therapists indicates that the former are much more concerned with elements of will and decision. (A study done by Vera Gatch, University of Oklahoma, as Ph.D. research.)

sistance and so on, but it holds that these dynamisms take their meaning from the existential situation of the patient's own immediate life. Speaking now in broader terms, the dynamism must be seen in the total existential context. For example, before repression is possible or conceivable, the person must have some possibility of accepting or rejecting—that is, some margin of freedom. The fundamental question is thus how a person *relates to* his freedom to actualize his potentialities in the first place, repression being one way of so relating.

Another characteristic of existential therapy is its emphasis on *presence*. This is related to *encounter*, which is a much more inclusive concept than "transference," Encounter—which leads to presence—includes such elements as esteem, the experience of friendship, erotic attraction at times, trust, et cetera, and transference, the last being one element in a total encounter. *Presence* implies that the encounter between the patient and therapist is taken as a real one in its total meaning. Existentially, truth always involves the relation of the person *to* something or someone. One can think of this as a "field"—the therapist is part of the patient's relationship field. This participating in the field which the patient creates (or the "world" which he builds) is our best avenue for understanding the patient; indeed, we cannot really *see* the patient unless we participate in this field. I believe any therapist is existential to the extent that, with his technical training and knowledge of transference and dynamisms and so on, he is still able to relate to the patient "as one existence communicating with another," to use Binswanger's phrase. This emphasis on relationship is in no way an oversimplification or short-cut, or at least *should* not be. It is not a substitute for discipline or thoroughness of training. It rather puts these things in their context—namely, the discipline and training are directed to understanding the human beings as human. The therapist, indeed, is assumedly an expert, and he should neither dodge this fact or play falsely modest about it; but if he is not first of all a human being, his expertness will be irrelevant and quite possibly harmful.

As we remarked above concerning memory, we now indicate with respect to insight and knowledge: *decision precedes knowledge and insight.* An insight does not simply "pop" up; it comes when the patient has at least begun to make the decisions necessary to living in a world with that insight. The patient cannot permit himself to get insight or self-knowledge until he is ready to take some orientation toward his life, to make some decision (not necessarily a momentous one; I speak of "decisive orientation") and has made the preliminary decisions along the way.

We shall make some final remarks about the ultimately serious, tragic aspects of life in relation to therapy. The therapist is doing the patient a disservice if he takes away from him the realization that it is entirely within the realm of possibility that he may fail, and that that may well be precisely what he is doing at this very moment. This point is important because patients tend to carry a never-quite-articulated belief (no doubt connected with childhood omnipotent beliefs associated with parents), that somehow the therapist will see that nothing harmful happens to them, and therefore they don't need to take their own existence seriously. The tendency prevails in much therapy to water down anxiety, despair, and the tragic aspects of life. It is very much to the credit of this approach that it confronts these tragic realities directly. In this connection the symbol of suicide as an ever-present possibility can have positive value; I am doubtful whether anyone ever takes his life with full seriousness until he realizes that it is entirely within his power to commit suicide but chooses himself not to.

It must also be added that the tendency to use existential concepts in the service of intellectualizing is especially to be guarded against. The terms, concepts and principles we have discussed can be used as a *defense* against confronting existential reality, just as readily as any other kinds of concepts. Perhaps, because these concepts refer to things which have to do with personal reality, they can the more seductively be used to give the illusion of reality. It helps always to come back to the existential touchstone of authenticity.

Dangers in the Relation of Existentialism to Psychotherapy

There must be an "understander" if there is to be understanding. The psychotherapist had best realize that he is seeing the patient through his own eyes, understanding the patient in his own way, which will always be limited and biased to some extent. If the therapist does not assume this but absolutizes his own perception and understanding, he will automatically dominate the patient by his own subjectivity, a danger against which Sartre has warned us. Then the therapist is playing God as surely as if he had an absolute technique. The existential therapist can overcome so far as possible his own tendency to strait jacket the patient by subjectivity by admitting his own bias and limitations to start with. Once these are admitted, the phenomenological approach can be of great help . . . in seeing and relating to the patient as he really is. . . .

. . . There cannot be any special "existential psychiatry," as

Leslie Farber has well remarked, any more than there can be Hegelian, Platonic, or Spinozan psychiatry. Existentialism is an *attitude*, an approach to human beings, rather than a special school or group. Like any philosophy, it has to do with the presuppositions underlying psychiatric and psychoanalytic technique.

It is doubtful, for example, whether it makes any sense to speak of an "existential psychotherapist" at this stage of the development of the movement. The existential approach is not a system of therapy—though it makes highly important contributions to therapy. It is not a set of techniques—though it may give birth to them. It is rather a concern with understanding the structure of the human being and his experience which to a greater or lesser extent should underlie *all* technique. . . .

You cannot analyze being, and if you could do so it would be a harmful thing to do. *Being* must be assumed in psychotherapy, not analyzed: an individual's being is shown, for example, in his right to exist as a person, his possibilities for self-respect and his ultimate freedom to choose his own way of life. All these must be assumed when we work with a patient, and if we cannot assume them about a given person, we should not work with him. To try to analyze these evidences of being is to violate the fundamental being of the person himself. Bringing our technical attitudes to bear on being itself is to repeat the same error for which existentialists criticize not only classical psychoanalysis but our whole culture, i.e., making the person subordinate to techniques. To analyze the "psyche" as in psychoanalysis is difficult enough and can and should be done only within limits. The blockages the person suffers which will not let him gain adequate self-esteem, for example, can be analyzed. But that is a far different thing from analyzing ontology, calling into question the fundamental qualities which constitute him as a human being. To analyze being is parallel to repressing it in the sense that it subordinates being to a technical attitude; except that analyzing is a little more harmful in that it gives the therapist a nice rationalization for his repression and relieves him of guilt for his failure to exhibit the reverence and humility with which being should rightly be regarded. (184-187)

Leslie H. Farber

Will and Willfulness in Hysteria

. . . Hysteria is a particular disorder of will whose principal expression is *willfulness*. . . . In willfulness the life of the will becomes distended, overweening, and obtrusive at the same time that its movements become increasingly separate, sovereign, and distinct from other aspects of spirit. And with distension of will which is relatively unrelieved, intellect is bound to suffer. I mean, of course, intellect in the large sense, including not only will's usual adversary, which is reason, but also imagination, humor, discretion, judgment. In willfulness, then, will pursues its own tyrannical course with reckless disdain for what we usually mean by content, unless that content be will itself. (231)

The theory that the stratagems themselves are witless manifestations of dark sexual forces—puppets whose strings are pulled by the libido—is welcomed by the hysteric because it absolves him of willful intent. He is *acted upon* by Nature who works her will on him. So long as both wills—his and Nature's—reside within his person, there can be no defeat; victory is his, whatever the outcome. Though the defeat of his will may have, in reality, brought him to treatment, this theory offers him a way of viewing that defeat as a victory for Nature's will, an outcome not too uncommon in the speculations of the 19th century. . . .

When this particular absorption with the willful possibilities of sex occurs at the feverish beginnings of psychotherapy it is apt to be called "positive transference" and mistakenly considered a good omen for cure. During this phase, before the two wills begin to oppose each other, the hysteric makes sexuality out of the therapist's science while the therapist makes science out of sexuality. In this affair the hysteric has the advantage, there being more sex to science than vice-versa. Moreover the therapist's disadvantage is increased by his habit, encouraged by psychoanalytic theory, of isolating the sexual function: whether his language is clinical or vernacular, he works on the brink of pornography. To serve pornography, sexuality must be torn from the larger human context and exalted into a life of its own. . . . Many activities that enjoy the name of distraction are actually the fictitious alternatives the will devises for sidestepping possible moral conflict. And in hysteria much of what is called by such names as "impulsivity" or "acting out" are more serious—even catastrophic—adventures invented by the will, alcohol being one of its most faithful accomplices in these escapades: it performs the double service of inflating the will at the same time as it dulls discrimination. . . .

When wholeness eludes us in its proper setting—in dialogue, so vital is it to our lives that we turn wildly to will, ready to grasp at any illusion of wholeness (however mindless or grotesque) the will conjures up for our reassurance. And caught in this illusion, delirious with well-being, we are convinced of the extraordinary keenness and clarity of our intellect. In point of fact, no state of mind so deadens—and injures—our faculties as our belief in this illusion of wholeness. The more dependent a person becomes on this illusion, the less able is he to experience true wholeness in dialogue, and at the point where he is no longer capable of dialogue he can be said to be *addicted* to his will. (235-237)

This feverish figure, endlessly assaulting the company, seeking to wrench the moment to some pretense of dialogue, is the image of the eternal stranger: that condition of man in which he is forever separated from his fellows, unknown and unaddressed—it is the figure of man's separated will posing as his total self. . . . It is true that we must live with hysteria, but we need not, I think, honor it. In fact, if we give it its rightful identification—as the sworn enemy of our capacity to be fully human—we may give ourselves a crucial advantage in the struggle we must constantly engage in to transcend it. (239-241)

Despair and the Life of Suicide

I find no mystery in the eagerness of those in despair to secure a physical diagnosis—say depression—and then offer themselves to pills or electric shock or lobotomy—anything which will spare them real contrition. But more mysterious to me is the willingness of those of our calling to accept the more demonic terms of despair, to conspire to relieve the despairer of his humanity through chemical, electrical or surgical means. (129)

. . . His definition of his condition as unendurable is very much a matter of choice, and thus, obviously, so is his suicide. What is interesting here is the despairer's effort to deny the fact of choice and, by extension, to deny responsibility for his suicidal act. . . .

. . . Those who are vulnerable to the worst torments of despair are also those who—because of what they were before falling into despair, and still, in the clutches of despair, potentially are—are seldom able quite to reach the demonic affirmation of self and the radical rejection of being toward which their despair strains. In some sense the despairer moves hazardously, despite distractions and entrenchment, toward a tragic, often excessively tragic, position in regard to the inauthentic in his life and in his relations with others. In other words, through his objectifications he may arrive at an extreme and radical concern over the very center of his being, creating in this way an abyss too wide and too deep for easy bridging. The very strategies of despair, and especially the logical strategies involved in the contemplation of suicide, reveal that there is some connection still linking them to life-outside-despair—perhaps only imagined, but imagined still—that despair is unable to sever. Despair would not be so anguished a condition as it is were it as wholly and hopelessly estranged as it believes itself to be. . . .

The Bargain with Death . . . The explanation for his response lies in what he believes is being promised him in return for the cooperation he so wholeheartedly supplies. What can this promise be but that self-expression, given free reign in this exceptional enterprise, will produce for him the dramatic representation of some uniqueness, some singularity of self with which life has seemingly so far failed to provide him, and of which his natural—un-self-engineered—death threatens to rob him? . . . All this is a dream of the will—a despairing attempt to affirm the self in a form in which the self has never been and can never be. (137-139)

The Therapeutic Despair

Buber's theory of confirmation can . . . help to distinguish between therapeutic dialogue and what he calls "genuine dialogue." As a quotidian affair stretching painfully through the years, the psychotherapy of schizophrenia has simply not been truthfully described. Reports not only give it order and meaning it does not possess; they also deprive it of the brutal tedium, exasperation, emptiness, futility—in short the agony of an existence in which dialogue is so fleeting as to be virtually nonexistent. . . .

. . . What of the weeks, months, years, when these two sit together for an hour a day, immersed in a silence broken only by obscure mouthings or posturings conveying no secure meaning; or by earnest professional adjurations which draw no response?

How much easier it would be during these desolate periods to abandon what must often seem a bitter mockery of relationship. But the patient has no choice, being captive to his illness and to the explicit rules of the institution. Nor does the therapist have much choice, at least if he is conscientious. Although he is more captive to his conscience than to the institution, conscience obliges him to agree with the unwritten assumption that his mere physical presence each day is necessarily preferable to his absence. Thus does it happen that two people "do time" together under circumstances which, could they be manufactured, would provide the police state with a frightening new torture.

With another kind of patient, the therapist might take refuge in his own thoughts. His silence might pass for that mirror-like impassivity which is still considered a virtue in the treatment of neurosis. But with a schizophrenic he has no such refuge. To deprive the patient of ordinary social responsiveness might drive him further from his fragmentary gestures toward his fellows. And silence faced with silence would be arbitrary, if not cruel. Because he knows this, the therapist finds his own silence a heavy burden. He is continually on guard against the double danger of silence and fear of silence, which he knows can easily sour into a clotted self-consciousness to be relieved at any cost. . . .

When faced with the inevitable despair, which I am suggesting must sooner or later overtake the conscientious therapist, it will not matter how indomitable or inventive may be his efforts to keep going: he cannot hope that his despair will be entirely unnoticed by his patient. Although perceptiveness may be severely impaired in the schizophrenic, he knows that it can never be extinguished—a knowledge which may, in fact, add the final straw to his desolation. What I would suggest here is a possibility which, since it has been overlooked, may offer some truth as well as solace. To the extent that the therapist becomes "present" for his patient, that patient is capable of pity for his friend's distress. . . . In response to the therapist's despair . . . the patient will often try to confirm the therapist's image of himself as therapist. And insofar as the therapist is sincerely dedicated to his work—paradoxically, just because he is so dedicated—this will also have the effect of confirming him as a fellow human being. (Once again [there is an] awesome split between the "human" and the "scientific.") . . . In therapy the paradox is inescapable that the man who is incapable of arousing pity will find it hard to help another.

All this means is that the therapist must be capable of feeling real despair, on another's behalf as well as—and I would stress the fact that we are not supermen— . . . on his own. In addition to the more strenuous virtues of courage and dedication, then, the therapist must be highly endowed with . . . imagination and perceptiveness: capable of imagining his own distress as well as the other's. . . .

. . . If we imagine such a powerful emotion as pity being aroused in the patient, we can see that for that moment, at least, he has ceased to be schizophrenic.

. . . Therapeutic sessions with the relatively controlled and civilized people . . . [called] neurotic simply do not give rise to such overwhelming despair as may evoke pity. There is ample room for both to confirm and be confirmed. And here we can no longer blink the fact that, human nature being what it is, the man who pours out his spiritual energy in confirming others will need more, and not less, confirmation of himself. (13-15)

With psychosis, not only are meanings elusive and discouragements ten times multiplied. A dimension of terror is added to our existence, as we learn to live with the insane possibility—which is, after all, one of the facts of madness—that meaning itself can be the mirage. To avoid this insanity, we grasp at every possibility of meaning as though it were the staunchest fact. (17)

Schizophrenia and the Mad Psychotherapist

In another paper, "The Therapeutic Despair," I attempted to describe the peculiar and painful nature of the therapeutic life with a schizophrenic patient—its emptiness, meaninglessness, lack of confirmation—in short, the circumstances which lead to a particular despair on the part of the therapist, which may evoke in the patient a response of pity for his doctor's plight. I suggested further that such pity might very well lead the patient to assuage the therapist's anguish through therapeutic movements intended to confirm the therapist as therapist. It seemed to me then, as it seems to me now, that despair is more or less intrinsic to the therapeutic life with schizophrenia, and moreover that such despair, if acknowledged rather than disowned, if contended with rather than evaded, *might* (the word is important) have a salutary effect on therapy. (209)

I would like only to suggest in passing that the avoidance of despair by reducing it to a merely "morbid" or "unhealthy" state of mind, thus refusing to conceive it as belonging inescapably, in some measure, to our lives as human beings—that such avoidance may be more malignant than despair itself. (It was Kierkegaard's belief, you will recall, that the worst of all despairs is that in which one does not know he is in despair.) It sometimes happens that despair itself provides the very conditions of seriousness and urgency which bring a man to ask those wholly authentic—we might call them tragic—questions about his own life and the meaning and measure of his particular human-ness. When despair is repudiated these questions go unasked, and it may be exactly here—in the failure to confront these questions—that there occurs a turning in one's development which is inauthentic. (217f.)

RELATION AND WILL

In spite of the fact that the intellectual life of the schizophrenic is as fearfully impoverished as his capacities for relation with others, we must assume that he is still human enough to hunger for relation, and, should it be even fleetingly achieved, to dread and be enraged by its loss. In a state so extreme much of his delusional and hallucinatory life will either reach for consummation, even glory, or else proclaim his repudiation of such a possibility with a web of corroborating though fantastic details. By his impoverishment he is reduced in his attempts at relation or in his repudiation of relation (and often both are intermingled) to what I choose to call his isolated will—or willfulness, if we define it as Webster does: namely, that state in which one is governed by will without yielding to reason; obstinate; perverse; stubborn. . . . I would say that willfulness not only accounts for much of the schizophrenic's behavior, but authors a great deal of his delusional material. Without the assistance of the imagination the will invents in its own image; this means that the will contrives plots in which will is pitted against will, its subject matter being, roughly, power. In delusion the willful one may be an outside agent with the schizophrenic as victim, but regardless of who is seen to be the willful agent and who the victim, the plot represents a crude example of what Yeats called the will doing the work of the imagination. . . .

To take but one example: a particular case of schizophrenic mutism may have begun in panic when talk led to such terrifying confusion about reality that distress, instead of being relieved, was not only perpetuated but intensified. But as his panic subsides, this person's muteness perhaps becomes—and may remain—a willful refusal to talk, in response to what he regards as the demand to talk being made on him by those about him. Reduced to his own will, the schizophrenic believes and perceives himself to be continually assailed by the willful demands of the world around him. Examples of schizophrenic willfulness, whether or not they had their antecedents in panic, and despite the often confusing nature of their delusional elaboration or justification, are numerous: the refusal to eat, waxy inflexibility or the refusal to move, untidiness and nakedness, even smearing—all these expressions may become willful responses to what seems to the schizophrenic to be willfulness on the part of those responsible for his care. Most of the gestures I have mentioned are those of rejection of relation, but it should be said that his sexual attempts to force intimacy can be equally willful—as with Frieda's masturbating patient—seeming almost assaultive in their grotesque lack of the nuances which usually assist the life of affection. . . .

Whether he [the therapist] is locked in frantic physical encounter with his patient or else trying, through monologue, to breach his patient's muteness, he is thrown back on his own isolated will in his efforts to provoke relationship. Even in defeat he may resort to a silence which is as willful as the silence of his patient. It can be said that both therapist and patient have a will to relation and a relationship of wills. . . . Relation, understood in any decent sense, cannot be willed: it happens or doesn't happen, depending on what human qualities are brought to the event: honesty, imagination, tact, humor, and so on. By contrast, the willful encounter—a far cry from the chancy and fleeting mutuality that occurs from time to time between people, and that we designate by the honorable term relation—will have a special binge-like excitement, even though its center is hollow. Its intensity is of the moment: unlike friendship, when the moment vanishes little remains. This is the reason the addictive possibilities of this therapeutic life are considerable. (In this regard it is no accident that two of the best known therapists in the field have attempted to give the experience of loneliness ontological status in the human condition.) As the therapist returns again and again to the excitements of this drama of wills that passes for relation, he becomes increasingly impatient of relation, although it is unlikely he will cease believing—and asserting—that the capacity for relation is his special power. Gradually, but not casually, he develops into an apostle of relation who can no longer abide relation. It is an unhappy fact that when, through drugs or life situation, one finds more and more scope for willfulness, those other human qualities I have mentioned are not merely held in abeyance but fall into the atrophy of disuse. And with such atrophy the ordinary amenities of the world become not only no longer sustaining but actually disturbing, making recourse to the drug ever more compelling. As the therapist continues to will what cannot be willed, those attributes of character to expand and harden will be precisely those public, self-assertive gestures which are inauthentic to the person he might have become. (224-226)

Viktor E. Frankl

From Death-Camp to Existentialism

Apparently, man must have an aim toward which he can constantly direct his life. He must accomplish concrete, personal tasks and fulfill concrete, personal demands; he must realize that unique meaning which each of us has to fulfill. Therefore, I consider it misleading to speak of "self-fulfillment" and "self-realization." For what is demanded of man is not primarily fulfillment and realization of *himself*, but, the actualization of specific tasks in his world—and only to the degree to which he accomplishes this actualization will he also fulfill himself: not *per intentionem* but *per effectum*.

Man's will-to-meaning represents the most human phenomenon possible—and its frustration does not signify something pathological, at least not in itself. A person is not necessarily sick if he thinks that his existence is meaningless. . . .

In my opinion and according to my personal convictions and experiences (be they clinical or metaclinical ones), the first and foremost aim of mental hygiene should be to stimulate man's will-to-meaning and to offer him concrete meaning potentialities. . . . Of course, this does not imply any imposition of the doctor's personal values on the patient: just the contrary. Since the logotherapist interprets his job mainly as the very education to responsibility, to the full awareness and consciousness of the very essence of human existence (i.e., responsibleness), he will certainly not impose his own values on the patient. He will try to develop the patient's sense of responsibility to the extent that the patient himself will spontaneously find his own personal life task. . . .

Such psychotherapy was not concocted in the philosopher's arm chair nor at the analyst's couch; it took shape in the hard school of air-raid shelters and bomb craters, in concentration camps and prisoner of war camps. There occur acute states of existential frustration—evanescence of any meaning to one's existence—which can become extremely dangerous. What I am thinking of are the "borderland" situations (*Grenzsituationen,* in the sense of Karl Jaspers). . . . Every age has its neuroses, and every age needs its own psychotherapy. (100-104)

Logotherapy is not a substitute for psychotherapy, but is its complement. Above all, it is destined to make the concept of man (underlying *each* kind of psychotherapeutic work) into a whole, an image of man in all his dimensions—including the noetic one. . . . Man becomes more and more like the image of the man he has been taught about. Man grows according to his interpretations of himself. . . . We have only to remember how in recent history the concept of man as "nothing but" the product of heredity and environment—or, as it was then termed, "blood and soil"—pushed us all into enormous disasters. I believe it to be a straight path from that homunculist image of man to the gas chambers of Auschwitz, Treblinka, and Maidanek. (108f.)

The Doctor and the Soul

Our aim must be to help our patient to achieve the highest possible activation of his life, to lead him, so to speak, from the state of a "*patiens*" to that of an "*agens.*" With this in view we must not only lead him to experience his existence as a constant effort to actualize values. We must also show him that the task he is responsible for is always a specific task. It is specific in a twin sense: one, that the task varies from person to person—in accord with the uniqueness of each person. Two, that it changes from hour to hour, in accord with the singularity of every situation. . . . We see, therefore, that the factors of uniqueness and singularity are essential constituents of the meaningfulness of human existence. To contemporary existentialist philosophy goes the honor of having shown that the existence of man is essentially concrete and subjective. It took the existentialist stress on these qualities to restore moral responsibility to the modern scene. Not for nothing has existentialist philosophy been termed the "summoning" philosophy. For the presentation of human life as singular and unique is an implicit summons to men to actualize in their own lives these unique and singular possibilities. (62f.)

The id, therefore, can never become a rival of the ego, can never be its opponent in any true sense, but only its opposite. For existence knows not struggle, only decision. The execution of an existential act ("existential consummation") is instantaneous, takes place at a point in time, and is therefore without extension (Palágyi); for that reason alone it could not be subject to causality, and therefore cannot be explained in terms of the dynamics of impulses. The moment we attempted to explain the ego-id relationship dynamically, we would at once be trapped in circular reasoning. Freud did in fact make this attempt when he began speaking of ego-drives. He was trying, that is, to derive the will dynamically from the instincts. But he failed—had to fail because of the contradiction inherent in this concept of ego-drives. The ego which decides, the ego of existential decision, necessarily eludes explanation in terms of instinctual or causal dynamics. As long as psychoanalysis continues to interpret the ego in this manner, continues to view it as drawing its energy from the id, it will cast no light on the problem of the ego, but will rather expose the bankruptcy of its whole concept. What is more, such an interpretation of the ego plays right into the hands of neurotics with their tendency toward "abdication of the ego." (101n.)

The logotherapist is not concerned with treating the individual symptom or the disease as such; rather, he sets out to transform the ego of the obsessional neurotic, the neurotic's attitude toward his neurosis. For it is this attitude which has built up the basic constitutional disturbance into clinical symptoms of illness. And this attitude, at least in milder cases or in the early stages, is quite subject to correction. Where the attitude itself has not as yet taken on the typical obsessional-neurotic rigidity, where it is not yet infiltrated, so to speak, by the basic disturbance, a change in its direction should still be possible. For at that point the patient is still faced with a "decision"—whether or not to go on to a fully developed obsessional neurosis. At one time in life every psychopath stands at the crossroads where he must decide between the mere disposition and its elaboration into actual psychopathy. Before this decision has been made he cannot properly be called a psychopath. (218)

. . . On the one hand the patient is not responsible for his obsessional "fancies," and on the other hand . . . he certainly is responsible for his attitude toward these fancies. For it is his attitude which converts the embarrassing fancies into torments when he "gets involved" with them, when he carries them further in his thoughts or, fearing them, fights them back. Here, too, positive logotherapeutic components must come into play in addition to the negative psychotherapeutic (in the narrower sense of the word) components. The patient will finally learn to ignore his obsessional neurosis and lead a meaningful life in spite of it. It is obvious that his turning toward his concrete life task facilitates his turning away from his obsessional thoughts. . . . (224)

The residue of freedom which is still present even in psychosis, in the patient's free attitude toward it, gives the patient the opportunity to realize attitudinal values. Insofar as he has freedom, he has responsibility. (240)

Partly objectively and partly subjectively, the schizophrenic experiences a restriction of the ego both qua consciousness and qua responsibility—he cannot assume the role of responsible subject (experience of pure objectness or principle of passivizing). In schizophrenia, then, the person's integral humanity is affected by the psychotic process. This is a basic distinction between the schizophrenic and the melancholiac. For the morbidity of the melancholiac could be understood in existential-analytic terms only as a shaping of the disease process by the human person—that is, as a mode of humanness. In the schizophrenic, however, existential analysis has shown that the person's very humanness is also affected, is itself shaped by the disease process. The popular concepts are right in viewing melancholia as a mere illness of the temperament and schizophrenia as an actual mental disease. As such, as a true disease "of the mind," schizophrenia—in contrast to obsessional neurosis—is a "creatural" affliction. Nevertheless, even for the schizophrenic there remains that residue of freedom toward fate and toward the disease which man always possesses, no matter how ill he may be, in all situations and at every moment of life, to the very last. (256f.)

Beyond Self-Actualization and Self-Expression

. . . It is never the task of the therapist to "give" a meaning to the life of the patient. It is up to the patient himself to "find" the concrete Meaning of his existence. The therapist merely assists him in this endeavor. That he must "find" the meaning implies that this meaning is to be discovered and not invented. It implies that the meaning of one's life is in a certain sense objective.

Unfortunately this objectivity is frequently neglected by some of those writers who call themselves existentialists. Though they never weary of repeating *ad nauseam* that man is "being in the world," they seem to forget that meaning is also "in the world" and thus not merely a subjective factor. It is more than a mere *self-expression,* or a projection of the self *into* the world. . . . Appointing self-realization as "the ultimate motive" would . . . devaluate the world and its objects to mere means to an end. As a matter of fact, A. H. Maslow explicitly contends that "the environment is no more than means to the person's self-actualizing ends." . . .

So now we must pose the crucial question whether or not man's *primary intention,* or even his *ultimate destination,* could ever be properly circumscribed by the term "self-actualization." I would venture a strictly negative response to this question. It appears to me to be quite obvious that self-actualization is an effect and cannot be the object of intention. Mirrored in this fact is the fundamental anthropological truth that self-transcendence is one of the basic features of human existence. Only as man withdraws from himself in the sense of releasing self-centered interest and attention will he gain an authentic mode of existence. This rule finds its clinical application (and clinical validation) in the logotherapeutic techniques of *de-reflection* and *paradoxical intention.* . . .

The potentialities of life are not indifferent *possibilities,* but must be seen in the light of meaning and values. At any given time only one of the possible choices of the individual fulfills *the necessity* of his life task. Herein is involved the challenge of each life situation—the challenge to responsibility. Man must make his choice concerning the mass of present potentials: which will be condemned to non-being and which one shall be actualized, and thus rescued for eternity. . . .

Potentialism involves an attempt to avoid this burden of responsibility. Under the pressure of time and in the face of life's transitoriness, man is often beguiled into believing that he can escape the necessity of making responsible choices. His efforts, however, are in vain, for wherever he turns, he is confronted with the exigencies of life and the inexorable demand—a demand rooted in some source beyond himself—to make meaningful and valuable and, thus, existential commitments. . . . The choice in question is a choice of the only potentiality, among many possibilities, which is *worth* actualizing. Thus the problem really just begins when potentialism ends. . . . This acceptance of finiteness is the precondition to mental health and human progress, while the inability to accept it is characteristic of the neurotic personality. (11-14)

Any philosophy or psychology which by its careful investigation of psychic phenomena in their richness and fullness deserves to be called a "phenomenological approach," must acknowledge the primordial fact that every true cognitive act implies the objectivity of the object. So, what is called the object, or to speak more generally, the world, is essentially more than a *mere self-expression of the subject.* To speak of the world as a mere "design" of the cognitive subject is to do injustice to the full phenomenon of the cognitive act which is the *self-transcendence of existence toward the world as an objective reality*. . . . The point of view, however, adopted by some of the existentialist writers blurs the objectivity of the object. . . . To them man is a being who, in all his cognitive acts and efforts, can never reach a real world. His world is but a design, projected by himself, and mirroring the structure of his being. . . . This kaleidoscopic epistemology presents a "world design" (*Weltentwurf*) wholly dependent upon man's "thrownness" (*Geworfenheit*)—a simple reflection of his subjective condition and structure. . . .

. . . An adequate view of man can only be properly formulated when it goes beyond homeostasis, beyond self-actualization —even beyond man himself!—to that transcendent sphere of human existence in which man chooses what he will do and what he will be in the midst of an objective world of meanings and values. (16f.)

On Logotherapy and Existential Analysis

As long as I have to examine a patient neurologically I have to "behave as if" he existed only in this dimension. But when I put my reflex hammer aside, I broaden my view again, I encounter him as man to man, I to Thou. I follow him into the fullness of dimensions, and into the wholeness of a human being. . . .

. . . Logotherapy focuses on the search for the meaning of human existence. Such a search is an important undertaking in psychotherapy since the lack of awareness of life's meaning is among the most important causes of emotional frustration in our time. But man's concern about a meaning in life, which should be worthy of life, is in itself by no means a sign of disease. Whether explicit or implicit, this is an intrinsically human question. . . . Today existential frustration seems to me to play at least as great a part in the formation of neuroses as the sexual one formerly did. (29f.)

The so-called life not worth living does not exist. And even the manifestations of psychosis conceal a real spiritual person, unassailable by mental disease. Only the possibilities of communication with the outside world and of self-expression are inhibited by the disease; the nucleus of man remains indestructible. The schizophrenic, as well as the manic-depressive, has a remnant of freedom with which he can confront his illness and realize himself, not only in spite of it but because of it. And if this were not the case it would be futile to be a psychiatrist. (36)

The Image of Man of Psychotherapy

Psychoanalysis in reality brings about an existential reorientation on the part of the patient, in so far as it does not simply miss its therapeutic result. Provided that one does not shudder at that so fashionable word, one can aptly speak of human meeting (*Begegnung*) as the actual agent in the modes of acting in psychoanalytic treatment. The so-called transference is also probably only a vehicle of such human meeting. . . . *Within the framework of psychotherapy, the methodology and technique applied at any given time is least effective of all: rather it is the human relationship between physician and patient* which is determining. . . . *The dream of half a century seems to me to have run its course, the dream in which what was held of value was a mechanics of the psyche and a technology of psychotherapy* or, in other words, an interpretation of psychic life on the basis of mechanisms and a therapy of psychic disorders with the help of techniques. (24f.)

Logotherapy is an authentic personalistic psychotherapy precisely to the extent that it does not concern itself with symptoms but tries to bring about a change in orientation, a personalistic reorientation with respect to the symptom. (34)

J. L. Moreno

Philosophy of the Third Psychiatric Revolution

II. "BEGEGNUNG": ENCOUNTER

In the search for a common matrix for all psychotherapies, I published in Vienna a few months before the outbreak of World War I a small publication, *Einladung zu einer Begegnung*. . . . *Begegnung* . . . means meeting, contact of bodies, confronting each other, facing each other, countering and battling, seeing and perceiving, touching and entering into each other, sharing and loving, communicating with each other in a primary, intuitive manner by speech or gesture, by kiss and embrace, becoming one —*una cum uno*. The word *Begegnung* contains the root for the word *gegen,* which means "against." It thus encompasses not only loving, but also hostile and threatening relationships. Encounter, which derives from the French *encontre,* is the nearest translation of *Begegnung*.

The German *zwischen-menschlich* and the English "interpersonal" or "interactional" are anemic notions compared to the living concept of encounter. *Begegnung conveys* that two or more persons meet not only to face one another, but to live and experience one another—as actors, each in his own right. It is not only an emotional rapport, like the professional meeting of a physician or therapist and patient, or an intellectual rapport, like teacher and student, or a scientific rapport, like a participant observer with his subject. . . .

The persons are there in space; they may meet for the first time, with all their strengths and weaknesses—human actors seething with spontaneity and zest. It is not *Einfühlung;* it is *Zweifühlung* (tele)—togetherness, sharing life. It is an intuitive reversal of roles, a realization of the self through the other; it is identity, the rare, unforgotten experience of total reciprocity. Or, as I described *Begegnung* more than forty years ago: "A meeting of two: eye to eye, face to face. And when you are near I will tear your eyes out and use them instead of mine, and you will tear my eyes out and use them instead of yours, then I will look at you with your eyes and you will look at me with mine." The encounter is extemporaneous, unstructured, unplanned, unrehearsed—it occurs on the spur of the moment. It is "in the moment" and "in the here." It can be thought of as the preamble, the universal frame of all forms of structured meeting, the common matrix of all the psychotherapies, from the total subordination of the patient (as in the hypnotic situation) to the superiority and autonomy of the protagonist (as in psychodrama).

Summing up, *Begegnung* is the sum total of interaction, a meeting of two or more persons, not in the dead past or imagined future, but in the here and now, *hic et nunc,* in the fullness of time —the real, concrete and complete situation for experience; it involves physical and psychic contact; it is an *I-to-I* relationship, not an *I-to-thou* relation—every *thou* is an I; a *thou* does not exist except in every *I;* it is the convergence of emotional, social and cosmic factors which occur in all age groups, but particularly in adolescence (*Begegnung syndrome*); it is the experience of identity and total reciprocity; but above all, psychodrama is the essence of the encounter. . . .

VI. TELIC SENSITIVITY

Telic reciprocity is the common characteristic of all encounter experience. It is the intuitive "click" between the participants—no words need be spoken between mother and infant, or two lovers. An intimate feeling envelops them; it is an uncanny sensitivity for each other which welds individuals into unity. In genuine love relations the partners share each other's cleverness as well as each other's limitations. Love is a telic relationship. Mother and infant or two lovers, *A* and *B*, do not only "identify," *they share in an act*. That is what "part"-icipation means.

In life itself we are expected to be sensitive to the feelings of the person with whom we are interacting at the time. Watching the behavior of partners and putting ourselves into their situations, mentally reversing roles with them, we are continuously getting clues as to how they expect us to act. In turn, we are giving them clues as to how we expect them to act. In many of the stereotyped and humdrum situations of life, it is insensitivity of partners for clues in significant situations which leads to serious interpersonal conflicts, often difficult to repair. . . .

The relation between therapist and patient, whether in individual or group psychotherapy, requires telic sensitivity. Telic sensitivity is "trainable." It is tele which establishes natural "correspondence" between therapist and patient. It is an absence of this factor in professional therapeutic relation which is responsible for therapeutic failures; it must be regained in order to make any technology work. Transference of the patient may relate him to a person who is not there; transference of the therapist may relate him to a patient who is not there. The result is that patient and therapist talk past each other, instead of to each other. Similarly, empathy and counterempathy do not add up to tele; they may run parallel, and never mix, that is, never become a telic relationship.

An individual with empathic sensitivity is able to penetrate and understand another individual, but this experience is possible without mutual love. If one partner empathizes with the other, he may be able to take advantage of her, be injurious or make her dependent upon himself because of his sheer ability to use his "empathic cunning." This is why training of empathic ability, as in the case of psychopathic individuals, frequently leads to the opposite of what is expected. . . .

Telic sensitivity is particularly important in psychodramatic production. . . . The director and auxiliary egos are confronted not only with which clues to use, but which clues to let "pass"; they have to let pass far more clues than they can use. The "timing" of the right clue is another aspect of the problem. Once the protagonist and auxiliary ego decide which clue is right and appropriate, they must rapidly use it before it is too late; otherwise, they may lose "contact" with each other. Adequate interpersonal communication results from the help which one individual can give to another at a certain moment and in a certain locus. . . .

The Dilemma of Existentialism, Daseinsanalyse and the Psychodrama

The need for establishing a better understanding between the phenomenologists, the existentialists and the empirical scientists has been, I believe, successfully bridged by sociometric theory. Psychodramatists have come to the new insights because of their preoccupation with therapeutic problems carrying the patient's autonomy in the process of treatment to a maximum. The patient becomes the chief guide in the research about him as well as in his cure. Two contradictory principles are operating in the therapeutic investigation. One is the utterly subjectivistic and existentialistic situations of the subject; the other is the objective requirements of the scientific method. The question is how to reconcile the two extreme positions. Sociometry and psychodrama have defined this methodological problem and have tried to solve it. "Existential validation" pays homage to the fact that any experience may be reciprocally satisfactory at the time of the consummation, here and now. The experience, for instance, of two lovers or two friends does not require any validation beyond the consent and enjoyment of the participants. If, in a sociometric test each individual discloses his preference on the test honestly, the test is perfectly reliable and valid. Psychotherapeutic methods, individual and group, depend upon genuine interaction between therapists and patients. Every session is a unique experience for the participants. Validation in individual and group psychotherapeutic practice is not imperative, as long as no pretense is made that generalizations can be drawn from whatever the events recorded, or that the future behavior of the participants can be predicted from the events. What matters is that the therapeutic experiences are valid for the participants themselves, at the time they take place. Indeed, a scientific validation would be meaningless for the participants, for the value of their experience is self-evident. But scientific and existential validation do not exclude one another, they can be constructed as a continuum. . . .

Silvano Arieti

Recent Conceptions and Misconceptions of Schizophrenia

One has the . . . feeling in reading [Binswanger's] . . . existentialist reports . . . that no attempt is made to change the patient. On the contrary, what occurs in the last stage of the illness is seen as the inevitable occurrence, like the last stanza of a poem, the last motive of a song, or the final act of a play. Everything is seen as fitting the world design, a superior symmetry. . . . The patient remains alone, in spite of the attempt made to understand the uniqueness of his experiences. We do not find in this report the caring endeavor of Frieda Fromm-Reichmann, who tries to help the patient to see why the therapist and he experience things in different ways. We do not recognize the attempts of Mme. Sechehaye to adapt herself to the psychotic world in order to trace back the deceitful meanders of the patient's symbolism; we do not detect Sullivan's attitude of the participant observer. As a matter of fact, we have the feeling that the existentialist psychiatrist does not participate at all. Like a spectator in the theater, he is not apathetic; he feels, admires, and suffers, but does not participate. He remains in the audience.

If . . . he becomes too enchanted by the scenery, in which he sees not only destruction but also the harmony of a world design, he may be at a loss in retrieving the little me in the patient, lost in all these flourishing stage settings. He may not be able to help the sufferer to reacquire his inner harmony, the real harmony. . . . If tragic failure is seen not as a possibility but as the ineluctable aspect of man, how can we not fail in our therapeutic endeavor? . . .

Actually the world design is the paranoid work itself. Had Binswanger selected more disintegrated or more regressed patients, he would not have been able to differentiate a world design, unless by the world design he were to mean the picture of progressive disintegration itself. (18-20)

What Is Effective in the Therapeutic Process?

Rather than to focus on how the past is effective in the present, the treatment must focus on how the present need *not* be the effect of the past. Although the past has to be uncovered, studied and understood, the reintegration of the psychotic will be based more on the realization of the patient of the present potentialities and on his trustful expectations of the future. . . .

. . . A new basic approach has to be resorted to, which . . . relies predominantly on the establishing of a new interpersonal contact with the therapist. . . . How will he reintegrate? How will the new interpersonal prototype benefit him? In the establishment of what I think may be called *basic trust*. . . .

Martin Buber defines trust as "a contact of the entire being with the one in whom one trusts." In Buber's terminology, it is this trust which permits the I-Thou relationship to exist. Psychologically this means that without others and trust in them there would be no I, no development of the self. . . . If you break the wall of mistrust a path is opened which will lead to reintegration. Obviously, the therapist cannot have this feeling for all patients but only for a minority of them and must limit himself to the treatment of these few, whom he likes very much, whom he wants to help at any cost, and in whom perhaps he sees an exaggeration of his own unsolved conflicts. . . .

. . . The most effective tool in the treatment of the psychotic is the creation of a certain feeling, atmosphere, based on the transference-countertransference relationship, on a prototypical I-Thou interpersonal relationship. In the spirit of this atmosphere, communication is reestablished, genetic interpretations are linked together, the social self is reintegrated. (31-33)

The Two Aspects of Schizophrenia

To use Buber's terminology, in this period of the life of the pre-schizophrenic, there is an intense I-Thou relationship. But the Thou is already pathological and cannot be entirely accepted by the I, cannot become a very consistent and well-integrated part of the I. This is the very beginning of the schizophrenic cleavage, this never-complete acceptance of the Thou, or of the social self, of that part of the self which originates from others. This Thou, which is not completely accepted or integrated, tends to remain or to become dissociated, something like a foreign body, something which is easily externalized, . . . in forms of projections and hallucinations. (405)

By becoming schizoid, the patient removes from his life that early intense relatedness which has been mentioned, and which was so destructive. He represses emotions to a certain extent and achieves several useful compromises. The bad images of the parents, which have remained half-conscious, are more tolerable because less anxiety-provoking; moreover, the self-image of being inadequate and worthless is also less anxiety-provoking and less traumatic. If one again follows Martin Buber's conceptions, it may be stated that during this period of adoption of a schizoid personality the I-Thou relationship is limited and constricted both quantitatively, in the sense that the relations involved are fewer and qualitatively, in the sense that the relatively few interpersonal relations left are less intense.

Let us remember, however, that an I-Thou relationship is maintained, even if limited. And here the writer wants to add something which was suggested by the application to psychiatry of Buber's basic formulations. Men do not have merely an I-Thou relationship but also an I-It relationship, that is, a relationship between the person and the inanimate world. This type of nonpersonal relationship is a normal component of life. However, the neurotic person who has difficulties in interpersonal relations, tries to change the I-Thou relationship into an I-It relationship. In other words, he tries to treat people as things; he depersonalizes them. For instance, people become machines, sex a biological phenomenon; human relations become scientific experiments, and so on. Even the analyst becomes a psychoanalytic machine which renders a service. Now, although this type of defense is found in many schizoid personalities, it is never, or almost never, found in the schizoids who become schizophrenics. The preschizophrenic schizoid is deprived of this neurotic mechanism. He cannot translate the personal into the impersonal. As a matter of fact, one sees the opposite process in operation toward the beginning of the overt psychotic illness. The impersonal tends to be personalized. Whatever happens is never attributed to chance or to physical events. Everything is anthropomorphized and seen as a consequence of a personal will.

The schizoid is not the only type of personality found in preschizophrenics. . . . People with stormy personalities have not found that detachment is a consistent protection against anxiety.

They do not like to restrict the I-Thou world, as the schizoid does, but want to retain it. In their attempt to gain parental approval and love, they have tried all types of attitudes toward the parents. At times they are extremely submissive and compliant, at times aggressive, at times very detached. They try all possible means of defense because, actually, no means offers a sure protection from anxiety. This variety of reactions has been enhanced by the inconsistency of the parents. The stormy personalities have acquired a capacity to change their attitudes toward life repeatedly, at times slowly, oftener suddenly and drastically. They continuously change their ways of relatedness, their I-Thou worlds, and do not develop strong senses of self-identity. They do not withdraw, they try to reach people, but every time they try, they are hurt. They often experience very strong conscious anxiety, which leads them repeatedly to crises. . . .

[The] . . . development of the projection mechanism in the paranoid type of schizophrenia may be viewed as consisting of three stages which succeed one another at different periods in the life of the patient.

First is the stage of introjection. The actions and attitudes of the parent are external and are being introjected. The I-Thou relationship is in the making, but has an unhealthy beginning on account of the pathogenic attitude of the parent. Second, is the stage of assimilation. The child has accepted the parent's attitude toward him. He sees, accuses and hates himself, as he feels the parents hated him. The Thou has become part of the I. But the Thou is unhealthy, and its assimilation produces low self-esteem and a shaky self-image. In other words, the I is unstable and liable to fragment. Third, is the stage of projection or the psychotic stage. Now, the I is fragmenting, and some fragments are externalized. This is accomplished by the patient's rejecting and projecting back to symbolic parents those attitudes toward himself he now rejects. The Thou is rejected. It is too unpleasant. The rest of the self is not going to accept it any longer. Self-condemnation is no longer part of the self; now condemnation comes from the persecutor. The persecutor is the Thou or a symbolic reproduction of the parent. But in order to remove the Thou, or the interpersonal world, which has caused so much torment, the patient remains with an impoverished and very sick I, a psychotic I. (407-410)

In order to avoid anxiety, in order to reject the Thou-world (the Thou which is in the I and which causes so much distress), the schizophrenic, after having vainly tried other less drastic ways, resorts or regresses to methods of thinking which preceded the development of the Thou-world in the course of evolution. The patient withdraws from a way of reasoning which is logical and is shared by society, and adopts an archaic or paleological way of thinking. He also withdraws from a system of symbolization shared with his fellow human beings, and adopts his own private symbols or paleosymbols. (413)

Carl R. Rogers

On Becoming a Person

. . . In my early professional years I was asking the question: How can I treat, or cure, or change this person? Now I would phrase the question in this way: How can I provide a relationship which this person may use for his own personal growth? . . .

No approach which relies upon knowledge, upon training, upon the acceptance of something that is *taught,* is of any use. These approaches seem so tempting and direct that I have, in the past, tried a great many of them. It is possible to explain a person to himself, to prescribe steps which should lead him forward, to train him in knowledge about a more satisfying mode of life. But such methods are, in my experience, futile and inconsequential. The most they can accomplish is some temporary change, which soon disappears, leaving the individual more than ever convinced of his inadequacy.

The failure of any such approach through the intellect has forced me to recognize that change appears to come about through *experience* in a *relationship*. . . . If I can provide a certain type of relationship, the other person will discover within himself the capacity to use that relationship for growth, and change and personal development will occur. . . .

I have found that the more I can be genuine in the relationship, the more helpful it will be. This means that I need to be aware of my own feelings, in so far as possible, rather than presenting an outward façade of one attitude, while actually holding another attitude at a deeper or unconscious level. Being genuine also involves the willingness to be and to express, in my words and my behavior, the various feelings and attitudes which exist in me. It is only in this way that the relationship can have *reality*, and reality seems deeply important as a first condition. It is only by providing the genuine reality which is in me, that the other person can successfully seek for the reality in him. I have found this to be true even when the attitudes I feel are not attitudes with which I am pleased, or attitudes which seem conducive to a good relationship. It seems extremely important to be real.

As a second condition, I find that the more acceptance and liking I feel toward this individual, the more I will be creating a relationship which he can use. By acceptance I mean a warm regard for him as a person of unconditional self-worth—of value no matter what his condition, his behavior, or his feelings. It means a respect and liking for him as a separate person, a willingness for him to possess his own feelings in his own way. It means an acceptance of and regard for his attitudes of the moment, no matter how negative or positive, no matter how much they may contradict other attitudes he has held in the past. This acceptance of each fluctuating aspect of this other person makes it for him a relationship of warmth and safety, and the safety of being liked and prized as a person seems a highly important element in a helping relationship.

I also find that the relationship is significant to the extent that I feel a continuing desire to understand—a sensitive empathy with each of the client's feelings and communications as they seem to him at that moment. Acceptance does not mean much until it involves understanding. It is only as I *understand* the feelings and thoughts which seem so horrible to you, or so weak, or so sentimental, or so bizarre—it is only as I see them as you see them, and accept them and you, that you can feel really free to explore all the hidden nooks and frightening crannies of your inner and often buried experience. This *freedom* is an important condition of the relationship. There is implied here a freedom to explore oneself at both conscious and unconscious levels, as rapidly as one can dare to embark on this dangerous quest. There is also a complete freedom from any type of moral or diagnostic evaluation, since all such evaluations are, I believe, always threatening.

Thus the relationship which I have found helpful is characterized by a sort of transparency on my part, in which my real feelings are evident; by an acceptance of this other person as a separate person with value in his own right; and by a deep empathic understanding which enables me to see his private world through his eyes. When these conditions are achieved, I become a companion to my client, accompanying him in the frightening search for himself, which he now feels free to undertake.

I am by no means always able to achieve this kind of relationship with another, and sometimes, even when I feel I have achieved it in myself, he may be too frightened to perceive what is being offered to him. But I would say that when I hold in myself the kind of attitudes I have described, and when the other person can to some degree experience these attitudes, then I believe that change and constructive personal development will *invariably* occur—and I include that word "invariably" only after long and careful consideration. . . .

. . . The individual will discover within himself the capacity to use this relationship for growth. . . . Gradually my experience has forced me to conclude that the individual has within himself the capacity and the tendency, latent if not evident, to move forward toward maturity. In a suitable psychological climate this tendency is released, and becomes actual rather than potential. It is evident in the capacity of the individual to understand those aspects of his life and of himself which are causing him pain and dissatisfaction, and understanding which probes beneath his conscious knowledge of himself into those experiences which he has hidden from himself because of their threatening nature. It shows itself in the tendency to reorganize his personality and his relationship to life in ways which are regarded as more mature. Whether one calls it a growth tendency, a drive toward self-actualization, or a forward-moving directional tendency, it is the mainspring of life, and is, in the last analysis, the tendency upon which all psychotherapy depends. It is the urge which is evident in all organic and human life—to expand, extend, become autonomous, develop, mature—the tendency to express and activate all the capacities of the organism, to the extent that such activation enhances the organism or the self. This tendency may become deeply buried under layer after layer of encrusted psychological defenses; it may be hidden behind elaborate façades which deny its existence; but it is my belief that it exists in every individual, and awaits only the proper conditions to be released and expressed. . . .

It is my hypothesis that in such a relationship the individual will reorganize himself at both the conscious and deeper levels of his personality in such a manner as to cope with life more constructively, more intelligently, and in a more socialized as well as a more satisfying way. . . . In such a relationship the individual becomes more integrated, more effective. He shows fewer of the characteristics which are usually termed neurotic or psychotic, and more of the characteristics of the healthy, well-functioning person. He changes his perception of himself, becoming more realistic in his views of self. He becomes more like the person he wishes to be. He values himself more highly. He is more self-confident and self-directing. He has a better understanding of himself, becomes more open to his experience, denies or represses less of his experience. He becomes more accepting in his attitudes toward others, seeing others as more similar to himself.

In his behavior he shows similar changes. He is less frustrated by stress, and recovers from stress more quickly. He becomes more mature in his everyday behavior as this is observed by friends. He is less defensive, more adaptive, more able to meet situations creatively. . . .

There seems every reason to suppose that the therapeutic relationship is only one instance of interpersonal relations, and that the same lawfulness governs all such relationships. Thus it seems reasonable to hypothesize that if the parent creates with his child a psychological climate such as we have described, then the child will become more self-directing, socialized, and mature. To the extent that the teacher creates such a relationship with his class, the student will become a self-initiated learner, more original, more self-disciplined, less anxious and other-directed. . . .

If I can create a relationship characterized on my part:

by a genuineness and transparency, in which I am my real feelings;
by a warm acceptance of and liking for the other person as a separate individual;
by a sensitive ability to see his world and himself as he sees them;

Then the other individual in the relationship:

will experience and understand aspects of himself which previously he has repressed;
will find himself becoming better integrated, more able to function effectively;
will become more similar to the person he would like to be;
will be more self-directing and self-confident;
will become more of a person, more unique and more self-expressive;
will be able to cope with the problems of life more adequately and more comfortably.

I believe that this statement holds whether I am speaking of my relationship with a client, with a group of students or staff members, with my family or children. (32-38)

Martin Buber, the existentialist philosopher of the University of Jerusalem, has a phrase, "confirming the other," which has had meaning for me. He says "Confirming means . . . accepting the whole potentiality of the other . . . I can recognize in him, know in him, the person he has been . . . *created* to become . . . I confirm him in myself, and then in him, in relation to this potentiality that . . . can now be developed, can evolve." If I accept the other person as something fixed, already diagnosed and classified, already shaped by his past, then I am doing my part to confirm this limited hypothesis. If I accept him as a process of becoming, then I am doing what I can to confirm or make real his potentialities.

It is at this point that I see Verplanck, Lindsley, and Skinner, working in operant conditioning, coming together with Buber, the philosopher or mystic. At least they come together in principle, in an odd way. If I see a relationship as only an opportunity to reinforce certain types of words or opinions in the other, then I tend to confirm him as an object—a basically mechanical, manipulable object. And if I see this as his potentiality, he tends to act in ways which support this hypothesis. If, on the other hand, I see a relationship as an opportunity to "reinforce" *all* that he is, the person that he is with all his existent potentialities, then he tends to act in ways which support *this* hypothesis. I have then—to use Buber's term—confirmed him as a living person, capable of creative inner development. Personally I prefer this second type of hypothesis. (55f.)

I have been astonished to find how accurately the Danish philosopher, Søren Kierkegaard, pictured the dilemma of the individual more than a century ago, with keen psychological insight. He points out that the most common despair is to be in despair at not choosing, or willing, to be one's self; but that the deepest form of despair is to choose "to be another than himself." On the other hand "to will to be that self which one truly is, is indeed the opposite of despair," and this choice is the deepest responsibility of man. As I read some of his writings I almost feel that he must have listened in on the statements made by our clients as they search and explore for the reality of self—often a painful and troubling search.

This exploration becomes even more disturbing when they find themselves involved in removing the false faces which they had not known were false faces. They begin to engage in the frightening task of exploring the turbulent and sometimes violent feelings within themselves. To remove a mask which you had thought was part of your real self can be a deeply disturbing experience, yet when there is freedom to think and feel and be, the individual moves toward such a goal. (110)

It seems that gradually, painfully, the individual explores what is behind the masks he presents to the world, and even behind the masks with which he has been deceiving himself. Deeply and often vividly he experiences the various elements of himself which have been hidden within. Thus to an increasing degree he becomes himself—not a façade of conformity to others, nor a cynical denial of all feeling, nor a front of intellectual rationality, but a living, breathing, feeling, fluctuating process—in short, he becomes a person. . . . In this process the individual becomes more open to his experience.

It is the opposite of defensiveness. . . . The individual becomes more openly aware of his own feelings and attitudes as they exist in him at an organic level. He also becomes more aware of reality as it exists outside of himself, instead of perceiving it in preconceived categories. . . . He is able to take in the evidence in a new situation, *as it is,* rather than distorting it to fit a pattern which he already holds. As you might expect, this increasing ability to be open to experience makes him far more realistic in dealing with new people, new situations, new problems. It means that his beliefs are not rigid, that he can tolerate ambiguity. He can receive much conflicting evidence without forcing closure upon the situation. This openness of awareness to what exists at *this moment* in oneself and in the *situation* is, I believe, an important element in the description of the person who emerges from therapy. (114-116)

A second characteristic of the persons who emerge from therapy is that the person increasingly discovers that his own organism is trustworthy, that it is a suitable instrument for discovering the most satisfying behavior in each immediate situation. . . . To the extent that this person is open to all of his experience, he has access to all of the available data in the situation, on which to base his behavior. He has knowledge of his own feelings and impulses, which are often complex and contradictory. He is freely able to sense the social demands, from the relatively rigid social "laws" to the desires of friends and family. He has access to his memories of similar situations, and the consequences of different behaviors in those situations. He has a relatively accurate perception of this existential situation in all of its complexity. He is better able to permit his total organism, his conscious thought participating, to consider, weigh and balance each stimulus, need, and demand, and its relative weight and intensity. Out of this complex weighing and balancing he is able to discover that course of action which seems to come closest to satisfying all his needs in the situation, long-range as well as immediate needs. . . .

There is a gradual growth of trust in, and even affection for the complex, rich, varied assortment of feelings and tendencies which exist in him at the organic level. Consciousness, instead of being the watchman over a dangerous and unpredictable lot of impulses, of which few can be permitted to see the light of day, becomes the comfortable inhabitant of a society of impulses and feelings and thoughts, which are discovered to be very satisfactorily self-governing when not fearfully guarded. . . . The individual increasingly comes to feel that this locus of evaluation lies within himself. Less and less does he look to others for approval or disapproval; for standards to live by; for decisions and choices. He recognizes that it rests within himself to choose; that the only question which matters is: "Am I living in a way which is deeply satisfying to me, and which truly expresses me?" This I think is perhaps *the* most important question for the creative individual. (118f.)

. . . A person is a fluid process, not a fixed and static entity; a flowing river of change, not a block of solid material; a continually changing constellation of potentialities, not a fixed quantity of traits. (124)

Persons or Science? A Philosophical Question

INTRODUCTORY NOTE

I am not a student of existential philosophy. I first became acquainted with the work of Søren Kierkegaard and that of Martin Buber at the insistence of some of the theological students at Chicago who were taking work with me. They were sure that I would find the thinking of these men congenial, and in this they were largely correct. (199)

Science always has to do with the other, the object. Various logicians of science, including Stevens, the psychologist, show that it is a basic element of science that it always has to do with the observable object, the observable other. This is true, even if the scientist is experimenting on himself, for to that degree he treats himself as the observable other. It never has anything to do with the experiencing me. Now does not this quality of science mean that it must forever be irrelevant to an experience such as therapy, which is intensely personal, highly subjective in its inwardness, and dependent entirely on the relationship of two individuals each of whom is an experiencing me? Science can of course study the events which occur, but always in a way which is irrelevant to what is occurring. An analogy would be to say that science can conduct an autopsy of the dead events of therapy, but by its very nature it can never enter into the living physiology of therapy. It is for this reason that therapists recognize—usually intuitively—that any advance in therapy, any fresh knowledge of it, any significant new hypotheses in regard to it—must come from the experience of therapists and clients, and can never come from science. . . .

Because science has as its field the "other," the "object," it means that everything it touches is transformed into an object. . . . A number of medical men feel some concern as to whether the increasing tendency to view the human organism as an object, in spite of its scientific efficacy, may not be unfortunate for the patient. . . . In therapy, both client and therapist become objects for dissection, but not persons with whom one enters a living relationship. . . . If we project ourselves into the future, and suppose that we had the answers to most of the questions which psychology investigates today, . . . we would find ourselves increasingly impelled to treat all others, and even ourselves, as objects. The knowledge of all human relationships would be so great that we would know it rather than live the relationships unreflectively. We see some foretaste of this in the attitude of sophisticated parents who know that affection "is good for the child." This knowledge frequently stands in the way of their being themselves, freely, unreflectively—affectionate or not. Thus the development of science in a field like therapy is either irrelevant to the experience, or may actually make it more difficult to live the relationship as a personal, experiential event.

The end result of science is to lead toward manipulation. . . . If we know all about how learning takes place, we use that knowledge to manipulate persons as objects . . . through advertisements, through propaganda, through prediction of their responses and the control of those responses. It is not too strong a statement to say that the growth of knowledge in the social sciences contains within itself a powerful tendency toward social control, toward control of the many by the few. An equally strong tendency is toward the weakening or destruction of the existential person. . . . (Skinner's *Walden Two* is a psychologist's picture of paradise . . . Huxley's *Brave New World*) . . . Thus, to put it bluntly, it seems that a developing social science (as now conceived and pursued) leads to social dictatorship and individual loss of personhood. . . .

In physical science it took centuries for the ethical issue to become crucial, but it has at last become so. In the social sciences the ethical issues arise much more quickly, because persons are involved. But in psychotherapy the issue arises most quickly and most deeply. Here is the maximizing of all that is subjective, inward, personal, here a relationship is lived, not examined, and a person, not an object, emerges; a person who feels, chooses, believes, acts, not as an automaton, but as a person. And here too is the ultimate in science . . . the reduction to hypotheses, and eventually to theorems, of all that has been regarded as most personal. . . . We must make a choice—an ethical, personal choice of values. We may do it by default, by not raising the question. We may be able to conserve both values—but choose we must. (211-215)

As observer I use all of the hunches which grow out of the living experience. To avoid deceiving myself as observer, to gain a more accurate picture of the order which exists, I make use of all the canons of science. Science is not an impersonal something, but simply a person living subjectively another phase of himself. A deeper understanding of therapy . . . may come from living it, or from observing it in accordance with the rules of science, or from the communication within the self between the two types of experience. . . . What I will do with the knowledge gained through scientific method—whether I will use it to understand, enhance, enrich, or use it to control, manipulate and destroy—is a matter of subjective choice dependent upon the values which have personal meaning for me. . . . If I am open to my experience and can permit all of the sensings of my intricate organism to be available to my awareness, then I am likely to use myself, my subjective experience, *and* my scientific knowledge, in ways which are realistically constructive.

This [new] . . . integration . . . reperceives the issue, by putting the subjective existential person, with the values which he holds, at the foundation and the root of the therapeutic relationship and of the scientific relationship. For science too, at its inception, is an "I-Thou" relationship with a person or persons. And only as a subjective person can I enter into either of these relationships. (223f.)

The Loneliness of Contemporary Man

What went wrong with her [Ellen West's] treatment? Here is an intelligent, sensitive young woman, seeking help. The prognosis, by modern standards, would seem very favorable. Why such complete failure? I am sure opinions differ, but I should like to state mine. The greatest weakness, in my opinion, is that no one involved in her treatment seems to have related to her as a *person;* a person worthy of respect, a person capable of autonomous choice, a person whose inner experiencing is a precious resource to be drawn upon and trusted. Rather, she seems to have been dealt with as an object. Her first analyst helps her to *see* her feelings, but not to experience them. This only makes her more of an object to herself, and still further estranges her from living in and drawing upon her experience. Quite wisely she says that the "analyst can give me discernment, but not healing." . . .

"I am isolated. I sit in a glass ball, I see people through a glass wall. I scream, but they do not hear me." What a desperate cry for a relationship between two persons. She never experienced what Buber has called "healing through meeting." There was no one who could meet her, accept her, as she was. (98f.)

For myself, I draw certain lessons from this case of Ellen West. The first is that in every respect in which we make an object of the person—whether by diagnosing him, analyzing him, or perceiving him impersonally in a case history—we stand in the way of our therapeutic goal. To make an object of a person has been helpful in treating physical ills. It has not been successful in treating psychological ills. We are deeply helpful only when we relate as persons, when we risk ourselves as persons in the relationship, when we experience the other as a person in his own right. Only then is there a meeting of a depth which dissolves the pain of aloneness in both client and therapist. (101)

Dialogue Between Martin Buber and Carl Rogers

Moderated by Maurice Friedman

APRIL 18, 1957
ANN ARBOR, MICHIGAN

CARL ROGERS: . . . How have you lived so deeply in interpersonal relationships and gained such an understanding of the human individual, without being a psychotherapist? (Buber laughs)

MARTIN BUBER: . . . When I was a student long ago I studied three terms psychiatry and what they call in Germany *Psychiatrische-Klinique*. I was most interested in the latter. . . . I studied it three terms: first with Flechzig in Leipzig, where there were students of Wundt. Afterwards in Berlin with Mendel, and a third term with Bleuler in Zürich, which was the most interesting of the three. . . .

About what mainly constituted what you ask, it was something other. It was just a certain inclination to meet people. And as far as possible, to, just to change if possible something in the *other*, but also to let *me* be changed by *him*. . . . I felt I had not the right to want to change another if I am not open to be changed by him as far as it is legitimate. . . . I *cannot* be so to speak above him and say, "No! I'm out of the play. *You* are mad." . . . There were two phases of it. The first phase went until the year 1918, meaning until I was about forty. And then, in 1918, I felt something rather strange. I felt that I had been strongly influenced by something that came to an end just then, meaning the First World War. . . . You may call this *imagining* the *real*. Imagining what was going on. This imagining, for four years, influenced me terribly. Just when it was finished, it finished by a certain episode in May, 1919, when a friend of mine, a great friend, a great man, was killed by the anti-revolutionary soldiers in a very barbaric way,[3] and I now again once more—and this was the last time—I was compelled to imagine just this killing, but not in an optical way alone, but may I say so, just with my *body*. And this was the decisive moment. . . . From now on, I had to give something more than just my inclination to exchange thoughts and feelings, and so on. I had to give the fruit of an experience. . . .

CARL ROGERS: . . . When I'm being effective as a therapist, I enter the relationship as a subjective person, not as a scrutinizer, not as a scientist. I feel, too, that when I am most effective, then somehow I am relatively whole in that relationship, or the word that has meaning to me is transparent. To be sure there may be many aspects of my life that aren't brought into the relationship, but what is brought into the relationship is transparent. There is nothing hidden. Then I think, too, that in such a relationship I

[3] Buber is referring to the German socialist and man of letters Gustav Landauer who was a leader in the first (non-communist) socialist government in Munich in 1919. *Cf.* Martin Buber, *Pointing the Way*, edited, translated, and with an introduction by Maurice Friedman (New York: Harper Torchbooks, 1963). "Recollection of a Death."

feel a real willingness for this other person *to be what he is.* I call that acceptance. I don't know that that's a very good word for it, but my meaning there is that I'm willing for him to possess the feelings he possesses, to hold the attitudes he holds, to be the person he is. And then another aspect of it which is important to me is that I think in those moments I am able to sense with a good deal of clarity the way his experience seems to him, really viewing it from within him, and yet without losing my own personhood or separateness in that. Then, if in addition to those things on *my* part, my client or the person with whom I'm working is able to sense something of those attitudes in me, then it seems to me that there is a real, experiential meeting of persons, in which each of us is changed. I think sometimes the client is changed more than I am, but I think both of us are changed in that kind of an experience. Now, I see that as having some resemblance to the sort of thing you have talked about in the I-Thou relationship. . . .

MARTIN BUBER: . . . A man coming to you for help . . . The essential difference between your role in this situation and his is obvious. He comes for help to you. You don't come for help to him. And not only this, but you are *able,* more or less, to help him. He can do different things to you, but not help you. And not this alone. You *see* him, *really.* I don't mean that you cannot be mistaken, but you *see* him, just as you said, as he *is.* He cannot, by far, cannot *see you.* Not only in the degree, but even in the kind of seeing. You are, of course, a very important person for him. But not a person whom he wants to see and to know and is able to. You're important for him. You're . . . he is floundering around, he comes to you. He is, may I say, entangled in your life, in your thoughts, in your being, your communication, and so on. But he is not interested in you as you. It cannot be. You are interested, you say so and you are right, in him as this person. This kind of detached presence he cannot have and give. . . .

You're on one side of the situation on the, may I say so, more or less active, and he in a more or less patient, not entirely active, not entirely passive, of course—but relatively. And this situation, let us now look on this common situation from your point of view and from his point of view. The same situation. You can see it, feel it, experience it from the two sides. From your side, seeing him, observing him, knowing him, helping him . . . from your side and from his side. You can experience, I would venture to say, bodily, his side of the situation. When you do, so to speak, something to him, you feel yourself touched first by what you do to him. He cannot do it at all. You are at your side and at his side at the same time. Here and there, or let's rather say, there and here. Where he is and where you are. He cannot be but where he is. And this, you will, you not only will, you want, your inner necessities may be as you are. I accept that. I have no objection at all. But the *situation* has an objection. You have necessarily another attitude to the situation than he has. You are able to do something that he is not able. You are not equals and cannot be. You have the great task, self-imposed—a great self-imposed task to supplement this need of his and to do rather more than in the normal situation. But, of course, there are limits, and I may be allowed to tell you certainly in your experience as a therapist, as a healing person or helping to healing, you must experience it again and again—the limits to simple humanity. To simple humanity meaning being I and my partner, so to speak, *alike* to one another, on the same plane. I see you *mean* being on the same plane, but you cannot. There is not only you, your mode of thinking, your mode of doing, there is also a certain situation—we are so and so—which may sometimes be tragic, even more terrible than what we call tragic. You *cannot* change this. Humanity, human will, human understanding, are not everything. There is some reality confronting us. We cannot forget it for a moment. . . .

CARL ROGERS: . . . It seems to me that when another person is really expressing himself and his experience and so on, I don't feel, in the way that you've described, different from him. . . . I feel as though in that moment his way of looking at his experience, distorted though it might be, is something I can look upon as having equal authority, equal validity with the way I see life and experience. It seems to me *that* really is the basis of helping, in a sense. . . . I think you're quite right, that there is an objective situation there, one that could be measured, one that is real, one that various people could agree upon if they examine the situation closely. But it has been my experience that that is reality when it is viewed from the outside, and that that really has *nothing* to do with the relationship that produces therapy. That is something immediate, equal, a meeting of two persons on an equal basis—even though, in the world of I-It, it could be seen as a very unequal relationship.

MARTIN BUBER: Now, Dr. Rogers, this is the first point where we must say to one another, "We disagree."

CARL ROGERS: OK.

MARTIN BUBER: You see, I cannot only look on you, on your part of things, on your experience. Let's take the case where I could talk to *him*, to the patient, too. I would, of course, hear from him a very different tale about this same moment. Now, you see,

I am not a therapist. I'm interested in you *and* in him. I must see the situation. I must see you and him in this dialogue bounded by tragedy. Sometimes, in many cases, a tragedy that can be overcome. Just in your method. I have no objection at all to your method, you see? There is no need to speak about it. But sometimes, method is not enough. You cannot do what is necessary to do. Now, let me ask you a question that seemingly has nothing to do with this, but it's the same point. You have certainly much to do with schizophrenics. Is it so?

CARL ROGERS: Some.

MARTIN BUBER: You have . . . have you also to do, let me say, with paranoiacs?

CARL ROGERS: Some.

MARTIN BUBER: Now, would you say that the situation is the same in the one case and in the other? Meaning, the situation as far as it has to do with the relationship between you and the other man. Is this relationship that you describe the same kind of relationship in the one case and in the other? . . .

CARL ROGERS: One of the things that I say very tentatively, because I realize this is opposed by a great weight of psychiatric and psychological opinion, I would say that there is no difference in the relationship that I form with a normal person, a schizophrenic, a paranoid—I don't really feel any difference. That doesn't mean, of course, that when. . . . Well, again, it's this question of looking at it from the outside. Looking at it from the outside, one can easily discern plenty of differences. But it seems to me that if therapy is effective, there is this same kind of meeting of persons no matter what the psychiatric label. . . . The moments in which people *do* change, are the moments in which perhaps the relationship is experienced the same on both sides. . . .

MARTIN BUBER: A very important point in my thinking is the problem of limits. Meaning, I do something, I try something, I will something, and I give all my thoughts in existence into this doing. And then I come at a certain moment to a wall, to a boundary, to a limit that I cannot, I *cannot* ignore. This is true, also, for what interests me more than anything, human effective dialogue. Meaning by dialogue not just a talking. Dialogue can be silence. We would perhaps, without the audience. I would recommend to do it without an audience. We could sit together, or rather walk together in silence and that could be a dialogue. But so, even in dialogue, full dialogue, there is a limit set. This is why I'm interested in paranoia. Here is a limit set for dialogue. It is sometimes very difficult to talk to a schizophrenic. In certain moments, as far as my experience with this, which is, of course, how may I say, dilettante?—I can talk to a schizophrenic as far as he is willing to let me into his particular world that is his own, and that in general he does not want to have you come in, or other people. But he lets some people in. And so he may let me in, too. But in the moment when he shuts himself, I cannot go on. And the same, only in a terrible, terribly strong manner, is the case with a paranoiac. He does not open himself and does not shut himself. He *is* shut. There is something else being done to him that shuts him. And this terribility of this fate I'm feeling very strongly because in the world of normal men, there are just analogous cases, when a sane man behaves, not to everyone, but behaves to some people *just so,* being *shut,* and the problem is if he can be opened, if he can open himself, and so on. And this is a problem for the human in general.

MAURICE FRIEDMAN: This is my role as moderator. I'm not quite satisfied as to . . . what extent it's an issue, to what extent . . . it may be a different use of terms, so let me ask Dr. Rogers one step further. As I understood, what Buber said was that the relationship is an I-Thou one, but not a fully reciprocal one, in the sense that while you have the meeting, nonetheless you see from his standpoint and he cannot see from yours. And in your response to that, you pointed again and again to the meeting that takes place and even to the change that may take place on both sides. But I didn't hear you ever point to the suggestion that he does not see from your standpoint, or that it is fully reciprocal in the sense that he also is helping you. And I wondered if this might not be perhaps just a difference if not of words, of viewpoint, where you were thinking of how you feel toward him, that he is an equal person and you respect him.

MARTIN BUBER: There remains a *decisive* difference. It's not a question of objecting to helping the other. It's one thing to help the other. He is a man wanting to help the other. And his attitude is this active, helping attitude. There is, I wish to say, a difference by the whole heaven, but I would prefer to say by the whole *hell,* a difference from your attitude. This is a man in health. A man *helped* cannot think, cannot imagine helping another. How could he?

CARL ROGERS: But that's where some of the difference arises. Because it seems to me again that in the most real moments of therapy I don't believe that this intention to help is any more than a substratum on my part either. Surely I wouldn't be doing this work if that wasn't part of my intention. And when I first see the client that's what I hope I will be able to do, is to be able to help him. And yet in the interchange of the moment, I don't think my mind is filled with the thought of "now I want to help you." It is much more "I want to understand you. What person are you behind that paranoid screen, or behind all these schizophrenic confusions, or behind all these masks that you wear in your real life. Who are you?" It seems to me that is a desire to meet a *person*, not "now I want to help." It seems to me that I've learned through my experience that when we *can* meet, then help does occur, but that's a by-product.

MAURICE FRIEDMAN: Dr. Rogers, would you not agree, though, that this is not fully reciprocal in the sense that that man does not have that attitude toward you, "I want to understand *you*. What sort of a person are *you*?"

CARL ROGERS: The only modification I made of that was that perhaps in the moment where real change takes place, then I wonder if it isn't reciprocal in the sense that I am able to see this individual as he is in that moment and he really senses my understanding and acceptance of him. And that I think is what is reciprocal and is perhaps what produces change.

MARTIN BUBER: You see, I, of course, am entirely with you as far as your experience goes. I cannot be with you as far as I have to look on the whole situation. Your experience and his. You see, you give him something in order to make him equal to you. You supplement his need in his relation to you. May I say so personally, out of a certain fullness you give him what he wants in order to be *able* to be, just for this moment, so to speak, on the same plane with you. But even that is very—it is a tangent. It is a tangent which may not last but one moment. It is not the situation as far as I see, not the situation of an hour; it is a situation of minutes. And these minutes are made possible by you. Not at all by him.

CARL ROGERS: That last I would thoroughly agree with—but I do sense some real disagreement there, because it seems to me that what I give him is permission to *be*. Which is a little different somehow from bestowing something on him.

MARTIN BUBER: I think no human being can give more than this. Making life possible for the other, if only for a moment. I'm with you. . . .

CARL ROGERS: . . . It seems to me that one of the most important types of meeting or relationship is the person's relationship to himself. In therapy again, which I have to draw on because that's my background of experience, there are some very vivid moments in which the individual is meeting some aspect of himself, a feeling which he has never recognized before, something of a meaning in himself that he has never known before. It could be any kind of thing. It may be his intense feeling of aloneness, or the terrible hurt he has felt, or something quite positive like his courage, and so on. But at any rate, in those moments, it seems to me that there is something that partakes of the same quality that I understand in a real meeting relationship. He is in his feeling and the feeling is in him. It is something that suffuses him. He has never experienced it before. In a very real sense, I think it could be described as a real meeting with an aspect of himself that he has never met before. Now I don't know whether that seems to you like stretching the concept you've used. I suppose I would just like to get your reaction to it. Whether to you that seems like a possible type of real relationship or a meeting? I'll push this one step further. I guess I have the feeling that it is when the person has met himself in that sense, probably in a good many different aspects, that then and perhaps only then, is he really capable of meeting another in an I-Thou relationship.

MARTIN BUBER: Now here we approach a problem of language. You call something dialogue that I cannot call so. But I can explain why I cannot call it so, why I would want another term between dialogue and monologue for this. Now for what I call dialogue, there is essentially necessary the moment of surprise. I mean. . . .

CARL ROGERS: You say "surprise"?

MARTIN BUBER: Yes, being surprised. A dialogue . . . let's take a rather trivial image. The dialogue is like a game of chess. The whole charm of chess is that I do not know and cannot know what my partner will do. I am surprised by what he does and on this surprise the whole play is based. Now you hint at this, that a man can surprise himself. But in a very different manner from how a person can surprise another person.

While the tape was being changed, Dr. Buber went on with his description of the characteristics of a true dialogue. A second feature is that in true meeting, or dialogue, that which is different in the other person, his otherness, is prized.

CARL ROGERS: The first two aspects of that . . . I hope that perhaps sometime I can play recordings of interviews for you to indicate how the surprise element can be there. That is, a person can be expressing something and then suddenly be hit by the meaning of that which has come from someplace in himself which he doesn't recognize. He really is *surprised* by himself. That can definitely happen. But the element that I see as being most foreign to your concept of dialogue is that it is quite true that this otherness in himself is not something to be prized. I think that in the kind of dialogue I'm talking about, within the person, that it is that otherness which probably would be broken down. . . .

MARTIN BUBER: And you see, may I add a technical matter? I have learned in the course of life to appreciate terms. And I think that in modern psychology, this does not exist in a sufficient measure. When I find something that is essentially different from another thing, I want a new term. I want a new concept. You see, for instance, modern psychology in general says about the unconscious that it is a certain mode of the psyche. It has no sense at all for me. If something is so different from . . . if two things are so different from one another as this strain of the soul, changing in every moment, where I cannot grasp anything when I try to grasp its way from one side—this *being* in pure time; and over against this what we call the unconscious, that is not a phenomenon at all, we have no access to it at all, we have only to deal with its effects and so on. We cannot say the first is psychic and the second is psychic; that the unconscious is something in which psychic and physiologic are, how may I say, mixed, it's not enough. They penetrate one another in such a manner that we see in relation to this the terms body and soul are so to speak late terms, late concepts, and concepts are never reality. Now, how can we comprehend this one concept?

CARL ROGERS: . . . As I see people coming together in relationships in therapy, I think that one of the things I have come to believe and feel and experience is that what I think of as human nature or basic human nature . . . is something that is really to be *trusted*. And it seems to me in some of your writings I catch something of that same feeling. At any rate, it's been very much my experience in therapy that one does not need to supply motivation toward the positive or toward the constructive. That exists in the individual. In other words, if we can release what is most basic in the individual, that it will be constructive. . . . It seems to me that orthodox psychoanalysis at least has held that when the individual is revealed, when you really get down to what is within the person, he consists mostly of instincts and attitudes and so on which must be *controlled*. That runs diametrically contrary to my own experience, which is that when you get to what is deepest in the individual, that is the very aspect that can most be trusted to be constructive or to tend toward socialization or toward the development of better inter-personal relationships. Does that have meaning for you?

MARTIN BUBER: When I have to do with, now let me say a problematic person, or just a sick person, a problematic person, a person that people call, or want to call, a bad person, . . . if I come near to the reality of this person, I experience it as a *polar* reality. . . . What you say may be trusted, I would say . . . stands in polar relation to what can be least trusted in this man. You cannot say and perhaps I differ from you in this point, you cannot say, "Oh, I detect in him just what can be trusted." I would say now when I see him when I grasp him more broadly and more deeply than before, I see his whole polarity and then I see how the worst in him and the best in him are dependent on one another attached to one another. And I can help, I may be able to help him just by helping him to change the relation between the poles. . . . There is not as we generally think in the soul of a man good and evil opposed. There is again and again in different manners a polarity, and the poles are not good and evil, but rather yes and no, rather acceptance and refusal. And we can strengthen, or we can help him strengthen, the one positive pole. And perhaps we can even strengthen the force of direction in him because this polarity is very often directionless. It is a chaotic state. We could bring a cosmic note into it. We can help put order, put a shape into this. Because I think the good, what we may call the good, is always only direction. Not a substance.

CARL ROGERS: And if I get the last portion of that particularly, you're saying that perhaps we can help the individual to strengthen the yes, that is to affirm life rather than refuse it. Is that . . . ?

MARTIN BUBER: You see, I differ only in this word, I would not say life. I would not put an object to it.

MAURICE FRIEDMAN: . . . When Dr. Rogers first asked Professor Buber about his attitude toward psychotherapy, he mentioned as one of the factors which entered into his approach to therapy, acceptance. Now, Professor Buber . . . often uses the term "confirmation." . . . Dr. Rogers writes about acceptance, in addition to saying that it is a warm regard for the other and a respect for his individuality, for him as a person of unconditional worth, that it means "an acceptance of and regard for his attitudes of the moment, no matter how much they may contradict other attitudes he has held in the past. And this acceptance of each fluctuating aspect of this other person makes it for him a relationship of warmth and safety." Now, I wonder whether Professor Buber would look on confirmation as similar to that, or would he see confirmation as including, perhaps, *not* being accepted, including some demand on the other that might mean in a sense a non-acceptance of his feelings at the moment in order to confirm him later.

MARTIN BUBER: I would say every true existential relationship between two persons begins with acceptance. By acceptance, I mean—perhaps the two concepts are not just alike—that by acceptance I mean being able to tell, or rather not to tell, but only to make it felt to the other person, that I accept him just as he is. I take you just as you are. Well, so, but it is not yet what I mean by confirming the other. Because accepting, this is just accepting how he ever is in this moment, in this actuality of his. Confirming means first of all, accepting the whole potentiality of the other and making even a decisive difference in his potentiality, and of course we can be mistaken again and again in this, but it's just a chance between human beings. I can recognize in him, know in him, more or less, the person he has been—I can say it only in this word—*created* to become. . . . And now I not only accept the other as he is, but I confirm him, in myself, and then in him, in relation to this potentiality that is meant by him and it can now be developed, it can evolve, it can answer the reality of life. He can do more or less to this scope but I can, too, do something. And this is with goals even deeper than acceptance. Let's take, for example, man and a woman, man and wife. He says, not expressly, but just by his whole relation to her, that "I accept you as you are." But this does *not* mean "I don't want you to change." But it says, "I discover in you just by my accepting love, I discover in you what you are meant to become." This is, of course, not anything to be expressed in massive terms. But it may be that it grows and grows with the years of common life. . . .

CARL ROGERS: . . . I think that sounds very much like this quality that is in the experience that I think of as acceptance, though I have tended to put it differently. I think that we do accept the individual *and* his potentiality. I think it's a real question whether we could accept the individual as he is, because often he is in pretty sad shape, if it were not for the fact that we also in some sense realize and recognize his potentiality. I guess I feel, too, that acceptance of the most complete sort, acceptance of this person as he is, is the strongest factor making for change that I know. In other words, I think that does release change or release potentiality to find that as I am, exactly as I am, I am fully accepted—then I can't help but change. Because then I feel there is no longer any need for defensive barriers, so then what takes over are the forward moving processes of life itself, I think.

MARTIN BUBER: I'm afraid I'm not so sure of that as you are, perhaps because I'm not a therapist. And I have necessarily to do with that problematic type. I cannot do in my relationship to him without this polarity. I cannot put this aside. As I said, I have to do with both men. I have to do with the problematic in him. And I have . . . there are cases when I must help him against himself. He wants my help against himself. He wants . . . you see, the first thing of all is that he trusts me. Yes, life has become baseless for him. He cannot tread on firm soil, on firm earth. He is so to say suspended in the air. And what does he want? What he wants is a being not only whom he can trust as a man trusts another, but a being that gives him now the certitude that "there *is* a soil, there *is* an existence. The world is not condemned to deprivation, degeneration, destruction. The world *can* be redeemed. *I* can be redeemed because there is this trust." And if this is reached, now I can help this man even in his struggle against himself. And this I can only do if I distinguish between accepting and confirming.

MAURICE FRIEDMAN: . . . My impression is that on the one hand there has been more insistence by Dr. Rogers on the fuller reciprocity of the I-Thou relation in therapy and less by Dr. Buber, but on the other, I get the impression that Dr. Rogers is more client-centered . . . more concerned with the becoming of the person. And he speaks in a recent article of being able to trust one's organism that it will find satisfaction, that it will express me. And he speaks of the locus of value as being inside one, whereas I get the impression from my encounter with Dr. Buber that he sees value as more in "the between." I wonder, is this a real issue between the two of you?

CARL ROGERS: . . . It seems to me that you could speak of the goal toward which therapy moves, and I guess the goal toward which maturity moves in an individual as being *becoming,* or being knowingly and acceptingly that which one most deeply is. That, too, expresses a real trust in the process which we are, that may not entirely be shared between us tonight.

MARTIN BUBER: . . . You speak about persons, and the concept "persons" is seemingly very near to the concept "individual." I would think that it is advisable to distinguish between them. An individual is just a certain uniqueness of a human being. And it can develop just by developing with uniqueness. This is what Jung calls individuation. He may become more and more an individual without making him more and more human. I have a lot of examples of man having become very very individual, very distinct of others, very developed in their such-and-such-ness without being at all what I would like to call a man. Individual is just this uniqueness, being able to be developed so and so. But a person, I would say, is an individual living really with the world. And with the world, I don't mean *in* the world. But just in *real contact,* in real reciprocity with the world in all the points in which the world can meet man. I don't say only with man, because sometimes we meet the world in other shapes than in that of man. But this is what I would call a person and if I may say expressly yes and no to certain phenomena, I'm *against* individuals and *for* persons. (209-221)

Hans Trüb

Individuation, Guilt, and Decision

Psychology as science *and psychology* as function know about the soul of man as about something in the third person. . . . They look down from above into the world of inner things, into the inner world of the individual. And they deal with its contents as with their "objects." They give names and they create classifications while carefully investigating the manifold connections and presenting them vividly in meaningful systems.

But the psychotherapist in his work with the ill is *essentially a human being.* As an individuality, he knows about the ever-enduring, meaningful *ground of creation* and about its lost and forgotten things, and as a man he feels himself indebted to and responsible for this, and he exerts himself to rediscover their secret meaning and to raise them anew to consciousness. For this psychology is to him an indispensable auxiliary function. . . . But he knows in the depths of his self that the secret meaning of these things that have been brought to consciousness first reveals itself *in the outgoing to the other.* Therefore he seeks and loves the human being in his patients and allows it . . . to come to him ever again. (550f.)

From the Self to the World

At this boundary, two things become clear to us: we must beware, in the first place, of seeing the psychic realm only in itself and thereupon forgetting the needful and helpful world and, in the second place, of conceiving the neurosis only as the effect of the psychic shortcomings of the age and the environment, and thereby denying the culpable failure of the human personality. True, the cure of the neurosis depends in the last analysis on the patient's carrying through the turning back personally with his soul and his taking the decisive first step into the world assigned to him. But at the same time it must also be stated with full clarity —and therein lies the paradox—that the psychotherapist cannot directly cure the neurosis as such, but at best only help to disentangle the psychic condition of the patient to the point at which the personal decision in favor of psychic commitment in that world falls due. . . .

The psychotherapist . . . has to embody as a substitute the community and its spiritual world which has denied itself to the neurotic and to which the latter in turn denies himself. It falls to his task to begin to reconstruct the interrupted dialogical relationship between this individual and the community in immediate meeting. This relation between physician and patient thus presents itself as a kind of cell in which the two partners together deliberately represent both universal distress and the sickness of the individual and carry it forward in personal dialogue to a cure. On this assumption, one can speak of a cure when the patient's psychic relationship to the world has been renewed and strengthened by these dialogues to such a degree that he can by himself arrive at an affirmation of that relationship in his own concrete realm of existence. The relationship of the "partners" in psychotherapy proves thereupon to be a prototype of the personal and thereby responsible relationship to the community which is to be resumed.

Thus the psychotherapist takes upon himself, as a substitute for the world which has denied itself [this opportunity], that helpful meeting (*Begegnung*) which the community owes the individual and whose absence is the cause of the neurotic's illness. He thereby answers as a mediator for the *possibility* of a meeting between this individual and his estranged community, and embraces in his role as mediator both sides of the relation which is to be restored. This double-edged responsibility, however, requires of him the complete commitment of his human personality in the dialogue with the individual partner.

Such a grave responsibility exposes the position of the psychotherapist to two dangers that must be taken seriously. Firstly, the physician may slip into an intimate relationship to the patient by construing the latter's newly awakened vitality as a personal inclination, thinking it applies to himself, and in this way narrowing the contractual partnership down to a private I-Thou relationship. . . . The second danger is that the physician—in order to escape the first danger—assumes the role of the objective practitioner, remaining with his own personality outside the above mentioned decision. Instead of initiating the dialogue between soul and world by the commitment of his own personality, he confronts the patient as a mere functionary of an other-oriented world, one who may indeed cure symptoms, but who by the same token reduces the course of the neurosis, striving for consciousness and cure, to silence. . . . By his own decision, [the psychotherapist who bases his task on the assumption of this profound responsibility] dares to take upon himself the debt of the community toward this individual whose ailment *is* the community, and, as substitute for the world, to find the freeing and the reuniting word in personal commitment. (43-45)

. . . Locked deep in his self, there also lives—and this is precisely the reason for his oppressive, personal guilt—the *ethos:* the dormant consciousness of his very own responsibility and the power to turn back.

The *ethos* is the hub of the man. In a certain sense it is the Archimedean point of his self-discovery which takes place outside of the closed ethical systems of his accustomed world. (54)

In the first phase the psychotherapist places himself personally on the side of the self-ensnared patient, leaving the claims of the world out of account. He meets him with love and understanding like an elder brother. And as a psychologist he . . . strives to let the patient's experience of himself become lucid and conscious and thus furthers to the best of his ability his process of individuation. In the second phase he steps over to the side of the implicated world and expects of the patient, by this time potentially healthy, that he now break out of self-incarceration and turn towards the world with his whole soul. . . .

It is therefore to be suggested to medical practice that every provisionally attained positive result of a self-discovery brought to light by psychological analysis be in each case immediately examined to see whether it can be elevated to the starting point of a new personal meeting with the world. (65f.)

Healing Through Meeting

Under the leadership of an exclusively introspective psychology, psychotherapy has gradually found its way into an impossible situation which can only be surveyed and escaped from an anthropological point of departure. We designate the required point of view "anthropological" in the sense that it takes into account the whole person, not only his psychic realm. "Psychology" is a way of looking at things . . . which is directed *only to psychic occurrences* as such and adequate only to them. But the encompassing nature of man in its entirety only becomes visible to us when we look openly at his situation in the world. Man's Self, . . . by which we understand the center of his personality, is *in actu* only as he discloses himself like a partner to the world. And so too the living sense of psychic processes, both healthy and pathological, is disclosed to us only from out of this self-disclosure.

The psychotherapist is thus enjoined to learn to know the patient and to recognize him in his partnership to the world. But—and this must be added at once—an objective knowledge by itself is not enough. In order to "discover" this patient as a whole person, the psychotherapist himself must enter into the partnership with him. This means: I do not truly recognize this other person *as a partner* so long as I make him an "objective" object of my cognition but only when I experience him as a partner *in my own meeting with him.* (19)

. . . With this we have touched on the central issue in psychotherapeutic treatment and cure: the idea of "eye to eye," a confrontation of partners which the physician summons up in personal meeting and thanks to which the restoration of the patient's capacity for meeting begins. (19f.)

The *self* of the neurotic person is and remains the self that it has, for better or worse, become: sealed in by its withdrawal from the world, distrustful, intractable. (26)

The human self is substantially designed for meeting and the opening out which takes place in meeting, and thus is defined personally. (39)

When I speak of "anthropology" in the indicated sense, I may gratefully refer to distinguished pioneers like Martin Buber, Franz Rosenzweig, Ferdinand Ebner, José Ortega y Gasset, Rudolf Pannwitz, Karl Jaspers, Viktor von Weizsäcker, Ludwig Binswanger, Ernst Michel, Eugen Rosenstock and—in a certain sense the father of all these—to Blaise Pascal and Søren Kierkegaard. (39)

By viewing the isolated patient from the beginning as one who has sacrificed his capacity for dialogue in withdrawing his self from meeting with the world, and by addressing him immediately, anthropological psychotherapy sets him up as a fellow human being, a Thou, the original partner in a fully human meeting. It seeks out this stubborn self, this introvert captive of the psyche, and will not release it. It summons this self by name as the one called upon to answer, the one personally responsible. And by addressing it in this manner, it challenges the self to disclose itself in its self and to individuate itself in the new dialogue with the physician-partner and beyond him in intercourse—and not merely the introverted kind—with the world. (42f.)

1. *Dialogical-anthropological procedure.* The physician posits, primarily in dialogic execution, that . . . "Thou" capable of being addressed in the patient which is identical with the "self" capable of answering. . . .

2. *Dialectic-psychological procedure.* The physician employs the contact with the patient on the level of consciousness in order to gain insight and admission to the irrational processes in his "unconscious." His primary purpose is to restore a system of organization to a "psyche" manifesting itself in contradictory fashion, that is, he exerts himself, by means of psychological analysis and semantic deciphering, to harmonize as it were "in themselves" the antitheses expressing themselves in the polarity of the conscious "I-complex" on the one hand and the autonomous complexes of the unconscious on the other. (44)

In the *basic anthropological attitude*, the physician addresses the patient in his self and by name as Thou, and thus directs him to the total dialogue.

This dialogical meeting is at once both starting-point and goal of our therapeutic effort. The true cure of the neurosis originates in it and is executed in it. That is: in the risk of this meeting, in its success or failure, the process of the cure is marked in its positive or negative aspect.

It is in the framework of this basic partnership relation that the psychic conflict tension, which derives from the contradiction of the conscious and unconscious psychic realms, arrives at a psychotherapeutic resolution. (45)

The neurotic man reacts, to be sure, to reality, often even very vehemently, but he no longer opens himself to it in his self or at most only with reservations. To this tendency of the self toward flight corresponds the profound dread, uncanny and inexplicable to the patient. . . . Out of this inexplicable dread, the patient constructs within himself a more or less complicated system of barely penetrable protections and defenses. . . . The uncovering by means of depth psychology of these inner psychic defense mechanisms can succeed in truly therapeutic fashion only if it possesses the key to the central understanding of these systems in the recognition of the self's *personally* executed flight from meeting—in view of what is every time a unique patient who is fatefully concerned. . . .

In the process of curing the neurosis, it is thus not simply, as an ideological personalism hastily concludes, a matter of dragging the self of the patient *without mediation* from its flight and resistance back to the dialogue with the world. Rather, the reconstruction of the capacity for dialogical meeting must go *hand in hand* with the methodically psychological effort to loosen and dismantle the complex defense mechanisms in the psychic realm of expression as fast as the recuperating self permits, in order thus to make the impeded psychic forces once more serviceable for the new meeting with the world. Without this supplemental assistance of depth psychology, what is dialogically expected of the patient's self in the meeting situation with the world would place too great a demand on it and expose it to the danger of regression. . . .

While the basic *dialogical* attitude [of the therapist] by no means excludes the basic *dialectical* attitude of the psychologist, focussing as this does on the contradictory multiplicity of the psyche, the latter is nevertheless coordinated with and subordinated to the partnership relation. . . .

Within the therapist, the psychologist's share in the process of the cure is substantially of a methodological sort, and therefore also subject to systematization in its procedures; the anthropological share, however, will not be systematized, for it is bound to the person-to-person meeting, each and every time unique, each and every time demanding a decision. . . .

The healing process of a neurosis takes place in practice only when the relationship of physician and patient is a real *partnership* from the beginning. The healing process takes place between *this* physician and *this* patient, in the totality of their personal confrontation. Reawakening and recuperation from within is possible only thanks to such meeting. In this structure the physician always substitutes for the world. In him the world assumes, by way of example, the form of a loving inclination which seeks to restore the patient's dispirited and mistrustful self to its original creature-like situation, to its new dialogical meeting with the forces of nature and history. (48-53)

Thus neuroses present themselves to us as more or less unsuccessful attempts to force and assert self-realization by means of the adequacy of one's own strength. . . .

In the neurotic person, however, there still stirs that profound "unrest of the heart" in which the original self, in need and expectation of transcendental assistance, secretly makes itself noticeable. In this unrest of the heart, the introverted defense mechanism, erected out of mistrust, finally becomes *questionable*. . . .

This is the therapeutic situation into which the physician is placed for the fulfillment of his task: to quiet and harmonize the psychic tension in the patient *not only according to the patient's wish,* but as a partner to penetrate to the personal basis of this person's being, to the *actual origin,* that is, of his elemental introversion which nourishes all neurosis. It is only out of this origin that a cure may be looked for once the self turns back and breaks through to the community of fellow-men. (56f.)

The physician allows himself to be drawn into the introversive process, that is he enters bravely into the suffering of the neurosis, and this not only as factually objectivizing psychologist, but fundamentally in the loving attitude of the helpful partner. . . .

In risking this personal commitment, even to the neurotic self-entanglement of the patient, the psychotherapist remains confident because he knows and keeps firmly in view the one true goal of the healing, the unlocking of the locked up person for the meeting with the world. Thanks to this goal he holds his own in the field of tension between this confused soul which is entrusted to him and the world, the partner he has to represent. In his alternating function, then, he answers imperturbably *both* for the patient *and* for the world. . . .

The willingness of the self to meet the world, the situation of a living dialogue, that is, between "within" and "without," should be striven for and furthered *simultaneously* with the effort to attain a psychic integration of the self. . . .

Our therapeutic effort therefore comes down in the last analysis to setting the neurotic patient, with his shattered confidence in life, back on his feet and on firm ground. . . . We therapists meet the patient not only in figures of his unconscious soul, to be conceived symbolically, but above all as bodily and personal representative of the world, his partner. . . . Only in the course of the *dialogically* conducted "psychological" cooperation do both things gradually awaken and grow in the patient: a new confidence in himself *and* confidence in the other person. (73-76)

Only mutual personal confidence assures the positive result of treatment of a neurosis. No matter how significant and reliable the self-illuminating insights achieved by the analysis of depth psychology may be in any given case for physician and patient, they demonstrate their curative force decisively only when the patient abandons once more the stand he consciously took during the analysis and throws himself *as himself* into the world, the world of real objects and meetings. . . . Only starting from their meeting as partners can the physician and the patient hold their ground, unshakable and with positive attitude, in the face of the cure's completion, which generally occurs unexpectedly and which in reality is equivalent to a leap over the abyss. (87f.)

The unconscious touched by us has and takes its origin from that absolute "no" of the rejected meeting behind whose mighty barrier a person's psychic necessity for true meeting with the world secretly dams itself up, falls back upon itself, and thus, as it were, coagulates into the "unconscious." (96)

Because of the unconsciousness of the images we are delivered up passively to the might of the reality of the real; by means of analysis, by making the images conscious, we are capable of meeting this reality of the world steadily. . . . Introspective analysis did not open up for us a world which has to compete with reality, it does not open up for us another reality *as a world* in which one might be able to live. Rather it puts us in possession of the *world of images* with which alone we are truly enabled to meet the one and only real world. (98f.)

It cannot suffice that I have an insight *for myself:* it is important that the insight arise *between* us, the participation in this insight by me and by you is important. One cannot convey truth to another, one finds it with one another. . . .

Following Rosenzweig, when we summon the person as person, we seek something which is in him from the beginning and yet disappeared in his youth. What is meant by the unconscious is precisely the personal element which is lost in the course of development, . . . which escapes consciousness. (103f.)

The recognition of the presence of another provides a yardstick for psychoanalytic work. . . . How far I must and may follow up psychological work with this person confronting me is always to be decided on the basis of the personal relationship. (110)

We experience this authenticity of the new about-face toward the world, if we experience it, as an autonomous act, bursting forth out of freedom, startling; we fear it, since it ends the rational procedure in the process of psychological realization, often in an abrupt manner. We hope for this result and yet stand before it in fear at the same time. For when it appears, the patient is lost to us at a blow as an object of treatment, and that which remains to be done proceeds from a fundamentally new point of departure. For now the problem lies *between* us. The situation from now on is an obviously dialogical one. (112f.)

Whether one wishes to show the patient something from the height of one's scientific superiority, or whether one does this in personal decisiveness are two entirely different things. The former leads simply into anonymous emptiness. . . . As psychotherapists we may not point to a truth which *we have* but only to a truth to be sought *between* us, between physician and patient. Only thus can we equalize again the enormous advantage which is given to us by the fact that the other one seeks us out and asks us in his need. (116).

Maurice Friedman

Problematic Rebel: An Image of Modern Man

The father is the first and often the most lasting image of man for the son. It not infrequently happens, however, that the father is not really present for the son, either because he is dead or absent or inattentive, or because he is in no sense a father, or because he is too weak or despicable for a son to be able to emulate him. In such a case the need for the father as the image of man remains and often leads to a lifetime search for a father who will supply an image of man as the actual father has not. Freud and modern psychoanalysts in general have only seen one aspect of this father-son relationship and have reduced it to fear of castration, introjection of the father's ideals and conscience, or even identification. The aspect which they have missed is the need that the son has for a relationship with the father which will help him find direction in the choices he must make between one way of life and another. This need is not for identification but dialogue, and it is not a conditioned formation or reaction but a free and even spontaneous response. At the same time, the other, conditioned reaction does enter in, and the relationship of father to son even in the most "normal" cases, must also be seen as a blend of the conditioned and the free, the "psychological" and the personal. (283f.)

. . . Every man stands, whether he knows it or not, in a continuous personal accountability so long as he lives. No man achieves a plane where he may not only approve of all he has been but may take for granted his responses to the new, unforeseen situation that awaits him. Our existence in time is characterized above all else by just this necessity of meeting the new face that the moment wears. In other words, the possibility of a final decision that is true of an ordinary trial is not true of our existence itself. "Only our concept of time makes it possible for us to speak of the Day of Judgment by that name," says Kafka in one of his aphorisms; "in reality it is a summary court in perpetual session." * If one thinks of guilt not in legal but in personal and existential terms, then it becomes impossible to say, . . . that one is completely innocent. The question of whether one's existence is authentic or inauthentic cannot be answered by the sum of one's actions, . . . nor by any objective standard that detaches guilt from one's personal existence itself. Neither is it merely a subjective or arbitrary matter, but the responsibility of the self in relation to the world. This responsibility cannot be judged from the standpoint of the world alone or of the self alone nor of any third party looking at the world and the self, but only within the relationship itself. "Only he who is a party can really judge," reads another Kafka aphorism, "but as a party he cannot judge. Hence it follows that there is no possibility of judgment in the world, only a glimmer of it." † This means too that man is accountable for his existence and is accountable alone, without any possibility of a "joint defense." "You are the problem. No scholar to be found far and wide," says Kafka in a remarkably Zen-like aphorism.‡ (347f.)

A man may defend himself against specific accusations of guilt, but when he has a sense of "boundless guilt" rooted in a deep feeling of worthlessness, a shame for his very existence, he can only take all accusations on himself. Everything that happens to such a person confirms his essential shame at being himself, and no amount of external success or social confirmation will do more than enable him to forget it temporarily. The only "immortality" such a man may know is the very shame which may do him to death but will not die itself, so much is it the very air that he breathes, the all too narrow and constricting ground upon which he walks! This "boundless guilt" represents that area in the depths where existential shame and existential guilt meet and interfuse. . . . It means a recognition of personal, existential guilt for what one's life has been. Since this guilt is not just a matter of specific acts, there is no point where one can accurately draw a line and say, "These acts were avoidable and these not;

* *The Great Wall of China*, "Reflections on Sin, Pain, Hope and the True Way," No. 38, p. 263.

† *Dearest Father*, "The Eight Octavo Notebooks," p. 76.

‡ *The Great Wall of China*, "Reflections," No. 19, p. 258.

these acts are a subject for guilt and these for shame." An important aspect of the problematic of guilt lies in this interrelationship of existential shame and existential guilt. (353f.)

Existential Psychotherapy and the Image of Man

PSYCHOTHERAPY AND THE IMAGE OF MAN

Each of the schools of psychotherapy has, with more or less clarity, its own image of man. That image stands in fruitful dialectic with the therapeutic practice of the members of the school, but it is not, for all that, a scientific product of that school. On the contrary, the far-reaching differences between the many schools of psychotherapy derive in part from the fact that implied in the positive goals they enunciate are different images of man. Man's nature is often taken by schools of psychotherapy to be itself the norm. Man should live according to his "nature," according to his "real self," and the like. However, it is also in man's nature to become ill. The very meaning of "health," therefore, implies some sense of what is authentic direction for man, for this particular person; it implies, in short, an image of man. Such terms as "health," "integration," "creativity," and "self-realization" not only imply an image of man, they usually imply essentially different ones for different schools and even different members of the same school.

In the "Philosophy of Life" chapter of his *New Introductory Lectures*, Freud writes:

> It cannot be supported for a moment that there can be some other way of regarding man aside from the scientific. For the spirit and the mind of man is a subject of investigation in exactly the same way as any non-human entity. The contribution of the science of psychoanalysis consists precisely in having extended research to the region of the mind. Any other . . . view of the mind has a purely emotional basis.

Many psychotherapists would take issue with Freud on this point. Looking on man in a purely "scientific" way similar to that which we bring to a non-human entity is not sufficient to understand man. It is necessary for the therapist to understand man to some extent from within through his own participation, through the fact that he himself is a person who must make basic decisions, that he confronts the other as a person and not merely as a scientific observer. C. G. Jung in *The Undiscovered Self* (1958) points out the difference between the psychotherapist when he is concerned with man in general, and therefore with statistics and scientific knowledge of man, and the same psychotherapist when he is concerned with the particular, unique individual before him and his concrete problems. The therapist, says Jung,

> is faced with the task of treating a sick person, who, especially in the case of psychic suffering, requires *individual understanding.* The more schematic the treatment is, the more resistances it—quite rightly—calls up in the patient, and the more the cure is jeopardized. . . . Today, over the whole field of medicine, it is recognized that the task of the doctor consists in treating the sick patient, not an abstract illness.*

This is not a question of a choice between the scientific generalization and the concrete individual, but of which direction is the primary one. Is the individual regarded as a collection of symptoms to be registered in the categories of a particular school or are the theories of the school regarded as primarily a means of returning again and again to the understanding of this unique person and his relation with his therapist? An increasingly important trend in psychotherapy suggests that the basic direction of movement should be toward the concrete person and his uniqueness and not toward subsuming the patient's symptoms under theoretical categories or adjusting him to some socially-derived view of the "ideal" man. This trend emphasizes the *image* of man as opposed to the *construct* of man, the understanding of man in his concrete uniqueness as opposed to the synthetic combination of analytical subcategories, such as Freud's division of the psyche into id, ego, and superego. The image of man retains the wholeness of the person; the construct displaces the center of man's existence from the person into separate factors which enter into but cannot in themselves constitute man's wholeness.

"THE BATTLE OVER THE IMAGE OF MAN"

"Below the level of those who regard existential therapy with interest as a new fad and those who approach it with hostile questions about technique," said Rollo May in opening the first conference on Existential Psychotherapy, "are those who approach it with an 'ontological hunger,' those who ask the ultimate questions about man, neurosis, health, and fulfillment." "Existential psychotherapy," says May in his introductory essay to *Existence,*† "is based on the assumption that it is possible to have a science of

* C. G. Jung, *The Undiscovered Self,* trans. by R. F. C. Hull (Boston: Little, Brown & Co., 1958), p. 12.

† Rollo May, Ernest Angel, Henri F. Ellenberger, Editors, *Existence: A New Dimension in Psychiatry and Psychology* (New York: Basic Books, 1958).

man which does not fragmentize man and destroy his humanity at the same moment as it studies him." In contrast to the tendency to make technique an end in itself, "existential technique should have flexibility and versatility," writes May, "varying from patient to patient and from one phase to another in treatment with the same patient." This means the recognition that the patient's commitment, his basic decision about his life, precedes his knowledge of himself. In fact, he cannot even permit himself to get insight or knowledge until he is ready to take a decisive orientation to life and has made the preliminary decisions along the way.

"The real battle," says Ludwig Binswanger of his argument with his lifelong friend Sigmund Freud, "is the battle over the image of man." Freud's genetic approach reduces human history to natural history. "Only human existence is genuinely historical," writes Binswanger. Hence Freud misses that in man which is specifically human. Psychoanalysis has developed its entire critique and interpretation on the basis of Freud's *homo natura* whose nature is driven instinctively and whose history is essentially formed by sexuality. "History becomes natural history, essential possibilities of human existing become genetic developmental processes."

One of the decisive aspects of this "battle over the image of man" is the problem of the relation between psychological necessity and personal freedom. Kierkegaard once remarked that one cannot judge another person, for no one knows how much of his action is suffering—a compulsion he must bear—and how much is temptation—a matter about which he has some real choice. This is not a theoretical question of "free will" versus "determinism," but a concrete question of the resources of a particular person in a particular situation. Probably even he himself will not know afterward to what extent he was able to respond to the situation with the spontaneity of the whole person and to what extent his action was the product of fragmentary and conditioned responses. He will have lost the situation in its presentness, its concreteness, its need for decision, lost it, perhaps, in a cloud of refashioned and rationalized memory. Psychotherapy has contributed an enormous amount to the understanding of the importance of determining factors, but also, since it is therapy and concerned with healing, it aims at freedom, at freeing man for a real response in the present situation to something which the therapist and the patient can recognize as reality. This is the place where the meeting of therapy and the image of man becomes truly decisive.

Freud's one-sided naturalist distortion of the image of man focuses on what man has to be, says Binswanger, and leaves out what he may and should become, his own freedom in relation to the psychological given. "Even the neurotic is not only a neurotic and man in general is not only one compelled." Existence does not lay its own ground, Binswanger points out in his analysis of "The Case of Ilse," but it is still left with freedom in relation to that ground: "That Ilse got just that father and mother was her destiny, received as a heritage and as a task; how to bear up under this destiny was the problem of her existence. Hence, in her 'father complex' both destiny and freedom were at work." Even such phenomena as repression and resistance must be understood from the aspect of the mixture of necessity and freedom, writes Rollo May.

Existential psychotherapy is more of an interplay of trends than a single trend. Its exponents make common cause with one another as much because of a common enemy—orthodox psychoanalysis—as because of an image of man which they share. Nonetheless, precisely through its awareness that "the battle is over the image of man," existential psychotherapy has made a decisive contribution to our understanding of the interrelationship of the image of man and psychotherapy. It has opened up genuine new directions of exploration, ranging from phenomenological analyses and the exploration of the world of the psychotic to a different understanding of the very meaning of such basic therapeutic terms as transference and healing. If it has tended, in so doing, to adopt images of man that are not only different from but even incompatible with each other, it has acted no differently than has "existentialism" itself. By attempting to apply existentialism to a field of enormous practical concern, moreover, existential psychotherapy has helped to bring out the issues that are implicit in existentialism but are often left unfaced.

PHENOMENOLOGY

. . . A particularly impressive part of *Existence* are the essays that analyze schizophrenia, hallucinations, and the world of the compulsive in terms of such phenomenological categories as temporality, spatiality, loss of distance, causality, and aesthesiology (theory of sensory experience). A distinctive contribution of existential psychotherapy, Rollo May points out, is that it places time in the center of the psychological picture and in so doing replaces the Freudian emphasis on the past, the realm of natural history, with the concern for the future, that mode alone in which the self, personality and, we would add, the image of man can be understood. In "Findings in a Case of Schizophrenic Depression," Eugene Minkowski demonstrates what happens to a man whose sense of the future is blocked. "Each day life began anew, like a solitary island in a gray sea of passing time." The normal synthetic view of time disintegrates and life is lived "in a succession of similar days which follow one another with a boundless monotony and sadness." This blocking of the future and fragmentation of the present is reminiscent of Samuel Beckett's play, *Waiting for Godot.* "The individual life impetus weakens, the synthesis of the human personality disintegrates; . . . there remains only the person face to face with a hostile universe."

Ludwig Binswanger places an analysis of temporality close to the center of his famous "Case of Ellen West." Ellen West was not Binswanger's own patient, but he had sufficient access to the records of her case to undertake an exhaustive analysis. Ellen West's existence is ruled by the past, encircled in a bare, empty present, and cut off from the future, writes Binswanger. Robbed of the authentic meaning of her life that only the future can give, Ellen West is driven to fill in time, to fill up the existential emptiness, through an insatiable animal greed that represents a desperate and always unsuccessful flight before the dread of nothingness. Binswanger also analyzes Ellen West in terms of a vertical axis of spatiality—the ethereal world, the terrestrial world, and the world of the tomb, or swamp. Binswanger shows how the loss of the ground on which to stand and work left her two conflicting worlds with the inevitable outcome of a dissipation of the ethereal world into empty possibility and the complete triumph of the world of the tomb.

Erwin W. Straus' essay in *Existence* on "Aesthesiology and Hallucinations" undertakes to analyze the relation of all the senses in order to reconstruct the world of the well person and that of the ill. Hallucinations, in his account, are "deformed modalities," "pathological variations of the basic relation I-and-the-*Other.*" The reciprocity of tactile experience is annulled. Voices address the patient yet remain anonymous. A world of hostile powers assaults him sexually yet remains at a distance. The barriers of his intimate life are levelled off and the innermost sphere of his existence invaded. Straus' conclusion is as disturbing to our ordinary way of feeling, or rather of not feeling, about the schizophrenic as it is to our ordinary way of thinking about him: "The schizophrenic does not withdraw from reality into a land of dreams; he is immersed in an alien reality with physiognomies which in the severest cases paralyze all action and cut off all communication."

THE WORLD-DESIGN

It is but a short step from Straus' phenomenological psychiatry to Binswanger's existential analysis, and the link between these two is Martin Heidegger's self-world ontology, itself derived from the phenomenology of his master Husserl. Binswanger, Medard Boss, and the other existential analysts take over from Heidegger the view of the self as capable of transcending itself and relating to the world, the world-design that results from this self-transcendence, or "being in the world," and the three realms of the *Eigenwelt* (one's relation to oneself), *Mitwelt* (one's relation to others), and *Umwelt* (one's natural environment). Being-in-the-world, according to Binswanger, has eliminated the fatal gap between subject and object, or self and world, and thus overcome "the fatal defect of all psychology" which reduces human existence to a mere subject of knowing. Now the way is open, Binswanger claims, for scientifically exact investigations of the modifications in mental disease of the essential structure of being-in-the-world. The result of such investigations is the discovery of the patient's world-design and with it the possibility of understanding from within even those patients with whom the therapist can establish no "emphatic" communication. "It is one of the most impressive achievements of existential analysis," writes Binswanger, "to have shown that even in the realm of subjectivity 'nothing is left to chance' but that a certain organized structure can be recognized from which each word, each idea, drawing, action, or gesture receives its peculiar imprint."

The real key, Binswanger suggests, is not the Oedipus complex, as it is for Freud, but the world-design that makes such a filial tie possible. This world-design stands outside the contrast conscious-unconscious. "It does not refer to anything psychic but to something which only makes possible the psychic fact." Existential analysis attempts to understand words, actions, and attitudes "from basic modes of human existence prior to the separation of body, soul, and mind, and of consciousness and unconsciousness." The issue between phenomenology and psychoanalysis essentially is whether actions, dreams, and speech directly reveal a meaning taken in the context of the personality, as Binswanger holds, or mask a *hidden* meaning, as Freud thinks, "an unconscious second person."

KIERKEGAARD'S "SICKNESS UNTO DEATH"

Binswanger describes Søren Kierkegaard's concept of "sickness unto death"—the "desperate" wish to be oneself and at the same time to be not oneself—as "one of the most important contributions to the purely 'anthropological' understanding of certain clinical forms of insanity, and particularly of schizophrenia." This "sickness unto death" he sees as central in the case of Ellen West. As was the case in her earlier defiance of her role as a woman, so now in her desperate conflict between a greed which would make her fat and a wish to be thin, Ellen West betrays the stubborn and defiant wish to be herself and not to be herself. "Fate wanted to have me fat and strong," said Ellen, "but I want to be thin and delicate." Ellen even gives a new twist here to the classic pattern of Jewish self-hate by equating being thin with a higher intellectual type and being fat with a bourgeois Jewish type. Ellen's wish to be thin is calamitous, says Binswanger, because it fixates her in the conflict between her ethereal world and the gloomy, dull, damp world of the swamp. Ellen's dread of becoming fat is only the end of the encirclement process by which her existence becomes closed to new possibilities. Ellen knows herself that she cannot live on if she does not succeed in "breaking the ban" and getting out of her preoccupation with self. Her existence, as a result, is "consecrated to death." Yet Binswanger sees Ellen's "freely chosen death" as in some sense a liberation from her "no exit" hell and a real, if tragic, entrance into authentic existence which "marks the victory of this existence over the power of 'hell.' "

Binswanger sees Ellen West's suicide as both "arbitrary act" and "necessary event." "Who will say where in this case guilt begins and 'fate' ends?" One of the most interesting aspects of this case, indeed, is its setting aside the customary notions that suicide is necessarily bad and that, in the case of a mentally ill person, it is necessarily purely a product of the sickness. The existential emptying or impoverishment of Ellen's existence was "nothing but a metamorphosis of freedom into compulsion," writes Binswanger, but her suicide itself was the final desperate breakthrough of the free personality:

> That this existence can once again break through its congealing, that once more it is able to burst the prison of pastness, to exchange it for the world of an authentic present, and so once more to become authentically and wholly itself—this testifies to the power of freedom in general which, to some degree, makes itself felt even in the insidious form of schizophrenia. (311)

One may wonder at Binswanger's confidence in the positive nature of Ellen's suicide, especially given his own statement that "love knows no answer to the question of whether Ellen West's suicide had to take place of fateful necessity or whether she had the possibility of escaping it."

THE I-THOU RELATIONSHIP

Binswanger adds to Heidegger's existence for the sake of *myself* the dimension of love. Binswanger acknowledges his indebtedness to Martin Buber for this mode of "meeting," or "encounter," and passage after passage in his works bear witness to the importance of this influence. Binswanger sees clearly that the I-Thou relation is an ontological reality and cannot be reduced to what takes place within each of the members of the relationship. At the same time, Binswanger's "dual mode" of love is less inclusive and more in danger of becoming a sentimentalized unity than Buber's dialogue, which includes relations of conflict and opposition so long as they are personal and reciprocal and each affirms the other in his own being.

For existential psychotherapy, the Freudian concept of "transference" is replaced by Buber's concept of "meeting," or "encounter," "an event occurring in a real relationship between two people," as May puts it. "When we are dealing with human beings," writes May, "no truth has reality by itself; it is always dependent upon the reality of the immediate relationship." If the therapist abstracts himself from his relationship with the patient and does not participate in it with real personal involvement, he will not even *see* the other person as he is. May goes so far as to define the therapist as "existential to the extent that, with all his technical training and his knowledge of transference and dynamisms, he is still able to relate to the patient as 'one existence communicating with another,' to use Binswanger's phrase." A prime difference between Freud's "transference" and the meeting of therapist and patient is that the latter, "far from being a revival of an ancient interpersonal relationship . . . works through the very fact of its novelty."

To Binswanger the dual mode of love and friendship forms the core of the normal existential experience. The singular mode is the autonomous individual, essentially related only to himself; the plural mode corresponds to the area of formal, impersonal relationships, competition, and struggle. This shades into the "anonymous mode," the mode of the individual living and acting in an anonymous collectivity. Binswanger analyzes the case of Ellen West in "I-Thou" terms. Ellen West's defiance and stubbornness exclude her from "the authentic I-Thou relationship of the being-with-one-another" and leave her to a world of interpersonal relations consisting of mere togetherness in which each seizes on the weak point of the other and tries to dominate him. Nonetheless, without a germ of true love, without at least that "readiness for Thou" which a number of lifelong relations and attachments showed that Ellen possessed, Ellen would not have suffered so much as she did from the emptiness and poverty of her existence. "To him who is completely empty of love, existence can become a burden but not a hell," writes Binswanger. Correspondingly, Binswanger sees Ellen's suicide as a breaking through the single mode and a triumph, despite all, of the dual mode of existence with its knowledge of a relationship beyond the isolated self. Even the way we must look at Ellen's suicide, Binswanger suggests, is given us through the I-Thou relationship which lifts us above the judgmental perspective of the plural mode of existence. The "uniting of human existence with the common ground which I and Thou share" is prior to the dichotomy of freedom and necessity, guilt and destiny.

"Even the reader of her case history," Binswanger remarks, "must have seen Ellen West not only as an object of interest but also as Thou." In reading this case, one does, indeed, get a vivid sense of Ellen West as a person with a developed inner life and a unique personal attitude and will. Her poetry, her travels, her social work, her experiences as a student, her relations with her cousin whom she eventually married, her pitiful efforts to combat her fear of becoming fat by eating almost nothing and sometimes taking as many as sixty laxatives a day, her touching appeal to her husband when she told him that if he loved her he would kill her, and the terrible choice that he had to make between leaving her in a clinic where no hope of cure or even relief was offered and taking her away to a home situation in which her suicide was almost certain—all these bring Ellen West before us not only as a case study but also as a person, a Thou.

HEIDEGGER VS. BUBER

There is, however, an issue between Heidegger and Buber of which Binswanger does not seem adequately aware. "Heidegger's 'existence' is monological," writes Martin Buber in "What is Man?". His man of authentic existence and "self-being" can no longer really live with man: he "knows a real life only in communication with himself." Even Heidegger's central category of solicitude, or care, does not take man beyond his radically isolated self-relationship to any real mutuality with another person in which one life is open to another. Heidegger's self is *a closed system*. . . . The basic issue between Heidegger and Buber is whether the reality of the self, and of ontology, is found in the ground of the self and its own "mature resolute existence" or whether it is found "between man and man." If the former, one can make use of existential categories of analysis since they will tell us something of a self that may be regarded in itself; if the latter, the self must be understood in dialogue with other selves, in the *between,* and never as an ontological entity understandable prior to its interhuman relations.

The issue between the two philosophers, therefore, is a much more radical one than the question of whether one may add the "I-Thou" relationship as one further existential category to those with which Heidegger has already provided us. We may ask, therefore, whether Binswanger has succeeded in his attempted synthesis of Heidegger's ontology and Buber's dialogue. From the standpoint of the latter, it is not admissible to substitute an ontological analysis of dialogue for dialogue itself. One of the main criticisms of Binswanger's existential analysis, as of existential psychotherapy in general, is that nowhere is this issue between Heidegger and Buber fully faced. Until it is, the very ground on which this form of psychotherapy rests is open to question.

A CRITIQUE OF EXISTENTIAL PSYCHOTHERAPY

One must also question Binswanger's claim that the existential analyst can communicate even with those schizophrenic patients with whom he cannot enter into an empathic relationship. Phenomenological analysis can certainly help in understanding, but such understanding is not the same as direct communication between one person and another. "To analyze phenomenologically the given being-in-the-world" does not necessarily mean real dialogue or understanding the other as a Thou, nor does "the degree of potential and real agreement between my world and his world determine the degree of possible communication," as Binswanger asserts. Binswanger's analytic-synthetic "world-design" cannot capture the uniqueness and wholeness of a person, for these are only revealed in the dialogue between I and Thou. Analysis of existence is not identical with existence; concern with existence does not give ready-made phenomenological categories a privileged position over the categories of Freud or any other psychologist. "The temptation to use existential concepts in the service of intellectualizing tendencies is especially to be guarded against," Rollo May rightly points out, "since, because they refer to things that have to do with the center of personal reality, these concepts can the more seductively give the illusion of dealing with reality."

A corollary of this tendency toward abstraction in existential psychotherapy is a general theoretical orientation. If technique follows understanding, as May asserts, then it should not hold, as he also claims, that the technique of the existential therapist need not be different, only the context of his therapy. One wonders in particular how so many existential analysts are able to use traditional Freudian techniques "on a fundamental existential basis." This seems particularly strange in the light of the expressed concern with the immediate life-situation of the patient as the starting point of therapy and the meeting of I and Thou as a basic element in therapy. "The configuration of self and world or self to self is not existential," Paul Goodman has remarked. "It is interpretation just in the Freudian sense. Real existential psychotherapy would try to do as far as possible without interpretations and stick to particular situations."

One must question, finally, Rollo May's assumption that a basically self-centered consciousness is the reality from which existential therapy must proceed, as well as his emphasis upon self-realization as the goal of such therapy. Unlike Binswanger, May makes self-awareness and self-consciousness the central element in being human, the experiencing of "I am" the *precondition* of therapy, and the grasping of one's self more basic than the relation of the self to the other. Similarly, guilt and neurosis arise, for May, primarily from failing to fulfill one's being and realize one's potentialities. May quotes Medard Boss:

> If you lock up potentialities you are guilty against (or *indebted to*) what is given you in your origin, in your "core." In this existential condition of being indebted and being guilty are founded all guilt feelings, in whatever thousand and one concrete forms and malformations they may appear in actuality. (53)

Boss' attempt to establish the ontological reality of guilt necessarily remains unconvincing because of the fundamental ambiguity of the phrase, "what is given you in your origin, in your 'core'." One's potential uniqueness may be given, but the direction in which one authenticates one's existence is not; one discovers it in constantly renewed decisions in response to the demand of concrete situations. When we are guilty, it is not because we have failed to realize our potentialities, which we cannot know in the abstract, but because we have failed to bring the resources we find available to us at a given moment into our response to a particular situation that calls us out. Our potentialities cannot be divorced from the discovery of our personal direction, and this comes not in the meeting of man with himself but with other men and with the image of man that he acquires through such meeting.* Our "real self," as Helen Lynd points out, is not a given that need only be freed from its social encrustations:

> Horney, Fromm, and even Sullivan at times, seem to assume that there is an already existent real or true or spontaneous self which can be evoked into active existence almost at will. There is a tacit assumption that somehow we know the dictates of the real self, and that we should live in terms of these rather than of a romanticized self-image or of the pseudo-self of other's expectations. But . . . such a real self is something to be discovered and created, not a given, but a lifelong endeavor.†

EXISTENTIAL GUILT

Although it has left its concept of guilt ambiguous through referring it back to the self's relationship to itself, existential psychotherapy has contributed to the growing awareness in contemporary psychotherapy that there *is* such a thing as "existential guilt." Certainly there is purely social and even neurotic guilt derived from a set of mores and taboos imposed upon the individual by parents and society and incorporated into an internalized "superego." But there is also real guilt, guilt which has to do with one's actual stance in the world and the way in which one goes out from it to relate to other people. Real guilt is neither subjective nor objective. It is dialogical—the inseparable corollary of one's personal responsibility, one's answerability for authenticating one's own existence and, by the same token, for responding to the partners of one's existence, the other persons with whom one lives. Where there is personal responsibility, there must also be the possibility of real guilt—guilt for failing to respond, for responding inadequately or too late, or without one's whole self. Such guilt is neither inner nor outer, nor is one answerable for it either to oneself alone or to society apart from oneself, but to that very bond between oneself and others through which one again and again discovers the direction in which one can authenticate one's existence. If a relation with another cannot be reduced to what goes on within each of the two persons, then the guilt which one person has toward a partner in relationship can-

* In his concluding remarks at the Conference on Existential Psychotherapy in New York City on April 22, 1961, Rollo May acknowledged that my criticism of him and the other thinkers represented in *Existence* is right. Referring to this present paper, which he had read in manuscript, he agreed that none of the existential psychologists and psychiatrists, not even Binswanger, had given adequate attention to the "between," Buber's I-Thou relation.

† Helen Merrell Lynd, *On Shame and the Search for Identity* (New York: Harcourt Brace & Co., 1958), p. 203.

not be reduced to the subjective guilt that he feels. "Existential guilt," writes Martin Buber, "occurs when someone injures an order of the human world whose foundations he knows and recognizes as those of his own existence and of all common human existence." Hence existential guilt transcends the realm of inner feelings and of the self's relation to itself. But the order of the human world that one injures is not an objective absolute: it is the sphere of the "interhuman" itself. This sphere and the guilt that arises in it cannot be identified with the taboos and restrictions of any particular culture and society.

> The totality of the order that a man knows to be injured or injurable by him transcends to some degree the totality of the parental and social taboos that bind him. The depth of the guilt feeling is not seldom connected with just that part of the guilt that cannot be ascribed to the taboo-offense, hence with the existential guilt.*

Guilt is an essential factor in the person's relations to others: it performs the necessary function of leading him to desire to set these relations to rights. It is actually here, in the real guilt of the person who has not responded to the legitimate claim and address of the world, that the possibility of transformation and healing lies.†

True guilt, of course, is not the neurotic, tormented self-preoccupation which so often goes by that name. "There is a sterile kind of heart searching," writes Buber, "which leads to nothing but self-torture, despair and still deeper enmeshment." This latter is not a true awareness, but a turning back on oneself which uses up the energies that one could spend in turning to the Thou. True guilt, in contrast, takes place between man and man. It has an ontic, superpersonal character of which the *feeling* of guilt is only the subjective and psychological counterpart. "Guilt does not reside in the human person. On the contrary, he stands in the most realistic sense in the guilt which envelops him." Similarly, the repression of guilt and the neuroses which result from this repression are not merely psychological phenomena but events between men.‡

* Martin Buber, "Guilt and Guilt Feelings," trans. by Maurice S. Friedman, *Psychiatry*, Vol. II, No. 2 (May 1957), p. 117.

† *Cf.* Hans Trüb, *Heilung aus der Begegnung. Eine Auseinandersetzung mit der Psychologie*, C. G. Jung, ed. by Ernst Michel and Arie Sborowitz (Stuttgart: Ernst Klett Verlag, 1952). Martin Buber, *Pointing the Way. Collected Essays*, Trans. and Ed. by Maurice Friedman (New York: Harper Torchbooks, 1963), "Healing through Meeting."

‡ Martin Buber, *Hasidism and Modern Man*, Ed. & Trans. by Maurice Friedman (New York: Horizon Press, 1958), "The Way of Man.

"HEALING THROUGH MEETING"

Real guilt is the beginning of ethos, or responsibility, writes the Swiss psychotherapist, Hans Trüb, but before the patient can become aware of it, he must be helped by the analyst to become aware of himself in general. This the analyst does through playing the part both of confidante and big-brother. He gives the neurotic the understanding the world has denied him and makes it more and more possible for him to step out of his self-imprisonment into a genuine relation with the analyst. In doing this, says Trüb, the analyst must avoid the intimacy of a private I-Thou relationship with the patient, on the one hand, and the temptation of dealing with the patient as an object, on the other.*

The analyst must see the illness of the patient as an illness of his relations with the world, writes Trüb. The roots of the neurosis lie both in the patient's closing himself off from the world and in the pattern of society itself and its rejection and non-confirmation of the patient. Consequently, the analyst must change at some point from the consoler who takes the part of the patient against the world to the person who puts before the patient the claim of the world. This change is necessary to complete the second part of the cure—that establishment of real relationship with the world which can only take place in the world itself. "On the analyst falls the task of preparing the way for the resumption in direct meeting of the interrupted dialogical relationship between the individual and the community." The psychotherapist must test the patient's finding of himself by the criterion of whether his self-realization can be the starting-point for a new personal meeting with the world. The patient must go forth whole in himself, but he must also recognize that it is not his own self but the world with which he must be concerned. This does not mean that the patient is simply integrated with or adjusted to the world. He does not cease to be a real person, responsible for himself, but at the same time he enters into responsible relationship with his community.† . . .

According to the Teachings of Hasidism," pp. 134ff.; Buber, *Pointing the Way,* "Healing through Meeting," p. 95f.

* Hans Trüb, *Heilung aus der Begegnung.*

† *Ibid.*

EXISTENTIAL ANALYSIS VS. HEALING THROUGH MEETING

Is "existential psychotherapy" "existential" in the sense that it takes over the phenomenological categories with which one or another group of phenomenologists or existentialists have analyzed human existence? Or is it "existential" in Kierkegaard's understanding of the term, namely as deriving from and pointing back to the concrete existence of the person? Both Binswanger and Trüb take over Buber's "I-Thou" terminology, but the one uses it in the service of a phenomenological analysis of the patient's "world-design" (who in the case of Ellen West is not even his own patient), whereas the other uses it as a means of *pointing* to the existential situation of the patient and the concrete meeting between patient and therapist. Which of these two applications of the I-Thou relation is "existential"—the one concerned with the extension of theory or the one concerned with therapy itself?

Binswanger's existential analysis tends to lead to still another *construct of man* to set over against those given us by the older schools of psychotherapy. The construct of man provided by existential analysis may be *existentialist,* but it is not truly *existential:* only an image of man is that. Only a psychotherapy which is existential in the sense of Kierkegaard and Buber—only a therapy which begins with the concrete existence of the person, with his wholeness and uniqueness, and with the healing that takes place through the meeting of therapist and patient—will point us toward the image of man. Existential psychotherapy is faced, in the last analysis, with the same issue that faces all the schools of psychotherapy: whether the starting point of therapy is to be found in the analytical category or the unique person—in the *construct of man* or the *image of man.* (286-296)

Part VII

ISSUES AND CONCLUSIONS

THE VALUE of an anthology lies precisely in the fact that a great many more questions and issues will occur to the reader than can be dealt with here, different ones, indeed, for each different reader. At the same time, there are certain broad issues that are objective and inescapable, and the form in which this "Critical Reader" has been organized should have served to bring these out. Since this whole book has been devoted to making these issues manifest, our final section on "Issues and Conclusions" can only serve to discuss briefly some of the issues that have not been dealt with explicitly, to summarize and clarify some of the central issues of intersubjectivity, ontology, and religion, and to put forward a few conclusions that, to the author at least, seem to emerge.

THE MEETING-POINT BETWEEN HEIDEGGER'S NAZISM AND HIS EXISTENTIALISM

The social thought of the existentialist thinkers might well form a section of this anthology in itself since Berdyaev, Buber, Camus, Maritain, and Sartre all have clearly articulated social philosophies, and most of the other existentialists have written on this subject. Such a section would be confronted with the question of to what extent the various socialist, communitarian, resistance, or other social philosophies are existentialist, to what extent merely philosophies of thinkers who are also existentialist. This subject as a whole would take us too far afield, but there is one particular question in connection with it that must be dealt with here. From 1933 until around 1936 Martin Heidegger was an active member of the Nazi party who identified himself with Hitler and the Nazi cause and who took part during his time as Rector of the University of Freiburg in all the S.A. activities that led to further persecution of the Jews and to the exclusion of Jewish professors, including fellow-disciples of his own Jewish teacher Edmund Husserl. What concerns us here is not the question of whether Heidegger was an active Nazi—a fact established and well-known, if not always understood in its full range—but whether, as many claim, Heidegger's political activities have no bearing on the meaning and value of his philosophy. We cannot, of course, dismiss a thought on the *ad hominem* ground that we disapprove of the thinker. But an existentialist philosopher who is concerned about authenticating his philosophy in his existence cannot fail to raise a question in our minds when he lends his life, thought, and work to such a movement as Nazism. In other words, we are not concerned with Heidegger's Nazi activities in themselves but whether there is any integral relation between them and his philosophy which casts further light on the meaning and implications of that philosophy.

To answer that question we must look at a selection of Heidegger's speeches and written statements during his Nazi period, which have been collected for us by the Swiss scholar Guido Schneeberger, plus some passages from his *Introduction to Metaphysics* (1936). We cannot fail to be struck in reading these selections by the integral relationship between Heidegger's Nazi terminology and his existentialist philosophy, particularly that of his later thought about Being. Nor can we fail to ask how Heidegger, whose central emphasis in *Being and Time* is on one's ownmost possibilities which must be realized in opposition to all tendencies to fall into the anonymity of the They, could have lent his thought to a totalitarianism that swallowed up and destroyed the unique individual in a way more terrible than any other in history. Whether these passages raise any essential question about Heidegger's ontology, the reader himself must be left to judge. The brief comments on this subject by Benedetto Croce, Günther Anders, Martin Buber, and others may aid in this judgment.

Guido Schneeberger

Supplement to Heidegger: Documents of His Life and Thought

47. "TRANSFER OF THE RECTORATE AT THE UNIVERSITY OF FREIBURG"

This . . . is the original common will for its being, and this in turn is the will for knowledge as the will for the historico-spiritual commission of the German nation. Knowledge and German destiny must above all come to power in the will for being; they will only come to power when faculties and student bodies expose knowledge to their innermost necessity and stand their ground for German destiny in its direst need. . . . To impose law upon oneself: that is the highest freedom. The much praised academic freedom will be banished from German universities; it was false, because only negating; it meant non-restriction in commission and omission. Now the concept of freedom of the German student will be restored to its truth. Henceforth three kinds of obligations will develop from it, and three duties of the German student body, first that to the ethnic community through the duty of labor, second that to the honor and fate of the nation through military service, and third to the spiritual commission of the German people through the duty of knowledge. . . . All powers and all faculties of the body must be developed through struggle, augmented in struggle, and maintained as struggle. We will fully understand the glory and greatness of the new start only when we consider this insight: all that is great stands in a storm. (*Freiburger Zeitung*, 150. *Jahrgang*, Nr. 145, 29. May 1933. *Abendausgabe* [evening edition] p. 6.) (54f.)

48. "THE CELEBRATION OF THE TRANSFER OF THE RECTORATE"

. . . The self-assertion of the University consists of its desire for a being of its own. . . . Knowledge . . . [in] its purest form . . . must by extreme simplification turn its attention to the unavoidable. The spirit which supports it is not to be conceived as *esprit* or *ratio* but as a primordial, conscious determination in favor of the nature of being. . . . Leadership . . . must possess the ability to walk alone; only thus can it create a following for itself. The German student body is ready for this following for it knows that true freedom exists only in the desire for law and obligation. The obligation to the ethnic community consists of the duty of labor, that to the honor of the nation in military service, while the spiritual commission is fulfilled in the duty of knowledge. Thus the university is the institution of higher learning which disciplines the leaders of the people through science. It is up to us whether we will ourselves a people, and the recent past has confirmed this will. (*Freiburger Studentenzeitung.* Edited by the *Freiburger Studentenschaft* with the notification of the academic authorities. Editor: Ernim Künzel. VIIth semester [XIV] Nr. 3, 1. June 1933, p. 2.) (56)

69. "THE UNIVERSITY IN THE NEW GERMANY" —AN ADDRESS BY PROF. MARTIN HEIDEGGER

Up to now, people have done *research* and *teaching* at the Universities as they had for decades previously. Teaching was supposed to emerge from the research, and one sought for a convenient harmonization between the two. It was only the point of view of the teacher which spoke out of this conception: no one concerned himself with the university as a community. Research became limitless and concealed its uncertainties behind the idea of the international progress of knowledge; teaching, deprived of goals, hid itself behind the rules of the examination schedules. . . . One must wage a sharp combat against this view in the Nazi spirit, which must not be allowed to suffocate through humanizing Christian conceptions which suppress its unconditional nature. . . . The *new courage* allows one to see all these perils clearly. Only it alone opens one's eyes to that which is coming and becoming. It compels every teacher and student to come to a *decision about the basic issues of knowledge,* and the decision is secular, for on it depends whether we Germans want to remain a knowing people in the highest sense. The new teaching which concerns us does not mean the amassing of insights, but letting others learn and making others learn. This means letting oneself be oppressed by the unknown and then becoming master over it in understanding knowledge, becoming certain with an eye for the essential. True research grows out of such teaching; it is bracketed with the whole by its being rooted in the people and its tie to the state. The student is forced out into the uncertainty of all things, upon which the necessity for commitment then bases itself. *Study must again mean taking a risk,* not a shelter for cowards. He who does not endure the struggle, remains down. The new courage must be conditioned into steadfastness, for the struggle for the educational strongholds of the leaders will take long. It will be fought with the energies of the new state which the people's chancellor Hitler will bring to reality. It must be fought without thought for one's own by a hardy generation which exists by constant testing and for the goal which it prescribed for itself. It is a struggle for the *form of the teacher* and the *leader* at the university. (*Heidelberger Neueste Nachrichten* . . . Nr. 150, 1. July 1933, p. 4.) (74f.)

79. MARTIN HEIDEGGER, "THE THREE OBLIGATIONS" ("LABOR, MILITARY SERVICE, KNOWLEDGE")

The *third obligation* of the student body is that toward the spiritual commission of the German people. This people effects its destiny by putting its history into the public domain of the supreme power of all world-forming powers of human existence, and by struggling ever more for its spiritual world. Thus exposed to the extreme questionability of its own existence, this people desires to be a spiritual people. It demands of itself and for itself a most high, wide and rich learning of the hardest clarity in its leaders and protectors. A student generation which dares an early entrance to manhood and spreads its volition over the future fate of the nation compels itself from the start to this learning. The duty of knowledge can no longer mean for it a dull and rapid breaking-in for a "polite" profession. Statesman and teacher, physician and judge, pastor and architect guide the ethnic-statist existence, they guard it and keep it sharpened in its fundamental relations to the world-forming powers of human existence; therefore these professions are turned over to the responsibility of the duty of knowledge together with the education for them. Knowledge is not in the service of the professions but vice versa: the professions effect and administer that highest and substantive knowledge of the people for the sake of its entire being. But this knowledge means for us not tranquilly taking cognizance of essences and values as such, but rather the sharpest sort of endangering of existence (*Dasein*) in the midst of the overpowering might of the existent. Because being is itself questionable, the people are forced into labor and battle and into a state to which the professions belong. (*Völkischer Beobachter, Kampfblatt der national-sozialistischen Bewegung*. South German edition. Munich. 46th volume, 201. Edition 20 July 1933, Supplement [p. 7 of the entire edition].) (92f.)

93. CROCE TO VOSSLER (MEANA, SEPTEMBER 1933)

I have finally read all of Heidegger's address, which is at once stupid and servile. I am not surprised at the success which his philosophizing may enjoy for a while: vacuous generalities always do, without producing anything. I too believe that he will hardly be able to have any sort of influence on politics. But he is dishonoring philosophy, and that also represents a damaging blow to politics, at least to future politics. (*Briefwechsel Benedetto Croce—Karl Vossler*. Suhrkamp Verlag. Berlin and Frankfurt/Main, 1955, pp. 342-345.) (111f.)

114. GERMAN STUDENTS!

The Nazi revolution carries with it the complete transformation of our German existence. It is up to you in this process to remain the ever striving, ever ready, ever tough and growing ones. Your desire for knowledge seeks to experience that which is essential, simple, great. Yours is the demand to be exposed to the closest constraints and the widest obligations. Be hard and authentic in your demands. Remain clear and sure in your refusals. Don't pervert hard-earned knowledge into vain private property. Guard it rather as the necessary patrimony of the leadership élite in the folk-vocations of the state. You can no longer be merely auditors. You are duty-bound to co-knowledge and co-operation in erecting the future institution of higher learning for the German spirit. Each one must first prove every talent and privilege and bring it into its right. This occurs through the power of militant involvement in the struggle of the entire nation for itself. May the desire for fealty reinforce itself with every passing day and hour. May your courage to sacrifice self for the rescue of the nature of our nation and the elevation of its innermost strength within its state grow ceaselessly. The rules of your being are not doctrines and "ideas." The Führer himself and he alone is German reality and its law, today and henceforth. Learn to realize ever more deeply: from now on each thing demands decision and every action accountability. Heil Hitler! Martin Heidegger, Rector. (*Freiburger Studentenzeitung* [. . .] VIIIth semester [XV], Nr. 1, 3. November 1933, p. 1.) (135f.)

132. PROF. DR. HEIDEGGER, FREIBURG IM BRESGAU: [ACKNOWLEDGEMENT TO ADOLF HITLER AND THE NAZI STATE]

The people wins back the *truth* of its will to Dasein, for truth is the revelation of that which a people in its actions and knowing makes sure, clear, and strong. Out of such truth arises the genuine will to knowledge. And this will to knowledge circumscribes the demand of knowledge. And from there the boundaries are finally drawn within which genuine questioning and investigating must prove and authenticate itself. From such an origin knowledge arises for us. It is bound to the necessity of the self-responsible people's Dasein. Knowledge is therefore the educative passion, bound in such necessity, to will to know in order to make known. *Being*-known, however, means to us: the things are powerful in clarity and determined to deed. . . .

We have freed ourselves from idolizing a system of thought without basis or force. We foresee the end of the philosophy that was in its service. We are sure of an uncompromisingly simple inquiry into the essence of being, with its clear hardness and its certainty legitimized by work. This inquiry by a national science has its innermost motivation in the original courage to grow or perish in the encounter with being. For this courage beckons to the fore, frees itself from what has preceded, dares the unaccustomed and the incalculable. For us inquiry is not the untrammeled play of curiosity. For us inquiry is not the idiosyncratic insistence upon equivocation at any price. For us inquiry means: exposing oneself to the loftiness of things and their laws; it means: not to lock out the terror of the unfettered or the confusion of darkness. On the other hand we do ask for this sort of inquiry, and we are not in the service of those who have become tired and of their comfortable seeking after convenient answers. We know that the courage of inquiry, the courage to experience and endure the abysses of existence, is already in itself a higher answer than every all-too-cheap information of artificially constructed systems of thought. . . . This revolution brings with it the *complete transformation of our German existence.* From now on each thing demands decision and every action accountability. (Acknowledgment of professors at the German universities and institutions of higher learning to Adolf Hitler and the Nazi state. Submitted by the Nazi Teachers Union [. . .] Dresden [1933], pp. 13f.) (149f.)

170. (MARTIN HEIDEGGER) NAZI SCHOOLING FOR KNOWLEDGE

. . . Our entire German reality has been altered by the Nazi state, in consequence of which all existing conception and thought also has to become something else. . . . What we hitherto have thought of as "knowledge" and "science" has acquired a new meaning. . . . Knowledge means *to know one's way* in the world in which we are individually and socially situated. . . . Knowledge means *being equal,* in decision and procedure, to whatever task may be laid upon us. . . . Knowledge means being *master* of the situation into which we are placed. . . . For knowledge it is decisive, not what and how much we know, but whether the knowledge is an indigenous one, oriented toward our circle of existence, and whether we answer for that which we know in action and deportment. . . . We distinguish between *authentic knowledge and apparent knowledge.* . . . For the man of this unheard-of will, our Führer Adolf Hitler, a triple "Sieg Heil!" (*Der Alemanne. Kampfblatt der Nationalsozialisten Oberbadens* [. . .] Series 33, 1. February, 1934, Evening edition, p. 9.) (200-202)

176. (A LETTER FROM HEIDEGGER TO THE REICHSFÜHRER OF THE GERMAN STUDENT BODY)

Freiburg im Breisgau, 6 February 1934

Dear Mr. Stäbel! . . . Today it became known through the press that the suspension of the CV organization Ripuaria has been lifted. The leader of the local student body, Herr von zu Mühlen, thereupon *had* to resign. This public triumph of Catholicism precisely here must in no case remain. It represents a damage to the entire effort than which no greater one could be conceived of at the moment. . . . Heil Hitler! Yours, Heidegger. [Hitherto unpublished.]

209. "THE MISERY OF GERMAN INTELLECTUALS" BY WERNER RINGS

. . . Toward the end of 1933, a German university did me the honor of informing me while abroad that I was excluded from any activity at German universities for four years because of "un-German" behavior; the letter bore the signature of the German philosopher Martin Heidegger. (*Neue Schweizer Rundschau.* Zürich. New Series. 13th volume, 8th fascicule, December, 1945, p. 466.) (264)

210. "NIHILISM AND EXISTENCE" BY GÜNTHER ANDERS

In spite of the fact that Heidegger's philosophy represents a technique of self-manipulation, while Hitler's represents one of mass manipulation, both converge in the first instance in their anti-democratic attitude. In both cases, this is not the aristocratic attitude well known from history, but that of the *nouveau arrivé*. Heidegger went to Plato for the theoretical underpinnings of this attitude; his distinction between the despised "one, they" and the "self" is in fact the Platonic distinction between *doxa* and *episteme* extended beyond the theoretical realm. "The Sophist" and "The Statesman," those Platonic dialogues which Heidegger loves best, are full of the politically anti-democratic consequences of this distinction. In "The Statesman" Plato's ideal is the "leader," and the law at worst the least of evils; thus its equation with the Führer by Heidegger could be as it were countersigned by classical philology. (*Die Neue Rundschau.* Stockholm. October, 1946, pp. 48-76 [pp. 50f., 75f.]. Later reprinted in *Die Stockholmer Neue Rundschau.* Selection. Suhrkamp Verlag formerly S. Fischer, Berlin and Frankfurt/Main 1949, pp. 96-124 [pp. 98f., and 123f.].) (266f.)

214. "MEMOIRS OF AN APOLITICAL WOMAN"

[Comments] on Simone de Beauvoir's *La force de l'âge* by François Bondy

They were able to spend time in Berlin even under Hitler, and calmly to read Husserl there without realizing that the philosopher with whose works they were occupied meantime was no longer permitted access to the library of his university because prohibited from doing so by his most prominent pupil, a partisan of the Third Reich. (*Neue Zürcher Zeitung.* 182nd volume, January 5, 1961, No. 412.) (272)

Martin Heidegger

An Introduction to Metaphysics (1936)

In opposition to this multiple misinterpretation of the spirit, we define the essence of the spirit briefly as follows (I shall quote from the address I delivered on the occasion of my appointment as rector, because of its succinct formulation): "Spirit is neither empty cleverness nor the irresponsible play of the wit, nor the boundless work of dismemberment carried on by the practical intelligence; much less is it world-reason; no, spirit is a fundamental, knowing resolve toward the essence of being." (Rektoratsrede, p. 13.) Spirit is the mobilization of the powers of the essent as such and as a whole. Where spirit prevails, the essent as such becomes always and at all times more essent. Thus the inquiry into the essent as such and as a whole, the asking of the question of being, is one of the essential and fundamental conditions for an awakening of the spirit and hence for an original world of historical being-there. It is indispensable if the peril of world darkening is to be forestalled and if our nation in the center of the Western world is to take on its historical mission. Here we can explain only in these broad outlines why the asking of the question of being is in itself through and through historical, and why, accordingly, our question as to whether being will remain a mere vapor for us or become the destiny of the West is anything but an exaggeration and a rhetorical figure. (40f.)

Because being is *logos, harmonia, alētheia, physics, phainesthai,* it does not show itself as one pleases. The true is not for every man but only for the strong. (112)

The works that are being peddled about nowadays as the philosophy of National Socialism but have nothing whatever to do with the inner truth and greatness of this movement (namely the encounter between global technology and modern man)—have all been written by men fishing in the troubled waters of "values" and "totalities." (166)

Martin Buber

Eclipse of God

[Heidegger writes:] "History exists only when the essence of truth is originally decided." But it is just his hour which he believes to be history, the very same hour whose problematics in its most inhuman manifestation led him astray. He has allied his thought, the thought of being, in which he takes part and to which he ascribes the power to make ready for the rise of the holy, to that hour which he has affirmed as history. He has bound his thought to his hour as no other philosopher has done. Can he, the existential thinker, despite all this, existentially wrestle, in opposition to the hour, for a freedom devoted to the eternal and gain it? Or must he succumb to the fate of the hour, and with it also to a "holy" to which no human holiness, no hallowed standing fast of man in the face of historical delusion, responsibly answers? (77)

EXISTENTIALISM AND SEX

Another issue that we should touch on, however lightly, is that of existentialism and sex. "Existentialist philosophies have not believed it necessary to concern themselves with sexuality," writes Jean-Paul Sartre in *Being and Nothingness*. "Heidegger, in particular, does not make the slightest allusion to it in his existential analytic with the result that his 'Dasein' appears to us as asexual." (383) What Sartre says is unquestionably true of Heidegger, but it is true only with qualification of other existentialist philosophers. Many of these show a keen awareness of the sexual, though this awareness is often a negative one that tends to regard sex *per se* as an obstacle to authentic existence. Kierkegaard's whole thought is based on sex, but he deals with the erotic as his lowest, aesthetic stage and pictures "the knight of infinite resignation" of the ethical stage as able to retain his love on a plane of perfect Platonic harmony without needing anything so gross as actual physical contact. Kierkegaard's "order of knighthood" in *Fear and Trembling*, which makes no distinction between man and woman, is a perfect example of that aspect of existential philosophy about which Sartre complains—the tendency to reduce sex to pure facticity and dismiss it from ontological concern. Berdyaev deals with sex in a more positive way than Kierkegaard, but he still tends to treat it with suspicion as that which binds the person over to objectification and slavery.[1]

Although it may no longer be true to say that Freud dominates the psychiatric thought of our time, it is certainly true that he dominates its approach to sex. While many people might quarrel with the central role that Freud ascribes to libidinal sexuality in the human psychic economy, few look at sex itself in basically other terms than that of Freud—namely, as an irrational, instinctual, and largely unconscious drive that must be understood in the first instance in terms of the biological needs of the individual organism and only secondarily and derivatively in terms of interpersonal relations. The significance of Sartre's approach to sex lies in the fact that, without any attempt to minimize its significance, he lifts it out of the Freudian categories to which we are accustomed and places it squarely within his own thought, with its emphasis upon the relation of the subject to himself and to others. He does not ignore the dark, swirling forces in man's being uncovered by the romantics and depth psychology, but he recognizes that human existence can never be reduced to a psychological state, a pure content of feeling, minus the attitude which the person has to that state or feeling. It is perhaps Sartre alone among the existentialists who has honored sex with a full-scale philosophical treatment—in his detailed and eminently concrete analyses in *Being and Nothingness*.

Sexual desire, to Sartre, is nothing other than the original attempt to get hold of the Other's free subjectivity through his objectivity-for-me. Sexual desire is not a psycho-physiological reaction but an original mode of realizing Being-for-Others. At the same time sexual desire is a dangerous sliding into sheer facticity. As a project for possessing the other as an object or possessing his freedom as a freedom subject to one's own, sexual desire is doomed to failure—a not surprising conclusion given the inherent instability of intersubjective relations in Sartre's world, where each by his look is constantly reducing the other to an object only to be reduced to an object himself by the look of others.

Martin Buber would certainly agree with Sartre that sex is human and not animal and that it cannot be divorced from our relations to others. He would further agree that sex begins in situation, that it represents a transcendence of the subject in relation to the other, and that it includes elements of sheer facticity. He is like Sartre also in his essentially positive attitude toward sex, which makes up a part of that "evil" urge with which one can and

[1] *Cf.* Berdyaev, *Slavery and Freedom*, pp. 222-237.

must respond to what meets one if one's existence is to be authentic. Buber calls this becoming a whole "a cruelly hazardous enterprise." It is, nonetheless, an enterprise that man can undertake; for man is not "a useless passion" for Buber, as he is for Sartre. As Sartre places sexuality in the interaction of the *for-itself* and the *in-itself*, so Buber places it in the interplay between I-Thou and I-It. Nowhere is the relationship between these two attitudes so intermingled and confused as precisely in this sphere, in which deception, illusion, and bad faith of every kind appear. Here, more than anywhere, monologue loves to mask itself as dialogue. In all the much-discussed erotic literature of the age, it is not love *between* the I and the Thou that is represented but the precious experience of the I that enjoys itself in the other without giving itself to the other.

But monologue, bad faith, seeming—the world of I-It—are not the only possibilities for Buber, as they are for Sartre. In true love the lovers receive the common event from both sides at once, "and for the first time understands in a bodily way what an event is." The lover does not assimilate the beloved into his own soul or attempt to possess her freedom. He vows her faithfully to himself and turns to her in her otherness, her independence, her self-reality, with all the power of intention of his own heart. This is not Sartre's otherness of the object nor even of the alien subject that makes me into an object. It is the otherness of the other who faces me as partner, who affirms me and contends with me, the other whose side of the sexual relationship I can experience in a quite concrete way through imagining the real. In avoiding sex and marriage as temptation to the finite, Kierkegaard sidestepped the possibility of authentic existence. There is scarcely a substitute for marriage, indeed, for teaching us the "vital acknowledgement of many-faced otherness." This acknowledgement begins in marriage with an experiencing of the other's relation to the sexual act far more radical than Sartre's incarnation of the other's freedom. Feeling the contact from two sides—with the palm of his hand and with the woman's skin—enjoyment is transformed into love, the other person is made present to him for all time, and "a mere elaboration of subjectivity is never again possible or tolerable to him." [2]

Viktor Frankl takes an approach to sexuality closely similar to Buber's:

> There is not the least thing to be objected to in the sexual drive as long as it is included in the personal realm: as soon and as long as the sexuality is *personalized*, personalized through love. By love we

[2] Buber, *Between Man and Man*, "Education," p. 96f.

> understand that human spiritual act that enables us to grasp another man in his being, in his suchness, in his uniqueness and particularity, but not only in his being and his suchness but also in his value, in what he shall become, and that means to affirm him. Love may be defined now as: being able to say Thou to someone—and beyond that to be able also to say Yes to him; personal love must now join the sexual drive to the spiritual person, it must personalize it. *Only an I that means a Thou can integrate the It.*[3]

For those who are not content to stop short with Sartre, Frankl's last sentence suggests a way in which we can make our own the unquestionably valuable insights of *both* Sartre's and Buber's approach to sexuality. Sartre keeps us aware of the demonic, tormented, sado-masochistic tendencies of sexual love, Buber of the transforming power of dialogue through which these tendencies are given direction and personal meaning. If we think of Sartre as a brilliant phenomenologist of sex in the I-It relationship, we shall have a much more concrete idea of just what that It is which must be integrated by the I that means a Thou.[4] Needless to say, the difference in the approach to sexuality not only of Sartre and Buber, but of Kierkegaard, Nietzsche, and Berdyaev is only a special case of the different understandings of intersubjectivity which have become clear to us from Part IV.

EXISTENTIALISM AND INTERSUBJECTIVITY

It was customary a few years ago for those in the know to use the new term "intersubjectivity" as if it were an adequate category in itself which essentially referred to the same thing, whoever used it. No attentive reader of Part IV of this book could make this mistake. The three philosophers who explicitly use this term—Husserl, Sartre, and Marcel—do so in as different a manner as is conceivable, and the broader range of those whom we have included under this heading—Camus, Jaspers, Merleau-Ponty, and Buber—make these differences still more radical.

To sharpen the issues involved, we shall restrict our comparison here to Husserl, Sartre, Heidegger, and Buber. Husserl sets as his problem how he can restrict knowledge to a "universal self-examination" or "egology," and still escape the Cartesian solipsism that makes it impossible for the isolated subject to know other subjects as anything other than objects. Despite Husserl's

[3] Viktor E. Frankl, *Das Menschenbild der Seelenheilkunde,* p. 91, my translation.

[4] For a full-scale comparison of these two approaches see Maurice Friedman, "Sex in Sartre and Buber," *Review of Existential Psychology and Psychiatry,* Vol. III, No. 2 (May, 1963).

elaboration of a world of intersubjectivity, I would agree with Sartre and Heidegger that Husserl does not really succeed. As he says himself, the first philosophical discipline for him is the "'solipsistically' reduced 'egology,' the egology of the primordially reduced ego. Then only would come intersubjective phenomenology, which is founded on that discipline." If one begins with the solipsistically reduced ego as one's foundation, one can never reach true intersubjectivity. To state that transcendence is already part of the intention of the ego does not change the fact that it is a "transcendence" which is included within the ego's field of knowing rather than a genuine encounter with something or someone other than oneself. To say that the alter-ego is given in an original pairing with the ego is also unconvincing since it is founded on an apperception of the other which sees him as an object and on an analogy to the other which assumes that one first experiences one's own and only then and thereby knows the not one's own.

The very notion of analogy limits the knowledge of the other to that in which he is similar to oneself. If this were not so, Husserl could not speak of "a living mutual wakening and an overlaying of each with the objective sense of the other" as leading, in the limiting case, to "complete 'likeness.'" "The outward conduct of someone who is angry or cheerful," he writes, "I easily understand from my own conduct under similar circumstances." How could *my* anger have preceded my recognition of the other ego? At whom would I be angry? Husserl actually assumes the thinking I first, thus making the other I a content of one's own consciousness. He never really distinguishes between "noetic" and "noematic" apperception. Other people remain for him a special case of other things. The "here" and "there" are not sufficient to understand the other man or woman, for he is more than just a location of a perceiving consciousness. Husserl leaves the perceiver himself a blank and allows no uniqueness but that of position. His identification of otherness with objectivity, his elimination in principle of anything that is not knowable by the subject, his affirmation of a transcendency which the ego acquires without ever leaving the starting point of its own sphere of consciousness, his definition of philosophical knowledge as "all-embracing self-investigation," and his assumption of a harmony of monads—all reveal the idealist thinker who can never allow the otherness of the other the same status as one's own subjectivity.

Husserl's "transcendental intersubjectivity" anticipates Sartre: "He experiences me forthwith as an Other for him, just as I experience him as *my* Other." At the same time, Sartre goes decisively beyond Husserl in substituting categories of existence for categories of knowledge and in replacing Husserl's "transcendental ego" by the concrete situation. For all this, there remains a serious question as to whether Sartre has escaped the solipsism with which he charges Husserl. Sartre's very categories of *for-itself* and *in-itself* tend to be an extension of the Cartesian mind-body dualism, and nowhere in Sartre is the danger of imprisonment in consciousness ever fully allayed. To Sartre, I know the other as a subject only when his presence affects me as an emptiness that limits my turning him into an object or when I become aware of the fact that he is trying to turn me into an object, just as I am trying to do to him. I do not really know the other subject directly but only as a part of my own consciousness and by indirect inference. Even the fact that I am aware of "the look" of the other does not in the least mean that I am aware of how the other really sees me. I see his eyes seeing me, but I do not see through his eyes. Many types of neurosis but also a great deal from our everyday experience illustrates this abundantly. Dostoevsky's *Notes from the Underground* and T. S. Eliot's early poem, "The Love Song of J. Alfred Prufrock," both portray men incapable of action and involvement because of their awareness of how others see them. Yet in both cases this awareness is an obviously distorted projection which bears little correspondence to reality. The Underground Man says of himself:

> I used to feel all hot down the back at the mere thought of the miserable appearance of my clothes and the wretchedness of my darting little figure. It was a most dreadful torture, an incessant, unbearable humiliation at the thought, which grew into an uninterrupted and most palpable sensation, that in the eyes of all those high society people, I was just a fly, an odious, obscene fly, more intelligent, more highly developed, more noble than anyone else (I had no doubts about that), but a fly that was always making way for everyone, a fly insulted and humiliated by everyone.[5]

Prufrock makes a similar confession and suffers from a similar inability to relate to another as person to person:

> And indeed there will be time
> To wonder, "Do I dare?" and, "Do I dare?"
> Time to turn back and descend the stair,
> With a bald spot in the middle of my hair—
> (They will say: "How his hair is growing thin!")
> My morning coat, my collar mounting firmly to the chin,

[5] *The Best Short Stories of Dostoevsky*, trans. with an Introduction by David Magarshack (New York: The Modern Library), p. 157.

My necktie rich and modest, but asserted by a simple pin—
(They will say: "But how his arms and legs are thin!") . . .

And I have known the eyes, already, known them all—
The eyes that fix you in a formulated phrase,
And when I am formulated, sprawling on a pin,
When I am pinned and wriggling on the wall,
Then how should I begin
To spit out all the butt-ends of my days and ways?
And how should I presume? . . .

I have heard the mermaids singing, each to each.

I do not think that they will sing to me.[6]

In Sartre too there is no "each to each." The possibility of a direct knowledge of the other as a Thou, the possibility of a full and direct mutuality is ruled out by him in advance and on principle. His world remains ultimately the world of the Cartesian *cogito* which he sees as the one certain starting-point for thought, and for him too "the universe of intersubjectivity" does not, in fact, transcend the world of isolated consciousness that divides each man off from the other.

Although Sartre's strictures against Heidegger's *Mitsein* as unduly general are telling ones, one might say that Heidegger is further along toward genuine intersubjectivity than Sartre in so far as his categories are really existential ones and do not suffer from that emphasis on the consciousness and perception of the other that make Sartre's intersubjectivity only a little less subjective than Husserl's. On the other hand, Heidegger is subject to the criticisms that Buber has made of "solicitude" as an essentially monological category. Even in so far as he does point to human togetherness, as Boss thinks, he makes no real distinction between that indirect sociality that Buber calls "I-It" and that direct sociality that he calls "the interhuman." Most of all, Heidegger's definition of existence as "toward death" makes it impossible for him to give "the between" any true ontological status. It is an indispensable ontic accompaniment of an existence which is in the last instance related essentially to itself. That this is so, despite Heidegger's emphasis upon *Dasein ist Mitsein*, becomes clear if we look once again at his definition of death in *Being and Time* as one's ownmost, not-to-be-outstripped, non-relational possibility:

6 *Collected Poems of T. S. Eliot* (New York: Harcourt Brace & Co., 1936), pp. 13f., 17.

> With death, Dasein stands before itself in its ownmost potentiality-for-Being. This is a possibility in which the issue is nothing less than Dasein's Being-in-the-world. Its death is the possibility of no-longer-being-able to be-there. If Dasein stands before itself as this possibility, it has been *fully* assigned to its ownmost potentiality-for-Being. When it stands before itself in this way, all its relations to any other Dasein have been undone. This ownmost non-relational possibility is at the same time the uttermost one. (294)

> The ownmost possibility is *non-relational.* Anticipation allows Dasein to understand that that potentiality-for-being in which its ownmost Being is an issue, must be taken over by Dasein alone. Death does not just "belong" to one's own Dasein in an undifferentiated way; death *lays claim* to it as an *individual* Dasein. The non-relational character of death, as understood in anticipation, individualizes Dasein down to itself. This individualizing is a way in which the "there" is disclosed for existence. It makes manifest that all Being-alongside the things with which we concern ourselves, and all Being with Others, will fail us when our ownmost potentiality-for-Being is the issue. Dasein can be *authentically itself* only if it makes this possible for itself of its own accord. (308f.)

If by this Heidegger meant only the fact that one dies alone, his statements would be unexceptionable. But having made existence toward death the very summit of authentic existence through which conscience recalls one to oneself, Heidegger can hardly be said to see authentic existence as ultimately intersubjective:

> When the call is understood with an existential kind of hearing, such understanding is more authentic the more non-relationally Dasein hears and understands its own Being-appealed-to, and the less the meaning of the call gets perverted by what one says or by what is fitting and accepted. (325)

Like Kierkegaard, Heidegger makes no distinction here between the relation to "the crowd" and that direct interhuman relation between man and man which deepens rather than endangers one's existence as a "single one." Like Kierkegaard, too, he sees the relation to others as only a secondary product of one's lonely relation to God (Kierkegaard) or to one's own anticipated death (Heidegger):

> As the non-relational possibility, death individualizes—but only in such a manner that, as the possibility which is not to be outstripped, it makes Dasein, as Being-with, have some understanding of the potentiality-for-Being of Others. (309)

As a result, it is as little possible for Heidegger as it is for Sartre to join Buber in the recognition that I become a self with other selves and am confirmed in my uniqueness through being made present by others in dialogue. Buber's I-Thou relationship is not to be confused with interpersonal relations in general, as we have seen. A man may have an I-Thou relationship with nature and art as well as other men. Also the I-Thou includes a reality of overagainstness, separateness, and "inner-worldly monastic solitude" quite foreign to Sullivan's definition of the self as entirely interpersonal. In the I-Thou relationship the partners are neither two nor one. Rather they stand in an interaction in which each becomes more deeply himself as he moves more fully to respond to the other. This includes for Buber not only life—"All real living is meeting"—but also, as we have seen in *Between Man and Man,* death:

> A great relation exists only between real persons. It can be strong as death, because it is stronger than solitude, because it breaches the barriers of a lofty solitude, subdues its strict law, and throws a bridge from self-being to self-being across the abyss of dread of the universe. (175)

It is characteristic of an issue that it may be understood objectively, but that it cannot be objectively removed. As we cannot approach Plato's theory of ideas as if Aristotle had never criticized them, so we cannot approach Husserl's intersubjectivity without the critique of Sartre nor Sartre's subject-object world without being aware of the critique of Buber. In this sense each successive thinker has served to sharpen the issue. Where Buber has made the issue of intersubjectivity sharpest of all the existentialist thinkers is his pointing to the "between" as the real ontological ground of existence, his typological distinction between I-Thou and I-It, and his understanding of the knowledge of dialogue as including not only direct contact and mutuality but also an experiencing of the other side. Even those existentialists who come closest to Buber's attitude to intersubjectivity—Marcel, Jaspers, and the later Camus—have failed to recognize how essential experiencing the other side is for the overcoming not only of the solipsistic predicament of the knowing subject but also for every type of relationship—from friendship and love to education, psychotherapy, and ethical action—in which the knowledge of the other's uniqueness alone enables us to meet and know him as a Thou.

To say that Buber has sharpened the issue of intersubjectivity is not to say that the reader need agree with Buber any more than he need agree with Aristotle's critique of Plato. But it should no longer be possible for the thoughtful person to lump together indiscriminately all attitudes toward intersubjectivity, to assert that Being-with really includes the I-Thou. Heidegger and Sartre see the ontological as essentially discovered in one's Dasein or the transcendence of facticity by consciousness, with the relations to others as an ontic dimension of the existence of self. Buber sees the ontological as found in the meeting between man and man and between man and world, with self-realization the indispensable accompaniment and corollary of the dialogue. The opposition between these two views points us to the issue at the heart of existentialism and intersubjectivity.

EXISTENTIALISM AS PHILOSOPHY AND EXISTENTIALISM AS LITERATURE

Another issue, one that has been present throughout this anthology, is the relation between existentialism as philosophy and existentialism as literature. Quite a number of our selections have been from literature—some from writers like Rilke and Kafka who have expressed their view of existence solely through the medium of literature, some from writers like Sartre, Camus, and Buber who have expressed their existentialism in both philosophy and literature. As far as we have found it useful to include selections of both types, there is nothing problematic in the relation of the two. Yet, if existentialism means a turning toward the particular and the concrete, we cannot help comparing the abstractness and abstruseness of a great many existentialist philosophies with the relatively greater concreteness and particularity of existentialist literature. On the other hand, since this is true of all literature, we must also ask whether "existentialist literature" is really not literature into which an existentialist philosophy has been read and for that reason less truly literature and less existential than non-existentialist literature!

There is a sense in which Franz Kafka is more truly existentialist than any of the existentialist philosophers. He not only stays close to the concrete in his existentialism, but he also never indulges in any metaphysics, positive or negative. He never goes outside the situation of the hero set in relation to a reality that transcends him—a reality that he can neither ignore nor comprehend but must come up against as best he may without any objective overview to guide him. If Kafka is a religious existentialist, he never falls into any theologizing that assumes something that is not given to him in his existence itself. If he is aware of the anxiety and emptiness of existence, he never hypostasizes that awareness into a negative metaphysics, such as Sartre's proclamation that God is dead and man condemned to be free.

When one thinks of a writer like Kafka, in fact, the question arises as to whether all existentialist philosophy is not bound to be essentialist by the very fact that it deals in conceptual counters—*Dasein, for-itself, I-Thou*—rather than in the truly unique. Even when those counters are understood as types that point back to the unique, one must concede that this pointing is a good deal less direct than that of existentialist literature, especially when that literature attains the opaque toughness that characterizes Kafka. This is not to deny the necessity and validity of existentialist philosophy as well as literature or to say that the inevitably essentialist elements in that philosophy rob it of all claim to be existentialist. But the philosophers themselves do not always seem to be aware that there is a limit to their claim and that speaking *about* existence is a long way from dealing with existence itself.

The problem becomes subtler still when we compare the existentialism of Sartre or Camus as expressed in philosophy and as expressed in literature. There is no denying the literary or philosophical talents of either man. Yet Sartre seems often to be reading his philosophy into his novels and plays while Camus seems most solid and most original in his literature. The extent to which one may find passages from Sartre's philosophy carried over almost verbatim in his novels has as its corollary the lack of a strong sense of development in Sartre's literature. His novels and plays are more like variations on a theme—many of them, like *The Flies*, *Nausea*, *No Exit*, *The Age of Reason*, and *The Devil and the Good Lord*—brilliant variations that confirm the hints of psychological astuteness with which his philosophy abounds. In Camus, on the other hand, there is a very important development from one stage of his literature to the next (for example, from *The Stranger* to *The Plague*)—a development regularly missed by those who make the mistake of using *The Myth of Sisyphus* as if it were some conceptual key to Camus' meaning in those novels. Camus' non-fiction works, however, lack the toughness and consistency of his literature. For all their insights, they never go beyond the level of philosophical essays to that of genuine systematic philosophy, as does the non-fiction of Sartre.

Another aspect of this problem is what the literature of an existentialist writer reveals concerning the meaning of his explicit philosophy. The somewhat heroic image of man taking on himself the responsibility of choosing an image of man for all men in Sartre's *Existentialism* is reflected with heightened tones in *The Flies*—a play which borrows the overtones of order and tragic meaning of the Greek tragedy of Orestes on which it is modeled.

In *Nausea, No Exit,* and *The Age of Reason,* in contrast, not only is this heroic cast entirely lacking but also the author himself seems to suggest that "the roads of freedom" lead inevitably to the inability to commit oneself to any meaningful direction or to choose any meaningful image of man. In Camus, on the other hand, the image of the rebel, diffuse and often inconsistent in *The Rebel,* becomes clear and forceful in *The Plague.*

These reflections are of importance here because they may throw some light on the problem we have raised. The work of Martin Buber illuminates this question in still a different way. Much of Buber's early philosophical writing, such as *Daniel, Events and Meetings, I and Thou,* and *Dialogue* is of a literary quality, either in the style, the form—occasionally actual dialogues or conversations—or in the interspersing of autobiographical anecdotes that illustrate concretely the points Buber is making. If much of Buber's later philosophy lacks this literary cast, he has never ceased to create literature in the form of retelling of legends and tales, translating the Bible, and writing a novel and a play. Not only has this literature occupied a lifetime, as in the case of the Tales of the Hasidim, but Buber himself has seen it also as the most effective way of teaching. Thus in *The Way of Man* he illustrates the wisdom that he has gleaned from his study of Hasidism through the interpretation of Hasidic tales; in *Images of Good and Evil* he interprets in the same way Biblical and Iranian Myths; and in *Right and Wrong* he offers an existentialist exegesis of five psalms. "I, myself, have no 'doctrine,'" writes Buber in the Foreword to his Hasidic chronicle-novel *For the Sake of Heaven.*

> My function is to point out realities of this order. He who expects of me a teaching other than a pointing out of this character, will always be disillusioned. And it would seem to me, indeed, that in this hour of history, the crucial thing is not to possess a fixed doctrine, but rather to recognize eternal reality and out of its depth to be able to face the reality of the present.[7]

The full significance of this "pointing" for our problem would be missed if we overlooked the fact that, concerned as he has been about creating *images* of man, Buber has also provided us in his latest philosophical stage (*The Knowledge of Man,* 1964) with a conceptual treatment of philosophical anthropology, or the problem of man. This means a recognition that a relatively abstract pointing is both necessary and valid for discovering and realizing existential truth.

7 Martin Buber, *For the Sake of Heaven. A Chronicle,* trans. by Ludwig Lewisohn (New York: Meridian Books, 1958), p. xiii.

PHENOMENOLOGICAL ANALYSIS OF EXISTENCE VERSUS POINTING TO THE CONCRETE

This whole problem of existentialism as philosophy and existentialism as literature can be seen as a special aspect of a still more basic problem that we have already come upon in our comparison of Binswanger's use of Buber with that of Trüb. That is, the relation between existentialism as phenomenological analysis of existence and existentialism as pointing to the concrete. In the existentialism of Merleau-Ponty, Heidegger, Sartre, Binswanger, and Tillich, the former dominates. In Kierkegaard, Marcel, Buber, Berdyaev, and Camus, it is the latter. In some, of course, like Kierkegaard, both aspects are present, and even in a thinker like Buber, typology often assumes a more dominant role than pointing to the unique. The differences between the existentialists on intersubjectivity and religion have been unclear to many who want to hold existentialism to be just one thing. However, it is here—in phenomenological analysis versus pointing to the concrete—that the greatest actual difficulty lies in understanding what existentialism is and in subsuming under one heading all those who are held to be existentialists.

In contrasting Binswanger's phenomenological application of Buber's I-Thou philosophy with Hans Trüb's practical application of it in therapy, I have suggested that this is an issue which existential psychotherapy must face. It is also an issue which existentialism as a whole must face. To face it does not mean a rejection of the one for the other but, rather, a decision as to which one is dominant. Phenomenological analysis is often as essentialist in its way as many of the philosophies it attacks: the forms of this analysis, while they allow openness to the phenomena, do not deal with the concrete in its uniqueness but in terms of world-designs that often superimpose a meaning rather than find one. Yet this analysis is undoubtedly valuable and illuminating, and it illustrates Tillich's point that one cannot and should not try to escape from all essentialism even in the most existentialist of philosophies. But when the analysis of the dead Ellen West as "Thou" takes the place of the meeting with a live Ellen West in therapy, then the existential itself has been submerged in the waters of a new essentialism.

Any pointing can be toward the concrete or away from it. The most abstract and systematic of "pointing" may justify itself existentially if it serves to point to the unique and concrete present from which it arose. Existentialism, as we have seen, is nothing new in the world's history, yet it has been necessary in modern times to make it explicit and articulated if it is to help us regain contact with that immediacy from which the very texture of modern life has increasingly alienated us. Hence Heidegger's "authenticity," Sartre's "bad faith," and Buber's "I-Thou" all have their place in this pointing. But there is always the danger—and the danger is great—that we shall relate to these new systems as we did to the old: as static systems of truth which we can use as substitutes for the direct meeting with the unexpected or the absurd. Once, when Martin Buber was speaking to a group of workers concerning the reality of faith, a man in the audience said impressively, in the words of the astronomer LaPlace, "I do not need this hypothesis God to be at home in the world." Buber thought it necessary to destroy the security of the man's naturalist world-view and, on the basis of modern physics, asked him what it was in the act of seeing red that held together the red-engendering oscillation there, the red-perceiving subject here, and the evanescent meeting between them. The man looked at him and said with equal impressiveness, "You are right." "I sat in front of him dismayed," Buber writes. He realized that he had led him to Pascal's "God of the Philosophers" rather than to the living God to whom one can say Thou. "I could not enter into the factory where the man worked, become his comrade, live with him, win his trust through real life-relationship." [8]

Why was Buber dismayed? His argument with the worker was not essentially different from the philosophy of dialogue that he has expounded in many books and that many unknown readers might relate to in just the way the worker did. Yet in this case the philosophy of dialogue did not serve to point to dialogue, but was accepted instead as a new "world-view" that would confirm the worker in the world of It. No amount of speaking, Buber realized, could take the place of that pointing that comes through "real life-relationship." The issue between phenomenological analysis and pointing to the concrete deepens, at this point, to the issue that must be placed before all existentialist thought, i.e., the relation of existentialist thought to life itself, the question of whether one can authenticate one's truth in one's everyday world. Those existentialists who insist on keeping their pointing as pointing and use anecdotes and literature to keep that pointing concrete are more existential than those who stop short at proliferating new categories for the analysis of existence. For the former as for the latter, however, the test of the ever-new verification of exis-

[8] Buber, *Eclipse of God*, "Report on Two Talks," trans. by Maurice Friedman, pp. 4-6.

tential truth in life is one that cannot be denied. It is for this reason that we have had to raise in this section the unpleasant question of the relation of Heidegger's philosophy to his activity and thought as a Nazi. But we shall not have learned anything from Kierkegaard's "Single One," Heidegger's "They," Sartre's "bad-faith," Buber's "seeming," or Camus' inauthentic hero of *The Fall* if we do not see this as a question that applies to *every* existentialist and to every man who takes existentialism seriously and tries to make one aspect or other of it his own.

ONTOLOGY AND RELIGION

Heidegger's attempt to get beyond "fundamental ontology" to metaphysics has brought him closer than he might realize to the traditional ontology that he attacks. On the other hand, Heidegger's statement that "every philosophy which revolves around an indirect or direct conception of 'transcendence' remains of necessity essentially an ontology, whether it achieves a new foundation of ontology or whether it assures us that it repudiates ontology as a conceptual freezing of experience" can be applied with justice to Jaspers. Long before I read this statement of Heidegger's I wrote of Jaspers' metaphysic:

> Recognizing the reading of the cipher as a dialogue between man and Transcendence which demands man's cooperation and involvement and is essentially dependent upon his becoming an authentic self, Jaspers contrasts the freedom, possibility, historicity, and uniqueness of the cipher with the non-historical, immutable, objective, and universal nature of ontology. Yet he then goes on to a series of statements which are really ontology in a new guise, as shown by his rejection of an immediate or personal relation with God and his "demand for the Godhead as the true Transcendence." This hidden ontology of Transcendence betrays Jaspers into the very objectification of the Absolute that he has ruled out. As the result of this objectification, the master of antinomies falls afoul of the fundamental antinomy whose tension is experienced in the lives of countless believing men—the conviction that one may have direct relationship with the Absolute and may address it as Thou without necessarily degrading it or reducing it to complete relatedness, and without blocking communication among men or laming man's independence—all of which Jaspers insists must take place if we do not "keep Transcendence pure in its hidden form and distance." But then he adds, in sublime contradiction (as if Godhead actually did communicate with man in a personal way), "God as Transcendent wants man to be himself." [9]

[9] Maurice Friedman, Review of *Jaspers' Metaphysics*. Based on Karl Jaspers' *Philosophie* (*Metaphysik*). By Adolph Lichtigfeld, *The Review of Religion*, Vol. XX, Nos. 1-2 (November, 1955), pp. 96-98.

There is one sense in which "the Encompassing" and "the Ground of Being" really do get beyond the subject-object relationship and ordinary ontology—when they are taken as a symbol of an ineffable reality which includes and transcends us. But when they are made an object of thought, a philosophical counter, a part of a system, they fall back into the subject-object relationship. This is what Tillich fails to recognize when he claims for his "God beyond God" that it is the ground of being that transcends both mysticism and the I-Thou relationship. It does so in thought only. In existential reality it falls below them to that abstract certainty of what is conceptually adequate but can never be immediately known. In this sense one may say that Tillich confuses the logical and the ontological, at one time using the "ground of being" as beyond the objectification of "primitive theism," at another using it as an ultimate concern that may be deduced even from the philosophies that most emphatically reject it. Knowing for Tillich is knowing in the relationship of faith, but at a still deeper level it is the knowledge which gives the ground for that relationship—the *gnosis* that takes refuge in comprehensive concepts. This is, at least in part, the issue between Tillich and Buber, who rests, as we have seen, with the paradox of the Absolute Person and finds it unnecessary, therefore, to transcend the I-Thou relation with God in order to guard against that naïve personalism that makes God into a person beside other persons. A comment of one of Tillich's closest friends and disciples, the late David E. Roberts, illuminates this dilemma not only in the existentialism of Tillich but in all "philosophical existentialism," if we may borrow Maritain's counterpoise to "existential existentialism":

> I have always been mystified as to how he could be so flexible, concrete, vital, and "close to home" on the one hand, and so schematic, abstract, abstruse, and remote on the other. . . . The schematic aspect . . . is an asset wherever it is used analytically and organizationally, that is, where it is used to clarify concepts and to show their interrelatedness. But it becomes a liability at the point where existential problems, after being high-lighted, are swallowed into an abyss. Somehow Tillich, like God, manages to engulf distinctions without blurring them. He fully realizes (again, no doubt, like God) that such problems are met, in so far as they ever are, by living rather than by constructing systems. But it is a weird experience, which I have undergone many times, to have problems answered with great sensitivity and patience, by being brought into connection with some relevant segment of the system, only to discover later that I do not happen to be the man who carries this system around in his head.[10]

[10] David E. Roberts, "Tillich's Doctrine of Man" in Charles W. Keg-

Along with unexistential system-building some will accuse the existentialists, systematic or not, of unnecessary abstruseness. Even apart from the problem of translation, this is all too often true. One sentence from Jaspers' *Philosophie* that it was necessary to delete for clarity's sake reads, "Wherever this unity exists the leap from the inconceivable to the absolutely unthinkable is evident." To some existentialism may seem just this: a "leap from the inconceivable to the absolutely unthinkable"! To others, however, despite the abstruseness into which some of its philosophers fall, existentialism will represent a range of meaningful ways in which human existence is being illuminated in our day. Despite all confusions and impreciseness (and these are not so great as the opponents of existentialism would like to make out), existentialism has an important continuing place in the philosophy and culture of our time. It offers modern man methods and subjects of "existential illumination" which are notably absent in those schools of modern philosophy that have from the outset excluded existential knowledge and the wholeness of man from their concern.

---

ley & Robert W. Bretall, editors, *The Theology of Paul Tillich,* Vol. I of *The Library of Living Theologians* (New York: The Macmillan Company, 1956), p. 130. *Cf.* Tillich's reply to Roberts on p. 329f.

BIBLIOGRAPHY OF SELECTIONS

Arieti, Silvano

"Recent Conceptions and Misconceptions of Schizophrenia," *American Journal of Psychotherapy,* Vol. XIV, No. 1 (January, 1960).
"The Two Aspects of Schizophrenia," *The Psychiatric Quarterly,* Vol. XXXI (July, 1957).
"What Is Effective in the Therapeutic Process?" *The American Journal of Psychoanalysis,* Vol. XVII, No. 1 (1957).

Basescu, Sabert

Comments on Medard Boss's "Anxiety, Guilt and Psychotherapeutic Liberation," *Review of Existential Psychology and Psychiatry,* Vol. II, No. 3 (September, 1962).

Berdyaev, Nicolas

The Beginning and the End. New York: Harper Torchbooks, 1957.
The Destiny of Man. New York: Harper Torchbooks, 1960.
The Divine and the Human. London: Geoffrey Bles, 1949.
Freedom and the Spirit. New York: Charles Scribner's Sons, 1935.
Slavery and Freedom. New York: Charles Scribner's Sons, 1944.
"Unground and Freedom," Introductory Essay to Jacob Boehme, *Six Theosophic Points.* (*See* citation below.)

Blakney, Raymond Bernard

Meister Eckhart. A Modern Translation. New York: Harper Torchbooks, 1957.

Binswanger, Ludwig

Basic Forms and Knowledge of Human Existence (*Grundformen und Erkenntnis menschlichen Daseins.* 3rd unchanged ed. Munich: Ernst Reinhardt Verlag, 1962). Selections translated for the first time here by Jacob Needleman.
Being-in-the-World. Selected Papers of Ludwig Binswanger. Edited and with a Critical Introduction by Jacob Needleman. New York: Basic Books, 1963.
"The Case of Lola Voss," in *Being-in-the-World,* trans. by Ernest Angel.
"Existential Analysis and Psychotherapy." In Hendrik M. Ruitenbeek, ed., *Psychoanalysis and Existential Philosophy.* New York: E. P. Dutton & Co. (paperback), 1962. Originally in Frieda Fromm-Reichmann and J. L. Moreno, eds., *Progress in Psychotherapy,* Vol. I. New York: Grune & Stratton, Inc., 1956.
"Extravagance," in *Being-in-the-World.*

"Freud's Conception of Man in the Light of Anthropology," in *Being-in-the-World.*

"Heidegger's Analytic of Existence and its Meaning for Psychiatry," in *Being-in-the-World.*

"Schizophrenie," in *Being-in-the-World.*

Boehme, Jacob

Six Theosophic Points and Other Writings. With an Introductory Essay, "Unground and Freedom," by Nicolas Berdyaev. Ann Arbor: The University of Michigan Press, Ann Arbor Paperbacks, 1958.

Boss, Medard

"Anxiety, Guilt and Psychotherapeutic Liberation," *Review of Existential Psychology and Psychiatry,* Vol. II, No. 3 (September, 1962).

" 'Daseinsanalysis' and Psychotherapy." In Ruitenbeek, *op. cit.* (See under Binswanger.) Originally in Jules H. Masserman and J. L. Moreno, editors, *Progress in Psychotherapy,* Vol. II. New York: Grune & Stratton, 1957.

Psychoanalysis and Daseinsanalysis. Trans. by Ludwig B. Lefebre. New York: Basic Books, 1963.

Buber, Martin

Between Man and Man. Trans. by Ronald Gregor Smith. Boston: Beacon Paperbacks, 1955.

"Distance and Relation." Trans. by Ronald Gregor Smith. *Psychiatry,* Vol. XX, No. 2 (May, 1957). Chapter II of Martin Buber, *The Knowledge of Man.*

Eclipse of God. Studies in the Relation between Religion and Philosophy. Trans. by Maurice Friedman *et al.* New York: Harper Torchbooks, 1957.

"Elements of the Interhuman." Trans. by Ronald Gregor Smith. *Psychiatry, loc. cit.* Chapter III of Martin Buber, *The Knowledge of Man.*

Good and Evil. Two Interpretations. New York: Charles Scribner's Sons, 1953. Scribner's Paperback, 1961.

"Guilt and Guilt Feelings." Trans. by Maurice Friedman. *Psychiatry, loc. cit.* Chapter VI of Martin Buber, *The Knowledge of Man.*

Hasidism and Modern Man. Edited & trans. with an Introduction by Maurice Friedman. New York: Horizon Press, 1958. Harper Torchbooks, 1964 or 1965.

The History of the Dialogical Principle (*"Nachwort"* to Martin Buber. *Die Schriften über das dialogische Prinzip.* Heidelberg: Verlag Lambert Schneider, 1954). Selections translated for the first time here by Maurice Friedman.

I and Thou. 2nd ed. with Postscript by the Author. Trans. by Ronald Gregor Smith. New York: Charles Scribner's Sons, 1958. Scribner's Paperback, 1960.

The Knowledge of Man. Edited with an Introductory Essay (Chapter I) by Maurice Friedman. Trans. by Maurice Friedman and Ronald Gregor Smith. New York: Harper and Bros., 1964. (Includes "Distance and Relation," "Elements of the Interhuman," "What Is Common to All," "The Word That is Spoken," "Guilt and Guilt Feelings," "Man and His Image-Work," and "Dialogue between Martin Buber and Carl Rogers.")

The Origin and Meaning of Hasidism. Edited and trans. with an Introduction by Maurice Friedman. New York: Horizon Press, 1960.

Pointing the Way. Edited & trans. with an Introduction by Maurice Friedman. New York: Harper Torchbooks, 1963.

"Productivity and Existence," *ibid.*

The Tales of Rabbi Nachman. Trans. by Maurice Friedman. New York: Horizon Press, 1956; Bloomington, Indiana: Indiana University Press, Midland Books, 1962.

The Tales of the Hasidim. The Early Masters. Trans. by Olga Marx. New York: Schocken Books, 1947. Schocken Paperbacks, 1961.

The Tales of the Hasidim. The Later Masters. Trans. by Olga Marx. New York: Schocken Books, 1948. Schocken Paperbacks, 1961.

"What Is Common to All." Trans. by Maurice Friedman. *The Review of Metaphysics,* Vol. XI, No. 3 (March, 1958). Chapter IV of Martin Buber, *The Knowledge of Man.*

"The Way of Man. According to the Teachings of the Hasidim," *Hasidism and Modern Man.* Also published separately with an Introduction by Maurice Friedman. Wallingford, Pa.: Pendle Hill Pamphlets, 1959.

Camus, Albert

The Myth of Sisyphus, And Other Essays. Trans. by Justin O'Brien. New York: Vintage Books, 1960.

Neither Victims Nor Executioners. Trans. by Dwight MacDonald. New York: *Liberation.* A *Liberation* Pamphlet, 1961. Reprinted from *Liberation,* February, 1960.

The Plague. Trans. by Stuart Gilbert. New York: Alfred A. Knopf, 1961.

The Rebel. An Essay on Man in Revolt. Trans. by Anthony Bower. New York: Vintage Books, 1956.

De Rosis, Louis

Comments on Medard Boss's "Anxiety, Guilt and Psychotherapeutic Liberation," *Review of Existential Psychology and Psychiatry, loc. cit.*

Dilthey, Wilhelm

Pattern and Meaning in History. Thoughts on History and Society. Edited with an Introduction by H. P. Rickman. New York: Harper Torchbooks, 1962.

"Selections" in H. A. Hodges, *Wilhelm Dilthey. An Introduction.* London: Routledge & Kegan Paul Ltd., 1944.

Dostoevsky, Fyodor

The Brothers Karamazov. Trans. by Constance Garnett. New York: The Modern Library, Illustrated Edition, 1943.

"Notes from the Underground," *The Best Short Stories of Dostoevsky.* Trans. with an Introduction by David Magarshack. New York: The Modern Library.

The Possessed. Trans. by Constance Garnett. New York: E. P. Dutton & Co., Everyman's Library, Volume II, 1931.

Ebner, Ferdinand

The Word and Spiritual Realities (*Das Wort und die geistigen Realitäten. Pneumatologische Fragmente.* Innsbruck: Brenner-Verlag,

1921. Reprinted in Ferdinand Ebner, *Fragmente, Aufsätze, Aphorismen. Zu einer Pneumatologie des Wortes.* Edited by Franz Seyr with an Introduction by Ludwig von Ficker. Munich: Kösel Verlag, 1963 [This is the first of a projected three-volume collection of Ebner's works.]). Selections translated for the first time here by Maurice Friedman.

Elkin, Henry

Comments on Medard Boss's "Anxiety, Guilt and Psychotherapeutic Liberation," *Review of Existential Psychology and Psychiatry, loc. cit.*

Fackenheim, Emil

"Schelling's Philosophy of Religion," *University of Toronto Quarterly,* Vol. XXII, No. 1 (October, 1952).

Farber, Leslie H.

Will and Willfulness. To be published in 1964 or 1965 by Basic Books, will include the four articles listed below.

"Despair and the Life of Suicide," *Review of Existential Psychology and Psychiatry,* Vol. II, No. 2 (May, 1962).

"Schizophrenia and the Mad Psychotherapist," *Review of Existential Psychology and Psychiatry,* Vol. II, No. 3, (September, 1962).

"The Therapeutic Despair," *Psychiatry,* Vol. XXI, No. 1 (February, 1958).

"Will and Willfulness in Hysteria," *Review of Existential Psychology and Psychiatry,* Vol. I, No. 3 (November, 1961).

Feuerbach, Ludwig

"Basic Principles of the Philosophy of the Future" (*Ludwig Feuerbach's Sämmtliche Werke,* Vol. II—*Philosophische Kritiken und Grundsätze, "Grundsätze der Philosophie der Zukunft"* (1843). Leipzig: Otto Wigand, 1846). Selections translated for the first time here by Leonie Sachs.

Frankl, Viktor E.

"Beyond Self-Actualization and Self-Expression," *Journal of Existential Psychiatry,* Vol. I, No. 1 (Spring, 1960).

The Doctor and the Soul. Trans. by Richard and Clara Winston. New York: Alfred A. Knopf, 1955.

From Death-Camp to Existentialism. A Psychiatrist's Path to a New Therapy. Trans. by Ilse Lasch. Boston: Beacon Press, 1959.

The Image of Man of Psychotherapy (*Das Menschenbild der Seelenheilkunde. Kritik des dynamischen Psychologismus.* Stuttgart: Hippokrates Verlag, 1959). Selections translated for the first time here by William Hallo.

"On Logotherapy and Existential Analysis," *The American Journal of Psychoanalysis,* Vol. XVIII, No. 1 (1958).

Freeman, Kathleen

Ancilla to The Pre-Socratic Philosophers. Oxford: Basil Blackwell, 1956.

Friedman, Maurice

"Dialogue between Martin Buber and Carl Rogers." Moderated by Maurice Friedman. *Psychologia* (Kyoto University), Vol. III, No. 4

(December, 1960). Appendix to Martin Buber, *The Knowledge of Man.*

"Existential Psychotherapy and the Image of Man," *Modern Age,* Vol. VI, No. 3 (Summer, 1962). To be reprinted in *Journal of Humanistic Psychology,* Fall, 1964.

Martin Buber: The Life of Dialogue. Chicago: The University of Chicago Press, 1955. Slightly revised and enlarged edition, New York: Harper Torchbooks, 1960.

Problematic Rebel: An Image of Modern Man. New York: Random House, 1963.

"Sex in Sartre and Buber," *Review of Existential Psychology and Psychiatry,* Vol. III, No. 2 (May, 1963).

Glatzer, Nahum N.

Franz Rosenzweig: His Life and Thought. New York: Schocken Books, 1953. Schocken Paperbacks, 1961.

Goldstein, Kurt

Human Nature in the Light of Psychopathology. New York: Schocken Paperbacks, 1963.

Heidegger, Martin

Being and Time. Trans. by John Macquarrie & Edward Robinson. New York: Harper & Row, 1963.

Existence and Being. With an Introduction by Werner Brock. Chicago: Henry Regnery Co., 1949. Gateway Books, 1960.

An Introduction to Metaphysics. Trans. by Ralph Manheim. New Haven: Yale University Press, 1959. New York: Doubleday Anchor Book, 1961.

Letter on Humanism (*Platons Lehre von der Wahrheit. Mit einem Brief über den "Humanismus."* Bern: A. Francke Verlag, 1947). Selections especially translated for this anthology by Edith Kern.

"Nietzsche's Statement God is Dead" ("*Nietzsche's Wort 'Gott ist Tot,'*" *Holzwege.* Frankfurt am Main: Vittorio Klostermann, 1950). Selections translated for the first time here by Edith Kern.

Of the Nature of the Ground (*Von Wesen des Grundes.* Frankfurt am Main: Vittorio Klostermann, 1955). Selection translated for the first time here by Edith Kern.

"The Time of the World Image" ("*Die Zeit des Weltbildes,*" *Holzwege.* Frankfurt am Main: Vittorio Klostermann, 1950). Selection translated for the first time here by Edith Kern.

"The Way Back into the Ground of Metaphysics." Trans. by Walter Kaufmann. In Walter Kaufmann, *Existentialism from Dostoevsky to Sartre.* New York: Meridian Books, 1956.

Herberg, Will

Four Existentialist Theologians. New York: Doubleday Anchor Book, 1958.

Husserl, Edmund

Cartesian Meditations. An Introduction to Phenomenology. Trans. by Dorion Cairns. The Hague: Martinus Nijhoff, 1960.

Janouch, Gustav

Conversations with Kafka. Notes and Reminiscences by Gustav Janouch with an Introduction by Max Brod. Trans. by Goronwy

Rees. London: Verschoyle; New York: Frederick A. Praeger, 1953.

Jaspers, Karl

The Perennial Scope of Philosophy. Trans. by Ralph Manheim. London: Routledge & Kegan Paul, 1950.

Philosophie, Vol. I—*Philosophische Weltorientierung;* Vol. II—*Existenzerhellung;* Vol. III—*Metaphysik.* Berlin: Springer Verlag, 1932. Selections translated here for the first time by Marga Franck and Arthur Newton in cooperation with Eva Reinitz Gossman and Maurice Friedman.

Psychologie der Weltanschauungen. Berlin: Springer Verlag, 1931. Passages translated here for the first time by Marga Franck and Arthur Newton in cooperation with Eva Reinitz Gossman and Maurice Friedman.

Reason and Anti-Reason in Our Time. Trans. by Stanley Godman. New Haven: Yale University Press, 1952.

Reason and Existenz. Five Lectures. Trans. with an Introduction by William Earle. New York: The Noonday Press, 1955. Noonday Paperback, 1957.

Kafka, Franz

Conversations with Kafka. See Janouch, Gustav.

Dearest Father. Stories and Other Writings. Trans. by Ernst Kaiser and Eithne Wilkins. New York: Schocken Books, 1954.

The Diaries of Franz Kafka, 1914-1923. Edited by Max Brod. Trans. by Martin Greenberg with the cooperation of Hannah Arendt. New York: Schocken Books, 1949.

Parables and Paradoxes, In German and English. New York: Schocken Paperbacks, 1961.

"Reflections on Sin, Pain, Hope, and the True Way," *The Great Wall of China. Stories and Reflections.* Trans. by Willa & Edwin Muir. New York: Schocken Books, 1946.

Kierkegaard, Søren

The Concept of Dread. Trans. with Introduction by Walter Lowrie. Princeton: Princeton University Press, 1944.

Concluding Unscientific Postscript. Trans. by David F. Swenson; completed with Introduction and Notes by Walter Lowrie. Princeton: Princeton University Press, 1941.

Fear and Trembling and *Sickness unto Death.* Trans. with Introductions and Notes by Walter Lowrie. New York: Doubleday Anchor Book, 1954. (Copyright 1951, 1954 by Princeton University Press.)

The Point of View. Trans. with Introduction by Walter Lowrie. London and New York: Oxford University Press, 1939.

Purity of Heart Is to Will One Thing. Spiritual Preparation for the Office of Confession. Trans. with an Introductory Essay by Douglas V. Steere. New York: Harper Torchbook, 1956.

Lynd, Helen Merrell

On Shame and the Search for Identity. New York: Harcourt, Brace, 1958. New York: Science Editions, 1961.

Marcel, Gabriel

Being and Having. Trans. by Katharine Farrer. Boston: Beacon Press, 1951.

Faith and Reality. Trans. by René Hague. Vol. I of *The Mystery of Being.* Chicago: Henry Regnery, Gateway Edition, 1960.

"I and Thou," In Paul Arthur Schilpp and Maurice Friedman, eds., *The Philosophy of Martin Buber.* The Library of Living Philosophers. Wilmette, Ill.: The Open Court Publishing Co., 1964.

Metaphysical Journal. Trans. by Bernard Wall. Chicago: Henry Regnery, 1952.

The Philosophy of Existentialism. Trans. by Manya Harari. New York: Philosophical Library, 1956. New York: The Citadel Press, 1961.

Reflection and Mystery. Trans. by G. S. Fraser. Vol. II of *The Mystery of Being.* Chicago: Henry Regnery, Gateway Edition, 1960.

Maritain, Jacques

Existence and the Existent. Trans. by Lewis Galantière and Gerald B. Phelan. New York: Pantheon Books, 1948. New York: Doubleday Image Book, 1956.

Marx, Karl

"Alienated Labor." Trans. by T. B. Bottomore. In Erich Fromm, *Marx's Concept of Man.* New York: Frederick Ungar, 1961.

May, Rollo

"The Context of Psychotherapy." In Morris I. Stein, ed., *Contemporary Psychotherapies.* New York: The Free Press of Glencoe, 1961.

"Dangers in the Relation of Existentialism to Psychotherapy." In Ruitenbeek, *op. cit.*

"Some Comments on Existential Psychotherapy," November, 1963, written expressly for this anthology.

"Existential Bases of Psychotherapy" in Rollo May, ed., *Existential Psychology.* New York: Random House Inc., 1961.

Existence. A New Dimension in Psychiatry and Psychology. Editor, with Ernest Angel and Henri F. Ellenberger. New York: Basic Books, 1958.

Meister Eckhart

See Blakney, Raymond.

Melville, Herman

Moby Dick. Introduction by Newton Arvin. New York: Rinehart & Co., 1948.

Merleau-Ponty, Maurice

Phenomenology of Perception. Trans. by Colin Smith. New York: The Humanities Press, 1962.

"What Is Phenomenology?" Trans. by John F. Bannan of the "Avant-Propos" of Merleau-Ponty's *Phénoménologie de la Perception. Cross Currents,* Vol. VI, No. 1 (Winter, 1956).

Moreno, J. L.

"The Dilemma of Existentialism, Daseinsanalyse and the Psychodrama, with Special Emphasis upon 'Existential' Validation," *International Journal of Sociometry and Sociatry,* Vol. I, No. 1 (September, 1956).

"The Philosophy of the Third Psychiatric Revolution." In Frieda Fromm-Reichmann and J. L. Moreno, *op. cit.*

The New Testament

Revised Standard Version. New York: Thomas Nelson & Sons, 1946.

Nietzsche, Friedrich

Thus Spake Zarathustra. Trans. by Thomas Common. New York: The Modern Library.

The Old Testament

Revised Standard Version. Vol. II. New York: Thomas Nelson & Sons, 1952.

Ortega y Gasset, José

"In Search of Goethe from Within." Trans. by Willard R. Trask. In William Phillips and Philip Rahv, editors, *The New Partisan Reader,* 1945-1953. New York: Harcourt, Brace, 1953.

Pascal, Blaise

The Thoughts of Pascal. Trans. from the Text of M. Auguste Molinier by C. Kegan Paul. London: George Bell & Sons, 1889.

Rilke, Rainer Maria

The Book of Hours. Poems from The Book of Hours, "Das Stundenbuch." Trans. by Babette Deutsch. Norfolk, Conn.: New Directions, 1941.

Duino Elegies. Trans. by J. B. Leishman and Stephen Spender. New York: W. W. Norton & Co., 1939.

Letters to a Young Poet. Trans. by M. D. Herter Norton. Revised Edition. New York: W. W. Norton & Co., 1954.

Rogers, Carl R.

"The Loneliness of Contemporary Man. As Seen in 'The Case of Ellen West.'" *Review of Existential Psychology and Psychiatry,* Vol. I, No. 2 (May, 1961).

On Becoming a Person. A Therapist's View of Psychotherapy. Boston: Houghton Mifflin, 1961.

Rosenzweig, Franz

"The New Thinking." Selections from Nahum N. Glatzer, *op. cit.*

The Star of Redemption (*Der Stern der Erlösung,* 3rd Edition, Part I—*"Die Elemente oder die immerwährende Vorwelt"*; Part II—*"Die Bahn oder die allzeiterneuerte Welt"*; Part III—*"Die Gestalt oder die ewige Überwelt."* [Pagination begins anew with each part.] Heidelberg: Verlag Lambert Schneider, 1954). Selections translated for the first time here by William Hallo.

Understanding the Sick and the Healthy. A View of World, Man, and God. Edited with an Introduction by N. N. Glatzer. New York: The Noonday Press, 1953.

Sartre, Jean-Paul

The Age of Reason. Trans. by Eric Sutton. New York: Bantam Books, 1959, by arrangement with Alfred A. Knopf.

Being and Nothingness. An Essay on Phenomenological Ontology.

Trans. with an Introduction by Hazel E. Barnes. New York: Philosophical Library, 1956.

"The Devil and the Good Lord," in *The Devil and the Good Lord & Two Other Plays*. Trans. by Kitty Black. New York: Alfred A. Knopf, 1960.

Existentialism. Trans. by Bernard Frechtman. New York: Philosophical Library, 1947.

"The Flies," in *No Exit and Three Other Plays*. Trans. by Stuart Gilbert. New York: Vintage Books, 1955.

"No Exit," *ibid.*

The Reprieve. Trans. by Eric Sutton. New York: Bantam Books, 1960 by arrangement with Alfred A. Knopf.

The Transcendence of the Ego. An Existentialist Theory of Consciousness. Trans. with an Introduction by Forrest Williams and Robert Kirkpatrick. New York: Noonday Paperbacks, 1957.

Schelling, Friedrich

Of Human Freedom. A Translation of F. W. J. Schelling's *Philosophische Untersuchungen über das Wesen der menschlichen Freiheit und die damit zusammenhängenden Gegenstände*. With a critical Introduction and Notes by James Gutmann. Chicago: The Open Court Publishing Co., 1936.

"The Philosophy of Revelation." *See* Fackenheim, Emil.

Schneeberger, Guido

Nachlese zu Heidegger. Dokumente zu Seinem Leben und Denken. With two Illustrations. Bern: 1962. Copyright and privately printed by Guido Schneeberger, Hochfeldstrasse 88, Bern, Switzerland. $2.75 (mailing costs included).

Straus, Erwin W.

The Primary World of Senses. Trans. by Jacob Needleman. New York: The Free Press of Glencoe, 1963.

Tillich, Paul

Biblical Religion and the Search for Ultimate Reality. Chicago: The University of Chicago Press, 1955.

The Courage to Be. New Haven: Yale University Press, 1952. Yale Paperbounds, 1959.

Dynamics of Faith. New York: Harper Torchbooks, 1958. (Copyright 1957 by Paul Tillich.)

Existence and the Christ. Vol. II of *Systematic Theology*. Chicago: The University of Chicago Press, 1957.

"Existentialism and Psychotherapy." *Review of Existential Psychology and Psychiatry*, Vol. I, No. 1 (January, 1961).

Systematic Theology, Vol. I. Chicago: The University of Chicago Press, 1951.

"The Theological Significance of Existentialism and Psychoanalysis," in Robert C. Kimball, ed., *Theology of Culture*. New York: Oxford University Press, 1959.

Trüb, Hans

"From the Self to the World" ("*Vom Selbst zur Welt.*" *Psyche*, Vol. I [1947], pp. 41-67). Selections translated for the first time here by William Hallo.

"Healing through Meeting" (*Heilung aus der Begegnung. Eine Auseinandersetzung mit der Psychologie C. G. Jungs*, edited by Ernst Michel and Arie Sborowitz with a Foreword [*Pointing the Way*, "Healing through Meeting"] by Martin Buber. Stuttgart: Ernst Klett Verlag, 1952). Selections translated for the first time here by William Hallo.

"Individuation, Guilt, and Decision" ("*Individuation, Schuld und Entscheidung. Über die Grenzen der Psychologie*," in Psychologischen Club Zürich, ed., *Die kulturelle Bedeutung der Komplexen Psychologie*. Berlin: Julius Springer Verlag, 1935). Selections translated for the first time here by Maurice Friedman.

Weizsäcker, Viktor von

Cases and Problems (*Fälle und Probleme. Anthropologische Vorlesungen in der medizinischen Klinik*. Stuttgart: Ferdinand Enke, 1947). Selections translated for the first time here by Katherina Englesing von Rhau in cooperation with Maurice Friedman.

Doctor and Patient (*Arzt und Kranker*, Vol. I. 3rd ed., Stuttgart: K. F. Koehler Verlag, 1949). Selections translated for the first time here by Katherina Englesing von Rhau in cooperation with Maurice Friedman.

The Unity of Perception and Movement (*Der Gestaltkreis. Theorie der Einheit von Wahrnehmen und Bewegen*, 4th ed. Stuttgart: Georg Thieme Verlag, 1950). Selections translated for the first time here by William Hallo.

Within and Beyond Medicine (*Diesseits und jenseits der Medizin. Arzt und Kranker—Neue Folge*. Stuttgart: K. F. Koehler Verlag, 1950). Selections translated for the first time here by Katherina Englesing von Rhau in cooperation with Maurice Friedman.